THE

HISTORY OF INDIA

THE

HISTORY OF INDIA.

BY

THE HON. MOUNTSTUART ELPHINSTONE

IN TWO VOLUMES

VOL. II.

GYAN

Published by

Gyan Publishing House
5, Ansari Road
Daryaganj, New Delhi-110002
Phone: 011-47034999, 9811692060
E-mail: books@gyanbooks.com

Distribution Network
gyanbooks.com
India, USA, Canada, UK, Australia

ISBN: 978-93-6280-044-2 (Set)
978-93-6280-757-1 (HB)
First Published, 1841

2nd Impression 2024

Printed at: Gyan Press, Delhi.

THE HISTORY OF INDIA, (VOL. II.)
Author: MOUNTSTUART ELPHINSTONE

THE

HISTORY OF INDIA.

BY

THE HON. MOUNTSTUART ELPHINSTONE.

VOL. II.

LONDON:
JOHN MURRAY, ALBEMARLE STREET

MDCCCXLIII.

CONTENTS

OF

THE SECOND VOLUME.

BOOK VI.

KINGS OF DELHI TO THE ACCESSION OF THE HOUSE OF TEIMUR.

(1206 TO 1526.)

CHAP. I. SLAVE KINGS.

(1206 TO 1288.)

A. D.		Page
1206.	Independence of India	1
	Kutb u dín	ib.
	Progress of a Túrki Slave	ib.
1210.	A'rám	3
1211.	Shams u dín Altamsh	ib.
1217.	Conquests of the Moguls under Chengíz Khán	4
1221.	King of Khárizm pursued into India	5
1223.	Returns to Persia	6
	State of Hindostan	8
1236.	Dealth of Altamsh	ib.
	Rukn u dín	9
	Sultána Rezia	10
	Her Virtues	ib.
	Her Weakness	11
	Rebellion	ib.
1239.	The Queen defeated and put to death	12
	Móizz u dín Behrám	ib.
	Mogul Irruption into the Panjáb	ib.
1241.	Alá u dín Masáúd	ib.
	Mogul Irruptions	ib.

A 2

A. D.		Page
1246.	Násir u dín Mahmúd - - - -	13
	Gheiás u din Bulbun Vizír - - - -	ib.
1253.	Removal of Bulbun - - - -	14
	Discontents and Intrigues - - - -	15
	Bulbun restored - - - - -	ib.
1266.	Gheiás u dín Bulbun - - - -	17
	Bulbun puts down the Influence of the Slaves -	ib.
	His Character - - - - -	ib.
1279.	Revolt of Bengal - - - - -	19
	Suppressed - - - - -	20
	Mogul Irruption - - - - -	ib.
	Victory and Death of the Heir Apparent - -	21
1286.	Death of Bulbun - - - - -	ib.
	Kei Kobád - - - - -	22
	Intrigues and Power of the Vizír - - -	ib.
	Massacre of Mogul Mercenaries - - -	ib.
	King's Interview with his Father - - -	23
	Murder of the Vizír - - - -	24
1288	The King dethroned and put to death - -	ib.

CHAP. II. HOUSE OF KHILJI.

(1288 TO 1321.)

1288.	Jelál u dín - - - - - -	26
	Mild Government of Jelál u dín - - -	ib.
	Vigour of Alá u dín, the King's nephew - -	28
1294.	Alá u dín's Invasion of the Deckan - -	29
	Submission of Deogíri - - - -	31
	Return to Hindostan - - - - -	32
1295.	Assassination of Jelál u dín - - -	33
	Singular Instance of Credulity and Injustice -	ib.
	Alá u dín - - - - - -	35
1297.	Expedition to Guzerát - - - -	36
	Mogul Incursions - - - -	37
1298.	Serious Invasion by the Moguls - - -	38
	Their Defeat at Delhi - - - -	ib.
1299.	Designs of the King's Nephew - - -	39
	He attempts to assassinate the King - -	ib.

A.D.		Page
1299.	His Failure and Death	40
1300.	Other Disturbances quelled	41
1303.	Capture of Chitór	42
1304;	1305. Unsuccessful Invasions of the Moguls	ib.
	Discontinuance of their Incursions	43
1306.	Expedition to the Deckan	ib.
	Story of the Princess Déwal Dévi	44
1309.	Failure of an Expedition to Telingána	46
1310.	Conquest of Carnáta	ib.
	Conquest of Maáber up to Cape Comorin	47
1311.	Massacre of Mogul Converts	48
1312.	Taking of Deogíri, and Conquest of Maharashtra	ib.
	Intrigues and Influence of Cáfúr	49
	Revolt of Guzerát	50
	Recovery of Chitór by the Rájpúts	ib.
1316.	Death of Alá u dín	ib.
	His Character	ib.
	His internal Policy	51
	Mobárik Khilji	53
1319.	Conquest of Malabár	54
	Influence of Khusru, and Ascendancy of a Hindú Party at Court	55
1321.	Murder of Mobárik, and Extirpation of his Family	ib.

Chap. III. House of Tóghlak, Seiads, and House of Lódi.

(1321 to 1526.)

House of Tóghlak — 1321 to 1412.

1321.	Gheiás u dín Tóghlak	57
1322.	Failure of an Expedition to Telingána	ib.
1323.	Conquest of Telingána, and Capture of Warangól, the Capital	58
1325.	Death of the King	ib.
	Mohammed Tóghlak	59
	Character of Mohammed Tóghlak	ib.
	Wild Schemes of Mohammed	61

A. D.		Page
1325.	Projected Conquest of Persia - - -	61
	Attempt to conquer China - - -	ib.
	Introduction of Paper Money - - -	62
	Tyranny and Exactions of the King - -	ib.
1338.	Rebellions - - - - -	63
1340.	Permanent revolt of Bengal and of the Coast of Coromandel - - - - -	ib.
1344.	Restoration of the Hindú Kingdoms of Carnáta and Telingána - - - - -	64
1345-6.	Other Rebellions - - - -	ib.
	Rebellion of the Mogul Troops in Guzerát - -	65
1347.	General Revolt of the Deckan - - -	ib.
	Vigour and Activity of the King - - -	ib.
1351.	Death of Mohammed Tóghlak - - -	66
	Removal of the Capital to Deogíri and other Caprices of Mohammed - - - - -	ib.
	Foreign Accounts of his Court and Government -	67
	The Mahometan Territory in India at its greatest Extent in this Reign - - - -	69
	Fírúz Tóghlak - - - - -	70
1356.	Independence of Bengal and the Deckan recognised	ib.
	The King's Infirmities - - - -	71
1385.	Rivalries at his Court - - - -	ib.
1388.	His Death - - - - -	72
	His Laws - - - - -	ib.
	His public Works - - - -	ib.
	Gheiás u dín Tóghlak II. - - -	74
1389.	Abubekr Tóghlak - - - -	ib.
1390.	Násir u dín Tóghlak - - - -	75
1394.	Mahmúd Tóghlak - - - -	ib.
	Dissolution of the Monarchy - - -	76
1398.	Invasion of Tamerlane - - - -	ib.
	Defeat of the Indian Army - - -	78
	Sack, Conflagration, and Massacre of Delhi -	79
1399.	Tamerlane retires from India - - -	80
	His Character - - - - -	ib.
	Anarchy at Delhi - - - -	8

GOVERNMENT OF THE SEIADS.

A. D.		Page
1414.	Seiad Khizr Khán	83
1421.	Seiad Mobárik	ib.
1435.	Seiad Mohammed	ib.
1444.	Seiad Alá u dín	ib.

HOUSE OF LÓDI.

1450.	Behlól Lódi	84
	Rise of the Family of Lódi	ib.
	Panjáb re-annexed to Delhi	ib.
1478.	Recovery of Júanpúr	85
1488.	Secander Lódi	ib.
	Good Administration of Secander	ib.
	His Bigotry	ib.
1517.	I'brahím Lódi	86
	Discontents and Rebellions	87
1524.	Invasion of Báber	ib.
	He retreats from Sirhind	88
1525.	Return of Báber (December)	89
1526.	Defeat and Death of I'brahím	ib.
	Occupation of Delhi and Agra	90

HOUSE OF TEIMUR.

BOOK VII.

FROM THE CONQUEST OF BÁBER TO THE ACCESSION OF AKBER.

CHAP. I. REIGN OF BÁBER.

Descent and early Life of Báber	93
His Wars and Adventures in his Youth	94
He is driven out of Transoxiana	98
Acquires the Kingdom of Cábul (1504)	100

A. D.		Page
	His Views on India	103
1526.	Báber's Proceedings after his Victory over Ibrahím	104
	Discontent of his Troops	105
	His War with Sanga, Rána of Méwár	106
1527,	March. Battle of Síkrí — Victory of Báber	109
	Settlement of the Country	110
1528.	Siege of Chándéri	111
	Afghán Insurrection	ib.
1529.	Defeat of the King of Bengal	113
	Sickness of Báber	114
	Intrigues regarding the Succession	115
1530,	Dec. 26. Death of Báber	117
	His Character	ib.

Chap. II. First Reign of Humáyun.

1531.	Arrangement with the King's Brothers	124
	Separation of Cábúl from India	ib.
	Afghán Insurrections in India	125
1532.	Disputes with Bahádur Sháh, King of Guzerát	ib.
1534.	Invasion and Conquest of Guzerát	126
1535.	Expulsion of the Moguls from Guzerát	128
	Early Life and Rise of Shír Khán Súr	129
	He obtains Possession of Behár	131
	Conquers Bengal	132
1537.	Humáyun marches against him	133
	Military Features of Behár and Bengal	ib.
1538,	January. Siege of Chunár	134
	Shír Khán's Plan for resisting the Invasion	135
1538,	June or July. Taking of Gour by Humáyun	136
	His difficulties during the rainy Season	ib.
	Active Operations of Shír Khán	ib.
	Retreat of Humáyun	137
	Shír Khán assumes the Title of King	ib.
	Intercepts Humáyun on his Retreat	ib.
1539,	June. Surprises him and disperses his Army	138
	Second Campaign	140
1540,	May. Final Defeat of Humáyun	ib.
	His Flight	ib.
1540,	July. Arrives at Lahór	141

A. D.		Page
	Fails in an attempt on Sind (1541-2)	141
	Seeks refuge in Jódpúr; which is refused	142
	Horrors of his march through the desert	143
	Is hospitably received at Amercót (1542)	144
	Birth of Akber (October 14. 1542)	ib.
	Second attempt on Sind	145
	Humáyun consents to retire to Candahár (1543)	146
	His Dangers in that Country	ib.
	His Flight to Persia	147

CHAP. III. SHÍR SHÁH AND OTHERS OF THE FAMILY OF SÚR.

1540.	Shír Sháh takes possession of all Humáyun's Dominions	149
1542.	Recovers Málwa	ib.
1543.	Massacres the Garrison of Ráisín	ib.
1544.	Invades Márwár	150
	Takes Chitór	151
1545.	Is killed at Cálinjer	ib.
	His Character	ib.
	His internal Improvements	ib.

Selím Sháh Súr.

	Selím supplants his elder Brother	152
1547.	Quells an obstinate Rebellion	153
1553.	Dies	154
	Account of a fanatical Sect	ib.

Mohammed Sháh Súr A'dili.

	Mohammed A'dili murders his Nephew and usurps the Throne	155
	His Vices and Incapacity	156
	Hému, a low Hindú, made Prime Minister	ib.
	Vigour and Talents of Hému	ib.
	Oppressive Measures of the King	ib.
1554.	Rebellions	157
	Separation of Delhi and the western Provinces	ib.
	Revolt of the Panjáb under Secander Súr	ib.
1555.	Revolt of Bengal	ib.

A. D.		Page
1555.	Revolt of Málwa - - - - -	157
1555, July.	Return of Humáyun - - -	158
	Success of Hému - - - - -	ib.
	His Defeat by Akber, and Death (1556) -	159
	Death of Mohammed A'dili (1557) - -	ib.

CHAP. IV. HUMÁYUN RESTORED.

	Reception of Humáyun in Persia (A. D. 1544) -	160
	Account of the Safavis or Sophis - - -	ib.
	Magnificence and Hospitality of Sháh Tahmasp -	ib.
	His Arrogance and Caprice - - -	161
	Forces Humáyun to profess the Shía religion -	ib.
	Sends an Army to restore Humáyun - -	165
	Taking of Candahár (September, 1545) - -	166
	Which is ceded to the Persians - - -	167
	Treacherously recovered by Humáyun after the Departure of the Persian army - - -	168
	Taking of Cábul - - - - -	169
	Expedition to Badakhshán - - - -	ib.
	Cámrán recovers Cábul - - - -	170
	Is driven out by Humáyun (April, 1547) - -	ib.
	Gives himself up to Humáyun, and is kindly treated (August, 1548) - - - -	171
	Humáyun invades Balkh (1549) - - -	ib.
	Fresh Rebellion of Cámrán - - -	ib.
	Calamitous Retreat from Balkh - - -	ib.
	Humáyun defeated by Cámrán, and deserted by his army (1550) - - - -	ib.
	Cámrán again expelled (1551) - - -	172
	Taken and blinded (September, 1553) - -	173
	Humáyun marches to recover India (January, 1555)	175
	Defeats Secander Súr - - - -	ib.
1555, July.	Takes Delhi and Agra - - -	ib.
1556, January.	His Death - - - -	176

BOOK VIII.

STATE OF INDIA UP TO THE ACCESSION OF AKBER.

CHAP. I. HISTORY OF THE INDEPENDENT STATES OF INDIA AFTER THE DISSOLUTION OF THE EMPIRE OF DELHI.

A. D.		Page
	States formed on the Dissolution of the Empire under Mahmúd Tóghlak - - - -	177
	Recovery of Telingána and Carnáta by the Hindús	178
	Further Dismemberment of the Empire - -	ib.

KINGDOMS OF THE DECKAN.

A. D.		Page
1347—1518.	Bahmani Kingdom of the Deckan - -	180
	Increased Intercourse with the Hindús - -	ib.
	Rivalry between the Shía and Sunni sects in the Court and Army - - - -	181
1489—1512.	States formed out of the Bahmani dominions - - - - - -	182
	Bijapúr - - - - - -	ib.
	Ahmednagar - - - - -	ib.
	Golcónda - - - - - -	183
	Berár - - - - - -	ib.
	Bidr - - - - - -	ib.
	Their history - - - - -	ib.
1565.	Battle of Tálicóta - - - - -	ib.
	Fall of the Kingdom of Bijáyanagar - -	184

KINGDOMS IN HINDOSTAN AND THE ADJOINING COUNTRIES.

	Page
Guzerát - - - - - -	185
Málwa - - - - - -	186
Other Mahometan kingdoms - - -	ib.
The Rájpút States. - - - -	ib.

A. D. Page

Change in the Condition of the Rájpúts after the Mahometan Conquests in India - - 186
State of the Rájpút Princes at the Accession of Akber - - - - - - 188
Méwár - - - - - - ib.
Márwár - - - - - - 189
Bíkanír - - - - - - 190
Jésalmér - - - - - - ib.
Ambér or Jeipúr - - - - - ib.
Háráuti - - - - - - 191
Petty States in the Desert - - - - ib.
Petty States on the East of the Table Land - ib.
Other unsubdued Tracts - - - - 192

CHAP. II. INTERNAL STATE OF INDIA.

Internal state of the Mahometan Empire 193
The King's Power - - - ib.
His Ministers - - - - ib.
Provinces - - - - 194
Army - - - - - ib.
Law (Mahometan and Common) - 195
Church - - - - 197
Moulavis - - - - 198
Fakírs - - - - - ib.
Superstitions - - - - 200
Sects - - - - 201
Hindús - - - - ib.
Conversions - - - - ib.
Revenue - - - - 202
Condition of the People - - 203
State of the Country - - - ib.
Towns and Commerce - - - 203
Coinage - - - - 207
Architecture - - - - 208
Manners - - - - 211
Mahometan Literature - - - 212
Language - - - - 213

BOOK IX.

AKBER.

Chap. I. From 1556 to 1586.

A. D.		Page
1556.	Accession of Akber - - - -	216
	Behrám Khán - - - - -	ib.
	Loss of Cábul - - - - -	217
1556,	November. Defeat and Death of Hému -	ib.
	Recovery of Delhi and Agra - - -	218
	Campaign in the Panjáb — Submission of Secander Súr - - - - - - -	ib.
	Arbitrary Government of Behrám Khán -	ib.
	General Discontent at Court - - -	219
1560,	March. Akber assumes the Government -	221
	Perplexity of Behrám - - - -	ib.
	He revolts - - - - -	ib.
1560,	September. His Submission and Pardon -	222
	His death - - - - -	ib.
	Difficult Situation of the young King -	ib.
	His Plan for restoring and consolidating the Empire	224
	Extent of his Territory - - - -	ib.
	Insubordination and Rebellions of his Officers	225
	Quelled, after a Struggle of Seven Years -	229
	Affairs of Cábul - - - - -	ib.
	Nominal Government of Prince Hakím, Akber's brother - - - - -	ib.
1566.	Hakím invades the Panjáb - - -	230
	Revolt of the Mírzas - - - -	231
	They fly to Guzerát - - - -	ib.
	Miscellaneous Occurrences - - -	ib.
1567.	Foreign Affairs — the Rájpúts - - -	233
1572,	1573. Conquest of Guzerát - - -	237
1575,	1576. Conquest of Bengal - - -	240
	State of that Province - - - -	242
1577.	Mutiny of the Troops in Bengal and Behár -	ib.
	Insurrection of the Afgháns in Bengal - -	243
	Final Settlement of the Province after fifteen Years of Disturbance (1592) - - - -	244

A. D.		Page
1579.	Revolt of Prince Hakím	244
	Reduction of Cábul	245
1581—1593.	Insurrection in Guzerát	ib.

CHAP. II. FROM 1586 TO THE DEATH OF AKBER.

1586.	Akber interferes in the Disputes of the Deckan	247
	Akber moves to Attok on the Indus	ib.
1586, 1587.	Conquest of Cashmír	ib.
	Wars with the north-eastern Afgháns	250
	Description of those Tribes and of their Country	ib.
	Sect of the Roushenías	253
	Destruction of the invading Army by the Eusofzeis (1586)	254
	Imperfect Settlement at the end of fifteen Years (1600)	259
1591.	Conquest of Sind	260
1594.	Recovery of Candahár	261
	Complete Settlement of Hindostan	262
1595.	Expedition to the Deckan	ib.
	Chánd Sultána	263
	Her Defence of Ahmednagar	264
1596.	Peace agreed on	265
	War renewed and extended to the whole of the Deckan	266
1599.	Akber goes in person to the Deckan	ib.
1600.	Death of Chánd Sultána	267
	Taking of Ahmednagar	ib.
1601.	Conquest of Cándésh	ib.
	Akber returns to Hindostan	268
	Refractory Conduct of his eldest Son, Selím (afterwards Jehángír)	ib.
1602.	Murder of A'bul Fazl	270
1603.	Reconciliation of Akber with Selím	271
	Continued Misconduct of Selím	272
	He is placed under Restraint and soon after released	273
	His Quarrels with his own Son, Khusru	ib.
	Death of Dániál, Akber's third Son	274
	Sickness of Akber	ib.
	Intrigues regarding the Succession	275

A. D. Page
Unsuccessful Combination to set aside Selím - 275
1605, 13th Oct. Death of Akber - - - 276
His Character - - - - - - 277

CHAP. III. INTERNAL POLICY.
His internal Policy, religious and civil - 280
His general Toleration and Impartiality - ib.
Progress of his religious Opinions - - ib.
Feizi - - - - - 281
His Translations from the Shanscrit - ib.
He superintends Translations from that and other Languages - - - 282
Abul Fazl - - - - - - ib.
Akber's Attachment to those Brothers - 283
Akber's religious and philosophical Conferences - - - - - 284
Religious System of Akber - - 286
His Discouragement of the Mahometan Peculiarities - - - - 289
His Restrictions on the Hindú Superstition ib.
His general Indulgence to Hindús - - 290
Discontents among the Mussulmans - 291
Limited Progress of his own Religion - 293
His civil Government — Revenue System - 294
Tódar Mal - - - - 299
Subahs or Governments, and their Establishments — military, judicial, and police - ib.
Reform and new Model of the Army - 301
Fortifications and public Works - - 304
Household and Court - - - 305

BOOK X.

JEHÁNGÍR — SHÁH JEHÁN.

CHAP. I. JEHÁNGIR.

(1605—1627.)

1605, State of India at the Accession of Jehángír - 310
Moderate Measures at the Commencement of his Reign - - - - - - ib.

A. D.		Page
1606.	Flight of Prince Khusru	312
	His Rebellion	ib.
	Quashed	313
	Barbarous Punishment of the Rebels	ib.
	Imprisonment of Khusru	ib.
1607.	Wars in Méwár and in the Deckan	314
1610.	Insurrection of a pretended Khusru	ib.
	Ill Success of the war in the Deckan	ib.
	Malik Amber	315
	He recovers Ahmednagar	ib.
	Marriage of the Emperor with Núr Jehán	ib.
	Her History	ib.
	Her Influence	319
	Combined Attack on Ahmednagar	320
1612.	Defeated by Malik Amber	ib.
	War with Méwár	321
1613.	Victories and Moderation of Sháh Jehán (Prince Khurram)	322
1614.	The Rána submits on honourable Terms	ib.
	Influence of Sháh Jehán	ib.
	Supported by Núr Jehán	323
	Insurrection in Cábul quelled	ib.
1615.	Embassy of Sir T. Roe	ib.
	His Account of the Empire, Court, and Character of Jehángír	ib.
	Prince Khusru	328
	Unpopularity of Sháh Jehán	ib.
	Prince Parvíz	329
1616.	Sháh Jehán declared Heir Apparent	ib.
	Sent to settle the Deckan	ib.
1616, October.	The Emperor moves to Mándu	ib.
	Sir T. Roe's Description of his March	ib.
1617.	Complete Success of Sháh Jehán	330
1617, Sept. to 1618, Sept.	Residence of the Emperor and Sháh Jéhán in Guzerát	ib.
1621.	Renewal of the Disturbances in the Deckan	331
	Sháh Jehán marches to quell them	ib.
	His Success in the Field	332
	He comes to Terms with Malik Amber	ib.
	Dangerous Illness of the Emperor	332

A. D.		Page
	Measures of Parvíz and Sháh Jehán - -	332
	Suspicious Death of Khusru - - -	ib.
	Alienation of the Empress from Sháh Jehán -	ib.
	Candahár taken by the Persians - - -	333
	Sháh Jehán ordered to retake it - - -	ib.
	His Reluctance to leave India - - -	334
	The Enterprise committed to Prince Shehriár -	ib.
	To whom most of Sháh Jehán's Troops are transferred - - - - - - -	ib.
	Mohábat Khán called to Court by the Empress -	ib.
1622.	Increased Distrust between the Emperor and Sháh Jehán - - - - -	335
1623.	Rebellion of Sháh Jehán - - - -	ib.
	Advance of the Emperor - - - -	ib.
	Retreat of Sháh Jehán - - - -	ib.
	Its Consequences - - - -	ib.
	Sháh Jehán retreats into Telingána - -	336
1624.	Makes his Way to Bengal - - -	ib.
	Obtains Possession of Bengal and Behár - -	ib.
	He is pursued by Prince Parvíz and Mohábat Khán	ib.
	Is defeated and flies to the Deckan - -	337
	State of the Deckan - - - -	ib.
	Sháh Jehán unites with Malik Amber - -	ib.
	Pressed by Parvíz and Mohábat Khán - -	ib.
	Deserted by his Army - - - -	338
1625.	Offers his Submission to the Emperor - -	ib.
	The Emperor marches against the Roushenías in Cábul - - - - - - -	ib.
	Persecution of Mohábat Khán by the Empress -	ib.
	His History - - - - - -	ib.
	He is summoned to Court - - -	339
	Brutal Treatment of his Son-in-law by the Emperor	ib.
1626,	March. Mohábat seizes on the Emperor's Person -	340
	Spirited Conduct of Núr Jehán - - -	342
	She attacks Mohábat's Camp - - -	343
	Is repulsed with heavy Loss - - -	344
	She joins the Emperor in his Confinement - -	ib.
	Insecurity of Mohábat's Power - - -	345
	Artifices of the Emperor - - - -	ib.
	Quarrel between the Rájpúts and the King's Troops	346

A. D. Page

Plots and Preparations of Núr Jehán - - 347
1626, September. Rescue of Jehángír - - - ib.
Terms granted to Mohábat Khán - - - - 348
He is sent against Sháh Jehán - - - ib.
1626, (end of.) He breaks with the Emperor, and joins Sháh Jehán - - - - - ib.
1627, October. Sickness and Death of Jehángír - - 349

Chap. II. Sháh Jehán till 1657.

1627, October. Asof Khán takes part with Sháh Jehán - 351
Imprisons the Empress - - - - ib.
Defeats Shehriár, who is put to Death - - ib.
1628, January. Sháh Jehán arrives from the Deckan, and is proclaimed at Agra - - - - 352
Local Disturbances - - - - 353
History of Khán Jehán Lódi - - - ib.
His Flight from Agra - - - - 355
His Proceedings in the Deckan - - - 356
1629, October. The Emperor marches against him - ib.
State of the Deckan - - - - ib.
Khán Jehán driven out of Ahmednagar - - 357
Pursued by A'zim Khán - - - - ib.
Fails in obtaining an Asylum at Bíjapúr - - ib.
His Ally, the King of Ahmednagar, defeated - 358
Khán Jehán flies from the Deckan - - ib.
1630. Is cut off in Bundélcand - - - - 359
Continuance of the War with Ahmednagar - ib.
Famine and Pestilence in the Deckan - - ib.
1631. The King of Bíjapúr joins the King of Ahmednagar ib.
Murder of the King of Ahmednagar by his Minister, Fatteh Khán - - - - - 360
Who submits to Sháh Jehán - - - ib.
War with Bíjapúr continues - - - ib.
1632. Tergiversation of Fatteh Khán - - - ib.
Siege of Bíjapúr - - - - 361
Failure of the Siege - - - - ib.
The Emperor returns to Delhi - - - ib.
1633, February. Final Surrender of Fatteh Khán - 362

A. D.		Page
1634.	Ill Success of the Operations in the Deckan	362
	Sháhji Bosla attempts to restore the King of Ahmednagar	363
1635,	November. The Emperor returns to the Deckan	ib.
	Failure of another Attempt on Bíjapúr	ib.
1636.	Peace with Bíjapúr	364
	Submission of Sháhjí Bosla	ib.
	The Emperor exacts a Tribute from Golcónda	ib.
1637.	Returns to Delhi	ib.
	Local Disturbances and Successes in Hindostan	365
	Recovery of Candahár	ib.
	Ali Merdán Khán	ib.
1644.	Invasion of Balkh	ib.
	Services of the Rájpúts in the Mountains of Hindú Cúsh	366
1645.	Sháh Jehán moves to Cábul	367
	Balkh reduced by Prince Morád and Ali Merdán Khán	ib.
	Overrun by the Usbeks from beyond the Oxus	ib.
1647.	Aurangzíb sent against them	ib.
	Is besieged in Balkh	ib.
	Sháh Jehán abandons his Conquest	368
	Disastrous Retreat of Aurangzíb	ib.
1648.	Candahár retaken by the Persians	ib.
1649.	Aurangzíb sent to recover it	369
	Fails in the Siege of Candahár	370
1652.	Second Attempt on Candahár under Aurangzíb	ib.
	Its Failure	371
	Great Expedition under Prince Dárá Shekó	ib.
	Siege of Candahár	ib.
1653.	November. Failure and Retreat of Dárá Shekó	372
	Death of the Vizír, Saád Ullah Khán	373
1655.	Renewal of the War in the Deckan under Aurangzíb	ib.
	Intrigues of Aurangzíb at Golcónda—Mír Jumla	ib.
	Treacherous Attack on Heiderábád by Aurangzíb	374
	Submission of the King of Golcónda	376
1656.	Unprovoked War with Bíjapúr	ib.

CHAP. III. FROM 1657 TO THE DEPOSAL OF SHÁH JEHÁN.

A. D.		Page
1657.	Dangerous Illness of the Emperor - - -	378
	Characters and Pretensions of his Sons - -	ib.
	Dárá Shekó - - - - -	ib.
	Shujá - - - - - -	379
	Aurangzíb - - - - -	ib.
	Morád - - - - - -	380
	Daughters of Sháh Jehán - - -	381
	Dárá administers the Government under the Emperor - - - - - -	ib.
	Rebellion of Shujá - - - -	382
	And of Morád - - - - -	ib.
	Cautious Measures of Aurangzíb - - -	ib.
	His Collusion with Mír Jumla - - -	ib.
	He marches to join Morád - - -	383
	Defensive Measures of Dárá - - -	384
	Sháh Jehán re-assumes the Government - -	ib.
	Shujá continues to advance on Agra - -	ib.
	Is defeated by Solimán, Son of Dárá, and returns to Bengal - - - - -	385
1658, April.	Aurangzíb and Morád defeat the Imperial Army under Jeswant Sing at Ujén - -	ib.
	Sháh Jehán's Anxiety for an Accommodation -	386
	Dárá marches from Agra to oppose his Brothers, against the Wish of Sháh Jehán - -	387
1658, June.	Is totally defeated - - - - -	ib.
	Dárá flies to Delhi - - - -	390
	Aurangzíb enters Agra - - - -	391
	Sháh Jehán adheres to the Cause of Dárá - -	ib.
	Is confined in his Palace - - - -	392
1658, August.	Aurangzíb imprisons Morád, and openly assumes the Government - - -	ib.
	High Prosperity of India under Sháh Jehán -	393
	Magnificence of Sháh Jehán - - -	396
	His Buildings - - - - -	397
	The Táj Mahal - - - - -	ib.
	His Economy - - - - -	399
	His personal Character - - - -	ib.

BOOK XI.

AURANGZÍB (OR ALAMGÍR).

CHAP. I. FROM 1658 TO 1662.

A. D. Page

Solimán deserted by Jei Sing and Dilír Khán - 400
Flies to Sirinagar and is made Prisoner by the Rája 401
1658, July. Aurangzíb marches from Delhi in pursuit of Dárá - - - - - - ib.
Dárá flies from Láhór - - - - 402
1658, November. Aurangzíb returns to Delhi - - ib.
Marches against Shujá, who is advancing from Bengal - - - - - - ib.
Treacherous Attack on his Baggage by Jeswant Sing - - - - - - - ib.
1659, January. Defeat of Shujá - - - 404
Jeswant Sing threatens Agra and flies to Márwár - ib.
Dárá Shekó appears in Guzerát, and is acknowledged in that Province - - - 405
He sets out to join Jeswant Sing - - - 406
Jeswant Sing is won over by Aurangzíb - - ib.
Abandons Dárá - - - - - - ib.
Dárá is attacked and defeated by Aurangzíb - 407
Disasters of his Flight to Guzerát - - - ib.
He is met by Bernier - - - - ib.
Ahmedábád shuts its Gates on him - - 408
He flies towards Sind - - - - ib.
He is betrayed by the Chief of Jún and delivered up to Aurangzíb - - - - 409
1659, July. He is brought to Delhi - - - ib.
Sympathy of the People - - - - 410
He is put to death - - - - - ib.
Operations against Shujá by Prince Sultán and Mír Jumla - - - - - - 411
1659, June. Prince Sultán goes over to Shujá - - 412
1660, January. Returns to his Allegiance - - ib.
And is imprisoned by his Father - - - ib.
Shujá flies to Aracán - - - - 413

A. D.		Page
	Uncertainty regarding his Fate - -	413
	Solimán given up by the Rája of Sirinagar	ib.
1661,	November. Morád murdered in his Prison	414
	Expedition of Mír Jumla to Assam -	415
1663,	March. Death of Mír Jumla - -	416
	Dangerous Illness of Aurangzíb - -	ib.
	Intrigues and Agitation - - -	ib.
	Firmness and Self-possession of Aurangzíb	417
1662,	December. His Recovery - -	ib.
	Disturbances in the Deckan - -	ib.
	Description of the Maratta Country -	ib.
	Account of the Nation - - -	420
	Rise of the Bosla Family - - -	422
	Sháhjí Bosla - - - -	424
	Sévají Bosla - - - -	ib.
	His Robberies - - - -	425
	His Adherents - - - -	ib.
	He surprises a Hill Fort - - -	ib.
	He usurps his Father's Jágír - -	426
	Obtains Possession of several Forts -	ib.
	Revolts against the Government of Bíjapúr	427
	Takes Possession of the Northern Concan (1648)	ib.
	His Attachment to the Hindú Religion -	428
	The Government of Bíjapúr seize Sháhjí as a Hostage for his Son (1649) - -	ib.
	Sháhjí released (1653) - - -	429
	Renewal of Sévají's Encroachments -	ib.
	Plunders the Mogul Provinces - -	430
	Obtains Forgiveness from Aurangzíb (1658)	ib.
	Afzal Khán sent against him from Bíjapúr	ib.
	Is assassinated by Sévají - - -	432
	And his Army dispersed (1659) - -	ib.
	Another Army sent from Bíjapúr - -	433
	The King of Bíjapúr takes the Field -	ib.
	Recovers most of Sévají's Conquests (1661)	ib.
	Sévají makes a very favourable Peace -	434
	Extent of his Territory - - -	ib.

Chapter II. From 1662 to 1681.

A. D.		Page
1662.	Sévají's Rupture with the Moguls	435
	Sháista Khán marches against him	ib.
	Occupies Púna	ib.
	Night Exploit of Sévají	ib.
	Prince Moazzim sent against him	437
1664, January.	Sévají plunders Surat	ib.
	Death of Sháhjí	ib.
	His Possessions in the South of India	ib.
	Maritime Exploits of Sévají	438
	Sévají assumes Sovereignty	ib.
	Rája Jei Sing sent against him	ib.
1665.	Submission of Sévají	439
	He co-operates with Jei Sing against Bíjapúr	440
	Goes to Delhi	ib.
	Haughty Reception by Aurangzíb	ib.
	Sévají escapes from Confinement	442
1666, December.	Arrives at Ráighar	443
	Death of Sháh Jehán	ib.
	Prosperous State of Aurangzíb's Empire	ib.
	Failure of Jei Sing's Attack on Bíjapúr	444
	His Death	445
	Return of Prince Moazzim and Jeswant Sing	ib.
	Progress of Sévají	ib.
	He makes Peace with the Emperor	ib.
	Levies Tribute on Bíjapúr and Golcónda	ib.
	His Internal Arrangements	446
	Schemes of Aurangzíb to entrap Sévají	447
	Aurangzíb breaks the Peace	448
	Sévají surprises Singhar	ib.
	Ravages the Mogul Territory	449
	Chout	ib.
1672.	Defeats the Moguls in a Field Action	450
	Khán Jehán made Viceroy of the Deckan	ib.
	Suspension of active Operations in the Deckan	450
1673—1675.	Aurangzíb occupied by a War with the north-eastern Afgháns	ib.
1676.	Aurangzíb returns to Delhi	453
	Insurrection of the Satnarámi Religionists	ib.

A. D.		Page
	Aurangzíb's Bigotry - - -	454
	His vexatious Treatment of the Hindús -	455
1677.	He revives the Jezía or Poll Tax on Infidels	457
	General Disaffection of the Hindús -	458
	Oppressive Measures against the Widow and Children of Rája Jeswant Sing - -	459
	They escape from Delhi - - -	ib.
	Combination of the Rájpúts - -	460
1679,	January. The Emperor marches against them	461
	Grants favourable Terms to the Rána of Méwár	ib.
1679,	July. The Rána breaks the Peace -	ib.
	Devastation of the Rájpút Country -	462
	Permanent Alienation of the Rájpúts -	ib.
	Prince Akber joins the Rájpúts with his Army	463
	Is proclaimed Emperor - - -	464
	Marches against Aurangzíb - -	ib.
	Dangerous Situation of the Emperor -	ib.
	His Presence of Mind - - - -	ib.
	Defection of Akber's army - -	465
	Akber flies to the Marattas - -	ib.
	Protracted War with the Rájpúts - -	466

CHAP. III. FROM 1681 TO 1698.

A. D.		Page
	Affairs of the Deckan resumed - -	468
	Sévají's Conquests from Bíjapúr - -	ib.
1675,	June. Is crowned at Ráighar with additional Solemnity - - - - -	ib.
	Makes an Incursion into the Mogul Territory	469
1675.	And first crosses the Nerbadda - -	ib.
	Sévají's Expedition to the South of India -	470
1677.	He takes Jinjí and Vellór, and recovers all his Father's Jágír in Mysore - -	471
1678.	The Moguls under Dilír Khán invade Golcónda	472
1679.	Lay Siege to Bíjapúr - - -	ib.
	Sévají's Son, Sambají, deserts to the Moguls	473
	He returns to his Father - - -	ib.
	Siege of Bíjapúr raised - - -	ib.
	Death of Sévají - - - -	474
	His Character - - - -	ib.
	Unsuccessful Attempt to set aside Sambají -	ib.

A. D.		Page
	He is acknowledged Rája	475
	Sambají's Cruelty	ib.
	His Obstinacy in besieging Jinjera	476
1681.	Joined by Prince Akber	ib.
	Plots against his Authority	ib.
	Executions	ib.
	Gives himself up to a Favourite, Calúsha	ib.
1682.	Fails at Jinjera	477
	Decline of his Affairs in the Deccan	ib.
1683.	Aurangzíb arrives in the Deccan	478
	His Views	ib.
1684.	His first Operations	479
	Destruction of Prince Moazzim's Army in the Concan	ib.
	Invasion of Bíjapúr	480
1685.	Sambají ravages the Country in the Emperor's Rear	ib.
	Failure of the Invasion of Bíjapúr	481
	Sambají plunders Baróch	ib.
	Aurangzíb invades Golcónda	482
	Makes Peace with the King	483
	Aurangzíb in Person moves against Bíjapúr	ib.
1686,	October 15. Takes the Capital and destroys the Monarchy	ib.
	Aurangzíb breaks the Peace with Golcónda	484
1687,	September. Takes the Capital and subverts the Monarchy	ib.
	Imprisons Prince Moazzim	ib.
	Effects of these Conquests	485
	Disordered State of the Deckan	ib.
1688.	Aurangzíb takes possession of Bijápúr and Golcónda, as far as Tanjore	486
	Inactivity of Sambají	ib.
	Prince Akber goes to Persia	ib.
	Sambají made Prisoner	487
1689,	August. Put to death	488
	Weakness of the Marattas	ib.
	Aurangzíb sends a Detachment to besiege Ráighar	489
	Regency of Rája Rám	ib.
1690.	Ráighar taken	ib.
	Rája Rám escapes to Jinjí	ib.
	Is proclaimed Rája	490

A. D.		Page
	System of Defence adopted by the Marattas	490
	Zulfikár Khán sent to reduce Jinjí	491
1692.	Marattas renew the War by desultory Operations under independent Leaders	492
	Comparison of the Mogul and Maratta Armies	493
1694.	Siege of Jinjí committed to Prince Cámbakhsh	497
	Disgust of Zulfikár	ib.
	He obstructs the Siege	498
1697.	Santají Górpara advances to raise the Siege	ib.
	Cámbakhsh placed under Restraint by Zulfikár	ib.
	Retreat of the Besiegers	499
	Aurangzíb cantons on the Bíma	ib.
	Releases Cámbakhsh	ib.
	Increased Disaffection of Zulfikár	500
	He renews the Siege, but protracts the Operations	ib.
	Resentment of the Emperor	ib.
1698,	January. Jinjí taken	ib.

CHAP. IV. FROM 1698 TO THE DEATH OF AURANGZÍB.

	Dissensions among the Marattas	501
	Murder of Santají Górpara	ib.
1699.	Rája Rám takes the Field in Person	ib.
	New Plan of Aurangzíb — a besieging and a pursuing Army	ib.
	Exhaustion of the Moguls	502
	Sieges by the Emperor in Person	ib.
1700.	Takes Sattára	503
	Death of Rája Rám	ib.
1701.	Aurangzíb goes on taking Forts	ib.
	Spirit and Perseverance of Aurangzíb	ib.
	Difficulties and Hardships to which he was exposed	504
	His indefatigable Industry	505
	His Attention to Details	ib.
	His Distrust of all around him	506
	His Management of his Sons and Courtiers	ib.
	Increased Disorders of the State	508
1702.	Successes of the Marattas	509
1705.	They begin to recover their Forts	ib.
	Exhausted State of the Army	ib.

A. D. Page
Disorder of the Finances - - - - 510
Grand Army hard pressed by the Marattas - ib.
1706. Retreats to Ahmednagar - - - - 511
Declining Health of the Emperor - - - 512
His Fears of encountering the Fate of Sháh Jehán ib.
His Suspicions of his Sons - - - 513
His Alarms at the Approach of Death - - ib.
1707, February. His Death - - - - 515
And Character - - - - - ib.
His Letters - - - - - 517
Miscellaneous Transactions - - - 518

BOOK XII.

SUCCESSORS OF AURANGZÍB.

Chap. I. To the Accession of Mohammed Sháh.

Bahádur Sháh.

Contest between Prince A'zim and his elder Brother, Prince Móazzim - - - - 521
1707, June. Victory of Móazzim, henceforward Bahádur Sháh - - - - - - ib.
Revolt of Prince Cámbakhsh in the Deckan - 522
1708, February. His Defeat and Death - - - ib.
Bahádur's Proceedings in the Deckan - - ib.
State of the Marattas - - - - ib.
Factions of Rája Sáho and Tára Bái - - ib.
Dáúd Khán Panni left in charge of the Deckan for Zulfikár Khán - - - - - 523
Makes a Truce with the Marattas - - 524
Transactions with the Rájpúts - - - ib.
1709. Peace with that Power - - - - 525
Rise of the Síks (end of the fifteenth Century) - ib.
Peaceful Character of their Sect - - - 526
Persecuted by the Mahometans (1606) - - ib.
Their Revolt - - - - - ib.
Guru Govind - - - - - 527

A. D.		Page
	He forms the Síks into a religious and military Commonwealth - - - -	527
	Their Doctrines and Manners - - -	ib.
	They are overpowered at first - - -	528
	Their Fanaticism - - - - -	529
	Their Successes, Ravages, and Cruelties under Bandu - - - - - - -	ib.
1710.	Bahádur marches against them - - -	530
	They are driven into the Hills - - -	ib.
	Escape of Bandu - - - - - -	ib.
1712,	February. Death of Bahádur Sháh - -	531
	Contest between his Sons - - -	ib.
	Artifices of Zulfikár Khán - - -	ib.
	He secures the Victory to Jehándár Sháh - -	ib.

Jehándár Sháh.

A. D.		Page
1712,	May or June. Accession of Jehándár Sháh -	532
	His Incapacity - - - - -	ib.
	Arrogance of Zulfikár Khán - - -	ib.
	General Discontent - - - -	ib.
	Revolt of Prince Farokhsír in Bengal - -	533
	He is supported by Abdullah and Hosén Ali, Governors of Behár and Allahábád - -	ib.
	Defeats the Imperial Army - - -	ib.
	Zulfikár betrays Jehándár Sháh to the Enemy -	ib.
1713,	February. But is put to death along with the Emperor - - - - - -	534

Farokhsír.

A. D.		Page
	Great Power of the Seiads Abdullah and Hosén Ali	ib.
	Jealousy of the Emperor - - - -	ib.
	His Intrigues - - - - -	535
	Hosén Ali sent against Ajít Sing, Rája of Márwár -	ib.
	Makes an honourable Peace - - -	ib.
	Increased Distrust - - - -	ib.
	Submission of the Emperor - - -	536
	Hosén Ali marches to settle the Deckan - -	ib.
	Farokhsír instigates Dáúd Khán Panni to resist him - - - - -	537
1716.	Defeat and Death of Dáúd Khán - - -	538

A. D. Page
Renewed Devastations of the Síks - - - 538
They are defeated and nearly extirpated - - ib.
Cruel Execution of Bandu - - - - 539
Progress of the Marattas - - - - ib.
Chín Kilich Khán (afterwards A'sof Jáh) - - 540
Ill success of Hosén Ali - - - - ib.
1717. He makes Peace with Rája Sáho, and submits to pay the *Chout* - - - - - 541
Farokhsír refuses to ratify the Treaty - - 542
State of the Court of Delhi — Abdullah Khán - ib.
Plots of Farokhsír - - - - ib.
Combination of great Nobles to support him - 544
His Levity and Irresolution - - - ib.
Disgusts his Confederates - - - 545
1718, December. Return of Hosén Ali, accompanied by 10,000 Marattas - - - - ib.
Farokhsír deposed and put to death - - 546
Nominal Emperors set up by the Seiads - - ib.
1719, February. Rafí u Dirját - - - - ib.
1719, May. Rafí u Doula - - - - ib.

CHAP. II. TO THE DEPARTURE OF NÁDIR SHÁH.

Mohammed Sháh.

1719, September. Mohammed Sháh - - - 547
General Indignation against the Seiads - - 548
Internal Dissensions of their Party - - ib.
Insurrections - - - - - - ib.
Proceedings of Asof Jáh - - - - 549
1720, April. He establishes his Power in the Deckan - 550
1720, June and July. Defeats the Armies of the Seiads - ib.
Alarm at Delhi - - - - - ib.
Prudent Conduct of Mohammed Sháh - - 551
His Plans against the Seiads - - - ib.
Mohammed Amín Khán - - - - ib.
Sádat Khán - - - - - ib.
Hosén Ali marches against Asof Jáh, accompanied by the Emperor - - - - 552
1720, October. Assassination of Hosén Ali - - ib.
The Emperor assumes the Government - - 553

A. D.		Page
	Difficult Situation of Abdullah Khán - -	553
	He sets up a new Emperor - - -	ib.
	Assembles an Army - - - - -	ib.
1720,	November. Is defeated and taken Prisoner -	554
1721.	Sudden Death of Mohammed Amín, the new Vizír	ib.
	Rapid Decline of the Monarchy - - -	555
1722,	January. Asof Jáh Vizír - - - -	556
	Indolence of the Emperor - - -	ib.
	His Favourites - - - - - -	ib.
	His Dislike to Asof Jáh - - - -	ib.
	Asof Jáh sent against the refractory Governor of Guzerát - - - - - -	ib.
	Quells the Insurrection and retains the Government of the Province - - - -	557
	Expedition against the Játs of Bhartpúr - -	ib.
	Disgust of Asof Jáh - - - -	558
1723,	October. He resigns his Office, and sets off for the Deckan - - - - - -	ib.
	The Emperor instigates Mobáriz Khán, Governor of Heiderábád, to supplant him - -	ib.
1724,	October. Mobáriz defeated and slain - -	ib.
	Asof Jáh's policy towards the Marattas - -	559
	Consolidation of the Maratta Government - -	ib.
	Bálají Wiswanát Péshwa - - - -	ib.
	Establishes the Government of Sáho - -	560
	Dies (October, 1720) - - - -	561
	His complicated Revenue System - - -	ib.
	His Motives - - - - - -	ib.
	Báji Ráo Péshwa - - - -	562
	His enterprising Policy - - - -	ib.
	Character of Sáho - - - -	563
	Of Báji Ráo - - - - - -	ib.
	Báji Ráo ravages Málwa - - - -	564
1725.	Obtains a Cession by the Governor of the *Chout* of Guzerát - - - - - -	ib.
1725—1729.	Asof Jáh foments the Dissensions of the Marattas - - - - - -	ib.
1729.	He is attacked, and compelled to make Concessions - - - - -	565

A. D. Page

1730. Accommodation between Sáho and his Rival, Samba - - - - - - - 566
Renewed Intrigues of Asof Jáh - - - ib.
Dábarí, a great Maratta Chief in Guzerát - - ib.
Marches to depose the Péshwa - - - 567
1731. Is anticipated by Báji Ráo, defeated, and killed - ib.
Moderation of Báji Ráo in settling Guzerát - ib.
Origin of the Families of Puár, Hólcar, and Sindia ib.
Compromise between Báji Ráo and Asof Jáh - 568
Rája Abhi Sing of Márwár, Viceroy of Guzerát - ib.
Procures the Assassination of Pílají Geikwár - 569
Retaliation of the Marattas - - - ib.
Abhi Sing retires to Márwár - - - 570
1732. Successes of Báji Ráo in Málwa - - - ib.
Obtains Possessions in Bundélcand - - 571
Rája Jei Sing (the 2d), Viceroy of Málwa - ib.
1734. His tacit Surrender of the Province to the Marattas ib.
1736. Báji Ráo increases his Demands - - - 572
Further Cessions by the Emperor - - - ib.
Alarm of Asof Jáh - - - - ib.
He is reconciled to the Emperor - - - ib.
1737. Báji Ráo appears before Delhi - - - 573
He retreats - - - - - - 574
Arrival of Asof Jáh at Delhi - - - ib.
Marches against Báji Ráo - - - ib.
Is attacked by Báji Ráo near Bópál - - 575
And constrained to make great Cessions on the Emperor's part - - - - - - 576
1738. Invasion of Nádir Sháh - - - - - ib.
Previous Transactions in Persia - - - ib.
Western Afgháns - - - - - - ib.
Ghiljeis - - - - - - - 578
Abdális (or Duránis) - - - - ib.
Revolt of the Ghiljeis (1708) - - - ib.
Conquest of Persia by the Ghiljeis (1720—1722) - 579
Their tyrannical Government - - - 581
Their Wars with the Turks and Russians - 583
Rise of Nádir Sháh - - - - ib.
He drives out the Ghiljeis, and recovers Khórásán from the Abdális (1729) - - - 584

A.D.		Page
	Renewed Invasion of the Abdális - -	585
	Nádir takes Herát (February, 1731) - -	ib.
	And gains the Attachment of the Abdális -	ib.
	He deposes Tahmasp Sháh (August, 1731) -	ib.
	Is himself elected King (February, 1736) - -	586
	He suppresses the Shía Religion - - -	ib.
	Invades the Ghiljeis - - - -	587
1738.	March. Takes Candahár - - - -	ib.
	His conciliatory Policy - - - -	588
1738.	His Difference with the Government of India -	ib.
	Supineness of the Court of Delhi - - -	589
	Nádir invades India - - - -	590
1739,	February. Defeats Mohammed Sháh - -	ib.
1739,	March. Advances to Delhi - - -	591
	Insurrection of the Inhabitants - - -	592
	General Massacre by the Persians - -	ib.
	Nádir's Extortions - - - -	594
	His Rapacity and Violence - - -	ib.
	He prepares to return - - - -	595
	The Country west of the Indus ceded to him -	ib.
1739,	May. Mohammed Sháh restored - - -	ib.
	Amount of the Treasures carried off by Nádir Sháh	ib.

CHAP. III. TO THE DEATH OF MOHAMMED SHÁH.

A.D.		Page
	Deplorable Condition of the Capital and of the Empire - - - - -	597
	Internal Dissensions - - - -	ib.
	Proceedings of the Marattas - - -	598
	Báji Ráo resumes offensive Operations - -	ib.
	Attacks Asof Jáh's Possessions - - -	ib.
1740.	Is repulsed by Asof's Son, Násir Jang - -	599
	Perplexed Affairs of Báji Ráo - - -	ib.
1740,	April. His Death. - - - -	ib.
	His Sons - - - - - -	ib.
	Wars in the Concan before Báji Ráo's Death -	600
	With A'ngria - - - - - -	ib.
	With the Abyssinians of Jinjera - - -	601
	With the Portuguese - - - -	ib.
	Bálají Ráo - - - - -	ib.

A. D.		Page
	Domestic Enemies of Báji Ráo - -	601
	The Pírti Nidhí, Ragují Bosla - -	602
	Damaji Geikwár - - - - -	ib.
	Their Intrigues to prevent Bálají succeeding to the Office of Péshwa - - -	603
1740,	August. Success of Bálají - -	604
1742.	Bálají marches into Málwa - -	ib.
	Revives his Father's Demands on the Court of Delhi	ib.
	Invasion of Bengal by Ragují Bosla -	ib.
	The Emperor purchases the Aid of Bálají by the formal Cession of Málwa - -	605
1743.	Bálají defeats and drives out Ragují -	606
	Fresh Combinations against the Péshwa -	ib.
	He buys over Ragují by liberal Cessions -	ib.
	Ragují again invades Bengal - -	ib.
	His General murdered by the Viceroy -	607
	He ultimately obtains the *Chout* of Bengal, and a Cession of Cattac (1751) - -	ib.
	Affairs of Asof Jáh - - -	ib.
	Revolt of Násir Jang (1741) - -	ib.
	Asof Jáh returns to the Deckan - -	ib.
1748.	His Death - - - - -	ib.
	Death of Sáho Rája (1749) - -	ib.
	Intrigues and Contests for the Succession -	608
	Boldness and Address of Bálají - -	ib.
	Alleged Abdication in favour of Bálají -	609
	Bálají takes Possession of the Government (1750)	610
	Marches against Salábat Jang, the son of Asof Jáh (March, 1751) - - - -	611
	He is recalled by the Insurrection of Tára Bái and Damají Geikwár - - - -	ib.
	Bálají seizes Damají by Treachery -	612
	Salábat Jang advances on Púna (December, 1751)	ib.
	Superiority of the Invaders — M. Bussy -	ib.
	Bálají is saved by a Mutiny of Salábat's Army -	ib.
	An Armistice concluded (1752) - -	613
	Transactions at Delhi resumed - -	ib.
	Rise of the Rohillas - - -	ib.
	The Emperor marches against them (1745) -	614

A. D. Page
Fresh Invasions from the Side of Persia - - 614
1748. Revolutions in that Country - - - ib.
Tyranny of Nádir Sháh - - - - ib.
His fears of the Shías - - - - 615
He puts out the Eyes of his Son - - - 616
His intolerable Cruelties - - - - ib.
His Favour to the Afgháns - - - ib.
He is assassinated by the Persians (June, 1747) - 617
Retreat of the Afgháns - - - - 618
Ahmed Khán Abdáli - - - - ib.
Ahmed crowned King at Candahár (October, 1747) 619
Changes the name of Abdális to Duránis - - ib.
His skilful Management of his unruly Subjects - ib.
His Views on India - - - - 620
He occupies the Panjáb - - - - ib.
He is repulsed by an Indian Army under Prince Ahmed, the Heir Apparent - - - ib.
1748, April. Death of Mohammed Sháh - - 621

Chap. IV. To the Extinction of the Mogul Empire.

Ahmed Sháh.

Internal Arrangements of the new King - - 622
1748, December. Attempts to subdue the Rohillas by Safdar Jang, the Vizír - - - - 623
1750. The Vizír marches against them in Person, and is defeated - - - - - ib.
1751. He calls in the Marattas - - - - ib.
Who compel the Rohillas to submit - - 624
Defeat of the Imperial Troops in Márwár - - ib.
Second Invasion of Ahmed Sháh Duráni - - ib.
1752. Cession of the Panjáb - - - - 625
Discontent of Safdar Jang, the Vizír - - ib.
He assassinates the Emperor's Favourite - - ib.
Ghází u dín the younger - - - - ib.
Resists the Vizír - - - - 626
Calls in the Marattas and expels the Vizír - - ib.
The Emperor plots against Ghází u dín - - ib.
1754. Is defeated and deposed - - - - 627

A'lamgír II.

A. D. Page

1754. June 2. Ghází u dín, Vizír - - - 627
His violent Government - - - - ib.
His Life in Danger in a Mutiny - - - ib.
His Suspicions of the Emperor - - - 628
1756. His treacherous Seizure of Ahmed Sháh Duráni's Governor of the Panjáb - - - ib.
Third Invasion of Ahmed Sháh - - - 629
He takes Delhi - - - - - ib.
Massacres and Exactions - - - - ib.
1757, June. His Return to his own Dominions - - 630
His Arrangements for the Protection of A'lamgír II. against Ghází u dín - - - - ib.
Najíb u doula, Minister - - - - ib.
Ghází u dín applies for the Assistance of the Marattas - - - - - - 631
Previous Transactions of that Nation - - ib.
Ragoba, the Péshwa's Brother, marches to support Ghází u dín - - - - - 632
1758. Takes Delhi - - - - - ib.
Escape of the Heir Apparent - - - ib.
And of Najíb u doula - - - - ib.
1758, May. Ragoba takes Possession of the Panjáb - ib.
Plans of the Marattas for the Conquest of Hindostan 633
General Combination of the Mahometan Princes - 634
The Marattas invade Róhilcand - - - ib.
1759, September. Fourth Invasion of Ahmed Sháh - ib.
Murder of A'lamgír II. by Ghází u dín - - 635
Events after the Death of A'lamgír II. - - ib.
The Maratta Troops in Hindostan dispersed by Ahmed Sháh - - - - - ib.
Power of the Marattas at its Zenith - - 637
Their Army - - - - - ib.
Great Preparations for the Contest in Hindostan - 638
Arrogance of the Commander Sedásheo Bháo - ib.
He takes Delhi - - - - - 639
Ahmed Sháh's Negotiation with Shujá u doula - 640
Who joins the Mahometan Confederacy - - 641
Ahmed Sháh marches against Sedásheo Bháo - ib.

A. D.		Page
1760,	October. His bold Passage of the Jamna	641
	Marattas retire to Pánipat and intrench their Camp	642
	Their Numbers	ib.
	Force under Ahmed Sháh	ib.
	Protracted Operations	643
	Failure of the Maratta Supplies	ib.
1761,	January 6. Battle of Pánipat	647
	Destruction of the Maratta Army	650
	Despondency of the Maratta Nation	651
	Death of the Péshwa	ib.
	Dissolution of the Mahometan Confederacy	652
	Extinction of the Mogul Empire	ib.

APPENDIX.

ON THE STATES FORMED ON THE DISSOLUTION OF THE EMPIRE OF DELHI.

Bahmani Kings of the Deckan.

1347.	Hassan Gangu, an Afghán of Delhi	653
	Wars with the Hindús	654
	Conquest of Rájamandri and Masulipatam	655
	Partial Conquest of the Concan	ib.

Dynasty of A'dil Sháh at Bíjapúr.

1489.	Founded by Eusof A'dil Sháh, a Turkish Slave	656
	Extent of the Kingdom	ib.
	Attempt to introduce the Shía Religion	657
	Religious Factions	ib.
	Rise of the Marattas	658
	Wars with the other Mahometan Kings	ib.
	League against Bijáyanagar	ib.
	Wars with the Portuguese	659

Dynasty of Nízám Sháh at Ahmednagar.

1490.	Founded by Ahmed, a Hindú Convert	ib.
	Religious Factions	660
	Wars with the other Kings of the Deckan	661
	Miscellaneous Facts	ib.
	Extent of the Kingdom	662

Dynasty of Kútb Sháh at Golcónda.

A. D. Page

1512. Founded by Kútb Kúli, a Túrkman Soldier - 662
Kútb professes the Shía Religion - - - 663
Extent of his Kingdom - - - - ib.
Conquests from the Hindús - - - ib.
Wars with the other Mahometan Kings - - ib.
1550. I'brahím, the fourth King - - - ib.
His Wars - - - - - 664
Conquests on the Coast of Coromandel - - ib.

Dynasty of Imád Sháh in Berár.

1484. Founded by Fatteh Ullah, descended from a converted Hindú - - - - - 665

Dynasty of Baríd Sháh at Bidr - - - - ib.

Guzerát.

Description of Guzerát - - - - 666
Original Extent of the Kingdom - - - 667
1396. Founded by Mozaffer, the Son of a Rájpút Convert 668
His Wars - - - - - - ib.
His Occupation and subsequent Evacuation of Málwa - - - - - - 669
1411. Ahmed Sháh - - - - - ib.
His Wars with Málwa and his Hindú Neighbours - ib.
And with other Mahometan Kings - - 670
Mohammed Sháh - - - - - 671
1451. Kútb Sháh - - - - - ib.
His Wars with Méwár - - - - ib.
Dáúd Khán - - - - - ib.
1459. Mahmúd Bégarra - - - - - ib.
His vigorous Government - - - - 672
He rescues the Bahmani King of the Deckan - ib.
Marches to the Indus - - - - ib.
Takes Girnár and Chámpanér - - - ib.
His Wars with Mahometan Kings - - 672
His maritime Power - - - - 673
1508. He co-operates with the Mamlúks of Egypt in a naval War with the Portuguese - - ib.
1511. Mozaffer II. - - - - - 674
Generosity to the King of Málwa - - - ib.
War with Sanga, Rána of Méwár - - - ib.

A. D.		Page
1526.	Bahádur - - - - - -	675
	Takes Part in the Wars of the Deckan - -	ib.
	His Supremacy acknowledged by the Kings of Cándésh, Berár, and Ahmednagar - -	ib.
1534.	Conquest of Málwa, and its Annexation to Guzerát	676
	Troubles in Málwa - - - - -	ib.
	War with Méwár - - - - -	677
	War with Humáyun and Expulsion of Bahádur -	ib.
1535.	Bahádur recovers his Kingdom - - -	ib.
	Disputes with the Portuguese at Diú - -	ib.
	Interview with the Portuguese Viceroy - -	678
	Death of Bahádur - - - -	ib.
	Mírán Mohammed Sháh - - - -	ib.
	Mahmúd III. - - - - -	679
	Ahmed II. - - - - -	ib.
1561.	Mozaffer III. - - - - - -	ib.
1572.	Guzerát conquered by Akber - - -	ib.

Málwa.

1401.	Founded by Diláwar, of a Family from Ghór -	680
	Wars in Hindostan and the Deckan - -	ib.
1512.	Mahmúd II. - - - - - -	681
	Ascendancy of Médni Rái, a Hindú Chief - -	ib.
	Mahmúd flies to Guzerát - - -	ib.
1519.	Is restored by Bahádur Sháh - - -	ib.
	Is defeated, taken Prisoner, and released by Sanga, Rána of Méwár - - - -	682
	His Ingratitude - - - - - -	ib.
1531.	He is defeated, and his Kingdom annexed to Guzerát	ib.

Candésh.

	Founded by Malik Rája, a Person of Arab Descent	ib.
	Prosperity of Cándésh - - - -	683
1599.	Conquered by Akber - - - -	ib.
1338—1576.	*Bengal* - - - - -	684
1394—1476.	*Jaunpúr* - - - -	685
	Sind - - - - - - -	ib.
	Multán - - - - - -	686

HISTORY

OF

INDIA.

BOOK VI.

KINGS OF DELHI, TO THE ACCESSION OF THE HOUSE OF TEIMUR, A.D. 1206 TO 1526.

CHAPTER I.

SLAVE KINGS.

Kutb u dín Eibak.

Independence of India.

FROM the death of Shaháb u dín, India became an independent kingdom; and after the disturbance occasioned by the dissolution of his empire had subsided, it ceased to have any connection with the countries beyond the Indus.

Progress of a Túrki slave.

The life of Kutb u dín, the founder of this new monarchy, affords a specimen of the history of the Túrki slaves, who rose to sovereignty throughout Asia, and who for a long time furnished a succession of rulers to India.

He was brought to Níshapúr in his infancy, and

purchased by a wealthy person, who had him instructed in Persian and Arabic. On his death, Kutb was sold to a merchant, who presented him to Shaháb u dín. He soon acquired his master's favour, and was in command of a body of horse, when, in some border warfare with the Kharizmians, he was taken prisoner on an occasion in which his gallantry had been conspicuous. Being afterwards recaptured, he was received with an increase of favour; and by his subsequent good conduct stood so high in his sovereign's estimation, that, after the defeat of the rája of Ajmír, he was left in charge of all the new conquests.

His master's subsequent successes were greatly promoted, as has been shown, by Kutb u dín's ability in his new station; and in process of time the conduct of affairs in Hindostan was almost entirely confided to his discretion. A natural manliness of character inherent in the Túrks gave to newly raised officers of that nation an estimation among the other great men which seldom falls to the lot of the creatures of princes; and Kutb u dín, instead of being an object of jealousy, seems to have been generally beloved for the frankness and generosity of his disposition.

Besides the friendships formed with the great, he strengthened himself by family connections with persons circumstanced like himself. He married the daughter of Eldóz; he gave his sister in marriage to Násir u dín Kubácha; and he afterwards bestowed his daughter on Altamsh, another rising slave, who afterwards succeeded to his throne.

CHAP. I.

Násir u dín from the first acknowledged his superiority, and held Sind of him, under the supremacy of Mahmúd of Ghór; but Eldóz, with whom ambition had more force than family ties, affected to treat India as if it were still a dependency of Ghazni, set out with an army to enforce his claim, and almost immediately gained possession of Láhór. He was soon after driven out by Kutb u dín, who followed up his success by the capture of Ghazni. A. D. 1205, A. H. 603. After being some time in possession, he was expelled in his turn by Eldóz, and spent the rest of his life in the government of his own dominions, where he left a permanent reputation as a just and virtuous ruler. He had only been four years on A. D. 1210, A. H. 607. the throne, but his administration had been known for the twenty years that he officiated as the representative of Shaháb u dín.

A'rám.

A'rám, his son, succeeded him. He showed no capacity, and was dethroned within a twelvemonth by his brother-in-law, Altamsh.

Shams u dín Altamsh.

It is related of Altamsh, probably after his elevation, A. D. 1211, A. H. 607. that he was of a noble family, but was sold, like Joseph, by his envious brothers. Sultán Shaháb u dín, unwilling to pay the price demanded for him, allowed Kutb u dín as a favour to purchase him for 50,000 pieces of silver. He passed through different stations, and was governor of Behár at the

BOOK VI.

time of his revolt. He was invited to the throne by a party; but a numerous body of Túrki chiefs were opposed to him, and he did not gain possession without a battle.

Eldóz, in his assumed superiority, gave him investiture unasked; but being soon after driven out of Ghazni by the king of Khárizm, he made an attempt to establish himself in India. He penetrated to Tanésar, and had even made a party in Altamsh's court, when he was defeated, was taken prisoner, and ended his days in confinement. A. D. 1215, A. H. 612.

Altamsh next marched against his wife's uncle, Násir u dín Kubácha, who had asserted his independence in Sind; but, although he displayed great activity and personal gallantry, he did not succeed in establishing his sovereignty.* A. D. 1217, A. H. 614.

At this time it seemed far from improbable that the Khárizmians would pursue their conquests into India, and Násir u dín had already been engaged with bodies of their troops which had approached the Indus.

Conquests of the Moguls under Chengíz Khán.

But all these alarms were suspended by an event which changed the whole face of Asia. Chengíz Khán, originally a petty chief among the Moguls, having subdued the three nations of Tartary, and swelled his bands with their united hordes, burst on the Mahometan kingdoms with an army that never was equalled in numbers either before or since.

* Forishta, in his History of Sind, vol. iv. p. 414., makes only one expedition; in his General History, vol. i. p. 208., he makes *two;* but in the second there is a confusion regarding the Khiljis which throws the whole into doubt.

This irruption of the Moguls was the greatest calamity that has fallen on mankind since the deluge. They had no religion to teach, and no seeds of improvement to sow, nor did they offer an alternative of conversion or tribute; their only object was to slaughter and destroy; and the only trace they left was in the devastation of every country which they visited. The storm first fell on the Sultan of Khárizm, who had drawn it on himself by the murder of Chengíz's ambassadors. His armies were defeated, his cities demolished, his country laid waste, and a great part of his subjects either massacred or reduced to slavery. He himself died of a broken heart, in an inaccessible retreat on an island in the Caspian, and his son and successor, Jelál u dín, was driven into the eastern extremity of his dominions.

This prince defended his country gallantly to the last. He gained a victory near Candahár, and another still further to the east; but these successes did not even retard his ruin. His last battle was on the Indus, where, after displaying the most obstinate valour, and witnessing the total destruction of his army, he swam the river with seven followers amidst a shower of arrows from his enemies, whom he left in admiration of his intrepidity.* A. D. 1221, A. H. 618.

King of Khárizm pursued into India.

In the course of the night and next day he was joined by 120 of his soldiers; and, before many days were passed, he had assembled 4000 horse.

* De Guignes, vol. iii. pp. 58, 59. D'Herbelot. Ferishta, vol. iv. p. 415.

BOOK VI.

The Moguls threatening to cross the Indus, he fled towards Delhi, and applied to Altamsh for assistance, or at least for an asylum. Altamsh sent a courteous answer, but was too prudent to draw on himself the resentment of the Moguls; and Jelál u dín, left to his own resources, formed an alliance with the Gakkars, drew together an army by means of plunder, and at length attacked Násir u dín Kubácha, and forced him to take refuge in Multán. After this he kept no measures with any one: he ravaged the country on the Indus; invaded and conquered Sind; and would, perhaps, have maintained himself in the possession of it, if some hopes in Persia had not induced him to pass into Kirmán.

Returns to Persia. A. D. 1223, A. H. 620.

Finding the Mogul armies withdrawn from Persia, he again established his power in that country, opposed them with vigour in a new invasion, and was killed at last in Mesopotamia, ten years after his passage of the Indus.*

During his abode in Sind, Ferishta relates that a Mogul army† came in pursuit of him, laid siege to Multán, and, being repelled by Násir u dín, continued their march to Sind, which Jelál u dín had quitted. They conducted themselves with their usual barbarity throughout; and finding provisions scarce in their camp before they departed, they put to death 10,000 Indian prisoners, when

* D'Herbelot, art. "Gelaleddin."

† Ferishta says, under Chaghatái Khán in person, but probably a detachment.

CHAP. I.

they would have been equally relieved by setting them free.

After he was delivered from this succession of enemies, Násir u dín was again invaded by Altamsh, who, this time, was more successful than before. Násir u dín was constrained to retreat to Bakkar; and on attempting, afterwards, to continue his course to Sind, he was drowned, with all his family, in a sudden squall on the Indus, and the whole of the territory subject to him submitted to the victor. A. D. 1225, A. H. 622.

The country to the south of Tatta seems to have maintained its independence from the time of Mohammed Cásim to that under discussion. It may, perhaps, have acknowledged the superiority of some of the intermediate dynasties during the interval, but the internal government was never out of the hands of the Súmera Rájpúts.

In the same year with this expedition to Sind, Altamsh marched against Bakhtiár Khilji, who looked on Behár and Bengal as his own conquest; and, though he professed obedience to Kutb u dín (to whose daughter he was married), openly disclaimed all dependence on his successor. Altamsh was successful in this undertaking; he deprived Bakhtiár of Behár (the government of which he conferred on his own son), and obliged him to hold Bengal under the crown of Delhi. Bakhtiár made a subsequent attempt to retrieve his losses, was defeated by the prince who governed Behár, and lost his life in the conflict.

BOOK VI.

A. D. 1226, A. H. 623, to A. D. 1232, A. H. 630.

Altamsh was now occupied for upwards of six years in reducing the part of Hindostan which had remained independent. He began by taking Rintambór, which, though so much in the line of former conquests, had been protected by its mountainous situation. He next took Mándu, a town of great extent and natural strength in Málwa; Gwálior, which had revolted, was next recovered; Bilsa was likewise taken; and the occupation of the ancient capital Ujén, with the destruction of its celebrated temple, completed the conquest of Málwa.

State of Hindostan.

All Hindostan, except some insulated portions, now acknowledged the government of Delhi; but the obedience of the different portions was in different degrees, from entire subjection to very imperfect dependence: and in this state, with various fluctuations, it remained till the end of the Mogul empire. In a succession of strong reigns, the subject country would greatly exceed the rest; and the princes who retained the internal government of their territories would be quite submissive and obedient in general politics: but two or three weak rulers would again throw all into confusion; new princes would start up, and the old ones would become unruly, till the next vigorous monarch had almost to begin the conquest anew.

Death of Altamsh. A. D. 1236, A. H. 633, Shaban 20.

After these victories Altamsh returned to Delhi, and died in April, 1236, as he was about to set out on a journey to Multán.

During the course of his reign he received investiture from the calif of Bagdad; the most authoritative recognition of a new government that could take place among Mussulmans.

His vizír was a man of great eminence, and had been long in one of the highest employments under the calif. The author of the "Jámá ul Hikáyát," a very popular collection of historical anecdotes in Persian, resided at his court.

The beautiful column called the Kutb, or Cútab Mínár, near Delhi, was completed in the reign of Altamsh. It is in the form of a minaret, with galleries; the shaft is fluted in a manner peculiar to itself, and ornamented with the richest effect. It is 242 feet high, although injured by an earthquake; and is still, I believe, the highest column in the world. Near it is an unfinished mosque, which for grandeur of design and elegance of execution is equal to any thing in India. It is ascribed in an inscription to Shaháb u dín Ghóri.

Rukn u dín.

At the death of Altamsh the contest with the Hindús was at an end; and the period which followed was occupied by a succession of plots, mutinies, and revolutions, equally destitute of present interest and permanent effects.

Rukn u dín, who succeeded his father, lavished his treasures on dancing-women, buffoons, and musicians, and left the government to his mother; and her tyranny and cruelty soon drove all ranks

BOOK VI.

into rebellion. He was deposed after a reign of seven months, and his sister Rezia was raised to the throne in his place.

Sultána Rezia.

A. D. 1236, A. H. 634. Her virtues,

"Rezia Bégum," says Ferishta, "was endowed with every princely virtue, and those who scrutinise her actions most severely will find in her no fault but that she was a woman."* If not distinguished for literature, she read the Koran correctly; and such was her talent for business, that Altamsh, when absent on his southern campaigns, left her in charge of his government in preference to his sons. Her conduct on the throne did not disappoint the expectations entertained of her. Of two separate factions which had concurred in dethroning her brother, one was opposed to the elevation of the Sultána. The vizír of the two last kings was at the head of the latter faction, and they were strong enough to appear before Delhi, and to defeat an army that was coming to its relief. But the queen's arts were more effectual than her arms. She succeeded so well in sowing dissensions among her enemies, that the whole confederacy dissolved, and left the individuals composing it at her mercy. Some were put to death, and others conciliated; and in a short time quiet was perfectly restored.

The internal administration of Rezia did not fall

* Briggs's Ferishta, vol. i. p. 217.

short of her political address. She appeared daily on her throne in the usual habit of a Sultan; gave audience to all comers, reformed the abuses which had crept in under the last government, revised the laws, decided suits of importance, and evinced all the qualities of a just and able sovereign. But her talents and virtues were insufficient to protect her from the effects of a single weakness. It was shown in the extraordinary marks of favour which she showered on her Master of the Horse; who, to make her partiality more degrading, was an Abyssinian slave. It does not appear that her fondness was criminal, since the greatest breach of decorum alleged against her is her allowing the Abyssinian to lift her on her horse. It was, however, imprudent in the highest degree; for, by raising her favourite to the office of Amír al O'mrá*, which gave him rank over all other courtiers, she at once disgusted her nobility, and furnished them with a plausible ground for exciting a clamour against her.

and weakness.

The first who openly rebelled was a Túrki chief called Altúnia. The queen immediately marched against his fort of Batinda; but her army mutinied, her favourite was killed in a tumult, and she herself, being made prisoner, was consigned to Altúnia, as the safest hands in which she could be placed; while her brother Behrám was raised to the vacant throne.

Rebellion.

* Literally "Commander of Commanders;" that is, General in Chief.

BOOK VI.

Rezia, when force failed her, had again recourse to art; and she so far gained over Altúnia by the influence of love or of ambition, that he agreed to marry her, and to assert her rights against his former confederates. Aided by her new consort, the queen assembled an army, and advanced to Delhi; and it was not till after two bloody battles that she was made prisoner along with her husband, and both were put to death. Her reign lasted for three years and six months.

The queen defeated and put to death.

Móizz u dín Behrám.

A. D. 1239, A. H. 637.

The new king endeavoured, by treachery and assassination, to rid himself of the nobles who, for their own purposes, had raised him to the throne. Before he had attained his end, his dominions were invaded by a body of Moguls, who penetrated to Láhór; and the assemblage of troops which followed led to new plots and seditions, which ended in his imprisonment and death, after he had reigned two years and two months.

Mogul irruption into the Panjáb.

Alá u dín Masáúd.

A. D. 1241, A. H. 639.

The reign of the next Sultan, a son of Rukn u dín, was a repetition of the same scenes, increased by the cruelty and licentiousness of the king, until at the end of little more than two years, he was deposed and put to death.

Mogul irruptions.

The only remarkable events of his reign were

two irruptions of the Moguls; the first through Tibet into Bengal, the only one recorded from that quarter during the period of authentic history; and the other by a division of the army of Mánku Khán into the north-western part of the kingdom. CHAP. I. A. D. 1244, A. H. 642.

The first of these invasions was defeated by the local officers; the second advanced no further than U'ch, on the joint rivers of the Panjáb to the south of Multán.

Násir u dín Mahmúd.

The twenty years' reign of Násir u dín was full of disturbances foreign and domestic, though none sufficient to overturn the government. A. D. 1246, A. H. 644.

He was the grandson of Altamsh, had been imprisoned immediately after that prince's death, and, though he had been for some time released and entrusted with a government, he retained the retired and studious habits of his youth. He reposed with entire confidence on the conduct of his vizír, whose name was Gheiás u dín Bulbun. This minister was a Túrki slave of Altamsh, and had been honoured by that monarch with the hand of one of his daughters, the aunt of the reigning king. Gheiás u dín Bulbun vizir.

The great danger was now from the Moguls, who were in possession of all the countries west of the Indus. To guard against it, Bulbun formed the frontier provinces into one great government, at the head of which he placed his relation, Shír Khán, who, like himself, had been a slave. He

BOOK VI.

then advised the king to proceed in person to the Panjáb. While in that province he severely chastised the Gakkars for their co-operation with the Moguls in their inroads, and compelled the jágírdárs*, who had long neglected their duty, to furnish their contingents with regularity.

He next turned his arms against different Hindú rájas, whom the weakness of the preceding reigns had tempted to revolt. In the first campaign he restored the royal authority in the country on both sides of the Jamna, from opposite Delhi to Cálinjer in Bundélcand; and in the three following years he settled the hilly country of Méwát, extending from near Delhi to the Chambal, the neighbouring territory of Rintambór, and the more remote one of Chitór. He afterwards took the strong fort of Narwar in Buldélcand, reduced Chandéri, and recovered all the revolted part of Málwa. In an interval of these expeditions he quelled a rebellion of the governor of U'ch; and, during the same period, Shír Khán, governor of the Panjáb, not only kept the Moguls out of his province, but invaded their territory and took possession of Ghazni.

A. D. 1247, A. H. 646, to A. D. 1250, A. H. 649.

Removal of Bulbun.

During most of these operations the king accompanied the army, and was the ostensible author of all its success. He nevertheless began to feel uneasy in the secondary place which he really occupied, and was induced by the insinuations of Imád u dín, an artful courtier, who had risen by

* Holders of land on military service. See Vol. I. p. 145.

the favour of the vizír, to remove that minister from his post, and to confer it on his secret accuser. CHAP. I.

All the vizír's immediate adherents were soon after displaced; and the misgovernment which followed created extensive discontents, and afforded a pretext to ten governors of provinces, who probably were in league with Gheiás, to unite their troops, and address a remonstrance to the king, followed up by a demand, in respectful but firm terms, for the dismission of the new minister. No mention was made of the displaced vizír, but the object of the confederacy was obvious; and, as resistance would have been hopeless, the king recalled Gheiás u dín, who thenceforth was the real head of the government. A. D. 1253, A. H. 651. Discontents and intrigues. Bulbun restored.

Imád u dín now raised a rebellion, in which he involved a relation of the king's; and although he was himself soon taken and put to death, yet a confederacy had been formed, including the Hindú rája of a place called Santúr and the king's governor of Sind. This rebellion was not entirely quelled till the end of the second year. A. D. 1255, A. H. 653, to A. D. 1257, A. H. 655.

During the same time another Mogul attack on the Panjáb was repelled, and an expedition was afterwards undertaken against the revolted governor of Karrah Mánikpúr. A more difficult task was to put down the inhabitants of Méwát. The vizír went against them, and it was not without great exertion and some danger that he vanquished them in battle, and ultimately reduced their country. Ten thousand of the insurgents are said to have A. D. 1258, A. H. 656.

BOOK VI.

been slain. The fierce and turbulent mountaineers of Méwát, though their frontier was within twenty-
A. D. 1259, A. H. 657. five miles of Delhi, were never entirely quieted until the establishment of the British government.

The last event of the reign was the arrival of an ambassador from Holáku Khán, grandson of Chengíz Khán, and himself a very powerful monarch. Every exertion was made to give him an honourable reception, and the splendour of the court is described as worthy of the best days of
A. D. 1266, A. H. 664. the monarchy. No other occurrence is recorded until the death of the king in February, 1266.

Násir u dín's private life was that of a Dervise. He defrayed all his personal expenses by copying books: his fare was of the humblest description, and was cooked by the queen, to whom he allowed no female servant; he had only one wife, and no concubines. He was an eminent patron of Persian literature. The "Tabakáti Násiri," a general history of Persia and India, which still retains the highest celebrity, was written at his court, and takes its name from him.

An instance is told of his temper and courtesy. On showing one of the books he had transcribed to a nobleman of his court, the nobleman pointed out several mistakes, which the king immediately corrected. When the nobleman was gone, he was observed to erase the corrections and restore the old reading; and when asked his reason, he said he knew that the copy was right all the time, but thought it better to make the corrections than to hurt the feelings of a well-intentioned adviser. CHAP. I.

*Gheiás u dín Bulbun.**

A. D. 1266, A. H. 664.

Bulbun being already in possession of all the powers of king, found no difficulty in assuming the title.

Bulbun puts down the influence of the slaves.

He had been brought up from infancy at the court of Altamsh, and had taken an active part in all the intrigues and revolutions of the succeeding reigns. During the life of Altamsh, he had entered into a covenant for mutual support with forty of the king's other slaves, most of whom had attained to high stations. Having gained his own object, he desired to put an end to a system which would have endangered the succession of his family. He therefore, on various pretexts, made away with his surviving confederates (some of them his own near connections by marriage); and he henceforth made it an invariable rule to confer no office but on men of family. So ostentatiously did he exercise his new policy, that he affected a repugnance even to ordinary intercourse with people of low origin. He also made it a rule to exclude Hindús from all offices of trust. All his other acts partook of the same contracted spirit. He established laws for the preservation of game round his capital;

His character.

* Often called Balín by English writers.

BOOK VI.

and having exceeded in wine in his early life, he severely punished even the moderate use of it after he had reformed. In cases of rebellion, not satisfied with chastising the leaders, as had been usual, he extended capital punishment to the meanest of their vassals and retainers. Stories are told of his inflexible justice; but they consist in publicly whipping governors of provinces, and sometimes having them beaten to death in his presence.

This narrow-minded and selfish tyrant was raised, by circumstances, to the appearance of a liberal and enlightened monarch. The horrors of the Mogul invasion drove men of eminence from the countries to which it extended; and Bulbun's being the only Mahometan government that was not subverted, his court was filled with illustrious exiles of that religion. He used to boast that no less than fifteen sovereign princes had been dependent on his hospitality: he gave the names of their territories to the streets which they inhabited; and his capital long preserved those memorials of Rúm, Ghór, Khárizm, Bagdad, and other kingdoms.

The number of literary fugitives was naturally still more considerable; and as the king's eldest son, Prince Mohammed, was a young man of the greatest accomplishments, his palace was the resort of all the famous authors of that age. The chief, among many names well known in Persian literature, was the poet Amír Khúsru; on the possession of whose society the prince was congratulated by

CHAP. I.

Sádí *, who sent him a copy of his works, and regretted that his extreme old age prevented his accepting an invitation to Delhi. Bulbun himself had a turn for pomp and magnificence; so that his court was surrounded by an external splendour which blinded strangers to its real character.

A. D. 1266, A. H. 665.

He was disturbed by Hindú insurrections on the banks of the Jamna and Ganges, as well as in the mountains of Júd and Méwát. They were created by banditti for the sake of plunder: and here his exterminating system, backed by the erection of garrisons and other prudent precautions, seems to have operated effectually. In Méwát he is said to have put 100,000 persons to the sword; but he also cut down the forest over a great extent of country; and, from that time, it afforded support to the husbandman, instead of an asylum to the robber.

Revolt of Bengal.

His only serious rebellion was in Bengal. The governor, Tógral, having made a successful expedition against Jájnagar beyond the river Megna †, had refused to send any portion of the booty to Delhi, and soon after assumed the title of king. He totally defeated the first army sent against him, on which the king hanged the unsuccessful

A. D. 1279, A. H. 678.

* The celebrated moral poet; perhaps the best author Persia ever produced.

† Now Tipperah (*Hamilton's Hindostan*, vol. i. p. 178.). Jájnagar has been taken for Jájpúr in Cattack, which never was the head place of a district. (See Mr. Stirling, *Asiatic Researches*, vol. xv. p. 274.)

BOOK VI.

general. Another army having been routed in spite of this severity, he at length moved in person to put down the rebellion. He acted on this occasion with the vigour and ability in which he never was deficient: he set out without waiting till the end of the periodical rains, marched straight to Súnárgong* (or Súndergong), then capital of the eastern district of Bengal, and struck such terror into the rebel, that he evacuated the open country, and withdrew, with a strong body of troops, into the forests. His retreat was discovered by one of the king's chiefs, who came unexpectedly on the camp, and, though at the head of only forty men, took the desperate resolution of entering it in open day. His small troop advanced without attracting observation till they reached Tógral's tent, when they rushed on with loud shouts. Tógral and those around him fled with precipitation, imagining the whole of the royal army was upon them: the panic spread to the troops; the whole dispersed in confusion; and Tógral himself was overtaken and slain as he was endeavouring to swim his horse over a river, on his flight towards Jájnagar.

Suppressed.

The king punished this rebellion with more than his usual severity, and was only prevented going on with his executions after he had returned to his capital, by the intercession of the Cázis, Muftis, and other learned and venerable men.

Mogul irruption.

Not long after this he had the misfortune to lose

* It has since been swept away by the Ganges. (Buchanan, quoted by Hamilton, *Hindostan*, vol. i. p. 187.)

his eldest son; a calamity to his people no less than to himself. The prince's death was worthy of the high character he had acquired. An army of Moguls belonging to Arghún Khán, then king of Persia, had invaded the Panjáb, and Prince Mohammed, who was governor of the province, hastened thither from the capital, where he had gone to meet his father. He defeated the invaders, and had recovered all the country they had overrun, when a fresh army arrived of chosen troops under a celebrated general named Teimúr Khán. A sanguinary conflict took place, and the prince gained a complete victory; but was killed by a body of the enemy, who had kept together during the pursuit. Amír Khúsru, the poet, his constant companion, was taken prisoner on the same occasion.

Victory and death of the heir apparent.

This loss drew tears from the meanest soldier in the army, and touched the heart even of Bulbun. That monarch had now reached his eightieth year, and was fast sinking under the affliction that had fallen on him, when he summoned his second son, Bakarra Khán, to attend him on his death-bed. His son, finding him in less immediate danger than he expected, returned, without leave, to his province of Bengal; and Bulbun was so much offended that he sent for Kei Khusru, the son of Prince Mohammed, and immediately declared him his heir. Soon after this act the king died. The ministers, desirous of averting a civil war, proclaimed Kei

Death of Bulbun.

BOOK VI.

Kobád, the son of Bakarra Khán, and restored Khusru to his father's government of Multán.

A. D. 1286, A. H. 685.

Both the losing claimants appeared to acquiesce in this arrangement, and Kei Kobád mounted the throne without opposition.

Kei Kobád.

A. D. 1286, A. H. 685.

Intrigues and power of the vizír.

The new king, who was in his eighteenth year at his accession, gave way, without restraint, to the pleasures natural to his age. He was encouraged in his vices by his vizír, Nizám u dín, who entertained hopes of securing the crown for himself. As Kei Khusru stood immediately in the way of his design, he took advantage of some imprudence on his part to render him an object of jealousy to the king; and being thus secure of impunity, he procured his assassination. By similar arts he brought about the death or disgrace of all the ministers who were not his own creatures; and, as his wife's ascendancy was as great in the harem as his was in the court, he held the king entirely cut off from all knowledge but what he thought proper to impart.

Massacre of Mogul mercenaries.

Many Mogul adventurers had, at this time, taken service at Delhi: it was an object to Nizám u dín to alienate these useful auxiliaries from the king; and he worked on that prince's fears by pretending a correspondence between them and their hostile countrymen, until he induced him to invite their chiefs to a banquet, and put them treacherously to death.

King's interview with his father.

Before his schemes were matured, he was interrupted by the approach of the king's father, Bakarra Khán, who, hearing of the state of affairs, marched with an army to look after the interests of his family. The vizír easily prevailed on the king to move out to oppose him; but, when the armies drew near, Bakarra Khán appealed so strongly to his son's affections that the minister could no longer prevent an interview. He endeavoured to frustrate the effects of it by imposing many humiliating ceremonies on Bakarra Khán, to all which that prince submitted; until, after repeated obeisances, he found the king remaining unmoved on his throne; when, shocked by this unnatural behaviour, he burst into tears. This sight overpowered all the king's resolutions: he leaped from his throne, and ran to throw himself at his father's feet; and, the father hastening to prevent him, he fell on his neck, and they remained for some minutes weeping in each other's arms, while the whole court was almost as much affected as themselves. When the first transport was over, Kei Kobád seated his father on the throne, and showed him every mark of love and reverence. All thoughts of war were now at an end; but, after repeated interviews, Bakarra Khán found that the vizír's vigilance, and his power over the enfeebled mind of the king, rendered it impossible to subvert his authority by peaceful means; and, being unwilling, or unable, to resort to force, he returned to Bengal, and left his son to his fate.

BOOK VI.

Kei Kobád plunged anew into all sorts of debauchery; and to such excess, that, at that early age, he entirely broke his constitution and brought on an attack of palsy. Being now driven on reflection, he perceived all the dangers of his situation; and, unable to rid himself of his minister by honourable means, he had recourse to the lessons with which he had been made familiar, and succeeded, before long, in taking him off by poison.

Murder of the vizír.

The removal of this predominating influence served only to let loose a number of other enemies, all eager to seize on the power which the king was unable himself to retain.

The ascendancy of the slaves about the court had been destroyed by the policy of Bulbun, and the contest was now between the principal military leaders; and, as the native Indians were not yet of sufficient importance to form a party, the only competitors were the Tartar chiefs and those of the old kingdom of Ghazni or Ghór. The Khiljis seem, from the ability of their chief, or some advantage of their own, to have been at the head of the latter class: they prevailed over the Tartars, and Jelál u dín Khilji was raised to the throne, after the way had been opened for him by the assassination of Kei Kobád.*

The king dethroned and put to death.

A. D. 1288, A. H. 687.

* Ferishta calls the competitors of the Khiljis, *Moguls;* but it is impossible to believe in the ascendancy of that tribe, any more than in the disappearance of the Turks, at so early a period. The pretender set up by the Tartars was, moreover,

the son of Kei Kobád, a natural object of choice to them for his Túrki descent, but of aversion to the Moguls for his father's massacre of their chiefs.

The succession of kings of Delhi which commenced with Kutb u dín, is by some considered as a continuation of the line of Ghór; but most oriental writers include those princes, along with E'ldőz and one or two others, in a dynasty to which they give the name of "the slaves of the Sultans of Ghór."

HOUSE OF KHILJI.

CHAP. II.

JELÁL U DÍN KHILJI.*

BOOK VI.

JELÁL U DÍN was seventy years of age when he came to the government.

A. D. 1288, A. H. 687.

He affected extreme regret at having his high office forced on him, and professed the utmost respect and attachment for the memory of Gheiás u dín. He over-acted humility so far as to refuse to enter the royal palace on horseback, and to stand at his usual station in the court instead of occupying the throne. But he kept the infant son of the late king in custody, and put him to death as soon as he felt strong enough for such a measure.

Mild government of Jelál u dín.

If this last atrocity be imputed to him on false grounds, which is not improbable, we should be inclined to acquit him of hypocrisy in all his former professions; for, during the rest of his reign, his lenity to his enemies, both open and secret,

* For the origin of the Khiljis, see Book V. Chap. II., note near the end of the chapter. Though Túrks by descent, they had been so long settled among the Afgháns that they had almost become identified with that people: but they probably mixed more with other nations, or at least with their Túrki brethren, and would be more civilised than the generality of Afghán mountaineers.

was carried even to a fault; and he continued to retain the simplicity of his manners, and to associate with his old friends on the same footing of familiarity that he did when a private man. He had frequent parties of those friends, together with men eminent for wit or literature; and, on those occasions, he carried conviviality beyond the limits of the Mahometan law, though never beyond those of sobriety.

He had soon occasion to display his clemency. Malik Jáju, a nephew of Gheiás u dín, rebelled against him in his government of Karrah, and was joined by all the adherents of the house of Bulbun. They were soon strong enough to march to Delhi, but were defeated by the king's second son, Arkalli Khán; and all the chiefs, including Malik Jáju, were made prisoners.

The king immediately released them all, and sent Malik Jáju to Multán, where he allowed him a liberal establishment for the rest of his days. He soon after showed equal magnanimity towards a body of chiefs of his own tribe, who were detected in a plot against his life. Unfortunately he did not confine his lenity to personal injuries, but allowed so general an impunity to offenders, that the whole frame of the government became relaxed; governors withheld their tribute, neglected their duty, and abused their power; the roads and highways were infested by robbers, and bands of plunderers and insurgents interrupted the communication between different parts of the kingdom.

BOOK VI.

A. D. 1292, A. H. 691.

He marched, himself, into Málwa, to quell an insurrection of a more general character. He was successful in the main; yet, from his aversion to shed blood, combined with the feebleness of age, he hesitated to attack the principal fortresses of the rebels, and left his suppression of the revolt incomplete. He showed more vigour soon after, on an invasion of the Panjáb by a numerous host of Moguls, whom he engaged in person, and totally defeated.

With characteristic moderation, he granted peace to the vanquished enemy, and allowed the wreck of their army to retire unmolested. Three thousand Moguls on this occasion joined his standard, and soon after embraced the Mahometan religion. A place in the suburbs of Delhi, still called Móghúlpúra, was assigned for their residence.

A. D. 1293, A. H. 692.

In the next year he made another march to Málwa, which was as inconclusive as the first. His own weakness, however, began, at this time, to be made up for by the energy of his nephew, Alá u dín, governor of Karrah, a man of vigour and ability, quite exempt from all the scruples which sometimes obstructed his uncle's success. Having obtained permission to act against the insurgents in Bundélcand and the east of Málwa, he not only restrained their turbulence, but took several forts which had before been left to dependent princes, and gained such a booty as enabled him to make considerable additions to his army. The king received the intelligence of his success with great

Vigour of Alá u dín, the king's nephew.

CHAP. II.

satisfaction; and, although his favourite wife endeavoured to put him on his guard against the ambition of Alá u dín, he gave him the government of Oud, in addition to that which he before possessed, and allowed him to assemble an army, and to entertain many of the old adherents of the Bulbun family.

Alá u dín's invasion of the Deckan. A. D. 1294, A. H. 693.

Alá u dín's first employment of his force justified his uncle's confidence, and opened a new æra in the history of India. He resolved to attempt the hitherto untried adventure of an invasion of the Deckan; and setting out with 8000 chosen horse from Karrah, made his way through the extensive forests that still fill the space between that place and Berár; threw the princes, whose country he was approaching, off their guard, by pretending to have left his uncle in disgust; and, having thus reached to E'lichpúr, he turned to the west, and proceeded, by rapid marches, to Deógíri, the main object of his expedition. Deógíri (now Doulatabad) was the capital of Rámdeó, a prince of so great power that the Mahometans look on him as king of the Deckan, and who, in fact, was rája of Maharashtra, or the country of the Marattas.

It was probably owing to the natural indolence of the Rajpúts, and their deeming it dishonourable to attack each other without warning, that the Mussulman invaders so often found them unprepared for defence. Their example seems to have infected the other Hindú chiefs; for, on this occasion, the rája was in all the security of profound peace. He had no troops about him; and his wife and son had gone out of the city to a neighbouring temple. In the consternation which ensued, Rámdeó preserved presence of mind sufficient to assemble a body of 3000 or 4000 citizens and domestics. With these he made head against the enemy, and afforded some little time for defensive arrangements. He was obliged to give way before long, and retired into the strong hill fort close to the city, into which some provisions had hastily been thrown. The town was taken without resistance, and was given up to pillage. The merchants were tortured to make them disclose the treasures (the first instance mentioned in Mussulman history of this species of barbarity); and forty elephants, with some thousand horses of the rája's, fell into the hands of the enemy. Meanwhile, the fort was invested; and Alá u dín, having given out that his army was only the advanced guard of the king's, the arrival of which would speedily render all opposition unavailing, the rája became impatient to come to terms, and had actually concluded a treaty very favourable to the invaders, when his son, who had escaped being shut up with his father, returned at the head of an army suddenly assembled, but far exceeding that of the Mussùlmans in numbers. Trusting to this superiority, he disregarded the remonstrances of his father, and attacked Alá u dín. The result would have gone hard with the invader, if a small body of troops which he had left to observe the garrison had not opportunely fallen on the enemy, and, being taken for the expected main army under the king, created a confusion which could not be retrieved. After this victory, Alá u dín raised his demands; and as the rája expected reinforcements from his allies, the affair might have been prolonged more than was safe for Alá u dín, had not the garrison unexpectedly discovered that, in the hurry of victualling the fort, sacks of salt had been taken by mistake instead of sacks of grain, and consequently that their provisions were already nearly exhausted. This discovery made the rája more compliant: he agreed to an immense payment in money and jewels, besides the cession of Elichpúr and its dependencies; after which Alá u dín drew off through Candésh into Málwa.

Submission of Deógíri.

Alá u dín's march to Deógíri was about 700 miles, great part of it through the mountains and forests of the Vindya range, which so completely separates Hindostan from the Deckan. The narrow and intricate paths, the want of supplies, and the danger of exposure to the arrows of the mountaineers, made the passage difficult for a small force, and impossible for a large one; while the entry into so great and populous a country as the Deckan with no more than 8000 men, seemed an act of rashness rather than courage.

To have surmounted these dangers, and obviated, by exploring a new route, the increased difficulty of returning by the same, give a high impression of the military talents of Alá u dín. The pretext

BOOK VI.

he used on his advance, that he was on his way to enter the service of the Hindú rája of Rájamandri, shows how much religious distinctions were weakened since the settlement of the Mahometans in India.

Return to Hindostan.

This expedition had been undertaken without leave; and as all communication had been cut off while it continued, Jelál u dín remained in suspense and anxiety, both as to the fate and the designs of his nephew; and when he heard that he was on his return, loaded with treasures and covered with glory, he felt nothing but delight at the intelligence. The more sagacious of his advisers took a different view of the matter; and, seeing fresh proofs of the daring spirit of Alá u dín, as well as of the resources at his disposal, they advised the king to adopt such measures of precaution as, without showing distrust, should prevent his assembling another army when the present should have dispersed to lay up their spoils. The generous temper of the king led him to disregard all these admonitions, and laid him open to the insidious designs of Alá u dín, who now affected alarm from the cabals of his enemies, and fear of the king's displeasure for his unauthorised expedition. He sent his brother, Alaf Khán, as crafty an intriguer as himself, and remarkable for his insinuating address, to deprecate his uncle's resentment, and induce him to meet Alá u dín in such a manner, as, under pretence of affording security to his nephew, should, in fact, leave none to himself. By degrees, he was persuaded to move with his army towards Karrah; then to advance with a small escort, and at last to cross the Ganges almost alone. Alá u dín fell at his feet, and the affectionate old man was patting him on the cheek, and reproaching him with having distrusted an uncle who had brought him up from his infancy and loved him better than his own sons, when Alá u dín made a signal to assassins posted for the purpose, who rushed forward and stabbed the king to the heart. His head was stuck on a spear and carried aloft through the camp and city. Ferishta shows a natural pleasure in relating the calamities which pursued the subordinate actors in this horrid tragedy to their graves; but that retribution affords little satisfaction while we continue to witness the uninterrupted prosperity of the parricide in whom the whole of this detestable act of perfidy had its rise.

Assassination of Jelál u dín. A. D. 1295, July 19. A. H. 695, Ramzan 17.

As Jelál u dín had reigned upwards of seven years, he must have been more than seventy-seven when he was killed.

A singular incident occurred in this reign, which shows the credulity of the Asiatics even at a period not remarkable for superstition. A dervise named Sidi Moula, a native of Persia, who had travelled through many countries, and was acquainted with most men of eminence in his day, arrived at Delhi, and instituted a school and an almshouse, where travellers, religious mendicants, and persons of all descriptions, were entertained at his expense. He

Singular instance of credulity and injustice.

BOOK VI.

lived on rice alone, and had neither wife nor slaves of either sex; yet his expenses were such as would have exceeded the means of the wealthiest nobleman. Besides his profuse dispensation of charity, he entertained the great men with splendour at his house, and did not hesitate to bestow sums of two or three thousand pieces of gold to relieve noble families in distress. Although he held some peculiar opinions, and among others never attended public worship, yet his piety remained unquestioned; and even among the suspicions to which his conduct gave birth, the cry of heresy was never raised against him. The first surmise regarding him was that he possessed the philosopher's stone; the next took a more dangerous form, and represented him as aiming at the crown; and this at last appeared in the definite shape of an accusation that he had prepared assassins to make away with the king, and had 10,000 of his votaries ready to profit by the confusion. The mysterious nature of the danger seems to have frightened the king out of his natural moderation. On the accusation of an alleged accomplice he apprehended Sidi Moula, and his most considerable associate; and, being unable to convict them on the evidence of one suspected witness, he ordered a large fire to be made on a plain before the town, to allow them to prove their innocence by an ordeal which they probably had appealed to. When the time came, the ministers raised their voices against the proceeding as equally opposed to Mahometan law and to natural reason; and the king giving way to their remonstrances, ordered the accused persons to be kept in confinement. As they were leading them away to prison, some Calenders (a sort of religious mendicants), countenanced, if not instigated, by the king, fell on Sidi Moula, and put him to death in the royal presence. With his last breath he protested his innocence, and denounced the curse that impended over his oppressor. Jelál u dín was greatly troubled at the moment: a dark whirlwind which happened just then to arise increased the general horror; and the death of the king's eldest son, which took place soon after, together with a failure of the rains and a famine which followed, as well as the awful termination of the monarch's own life, and the exclusion of his immediate family from the throne, were ascribed to the Divine vengeance for this act of impiety and injustice.

Alá u dín.

When the accounts of the late king's death reached Delhi, his widow made a feeble attempt to set up her own son, an infant, in his place: on the approach of Alá u dín she fled to Multán, where the only other surviving son of Jelál u dín was governor; but the whole family were inveigled from this asylum by means of a fallacious promise, when the two princes were put to death and the queen imprisoned. A. D. 1295, A. H. 695.

Alá u dín studiously endeavoured to recover the

BOOK VI.

goodwill of his people, by his just exercise of the power he had obtained by so many atrocities. He was liberal in bestowing wealth and honours, and was profuse in gifts as well as in shows and magnificence: but as in the midst of his course of conciliation he could not refrain from acts of rapacity, and never repressed his arbitrary temper, he was only partially successful in his attempts to gain popularity; and although his reign was long and glorious, he was always disturbed by conspiracies and rebellions, and disquieted by suspicions even of his own family and of those most trusted by him.

A. D. 1297, A. H. 697. Expedition to Guzerát.

His first great undertaking was an expedition to Guzerát. Shaháb u dín's garrison had long been withdrawn, and the rája had recovered his independence. The present conquest was final. Alif Khán, the king's brother, and his vizír, Núsrat Khán, who were at the head of the army, almost immediately took possession of the province; the rája flying to Báglána, the nearest part of the Deckan.

A harsh attempt to compel the troops to give up their plunder, while on their return towards Delhi, brought on a dangerous mutiny, in which the vizír's brother and the king's nephew lost their lives. It was at last quelled, and many of the mutineers were killed; the survivors took refuge with the rája of Rintambór. Their families, including the women and children, were massacred by the king's order. The fugitives themselves,

CHAP. II.

who appear to have been Mogul converts (always the chief actors in scenes of turbulence in those days), were put to death when Rintambór was taken.*

Mogul incursions.

During the preceding year an incursion of the Moguls into the Panjáb had been repulsed with loss; and another, equally unsuccessful, took place about this time. It was followed up by a more serious invasion, apparently designed for conquest as well as plunder.† The commander was Kutlugh

* The emperor Báber, who, though a Túrk, was himself descended by the mother's side from Mogul ancestors, gives the following account of the Moguls in his service: — "The horde of Moguls have uniformly been the authors of every kind of mischief and devastation: down to the present time they have five times rebelled against me." (*Erskine's Báber*, p. 69.)

† At least eleven of these invasions are mentioned by Ferishta, not one of which is noticed by De Guignes, D'Herbelot, or Price, in their accounts of the Mogul transactions; and although there is a long list in D'Ohson (vol. iv. p. 559.), yet they are all given on the authority of Ferishta.

It is not improbable that the cruel ravages by which they were marked may have led the Indian historians to overrate the importance of the ordinary incursions; but, in some instances, especially in the present one, the silence of the European writers may perhaps be ascribed to the imperfect information they possess respecting Mogul affairs in the east of Persia and in Transoxiana.

The commander of the last expedition is called Chóldí Khán by Ferishta; and Touldai Khán was one of the officers of Gházán Khán, then king of Persia. (Price, vol. ii. p. 605.)

The most conspicuous general of the same monarch was Kutlugh Sháh, who was at Herát in this year, A. D. 1297 (Price, vol. ii. p. 616., and De Guignes, vol. iii. p. 270.), and might possibly have led an expedition to India, though circumstances make it improbable. Opposed to this coincidence of

BOOK VI.

Serious invasion by the Moguls.

Khán, whom Ferishta describes as the son of Dáúd Khán, king of Transoxiana. He marched straight to Delhi, the Indian army which had been sent to oppose him retreating as he advanced, and the whole population of the surrounding country flying to the capital.

So great was the crowd of fugitives that all communication through the streets was interrupted; the provisions were almost immediately consumed, and in a few days famine was added to the miseries and terrors of the inhabitants.

Alá u dín was forced in these circumstances to give up his intention of declining an action. He moved out at the head of all the troops he could collect; and Ferishta alleges that the number of men assembled on both sides exceeded all that ever appeared in one place in India up to the time when he wrote.

Their defeat at Delhi.

This most important contest was gained by Alá u dín, almost entirely from the skill displayed by Zafar Khán, who was before the most distinguished of his generals. But the great services of that

---

names, which would lead us to suppose these invasions to have been made by the Moguls of Persia, is the positive assertion of Ferishta, that they and all the subsequent inroads originated in Dáúd Khán, king of Transoxiana, who, by his account, was the father of Kutlugh Khán. Dáúd Khán is evidently the Doizi or Davat Khán mentioned by De Guignes (vol. iii. p. 311., and note) as king of Transoxiana; and Kutlugh is so common a Mogul name, that two persons may very probably have borne it at the same time. There does not, therefore, seem to be any ground for doubting Ferishta's account.

gallant chief had already rendered him an object of jealousy to Alá u dín, and no less to Alíf Khán, who purposely left him unsupported during the pursuit; and the Moguls, perceiving his reduced numbers, turned upon him and cut him to pieces, with his detachment, after a resistance worthy of his former exploits.

A. D. 1299, A. H. 699.

About a year after this deliverance, Alá u dín dispatched an army, under his brother and the vizír, to reduce the hill fort of Rintambór.* They took a place called Jháyin, not far from Rintambór, and proceeded to lay siege to that fortress. In the commencement of the operations the vizír was killed by a stone from an engine; and the garrison, making a sally, compelled the besiegers to fall back on Jháyin, and wait for reinforcements from Delhi. Alá u dín, on this, determined to prosecute the siege in person, and had made some progress on his march, when he had nearly fallen a victim to a crime of which he had himself set the example. His nephew, Prince Solimán, who held one of the highest offices in the state, reflecting on the resemblance between his own situation and that from which the present king had risen to the throne, was led to think that a similar attempt on his part might be attended with equal success. A favourable opportunity soon presented itself, when

Designs of the king's nephew.

He attempts to assassinate the king.

* It does not appear when this place was lost. It was besieged by insurgents, and defended by the king of Delhi's troops, in A. D. 1259.

BOOK VI.

the king was hunting at a distance from the camp, and was left with only two or three attendants, in consequence of the occupations of the chase. At this moment, Solimán approached him with some of the newly converted Moguls; and before he had any suspicion of their purpose, they discharged their arrows at him with such effect that he fell senseless on the ground. Solimán, conceiving that his object was accomplished, gallopped directly to the camp, announced the king's death, and his own accession, and directed himself to be formally proclaimed. While he was seated on his throne, and receiving the homage of the great officers, Alá u dín came gradually to himself; and, after his wounds were bound up, determined to proceed to join his brother at Jháyin. He was dissuaded from this by one of his officers, who advised him not to give his nephew time to establish his authority, but to show himself to the army, whose fidelity he had no reason to distrust. Alá u dín saw the wisdom of his advice, and mounting his horse, wounded as he was, he proceeded towards the camp. He met some foraging parties on his way, by which his retinue was increased to about 500 horse. With this escort he presented himself on an eminence, in full view of the camp, and displayed the white umbrella, which was then the sign of sovereignty. He was no sooner perceived than the whole army flocked to join him; and the usurper, finding him-

His failure and death.

self left almost alone, mounted his horse, and sought for safety in a precipitate flight. He was overtaken, and his head brought to the king, who put the other conspirators to death.

Other disturbances quelled.

The king then proceeded to join his brother, and soon after resumed the siege of Rintambór. But his utmost efforts were insufficient to take the place; and, before long, he received intelligence of the revolt of two of his other nephews, at Badáyun. He did not think it necessary to move himself on this occasion: he suppressed the rebellion by means of his officers; and when his nephews were sent to him, he first put out their eyes, and afterwards ordered them to be beheaded.

The ill success of these rebellions did not prevent the occurrence of another of a still more extraordinary character. Háji Moula, a young slave of one of the principal families in Delhi, took advantage of some discontent against the chief magistrate of police to collect a mob and put him to death, under pretence of an order from the king; and having thus got a body of infuriated followers, he proceeded to take possession of the city, to release the prisoners, distribute the royal arms and treasures among his adherents, and to set up a prince of the royal family for king. The decided conduct of a local officer prevented the ill effects of this explosion. He contrived to introduce a body of troops into the capital, killed Háji Moula, dispersed his rabble, and put his new king to death.

Many executions followed by the king's order; and, amongst others, the whole family of Háji

BOOK VI.

Moula's former master, men, women, and children, were slaughtered, without a charge against them.

At length, Rintambór fell after a siege of more than a year. The rája, with his family, and the garrison, were put to the sword.

A. D. 1300, A. H. 700. A. D. 1303, A. H. 703. Capture of Chitór.

In the year 1303, Alá u dín went, in person, against Chitór, a celebrated hill fort in Méwár, and the principal seat of the Rájpút tribe of Sesódia. He took the fort, made the rája prisoner, and left the eldest of his own sons as governor. Next year the rája escaped, and made himself so formidable, that Alá u dín found it prudent to make over the fort to another Rájpút prince, named Máldeó, who, by Ferishta's account, was a nephew of the rája, but who is represented by the Rájpúts as a person of another family. Máldeó remained tributary to Delhi until near the end of Alá u dín's reign, when he was expelled by Hamír, a son of the former rája.*

Unsuccessful invasions of the Moguls.

Alá u dín was recalled from these conquests by a new Mogul invasion and another attack on Delhi. His force was so much weakened by detachments, that when he arrived at the capital he was unable to meet the enemy in the field, and obliged to intrench his camp.

The Moguls, who, probably, were not prepared for protracted operations, withdrew without a

* The descendant of this family is now rána of Oudipúr, the chief of the Rájpút princes.

CHAP. II.

battle; and their retreat was ascribed, by the piety of the age, to a panic sent among them on the prayer of Nizám u dín Oulia, a celebrated saint then alive.

A. D. 1304-5, A. H. 704-5.

In the next two years there were three Mogul inroads, one of which penetrated, by the north of the Panjáb, into Róhilcand.

On all those occasions the prisoners were sent to Delhi, where the chiefs were trampled to death by elephants, and the men butchered in cold blood.*

Discontinuance of their incursions.

These were the last Mogul invasions for many years.

Expedition to the Deckan.

Though Alá u dín's continual occupation since his accession had, in some measure, withdrawn his attention from the Deckan, he had not forgotten the scene of his early exploits. At the time of his own expedition to Chitór (A. D. 1303, A. H. 703), he sent an army through Bengal, to attack Warangól, the capital of Télingána, situated to the south of the river Godáveri; and he now prepared a great force, for the purpose of reducing the rája of Deógíri, who had, of late, withheld his tribute. Malik Cáfúr, who commanded this army, was a eunuch, and had been the slave of a merchant at Cambay, from whom he was taken, by force, during the conquest of Guzerát. Having come into the king's possession, he so completely won his master's affections that he rose to the highest offices, and excited the utmost disgust

* Ferishta says 9000 on one occasion.

BOOK VI.

A. D. 1306, A. H. 706.

among the nobles by his rapid promotion from so base an origin. He now proceeded through Málwa, and by Sultánpúr in Cándésh, to Deógíri. Before he commenced the siege, he overran the greater part of the Maratta country; and so impressed Rám Deó with the impossibility of resistance, that he came out of his fortress, and agreed to accompany Cáfúr to Delhi. He was there received with favour, returned loaded with honours, and from that time forward remained faithful to the Mussulmans. A circumstance occurred during this expedition which deserves to be mentioned.

Story of the Princess Déwal Dévi.

Alp Khán, governor of Guzerát (who must be distinguished from A'lif Khán, the king's brother), had been directed to march to Deógíri, to cooperate with Cáfúr. His road lay through Báglána, where the fugitive rája of Guzerát had taken refuge, as has been related. This rája's wife, Cáula Dévi, had been taken prisoner during his flight, and having been carried to Alá u dín's harem, had gained a great share of his favour by her beauty and talents. On hearing of the intended march of these forces, she entreated that means might be taken to recover her daughter by the rája, who still remained with the exile prince. Alp Khán was enjoined to attend to this object, and endeavoured, by the offer of favourable terms, to prevail on the rája to give up his daughter. The rája rejected his overtures, and Alp Khán marched against him. The princess, whose name was Déwal Dévi*, had long been sued for by the son of Rám Deó, the rája of Deógíri; but her father, considering a Maratta, however high in station, as an unworthy match for the daughter of a Rájpút, had rejected all his offers. In the present extremity, however, he gave a reluctant consent, and the princess was sent off, with an escort, to Deógíri. Immediately after her departure, Alp Khán succeeded in defeating and dispersing the rája's army. His victory afforded him little satisfaction, when he found that the princess had escaped him; and knowing the influence of Cáula Dévi, and the impetuous temper of the king, he gave up his whole attention to the means of accomplishing an object which they had both so much at heart. His utmost efforts were not attended with success; and he had arrived within a march of Deógíri without hearing any tidings of the princess, when a party who had gone from his camp to see the caves of Ellóra happened, by mere chance, to fall in with her escort; and being under the necessity of fighting in self-defence, they dispersed the escort, and captured the princess, before they were aware of the importance of their acquisition. Alp Khán, delighted with his prize, immediately marched with her to Delhi. Her beauty made such an impression on the king's eldest son, Khizr Khán, that he soon after married her; and their loves are the subject of a celebrated Persian poem, by Amír Khusru.

This incident is remarkable, as showing the intermixture which had already taken place between

BOOK VI.

the Hindús and Mahometans; and also as leading to the first mention of the caves of Ellóra, which have been compared, as works of labour, to the pyramids of Egypt, and which, in reality, far surpass them as specimens of art.

During this expedition of Cáfúr, the king, in person, reduced Jhálór and Sewána, places in Márwár, to the north of Guzerát.

A. D. 1309, A. H. 709. Failure of an expedition to Télingána.

After the return of Cáfúr, according to Ferishta, Alá u dín received accounts of the failure of his expedition to Warangól. He had been induced to send it by an unexplored route from Bengal, in consequence of the solicitation of the rája of Orissa, who had become jealous of the extension of his neighbour's power.* It is not recorded how it failed, or how the contest was so long protracted. Cáfúr was sent to retrieve the disaster. He marched by Deógíri, ravaged the north of Télingána, gained a great victory in the field, took the strong fort of Warangól after a siege of some months, and compelled the rája to pay a large contribution and submit to permanent tribute.

A. D. 1310, A. H. 710. Conquest of Carnáta.

Next year Cáfúr was again sent to the Deckan, against the Belál rája of Carnáta.† He marched by Deógíri, crossed the Godáveri, at Peitan, and penetrated, after a great battle, to Dwára Samúdra, the capital, which he took; and, having made the

* Wilson's Introduction to the Mackenzie Catalogue, p. cxxxii. For an account of the principality of Warangól, see book iv. chap. 2.

† See book iv. chap. 2.

rája prisoner, put an end to the dynasty of Belál.*

and of Maáber, up to Cape Comorin.

He does not appear to have invaded the western part of the Belál possessions; but he reduced the whole of their eastern territory, including Maáber on the sea-coast, as far south as Rámeshwar, or Adam's Bridge, opposite Ceylon. He there built a mosque, which was still standing when Ferishta wrote.†

* Wilson's Introduction to the Mackenzie Collection, p. cxiii. Dwára Samúdra was situated in the heart of Carnáta, about 100 miles north-west of Seringapatam, where its ruins still remain. (*Buchanan's Journey*, vol. iii. p. 391.)

† Briggs's Ferishta, vol. i. p. 373. Maáber (the place of crossing over) has very generally been supposed to be Malabár, as well from the resemblance of the names as from the position of the latter country in reference to Arabia; but there is no doubt that the appellation really applies to the tract on the opposite coast, extending north from Rámeshwar. (See *Marsden's Marco Polo*, p. 626. note.) That Maáber in this sense was included in the Belál kingdom, appears from Professor Wilson's Introduction to the Mackenzie Collection, vol. i. p. cxi. It remained united to Delhi for twenty or thirty years, till near the middle of the fourteenth century; about which time Ibn Batúta crossed from Ceylon to Maáber, and found it in the possession of a Mahometan family, who had shortly before acquired it, in consequence of the revolt of Jelál u dín Hasan, a sheríf or seiad, who had been a subject of Mohammed Tóghlak. The revolt of Seiad Hasan in Maáber against Mohammed Tóghlak is also mentioned by Ferishta. (Briggs, vol. i. p. 423.) It is not probable that Cáfúr conquered the western territory of the Belála; because it appears from Wilks's *Mysore* that the remains of that family retired to Tónúr near Seringapatam; and Ibn Batúta found Malabár (which he visited on his way to, and on his return from, Maáber) in the hands of Hindú princes, except Honáwar, which was held by a Mussulman under the

BOOK VI.

After this expedition, Cáfúr returned, with vast treasures, to Delhi.*

Massacre of Mogul converts.

A. D. 1311, A. H. 711.

It seems to have been about this time that Alá u dín at once discharged the whole of the Mogul converts from his service. Though habitually turbulent, they seem to have given no immediate occasion for this violent and imprudent measure. Being now driven to despair, some of them entered on a plot to assassinate the king; and on its being detected, the king ordered the whole of them (amounting, according to Ferishta, to 15,000) to be massacred, and their families to be sold for slaves.

A. D. 1312, A. H. 712.

Taking of Deógíri, and conquest of Maharashtra.

Rám Deó had died before, or during, Cáfúr's last expedition; and his son, who succeeded him, was already suspected of disaffection. He now withheld his tribute; and some disturbances having likewise taken place in Carnáta, Cáfúr once more set out to quell them. He put the rája of Deógíri to death, and carried his arms over all Maharashtra and Carnáta, compelling those princes who still retained their territories to pay tribute; and, after

sovereignty of a Hindú. The Mussulman religion had been introduced in that quarter from Arabia, some centuries before Alá u dín's invasion of the Deckan; and it did not become the dominant one until the conquest of Malabár by Heider Ali.

* Ferishta states that, at this time, there was no silver coinage in the Carnatic; and Colonel Briggs observes that the same was true, to a certain extent, till very lately: the common coin was the pagoda, and there was a small coin called a gold fanam, as low in value as a sixpence.

accomplishing all the objects of his expedition, he returned again to Delhi.

Intrigues and influence of Cáfúr.

Alá u dín's constitution had by this time yielded to a long course of intemperance. His ill health made him more suspicious and irritable than ever; and, like most people who distrust the bulk of mankind, he was the dupe of one artful individual. This was Cáfúr, the extent of whose abilities was equalled by the depravity of his principles. The use he made of his influence was to destroy all who he thought might rival him in favour, and afterwards to irritate the king against his sons, and the queen their mother, who might otherwise have found means to reconcile him to his children. Cáfúr first encouraged him in the notion that he was slighted and neglected by them in his illness, and at last infused suspicions that they were plotting against his life. Alá u dín, notwithstanding his unfeeling nature, seems to have had some affection for his offspring; so that it was not till near his end that Cáfúr prevailed on him, by innumerable artifices, to commit the two eldest princes and the queen to prison. At the same time Cáfúr procured an order to make away with Alp Khán, whose power he dreaded, and thus to remove the only remaining obstacle to his seizing on the government on his master's death.

Meanwhile the king's blind subjection to his favourite, and the increased tyranny of his administration, excited general discontent. The nobles of the court were disgusted. Guzerát broke into

BOOK VI.

Revolt of Guzerát. Recovery of Chitór by the Rájpúts.

open rebellion. It was at this time that Chitór was recovered by rána Hamír; and Harpál, the son-in-law of Rámdeó, raised an extensive insurrection in the Deckan, and expelled many Mahometan garrisons.

Death of Alá u dín. A. D. 1316, Dec. 19. A. H. 716, Shawál 6.

The paroxysms of rage produced by a succession of these tidings increased the king's sufferings, and soon brought him to the brink of the grave. His end is said to have been accelerated by poison, administered by Cáfúr.

His character.

So great is the effect of vigour in a despotism, that although Alá u dín was ignorant and capricious, as well as cruel and tyrannical, yet his foreign conquests were among the greatest ever made in India, and his internal administration, in spite of many absurd and oppressive measures, was, on the whole, equally successful. Quiet and security prevailed throughout the provinces; wealth increased, and showed itself in public and private buildings, and in other forms of luxury and improvement. Alá u dín was so absolutely illiterate, that he began to learn to read after he had been for some time on the throne; yet so arrogant, that his most experienced ministers durst not venture to contradict him, and the best informed men about his court were careful to keep down their knowledge to the level of his acquirements. Nor did this presumption wear off with his youth: it increased in his latter days to such a pitch, that every word he uttered was considered as irrevocable. In the commencement of his career of prosperity, he enter-

CHAP. II.

tained thoughts of setting up for a prophet, and founding a new religion; and when he had laid aside that fancy, he assumed the title of "The Second Alexander," and publicly discussed a project of universal conquest.

His internal policy.

Some curious features are preserved of his policy, and that of his age.

At the time when he had been so often threatened by conspiracies, he called his counsellors together to consider the causes and the remedy. They traced his danger to three principal sources: —convivial meetings, where men opened their secret thoughts to each other; connections between great nobles, especially by intermarriages; and, above all, the unequal distribution of property, and the accumulation of wealth by governors of provinces. The king concurred in these opinions: he forbade the use of wine, and prohibited all private meetings and political discussions among the nobles of his court, till, at length, no man could entertain his friends without a written order from the vizír. No marriage among the nobility was allowed without a licence from the crown. Farmers were limited to a certain quantity of land, and a certain number of cattle and servants. Graziers, in like manner, were restricted as to the number of their flocks and herds. Official emoluments were reduced; the land tax was increased, and more rigorously exacted; and, at last, the king became so rapacious, that the private property both of Mussulmans and Hindús was confiscated without a cause, so that men were almost reduced to a level over all the empire.*

Among other measures of Alá u dín's, one was for fixing rates for the prices of all articles. This plan originated in a wish to reduce the pay of the troops, which the king thought would be unjust unless the expense of living was lowered likewise. Accordingly, prices were fixed for grain, cattle, horses, &c., and for all other commodities, which were classed for the purpose.† Everything was included except labour. Public granaries were constructed; importation was encouraged; exportation forbidden; money was advanced to merchants to enable them to import goods. Wholesale purchases were not allowed; hours were fixed for opening and shutting shops; and the whole was rendered effective by public reports to the king, and the employment of spies and informers to detect breaches of the regulation.

A dearth which ensued soon after occasioned a relaxation in enforcing the rules about grain; and the others, though not rescinded till the next reign, were probably in a great measure neglected after the king had cooled on his scheme.

One of Alá u dín's maxims was, that "religion

* It is difficult to reconcile this statement, the last words of which are Ferishta's, with the same author's glowing account of the general prosperity; but it is probable the unfavourable picture only applies to the last years of the reign.

† Tables of the prices are given in Ferishta, and would be interesting if the value of the coins could be better ascertained.

had no connection with civil government, but was only the business, or rather amusement, of private life;" and another, that "the will of a wise prince was better than the opinions of variable bodies of men."

Alá u dín had reigned upwards of twenty years.

Mobárik Khilji.

On the death of Alá u dín, Cáfúr produced a pretended will of that prince, appointing his youngest son, an infant, to be his successor, under the guardianship of Cáfúr.

Having thus gained possession of the government, Cáfúr put out the eyes of the king's two eldest sons, and not long after sent assassins to murder the third son, Mobárik. The assassins, however, were won over and induced to spare him; and before Cáfúr had time to take further measures, he was himself assassinated by the royal guard, headed by their commander and his lieutenant.

Mobárik was immediately raised to the government. He did not assume the title of king for two months, at the end of which time he deprived his infant brother of sight, and sent him to a hill fort for life. A. D. 1317, March 22. A. H. 717, Moharrem 7.

He next put to death the two officers who had placed him on the throne, and broke up the guard. He raised several of his slaves to high rank and office, and made one of them, a converted Hindú, to whom he gave the title of Khusru Khán, his

BOOK VI.

vizír; so that his first acts gave an earnest of the bloody and licentious reign that was to follow.

These misdeeds were not entirely unmixed with good actions; he set free all prisoners, to the number of 17,000; a sweeping measure, which could only have been commendable after a reign like the preceding. He restored the lands confiscated by Alá u dín, removed his oppressive taxes, and abolished his restrictions on trade and property.

His military proceedings in the early part of his reign were not less meritorious. He sent an army to reduce Guzerát, and marched, himself, to the Deckan, where he took Harpál prisoner, and in-

A. D. 1318, A. H. 718.

humanly ordered him to be flayed alive. Having completely restored tranquillity, he returned to Delhi, and gave himself up to a course of the most degrading and odious debauchery. One of his amusements was to accompany a troop of actresses in a female habit, and to dance along with them at the houses of the nobility. He was in a constant state of intoxication; and his chief delight appeared to be to display his worst vices to the public. It is not surprising that under such a prince there should be a continual succession of conspiracies and rebellions; each of which was followed by tortures and executions, and each gave rise to fresh suspicions, and additional acts of tyranny.

Conquest of Malabár.

During his expedition to the Deckan, he sent his favourite Khusru to conquer Malabár, which he effected in the course of a year, and brought a great treasure to Delhi. The whole administration of the government was then confided to him, and every man's life and fortune was at his mercy. He put some of the nobility to death, and struck such a terror into the rest, that they thought themselves fortunate in being allowed to quit the court, and leave the king to the machinations of his favourite. The opportunity was not lost on Khusru, who surrounded the king with his creatures, and filled the capital with Hindú troops of his own cast, until at length, when his plot was matured, he perpetrated the murder of his infatuated master, and at once assumed the vacant throne. He put to death all the survivors of the family of Alá u dín, and transferred Déwal Dévi to his own seraglio. His other measures were in the same spirit. But, notwithstanding his infamous character and his manifold crimes, he did not fail to obtain adherents, and to strengthen his party. He not only brought his own low creatures into power, but endeavoured to gain over the established nobles, by investing them with some of the highest offices. Among this number was Júna Khán, the son of Gházi Khán Tóghlak, governor of the Panjáb, whose reputation and influence made it of the utmost consequence to conciliate him. In this Khusru failed. Júna Khán fled from court, and Gházi Khán went into open rebellion; and, marching to Delhi with the veteran troops of the frontier, he gained a victory over the dissolute and ill-commanded bands opposed to him, and put an end to the reign and life of the usurper, to the universal joy of the people.

CHAP. II.

A. D. 1318, A. H. 719. Influence of Khusru, and ascendancy of a Hindú party at court.

A. D. 1321. March 24. A. H. 721, Rabi ul áwal. Murder of Mobárik, and extirpation of his family.

A. D. 1321. Aug. 22. A. H. 721, Rejéb 30.

BOOK VI.

On entering Delhi, Gházi Khán made a declaration that his only object was to deliver the country from oppression, and that he was willing to place any of the royal line on the throne. No member of the Khilji family was found to have survived, and Tóghlak was himself proclaimed under the title of Gheiás u dín.

CHAP. III.

HOUSE OF TÓGHLAK, SEIADS, AND HOUSE OF LÓDI.

HOUSE OF TÓGHLAK.

Gheiás u dín Tóghlak.

CHAP. III.

Gheiás u dín Tóghlak was the son of a Turkí slave of Gheiás u dín *Bulbun*, by an Indian mother.

A. D. 1321, A. H. 721.

His whole reign was as commendable as his accession was blameless. He began by restoring order in his internal administration, and by putting his frontier in an effective state of defence against the Moguls. He then sent his son, Júna Khán, to settle the Deckan, where affairs had fallen into disorder. Júna Khán's operations were successful, until he reached Warangól, on the fortifications of which place he was unable to make any impression: the siege was protracted until the setting in of the hot winds, and perhaps till the first burst of the rainy season; a malignant distemper broke out in his camp; and his troops, already depressed by these disasters, were alarmed by false reports of the death of the king, and a revolution at Delhi. At length, some of his principal officers deserted him with their troops; and the prince himself, endeavouring to retreat with the rest, was pressed by

A. D. 1322, A. H. 722

Failure of an expedition to Telingána.

the Hindús, and pursued with great slaughter, towards Doulatábád. He only brought back 3000 horse, out of his whole army, to Delhi. Júna Khán proved himself so indiscreet and self-willed in his own reign, that it is difficult to help ascribing a share of his failure, in this instance, to himself.

Conquest of Telingána. Capture of Warangól, the capital. A. D. 1323, A. H. 723.

He was more successful in his next attempt; he took Bidr, a place of strength and importance; and afterwards reduced Warangól, and brought the rája prisoner to Delhi.*

A. D. 1324-5. A. H. 724-5.

After this the king proceeded in person to Bengal, where Bakarra Khán, the father of the former king, Kei Kobád, still retained his government, after a lapse of forty years. He was now confirmed in possession, and permitted the use of royal ornaments, by the son of his father's former slave.

The king also settled some disturbances in Súnárgong (now Dacca †), which seems to have been a province independent of Bengal. On his way back, he reduced Tirhút (formerly Mithila), and took the rája prisoner.

Death of the king.

As he approached the capital, he was met by his eldest son Júna Khán, who received him with magnificence in a wooden pavilion erected for the occasion. During the ceremonies, the building gave way, and the king, with five other persons, was crushed in its fall. This misfortune may have been purely accidental; but the unusualness of erecting

* The rája was afterwards released and restored.

† Hamilton's Hindostan, vol. i. p. 187.

such a structure at all, the opportune absence of the eldest prince at the moment, and the circumstance of the second, who was his father's favourite, being involved in the same calamity, fixed strong suspicions on the successor, in whose favour every thing turned out so well.*

CHAP. III.

A. D. 1325, February. A. H. 725, Rabi ul áwal.

The fort or castle of Tóghlakábád, which is remarkable even at Delhi for its massive grandeur, was built by Gheiás u dín.

Mohammed Tóghlak.

A. D. 1325, A. H. 725. Character of Mohammed Tóghlak.

Júna Khán, who assumed the name of Sultán Mohammed, took possession of his dignity with extraordinary magnificence; and distributed gifts and pensions to his friends, and to men of learning, with a profusion never before equalled.

He established hospitals and almshouses on the same liberal scale; and throughout his whole reign his munificence to the learned was such as to deserve and to obtain their warmest expressions of praise.

It is admitted, on all hands, that he was the most eloquent and accomplished prince of his age. His letters, both in Arabic and Persian, were admired for their elegance, long after he had ceased to reign. His memory was extraordinary; and besides a thorough knowledge of logic, and the philosophy of the Greeks, he was much attached to mathematics and to physical science; and used

* See *Ibn Batuta*, p. 130.

himself to attend sick persons, for the purpose of watching the symptoms of any extraordinary disease. He was regular in his devotions, abstained from wine, and conformed in his private life to all the moral precepts of his religion. In war he was distinguished for his gallantry and personal activity; so that his contemporaries were justified in esteeming him as one of the wonders of the age.

Yet the whole of these splendid talents and accomplishments were given to him in vain: they were accompanied by a perversion of judgment which, after every allowance for the intoxication of absolute power, leaves us in doubt whether he was not affected by some degree of insanity. His whole life was spent in pursuing visionary schemes, by means equally irrational, and with a total disregard of the sufferings which they occasioned to his subjects; and its results were more calamitous than those of any other Indian reign.

His first act was one which neither his virtues nor defects would have led us to anticipate. An army of Moguls, under a very celebrated general, Teimúrshín Khán, having entered the Panjáb, he bought them off by the payment of an immense contribution; and this first instance of such policy in India was not, as might have been expected, followed by fresh invasions.

His next measure was equally inconsistent with his character; for it was perfectly rational and well-judged. He completed the reduction of the

Deckan, and brought his most remote provinces into as good order as those near his capital.

Wild schemes of Mohammed.

He then plunged into the career which seemed naturally suited to his genius.

Projected conquest of Persia.

He first determined on the conquest of Persia; and assembled a vast army*; which, after it had consumed his treasures, dispersed for want of pay, and carried pillage and ruin to every quarter.

Attempt to conquer China.

His next undertaking was to conquer China, and fill his exhausted coffers with the plunder of that rich monarchy. With this view he sent an army of 100,000 men through the Hémaláya mountains; but when the passage was effected, the Indians found a powerful Chinese army assembled on the frontier, with which theirs, reduced in numbers, and exhausted by fatigue, was unable to cope. Their provisions likewise failed; and the approach of the rainy season did not admit of a moment's delay in falling back.

During their retreat they were harassed by the mountaineers, slaughtered by the pursuing enemy, and worn out by famine. The Chinese were at last checked by the torrents of rain which began to fall, and the Indians, in time, made their way through the mountains; but they now found the low country inundated, and the hills covered with impervious jungle. So terrible were the calamities of their retreat, that at the end of fifteen days scarcely a man was left to tell the tale; and many

* Ferishta makes it amount to 370,000 horse.

BOOK VI.

of those who had been left behind in garrisons, as the army advanced, were put to death by the king, as if they had contributed to the failure of this ill-starred expedition.

Introduction of paper money.

As this expedient had failed to relieve the king's wants, he had recourse to another, almost equally ill-contrived. He had heard of the use of paper money in China, and he now introduced the system into his own dominions, substituting copper tokens for paper. The king's insolvency, and the instability of his government, destroyed the credit of his tokens from the first; foreign merchants refused to take them, and all attempts at compulsion were evaded, even at home: trade, in consequence, was at a stand; and confusion and distress were spread throughout all ranks. The king gained, to appearance, in the payment of his debts, but his receipts were diminished in the same proportion; the roots of his revenue were struck at by the impoverished condition of his subjects; and the result of all this sacrifice of the fortunes of the people was to leave his own in greater embarrassment than ever.

Tyranny and exactions of the king.

The king's exactions, which were always excessive, were now rendered intolerable by the urgency of his necessities: the husbandmen abandoned their fields, fled to the woods, and, in many places, maintained themselves by rapine; many towns were likewise deserted, and Mohammed, driven to fury by the disorders which he had himself occasioned, revenged himself by a measure which surpassed all his other enormities. He ordered out his army as if for a grand hunt, surrounded an extensive tract of country, as is usual on the great scale of the Indian chace, and then gave orders that the circle should close towards the centre, and that all within it (mostly inoffensive peasants) should be slaughtered like wild beasts. This sort of hunt was more than once repeated; and on a subsequent occasion there was a general massacre of the inhabitants of the great city of Canouj. These horrors led in due time to famine, and the miseries of the country exceeded all power of description.

Rebellions.

A. D. 1338, A. H. 739.

All this oppression was not allowed to pass without attempts to shake it off. Mohammed's own nephew first revolted in Málwa; and, being pursued by the king into the Deckan, was taken and flayed alive. Malik Beirám, the old friend of the king's father, whom he had helped to mount the throne, next rebelled in the Panjáb, and was also subdued and put to death.

A. D. 1339, A. H. 740.

Permanent revolt of Bengal, about A. D. 1340, A. H. 741; and of the coast of Coromandel.

Bengal soon after revolted under a Mussulman officer, and was never again subdued. The country on the coast of Coromandel almost immediately followed the example, and had the same success.

The king went in person to put down this last rebellion; but his army was attacked by a pestilence at Warangól, and suffered so much by its ravages, that he was obliged to return to Deógíri. On his way he had occasion to have a tooth drawn, and

BOOK VI.

he buried it, with great ceremony, under a magnificent tomb.

Meanwhile the Afgháns crossed the Indus and ravaged the Panjáb; when they retired, they were succeeded by the Gakkars, who took Láhór, and completed the ruin of the province.

Restoration of the Hindú kingdoms of Carnáta and Telingána. A. D. 1344, A. H. 744.

The rájas of Carnáta and Telingána now formed a combination to recover their independence. The former was the founder of a new dynasty, erected on the ruins of that of Belál, which fixed its capital at Bijáyanagar, and maintained a nearly equal struggle with the Mussulmans until near the end of the sixteenth century; the latter regained possession of Warangól, while Mohammed's garrisons were expelled from every part of their dominions.

Other rebellions.

The famine in Hindostan being at this time at its height, the governor of Sambal became unable to collect his revenue, and, dreading the king's violence, went into rebellion. He was soon crushed, as was a similar insurgent at Bidr in the Deckan; but a new rebellion almost immediately followed in the latter place by one of the chiefs of converted Moguls, or, as they were now called, Amír Jadída, or new nobility. The present revolt was quashed, but their other chiefs remained as ready as ever to profit by any new disturbance.

A. D. 1345, A. H. 745.

A. D. 1346, A. H. 746.

The next rebellion was that of Ein ul Múlk, who, being removed from his government of Oud to that of the Deckan, suspected the king's intentions, and threw off his allegiance. He was

CHAP. III.

soon reduced, and, contrary to all expectation, was pardoned, and restored to his office.

The governor of the Deckan, who had hitherto made head against his continually increasing difficulties, was afterwards removed; and the country was placed under the king's son-in-law, Imád ul Mulk, while a great addition was laid on the revenue of the province.

Málwa likewise was put under a new governor of low origin, who showed his zeal by a treacherous massacre of seventy of the Mogul Amírs; on which the officers of the same nation in Guzerát prevailed on the rest of the troops to join them in rebellion. The king suppressed this insurrection in person, and ravaged his own province as if it had been an enemy's, giving up the rich towns of Cambay and Surat to plunder.

Rebellion of the Mogul troops in Guzerát.

A. D. 1347, A. H. 748.

Some of the rebels of Guzerát, having taken refuge in the Deckan, were protected by the Mogul Amírs in that province; which Mohammed so highly resented that he ordered those chiefs to be made prisoners. They soon after effected their escape, raised a general rebellion, and proclaimed Ismáel Khán, an Afghán general, king. Mohammed Tóghlak, with a courage and activity worthy of a better cause, hastened to the Deckan, defeated the insurgents, and shut up the chiefs and their king in the fort of Deógíri. Before he could complete his success by the capture of that fortress, his presence was required by a new revolt of Guzerát; and as he was marching to suppress it,

General revolt of the Deckan.

Vigour and activity of the king.

BOOK VI.

the people of the Deckan rose on his rear, and plundered his baggage and elephants. The disturbance in Guzerát was, however, got under, and the chiefs compelled to take refuge with the Rájpút princes of Tatta in Sind, when intelligence arrived from the Deckan that things had there assumed a more formidable shape than ever. The rebel king had abdicated in favour of Hasan Gangu (who founded the new dynasty of Bahmani), and under his auspices the insurgents had defeated and slain Mohammed's son-in-law, Imád ul Mulk, and not only recovered the Deckan, but induced the governor of Málwa to join in their insurrection. Mohammed, now sensible of his error in hastening to oppose every new revolt, and not first settling that on hand, determined to place Guzerát on a secure footing before he ventured to confront the increased difficulties which threatened him in the Deckan. Although already in precarious health, he set out after the fugitives to Sind. He was opposed by the rebels on the Indus, but crossed the river in defiance of them, and had reached Tatta, when he had an accession of illness, and died in that city, leaving the reputation of one of the most accomplished princes and most furious tyrants that ever adorned or disgraced human nature.

Death of Mohammed Tóghlak. A. D. 1351, March 20. A. H. 752, Moharram 21.

Among the many projects of Mohammed, none occasioned so much misery, or gave rise to so much complaint, as that of transferring the capital from Delhi to Deógíri. The design was by no means

Removal of the capital to Deógíri, and other caprices of

CHAP. III.

Mohammed.

unreasonable in itself, if it had been begun without precipitancy, and conducted with steadiness. But Mohammed, as soon as the fancy struck him, ordered the whole of the inhabitants of Delhi to remove to Deógíri, to which he gave the name of Doulatábád.* After this the people were twice permitted to return to Delhi, and twice compelled, on pain of death, to leave it: one of these movements took place during a famine, and caused a prodigious loss of life, and all were attended with ruin and distress to thousands. The plan entirely failed in the end.

Another of his whims was to acknowledge the sovereignty of the nominal caliph in Egypt, to solicit investiture from him, and strike out of the list of kings all who had not received a similar confirmation of their title.

Another very expensive one was to divide the country into districts of sixty miles square, that the cultivation might be carried on under the management of the government.

Foreign accounts of his court and government.

Many particulars regarding this reign are given by Ibn Batúta, a native of Tangiers, who travelled over all Asia, and visited the court of Mohammed about A.D. 1341, and who could have no interest

* On this occasion he completed the present fort, which still affords a stupendous proof of the great scale of his undertakings. The rock round the hill is cut perfectly smooth and perpendicular for 180 feet, — the only entrance being through a winding passage in the heart of the rock. The whole is surrounded by a broad and deep ditch, cut also in the solid rock.

in misrepresentation, as he wrote after his return to Africa. He confirms to their full extent the native accounts both of the king's talents and of his crimes, and gives exactly such a picture of mixed magnificence and desolation as one would expect under such a sovereign. He found an admirably regulated horse and foot post from the frontiers to the capital, while the country was so disturbed as to make travelling unsafe. He describes Delhi as a most magnificent city, its mosque and walls without an equal on earth; but, although the king was then re-peopling it, it was almost a desert. " The greatest city in the world (he says) had the fewest inhabitants."

The king being absent, he was carried, with some other noble and learned strangers, who arrived along with him, to the court of the queen-mother, where they were received and entertained with respect and attention, and dismissed with robes of honour. He had a house allotted him, with an ample supply of provisions and every thing he could desire, and 2000 dínárs were given to him " to pay for his washing."

His daughter happening to die, it was privately reported to the king by post; and when the funeral took place, he was surprised to find it attended by the vizír, and performed with all the ceremonies usual for the nobles of the country. The queen-mother sent for his wife to console her, and presented her with dresses and ornaments.

The king's own manners, when he returned,

were as courteous as his previous proceedings. Ibn Batúta went out to meet him, and was graciously received, the king taking him by the hand and promising him every kindness. He afterwards made him a judge, conversed with him in Arabic on the duties of the office; and when Ibn Batúta hesitated, on account of his ignorance of the Indian language, the king, though somewhat ruffled by his starting difficulties, answered his objections with temper, and assigned him a most liberal salary. He afterwards paid his debts, to the amount of 55,000 dínárs, on his requesting it in an Arabic poem.* But Ibn Batúta soon found the dangerous ground he stood on. A particular dervise near Delhi falling under the king's suspicions, he immediately put him to death, and seized all persons who had frequented his cell. Among the number was Ibn Batúta, who was one of the very few who escaped with their lives. After this, he took an early opportunity of resigning his office; but the king, instead of being offended, attached him to an embassy which he was sending to China, in return for a very splendid one which had just reached his court.

The Mahometan territory in India at its greatest extent in this reign.

The Mahometan empire to the east of the Indus was more extensive in the early part of this king's reign than it ever was at any other period, but the provinces now lost were not all retrieved till the time of Aurangzíb; and, even in those which did

* The dínár, at this period, seems to have been a very small coin; but I do not know its precise value.

BOOK VI.

not revolt, the royal authority received a shock from which it did not recover till the accession of the Mogul dynasty.

There is in general so little scruple about getting rid of a bad king in the East, that it is seldom such extensive mischief is brought about by the misgovernment of one man.

Fírúz Tóghlak.

A. D. 1351, A. H. 752.

On the death of Mohammed Tóghlak the army fell into disorders, in which, as usual, the Moguls were the principal actors. The Indian chiefs (now mentioned for the first time) succeeded in repressing them, and raised Fírúz u dín, the late king's nephew, to the throne. He left a detachment to settle Sind, and marched along the Indus to U'ch, and thence to Delhi, where he overcame an opposition set up in the name of a child, the real or supposititious son of his predecessor.

A. D. 1353, A. H. 754.

Three years after his accession he made an attempt to recover Bengal, and overran the whole province, but was not able to reduce his enemy, until the rains setting in compelled him to retreat.

A. D. 1356, A. H. 757. Independence of Bengal and the Deckan recognised.

At a later period he received embassies both from Bengal and the Deckan, and thus acknowledged the independence of both monarchs; though, perhaps, without renouncing his nominal superiority. Whether the treaty with Bengal was merely personal, or whether the death of the first king was a temptation for infringing it, we find

CHAP. III.

the war almost immediately renewed with his successor, Secander, against whom Fírúz marched in person to the extreme south-east of Bengal. He afterwards renewed his treaty with Secander, whose independence was no longer questioned. Several years after this adjustment, some provocation from Jám Báni, the Rájpút prince of Tatta, induced the king to march in person to Sind; and although his expedition was unsuccessful, his failure was softened by the nominal submission of the Jám. From Sind he went to Guzerát, where he left a new governor. In the course of a few years the death of this officer led to another appointment and a rebellion of no long duration.

A. D. 1372, A. H. 773.

The king's infirmities. A. D. 1385, A. H. 787.

Other affairs of less importance kept Fírúz in activity till A. D. 1385, when, having reached his eighty-seventh year, he became incapable, from his infirmities, of conducting his government, and it fell by degrees entirely into the hands of his vizír.

Rivalries at his court.

The enjoyment of power tempted that minister to secure its permanence by plotting against the heir apparent. He had nearly succeeded, through the usual calumnies, in paving his way to the succession by the removal of the king's eldest son, when that prince took the bold measure of secretly introducing himself into the seraglio, and throwing himself on the affection of his father. Fírúz, either from conviction or weakness, gave up the vizír, and soon after openly invested his son with the whole powers of the state.

The prince, whose name was Násir u dín,

BOOK VI.

showed so little ability in the exercise of his authority, that in little more than a year he was displaced by two of his cousins. They raised a sedition in the capital, and, making use of the name of the old king, whose person they had secured, obliged Násir u dín to fly to the mountains of Sarmór, between the upper courses of the Jamna and Satlaj. They then announced that Fírúz had abdicated in favour of his grandson, Gheiás u dín.

His death. A. D. 1388, Oct. 23. A. H. 790, Rámzán 3.

Almost immediately after this revolution Fírúz died at the age of ninety.

His laws.

His reign, though not brilliant in other respects, was distinguished for the enlightened spirit of his regulations, and the extent and utility of his public works. He limited the number of capital punishments, and put a stop to the use of torture and the practice of mutilation; which last prohibition was the more meritorious as it was at variance with the Mahometan law. He abolished a great number of vexatious taxes and fees; put an end to all fluctuating and precarious imposts, and fixed the revenues in such a manner as to leave as little discretion as possible to the collectors, and to give precision and publicity to the demands of the state. He in some measure fell into the spirit of his times in punishing atheism by banishment, but showed his usual good sense in discouraging luxury in apparel by his own example rather than by sumptuary laws.

His public works.

The following list is given of his public works, for the maintenance of which lands were assigned:

50 dams across rivers, to promote irrigation; 40 mosques; 30 colleges; 100 caravanserais; 30 reservoirs for irrigation; 100 hospitals; 100 public baths; 150 bridges; besides many other edifices for pleasure or ornament.

The round numbers, as well as the amount of some of the items, suggest doubts of the accuracy of this list; but the works of Fírúz that still remain afford sufficient evidence of the magnitude of his undertakings. The most considerable of these is not specified in the list: it is a canal from the point in the Jamna where it leaves the mountains, by Cárnál, to Hánsi and Hissár. It reaches to the river Gágar, and in former times was again connected with the Satlaj, the nearest of the rivers of the Panjáb. It seems to have been intended for irrigation; but as it has been disused, perhaps, since the death of Fírúz, we can only judge of it by the part restored by the British government, which takes in the whole to beyond Hissár, a distance of 200 miles. This portion now turns mills for grinding corn (which before were not used in India), and is also employed in saw-mills and oil and sugar mills. It floats down rafts of wood from the mountains, and is capable of conveying merchandise in boats of a certain construction; but its great object is irrigation, by means of which it has fertilised a large tract, and turned the inhabitants from pastoral life to agriculture.*

* Major Colvin, *Journal of the Asiatic Society of Bengal*, vol. ii. p. 105.

BOOK VI.

Gheiás u dín Tóghlak II.

A. D. 1389, February. A. H. 791, Saffar.

Gheiás u dín soon quarrelled with his kinsmen, by whom he had been raised; and was deposed and murdered at the end of five months.

Abubekr Tóghlak.

A. D. 1389, November. A. H. 792, Zi Haj.

A. D. 1390, August. A. H. 793, Rámzán.

Abubekr, grandson of Fírúz by another son, was next made king, and had reigned for a year, when Násir u dín left the mountains, where he had remained since his expulsion, returned at the head of an army, and recovered the capital. A contest followed, and lasted for several months, during which time Delhi was more than once lost and recovered, until at length Násir u dín obtained permanent possession, and soon after made his rival prisoner. It was a remarkable circumstance in this contest, that a Hindú chief named Rái Sarwar was among the most important of the adherents of Násir, and that the Hindús of Méwát took an active part for his opponent. The household troops, who were all foreigners, having shown particular hostility to the conqueror, were banished the city; and as some endeavoured to conceal their character, recourse was had to a test like the Jewish Shiboleth, and all were treated as foreigners who could not pronounce a certain letter peculiar to the languages of Hindostan. From these circumstances we may judge of the increased importance of the

Hindús, and of the *native* Mahometans, since the separation of the kingdoms of Ghór and India. CHAP. III.

Násir u dín Tóghlak.

The second reign of Násir u dín, though it presented a scene of general disorder, was marked by few great events.

Farhat ul Mulk, the governor of Guzerát, revolted, and was reduced by Mozaffer Khán, who revolted himself in the next reign. There was also a rebellion of Ráhtór Rájpúts beyond the Jamna; and the weakness into which the royal authority had fallen became every where apparent.

This king's vizír was a Hindú convert, and was put to death on the accusation of his own nephew, an unconverted Hindú.

On the death of Násir u dín, his son Humáyun succeeded, but died at the end of forty-five days, when his younger brother Mahmúd was placed on the throne.

Mahmúd Tóghlak.

The young king was a minor, and little qualified to restore the lost authority of the crown. Mozaffer Khán, the governor of Guzerat, began to act as an independent prince. Málwa, which had been reannexed to the crown after the separation of the Deckan, now permanently threw off the yoke, as did the little province of Cándésh; A. D. 1394, A. H. 795.

BOOK VI.

and these new kingdoms remained independent until the time of Akber.

Dissolution of the monarchy.

The king's own vizír also seized on the province of Júanpúr, and founded a kingdom. Meanwhile the capital was torn by sanguinary broils between factions. The remaining provinces looked on with indifference, or fell into disputes among themselves; and while the attention of all parties was absorbed in these fierce commotions, the invasion of Tamerlane burst upon their heads and overwhelmed the contending parties in one common ruin.

Invasion of Tamerlane.

Tamerlane had united the hordes of Tartary in the same manner, though not to the same extent, as Chengíz Khán; and, like him, he had carried his destructive inroads into all the surrounding countries. Though a Túrk and a Mussulman *, and born in a comparatively civilised country, he was almost as barbarous in his mode of war, and at least as short-sighted in his policy, as the Mogul. His empire was even more transient, since he did not attempt to retain the greater part of the countries he overran; and if some of the fragments that remained to his family became flourishing provinces, it was because the character of his descend-

* Tamerlane, or the Amír Teimúr, as he is called in Asia, was born at Késh, near Samarcand, where the languages are Túrki and Persian, and where his family had been settled for 200 years. He claimed a remote descent from the same stock with Chengíz Khán; but all that is certain is, that his grandfather was chief of the tribe of Berlás.

ants formed almost a contrast to his own. He had conquered Persia and Transoxiana, and ravaged Tartary, Georgia, and Mesopotamia, with parts of Russia and Siberia, before he turned his arms, without the pretext of a quarrel, on the distracted empire of Hindostan.

A. D. 1398, A. H. 800.

Early in the spring of A. D. 1398*, Pír Mohammed, the grandson of Tamerlane, who had been employed in reducing the Afgháns in the mountains of Solimán, crossed the Indus in a line with U'ch, and soon after laid siege to Multán; an operation which occupied him for upwards of six months.

Meanwhile, Tamerlane passed Hindú Cúsh by the usual route to Cábul†; left that city in August, and marched by Haryúb and Bannu to Dínkót on the Indus.‡ He crossed that river by a bridge of rafts and reeds, and marched to the Hydaspes, and down its banks to Tulamba, reducing the country as he passed. He levied a heavy contribution on Tulamba, which was afterwards sacked, and the inhabitants massacred by the troops, — it is said, without his orders.

By this time, Pír Mohammed had taken Multán by blockade; but the rains having set in, he lost his horses, and was at length obliged to shut him-

* Tamerlane's proceedings are from Price, vol. iii. p. 219, &c. Rennel's Memoir, p. 115, &c., and Briggs's Ferishta.

† His previous expedition into the mountains of the Síapósh Cáfirs will be read with interest in Price, from Mírkhónd.

‡ The exact position of Dínkót is not known, but it must be to the south of the salt range.

BOOK VI.

A. D. 1398, Oct. 25. self up in the town. On the approach of Tamerlane, he set out to meet him, leaving a garrison in Multán, and joined his father on the Gára or Satlaj.

Tamerlane thence proceeded with a light detachment to Adjudin, where he met with no sort of resistance; and as the town was famous for the tomb of a Mahometan saint, "out of respect for his memory, he spared the few inhabitants who remained in the place." He then proceeded to Batnér, and massacred the country people who

Nov. 9. had taken refuge under the walls. The place afterwards surrendered on terms; but, by one of those mistakes which so constantly accompanied Tamerlane's capitulations, the town was burned, and all the inhabitants put to the sword. He then marched to Sámána, where he joined his main body, having slaughtered the inhabitants of every place he passed. From Sámána the towns were deserted, and consequently there were no more general massacres. Many prisoners were, however, taken; and on reaching Delhi, Tamerlane put to

Dec. 12. death all of them above fifteen years of age (to the number, according to the exaggerated accounts of the Mussulman historians, of 100,000).

Defeat of the Indian army.

The Indian army, which was inferior in numbers, and divided in councils, being defeated and driven into the town, Mahmúd Tóghlak fled to Guzerát; Delhi surrendered under a solemn pro-

Dec. 17. mise of protection; and Tamerlane was publicly proclaimed emperor of India.

CHAP. III.

Sack, conflagration, and massacre of Delhi.

What follows is so constant a concomitant of Tamerlane's promises of protection, that we are at a loss whether to ascribe it to systematic perfidy, or to the habitual ferocity and insubordination of the troops. On this occasion, the most credible accounts attribute *the commencement* to the latter cause. Plunder and violence brought on resistance: "this led to a general massacre; some streets were rendered impassable by heaps of dead; and the gates being forced, the whole Mogul army gained admittance, and a scene of horror ensued easier to be imagined than described." *

For five days Tamerlane remained a tranquil spectator of the sack and conflagration of the city, and during that time he was celebrating a feast in honour of his victory. When the troops were wearied with slaughter, and nothing was left to plunder, he gave orders for the prosecution of his march; and on the day of his departure he "offered up to the Divine Majesty *the sincere and humble tribute of grateful praise* in the noble mosque of polished marble," erected on the banks of the Jamna by Fírúz.† A. D. 1398, Dec. 31.

The booty carried off from Delhi is said to have been very great; and innumerable men and women of all ranks were dragged into slavery. Tamerlane secured to himself the masons and workers in stone and marble, for the purpose of constructing a mosque at Samarcand.

* Briggs's Ferishta. † Price, apparently from Mírkhónd.

BOOK VI.

Tamerlane retires from India.

He then marched to Mírat, where there was a general massacre; and afterwards crossed the Ganges, and proceeded up its banks to near Hardwár, where that river leaves the mountains. Several affairs took place with bodies of Hindús in the skirts of the hills, in which Tamerlane exposed his person like a private soldier, and underwent fatigues the more extraordinary as he had reached the age of sixty-three. He marched along the foot of the mountains to Jammu (or Jummoo, north of Láhór); then turned to the south, fell into the route by which he first advanced, and quitted India, leaving anarchy, famine, and pestilence behind him.*

A. D. 1399, March. A. H. 801.

His character.

We must estimate Tamerlane's character from his actions, and not from the motives assigned to him by panegyrists, nor from maxims drawn up by his orders according to his idea of a perfect government. His own memoirs of his life throw a true light on his character.† They are written in the plain and picturesque style of Túrki autobiography; and if there was a doubt that they were from Tamerlane's dictation, it would be removed by the unconscious simplicity with which he relates his own intrigues and perfidy; taking credit all the time for an excess of goodness and sincerity which the boldest flatterer would not have ventured to

* About the 10th of March, 1399, A. H. 801. He was now marching on his famous expedition against Bajazet.

† Mulfuzát Timúri, translated by Major Stewart.

CHAP. III.

ascribe to him. The mixture also of cant and hypocrisy, with real superstition and devotion, could not have been exhibited by any hand but his own; and these traits, with his courage, prudence, and address, his perfect knowledge of mankind, and his boldness in practising on their weakness, make one of the most extraordinary pictures ever presented to the world. The commanding language of barbarous conquerors, contrasted with the evasions of the princes whom they threaten, leads us to figure them as rude and artless soldiers; but the essential character of Tamerlane was that of a wily politician; and probably it was to similar talents that the other Tartar conquerors owed their ascendancy over so many chiefs, who were their equals in merely military qualities.

There is a resemblance between the histories of Chengíz Khán and Tamerlane; but of those two enemies of mankind, the first was perhaps the most violent, and the second the most perfidious.

Anarchy at Delhi.

For two months after Tamerlane's departure Delhi remained without a government, and almost without inhabitants. A struggle then took place for the possession of it, in which a chief named Ecbál, who had been in power under Mahmúd, was at last successful. He failed in various attempts to extend his authority beyond the districts round the capital; and, at last, was killed on a distant expedition towards Multán.

A. D. 1400, A. H. 802.

Mahmúd had returned from Guzerát, and for some time lived as a pensioner at Delhi; then at

BOOK VI.

Canouj, a city belonging to the king of Júanpúr, on which Ecbál made several attempts; at last, on

A. D. 1405, A. H. 808. that chief's death, he was restored to the possession

A. D. 1412, A. H. 814. of Delhi. He died there after a nominal reign of twenty years, and was succeeded by Doulat Khán Lódi; who, at the end of fifteen months, was

A. D. 1414, A. H. 817. expelled by Khizr Khán, the governor of the Panjáb.

CHAP. III.

GOVERNMENT OF THE SEIADS.

Seiad Khizr Khán. A. D. 1414, A. H. 817.

Seiad Mobárik. A. D. 1421, A. H. 824.

Seiad Mohammed. A. D. 1435, A. H. 839.

Seiad Alá u dín. A. D. 1444, A. H. 849.

For thirty-six years after this, there was no kingdom of India, either in name or in reality. Khizr Khán affected to regard Tamerlane as emperor, and to govern in his name, without the title or forms of royalty. He was a descendant of the Prophet, though himself a native of India; and, with three of his descendants who succeeded him, forms what is called the dynasty of the Seiads. He obtained scarcely any territory with Delhi: his original province of the Panjáb soon revolted; and his family had to struggle for the possession of a part of it during the whole period of their government. They, however, made some spirited attempts to extend their territory, and made incursions into Malwa and the borders of Rájpútána; but in the time of Seiad Alá u dín, the last of the race, the frontier came in one place to within a mile of the city walls, and nowhere extended beyond twelve. But Alá u dín possessed Budáyun, a town about one hundred miles east of Delhi, and to it he at length retired, making over his former capital and his pretensions to Behlól Khán Lódi, who assumed the title of king.

A. D. 1450, A. H. 854.

BOOK VI.

HOUSE OF LO'DI.

Behlól Lódi.

Rise of the family of Lódi.

The ancestors of Behlól had been enriched by commerce, and his grandfather was governor of Multán under Fírúz Tóghlak, who was the first great patron of the Afgháns. Behlól's father and several of his uncles held commands under the Seiad rulers; and one of them, Islám Khán, was so considerable that he had 12,000 men of his own nation in his pay. The power of the family, together with the calumnies of a disaffected relation, at length excited the jealousy of Seiad Mohammed, and the Lódis were persecuted and driven into the hills. They continued to resist the Seiad's authority, until Behlól had an opportunity of occupying, first, Sirhind, and afterwards the whole of the Panjáb.

Behlól had been invited to Delhi by Hamíd, the vizír of his predecessor, but finding himself overshadowed by this powerful subject, he seized his person by a stratagem, and after he had broken his influence, allowed him to retire to private life.

Panjáb re-annexed to Delhi.

Behlól's accession again brought back the Panjáb to Delhi. Multán had become independent during the time of the Seiads, and Behlól had marched against it, when he was recalled by an attack of the king of Júanpúr, who had laid siege to Delhi. A war now commenced with that prince, which was continued, with short intervals of hollow peace, for twenty-six years, and ended in the conquest of Júanpúr, which was permanently reannexed to Delhi. Behlól survived this long war for ten years, and made other conquests on a smaller scale; so that at his death he left a territory extending from the Jamna to the Hémaláya mountains as far east as Benáres, besides a tract on the west of the Jamna extending to Bundélcand.

A. D. 1452. A. H. 856.

Recovery of Júanpúr. A. D. 1478. A. H. 883.

A. D. 1488. A. H. 894.

Secander Lódi.

Secander's accession was disputed by some chiefs on the part of his infant nephew. It was afterwards contested in the field by two of his brothers, one of whom maintained an obstinate struggle. Secander was successful on all these occasions, and treated the inferior rebels with clemency, and his relations with affection. He reannexed Behár as far as the frontiers of Bengal to Delhi, and also extended his territories in the direction of Bundélcand. His internal administration was just and vigorous; and he seems, in all other respects, to have been a mild and excellent prince. But he was one of the few bigots who have sat on the throne of India. He destroyed the temples in towns and forts that he took from Hindús, and he forbade that people performing pilgrimages, and

Good administration of Secander.

His bigotry.

BOOK VI.

bathing on certain festivals at places on the sacred streams within his own dominions. On one occasion he carried his zeal to cruelty and injustice; for a Bramin having been active in propagating the doctrine that "all religions, if sincerely practised, were equally acceptable to God," he summoned him to defend this opinion in his presence, against twelve Mahometan divines; and, on his refusing to renounce his tolerant maxims, put him to death. *

A holy man of his own religion having remonstrated with him on his prohibition of pilgrimages, Secander drew his sword, exclaiming, "Wretch, do you defend idolatry?" He was appeased by the answer,—"No; but I maintain that kings ought not to persecute their subjects."

When marching against one of his brothers, a Calender addressed him with prayers for his success, on which he said, "Pray for victory to him who will best promote the good of his subjects."

Secander was a poet, and was a great patron of letters. He died at Agra, after a reign of twenty-eight years.

I'brahim Lódi.

I'brahím, who succeeded, had none of his father's virtues. He disgusted his tribe by his pride, and

* The Bramin was, probably, a disciple of Kabír, a Hindú philosopher, who taught similar doctrines at an earlier period in this century. (See Professor Wilson, *Asiatic Researches*, vol. xvi. p. 55.)

alarmed his chiefs by his suspicious and tyrannical temper. From these causes his reign was continually disturbed by rebellions. At the commencement of it one of his brothers was proclaimed king at Júanpúr, was subdued in the course of a twelvemonth, and was privately executed by I'brahím, who imprisoned his other brothers for life. A chief named Islám Khán next rebelled, and was killed in battle. Several men of rank and governors of provinces were executed for their share in these transactions. Others were put to death on suspicion; some were secretly made away with after being imprisoned; and one was assassinated at the seat of his government. These proceedings spread general distrust and disaffection; various chiefs revolted, and the whole of the eastern part of I'brahím's dominions threw off its obedience, and formed a separate state under Deria Khán Lohání, whose son afterwards took the title of king. Doulat Khán Lódi, the governor of the Panjáb, dreading the fate of so many other chiefs, revolted, and called in the aid of Báber, who had for some time reigned in Cábul. Báber had before invaded the Panjáb, which he claimed as part of the inheritance of Tamerlane, and he now gladly availed himself of this invitation; but some other Afghán chiefs, either from attachment to I'brahím or aversion to a foreigner, drove out Doulat Khán, and opposed Báber in the field. They were totally defeated near Láhór, and that city was reduced to ashes by the victors. Díbálpúr was next stormed, and the

Discontents and rebellions. (margin, beside "tinually disturbed by rebellions")

Invasion of Báber. (margin, beside "whose son afterwards took the title of king")

A. D. 1524, A. H. 930. (margin, beside "Báber in the field")

garrison put to the sword; and at this place Báber was joined by Doulat Khán. He had reason, soon after, to suspect the intentions of this person, and threw him and his sons into confinement. Relenting, subsequently, he released them, treated them honourably, and granted them a jágír. He did not, however, succeed in removing their distrust: by the time he had reached Sirhind on his advance towards Delhi, Doulat Khán and one of his sons revolted and fled to the hills.* Unwilling to leave such dangerous enemies behind him, Báber determined to return to Cábul. He nevertheless kept his hold on the country he had reduced, and left persons on whom he could depend in the principal places. At Díbálpúr he left Alá u dín, an uncle of King I'brahím, who seems to have escaped from confinement, and who had joined Báber. Doulat Khán now returned to the Panjáb, and overrun great part of it, Alá u dín flying to Cábul; but in the end Doulat Khán was entirely defeated by one of Báber's generals; and as that monarch himself was engaged in defending Balkh against the Uzbeks, he sent Alá u dín to India, with orders to his own chiefs to assist him. Thus supported, Alá u dín advanced to Delhi, and from the general disaffection his army was soon swelled to 40,000 men. With this force he engaged I'bra-

He retreats from Sirhind.

* The other son, whose name was Diláwar, adhered to Báber, and had a high place in his confidence. He had the title of Khán Khánán, the second in the court of Delhi, and continued to be a person of great authority in his reign and Humáyun's.

him under the walls of Delhi, and was totally defeated. By this time, Báber had settled Balkh, and was advanced as far as Láhór on his way into India. From Láhór he marched into the hills in pursuit of Doulat Khán, who submitted and gave up his fort *; after which Báber continued his route through the hills to Rópúr on the Satlaj, above Lodiána, and from thence nearly by the direct road to Delhi. At Pánípat he found himself in the neighbourhood of I'brahím, who had come out to meet him at the head of an army amounting, as it was represented to Báber, to 100,000 men, with 1000 elephants. On the approach of this force, Báber took up a position, linked his guns together by ropes of twisted leather, and lined them with infantry further protected by breastworks. He likewise strengthened his flanks with fieldworks of earth and fascines. His army, including followers, amounted to no more than 12,000 men. When I'brahím drew near, he also fortified his position; but had not steadiness enough to adhere to his plan of awaiting an attack, and in a few days led out his army to storm Báber's lines. As soon as he was engaged with the front, Báber ordered his right and left wings to attack the flanks and rear of the enemy. They accordingly advanced and plied them with their arrows; until the Indian

Return of Báber, December.

Defeat and death of I'brahím. A. D. 1526, April 21.

* His son Gházi Khán fled, and Báber took possession of his library, in which he found a number of valuable books. One would have thought the Korán a sufficient library for an Afghán chief of those days.

BOOK VI.

troops, after attempting, in a few feeble charges, to drive them off, fell into disorder, when Báber, who had hitherto been annoying them with his cannon, ordered his centre to move forward, and completed the rout of the enemy. I'brahím was killed, and the Indian army, having been nearly surrounded during the battle, suffered prodigious loss in the defeat. Báber judged from observation that 15,000 or 16,000 lay dead on the field, of whom 5000 or 6000 lay in one spot around their king. The Indians reported that not less than 40,000 perished in the battle and pursuit.

This action does not give a high idea of the military character of either party. It lasted from soon after sunrise till noon, during which period, Báber observes, with satisfaction, that his guns were discharged *many times* to good purpose. The service of artillery would not in that age have been much better in Europe; but although Báber's plan of harassing the enemy's flanks and rear with arrows seems to be justified by its success, it does not appear remarkable either for skill or spirit, or likely to have been carried on with impunity against an active enemy.

Occupation of Delhi and Agra. May 10.

Delhi was surrendered, and Báber advanced and took possession of Agra, which had lately been the royal residence.

From a list of I'brahím's nobles given by Ferishta, they appear all to have been of the Afghán tribes of Lódi or Lohání, or of that called Fermuli, who were mixed with the Afgháns, like the

Khiljis, if indeed they are not a portion of the latter people.

The rája * of Gwáliór, who was reduced to submission during the last reign, accompanied I'brahím's army, and fell along with him in the battle.

Báber reviews his own conquest with much complacency, and compares it to those of Sultán Mahmúd and Shaháb u dín; and although we must not confound the acquisition of the few distracted provinces held by I'brahím with the subjugation of India, yet it must be admitted that his enterprise was as glorious in its achievement as it was memorable in its effects. His force seemed insufficient even to occupy the territory he had to subdue, and it was drawn with difficulty from his own dominions, still threatened by the Uzbeks, whose power the combined force of the whole house of Tamerlane had proved unable to withstand.

Báber's conduct to the places where he met with resistance was as inhuman as that of Tamerlane, who was naturally his model.

The smallness of his force was some justification of the means he took to strike a terror; but the invariable practice of his country is the best palliation for him. His natural disposition was remarkably humane; and although we cannot help being shocked at these occurrences, and at two or three cruel executions mentioned in his memoirs,

* Ibn Batuta, p. 133.

BOOK VI.

yet they prove no more against his personal character in this respect, than his slaughtering Gauls or crucifying pirates against Cæsar's clemency.

Báber was the founder of a line of kings under whom India rose to the highest pitch of prosperity; and out of the ruins of whose empire all the existing states in that country are composed.

HOUSE OF TEIMU'R.

BOOK VII.

FROM THE CONQUEST OF BÁBER TO THE ACCESSION OF AKBER.

CHAP. I.

REIGN OF BÁBER.

CHAP. I.

Descent and early life of Báber.

THE early life of Báber was a tissue of surprising vicissitudes and romantic adventures.* He was the sixth in descent from Tamerlane. The extensive dominions of his grandfather, Abusaíd, were shared by the numerous sons of that monarch. One of them, Ahmed Mírza, obtained Samarcand and Bokhára; Balkh or Bactria fell to another, Mahmúd Mírza; and Cábul to a third, whose name was Ulugh Bég. O'mar Shékh Mírza, the fourth son, and the father of Báber, had at first been in charge of Cábul; but was transferred during his father's lifetime to Ferghána, on the upper course of the Jaxartes, a small but rich and beautiful country, of which Báber always speaks with fondness. The mother of Báber was a *Mogul*, the sister

* The account of Báber is taken from his own Memoirs, translated by Mr. Erskine. It differs, in some respects, from that given by Ferishta.

BOOK VII.

of Mahmúd Khán, a descendant of Chaghatái Khán, and head of *his* branch of the empire of Chengíz Khán. This connection does not seem to have inspired any attachment on the part of Báber towards the Mogul nation, of whom he never speaks in his memoirs but with contempt and aversion.*

His wars and adventures in his youth.

Báber was only twelve years old at the death of his father and his own accession (A. D. 1494). O'mar Shékh Mírza had just been involved in a war with his brother, Ahmed Mírza, of Samarcand, and his brother-in-law, Mahmúd Khán, the Mogul; and those princes showed no disposition to relent in favour of their youthful nephew. They, howver, failed entirely in an attack on his capital; ande shortly after Ahmed Mírza died. He was succeeded by his brother, the king of Bactria. He also died soon after, and was succeeded by his son, Báisánghar Mírza. Confusions ensued, and Báber was induced to attempt the conquest of Samarcand for himself. Though he had for some time conducted his own government, he was as yet only fifteen; and considering that circumstance, together with the insignificance of his means, it is much less

* "Under these circumstances," observes Mr. Erskine, "it may seem one of the strangest caprices of fortune, that the empire which he founded in India should have been called, both in the country and by foreigners, the empire of the Moguls; thus taking its name from a race which he detested." (*Erskine's Baber*, p. 236.) The reason is, that the Indians call all northern Mussulmans, except the Afgháns, Moguls: they now apply the term particularly to the Persians.

surprising that he more than once failed in this undertaking, than that his spirit and perseverance were at last rewarded with success (A.D. 1497).

The possession of the capital of Tamerlane, which seemed a step to the sovereignty of all Transoxiana, proved in itself to be more than Báber had strength to maintain. The country of Samarcand was exhausted by long disorders, and afforded no means of paying his troops, who, in consequence, began to desert in great numbers. They spread their discontent among those left in Ferghána, and at last openly revolted, under Ahmed Tambol, one of Báber's principal leaders, in the name of his younger brother, Jehángír Mírza. Such a rebellion at home allowed no time for delay, and Báber left Samarcand, after a reign of a hundred days: on his departure the inhabitants immediately threw off their obedience to him. An unfortunate illness, which he with difficulty survived, so retarded his operations, that, by the time he had abandoned Samarcand, he found he had lost his hereditary dominions. On this he had recourse to his Mogul uncle, and sometimes with slender aid from him, but oftener with his own resources alone, he made various attempts, not without partial success, both on Samarcand and Ferghána. At length, in 1499, he succeeded in recovering his native kingdom; but he had not entirely subdued the rebels when he was tempted by strong invitations from Samarcand to set out for that capital. Before he reached his destination, he learned that both Samarcand

and Bokhára were occupied by the Uzbeks, then founding the dominion which they still possess over Transoxiana.*

Meanwhile Tambol had again seized on Ferghána, and Báber was compelled to take refuge in the almost inaccessible mountains to the south of that country. While there, he learned that Sheibáni Khán, the chief of the Uzbeks, had left Samarcand on an expedition; and with characteristic spirit of enterprise he determined to avail himself of the opportunity to attempt to surprise that city. He set off with only 240 men; escaladed the walls in the night; overpowered the guards, and magnified the impression of his numbers by boldness and rapidity, until the citizens rose in his favour, and massacred the Uzbeks wherever they were to be found. Sheibáni Khán hastened back on this intelligence, but found the gates shut against him, and ultimately withdrew to Bokhára.

The whole of Sogdiana now declared for Báber. He remained for six months in quiet possession, and employed the interval in endeavours to form a combination among the neighbouring princes, by impressing them with a sense of their danger from the Uzbeks. His exertions were fruitless; and he was obliged to encounter alone the whole power of

* The Uzbeks (so called from one of their kháns) were a mass of tribes of Túrki, Mogúl, and probably of Fennic origin, moulded into one people, but with a great preponderance of Túrks. They had before been settled on the Jaik, and had been in possession of a large tract in Siberia. (*Erskine's Baber*, Introduction, pp. lix. lx.)

Sheibáni. The hopes of success, which even then he continued to cherish, were frustrated by the baseness of some Mogul auxiliaries, who left the battle for the purpose of plundering his baggage. The consequence was a total defeat; and Báber was obliged to retire with the few troops that adhered to him within the walls of Samarcand. He resolved to defend that place to the last extremity, and repelled various assaults that were made on him by the Uzbeks. Sheibáni had then recourse to a blockade, and in four months reduced his enemies to all the miseries of famine. The inhabitants perished in great numbers; the soldiers let themselves down from the walls and deserted; and Báber, who had shared in all the privations of the people, was compelled at last to evacuate the town.

After this he spent nearly two years in the utmost poverty and distress, sometimes in the mountains, and oftener in his uncle's camp, where he remained in such a state of destitution that his very servants left him from absolute want. He seems to have been almost reduced to despondency by his repeated misfortunes, and once resolved to withdraw to China, and pass his life in obscurity and retirement. Occasional openings in Ferghána served to keep alive his hopes; and at length, with the help of his uncle, he recovered the capital, and was joined by his brother Jehángír, who had hitherto been his nominal rival. Tambol, in this strait, called in the formidable aid of the Uzbeks.

BOOK VII.

Báber was overpowered, compelled to fly after a desperate conflict in the streets, and so hotly pursued that his companions, one by one, fell into the hands of the enemy, and his own horse was so much exhausted that he was overtaken by two of Tambol's soldiers. They endeavoured to persuade him to surrender; and Báber, while he kept up the parley, continued to push on towards the mountains. At length he thought he had succeeded, by arguments and entreaties, in bringing over the pursuers to his interest, and they took a solemn oath to share his fortunes; but, whether they were originally insincere, or lost heart when they contemplated the prospect before them, they ended by betraying Báber to his enemies; and it was with the utmost difficulty that he again recovered his freedom. He only escaped to a condition almost as hopeless as captivity. His uncle's Mogul army had been defeated by Sheibáni, and himself made prisoner; while the whole of Transoxiana, except that annexed to Bactria, fell into the hands of the Uzbeks. All his prospects being thus extinguished, Báber bade a last farewell to his native country of Ferghána, and set out to try his fortune in new scenes beyond the range of Hindú Cush.

He is driven out of Transoxiana.

After all that he had done and suffered (enough to fill up an eventful life) Báber was yet only in his twenty-third year. He bore his numerous reverses with the elasticity of youth. He himself tells us that he often shed many tears, and composed many melancholy verses; but in general his cheerful temper buoyed him up, and enabled him to enjoy the present and to entertain favourable prospects of the future. He says he never had more perfect pleasure than for a few days after he evacuated Samarcand, when he first got a full meal, a quiet night's rest, and a temporary freedom from labour and anxiety. He had often similar moments of enjoyment, thanks to his sociable habits and his relish for simple pleasures. He pauses, in relating one of his desperate expeditions, to describe a particular sort of melon with which he had been struck: if ever he had an interval of rest he was occupied with plants and gardening; and during all his marches, in peace or war, flowers and trees and cheerful landscapes were never thrown away on him. It may be because others have not opened their hearts as he has done, but there certainly is no person in Asiatic history into whose tastes and feelings we can enter as into Báber's.

Bactria was now in the hands of Khusru Sháh, a favourite of Báber's late uncle, and afterwards minister to his cousin, Báisanghar Mírza, the same whom he had driven out of Samarcand. Khusru Sháh had since murdered his master, and was in possession of what remained of his dominions. He endeavoured to conciliate Báber, and received him with a show of hospitality when he entered his territory. His professions arose from a sense of his own insecurity; it was not long ere all the Moguls in his employment proffered their services

BOOK VII.

to Báber; and, before they had openly declared themselves, Khusru's own brother, Báki, came over to the same side, and was followed by the whole of the army. When Báber approached Khusru's frontier he had between two and three hundred followers, many of them armed with clubs; and only two tents, the best of which was allotted to his mother. He now set out to invade Cábul at the head of a regular and well equipped army. His uncle, Ulugh Bég, the king of that country, had expired two years before; his son and successor had been expelled by his minister; and *he*, in his turn, had been dispossessed by the Mogul or Túrki family of Arghún, who had been for some time in possession of Candahár. Báber occupied Cábul almost without opposition (A. D. 1504); and, regarding the original owner as completely ejected, he took possession in his own name, and subsequently resisted an attempt of his cousin to regain his inheritance. He afterwards lost Bactria; which was recovered by Khusru Sháh, and ultimately conquered by the Uzbeks. Báber's connection with the country beyond the mountains was therefore entirely cut off. He was now king of Cábul, over which country he reigned for twenty-two years, before his conquest of India; and which was enjoyed by his descendants till the end of the seventeenth century.

Acquires the kingdom of Cábul.

But though Báber had gained a fixed establishment, he was by no means in a state of repose. He had, in fact, only changed the character of his toils and perils. He was still threatened from without by an enemy who had hitherto proved irresistible; and within, a great part of his territory was in the hands of independent tribes, and so strong that he could not hope to subdue it; while part of the rest was possessed by personal enemies and rivals. His title was doubtful; he had no minister whom he could trust; his brother Jehángír had but lately joined him after having been long in rebellion; and his army was an assemblage of adventurers, strangers to him and traitors to their former masters.

His first years were spent in the conquest of Candahár, in expeditions into the mountains of the Afgháns and Hazárehs, and in a dangerous journey to Herát to concert measures with that branch of the house of Tamerlane for their common defence against the Uzbeks. On these occasions he underwent the usual risks and more than the usual hardships of war, and had once nearly perished in the snow during a winter march through the mountains of the Hazárehs.

In this period his brother Jehángír revolted (A. D. 1506); but was subdued and pardoned: a more serious insurrection took place while he was at Herát, when his Mogul troops set up one of his cousins as king, who was also defeated and pardoned (A. D. 1507); and he was afterwards brought to the brink of ruin by a conspiracy of the Moguls, who had come over from Khusru Sháh. These men, from two to three thousand in number, gave

BOOK VII.

the first sign of their disaffection by an attempt to seize Báber's person; and when he had escaped and fled from Cábul, they called in Abdu Rizák the son of Ulugh Bég, whom Báber had supplanted in the government (A. D. 1508). The right of this young man had probably little influence; for all the princes of the house of Tamerlane seemed to consider that conqueror's dominions as a common prize, from which each might take what share he could: his strength lay in the connections he possessed in a country where his father had reigned; and those were so powerful that Báber found himself deserted by the whole of his troops except about 500 men. A moment's despondency, at this crisis, would have been fatal; but Báber made up for his small force by the boldness and activity of his enterprises: he led his troops to repeated encounters, exposed himself in the hottest of every engagement, and, almost entirely by his personal courage and exertions, at last retrieved his affairs.*

His most important wars were with his old enemies the Uzbeks. Sheibáni Khán, after the conquest of Transoxiana, invaded Khorásán, took Herát, and extinguished the principal branch of the house of Tamerlane. He then advanced to Candahár and took the city. He was drawn off by distant troubles before he had reduced the citadel;

* Mr. Erskine, from Kháfi Khán and Ferishta. Báber's Memoirs break off in the beginning of the insurrection, and are not resumed for some years. The intervening portion seems never to have been written. (*Erskine's Baber*, p. 236.)

CHAP. I.

but left it so weakened that it fell into the hands of its old possessors the Arghúns, who had remained in the neighbourhood, and who now retained it for several years (from A. D. 1507 to 1522). What might have been Báber's fortune if the Uzbeks had continued their progress, it is not easy to surmise. It is possible he might have shared the fate of so many princes of his family, had not Sheibáni Khán encountered a new enemy whose success put a stop to the career of Tartar conquest. This was Sháh Ismáel Saffavi, king of Persia, with whom Sheibáni went to war about this time, and by whom he was totally defeated and slain (A. D. 1510).

His death opened a new field to Báber, or rather recalled him to that which had been the scene of his earliest exploits. He immediately occupied Bactria, made an alliance with Sháh Ismáel, and, with the aid of a Persian force, took Bokhára, and again obtained possession of Samarcand (A. D. 1511).

But he was destined never to be long successful in Transoxiana: before the end of a twelvemonth he was driven out of Samarcand by the Uzbeks; and, although he maintained the contest, with the support of the Persians, for two years longer, yet he at last suffered a total defeat, and lost all his acquisitions except Bactria (A. D. 1514).

His views on India.

It was after this failure that he turned his serious attention to India, and began those enterprises, the result of which has already been related.

A. D. 1526, A. H. 933.

After the taking of Agra, Báber's first act was

BOOK VII.

Báber's proceedings after his victory over I'brahím.

to distribute the captured treasures to his adherents. He gave his son Humáyun a diamond, which was esteemed one of the finest in the world; and he sent a present of a sháhrukhi each to every man, woman, and child, slave or free, in the country of Cábul. *

But, although in possession of the capital, Báber was far from having conquered the kingdom. He only occupied the part to the north-west of Delhi, with a narrow tract along the Jamna to Agra. The whole of the country to the east of the Ganges had become independent in I'brahím's time under Deria Khán Loháni. His son took the title of king by the name of Mohammed Sháh Loháni, and seems to have possessed Behár on both sides of the Ganges. Many places on the west of the Jamna had also been in rebellion in I'brahím's time, and many of those which had been obedient now held out under the Afghán and Fermuli chiefs belonging to the late government. Nor was this the only opposition with which Báber had to contend: a strong dislike and hostility at first subsisted between his troops and the Indians, the villages round his camp were deserted, and it became a matter of

* The sháhrukhi is only 10*d.* or 11*d.*; but the whole sum must have been very great; and this injudicious expenditure justifies the nickname of "the Calender" given to him at the time, from a religious order, whose practice it is to keep nothing for to-morrow. He could not always have been so profuse, though always generous; for after he once got Cábul, we hear of no financial embarrassments.

Discontent of his troops.

great difficulty to procure grain or forage for the army. In addition to this, the summer, always nearly intolerable to natives of cold countries, was in that year unusually oppressive, and so affected his troops that all ranks began to murmur, and at length to clamour to be led back to Cábul: some even made preparations for returning without leave. On this, Báber assembled the officers, and pointed out to them that, as the conquest of India had long been the great object of their labours, it would be weakness and disgrace to abandon it now that it was achieved; that *he*, therefore, was determined to remain in India; that all who chose to return were at liberty to do so at once; but that henceforth he would hear of no remonstrances against his resolution. This address induced the greater part to give up their discontents. Khája Kilán, however, one of his best and most confidential chiefs, was among those that decided to return, and was accordingly appointed to a government beyond the Indus, and dismissed with honour to his new charge.

The determination so strongly expressed had an effect even on the enemy; and many, who had hitherto expected Báber to withdraw as Tamerlane had done, now made their submission: detachments were sent to reduce others; and, in the course of the next four months, not only had the country held by Sultán I'brahím been secured, but all the revolted provinces ever possessed by the house of Lódi, including the former kingdom of

BOOK VII.

Júanpúr, were brought into subjection by an army under Prince Humáyun, Báber's eldest son.

A. D. 1526, July to Oct. A. H. 932.

The last places which submitted were Biána, Dhulpúr on the Chambal, and Gwaliór beyond that river.

His war with Sanga, rána of Méwár.

After he had thus been acknowledged by all the Mussulmans, Báber had to commence a war with the Hindús, who, contrary to their usual practice, were on this occasion the aggressors.

Hamír Sing, the Rájpút prince who recovered Chitór in the reign of Alá u dín Khilji (A. D. 1316), had, in the course of a long reign, re-established the Rájpút dominion over all Méwár; to which his son had added Ajmír.* After the separation of Málwa from Delhi the new kings of that country were engaged in frequent hostilities with the rájas of Méwár; and, immediately before the time of Báber, Mahmúd, king of Málwa, had been defeated and taken prisoner by Sanga, the Rájpút prince † (A. D. 1519).

Sanga, the sixth in succession from Hamír, possessed all the hereditary dominions of Méwár, and likewise held the eastern part of Málwa as far as Bilsa and Chándéri ‡, in dependence. He was recognised as their leader by the rájas of Márwár, and Jeipúr, and all the other Rájpút princes. §

Being a natural enemy to the king of Delhi, he had opened a friendly communication with Báber

* Colonel Tod's Rajputána, vol. i. p. 274.

† Briggs's Ferishta, vol. iv. p. 261.

‡ Báber's Memoirs, p. 312.

§ Colonel Tod, vol. i. p. 299.

while he was advancing against I'brahím, and for the same reason he began to form combinations against him as soon as he found him established in the former position of that prince. Besides his Hindú allies, Sanga was on this occasion accompanied by Mahmúd, a prince of the house of Lódi, who had assumed the title of king, and, though possessed of no territory, was followed by 10,000 adherents. The Lódi chiefs formerly driven out by Humáyun also returned to their former possessions, or raised men in other places to co-operate with the rája. Great efforts were made on both sides to secure the alliance of Hasan Khán, rája of Méwát, who, by his name, must have been a converted Hindú. His territory is that hilly tract extending towards the river Chambal, from within twenty-five miles of Delhi, and including the petty state which is now called Machéri or Alwar.

The son of this chief being a hostage in Báber's hands, he adopted the liberal policy of sending him to his father as the true way to gain his sincere co-operation. His generosity did not make the desired impression; for Hasan Khán was no sooner set at ease about his son than he openly joined the enemy. Rája Sanga immediately advanced to support his ally, and soon arrived at Biána, within fifty miles of Agra. He drove the garrison of that place, with loss, into their fort, and cut off all communication between them and the capital. Báber, on this, sent forward a detachment to observe the enemy, and soon after moved out with all his

BOOK VII.

forces. He had reached Síkrí*, about twenty miles from Agra, when he found himself in the neighbourhood of the Hindú army. His advanced guard was immediately attacked; and though reinforced from the main body, was defeated with heavy loss. If the rája had pressed on during the first panic, it is probable he would have obtained an easy victory: he chose to withdraw to his encampment after his success, and thus allowed Báber ample time to take

February 18 or 19.

up a position and to fortify his camp, so as to make it a difficult matter to assail him.

Báber's troops had looked on this contest in a very serious light from the first; and the reports of fugitives, together with the disaster which had taken place almost before their eyes, had made a very deep impression on them; when, by ill luck, a celebrated astrologer arrived from Cábul, and loudly announced, from the aspect of Mars, the certain defeat of the king's army, which happened to be in the quarter opposite to that planet. The consternation occasioned by these real and imaginary terrors was so general that even the officers of the highest rank were infected, lost all courage and decision in council, and could scarcely even maintain an appearance of firmness before their men. Báber's Indian troops began to desert; some of them went over to the enemy; and the rest of the army, though faithful, was completely dispirited and alarmed. Báber himself, though he despised

* Now Fattehpúr Síkrí.

the prediction of the astrologer, was not insensible to the dangers of his situation: he tells us that he repented of his sins, forswore wine, and gave away his gold and silver drinking vessels to the poor; he also made a vow to let his beard grow, and promised to remit the stamp tax on all Mussulmans, if it should please God to give him victory. But he was too much used to danger to be depressed; and that he might infuse some of his own spirit into his troops, he assembled his officers of all ranks, and without touching on the usual topics of necessity, or of spoil and conquests,—scarcely even on that of religion,—he made a direct appeal to their sense of honour, and set the chance of glory against the risk of death. His theme seems to have been well chosen, for the whole assembly answered him with one voice, and accompanied their acclamations with an oath on the Koran to conquer or die. This scene revived the courage of the army; and, as every day brought in accounts of some fresh disorder in the provinces, Báber determined no longer to avoid an action, but to bring things to an immediate crisis. With this view, he drew up his army in front of his intrenchments, and, after arranging his guns, and making his other preparations, he gallopped along the line from right to left, animating his soldiers by short addresses, and instructing the officers how to conduct themselves in the battle. The Hindús, it appears, were equally ready for a decisive effort; but so anxious is Báber to do justice to the great occasion, that,

Battle of Síkrí; victory of Báber.

BOOK VII.

instead of his own account of the action, he gives us the elaborate despatch of his secretary, from which we can barely discover, in many pages of

A. D. 1527, March 16. A. H. 933, Jamádi u Sáni 13.

flowery declamation, that Báber gained a great victory, that Rája Sanga escaped with difficulty, and that Hasan Khán and many other chiefs were slain. Báber (to return to his own narrative) could now relieve his heart by a torrent of abuse against the astrologer, who came to congratulate him on his victory, and whom he inveighed against as a perverse, conceited, and insufferable evil-speaker: he was an old servant, however, and Báber made him a liberal present, while he desired him to quit his dominions.

Settlement of the country.

After this victory, Báber proceeded to reduce Méwát, and brought it into greater order than it ever had been in under the former government. Having promised, before the great battle, that he would allow any one who pleased leave of absence to Cábul, he formed all who desired to avail themselves of that permission into a detachment, and sent them back under the command of Humáyun.

He spent the next six months in internal arrangements, and restoring order throughout the provinces that had been disturbed during the doubtful period of his contest with Rája Sanga; and by the end of the year his authority was everywhere re-established, except in Oud, beyond the Ganges. A body of Afgháns still remained in arms in that province, and a detachment had been sent against them.

About the beginning of the next year Báber marched against Chándéri, on the borders of Bundélcand and Málwa. It was held by Médni Rái, a Rájpút chief who had risen to great power under Mahmúd II., king of Málwa. He had afterwards usurped the government; and, on being expelled by Mahmúd with the aid of the king of Guzerát, established himself at Chándéri, under the protection of Rája Sanga. He had made good his retreat after the late battle, and now offered a desperate resistance. But the Rájpúts, as usual, showed more valour than skill or perseverance. On the second day of the siege they gave up all for lost, and Báber witnessed one of those extraordinary instances of self-devotion which are so common in Rájpút history. His troops had already mounted the works, when the garrison put their women to death, and rushed forth naked, not to conquer, but to die. They drove the Mussulmans before them, leaped from the ramparts, and continued their charge with unabated fury until they were overpowered and destroyed: 200 or 300 had remained to defend Médni Rái's house, most of whom slew each other, each contending who should be the first victim.

CHAP. I.

A. D. 1528, A. H. 934. Siege of Chándéri.

A. D. 1528, January 20.

During the siege of Chándéri, Báber received intelligence of the defeat of his detachment in Oud by an Afghán chief named Bában, or Bibán, and immediately marched, himself, in that direction. The Afgháns having taken post at the passage of the Ganges, Báber threw a bridge over the river,

Afghán insurrection.

under the fire of his artillery, and ultimately compelled the enemy to retire beyond the Gógra, whither he marched in pursuit of them. He seems to have compelled the rebels to take refuge in the territories of the king of Bengal, and it was probably on this occasion that he reduced Behár; if that was not done before by Humáyun: but in this place there is an interruption in the Memoirs, which is not filled up by any other historian.

For some months after this, Báber seems to have been in bad health, and to have indulged in a longer course of relaxation than often fell to his lot. His Memoirs (which are now resumed) are filled with descriptions of Hindú forts and temples, and of fountains and cascades that he had visited; as well as of his own gardens and improvements, and of the jugglers, wrestlers, and other sources of amusement peculiar to India.

Even during this period he made the important acquisition of the fort of Rintambór: it was made over to him by the second son of Rája Sanga, that prince having died, and having been succeeded by the eldest son.

His attention was at last effectually roused by the intelligence that the province of Behár had been seized on by Sultán Mahmúd, the same Lódi prince who had been present at the defeat of Rája Sánga. Mahmúd seems to have been supported from Bengal; and being joined by the Afgháns in Behár and the adjoining provinces, his army soon swelled to such an extent as to be called

100,000 men. With this force he had advanced to Benáres by the time when Báber reached the junction of the Jamna and Ganges, now Allahabad. The approach of Báber, however, dissolved this hasty assemblage, which was already a prey to dissension. They had attempted to storm the hill fort of Chunár; and a repulse they met with, though not in itself considerable, was sufficient, in the present state of their minds, to break up the army. Mahmúd retreated with such portion as he could keep together. He took up a position behind the river Són (Soane); and many of the chiefs who had quitted him made their submission to Báber. Báber continued his advance; and Mahmúd, finding it in vain to oppose him, sought for safety in flight.

Defeat of the king of Bengal.

All Behár south of the Ganges was now in Báber's hands; North Behár was still in possession of the king of Bengal, who had a considerable army on foot in that quarter. His object appears to have been to have retained that portion of the Delhi territories without quarrelling with the possessor of the rest; and he kept an ambassador in Báber's camp, to amuse him with negotiations, until Báber lost patience, crossed the Ganges, and advanced against the Bengalese army.

He had still to pass the river Gógra, on which the enemy were encamped, near its junction with the Ganges. He was, however, well provided with boats, and drove away those of the Bengalese, which might otherwise have obstructed his passage.

The Bengalese then moved down to oppose his crossing, and a cannonade was kept up on both sides. As Báber's divisions landed in succession, they charged the different parties opposed to them, and at last drove the enemy from the field. Soon after this the king of Bengal consented to terms of peace. Báber was preparing to return to Agra, when he heard that a body of Afgháns, who had separated from the Bengal army, under Bában and another chief, named Báyazid, had crossed the Gógra, and taken Luknow. He immediately marched in that direction; and, on the retreat of the Afgháns, sent a detachment in pursuit of them. It followed them across the Ganges and Jamna, and had completely dispersed them in Bundélcand, when the setting in of the rainy season put an end to all operations.

Sickness of Báber.

For the last fifteen months of his life Báber's health seems to have been greatly broken: the silence of his diary gives a proof of his diminished activity, and some circumstances lead to a belief that his authority began to be weakened by the prospect of its speedy cessation. Humáyun left his government of Badakhshán without leave, and Khalífa, Báber's prime minister, on being selected to replace him, found means to excuse himself, and remain at court. Notwithstanding Humáyun's unlooked for return, he was affectionately received; and a dangerous illness, with which he was soon after attacked, was the immediate cause of the death of Báber.

When it was announced to him that the physicians had given over all their efforts, declaring that medicine could no longer avail, Báber seized on the only hope that remained, and, in conformity with a superstition which still prevails in the East, he determined to devote his own life for that of his son. His friends, who had as little doubt of the efficacy of this substitution as he had himself, entreated him to forbear from a sacrifice involving the happiness of so many; but Báber's resolution was unmoved. He walked three times round the bed of the dying prince (a solemnity usual on such occasions), and then spent some moments in earnest prayer to God; at the end of which, he was filled with such assurance, that he more than once exclaimed, "I have borne it away — I have borne it away!" and so powerful was the impression both on his mind and his son's, that all the historians agree that Humáyun began from that time to recover, while it is certain that Báber, who was already ill, and whose health must have been severely shaken by his anxiety and agitation, began visibly to decline. It soon became evident that his end was approaching. He called his sons and ministers about him, explained his dying wishes, and enjoined concord among all, and affection among his children. But Khalífa, his minister, whose influence, for some unexplained reason, was, at that time, irresistible, had already resolved to overturn the dearest of his plans. Desirous of keeping power in his own hands, he determined to

Intrigues regarding the succession.

BOOK VII.

set aside Báber's own sons, and to give the crown to his son-in-law, Mehdi Khája, a young man whose thoughtless and flighty disposition made it seem easy to keep him in perpetual dependence.* Mehdi Khája was at no pains to undeceive him in these expectations, and was now considered by himself and others as assured of the succession the moment that Báber should breathe his last. As that moment approached, however, he was suddenly seized by Khalífa, put into confinement, and cut off from all communication with those around. The cause of this revolution is explained in a narrative referred to by Mr. Erskine, which is given on the authority of Mohammed Mokím, the father of the author. Khalífa, it seems, was on a visit to Mehdi Khája, with no person present but Mokím: he was suddenly summoned to Báber, who lay at the last extremity. Mehdi Khája attended him with great respect to the door, and stood looking after him, so that Mokím could not follow without pushing by him. "As soon as Khalífa was fairly gone, he muttered to himself, 'God willing, I will soon flay your hide off, old boy;' and, turning round at the same instant, saw my father. He was quite confounded; but, immediately seizing my

* Khalífa was one of Báber's old officers; but it is not easy to conjecture how he could acquire so inordinate a power under so able a sovereign as Báber, and with an experienced heir-apparent like Humáyun. Equally extraordinary does it seem that, from this time forward, he disappears, and is not mentioned in Ferishta or Abul Fazl, either under his own name of Khalífa, or his title of Nizám u dín.

CHAP. I.

father's ear, with a convulsive eagerness, twisted it round, and said, hurriedly, 'You, Tájik! the red tongue often gives the green head to the winds.'" Mokím lost no time in apprising Khalífa of what had passed; and the result was, his immediately transferring his allegiance to Humáyun.

Death of Báber.

In the midst of these intrigues, with which he was probably unacquainted, Báber expired, — the most admirable, though not the most powerful, prince that ever reigned in Asia. He died, at Agra, in the fiftieth year of his age, and the thirty-eighth of his reign. His body was buried, by his own desire, at Cábul, and on a spot which it is probable that he had himself selected.*

A. D. 1530, Dec. 26. A. H. 937.

His character.

Báber's character is best shown in his actions; but something remains to be said of his private life and his writings. His memoirs are almost singular in their own nature, and perfectly so if we consider the circumstances of the writer. They contain a minute account of the life of a great Tartar monarch, along with a natural effusion of his opinions and feelings, free from disguise and reserve, and no less free from all affectation of extreme frankness and candour.†

* "He had directed his body to be interred in this place, to him the choicest in his wide dominions." .... "A running and clear stream yet waters the fragrant flowers of the cemetery, which is the great holyday resort of the people of Cábul. In the front of the grave is a small but chaste mosque of white marble." .... "There is a noble prospect from the hill that overlooks Báber's tomb," &c. &c. (*Burnes's Travels*, vol. i. p. 141.)

† In this last respect, they are a contrast to those of Tamer-

BOOK VII.

The style is plain and manly, as well as lively and picturesque; and being the work of a man of genius and observation, it presents his countrymen and contemporaries, in their appearance, manners, pursuits, and actions, as clearly as in a mirror. In this respect it is almost the only specimen of real history in Asia; for the ordinary writers, though they give pompous accounts of the deeds and ceremonies of the great, are apt to omit the lives and manners even of that class; while every thing beneath their level is left entirely out of sight. In Báber, the figures, dress, tastes, and habits of each individual introduced are described with such minuteness and reality, that we seem to live among them, and to know their persons as well as we do their characters.* His description of the countries he visited, their scenery, climate, productions, and works of art and industry, are more full and accurate than will, perhaps, be found, in equal space, in any modern traveller; and, considering the cir-

lane, which, with all their simplicity of language, are evidently written for effect. "One day, having unintentionally trodden on an ant, I felt as if my foot had lost all its power." (*Memoirs of Teimur*, p. 30.) Who can imagine this to be natural, even if the author had been a Bramin ascetic, instead of the most sanguinary of conquerors?

* These portraits, however, are necessarily confined to the inhabitants of the courts and camps where Báber passed his days: in the countries which he has so well delineated, he only gives such remarkable particulars about the natives as would strike a stranger, without attempting a detailed account of their way of life, with which he must necessarily have been unacquainted.

cumstances in which they were compiled, are truly surprising.*

But the great charm of the work is in the character of the author, whom we find, after all the trials of a long life, retaining the same kind and affectionate heart, and the same easy and sociable temper, with which he set out on his career, and in whom the possession of power and grandeur had neither blunted the delicacy of his taste, nor diminished his sensibility to the enjoyment of nature and imagination.

"It is a relief," says his translator, "in the midst of the pompous coldness of Asiatic history, to find a king who can weep for days, and tell us that he wept for the playmate of his boyhood." He speaks with as much interest of his mother and female relations as if he had never quitted their fireside; and his friends make almost as great a figure in the personal part of his narrative as he does himself. He repeats their sayings, records their accidents and illnesses, relates their adventures, and sometimes jokes on their eccentricities.

After a letter, on the affairs of his government, to his most confidential counsellor, Khája Kilán (then at Cábul), he tells him little anecdotes of their common acquaintances, which he thinks will

* Compare his descriptions of the countries through which he fought his way with those of Ibn Batúta, himself a writer of remarkable merit, and a professed traveller and inquirer. Or compare his geography with that of any Asiatic who has written expressly on the science.

BOOK VII.

amuse him, and adds, "For God's sake excuse all these fooleries, and do not think the worse of me for them." He endeavours afterwards to persuade Khája Kilán to leave off wine, as he had done; and says, in substance, "Drinking was a very pleasant thing with our old friends and companions; but now that you have only Shír Ahmed and Heider Kúli to take your wine with, it can be no great sacrifice to leave it off." In the same letter, he says how much he envies his friend his residence at Cábul, and adds, "They, very recently, brought me a single musk melon *: while cutting it up, I felt myself affected with a strong feeling of loneliness, and a sense of my exile from my native country, and I could not help shedding tears while I was eating it."

It would have been fortunate if Báber had left off wine sooner, for there seems good reason to think his indulgence in it tended to shorten his days. Many a drinking party is recorded in his memoirs, with at least as much interest as his battles or negotiations; and unsuitable as they are to his station, they are not the least agreeable scenes in Báber's history. The perfect ease and familiarity among the company makes one forget the prince in the man; and the temptations that generally lead to those excesses — a shady wood, a hill with a fine prospect, or the idleness of a boat floating down a river; together with the amuse-

* This fruit had not then been introduced into India.

ments with which they are accompanied, extemporary verses, recitations in Túrki and Persian, with sometimes a song, and often a contest of repartee — take away all the coarseness that might attach to such scenes of dissipation.

The unsettled nature of his life is shown by his observing, near the end of it, that since he was eleven years old he had never kept the fast of the Rámzán twice in any one place; and the time not spent in war and travelling was occupied in hunting and other sports, or in long excursions on horseback about the country. On his last journey, after his health had begun to fail, he rode, in two days, from Calpí to Agra (160 miles), without any particular motive for dispatch; and on the same journey he swam twice across the Ganges, as he said he had done with every other river he had met with. His mind was as active as his body: besides the business of the kingdom, he was constantly taken up with aqueducts, reservoirs, and other improvements, as well as introducing new fruits and other productions of remote countries. Yet he found time to compose many elegant Persian poems and a collection of Túrki compositions, which are mentioned as giving him a high rank among the poets of his own country.*

* Almost all that has been said of Báber has been drawn from Mr. Erskine's admirable translation of his Memoirs from the Túrki. The notes and supplements which accompany that work remove the obscurities which, without such assistance, would beset us in every page; and the preliminary dissertation

gives a complete view of the state of Asia in Báber's time, and contains the best account of the geography of the countries which were the scene of his exploits, and the clearest exposition of the divisions of the Tartar nations. The translation seems to have imbibed the very spirit of the original. The style is singularly happy, strikingly characteristic, though perfectly natural, and equally remote from the usual inflated language of the East, and from the imitation of scriptural simplicity into which other translators of similar works have fallen.

CHAP. II.

FIRST REIGN OF HUMÁYUN.

Báber left three sons besides Humáyun; Cámrán, Hindál, and Mírza Askari.*

* The narrative of the reign of Humáyun (where not otherwise specified) is taken from Ferishta, the Memoirs of Humáyun, and Abul Fazl. Ferishta is peculiarly defective at this period, which was too remote to admit of his conversing with eye-witnesses, and too recent to allow him to benefit by written histories.

The Memoirs are written by a person named Jouher, who was a menial servant of Humáyun, and whose duty it was to carry an ewer for his master to wash his hands. He was in constant attendance on Humáyun, and although unacquainted with his political relations and secret designs, was a minute and correct observer of all that came within his reach, and describes what he saw with simplicity and distinctness. He was devoted to Humáyun, and anxious to put all his actions in the most favourable light; but he seldom imagined that any thing in his master's conduct required either concealment or apology. Abul Fazl was the well-known minister and favourite of Akber, and was a man of enlarged views and extraordinary talents; but he was a professed rhetorician, and is still the model of the unnatural style which is so much admired in India; he was, besides, a most assiduous courtier, eager to extol the virtues, to gloss over the crimes, and to preserve the dignity of his master and those in whom he was interested. His dates and his general statement of events are valuable; but he requires constant attention, not so much to guard against his barefaced partiality, as against the prejudice which he draws on his favourites by his fawning and fulsome commendations of them, and against the suspicions which he excites by his dishonest way of telling a story, even in cases where the action related was innocent or

BOOK VII.

Arrangements of the king's brother.

Cámrán was governor of Cábul and Candahár, and the other two were unemployed in India. From his having assigned no shares to his younger children, it is probable that Báber did not intend to divide the empire: but Cámrán showed no disposition to give way to his brother; and as he was in possession of a strong and warlike country among the hereditary subjects of his family, he had a great advantage over Humáyun, who could not assemble an army without evacuating his new and disaffected provinces.

Separation of Cábul from India.

In these circumstances, Humáyun thought it prudent to yield with a good grace, and give up the Panjab and the country on the Indus, in addition to Cámrán's former territories. At the same time he gave the government of Sambal to Hindál, and that of Méwát to Mírza Askari. By the cession to Cámrán, Humáyun was left to govern a new conquest, while he was deprived of the resources by which it had been gained, and by which it might have been retained; but as he still possessed Báber's veteran army, and profited by the impression of his power, the effects of the dismemberment did not at first appear.

---

excusable. His narrative is florid, feeble, and indistinct; overloaded with commonplace reflections and pious effusions, generally ending in a compliment to his patron. In this part of his writings I have generally availed myself of Major Price's History, which, though it does not profess to be a translation, is often a literal version, and always a full and faithful abstract of the original.

CHAP. II.

Afghán insurrections in India.

Humáyun was engaged in the siege of Cálanjer, in Bundélcand, when he received intelligence that Bában and Báyazíd, the Afghán chiefs, whose party was formerly broken up by Báber, were again in rebellion in Júanpúr. He defeated and dispersed this assemblage; and then went against the hill fort of Chunár, near Benáres, at that time held by his future rival, Shír Khán. Shír Khán submitted on condition of retaining the fort, and Humáyun returned to Agra.

A. D. 1532, A. H. 939.

Disputes with Bahádur Sháh, king of Guzerát.

Some time before this period, a brother-in-law of Humáyun's, who had been engaged in plots against his life and government, had taken refuge with Bahádur Sháh, king of Guzerát; and the refusal of that monarch to comply with Humáyun's demand for his surrender led to irritation and hostile feelings between the two kings. Bahádur, whose native kingdom always occupied a high rank among those formed out of the fragments of the empire of Delhi, had lately extended his power much beyond its former limits. The kings of Cándésh, Bérár, and Ahmednagar had agreed to do him homage for their crowns; and he had completely conquered the kingdom of Málwa, and annexed it to his own.

A. D. 1532, A. H. 940.

While his discussion with Humáyun was at its height, Alá u dín, the uncle of Sultán I'brahím Lódi, who acted so conspicuous a part in the former reign, having quitted the residence assigned to him by Báber, in Badakhshán, threw himself on the protection of the king of Guzerát; and Ba-

BOOK VII.

hádúr, whose family had risen to greatness under the house of Lódi, and who had himself found an asylum at the court of I'brahím, being at once incited by favour for his hereditary patrons, resentment at Humáyun, and pride in his own power and prosperity, was tempted into measures as inconsistent with sound policy as with justice. Without any open declaration of war with Humáyun, he liberally supplied Alá u dín with money, and enabled him, in a very short time, to assemble a large force, and to send it against Agra, under his son, Tátár Khán. This army, so hastily collected, was as speedily dispersed; and Tátár Khán fell in battle, at the head of a division which remained faithful in the general desertion.

A. D. 1534, A. H. 941.

Invasion and conquest of Guzerát.

Encouraged by this success, or, perhaps, in pursuance of plans already determined on, Humáyun marched from Agra to revenge the injury he had received from Bahádur Sháh. That prince was now at war with the rána of Méwár, and being entirely occupied by the siege of Chitór, was particularly exposed to the attack of an enemy; but Humáyun, moved by his remonstrances against the impiety of molesting a Mussulman prince while engaged in war with the infidels, or influenced by his own dilatory habits, retarded his march, until the place was taken, and the besieger prepared to receive him in an intrenched camp at Mandesór. Bahádur had chosen this course on account of the superiority of his artillery, commanded by a Constantinopolitan Turk, and partly

A. D. 1534, November. A. H. 941, Jamádi al awal.

A. D. 1535, March. A. H. 941, Rámzán.

served by Portuguese prisoners. These advantages availed him little; his position was rendered untenable by the enemy's cutting off his supplies; and, finding that famine would soon force him to surrender, he blew up his guns, and fled in the night, almost alone, to Mándu, leaving his army to provide for its own safety.

The army immediately dispersed, and Bahádur, being hard pressed at Mándu, continued his flight to Chámpanér, and thence to the sea-port of Cambay. Humáyun was by this time in pursuit of him in person, with a light detachment, and reached Cambay on the evening of the day on which Bahádur had quitted it for his final place of refuge at Diú, in the most remote part of the peninsula of Guzerát.*

Having failed in his immediate object, Humáyun quitted the peninsula, and proceeded to occupy the settled part of Guzerát. He soon obtained possession of the open country, but the year was well advanced before the hill fort of Chámpanér fell into his hands. It was scaled in the

* When Humáyun was encamped at Cambay, he was exposed to considerable danger from a night attack of a body of Cúlis, a forest tribe still famous for similar exploits in Guzerát. They made their way with so much silence and intelligence into the camp, that they surprised Humáyun's own tent and carried off his baggage and books, among which was a remarkable copy of the "History of Tamerlane," the loss and subsequent recovery of which are thought worthy of being recorded by the historians of those times. Humáyun, by way of retaliating the insult he had received from these lawless mountaineers, gave up the unoffending town of Cambay to plunder.

BOOK VII.

A. D. 1535, August. A. H. 942, Safar.

night, with the help of steel spikes fixed in an almost perpendicular rock, by 300 chosen men, who climbed up, one by one, during an attack made on one of the gates by the army. Humáyun himself was among the 300.*

Expulsion of the Moguls from Guzerát.

Soon after the taking of Chámpanér, Humáyun received accounts of the commencement of those troubles which ended in the successful revolt of Shír Khán. He set off for Agra, leaving his brother, Mírza Askari, in charge of his new conquests; and had scarcely quitted Guzerát, when dissensions broke out among the officers left behind; discontents and intrigues ensued, and ended in some project for raising Mírza Askari to the throne. Bahádur profited by these disorders; and to such a state of weakness were the invaders reduced, that

A. D. 1535-6 A. H. 942.

they gave up Guzerát, without a struggle; and evacuated Málwa, which was not even threatened.†

* When the fort was taken, it was found that the place where Bahádur's treasure was concealed was known only to one officer, and it was suggested to have recourse to torture to make him disclose the secret; but Humáyun said they had much better have recourse to wine, and directed that the officer should be well treated, and invited to an entertainment by one of his own chiefs. Accordingly, when his heart was softened by kindness and warmed with good cheer, the officer made no scruple to tell his entertainer, that if the water were drawn off from a certain reservoir, the treasure would be found in a vault beneath it; and his instructions being complied with, a large amount of gold and silver was found as he had described.

† Ferishta, vols. ii. and iv. Price, vol. iv. Memoirs of Humáyun. Bird's History of Guzerát. Paper by Col. Miles, *Bombay Literary Transactions*, vol. i.

CHAP. II.

Early life and rise of Shír Khán Súr.

Humáyun had not been long returned to his capital before he set out against Shír Khán.* This person†, who was soon to act so great a part, was the grandson of I'brahím Khán, a native of Afghánistán. I'brahím claimed to be descended of the family (though probably only of the tribe) of the kings of Ghór, and both he and his son Hasan were married into noble families of their own nation. Hasan held a jágír at Sahserám, in Behár, for the maintenance of 500 horse. He had two sons by his Afghán wife, Shír Khán and Nizám

* He marched in the month of Safar, but the year is uncertain: the "Tárikhi Shír Sháh" says A. H. 942 (A. D. 1535); and the "Mantakhib al Towárikh," as well as Ferishta, A. H. 943 (A. D. 1536). The former date, 942, is impossible, because Humáyun took the fort of Chámpanér in Guzerát in that very month and year. The other year, 943, is improbable, as it allows only a twelvemonth for the final settlement of Guzerát and Málwa, besides the return to Delhi and the preparations for the war with Shír Khàn; while it leaves a year and a half for Humáyun's march of 350 miles through his own dominions to Chúnár. I should therefore suppose that his march took place in Safar, A. H. 944 (July 1537).

† This account of Shír Sháh is compiled from Ferishta, vols. i., ii., iv., from Erskine's *Baber*, and from Abul Fazl in Price, vol. iv. Ferishta gives a connected history of Shír Sháh (vol. ii. p. 98.), which, though it appears to be written with perfect impartiality, is extremely confused from inattention to dates; the different expeditions of Báber being mixed up with those of Humáyun in such a manner as to make them quite inexplicable without other aid. This aid he himself partially supplies under the reigns of I'brahím, Báber, and Humáyun; but more is derived from Báber's own Memoirs. Abul Fazl also furnishes several facts, though his general narrative is a mere invective against Shír Sháh, such as might have been expected from the minister of Humáyun's son.

Khán; but he was led, by the arts of a concubine, to slight his wife, and neglect her children; and as soon as Shír Khán was of an age to act for himself, he left his father, went to Júanpúr, and entered as a private soldier into the service of the governor. His father applied to the governor to send him home for his education, but Shír Khán urged that there were more opportunities of education at Júanpúr than at Sahserám; and he seems to have been in earnest in his preference, for he devoted himself to study, made himself familiar with history and poetry, and could repeat all the poems of Sádi from memory, besides acquiring a general knowledge of other branches of information. He was subsequently restored to favour by his father, and managed his jágír, until Solimán, the son of his step-mother, had grown up. After this he found his situation so unpleasant, that he went off with his full brother, Nizám, and entered into the service of Sultán Secander, who was then king.* He remained at Delhi until his father died, when the jágír of Sahserám was conferred on him; and after the defeat of Sultán I'brahím (A. D. 1526), he was active in the service of Mohammed Sháh Lohání, who set up for king of Júanpúr and Behár. He was for some time in favour with this prince, but being again deprived of his paternal jágír by the intrigues of his half brother, Solimán, he left the court in disgust, and joined Junid, the governor of

* Secander died in A. D. 1517.

Júanpúr, on the part of Báber (A. D. 1527). By the assistance of Juníd, he assembled a body of adventurers in the hills of Behár, recovered his own jágír, and carried on attacks and depredations on the territory of Mohammed Sháh Loháni, professing himself a subject of Báber. About this time (A. D. 1528), he waited on that monarch, accompanied him to Chándéri, and was confirmed in his possessions, and intrusted with a command in Behár, on the part of the emperor.

Next year (1529) Mahmúd Lódi took Behár; and Shír Khán, either from necessity, or an inclination to the cause of his nation, joined the Lódi standard. On the dispersion of Mahmúd's army, he was one of the many chiefs who made their submission to Báber (April 1529).* Mohammed Sháh Loháni was now dead; and his son Jelál, who was a minor, in charge of his mother, and at that time accompanying the Bengal army, made his submission also, and was invested with considerable powers, on the part of the emperor. He was still, however, under the management of his mother, Dúdú, over whom Shír Khán acquired such an ascendancy, that, on her death, Jelál was left in entire dependence on that ambitious chief. Shír Khán now made himself master of Behár, and also obtained possession of the fort of Chunár, as, at this or some subsequent period, he did of the still more important fortress of Rohtás.†

He obtains possession of Behár.

* Erskine's Báber, p. 408.

† Rohtás was taken by treachery from a Hindú rája. Shír

BOOK VII.

These rapid advances to power were made in the early part of Humáyun's reign; and as soon as that prince had settled his discussions with Cámrán, and had time to attend to his interests in the provinces, he marched against Chunár, as has been already stated (1532). He, however, was content with the recognition of his title, and the service of a body of horse, under Shír Khán's son; and this young man took an opportunity to withdraw when the king began his march against Bahádur Sháh. Humáyun, thenceforward, was fully occupied in Guzerát; and before his return, Shír Khán had got complete possession of Behár, had invaded Bengal, and had made great progress in the conquest of that rich kingdom.

And conquers Bengal.

His war with Bengal was occasioned by Jelál Lohání, who had called in the aid of the king of that country to relieve him from the control of Shír Khán, and, by his means, had at one time nearly succeeded in his object; but Shír Khán soon retrieved his losses, repelled the attack on himself, and laid siege to Gour, the capital of the hostile king.

Khán persuaded him to give an asylum to his family, and then introduced armed soldiers in the covered litters, which were supposed to conceal the women. This stratagem, which has so fabulous an appearance, was thought sufficiently plausible in modern times to be employed by M. Bussy to conceal the treachery of a governor who admitted him into the strong fort of Doulatábád.

He was engaged in this enterprise when Humáyun returned; and that prince could not fail to perceive, at once, the advantage of attacking him while thus embarrassed, and the danger of allowing him to consolidate his power.

Humáyun marches against him.

With those views, he marched at the head of a powerful army from Agra, and advanced through a peaceful country, till he reached Chunár, near Benáres.

Military features of Behár and Bengal.

But Shír Khán was well aware of all the danger of his situation, and laid his plans for averting it with a foresight and combination of which we have no example in the previous history of India.

His first object was to gain time to complete the conquest of Bengal, before he should be disturbed by a new enemy. For this purpose he threw a strong garrison into Chunár, and provided it with all the means of retarding the advance of Humáyun, by an obstinate defence.

This fort stands on a rock, close to the Ganges, and is, as it were, a detached portion of the Vindya mountains, which extend to the same river near Mírzápúr. From that neighbourhood the hills recede westward, by the fort of Rohtás and Shírgháti, and do not approach the river again until near Bhágalpúr, after which they run straight south, leaving the Ganges at a great distance. These hills, therefore, cover the whole of the south-west of Behár and Bengal, and shut up the road along the south bank of the Ganges, in two places; one near Chunár, and the other at Sícragalli, east

BOOK VII.

of Bhágalpúr. The hills themselves are not high, but poor and covered with woods.

As Humáyun marched along the Ganges, and made use of that river to convey his guns and stores, it was necessary for him to begin with the siege of Chunár.* After investing the place, he endeavoured to mine such parts of the walls as were accessible on the land side, and also brought floating batteries, constructed for the purpose, to bear upon the face towards the river. Notwithstanding all these preparations, his attack failed; the garrison, however, having already held out for several months, and knowing that they had no prospect of relief, at length surrendered. The siege had been conducted by Rúmi Khán, the Constantinopolitan Turk, who brought Bahádur Sháh of Guzerat's ordnance to so high a state, and who had since entered into the service of Humáyun; and so much importance was attached to the knowledge of the service of artillery in those days, that the right hands of all the gunners in the garrison, to the number of 300, were cut off, either

Siege of Chunár.

* The Memoirs of Humáyun say that the army reached Chunár on the Shabí Bárát (Shábán 15th) of A. H. 945, January, 1539; but this would leave only six months for the conquest of Bengal and all the other operations till Humayun's defeat in Safar, 946 (June, 1539). I conclude, therefore, that the memoir writer, who scarcely ever gives a date, may have mistaken the year, although he has remembered the festival, and that the siege began 15th Shábán, 944 (January 8th, 1538). All accounts agree that the siege lasted several months; some say six months.

to disable them for the future, or in revenge for the loss they had occasioned.

After the taking of Chunár, Humáyun pushed his march along the Ganges. Before reaching Patna, he was met by Mahmúd, king of Bengal, who had just been driven from his dominions, and was still suffering from a wound he had received in his last defeat.

As he approached the defile of Sícragali, he sent on a strong detachment to take possession of it. They found it already occupied by Jelál Khán, the son of Shír Khán, who attacked and repulsed them with considerable loss. Humáyun hastened on with his main body to retrieve this check, but was agreeably surprised to find the pass deserted, and the road open to the capital of Bengal.

Shír Khán's plan for resisting the invasion.

It was no part of Shír Khán's plan to cope with the superior of force Humáyun in this stage of the campaign. His design from the first was to retire to the hilly tract on the south-west; and with this view he had removed his family, and all that he possesssed of value, to Rohtás. The protacted siege of Chunár had enabled him to reduce Gour, and to defeat Mahmúd in a conclusive battle. He had still required time to remove the captured treasure and stores to Rohtás, and to dispose of the open country in the manner that suited his views. Jelál Khán had therefore been instructed to delay Humáyun at the pass, but to avoid any serious encounter, and to join his father in the

BOOK VII.

Taking of Gour by Humáyun. His difficulties during the rainy season.

hills. Humáyun accordingly took possession of Gour* without further opposition. But the rains had by this time attained their height: the Delta of the Ganges was one vast sheet of water; and in the country beyond the reach of inundation every brook and channel was become an impassable flood. It was impossible to carry on operations in Bengal, and scarcely less difficult to keep up a communication with upper India. This forced inactivity lasted for several months, during which time the spirit of the soldiers sank under the moist and sultry climate, and their numbers were thinned by the sickly season that follows the heavy rains. No sooner were the roads open, than they began to desert in numbers; and Prince Hindál, who had been left in North Behár, went off even before the rains had ceased.

Active operations of Shír Khán.

Meanwhile Shír Khán issued from his retreat, took possession of Behár and Benáres, recovered Chunár, laid siege to Júanpúr, and pushed his detachments up the Ganges as far as Canóuj. Thus, when the season for military operations commenced, Humáyun found his communication with his capital again intercepted, and himself left with no alternative but to trust his new conquest to the charge of a weak detachment, and endeavour to

* Probably June or July, 1538. Abul Fazl states that Bengal was conquered in A. H. 945. That year began on May 30th, 1538; but it appears that Humáyun had met with rain before he left Behár, where the rainy season does not commence till June.

force his way to Agra with the rest of his reduced army.

Retreat of Humáyun.

He for some time hesitated to adopt this decided measure, and the dry season was half over before he set out on his retreat. He sent on a considerable body before he himself began his march, under the command of Khán Khánán Lodi, one of Báber's principal generals. By the time this force reached Monghír, it was surprised and defeated by a detachment sent by Shír, who was now as enterprising as he had before been cautious; and who, to show his confidence in the result of his operations, had already assumed the title of king.

Shír Khán assumes the title of king.

If Humáyun had not before had sufficient motives for extricating himself from his present situation, the accounts he was daily receiving of the progress of affairs at Agra must have filled him with impatience: but by the time he had passed Baxar, between Patna and Benáres, he found that Shír Sháh had raised the siege of Júanpúr, and was come by forced marches to intercept his retreat. Shír Sháh had made a march of thirty-five miles on that day, and Humáyun was advised to attack him before his troops had time to refresh. The step seemed too hazardous to be adopted at once; and next day he found Shír intrenched in such a manner that he could neither be passed nor attacked with any prospect of success. Humáyun, therefore, intrenched in his turn, and began to collect boats and form a bridge across the Ganges,

Intercepts Humáyun on his retreat.

BOOK VII.

so as to pursue his retreat along the opposite bank. Shír Sháh, to whom every delay was an advantage, allowed him to go on for nearly two months; when, the bridge of boats being nearly completed, Shír Sháh one day left his camp standing and occupied by a sufficient force to conceal his movement from the enemy, while he himself, with the choice of his army, made a secret march to the rear of Humáyun's position, and, returning in the night, attacked him in three columns about daybreak, and completely surprised his camp. Humáyun had only time to leap on horseback, and, though himself disposed to make one effort, at least, against the enemy, he was urged by those around him to provide for his own safety; and one of his principal officers, seizing his reins, in a manner compelled him to make his way to the river-side. The bridge, as has been mentioned, was not finished; and as Humáyun had not a moment for deliberation, he plunged at once into the Ganges. Before he reached the opposite bank his horse was exhausted, and sunk into the stream; and Humáyun himself must have met with the same fate, if he had not been saved by a water-carrier who was crossing with the aid of the skin used to hold water, which he had inflated like a bladder, and which enabled him to support the king's weight as well as his own. Thus rescued, Humáyun pursued his flight, with a very small retinue, to Calpí, and thence proceeded to Agra, almost the whole of his army having been cut off by the enemy or drowned

Surprises him, and disperses his army.

in the river. Humáyun's queen, whom it had been the object of his last exertion to save, had already been surrounded, and fell into the hands of the enemy: she was treated by Shír Sháh with scrupulous delicacy and attention, and was sent on the first opportunity to a place of safety. This tremendous disaster took place in the end of June, 1539.* A. H. 946, Safar 6. A. D. 1539, June 26.

Humáyun's presence, discomfited as he was, was of essential importance at Agra. While he was shut up in Bengal, Prince Hindál had begun to collect adherents at Agra, and being afterwards joined by the fugitives from Bengal, he went into open rebellion; while Prince Cámrán, on being applied to by the king's representatives, immediately set out from Cábul, professedly to support Humáyun's interests, but in reality to be at hand to profit by any opportunity of advancing his own. The arrival of Humáyun put a stop to all those designs. He pardoned Hindál at the intercession of Cámrán; and the three brothers united their exertions to arrest the progress of their common enemy.

* Most writers ascribe Humáyun's defeat to treachery, and say that Shír Sháh attacked him during an armistice, or even after a peace had been signed. This account, in itself, does not seem improbable; but that given by Major Price from Abul Fazl, although it occasionally applies opprobrious epithets to the enemy of Humáyun, does great justice to Shír Sháh in the facts, and asserts, on this occasion, that he delayed Humayún's retreat by amusing him with negotiations, but never professed to suspend his hostility, and was entirely indebted to his military skill for the success of his stratagem.

BOOK VII.

While Humáyun was occupied in repairing his losses, Shír Sháh contented himself with retaining his acquisitions in Hindostan, and proceeded to recover possession of Bengal, and to put all his former territories into a state of order.

A. D. 1540, April. A. H. 946, Zíl Caádah.

Eight or nine months were employed on both sides in these transactions. Towards the end of the Mahometan year, Humáyun once more moved from Agra, his own army being strengthened by a reinforcement of 3000 men belonging to Cámrán, who himself retired to Láhór. By this time Shír Sháh had reached the Ganges opposite Canouj; and both parties seemed unwilling to offer an advantage to the other; until at length Sultán Mírza (a prince of the family of Tamerlane who had before been in rebellion) deserted from Humáyun's camp with his followers; and the example was so likely to be followed, that Humáyun determined to bring the contest to an issue, and crossed the Ganges, by a bridge of boats which he had constructed. A general action ensued, in which Humáyun's army was entirely defeated and driven into the Ganges. Humáyun himself was in imminent danger: his horse was wounded; and he must have been killed or taken, if he had not fortunately found an elephant, on which he mounted: even then the driver could not be prevailed on to attempt to swim the Ganges; and the king was obliged to throw him from his seat on the neck, and give his place to an eunuch whom he had found on the elephant, and who now guided the animal

Second campaign.

Final defeat of Humáyun.

A. D. 1540, May 16. A. H. 947, Moharram 10.

His flight.

across the stream. The opposite bank was too steep for the elephant to ascend; and Humáyun must still have perished, if two soldiers, who happened to have gained that part of the shore, had not tied their turbans together and thrown one end to him, so as to enable him to make good his landing. Before long he was joined by his brothers, the princes Hindál and Askeri, and also by some troops, and all together made their way to Agra, after a narrow escape from being plundered by the villagers on their road.

He arrives at Láhór. A. D. 1540, July 5. A. H. 947, Rabi al Awal.

All hope of further resistance was now at an end; and they had scarcely time to remove the royal family and the most portable part of the treasures from Agra and Delhi, and to escape to Cámrán at Láhor.

Even there Humáyun was no welcome guest. Cámrán was equally afraid of being supplanted by him at home, and of being involved in his quarrel with Shír Sháh, and lost no time in making his peace with the conqueror, to whom he ceded the Panjáb, and retired, himself, to Cabul, leaving Humáyun to provide as he could for his own safety.

A. D. 1540, end of Oct. A. H. 947, Jamádi al Awal.

Fails in an attempt on Sind.

The deserted monarch turned his thoughts to Sind, the province which adjoined to Cámrán's territories on the south. It was in the hands of Husén, the head of the family of Arghún, who had been driven out of Candahár by Báber; and as it had once belonged to Delhi, Humáyun hoped that he might still find some means of inducing it to recognise his authority.

BOOK VII.

But there was nothing in Humáyun's character to promise him such an ascendancy.

Though not deficient in intelligence, he had little energy; and, though free from vices and violent passions, he was no less devoid of principles and affections. By nature he was more inclined to ease than ambition; yet as he had been brought up under Báber, and accustomed to bodily and mental exertion, he never was entirely wanting to the exigencies of his situation, or quite lost the advantages of his birth and pretensions, though he never turned them to the best account.

He passed into the Arghún territories through U'ch; but after a year and a half of fruitless negotiations, and no less fruitless hostilities (during which he attempted the sieges of Bakkar and Sehwán), he found his funds expended, and the resources of the country exhausted, and was deserted by the adventurers he had collected, just as Husén Arghún was advancing to attack him.

Seeks refuge in Jódpúr;

In this extremity he fled to U'ch, and resolved, as a last resource, to throw himself on the protection of Máldeó, rája of Márwár, whom he supposed to be favourably disposed towards him; but when, after a journey over the desert, in which he lost many of his followers from thirst and fatigue, he had reached the neighbourhood of Jódpúr, he found that the rája was much less inclined to assist him than to deliver him up to his enemies, and was obliged again to seek comparative safety in the dreary sands from which he had just

which is refused.

emerged. His present object was to make his way to Amercót, a fort in the desert not far from the Indus; and in this journey he had a more desolate tract than ever to pass, and had greater evils to encounter than any he had yet experienced. Before he quitted the inhabited country, the villagers repelled all approaches to their water, which was to them a precious possession; and it was not without a conflict and bloodshed that his followers were able to slake their thirst. And all this was but a prelude to scenes of greater distress. His small train was encumbered by the presence of the women of his family; and they had already left the last trace of human culture behind, and were struggling with thirst in the heart of the desert, when, one morning, after a night of fatigue, they perceived that their march was followed by a considerable body of horse; and the worst apprehensions seem to be realised when they found it was commanded by the son of Máldeó, and was sent to chastise their intrusion into his territory.

Horrors of his march through the desert.

These new enemies closed in on the exhausted party, cut off those who attempted resistance, and drove the rest before them; while another detachment pushed forward and took possession of the wells, on which the only remaining hope even of temporary relief was founded.

The calamities of the fugitives seemed now drawing to a close; but the Rájpúts had no intention of destroying them; and when all hope appeared to be extinguished, the rája's son advanced

BOOK VII.

with a white flag, and after reproaching them with having entered his father's territory without leave, and with having killed kine in a Hindú country, supplied them with water for their immediate relief, and allowed them to proceed without further molestation. But the natural horrors of the desert still remained; several marches were still to be accomplished; and it was not till they had again endured the torments of thirst, and witnessed the miserable death of many of their companions, that Humáyun, with seven mounted attendants, at length found entrance to Amercót. The straggling survivors of his party assembled at the same place.

Is hospitably received at Amercót.

At Amercót he, at last, found a friend. The chief, whose name was Rána Persád, not only received him with respect and hospitality, but offered his assistance in another attempt to gain an establishment in Sind.

Birth of Akber.

It was this period of depression and affliction that gave birth to Akber, a prince destined to raise the Indian empire to the greatest lustre that it ever enjoyed (Oct. 14. 1542). During his residence beyond the Indus, Humáyun had been struck with the beauty of a young lady whom he saw at an entertainment given to him, in the women's apartment, by his step-mother, the mother of prince Hindál. He found she was the daughter of a Seiad, a native of Jám, in Khorásán *, and formerly pre-

* Price, vol. iv. pp. 760. 840. Memoirs of Humáyun, p. 31.

ceptor to that prince, that her name was Hamída, and that she was not yet betrothed; and so strong was the impression made on him, that, in spite of the angry remonstrances of his brother, he almost immediately married her. She was far advanced in her pregnancy during the march to Amercót, and it was with the utmost difficulty that she was conveyed through the hardships of the desert.

Second attempt on Sind.

Humáyun had marched for Sind the day before the birth of Akber. It is usual on such occasions for the father to give presents among his friends. Humáyun had no presents to give, except one pod of musk, which he broke up when the news reached him, and distributed among his adherents, with a wish that his son's fame might be diffused throughout the world like the odour of that perfume.

He was accompanied on this expedition by Rána Persád with a considerable body of Rájpúts, and he had again collected 100 Moguls of his own. With this force they proceeded to Jún in Sind.* They took the place after an action with the officer in charge; and though harassed by attacks from the troops of the Arghúns, they were joined by the neighbouring Hindú princes, and formed an army estimated by the author of the Memoirs at 15,000 horse.

But Humáyun's ill fortune, or ill management, continued to attend him. The rája, after giving

* Probably Jún (or Jiún) on a branch of the Indus, half way between Tatta and Amercót. (See the map to Dr. Burnes's Account of Sind.)

decisive proofs of his fidelity, was affronted by a Mogul, and got so little redress on complaining, that he quitted the camp in indignation, and was followed by all his Hindú friends.

Humáyun consents to retire to Candahár.

In consequence of this defection, Humáyun was left almost alone to contend with Husén Arghún, who was advancing against him. He, nevertheless, threw up intrenchments, and defended himself as well as he could; till Husén Arghún, glad to get rid of him on any terms, consented to allow him to withdraw, and even to assist him on his journey, if he would immediately set out for Candahár. These terms being settled, Humáyun began his march towards his native kingdom (July 9. 1543).

His dangers in that country.

His younger brothers had long quitted him, after occasioning him much annoyance from their restless disposition; and Candahár was then held by Mírza Askari on the part of Cámrán. Humáyun's object probably was to bring that prince over to his side, or to take the chances of gaining possession in some other way. His professed intention, however, was to leave his son at Candahár, and proceed himself on a pilgrimage to Mecca.*

When he had reached Shál, about 130 miles south of Candahár, a horseman, sent by one of his

* Some unexplained delay must have occurred between Jún and Sehwán. The whole distance from Jún to Shál is under 450 miles; and the journey from Sehwán to Shál appears, by the Memoirs, to have been made in nine days; yet the whole time, from Jún to Shál, was five months (from Rabi a Sáni, July 9th, to the middle of Rámzán, about December 10th).

old adherents, gallopped up to his tent, sprung from his horse, and, without quitting the bridle, rushed into the tent, and announced that Mírza Askari was close at hand, with the design of making Humáyun prisoner. So little was he prepared for this intelligence, that he had only time to place his queen on his own horse, and was obliged to leave her child to the compassion of his uncle. Mírza Askari soon after arrived. He pretended to have come with friendly intentions, treated his infant nephew with affection, and removed the whole party to Candahár (Dec. 14. 1543). Meanwhile Humáyun, accompanied by forty-two followers, escaped to the Garmsír, and thence to Sístán, which was then under the Persian government. He was received with great respect by the governor, and sent on to Herát, to wait the orders of the king of Persia. At the latter city he was joined by several of his partisans from Candahár.

His flight to Persia.

Three years had elapsed since his first arrival in Sind, of which eighteen months had been occupied in his negotiations and military attempts in that country. Six months were spent in his journeys to the eastward of the Indus; and a year in his residence at Jún and his journey to Candahár. In his military affairs he had shown no want of personal courage, but great deficiency in enterprise; and he had gone through his subsequent calamities with cheerfulness that approached to magnanimity.

His temper was put to many trials; for, as delicacy and subordination cannot be kept up under great sufferings, he was often exposed to instances of ill humour and disrespect from his followers. He was more than once refused a horse when it was almost necessary to his safety. A boat, which he had prepared to convey his family, on his flight, across the Indus, was seized by one of his chiefs; and, during the terrible march to Amercót, an officer, who had lent his horse to the mother of Akber, on finding his own exhausted, compelled her to dismount; and Humáyun was obliged to give her *his*, and proceed on foot till he met with a baggage camel. On the other hand, he sometimes showed little consideration for his followers. When he reached Amercót, and was under the protection of the rája, he suddenly seized the baggage of his adherents, and even ripped open their saddles to discover their property, of which he took half to supply his own exigencies. At the end of one of his first marches towards Jódpúr, where he had lost many of his party in the desert, he loaded all the cattle, even his own horses, with water, to relieve the survivors who might be unable to come on; and as he went part of the way back himself, he found a Mogul merchant, to whom he owed a large sum of money, lying in the last stage of exhaustion, when, with a hard-hearted pleasantry, he refused to give him a drop of water until he had cancelled his debt before legal witnesses; and it does not appear that he ever relieved the poor man from the consequences of this forced remission.

CHAP. III.

SHÍR SHÁH, AND OTHERS OF THE FAMILY OF SÚR.

CHAP. III.

A. D. 1540, A. H. 947.

THE ultimate success of the house of Teimúr, and the great celebrity which they afterwards obtained, have occasioned Shír Sháh to be regarded as an usurper. Yet, as he was born in India, and expelled a foreign family who had only been fourteen years in possession, his claim was, in reality, more conformable to justice than those of most founders of dynasties in that country.

Shír Sháh takes possession of all Humáyun's dominions.

The retreat of Cámrán seems to have been concerted with Shír Sháh, for he had no sooner withdrawn than the latter monarch took possession of the whole of the Panjáb. After settling the province, and founding the famous fort of Róhtás, on the Hydaspes, which he named after that in Behár, he returned to Agra, and was soon called to subdue the revolt of his own governor of Bengal. He made such a division of that province for the future as to guard against a repetition of disturbance.

Recovers Málwa.

A. D. 1542, A. H. 949. A. D. 1543, A. H. 950.

In the course of the next year he conquered Málwa; and in that succeeding he reduced the fort of Ráisín, which was held by the son of Silhadi, a Hindú chief, who had enjoyed great authority under the government of Bahádur Sháh.

Massacres the garrison of Ráisín.

The garrison surrendered on terms; but when they had left the fort, the capitulation was declared null on the authority of the legal opinion of some Mahometan lawyers; and the Hindús, who had confided to the faith of their engagement, were attacked and cut to pieces after a brave resistance. No motive can be discovered for this act of treachery and cruelty. There was no example to make or injury to revenge, and the days of religious fury were long since gone by; yet there is no action so atrocious in the history of any Mahometan prince in India, except Tamerlane.

A. D. 1544, A. H. 951. Invades Márwár.

Next year, Shír invaded Márwár with an army of 80,000 men. Máldéo, rája of that country, was in the height of his power, and derived additional strength from the sterility of his territory and the want of water in many parts of it. Although he had only 50,000 men to oppose to the superior numbers of his antagonist, he appears, at first, to have overawed the invader. Shír remained for a month, halted within a short distance of his army; but succeeded, at last, by the usual trick of letters written on purpose to be intercepted, in exciting the rája's suspicions of his chiefs, and thus inducing him to commence a retreat. One of those chiefs, indignant at the imputation, determined, in the Rájpút spirit of honour, to wipe it off at any risk. He quitted the army with his own tribe, consisting of only 12,000 men, and fell with such impetuosity on Shír Sháh, who was unprepared for so vigorous an effort, that he threw his camp into confusion; and so nearly gained the victory, that Shír Sháh, when he had, at last, succeeded in repulsing the assailants, declared that he had nearly lost the empire of India for a handful of millet; alluding to the poverty of the country and the low quality of its produce.

Takes Chitór. Is killed at Calinjer.

After this he reduced the Rána of Mewár to submission, and subsequently laid siege to Cálinjer. He was here overtaken by a just retribution for his breach of faith at Ráisín; for the rája refused to enter into terms which he could not be sure would be observed; and as Shír was superintending the batteries, he was involved in the explosion of a magazine, which had been struck by the enemy's shot, and was so scorched, that, although he survived for some hours, his recovery was hopeless from the first, and towards evening he expired.

In the midst of his agonies, he continued to direct the operations of the siege; and when intelligence was brought to him that the place was taken, he exclaimed, "Thanks be to Almighty God!" and never spoke again.

A. D. 1545, May 22. A. H. 952, Rabi ul Awal.

His character.

Shír Sháh appears to have been a prince of consummate prudence and ability. His ambition was always too strong for his principles, and in the massacre at Ráisín, he had not even that passion to plead; but towards his subjects, his measures were as benevolent in their intention as wise in their conduct. Notwithstanding his short reign and constant activity in the field, he brought his territories into the highest order, and introduced many improvements in his civil government. Abul Fazl affects to deride his institutions, which he re-

His internal improvements.

BOOK VII.

presents as a revival of those of Alá u dín; nevertheless, most of them remained after the downfal of his dynasty, and are spoken of by the same author, along with many others of former sovereigns, as original conceptions of his master, Akber. Another author, who wrote under Akber*, states that Shír Sháh made a high road, extending for four months' journey, from Bengal to the western Rohtás, near the Indus, with caravanserais at every stage, and wells at every mile and a half; there was an Imám and a Muezzin at every mosque, and provisions for the poor at every caravanserai, with attendants of proper casts for Hindús as well as Mussulmans. The road was planted with rows of trees, for shade; and in many places was in the state described when the author saw it after it had stood for fifty-two years.

Shír Sháh was buried at Sahserám, where his stately mausoleum is still to be seen, standing in the centre of an artificial piece of water a mile in circumference, which is faced by walls of cut stone, with flights of steps descending to the water.

Selím Sháh Súr.

A. D. 1545, May 25. A. H. 952, Rabí ul awal 15. Selím supplants his elder brother.

A'dil Khán was the eldest son of Shír Sháh, and had been recognised as his heir by that king. He was a prince of a feeble character, while his second brother, Jelál Khán, was a man of known abilities,

* In the "Muntakhib ul Tawárikh," written in A. H. 1004, A. D. 1594-5.

and had distinguished himself as a soldier in his father's wars. For these reasons, most of the chiefs were disposed to support Jelál; and four of the principal of them having pledged their faith to A'dil for his personal safety, and for his receiving an adequate provision, he was induced to abdicate in favour of his brother. Jelál accordingly was proclaimed by the title of Selím Sháh, and a tract of country near Biána was assigned to A'dil. He soon after took alarm at some proceedings of Selím; and he seems to have had good grounds for his suspicions, as Khowás Khán, the principal general of Shír Sháh, and one of the four chiefs who were security for the late agreement, took A'dil under his protection, revolted from the king, and marched straight to the capital for the purpose of deposing him. Selím had much to fear from disaffection at home as well as from the declared rebels; but he anticipated all movements against him by his promptitude and firmness, defeated the enemy, and in time entirely crushed the rebellion. A'dil fled to Behár, and was never more heard of.

Quells an obstinate rebellion.

The nobles who had been secretly engaged in the conspiracy did not feel that their failure to take part with it had saved them from the suspicions of the king. One was convicted and punished; and the others began to plot anew, and took arms for their own protection, without setting up any competitor for the crown.

The contest on this occasion took place in the Panjáb. The rebels were again defeated. They

BOOK VII.

Till A. D. 1547, A. H. 954.

retired among the Gakkars; by the strength of whose country, and the support of the Afghán tribe of Niázi, they were able to keep alive the insurrection for two years.

The rest of Selím's reign was passed in tranquillity. On one occasion, indeed, he was informed that King Humáyun, who had recovered Cábul, had actually crossed the Indus to attack him. Selím happened to be indisposed at the time, and was sitting under the application of leeches; but he started up on the instannt, directed an immediate march, and was encamped six miles from Delhi before evening. If alarm had any share in this display of energy, it was ill founded: Humáyun had only crossed for local purposes, and almost immediately retired to Cábul.

Dies. A. D. 1553, A. H. 960.

Selím Sháh died after a reign of nine years. He was an improver, like his father, but rather in public works than in laws. One division of the royal palace at Delhi was built by him; and although Humáyun ordered it to be called Núrghar, by which name only it can be mentioned at court, it still retains that of Selímghar every where but in the royal presence.

Account of a fanatical sect.

In this king's reign there appeared at Biána a sectary, named Shékh Allái, who preached the doctrines of the Gheir Mehdis, and by his earnest zeal and persuasive eloquence soon induced many persons to join him. They threw their property into a common stock; and some even left their families and devoted themselves to the shékh.

Khowás Khán, the great general whose rebellion has been mentioned, was at one time among their number. At first, the shékh's fanaticism was inoffensive; but some of his followers went beyond all tolerable bounds: they thought it was their duty to interfere whenever they saw a man in any act of sin, and if he did not attend to their remonstrance, to put him to death. The civil government, as well as the Mahometan lawyers, thought it now high time to interpose. The shékh was tried, and condemned to death; but the king remitted his sentence, and banished him to Hindia on the Nerbadda. This only spread the infection of his doctrines: he converted the governor and the garrison, and was making greater progress than ever, when he was recalled to the capital. The king was importuned by the Múllas to put him to death; and, after many delays, he ordered him to be whipped, and then left to consider whether he would recant his errors: the shékh had, previously, been seized by an epidemic then prevailing, and was so reduced that he expired at the third lash. His sect created no disturbance, and seems to have melted away.

Mohammed Sháh Súr A'dili.

On Selím's death, his son, a boy of twelve years old, was murdered by his uncle, Mohammed Khán, who usurped his throne under the title of Mohammed A'dil Sháh, but is better known by that of

A. D. 1553, A. H. 960. Mohammed A'dili murders his nephew,

and usurps the throne. His vices and incapacity.

A'dili. His character was not such as to efface the memory of his crime; he was grossly ignorant, fond of coarse debauchery and low society, and as despicable from his incapacity as he was odious for his vices.

Hému, a low Hindú, made prime minister.

Vigour and talents of Hému.

He committed the conduct of his government to one Hému, a Hindú, who had once kept a small shop, and whose appearance is said to have been meaner than his origin. Yet, with all these external disadvantages, Hému had abilities and force of mind sufficient to maintain his ascendancy amidst a proud and martial nobility, and to prevent the dissolution of the government, weighed down as it was by the follies and iniquities of its head.

Oppressive measures of the king.

A'dili was scarcely seated on his throne before he had dissipated his treasures by the most indiscriminate profusion. When he had nothing of his own to give, he resumed the governments and jágírs of his nobles, and bestowed them on his favourites. As the Afghána are never very capable of subordination, and are particularly jealous of any slight, the sufferers by these resumptions bore their wrongs with great impatience. On one occasion, when the king transferred the lands held by a military chief to an upstart whom he favoured, the son of the dispossessed chief started forward, and exclaimed, "What! is my father's estate to be given to a seller of dogs?" An attempt was made to force him out of the court; and the person to whom the grant had been made seized him by the throat for the purpose, when the young man drew his dagger, and laid the aggressor dead at his feet. Being now attacked on all sides, he ran at the king, who leaped from his throne, and had scarce a moment to pass into his seraglio when the assassin was at the door. The king, however, was able to draw the bolt, and was soon delivered from his danger by the death of his assailant. The ill consequences of the affair did not end here. On the same day, one of the principal nobles fled from the court, and, being joined by other malecontents, set up the standard of revolt near Chunár. The king marched against the rebels; but though he defeated them in action, his affairs were little improved by his success; for I'brahím Súr, a person of his own family, seized on Delhi and Agra; and the king, after a vain attempt to expel him, was forced to leave him in possession, and confine himself to the eastern portion of his dominions. This example of successful rebellion was not lost on the spectators. Secander Súr, another nephew of Shír Sháh, proclaimed himself king in the Panjáb, advanced on I'brahím, defeated him in action, and constrained him to leave Delhi and Agra. I'brahím was now driven in on the territory still in the hands of A'dili. He was met and defeated by Hému, and pursued to Biána, were he would have been captured had not Hému's attention been called off by a rebellion of Bengal. The usurper in this case was Mohammed Súr, who had been intrusted with the government of the province. By the time Hému had joined his master, he heard that Málwa

A. D. 1554. A. H. 961. Rebellions.

Separation of Delhi and the western provinces.

Revolt of the Panjáb under Secander Súr.

Revolt of Bengal.

Revolt of Málwa.

had also revolted, and that Humáyun, having again entered India, had defeated Secander, and had taken Delhi and Agra.

Notwithstanding this disastrous intelligence, Hému persevered in opposing the new king of Bengal, who had advanced to some distance from his usurped territory. Hému was again victorious, and Mohammed Súr fell in the battle.

Return of Humáyun.

The rebellions in other quarters still continued; but the most imminent danger that presented itself was from Humáyun at Agra. While preparing to engage in this new contest, Hému heard of the death of his enemy and the accession of Akber, who was then in the Panjáb. Deriving fresh courage from this change, Hému deposited his nominal king at Chunár, and set off with 30,000 men to recover the capital. His numbers increased as he advanced through a friendly country: Agra was taken after a siege, and all the Mogul troops who had been with Humáyun were assembled under Tardi Bég at Delhi. Having been defeated in the field, Tardi Bég precipitately abandoned the city; and Hému now prepared to march to Láhór, and give the last blow to the apparently discomfited invaders.

Success of Hému.

The general opinion in Akber's camp was in favour of a retreat to Cábul; but Akber, who was only in his thirteenth year, left the whole conduct of affairs to Behrám Khán; and the intrepid character of that officer preserved the hopes of the house of Teimúr. Rejecting the timid counsels of

CHAP. III.

the other chiefs, Behrám advanced against Hému with a greatly inferior force; and after a desperate battle at Pánípat, in which Hému showed the most heroic courage, the Indian army was defeated, and Hému taken prisoner (November 5. 1556).

His defeat by Akber, and death.

With Hému A'dili lost all hope of recovering his dominions: he continued to reign for some time longer, till he was killed in a battle with a new pretender in Bengal.

Death of Mohammed A'dili.

CHAP. IV.

HUMÁYUN RESTORED.

BOOK VII.

Reception of Humáyun in Persia.

Account of the Safavis (or Sophis.)

At the time when Humáyun entered Persia the throne was occupied by Sháh Tahmasp, the second of the Safavi (or Sophi) kings. His father was descended from a family of dervises, which had derived importance and influence from its sanctity, and was still principally supported by the enthusiasm of the nation for the Shiá religion, which had been widely disseminated by the family, and formally established in Persia by Sháh Ismáel, the first king of the race. Though the Shiás and Sunnís differ less than Catholics and Protestants, their mutual animosity is much more bitter; and the attachment of the Persians to *their* sect is national as well as religious; the Shiá faith being professed in no great kingdom but theirs. Coming so early in the succession to its founder, Sháh Tahmasp was not only a devout adherent but an ardent apostle of this new religion; and it was by his feelings in that respect that he was, in a great measure, actuated in his conduct to Humáyun. The intercourse between those princes was highly characteristic of Asiatic despots.

Magnificence and hospitality of Sháh Tahmasp.

Humáyun's reception was marked with every circumstance of hospitality and magnificence. The governor of every province received him with the highest honour, and the people of every city came in a body to meet him; he was lodged in the king's palaces, and entertained with regal splendour; but in the midst of this studied respect, he was treated with little delicacy, and all semblance of generosity disappeared as often as he disputed the will of the Persian monarch, or became in any way obnoxious to his pride or caprice. Though welcomed from the moment of his arrival, he was not allowed to approach the capital; and many months elapsed before he was admitted to an interview with the king. During this interval, he sent his most confidential officer, Behrám Khán, on a mission to Sháh Tahmasp; and it was through a circumstance in the treatment of his envoy that he was first reminded how completely he was in the power of another.

His arrogance and caprice.

More effectually to unite his followers by some visible symbol, the first Safavi had made them wear a particular description of cap; from which the Persians took the name they now bear. This sectarian distinction was an object of as much aversion to the other Mahometans as a rosary and crucifix would have been to a Calvinist of the seventeenth century.*

Forces Humáyun to profess the Shía religion.

On one occasion of Behrám's attendance at

* The Persians generally call themselves Kazlbásh, or Redhead, from the colour of this cap. Báber attempted to introduce it among his troops at a time when he depended on the good will of the Persians; but the measure, though unaccompanied with any religious innovation, was so unpopular as to produce a dangerous disaffection to his government. (See Erskine's *Báber*, p. 244.)

court, the king desired him to wear the cap; and on Behrám's representing that he was the servant of another prince, and was not at liberty to act without orders, Tahmasp told him "he might do as he pleased," but gave evident signs of great displeasure; and, sending for some offenders, ordered them to be beheaded on the spot, with a view to strike a terror into the refractory ambassador.

Sháh Tahmasp's meeting with Humáyun was on terms of perfect equality, and in every way suitable to his own grandeur and the dignity of his guest. Yet the two kings were scarcely seated, when Tahmasp told the king of India that he must adopt the disputed cap; and Humáyun, to whom the demand was not unexpected, at once consented with an appropriate compliment. His assuming it was announced by a triumphal flourish from the king of Persia's band, and welcomed by a general salutation to both monarchs by the Persian courtiers. Some more private conversation probably passed on the subject of religion, in which Humáyun was not so compliant; for next day, when Tahmasp was passing Humáyun's palace on a journey, the latter prince went to the gate to salute him, but the Persian passed on without noticing him, and left Humáyun mortified and humiliated. Some days after, when a large supply of firewood was sent to Humáyun, it was accompanied by a message that it should serve for his funeral pile if he refused to embrace the Shiá religion. To this the exiled prince replied with humility, but with firmness, and requested leave to proceed on his pilgrimage; but Tahmasp was inexorable, declaring that he was determined to extirpate the Sunnís, and that Humáyun must adopt the religion of the country he had voluntarily entered, or take the consequences.

After all this intimidation, a cázi deputed by Sháh Tahmasp to confer with him presented Humáyun with three papers, and told him he might take his choice which he would sign. Humáyun rejected them in succession, with indignation, and at one time started up to call his attendants. His anger was composed by the cázi, who conducted his negotiation with kindness as well as with address, and succeeded in convincing him that, although he might give up his own life for his religion, he had no right to sacrifice those of his adherents; and that his duty as well as his interest called on him to comply with a demand which he had no means of effectually resisting.

The memoir writer does not mention, and may not have known, the contents of the paper; and Abul Fazl, with courtly dexterity, passes over the whole subject of religion, and scarcely hints at a temporary misunderstanding between the kings; but it seems clear that it must have contained a profession of the Shía religion, and a promise to introduce it into India, as well as an engagement to cede the frontier province or kingdom of Candahár. This last article was carried into effect;

BOOK VII.

and it was probably a sense of the impossibility of fulfilling the other that made Humáyun so indifferent to a rupture with Persia, when the period of performance drew near. That Humáyun himself professed to have been converted appears from a pilgrimage which he made to the tomb of Shékh Safi at Ardebíl, a mark of respect not very consistent with the character of a professed Sunni.*

After the contest about this paper, Humáyun was neglected for two months; and when Tahmasp renewed his attentions, they were not unmixed with ebullitions of an overbearing temper on points unconnected with the favourite topic of religion. Tahmasp had heard from some of Humáyun's enemies, that, during that monarch's prosperity, on some practice of divination to discover the destiny of reigning princes, he had placed the king of Persia in a class inferior to that in which he ranked himself. Tahmasp now took him to task for this assumption, and, on Humáyun's endeavouring to explain his reasons, told him that it was through such arrogance that he came to be driven out of his kingdom by peasants, and to leave his women and his child in the hands of his enemies.

Nevertheless the public conduct of the king of

* The "Muntakhib ul Tawárikh" states that the paper contained the Shiá confession of faith, and that Humáyun complied with the demand for his accepting it by reading it aloud without any other sign of assent or dissent. The same book adds, that he adopted the Shiá mode of reciting a portion of the public prayers, which is the most contested point between the two sects.

Persia continued to be as cordial and as generous as ever. He gave great hunting and drinking parties in honour of Humáyun; and, when the time of that prince's departure approached, he loaded him with attentions, and on one occasion laid his hand on his heart and entreated his guest to forgive him if he had ever failed in what was due to him. He then dismissed Humáyun, with a promise that 12,000 horse should be ready to join him in Sístán. But the two kings were not destined to part without one more explosion of temper from the king of Persia. Instead of marching straight to the frontier, Humáyun loitered about different places which he wished to visit, until he was overtaken by Tahmasp who was moving on some business through his dominions. He no sooner saw Humáyun's tents than he exclaimed, "What! has he not yet left this country?" and sent a messenger to direct him to make a march of twelve farsakhs (upwards of forty miles) without a moment's delay.

Sends an army to restore Humáyun.

In Sístán, Humáyun found 14,000 horse (instead of the 12,000 promised), under the command of the king's son, Morád Mírza. Cámrán was still in possession of Cábul. Candahár had been surprised by Hindál, but retaken; and that prince had been forgiven by his brother, and was now governor of Ghazni, the government of Candahár being intrusted to Mírza Askeri. Cámrán h d also taken Badakhshán from his relation, Solimán, who had been placed there by Báber: it com-

BOOK VII.

prehended the south of Bactria; the northern part of that province, including Balkh, was in the hands of the Uzbegs. Shír Sháh was still alive, and there was little to be hoped from an invasion of Hindostán.

Humáyun's own troops, while in Persia, only amounted to 700 men, and they were probably not more numerous when he marched with the Persian force against the fort of Bóst, on the river Hélmand. That place soon surrendered, and the force advanced unobstructed to Candahár (March, 1545).

The eagerness of the Persians, and their fear that Mírza Askeri might escape with his treasures, led them at first to a tumultuary attack, which was repelled by the garrison, and the siege was then opened in form. It lasted for more than five months, during which time Humáyun sent Behrám Khán to Cábul to endeavour to bring Cámrán to terms. His mission was unsuccessful; and as for a long time none of the chiefs or inhabitants of the country joined Humáyun, the Persians began to be disheartened, and to talk of returning to their own country. At length things took a favourable turn: deserters of different ranks came in from Cábul; and the garrison of Candahár being reduced to distress for subsistence, many of the troops composing it escaped to their own homes, while others let themselves down from the walls and came over to the besiegers.

Taking of Candahár;

Mírza Askeri was now obliged to surrender;

and, by the intervention of his aunt, the sister of Báber, he obtained a promise of pardon from his brother (September, 1545). But Humáyun's heart seems to have been hardened by his long misfortunes and disappointments; and his proceedings, which formerly were chiefly to be blamed for weakness, began to assume a darker character. Askeri was compelled to make his appearance before the conqueror with his sword hung naked from his neck, and to display his submission in the most humiliating forms. When this was over, Humáyun with seeming generosity placed him by his side, and showed him every mark of forgiveness and returning kindness. A great entertainment was given to celebrate the reconciliation; but when the festivity was at its height, and all fears and suspicions had been laid aside, some orders which Askeri had written to the Belóch chiefs for apprehending Humáyun during his flight to Persia were produced; and, on pretext of this long past act of enmity, he was made prisoner, and kept in chains for nearly three years.

which is ceded to the Persians,

The fort and treasures were made over to the Persians, on which the greater part of their troops returned home; and the garrison which was left under Morád Mírza began, according to Abul Fazl, to oppress the inhabitants. Abul Fazl enters on a long apologetical narrative of the events that followed; which, for its own cant and hypocrisy, as well as the perfidy of the acts it defends, is not surpassed by any thing even in the Memoirs of

BOOK VII.

but treacherously recovered by Humáyun, after the departure of the Persian army.

Tamerlane. The sum is, that the Persian prince having suddenly died, Humáyun, still professing the most fervent attachment to Sháh Tahmasp, obtained admission on friendly terms into the city, slaughtered many of the garrison, and made an extraordinary merit of allowing the rest to return to their own country.*

It is probable that the sophistical pretexts of Abul Fazl are not chargeable to Humáyun, who might plead that he was not bound to observe an

* The following is a specimen of Abul Fazl's manner of relating a story like the present. It is from Col. Price's version, and, though not literal, gives the spirit of the original. After enlarging on the complaints of the people of Candahár (who had never been subject to Humáyun) against the officers of their present sovereign the king of Persia, he goes on: "The generous monarch felt himself under considerable embarrassment, lest, in satisfying the demands of justice by inflicting punishment on the oppressors, he might give offence to his good ally, the king of Persia; or by suffering the guilty to escape entirely unpunished, they might be encouraged to extend their malpractices a hundred fold against the unfortunates still subject to their authority, his conscience pretty distinctly reminding him that by this latter course he should most surely incur the just vengeance of an offended God." On mature consideration of the risks of a quarrel, Humáyun stifled the reproaches of his conscience, until Morád Mírza's death afforded an opportunity for executing his design. Even then he absolutely refused to endanger the lives of the sháh's troops by giving them any notice of his hostile intentions, and only consented to lull them into security, and surprise them when they were off their guard. He begged permission of the governor to send Mírza Askeri, under an escort, to be kept prisoner in Candahár. The Persian gave his consent without hesitation; and the escort being secretly supported by other detachments, seized one of the gates, on which a conflict ensued, and many of the garrison were put to the sword. (Price, vol. iv. p. 89.)

engagement wrung from him by force. This argument, however, if admissible, as far as relates to his conversion, does not apply to the cession of Candahár. *That* was the price of the assistance of the king of Persia; and by availing himself of that assistance, after he was free from restraint, he ratified his engagement anew; and his infraction of it, especially with the concomitant circumstances, must leave him under the stigma of treachery, though not, perhaps, of ingratitude.

Taking of Cábul.

After the occupation of Candahár, Humáyun marched for Cábul, although the winter had already set in with extraordinary severity. As he advanced, he was joined by his brother Hindál; and afterwards by other deserters, in such numbers that, when he reached Cábul, Cámrán found it impossible to resist, and fled to Bakkar on the Indus, where he threw himself on the protection of Husén Arghún, prince of Sind. Humáyun entered Cábul, and recovered his son Akber, now between two and three years of age.

Expedition to Badakhshán.

After remaining for some months at Cábul, Humáyun set out to recover Badakhshán, which was again in the hands of Mírza Sólimán. Before his departure, he thought it prudent to put his cousin, Yádgár Mírza, who had just joined him, and was suspected of fresh intrigues, to death. What is remarkable in this event is, that the governor of Cábul flatly refused to carry the order into execution, and that Humáyun directed another person to perform it without inflicting any punishment on the governor.

BOOK VII.

Cámrán recovers Cábul.

While Humáyun was at Badakhshán, where he remained for many months, Cámrán returned from Sind and surprised Cábul. Humáyun marched against him in the dead of winter, defeated his troops, and drove him within the walls. On this and all subsequent occasions during the siege, Humáyun put his prisoners to death in cold blood, which Cámrán retaliated by still greater cruelties, and even threatened to expose young Akber, who had again fallen into his hands, to the fire of the cannon, if they continued to batter the town.*

Is driven out by Humáyun.

At length Cámrán was compelled to quit Cábul (April, 1547). He made his escape in the night, and fled to Górí, in the south of Bactria. Being, after some time, dislodged from thence by a detachment of Humáyun's, he had recourse to the Uzbeks at Balkh, and by their aid he recovered Badakhshán. During these operations, the summer passed, and Humáyun was constrained by the snow to defer his march from Cábul until the next spring. He then set out for Badakhshán, where

* Abul Fazl states that Cámrán did actually expose Akber without giving the least notice; and that it was only by the direct interposition of Providence, shown in miracles, of which he relates the particulars, that the destruction of the royal infant was averted. The account given in the text of this one fact is from the memoir writer; that author passes over most of the other atrocities on both sides; but on that subject I am afraid there is no reason for distrusting Abul Fazl. The memoir writer mentions that Cábul was given up to plunder, after the flight of Cámrán, as a punishment for the infidelity of the inhabitants; which is not noticed by Abul Fazl.

Cámrán was defeated, driven into Tálekán, and, being disappointed of the assistance he expected from the Uzbeks, reduced to surrender (August, 1548). On this occasion, Humáyun behaved with perfect good faith and humanity: he treated Cámrán with great kindness; and three of the brothers being now together, he released the fourth, Mírza Askeri, and they all assembled at a feast, where they *ate salt* together, and were, for the time, entirely reconciled.

Gives himself up to Humáyun, and is kindly treated.

After this Humáyun returned to Cábul. Next spring (1549), he set out to attack the Uzbeks in Balkh; and he appears at last to have acquired a sufficient spirit of enterprise; for, having taken the small fort of Eibak, he immediately began to hold consultations about the conquest of Transoxiana: but, at the moment of his reaching Balkh, where he had beat off a sally of the garrison, he received intelligence that Cámrán had rebelled, and was threatening Cábul; and, on commencing his march on his return to his capital, he was so pressed by the Uzbeks that his retreat soon became a flight, and it was with difficulty that his troops made their way, in total confusion and disorder, to a place of safety. This calamity shook the fidelity of his remaining adherents; and, in a battle which took place soon after, some of his greatest chiefs deserted him; and he had nearly lost his life in the defeat which followed. On this occasion, he was wounded by a soldier of Cámrán, who was about to repeat the blow, when Humáyun called out, "You

Humáyun invades Balkh.

Fresh rebellion of Cámrán.

Calamitous retreat from Balkh.

Humáyun defeated by Cámrán, and deserted by his army.

wretch! how dare you?" and the man was so confounded by the stern look of the king, that he dropped his arm, and allowed his wounded antagonist to retire (middle of 1550). Humáyun now fled with only eleven attendants, among whom was Jouher, the author of the Memoirs. He underwent many hardships, and for some time suffered from his wound: in the end he reached Badakhshán, where Mírza Sóliman, for the first time, zealously supported him. On his flight, Cámrán again took Cábul, and Akber once more fell into his hands. But in a subsequent battle, fortune proved favourable to Humáyun; Cámrán was obliged to take refuge with an Afghán tribe in the mountains of Kheiber; Cábul was taken, and all the open country restored to obedience (1551).

Cámrán again expelled.

The king soon after marched against the Khalíls, the tribe that had harboured Cámrán. He was attacked in the night by those mountaineers: his brother Hindál was killed, and he was obliged to take refuge in Bésút, a small fort in the pass between Pesháwer and Cábul. The Afgháns did not follow up their advantage; and while Cámrán was feasted in turn by successive tribes, Humáyun again took the field, defeated the Afgháns, and compelled Cámrán to fly to India; where he sought an asylum with Sultán Selím, the successor of Shír Sháh (1552). Receiving no encouragement in that quarter, he fled to the Sultán of the Gakkars, and was ultimately betrayed by him to Humáyun,

CHAP. IV.

three years after his last expulsion from Cábul* (September, 1553).

Taken, A. D. 1553, September. A. H. 961, Rámzán;

Though Cámrán's repeated offences would have justified his immediate execution, they do not in the least reconcile us to the treatment he received when given up.

Humáyun had come into the Gakkar territory to receive the prisoner; and Cámrán, when brought before him, advanced with great humility; but Humáyun received him graciously, seated him on his right hand, and soon after, some water melon being handed round, he gave half of the piece he had taken to his brother. In the evening there was an entertainment, with singers, and the "night was passed" in "jollity and carousing."† Next day passed in the same manner: during the course of it, some of his counsellors asked Humáyun what he intended to do with his brother? and he answered, "Let us first satisfy the Gakkar chief, and then I will do what is thought proper."

and blinded.

On the third day the Gakkar chief was satisfied; and it was determined that Cámrán should be blinded. The author of the Memoirs, having been ordered to attend on the prince, describes the particulars of his misfortune. At first, no person was willing to undertake the duty, and the king had given the order just as he was setting off on his march. One officer rode after him, and told him in Túrki the difficulty that had arisen; on which the king reviled him, and asked why he had not done

* Memoirs, p. 105.

† Ibid. p. 104.

it himself? On the officer's return, the order was made known to Cámrán with many expressions of sorrow, and the operation was performed by piercing his eyes repeatedly with a lancet. Cámrán bore the torture without a groan, until lemon juice and salt were squeezed into his eyes, when he called out, "O Lord, my God! whatever sins I have committed have been amply punished in this world; have compassion on me in the next."

After witnessing this part of the scene, the author could no longer remain: he went on to the camp, and sat down in his tent in a very melancholy mood. On this the king sent for him, and asked why he had come away without orders? The author replied that the business was completed, and the king told him he need not go back; and immediately gave him an order about some trifling business, without further noticing what had passed. He probably felt more shame than pleasure at the intelligence; and, indeed, the circumstances are important, rather as showing the effects of his situation than his own disposition, of which they are not otherwise characteristic than in the indecision and the wish to go on smoothly to the last. He was not naturally either cunning or cruel; and if he had been a limited monarch in Europe, he would most likely not have been more treacherous or bloody than Charles II.

Cámrán, now no longer dangerous, was permitted to go to Mecca, where he soon after died.

After this transaction, Humáyun was desirous of

proceeding to Cashmír; but, hearing of the advance of Selím Sháh, he retreated to Cábul, and spent the next year at that place and Candahár.

In the mean time, Selím Sháh had died; and the misgovernment of his successor had broken up his territories into five portions, in each of which there was a separate king.

Secander Sháh, to whose share the Panjáb had fallen, had since attacked I'brahím, the usurper of Delhi and Agra, and had driven him from his territories, while A'dili, the real sovereign, was carrying on operations against both. Circumstances could not, therefore, have been more favourable to Humáyun; but the recollection of former misfortunes seems to have excited gloomy forebodings about India; and it was not till he was encouraged by omens as well as arguments, that Humáyun could make up his mind to the enterprise. When he had undertaken it, he executed it with alacrity: he set out from Cábul with 15,000 horse (January, 1555): he invaded the Panjáb, defeated Secander's governor, and took possession of Láhór, where he remained for some time to settle the province.

Humáyun marches to recover India.

At Sirhind he engaged Secander, who had advanced to meet him at the head of a large army. Humáyun gained a decided victory, and immediately took possession of Delhi and Agra, while Secander fled to the mountains under Hémaláya.

Defeats Secander Súr.

Takes Delhi and Agra.

The latter prince, not long after, again issued from his retreat, and Behrám Khán was sent along with Prince Akber to the Panjáb to oppose him.

BOOK VII.

His death.

Humáyun, though thus restored to his capital, had recovered but a small portion of his original dominions, and even that he did not live to enjoy. In less than six months after his return to Delhi, he met with an accident which occasioned his almost immediate death. He had been walking on the terrace of his library, and was descending the stairs (which, in such situations, are narrow steps on the outside of the building, and only guarded by an ornamental parapet about a foot high). Hearing the call to prayers from the minarets, he stopped, as is usual on such occasions, repeated the creed, and sat down on the steps till the crier had done. He then endeavoured to rise, supporting himself on his staff; the staff slipped on the polished marble of the steps, and the king fell headlong over the parapet. He was stunned at the time; and, although he soon recovered his senses, the injury he had received was beyond cure. On the fourth day after his accident he expired, in the forty-ninth year of his age, and twenty-sixth of his reign, including the sixteen years of his banishment from his capital.

His unsettled reign left little time for internal improvements; and it is marked by no domestic event of importance, except the death of the celebrated Persian historian, Khóndemír, who had come to Báber's court soon after his invasion of India, and died in the camp of Humáyun during his expedition to Guzerát.

BOOK VIII.

STATE OF INDIA UP TO THE ACCESSION OF AKBER.

CHAP. I.

HISTORY OF THE INDEPENDENT STATES OF INDIA AFTER THE DISSOLUTION OF THE EMPIRE OF DELHI.

As we have reached the epoch at which the whole of India was formed into one empire, and a considerable alteration was made in the relations of different classes of the inhabitants, the time seems suitable for reviewing the preceding transactions of the separate communities, and ascertaining their actual condition at the commencement of the change.

States formed on the dissolution of the empire under Mahmúd Tóghlak.

The empire of Delhi, in the reign of Mohammed Tóghlak, extended to the Hémaláya mountains on the north-east, and to the Indus on the north-west; on the east and west it reached the sea; and on the south it might be said to include the whole of the peninsula, except a long narrow tract on the south-west, the frontier of which would be imperfectly marked by a line drawn from Bombay to

BOOK VIII.

Ramêshwar. But within these limits, one large space was unsubdued and another unexplored.

This last was the kingdom of Orissa, a tract of forest which extended nearly from the mouth of the Ganges to that of the Godáveri, something less than 500 miles, and ran inland for a depth of from 300 to 400 miles. The imperfectly conquered part was the Rájpút territory, a still more extensive tract in the north-west of India.

Recovery of Télingána and Carnáta by the Hindús.

During the disorders produced by the misgovernment of Mohammed Tóghlak, the rájas of Télingána and Carnáta restored those territories to the Hindús. The former prince had not long before been driven from Warangól, and compelled to retire to the south; and he now returned to reoccupy his old possessions. The other was of a new family, who set themselves up in the place of the Beláls, and fixed their capital at Bijáyanagar, on the Tumbrada. These two rájas soon reduced the Mussulman frontier to the Kishna on the south, and the meridian of Heiderábád on the east. They also brought the more southern parts of the peninsula into dependence, and formed states capable of contending on equal terms with their Mahometan neighbours. The western state, that of Bijáyanagar was the most considerable from the first. It was of much longer duration than the other, and before its fall had attained a pitch of power and splendour, not, perhaps, surpassed by any previous Hindú dynasty since the Mahometan invasion.

Further dismember-

This re-conquest, which took place in A. D. 1344,

CHAP. I.

ment of the empire.

was preceded by the revolt of Bengal (about A. D. 1340); and succeeded (in A. D. 1347) by the grand rebellion of the Deckan, by which the power of Delhi was driven across the Nerbadda.

The death of Mohammed Tóghlak (A. D. 1351) for a time put a stop to further dismemberment; but towards the end of the century, during the minority of Mahmúd (the last Tóghlak king), Guzerát, Málwa, and Júanpúr proclaimed their independence; the latter kingdom being formed of the country on the Ganges, from Bengal to the centre of Oud. The invasion of Tamerlane soon followed (A. D. 1398): the remaining provinces threw off the yoke; and the territory of Delhi was reduced to a few miles near the capital.

The recovery of some parts of these lost dominions has already been related; and I shall now explain their progress during the intermediate period, and the position in which they stood at the accession of Akber.*

The first place is claimed by the kingdoms of the Deckan.

* As the particular transactions of these separate kingdoms are not essential to the general history of India, I have thrown them into an Appendix, and confined the text to an outline and the results.

KINGDOMS OF THE DECKAN.

Bahmani kingdom of the Deckan. A. D. 1347, until A. D. 1518.

Hasan Gangu, who headed the successful revolt against Mohammed Tóghlak, transmitted his crown to his descendants, who reigned for thirteen generations and for 171 years.

The Hindú rájas of Bijáyanagar and Warangól were the allies of the new monarchy in its resistance to the emperor of Delhi; but when delivered from their common enemy, their natural antipathy revived. The struggle was of long duration, but the Mahometans were the gainers in the end. During the rule of the house of Bahmani, they conquered the country between the Kishna and Tumbadra from Bijáyanagar, and entirely subverted the kingdom of Warangól; and immediately before their fall, they had gained a territory in Orissa, and had extended their conquests on the east coast as far as Masulipatam, and on the west as far as Goa.

Increased intercourse with the Hindús.

These long wars on tolerably equal terms, together with occasional alliances against common enemies, seem to have had some effect in mitigating the overbearing conduct of the Mussulmans towards the Hindús. Men of both religions entered freely into each others service: the flower of the king of

Málwa's army, during an invasion of the Bahmani territories, is said to have consisted of 12,000 Afgháns *and Rájpúts*, while Deó Ráj, rája of Bijáyanagar recruited Mahometans, assigned lands to their chiefs, and built a mosque at his capital expressly for their encouragement.

Rivalry between the Shía and Sunni sects in the court and army.

The domestic history of the Bahmani dynasty was much influenced by the rivalry between the foreign and native troops. In most Asiatic despotisms the king first trusts to the army against the people, and then to a body of foreign household troops, or Mamlúks, against the rest of the army; and these Mamlúks, in the end, usurp the government. In the Deckan the course was different; the army which placed the Bahmani dynasty on the throne was chiefly composed of foreigners, and there seems to have been no guard more trusted to than the rest. In time, the native troops increased in number, and so nicely balanced the foreigners, that neither party ever obtained a permanent influence over the government.

At the time of the separation from Delhi, many of the foreign troops were probably Mogul converts; in later times, according to Ferishta, they consisted of Persians and Túrks, Georgians, Circassians, Calmucs, and other Tartars; the greater part of them were of the Shía sect; and the contest with the native troops was probably more between Shías and Sunnis than between parties arising from difference of race. The native party, or Deccanis as they were called, were always joined

BOOK VIII.

by the Abyssinian mercenaries, who came in numbers by the sea ports on the western coast*, and who may be presumed to have been Sunnis.

These parties reached the highest pitch of animosity in the reign of Alá u dín II., in A. D. 1437. They occasioned continual jealousy and distraction, and were as injurious to the government by their intrigues at court as by their want of co-operation on service. They were kept in control under vigorous administrations; but towards the end of the dynasty, Mahmúd, a weak prince, was alternately the tool of the foreigners, whose chief was Eusof A'dil Khán, a Túrk, and of the Deccanis, then under Nizám ul Múlk Behri, the son of a converted Hindú.

States formed out of the Bahami dominions. A. D. 1489—1512.

Bijapúr.

The Deccanis having gained the ascendency, Eusof A'dil retired to his government of Bíjapúr, where he subsequently took the title of king, and founded the dynasty of Adil Sháh.

Ahmednagar.

Nizám ul Múlk being afterwards assassinated by Kásim Baríd, a Túrk, his son Ahmed set up a separate dynasty called Nizám Sháh, the capital of which was Ahmednagar.

Kasim Baríd was now the master at the court of Mahmúd; and two other great chiefs became independent, although they did not, for some time, take the title of king. These were, Kútb Kúli, a Turkman, from Persia, and Imád ul Mulk, descended from Hindú converts: the former founded

* The Persian or Mogul party also chiefly received their recruits by sea. It is difficult to account for the little influx of Arabs.

the dynasty of Kútb Sháh, at Golconda, close to Heiderabad; and the latter that of Imád Sháh, at E'lichpúr in Berár. Amír Baríd, the son of Kásim, governed for some time under a succession of pageants: at length he threw off the mask, and was first of the Barid kings of Bidr, the family of Bahmani being thenceforth no longer mentioned.

Golcónda. Berár. Bidr.

Their history.

The internal strife between Shías and Sunnis which continued after the formation of these kingdoms, their wars and alliances among themselves and with the neighbouring Mahometan princes towards the North, give sufficient variety to their history during the period for which they lasted, but lose all their importance when the whole merged in the empire of the House of Teimur.

Their conquests from the Hindús had more permanent effects. The rája of Bijáyanagar long maintained his place among the powers of the Deckan, taking part in the wars and confederacies of the Mahometan kings; but at length, in 1565, the Musssulmans became jealous of the power and presumption of the infidel ruler, and formed a league against Rám Rája the prince on the throne at the time. A great battle took place on the Kishna near Tálicót, which for the numbers engaged, the fierceness of the conflict, and the importance of the stake, resembled those of the early Mahometan invaders. The barbarous spirit of those days seemed also to be renewed in it; for, on the defeat of the Hindús, their old and brave rája, being taken prisoner, was put to death in cold

A. D. 1565, Jan. 25. A. H. 972, Jamadi u Sani 20.

Battle of Tálicóta.

BOOK VIII.

blood, and his head was kept till lately at Bíjapúr as a trophy.

Fall of the kingdom of Bijáyanagar.

This battle destroyed the monarchy of Bijáyanagar, which, at that time, comprehended almost all the south of India. But it added little to the territories of the victors; their mutual jealousies prevented each from much extending his frontier; and the country fell into the hands of petty princes, or of those insurgent officers of the old government, since so well known as zemíndárs or poligars.*

The kings of Golconda were more fortunate in their separate conquests. They completely subdued all Warangól, which had made efforts at independence, and reduced other parts of Telingána and Carnáta, as far as the river Penár. These acquisitions by no means extended to the recovery of the country lost by Mohammed Tóghlak; but were all that were made by the Mussulmans until the time of Aurangzib.

* Briggs's Ferishta, vol. iii. pp. 127. and 414. Wilson, Mackenzie Collection, vol. i. p. cli. Wilkes's Mysore, vol. i. p. 18. The brother of the late rája removed his residence further east, and finally settled at Chandragíri, about seventy miles north-west of Madras, at which last place his descendant first granted a settlement to the English, in A. D. 1640. Rennell's Hindostan, p. 291.

KINGDOMS IN HINDOSTAN AND THE ADJOINING COUNTRIES.

Guzerát and Málwa became independent during the reign of Mahmúd Tóghlak, and probably assumed the name of kingdoms after that title was abolished in Delhi, on the invasion of Tamerlane. Candésh, which had not joined the rebellion in the Deckan, afterwards followed the example of its northern neighbours.

But although the revolt of the three provinces was simultaneous, it was not made in concert; and whatever connection afterwards subsisted between their histories arose out of their wars rather than their alliances.

Guzerát.

The territory of the kings of Guzerát, though rich, was small, encroached on by hills and forests, filled with predatory tribes, and surrounded by powerful enemies. Yet they were the most conspicuous of all the minor kings after the extinction of the Bahmani dynasty.

They twice conquered Málwa, and finally annexed that kingdom to their own: they repeatedly defeated the Rájpúts of Méwár, and took their famous capital of Chitór: they established a sort of supremacy over Cándésh, and even received

BOOK VIII.

the homage of the kings of Admednagar and Berár: on one occasion they carried their arms to the Indus; and they were more than once engaged in maritime wars with the Portuguese, which make a figure in the history of that nation.

Their territory was occupied, as has been related, by Humáyun, but was recovered in the confusions which soon followed, and was independent at the accession of Akber.

Málwa.

Málwa was engaged in frequent wars with all its neighbours in Hindostan and the Deckan; but the most remarkable part of its history was the ascendency obtained by a Hindú chief, who by his courage and abilities rescued the king from many difficulties, but at last engrossed all the powers of the state, filled all offices with Rájpúts, and was only dispossessed by the march of the king of Guzerát to the assistance of his brother Mahometan.

Other Mahometan kingdoms.

Cándésh, Bengal, Juanpúr, Sind and Multán, were all independent at the accession of Akber; but their separate history is of little moment.

The Rájpút States.

The states yet mentioned were all fragments of the empire of Mohammed Tóghlak; but a portion of the original princes of India still remained unconquered, and are acknowledged as sovereign states even to the present day.

Change in the condition of the Rájpúts after the Mahometan con-

The Rájpúts, who at the time of Sultán Mahmúd's invasion were in possession of all the governments of India, sunk into the mass of the population as those governments were overturned;

and no longer appeared *as rulers*, except in places where the strength of the country afforded some protection against the Mussulman arms.

quests in India.

Those on the Jamna and Ganges, and in general in all the completely conquered tracts, became what they are now; and, though they still retained their high spirit and military figure, had adapted their habits to agriculture, and no longer aspired to a share in the government of the country.

The remains of Rájpút independence were preserved on the table land in the centre of Hindostan, and in the sandy tract stretching west from it to the Indus. Their exemption from the encroachment of the Mussulmans was in proportion to the strength of the country. Méwát, Bundélcand, Bághélcand, &c. lie on the slope towards the Jamna, and, though close to the level country on that river, are rough and broken: it is there that we find the tributaries so often in insurrection, and there also are the forts of Rintimbór, Gwáliór, Cálinjer, &c., the taking and retaking of some of which seem to occur in almost every reign. The open part of the table land is partially protected by this tract: it is easier of access from the north about Jeipúr, which principality has always been submissive. Ajmír and Málwa, on the open part of the table land, were early conquered and easily retained. The east part of the rána of Oudipúr's country (or Méwár) was equally defenceless, but he had an inexpugna-

BOOK VIII.

ble retreat in the A'ravali mountains, and in the hills and forests connected with them, which form the northern boundary of Guzerát. The rája of Jódpúr (or Márwár), with his kinsman the rája of Bíkanér, the rája of Jésalmér, and some smaller rájas, were protected by the desert, with which the fertile parts of their territories are interspersed or surrounded.

The government of the Rájpúts, partly feudal and partly clannish, their high sense of honour, and their strong mutual attachment, have already been explained *, and had not degenerated in Akber's time.

State of the Rájpút princes at the accession of Akber Méwár.

The state of the different governments, at the accession of that monarch, was as follows: —

The family and tribe of the rána of Oudipúr (which were first called Ghelót, and afterwards Sesódia,) are said to be descended from Rámá, and, consequently, to draw their origin from Oud. They were afterwards settled in the peninsula of Guzerat, from whence they moved to I'dar, in the hills north of that province; and ultimately established themselves at Chitór, Colonel Tod thinks early in the eighth century of our æra. They make no figure in history until A.D. 1303, when Chitór was taken by Alá u dín, and almost immediately after recovered by the rána. Hamír, by whom that exploit was performed, had a series of able successors, and by their means Méwár attained

* See Vol. I. p. 606.

the ascendency among the Rájpúts, which enabled Sanga to bring them all into the field against Báber.

The great defeat sustained in that contest weakened the power of Sanga's family, and at a later period it was so much reduced by the incapacity of his grandson, Bicarmajít, that Bahádur, king of Guzerát, was able to take Chitór, and would have turned his success to account, but for his defeat by Humáyun, which immediately followed the capture of Chitór. From that time till the accession of Akber, the ránas remained in quiet possession of their territory, and retained their high rank among the Rájpút princes, though they never recovered their political ascendency, and were compelled, in the reign of Shír Sháh, to acknowledge the sovereignty of the king of Delhi.

Márwár.

The next Rájpút state in importance was that of the Ráhtórs in Márwár, the capital of which was Jódpúr. The Ráhtórs were in possession of Canouj when that kingdom was subverted by Shaháb u dín in A. D. 1194. After the conquest, part of the Ráhtórs remained on the Ganges, and occasionally revolted against the Mussulmans, until they became reconciled to the yoke; but another portion, under two grandsons of the last king, preferred their liberty to their country, and retired to the desert between the table land and the Indus. They there subdued the old inhabitants of the race of Jats, dispossessed some small tribes of Rájpúts, who had preceded them as colonists, and soon formed an extensive and powerful principality. A younger branch of the royal family at a later period (A.D. 1459) founded the separate state of Bíkanír, and occupied an additional portion of the desert. The Ráhtórs do not seem to have been molested by the Mussulmans until the expedition of Shír Sháh against Máldeó, and probably recovered their independence after that storm was blown over. Máldeó was still alive in the beginning of Akber's reign.

Bíkanír.

Jésalmér.

In the western part of the desert were the Bháttis, under the rája of Jésalmér. The Bháttis claim to be of the tribe of Yádu, and consequently derived from Mattra on the Jamna. They were part of Crishna's colony in Guzerát, and were expelled after the death of that hero. They then retired towards the Indus, and are lost in an unusually thick cloud of Rájpút fable, until they appear at Tánót, north of Jésalmér, and within fifty miles of the Indus. From this period (which Colonel Tod thinks was in A. D. 731) their annals assume a historical character, but are marked by no important event, except the removal of their capital, in A. D. 1156, to Jésalmér. They came very little in contact with the Mussulmans till after Akber's time.

Ambér or Jeipúr.

The rájas of Ambér, or Jeipúr, of the tribe of Cachwahá, have, in modern times, stood on an equality with the rána of Oudipúr and the rája of Jódpúr; but their rise into distinction is since the accession of Akber. They were ancient feudatories of Ajmír, and probably remained in submission to the Mahometans after the conquest of that kingdom. They may have increased their consequence during the weakness of the neighbouring governments in the fifteenth century, for they must have been held in consideration when Akber married the rája's daughter.

Háráuti.

The rájas of the tribe of Hára, who give their name to Háráuti, claim descent from the family that ruled in Ajmír before the Mahometans; and settled in their present possessions, of which Búndi was then the capital, in A. D. 1342. They were in some degree of feudal dependence on Oudipúr. They are not noticed in Mahometan history till just before Akber, when the reigning rája obtained the famous fort of Rintimbór from the governor who had held it for the Afghán kings.

Petty states in the desert.

Besides these greater states, there were several petty principalities, as the Chouháns of Párker, the Sódas of Amercót, &c., which, being in the extreme west of the desert, were beyond the reach of Mussulman invaders; and those of Siróhi Jhálór, &c., which, lying in the fertile tract beneath the A'ravalli mountains, and on one road from Ajmír to Guzerát, were liable to constant invasion and exaction of tribute.

Petty states on the east of the table land.

On the eastern slope of the table land, Méwát, Gwáliór, Narwar, Panna, Orcha, Chandéri, and other places in Bundélcand, had been repeatedly attacked by Báber and Shír Sháh, and were all

BOOK VIII.

tributary at the time of Akber's accession. They were mostly held by old Rájpút families.

Other unsubdued tracts.

The petty states under the Hémaláya mountains, from Cashmír inclusive to the Bay of Bengal, were independent under sovereigns of their own.

Many mountain and forest tribes throughout India were unsubdued, though they could scarcely be called independent: they were left out of the pale of society, which they sometimes disturbed by their depredations.

CHAP. II.

INTERNAL STATE OF INDIA.

CHAP. II.

Internal state of the Mahometan empire.

Of the internal state of the Mahometan empire in India we have no means of obtaining more than a slight view.

The king's power.

By the theory of the Mahometan law, the ruler of the faithful should be elected by the congregation, and might be deposed for any flagrant violation of the precepts of the Korán; but, in practice, the king's office was hereditary, and his power absolute. He was considered as bound to observe the Mahometan law; but neither the U'lemá nor any other public body had the means of enforcing his obedience to it: the municipal institutions of villages, some local jurisdictions which will be mentioned, and some other means of passive resistance, obstructed his will on ordinary occasions; but when he was determined to persevere, there was no remedy short of rebellion.

His ministers.

The duties of vizír, or prime minister, varied according to the abilities of the individual and the activity of the king. In some cases he was an uncontrolled vicegerent; in others, only the chief among the ministers. The others had their departments, but not very strictly defined.

The kings were easy of access: they inquired into petitions, and transacted a great deal of business in the daily assemblies of their court; which, although it must have caused some confusion and loss of time, afforded them the advantage of information from many quarters, besides giving publicity to their decisions and their principles of government.

Provinces.

The governors of provinces exercised, each within his jurisdiction, all the executive powers of the state. Several of the subordinate officers were appointed by the king, but all were under the orders of the governor. In most provinces there were Hindú chiefs who retained a hereditary jurisdiction; the most submissive of this class paid their revenue and furnished the aid of their troops and militia to the governor, and were subject to his control in cases where he thought it necessary, but were not interfered with in the ordinary course of their administration: the most independent only yielded a general obedience to the government, and afforded their aid to keep the peace; but these last were confined to strong countries, or large tracts bordering on a province.*

Army.

Part of the army were men hired singly by the

* It was to these hereditary chiefs that the term zemíndár was originally applied. The pride of the Mussulmans extended it to independent princes (like those of Oudipúr and Jódpúr), whom they affected to consider as subordinate to their government; but it is only in comparatively modern times that it has been extended *downwards*, so as to include persons holding assignments of the government revenue, as well as district and village officers.—(See Mr. Stirling, *Asiatic Researches*, vol. xv. p. 239.)

king, and mounted on his horses, but the greater number probably brought their own horses and arms; and these last would often come in parties, large or small, under leaders of their own. There was no feudal authority under the kings of Delhi. Fírúz Sháh Tóghlak is said to have been the first that assigned land in lieu of pay; and Alá u dín is said to have been extremely on his guard against all grants, as tending to the independence of his officers.*

Most governors had under them some portion of the regular army, in addition to their local troops; and in case of disturbance, reinforcements were sent under separate commanders, who, when the force was considerable, were nearly on an equality with the governor.

At other times governors were summoned to contribute to the formation of armies, and on those occasions they collected the contingents of their zemíndárs, took away as many as could be spared of the troops of the province, and, if their situation was favourable, recruited new ones for the occasion.

Law.

By the original theory of Mahometan government the law was independent of the state, or, rather, the state was dependent on the law. The calif was not excluded from a control over the administration of justice; but in that, and even in his military and political transactions, he was to be

* History of Fírúz Sháh, by Shamsí Surájí.

BOOK VIII.

guided by the rules of the Korán, and the decisions and practice of the Prophet, and of his own predecessors. Before long, the accumulation of decisions and the writings of learned lawyers contributed to form a great body of jurisprudence, the interpretation of which required a distinct profession. At the same time the extension of the Mussulman conquests gave rise to a sort of common law; not derived from the Korán, but from the custom of the country and the discretion of the kings. From these separate sources arose two distinct classes of tribunals: those of the cázis, which recognised the Mahometan law alone, and which only acted on application, and by fixed rules of procedure; and those of the officers of government, whose authority was arbitrary and undefined.

Civil trials, about marriage, adoption, inheritance, and, generally speaking, all questions regarding private property, ought properly to come before the cázi; who ought also to try all offences that did not threaten the safety of the state or the public tranquillity.

The jurisdiction of the king's officers was not so well defined. We may presume that their interference in civil cases would be rightly exercised in causes between servants of the government, and where there were parties of such power as to be beyond the reach of the cázi; they might reasonably be expected also to supply the defects of the Mahometan law in the case of Hindús; and the revenue officers would be natural umpires in many disputes about land. In criminal cases, rebels, conspirators, and highway robbers, as well as persons embezzling public money, or otherwise offending directly against the state, fell under the lawful jurisdiction of the same functionaries. In general, however, the governors and their officers were not scrupulous in confining themselves to those classes of trials. They received all complaints that were made to them, giving summary decisions in many cases, and referring those that turned on points of Mahometan law to the cázi, to whom also all causes that did not excite interest or promise profit would be left. The power of the cázis varied in different reigns. At some times we see the office, even in provincial courts, filled by men of celebrity; and at those times, we must conclude, their authority was respected, as appeared likewise from the occasional resistance of the cázis to the governors: at others it probably sunk nearly to its present level, when the duty is reduced to performing marriages, registering and authenticating deeds, and similar unimportant functions.

Church.

There was no church establishment, or, rather, no church government: every man, king or subject, who founded a mosque, left funds to maintain the priest (imám) and other persons required for public worship. Assignments were also made to holy men and their successors, and even to their tombs.

There was in each district an officer called sadr, whose business it was to see that the objects of all

BOOK VIII.

these grants, or at least those made by the crown, were carried into effect; and there was a sadr u sadúr at the head of all the sadrs: their jurisdiction was only over the application of the funds; the succession was settled by the original grantor, and generally depended on the choice of the incumbent, regulated by the opinion of the learned of the neighbourhood.

Moulavis.

Though there was no organised body of clergy, there was a class (called moulavis or mullahs) from which judges, lawyers, and ministers of religion were generally or always taken. But these were rather *graduates* in law and divinity than ecclesiastics. The degree was conferred by a meeting of some of the recognised members of the class, who were supposed to ascertain the learning and fitness of an individual, and who formally invested him with his new character, by tying on a peculiar kind of turban. He was bound by no vows, and was subject to no superior, but was controlled by public opinion and the hopes of preferment alone.

Fakírs.

Distinct from the ministers of religion was a numerous class of monkish devotees, called dervises in Persia, but in India more frequently fakírs. This is an excrescence on the Mahometan system, originating in the sanctity of particular persons. At first there were no saints, and the earliest instances of elevation to that character were in the case of martyrs, or of distinguished champions of the faith who fell in battle. By degrees, austere and religious lives led to this sort of canonisation which was conferred by public opinion, and generally on living men. These saints were followed by disciples, who, by degrees, formed orders, always distinguished by some watchword and some form of initiation, and sometimes by peculiarities of dress or observances. Many of these became early extinct, while others branched out into new orders. Small numbers of fakírs lived with their chiefs, and others were drawn together by charitable distributions, &c.; but they had no monasteries like the Hindús.

The most eminent among the saints were not impostors, although their followers might magnify the prophetic character of their predictions and the miraculous effects of their prayers: in later times, however, there was a lower class of fakírs, who supported their claims to supernatural powers by tricks with magnets, phosphorus, &c., and by legerdemain. Of the higher description many were treated with the utmost reverence even by kings; and, although professing poverty and abstinence, were accustomed to live in great splendour, or at least to distribute vast sums in charity*: and they often acquired such influence as to excite the jealousy of the government. Several instances occur of men of great sanctity being put to death for real or suspected plots against the state.†

* Bahá u dín Zakaríah, who died in the beginning of the fourteenth century, and is still one of the most revered saints, left enormous wealth to his heirs. (Briggs's *Ferishta*, vol. i. p. 377.)

† Ibn Batúta, in the middle of the thirteenth century, fur-

BOOK VIII.

The most flourishing period for these holy men was the thirteenth and the beginning of the fourteenth centuries. Many saints of those and later times are still revered, and are the objects of vows and pilgrimages; but the fakírs, their followers, though perhaps respected at first, have long lost their influence.

Superstitions.

Many of the superstitions of the age were unconnected with, and even opposed to, religion. Not only was the faith unbounded in astrology, divination, magic, and other arts discouraged by Mahomet; but even practices of the Hindús, and prejudices originating in their religion, began to gain ground. The miracles of their jógis are related by orthodox writers with as perfect a conviction as could have been given to those in the Korán; witchcraft was universally believed; omens and dreams were paid the greatest attention to; and this credulity was not influenced by the prevalence of scepticism in religion; it was admitted even by Akber, and exercised absolute sway over his son, while it was by no one treated so con-

nishes examples of all these kinds. A great fakír put to death for a conspiracy in his time has been mentioned. He met several really holy men who made no pretensions; but he also met one who pretended to live almost without nourishment, and another who professed to remember a calif who died near 100 years before. The first of these also told Ibn Batúta's thoughts, and foretold events: another fakír had seven foxes that followed him like dogs, and a lion that lived in harmony with an antelope. For an account of the orders, the method of initiation, and the principal saints, see Herklot's *Kánúni Islám*.

temptuously as by the bigoted Aurangzíb. The Shía religion never made any progress in Hindostan, as it did in the Deckan: there were no sectarian animosities, and, altogether, there was more superstition than fanaticism. The Hindús were regarded with some contempt, but with no hostility. They were liable to a capitation tax (jezía) and some other invidious distinctions, but were not molested in the exercise of their religion. The Hindús who are mentioned as military commanders may perhaps have been zemíndárs, heading their contingents, and not officers appointed by the crown: there is no doubt, however, that many were employed in civil offices, especially of revenue and accounts*; and we have seen that Hému and Médni Rái were intrusted with all the powers of their respective governments, and that under Mobárik Khilji the whole spirit of the court and administration was Hindú.

Sects.

Hindús.

Conversions.

It is difficult to form an opinion as to the period when the conversions of Hindús were chiefly accomplished, or in what circumstances they were brought about. The actual state of the population affords us little light. The largest proportion of Mussulmans to Hindús is probably in the remote districts in the east of Bengal; while about the Mahometan capitals of Delhi and Agra it is much less considerable.†

* Baber informs us that when he arrived in India, "the officers of revenue, merchants, and workpeople were all Hindus." (Erskine's *Baber*, p. 232.)

† In Bengal, east of the Ganges, they are more than one half

BOOK VIII.

The terror of the arms of the Mahometans, and the novelty of their doctrines, led many to change their religion at first; but when these were succeeded by controversial discussion and more moderate intolerance, a spirit opposed to conversion would naturally arise.

The whole of the Mussulmans in India at the present moment do not exceed one eighth of the population; and, after allowing for the great and long-continued immigration, and for the natural increase, during eight centuries, of a favoured class whose circumstances gave great facility in rearing families, the number left for converts would not be very great. Even if the whole eighth part of the population were converts, the proportion would be surprisingly small compared to other Mahometan countries.*

Revenue.

The revenue system was probably the same as now exists, and as existed under the Hindús; for the alterations attempted by Shír Sháh, and accomplished by Akber, were not designed to change the system, but to render it more perfect. The confusion of new conquests, and the ignorance of

---

of the population. In most parts of Bengal they are one fourth; but in the west of Behár and in Benáres, not above one twentieth. See Lord Wellesley's interrogatories, in 1801, laid before parliament. Buchanan makes the Mahometans in the west of Behár one thirteenth.

* The proportion of one eighth is from Hamilton's Description of Hindostan, vol. i. p. 25. He does not give his authority, but he is supported by the common opinion.

foreign rulers, must, however, have led to many abuses and exactions.

Condition of the people.

The condition of the people in ordinary times does not appear to have borne the marks of oppression. The historian of Fírúz Sháh (A. D. 1351 to 1394) expatiates on the happy state of the ryots, the goodness of their houses and furniture, and the general use of gold and silver ornaments by their women. He is a panegyrical writer, and not much to be trusted; but he says, among other things, that every ryot had a good bedstead and a neat garden; and the mere mention of such circumstances shows a more minute attention to the comforts of the people than would be met with in a modern author.

State of the country.

The general state of the country must, no doubt, have been flourishing. Nicolo di Conti, who travelled about A. D. 1420*, speaks highly of what he saw about Guzerát, and found the banks of the Ganges (or perhaps the Megna) covered with towns, amidst beautiful gardens and orchards, and passed four famous cities before he reached Maarazia, which he describes as a powerful city filled with gold, silver, and precious stones. Barbosa and Bartema, who travelled in the first years of the sixteenth century, corroborate those accounts. The former, in particular, describes Cambay as a remarkably well-built city, in a beautiful and fertile country, filled with merchants of all nations, and

Towns and commerce.

* Ramusio, vol. i. p. 359.

BOOK VIII.

with artisans and manufacturers like those of Flanders.* Even Ibn Batúta, who travelled during the anarchy and oppression of Mohammed Tóghlak's reign (about 1440 or 1450), though insurrections were raging in most parts through which he passed, enumerates many large and populous towns and cities, and gives a high impression of the state in which the country must have been before it fell into disorder.

Báber, in the beginning of the sixteenth century, although he regards Hindostan with the same dislike that Europeans still feel, speaks of it as a rich and noble country, abounding in gold and silver†; and expresses his astonishment at the swarming population, and the innumerable workmen in every trade and profession.‡

* Barbosa is in Ramusio, vol. i. p. 288., and Bartema, in the same volume, p. 147. Cesare Federici, in 1563, gives a similar account of Guzerát, Ramusio, vol. iii. p. 386. (edition of 1606), and Hackluyt, vol. ii. p. 343.

† Erskine's Baber, pp. 310. 333.

‡ Ibid. pp. 315. 334. To all these accounts of the flourishing state of the country, it is natural to oppose the statement of Báber, that in his time elephants abounded about Calpí and in Karrah and Mánikpúr (Erskine's *Báber*, p. 315.), and the fact of Akber's falling in with a herd of those animals near Coláras in the east of Malwa (Briggs's *Ferishta*, vol. ii. p. 216.); from which we might suppose that those places were then amidst forests which have since been cleared away. I am disposed to think, however, that the disappearance of the elephants is to be ascribed to the activity of the Mahometan hunters, and not to the improvement of the country. Ibn Batúta, who wrote near two centuries before Báber, expressly says that Karrah and Mánikpúr were the two most populous districts in India

The part of India still retained by the Hindús was nowise inferior to that possessed by the Mahometans. Besides the writers already mentioned, Abdurizák, an ambassador from the grandson of Tamerlane, visited the south of India in A. D. 1442 * ; and all concur in giving the impression of a prosperous country.

Those of them who visited Bijáyanagar are unbounded in their admiration of the extent and grandeur of that city; their descriptions of which, and of the wealth of the inhabitants and the pomp of the rája, are equal to those given by others of Delhi and Canouj.†

Other populous towns are mentioned; and Ibn Batúta speaks of Madura, at the extremity of the peninsula (then recently conquered by the Ma-

(Lee's *Ibn Batúta*, p. 119.); small tracts of hills and jungle would be enough to shelter elephants, who would spread over the cultivated country for food; and that there is no necessary connection between the residence of such animals and the absence of population, appears from the facts that the rhinoceros is still common in the Rájmahal hills, close to the populous lands of Bengal, while in the vast forest on the east of Berár there are neither rhinoceroses nor elephants, except a few of the last, which are supposed to be tame ones which have escaped.

* Murray's Discoveries in Asia, vol. ii. p. 18.

† Abdurizák's description of Bijáyanagar is so glowing, that it is scarcely surpassed by that in the story of Prince Ahmed in the "Arabian Nights," which appears to be taken from it. Conti is so extravagant as to say that it is sixty miles in circumference. Bartema says seven miles; but adds, that it is very like Milan.

BOOK VIII.

hometans) as a city like Delhi. The same author says, that through the whole of Malabár, for two month's journey, there was not a span free from cultivation: every body had a garden, with his house placed in the middle of it, and a wooden fence round the whole.*

The sea ports, above all, seem to have attracted admiration. Those on both coasts are described as large cities, the resort and habitation of merchants from every part of the world, and carrying on trade with Africa, Arabia, Persia, and China.† A great home trade was likewise carried on along the coast, and into the interior.

The adulation of the historians of later kings has had a tendency to depreciate the state of improvement attained under the early dynasties. One claims the institution of posts for his hero, another the establishment of highways with caravanserais and rows of trees; and Abul Fazl has been the occasion of most of the useful inventions in India being ascribed to Akber. But we have seen from Ibn Batúta that regular horse as well as foot posts existed under Mohammed Tóghlak; and foot posts, to a certain extent, must be coeval with village establishments.‡ The roads may have been improved

* Lee's Ibn Batúta, p. 166.

† Besides ships from Persia, Arabia, and other neighbouring countries, some of the ports of Malabár were frequented by large junks from China. (*Ibn Batúta*, pp. 169. 172.)

‡ Each village has a public messenger; and economy as well as dispatch would suggest to the head of a district to send his

by Shír Sháh; but Ibn Batúta, 200 years before his time, found the highways shaded by trees, with resting-houses and wells at regular intervals along a great part of the coast of Malabár, then under the Hindús; and in an inscription lately discovered*, which there is every reason to think is of the third century *before* Christ, there is an especial order by the king for digging wells and planting trees along the public highways.

Coinage.

It has been said (though not by Abul Fazl) that Akber first coined silver or gold money. The assertion is inconsistent with all history: if the Hindús had not a coinage in those metals earlier, they at least adopted it from the Bactrian Greeks† about the beginning of the Christian æra. The Ghaznavites could not have dropped a practice observed by the Samánis and the califs; and the second coin in Mr. Marsden's collection, belonging to the Delhi kings, is a silver one of Altamsh, who died in 1235.‡

If the value of the coins at different periods can be fixed at all, it can only be after a long inquiry by a person accustomed to such subjects.§ The

letters and orders by their means from village to village along the road.

* See Vol. I. pp. 394. 265.

† Mr. Prinsep's Useful Tables, p. 15., and his Researches in the *Journal of the Asiatic Society of Calcutta.*

‡ Marsden's Numismata Orientalia, p. 521.

§ Some notion of the fluctuations in this respect may be formed from the following statements:—The dínár under the califs was about equal to 10*s.* 8*d.* (Marsden's *Numismata,*

BOOK VIII.

first princes used dínárs and dirhems, like the califs; these were succeeded by tankhas, divided into dáms or jítals. Shír Sháh changed the name of tankha to that of rupeia, or rupee, which was adopted by Akber; and the latter prince fixed the weight and relative value of money on a scale which remained unaltered till the dissolution of the Mogul empire, and is the basis of that now in use.

Architecture.

We are enabled, in some degree, to judge of the progress of the early Mussulmans by the specimens

---

p. xvii.) In Ibn Batúta's time a western dínár was to an eastern as 4 to 1, and an eastern dínár seems to have been one tenth of a tankha, which, even supposing the tankha of that day to be equal to a rupee of Akber, would be only $2\frac{1}{4}$*d.* (*Ibn Batúta*, p. 149.) A modern dínár, in Cábul, is so small, that it takes 200 to make an abássi, a coin of less value than a shilling. The tankha is said by Ferishta (vol. i. p. 360.) to have been, in Alá u din's time, equal to fifty jítals (a copper coin which some said was equal to a peisa), and in Mohammed Tóghlak's time it was so debased as to be worth no more than 16 peisas. The tankha appears to be the coin represented by the modern rupee, and perhaps, when at its proper standard, was about the same value. The rupee of Akber contained 174·5 grains of pure silver, and was divided into 40 dáms or peisas of ($191\frac{1}{2}$ grains of copper each). The dám was divided into 25 jítals (probably a nominal coin). Queen Elizabeth's shilling contained 88·8 grains of pure silver; Akber's rupee, therefore, was worth 1*s.* $11\frac{1}{2}$*d.* of English money of his time. Akber's standard remained almost unaltered, all over the Mogul dominions, until the breaking up of the empire in the middle of the last century, when numerous mints sprung up and issued much debased money. The rupee that now circulates in the Company's territories contains 176 grains of pure silver, and exchanges for 64 peisas, containing 100 grains of copper each.

they have left of their architecture. The arches of the unfinished mosque near the Kutb Mínár, besides their height and the rich ornamental inscriptions with which they are covered, deserve mention, as early instances of the pointed arch.* The centre arch appears, by the inscription, to have been finished in A.H. 594, A.D. 1197. Many of the buildings of the later princes before Akber have small pointed arches, and seem to betray the incapacity of the builders to erect a dome of any size. Their mosques are composed of a collection of small cupolas, each resting on four pillars; so that the whole mosque is only a succession of alleys between ranges of pillars, with no clear space of any extent.

It is probable, however, that this form may have been retained, as that originally appropriated for mosques, by architects capable of constructing large cupolas. The Black Mosque at Delhi, for instance, is in the ancient style, though built in A.D. 1387, under Fírúz Tóghlak; while the tomb of Gheiás u dín Tóghlak, who died in A.D. 1325, is covered with one cupola of considerable magnitude.†

* The Kutb Mínár, finished by Altamsh between A. D. 1210 and A. D. 1236, has pointed arches in the doors. By examining the ruins of old and new Delhi alone, a view of the progress of Indian architecture might be made out which would throw light on the history of the art in the East.

† The dome was, no doubt, borrowed from the buildings of the Greek empire; but the mosques erected after it had once

BOOK VIII.

The domes at first are low and flat; they gradually gain elevation till the time of Jehángír, or Sháh Jehán, when they take in considerably more than half of a sphere, and are raised upon a cylinder. The arches, also, are different at different times: the early ones are plain Gothic arches; the latest ones are ogee and horse-shoe arches, feathered all round. The buildings after Akber's accession are much lighter, as well as more lofty and more splendid, than those of an earlier date; which, on the other hand, make a strong impression from their massive and austere character.*

Though the constant use of the pointed arch, the nature of the tracery, and some other particulars, create a resemblance between the Gothic and Indian architecture which strikes every one at first sight, yet the frequency and importance of domes, and the prevalence of horizontal lines in the Indian, make an essential difference between the styles. The more ancient buildings in particular, which in other respects are most like the Gothic, are marked by a bold and unbroken cornice formed of flat stones, projecting very far, and supported by deep brackets or modilions of the same material.

---

been fully established in India are incomparably superior in the elegance of their exterior to St. Sophia.

* "These Patans built like giants, and finished their work like jewellers. Yet the ornaments, florid as they are in their proper places, are never thrown away, or allowed to interfere with the general severe and solemn character of their edifices." (*Bishop Heber's Journal*, vol. i. p. 565.)

Even the abundance of turrets and pinnacles does not increase the resemblance to the Gothic; for they seldom taper at all, and never much; and they always end in a dome, which sometimes bulges out beyond the circumference of the turret.

Manners.

The early Mussulmans were stout and ruddy men dressed in short tunics of thick cloth, and always in boots. Those of Aurangzíb's time were generally slender, dark, and sallow, and wore long white gowns of the thinnest muslin, which spread out from the waist in innumerable folds, and scarcely showed the naked foot and embroidered slipper. It is difficult to ascertain the gradation by which this change, and a corresponding alteration in manners, were effected.

It must have *begun* soon after the dissolution of the connection with Ghazni and Ghór. Ibn Batúta, in the middle of the fourteenth century, mentions the use of bítel, and notices peculiarities in the cookery, and what he calls *oddity* in the manners; and Báber, early in the sixteenth, is shocked to find every thing so unlike what he is used to.*

* Baber's account is amusing, being written with all the violent prejudice still felt by persons just arrived from Cábul or from Europe. "Hindostan is a country that has few pleasures to recommend it. The people are not handsome. They have no idea of the charms of friendly society, of frankly mixing together, or of familiar intercourse. They have no genius, no comprehension of mind, no politeness of manners, no kindness, no fellow-feeling, no ingenuity or mechanical invention in planning or executing their handicraft works, no skill or knowledge in design or architecture; they have no good horses, no good flesh, no grapes or musk melons, no good fruits, no ice or

BOOK VIII.

It is probable that the greatest alteration took place after the accession of the house of Teimúr, when the influx of foreigners was stopped by hostile feelings towards the Uzbeks and Afgháns, and by religious prejudices against the Persians.* It was the direct policy of Akber that the manners of the Mahometans should assimilate to those of the original natives.

This mixture probably softened the manners of the people from the first; but it was some time before it had any effect on the government. There were many more instances of cruelty and perfidy under the slave kings than in the time of Mahmúd and his successors. Such atrocities under the succeeding dynasties were generally owing to the tyrannical disposition of an individual, or the revolts of foreign troops; and under most of the princes of the house of Teimúr, the general character of the government approached to the mildness and moderation of European sovereignties.

Mahometan literature.

Purely Mahometan literature flourished most in India during the period to which we are now ad-

---

cold water, no good food or bread in their bázárs, no baths or colleges, no candles, no torches, not a candlestick." He then goes on to ridicule their clumsy substitutes for the last useful articles. (*Erskine's Báber*, p. 333.)

* So complete was the separation at last, that Aurangzíb treats the Persians (the original models of the Indian Mussulmans) as rude barbarians, and hardly ever mentions their name without a rhyming addition, which may be translated, "monsters of the wilds."

verting, and fell off after the accession of Akber. Improvements in science were, doubtless, obtained from Hindú and European sources; but, I believe, there is no eminent specimen of Persian composition in India after the epoch mentioned.

The great superiority of Mahometan writers over their predecessors in Shanscrit is in history, and is derived from the Arabs. Though often verbose on ordinary topics, and silent on those of interest, deficient in critical skill and philosophical spirit, and not exempt from occasional puerility and exaggeration, their histories always present a connected narrative of the progress of events, show a knowledge of geography, a minute attention to dates, and a laudable readiness to quote authorities, which place them immeasurably above the vague fables of the Bramins.

Language.

It is surprising that so little is known of the modern language of the Indian Mahometans.

After the founding of the kingdom of Delhi, the conversation of their wives and children, as well as their continual intercourse with the natives, must have taught the conquerors to speak the language of the country, in which most of the roots were Shanscrit, but the forms and inflexions more like modern Hindostáni. It is not likely that this language remained long unmixed; though the progress of its change into that now spoken has not yet been traced by any orientalist.

It is stated by a modern Mahometan writer *,

* Quoted in Dr. Gilchrist's Hindostáni Philology.

BOOK VIII.

that the language took its present form during Teimúr's invasion; and, although it cannot be supposed that an incursion which lasted less than a year, and left no traces but in blood, could affect the language of a nation, yet it is not improbable that the beginning of the fifteenth century may have formed a marked epoch in the progress of Hindostáni.

It could have made little progress before the end of the twelfth century, as it is formed on the Indian dialect of Canouj, and not on that of the Panjáb, the only province previously occupied.*

The use of this mixed language in composition must have been of a later date; for though Mr. Colebrooke mentions a Hindú poet who wrote at Ambér (or Jeipúr) about the beginning of the sixteenth century, and who sometimes borrowed words from the Persian; yet he states that even Mahometan poets at first wrote in the pure local dialect above mentioned, which, he says, was called Hindí or Hindevi; and the specimens given in a Persian book on the poets of India (written in A. D. 1752), although all composed by Mahometans, do not introduce Persian or Arabic till near the end of the series.

The earliest of the celebrated poets in modern Hindostáni is Wali, who wrote in the middle of the seventeenth century. He is followed by a long train down to the present time. Their composi-

* Mr. Colebrooke, *Asiatic Researches*, vol. vii. p. 220.

tions are, in general, mere imitations of the Persians. It is probable, however, that they had the merit of introducing satires on manners and domestic life in Asia; for those of the Arabs and Persians seem to have been invectives against individuals, like Ferdousi's against Mahmúd. The best author in this branch of poetry is Souda, who lived late in the last century.

The other dialects (as those of Bengal, Guzerát, &c.), and also the languages of the Deckan, have admitted Persian and Arabic words in great numbers, but without forming a new language like the Hindostáni.

BOOK IX.

AKBER.

CHAP. I.

FROM 1556 TO 1586.

BOOK IX.

A. D. 1556, A. H. 963. Accession of Akber.

Akber was only thirteen years and four months old at his father's death, and though unusually manly and intelligent for his age, was obviously incapable of administering the government. He had been sent by Humáyun as the nominal head of the army in the Panjáb, but the real command was vested in Behrám Khán; and the same relation was preserved after Akber's accession. Behrám received a title equivalent to that of "the king's father *," and was invested with the unlimited exercise of all the powers of sovereignty.

Behrám Khán.

The nobleman thus trusted was a Túrkman by birth, and had been a distinguished officer under Humáyun before his expulsion from India. In the final defeat of that monarch by Shír Sháh, Behrám was separated from his master, and made

* It was "Khán Bábá," which is the Persian for the title of Atábek, so common among the Túrks, both meaning "Lord Father."

his way, after a long series of dangers and adventures, through Guzerát to Sind, where he joined Humáyun, in the third year after his expulsion. He was received with joy by the whole of the exiled party, who seem already to have rightly estimated his value in times of difficulty. He became thenceforward the most confidential of Humáyun's officers; and it would have been better for the affairs of his sovereign if they had borne more of the impress of his determined character.

Loss of Cábul.

At the time of Humáyun's death, Behrám was engaged in putting an end to the resistance of Secander Súr, who had retired to the skirts of the northern mountains, and still retained his pretensions to be king of Delhi and the Panjáb. He had scarcely time to arrange the new government, when he received intelligence that Mírzá Solimán of Badakhshán had taken possession of Cábul and all that part of Humáyun's late dominions; and while he was considering the means of repairing this disaster, he learned that Hému had set out with an army on the part of Sultán A'dili, for the double purpose of expelling the Moguls and reducing the rebellion of Secander Súr. The result of this contest has been already told.* The Afgháns were defeated; and Hému, who fought with desperate valour, and had continued to resist after he had received a mortal wound from an arrow through the eye, at length fell senseless on his elephant,

A. D. 1556, Nov. 5.; A. H. 964, Moharram 2.

Defeat and death of Hému.

* See p. 159.

BOOK IX.

and was taken prisoner and brought to Akber's tent. Behrám was desirous that Akber should give him the first wound, and thus, by imbruing his sword in the blood of so distinguished an infidel, should establish his right to the envied title of "Ghází," or "Champion of the Faith;" but the spirited boy refused to strike a wounded enemy, and Behrám, irritated by his scruples, himself cut off the captive's head at a blow.

Recovery of Delhi and Agra.

Campaign in the Panjáb.

Submission of Secander Súr.

Akber soon after took possession of Delhi and Agra. He was, before long, obliged to return to the Panjáb, by intelligence that Secander Súr had issued from the mountains and possessed himself of a great portion of the province. The plain country was easily recovered, and Secander retired to the strong fort of Mánkót. He defended that place with obstinacy; and it was not till after eight months' operations that he capitulated, and was allowed to retire to Bengal, which was still held by an officer of the Afghán dynasty.

Arbitrary government of Behrám Khán.

The real restoration of the house of Tamerlane may be dated from this period: it had been brought about entirely through the exertions of Behrám Khán, whose power was now at the highest pitch ever reached by a subject, and already began to show distant indications of decline.

Behrám's military talents, and the boldness and vigour of his government, had enabled him to surmount external difficulties under which a less determined leader would have sunk; and even his arbitrary and inflexible disposition was essential to the maintenance of subordination in an army of adventurers, whose disorders Humáyun had never been able to repress, and which must soon have overturned the government after it fell into the hands of a minor.

His domination was therefore submitted to without a murmur as long as the general safety depended on his exercise of it; but when the fear of immediate destruction was removed, the pressure of his rule began to be felt, and was rendered more intolerable by some of the vices of his nature. His temper was harsh and severe, his manners haughty and overbearing. He was jealous of his authority to the last degree, exacted unbounded obedience and respect, and could not suffer the smallest pretension to power or influence derived from any source but his favour.

General discontent at court.

These qualities soon raised up a host of enemies, and, in time, alienated the mind of the king, now advancing towards manhood, and impatient of the insignificance to which he was reduced by the dictatorial proceedings of his minister.

His indignation was increased by the injustice of some of Behrám's acts of power. As early as the battle with Hému, Behrám took advantage of Akber's absence on a hawking party, to put to death Tardi Bég, the former governor of Delhi, without even the ceremony of taking the king's orders on so solemn an occasion. The victim had been one of Báber's favourite companions, and had accompanied Humáyun in all his wanderings, but had no

BOOK IX.

doubt exposed himself to punishment for his premature evacuation of Delhi. One day, while Akber was amusing himself with an elephant fight, one of these animals ran off the field, pursued by its antagonist, and followed by a promiscuous crowd of spectators: it rushed through the tents of Behrám, some of which were thrown down; thus exposing the minister himself to danger, while it threw all around him into the utmost confusion and alarm. Irritated by this seeming affront, and perhaps suspecting a secret design against his life, Behrám ordered the elephant driver to be put to death, and for some time maintained a reserved and sullen demeanour towards the king himself. A nobleman of consequence enough to oppose Behrám was put to death on some slight charge by that minister. The king's own tutor, Pír Mohammed Khán, narrowly escaped the same fate, and was banished, on pretence of a pilgrimage to Mecca. Those about the king's person were constantly harassed by Behrám's distrustful temper, and were provoked by his persecutions to realize his suspicions of their enmity. At length Akber was driven to make an effort to deliver himself from the thraldom in which he lived. He concerted a plan with those around him, and took occasion, when on a hunting party, to make an unexpected journey to Delhi, on the plea of a sudden illness of his mother. He was no sooner beyond the sphere of the minister's influence, than he issued a proclamation, announcing that he had taken the go-

A. D. 1560, March; A. H. 667, Jemadi ul Akhir 28.

vernment into his own hands, and forbidding obedience to orders issued by any other than his authority. Behrám's eyes were opened by these proceedings; and he exerted himself, when too late, to recover the king's confidence. He sent two of his principal adherents to court; but Akber, nowise mollified by this submission, refused to see the envoys, and soon after committed them to prison.

Akber assumes the government.

Perplexity of Behrám.

This open separation was not long in producing its natural effect: all ranks forsook the falling minister, to court the sovereign, from whose youthful virtues, and even weaknesses, they expected a happy contrast to the strict control of Behrám.

The minister, thus left to his own resources, meditated various schemes for retrieving his power: he once thought of seizing the king's person, and afterwards of setting up an independent principality in Málwa; but the support he met with did not encourage him, and he probably was at heart reluctant to draw his sword against the son of his old master; he therefore set off for Nágór, with the avowed intention of embarking in Guzerát for Mecca.

At Nágór he lingered, as if in hopes of some change in his fortunes, until he received a message from Akber, dismissing him from his office, and directing him to proceed on his pilgrimage without delay. On this he sent his standards, kettle-drums, and other ensigns of authority to the king, and set out, in a private character, on his way to Guzerát;

He revolts.

BOOK IX.

but, irritated at some further proceedings of Akber, he again changed his mind, assembled a body of troops, and, going openly into insurrection, attempted an invasion of the Panjáb. He was disappointed in his reception in that province. Akber moved against him in person, and sent detachments to intercept him; he was defeated by one of those detachments, constrained to fly to the hills, and at length reduced to throw himself on the king's mercy. Akber did not, on this occasion, forget the great services of his former minister. He sent his principal nobility to meet him at some distance, and to conduct him at once to the royal tent. When Behrám appeared in Akber's presence, he threw himself at his feet, and, moved by former recollections, began to sob aloud. Akber instantly raised him with his own hand, seated him on his right, and, after investing him with a dress of honour, gave him his choice of one of the principal governments under the crown, a high station at court, or an honourable dismissal on his pilgrimage to Mecca. Behrám's pride and prudence equally counselled the latter course. He was assigned a liberal pension, and proceeded to Guzerát; but, while he was preparing for his embarkation, he was assassinated by an Afghán, whose father he had killed in battle during the reign of Humáyun.

A. D. 1560, September; A. H. 968, Moharram.

His submission and pardon.

His death.

Difficult situation of the young king.

The charge which Akber had now taken on himself seemed beyond the strength of a youth of eighteen; but the young king was possessed of more than usual advantages, both from nature and education.

He was born in the midst of hardships, and brought up in captivity. His courage was exercised in his father's wars, and his prudence called forth by the delicacy of his situation during the ascendancy of Behrám. He was engaging in his manners, well formed in his person, excelled in all exercises of strength and agility, and showed exuberant courage even in his amusements, as in taming unbroken horses and elephants, and in rash encounters with tigers and other wild beasts. Yet, with this disposition, and a passionate love of glory, he founded his hopes of fame at least as much on the wisdom and liberality of his government as on its military success.

It required all his great qualities to maintain him in the situation in which he was placed.

Of all the dynasties that had yet ruled in India, that of Tamerlane was the weakest and the most insecure in its foundations. The houses of Ghazni and Ghór depended on their native kingdom, which was contiguous to their Indian conquest; and the slave dynasties were supported by the continual influx of their countrymen; but, though Báber had been in some measure naturalised in Cábul, yet the separation of that country under Cámrán had broken its connection with India, and the rivalry of an Afghán dynasty turned the most warlike part of its inhabitants, as well as of the Indian Mussulmans, into enemies. The only adherents of the

BOOK IX.

house of Tamerlane were a body of adventurers, whose sole bond of union was their common advantage during success.

The weakness arising from this want of natural support had been shown in the easy expulsion of Humáyun, and was still felt in the early part of the reign of his son.

His plan for restoring and consolidating the empire.

It was probably by these considerations, joined to a generous and candid nature, that Akber was led to form the noble design of putting himself at the head of the whole Indian nation, and forming the inhabitants of that vast territory, without distinction of race or religion, into one community.

This policy was steadily pursued throughout his reign. He admitted Hindús to every degree of power, and Mussulmans of every party to the highest stations in the service, according to their rank and merit; until, as far as his dominions extended, they were filled with a loyal and united people.

But these were the fruits of time; and the first calls on Akber's attention were of an urgent nature:—

1. To establish his authority over his chiefs.
2. To recover the dominions of the crown.
3. To restore, in the internal administration of them, that order which had been lost amidst so many revolutions.

Extent of his territory.

In the first years of Akber's reign, his territory was confined to the Panjáb and the country round Delhi and Agra. In the third year, he acquired

Ajmír without a battle; early in the fourth, he obtained the fort of Guáliór; and, not long before Behrám's fall, he had driven the Afgháns out of Lucknow, and the country on the Ganges as far east as Júanpúr.

CHAP. I.

A. D. 1559, A. H. 966.

Insubordination and rebellions of his officers.

The adherents of the house of Súr that still remained in those parts were under Shír Sháh II., a son of the last king, A'dili; and, soon after Akber took charge of his own government, that prince advanced with a considerable army to Júanpúr, in the hope of recovering his dominions. He was totally defeated by Khán Zemán, a chief of Akber's; but the victor, despising the youth and feeble resources of his master, withheld the king's share of the booty, and showed so great a spirit of independence that Akber found it necessary to proceed in person towards the residence of the refractory governor. His presence produced more dutiful behaviour, but the disposition to insubordination was only kept under for the time.

A. D. 1560, A. H. 968.

The next affectation of independence was in Málwa. That province had remained in possession of Báz Bahádur, one of the officers of the Afghán kings, and an attempt had been made to dispossess him during the administration of Behrám Khán. The undertaking was renewed with more vigour by Akber. A'dam Khán, the officer employed, succeeded in defeating and expelling Báz Bahádur*,

* An affecting incident occurred on this occasion. Báz Bahádur had a Hindú mistress, who is said to have been one of the most beautiful women ever seen in India. She was as

BOOK IX.

but was as little disposed as Khán Zemán to part with the fruits of his victory.

Akber did not wait for any open act of mutiny: he disconcerted the ill designs of his general by a
A. D. 1560, May; A. H. 968, Shábán.
rapid march to his camp; and A'dam Khán, unprepared for so sudden a crisis, lost no time in making his submission: his offence was readily pardoned; but he was soon after removed from his government, which was given to the king's former tutor, Pír Mohammed Khán. This man, bred to letters, showed none of the virtues to be expected, either from his old profession or his present station. He was invaded by Báz Bahádur; and, although he gained considerable successes at first, he stained them by the massacre of the inhabitants of two cities of which he had obtained possession, and was ultimately defeated and drowned in the Nerbadda; the whole province falling into the hands of its old
A. D. 1561, A. H. 969.
possessor. Báz Bahádur was finally subdued by Abdulla Khán Uzbek, whom Akber immediately sent against him. At a subsequent period, he entered the service of the emperor, whose liberal

accomplished as she was fair, and was celebrated for her verses in the Hindú language. She fell into the hands of A'dam Khán on the flight of Báz Bahádur; and finding herself unable to resist his importunities and threatened violence, she appointed an hour to receive him, put on her most splendid dress, on which she sprinkled the richest perfumes, and lay down on a couch with her mantle drawn over her face. Her attendants thought that she had fallen asleep, but on endeavouring to wake her on the approach of the Khán, they found she had taken poison, and was already dead. (*Kháfi Khán.*)

policy always left that resource for his conquered enemies.

The ungovernable spirit of A'dam Khán was not tamed by his removal from power; for, on some subsequent rivalry with Akber's vizír, he stabbed him, while at prayers, in a room adjoining to that occupied by the young king. Akber ran out on hearing the disturbance, and his first impulse was to revenge the death of his minister with his own hand: he restrained himself sufficiently to sheath his sword, but ordered the murderer to be thrown from the lofty building where his offence took place. Nor was Abdullah Khán less unruly in his government of Málwa: within a little more than a year of the conquest of the province, he obliged Akber to move against him in person; and having in vain attempted to oppose the royal army, he fled to Guzérat, and took refuge with the king of that country. His fate was viewed with dissatisfaction by several other Uzbeks, who occupied commands in Akber's army. They suspected that the young monarch was actuated by a dislike to their race, such as a descendant of Baber might well be supposed to entertain; and they shared with many military leaders in their impatience of the subordination to which their class was about to be reduced. In this spirit they revolted, and were joined by Khán Zemán, before mentioned, and by Asof Khán, another nobleman, who had lately distinguished himself by the conquest of Garrah, a principality on the Nerbadda, bordering

A. D. 1562, A. H. 970.

A. D. 1563, A. H. 970-1.

A. D. 1564, A. H. 972.

on Bundélcand. It was governed by a queen, who opposed the Mahometan general in an unsuccessful action, when, seeing her army routed, and being herself severely wounded, she avoided falling into the hands of the enemy by stabbing herself with her dagger. Her treasures, which were of great value, fell into the hands of Asof Khán; he secreted the greater part, and the detection of this embezzlement was the immediate cause of his revolt.

The war with these rebels was attended with various success, and with alternate submission and renewed defection on the part of more than one of the chiefs. It occupied Akber for more than two years; and was concluded by an act of courage very characteristic of the conqueror. Akber had made great progress in reducing the rebellion, when he was drawn off by an invasion of the Panjáb, under his brother Hakím. This occupied him for several months; and on his return, he found the rebels had recovered their ground, and were in possession of most parts of the Subahs of Oud and Allahábád. He marched against them without delay, though it was the height of the rainy season; drove them across the Ganges; and when they thought themselves secure behind that swollen river, he made a forced march through a flooded country, swam the Ganges at nightfall with his advanced guard of not 2000 men on horses and elephants, and, after lying concealed during the night, attacked the enemy about sunrise. The rebels, though aware of the approach of a small body of horse, were quite unprepared for an attack; and Khán Zemán having been killed, and another principal chief unhorsed and made prisoner, in the first confusion, they lost all the advantage of their numbers, fell into complete disorder, and soon after dispersed and fled in all directions.

Quelled after a struggle of seven years.

The invasion from Cábul which had interrupted Akber's operations, had its origin in much earlier events. Two of Akber's chiefs, Abul Máalí and Sherf u dín, had revolted at Nágór, before the Uzbek rebellion (in A. D. 1561, A. H. 969), had defeated the king's troops, and advanced towards Delhi: they were afterwards driven back in their turn, and forced to seek for safety beyond the Indus. They retired with the remains of their force to Cábul, where circumstances secured them a favourable reception.

Affairs of Cábul.

That kingdom was left at the death of Humáyun under the nominal government of his infant son, Mírza Hakín, and immediately after was overrun, as has been mentioned *, by his relation, Sólimán of Badakhshan; and, though soon afterwards recovered, was never really in obedience to Akber. The government was in the hands of the prince's mother, who maintained her difficult position with ability, though not more exposed to danger from foreign enemies than from the plots and usurpations of her own ministers.

Nominal government of Prince Hakím, Akber's brother.

* See p. 217.

She had recently been delivered from a crisis of the latter description, when she was joined by the rebellious chiefs from India; and before long she was induced to confide the control of her affairs to Abul Máalí. That adventurer at first showed himself a useful minister; but his secret views were directed to objects very different from the establishment of the Bégum's authority, and as soon as he had himself formed a party in the kingdom, he had her assassinated, and took the government into his own hands. The aid of Mírza Sólimán was now invoked, and the result was the defeat and death of Abul Máalí (1563). Mirza Sólimán affected to leave his young relation in possession of Cábul, but really placed him under the tutelage of one of his dependents, whose yoke was so irksome that Mírza Hakím rose against it; and, after a struggle with Sólimán, was overcome and chased out of Cábul. This took place in the last year of the war with the Uzbek chiefs; and Hakím, although he had received such assistance as the times admitted from Akber, yet, conceiving his brother's hands to be fully occupied with the rebellion, at once resolved to indemnify himself at his expense, seized on Láhór, and took possession of the greater part of the Panjáb. This invasion ended in the expulsion of Prince Hakím from India (November, 1566); and an opportune change of circumstances at the same moment opened the way for his return to Cábul, of which country he remained for a considerable period in undisturbed possession.

Hakím invades the Panjáb.

Revolt of the Mírzas.

During these transactions, and before the final close of the operations against the Uzbeks, another revolt had taken place in India, which ultimately led to important consequences. Sultán Mírza, a prince of the house of Tamerlane, had come to India with Báber; he had rebelled against Humáyun, and though subdued and pardoned, his four sons and three nephews took advantage of the general disturbance just mentioned, and revolted at Sambal, the government which had been assigned to their father. At first they were overpowered without an effort; and the danger from them seemed to be completely at an end, when they were compelled to fly to Guzerát (1566): yet they there sowed the seeds of future troubles, which only ended with the subjugation of the kingdom.

They fly to Guzerát.

Miscellaneous occurrences.

Some instances occurred during the disturbances above related, which, although they had no important results, yet serve to show the state of society at the time.

During the insurrection of Sherf u dín, as Akber was going in procession to a celebrated shrine, an archer, who it afterwards appeared belonged to the rebel chief, mixed with the spectators, and, pretending to discharge his arrow at a bird which was flying over him, suddenly brought it down in the direction of the emperor, and lodged it some inches deep in his shoulder. He was instantly seized, and Akber was intreated to put off his execution, and to extort a disclosure of the name of his instigator; but he said that a confession in such

BOOK IX.

circumstances was more likely to criminate the innocent than the guilty, and allowed the punishment to take its course.* On another occasion, Khója Móazzim, a near relation of Akber through his mother, had given way to a violent temper, and treated his wife with such brutality, that her relations applied to Akber to intercede with him, and prevail on him to leave her with her mother when he was about to remove to his jágír. Akber took an opportunity, while going out on a hunting party, to pay him a visit in his house near Delhi; but the monster guessed his design, and and running to his female apartment before Akber had alighted, stabbed his wife to the heart, and threw the bloody dagger from the window among the king's attendants. When Akber entered the house he found him armed for resistance, and narrowly escaped death from one of his slaves, who was cut down as he was making a blow at the emperor. Akber, incensed at these atrocities, ordered Móazzim to be thrown headlong into the Jamna: he did not immediately sink; and Akber relented and ordered him to be taken out and imprisoned in Gwáliór, where he soon after died a maniac.†

On one of Akber's marches he found two great bodies of Hindú devotees prepared, according to their custom ‡, to contend sword in hand for the possession of a place for bathing during a great

* Kháfi Khán. Akbernámeh.

† Akbernámeh.

‡ See Vol. I. p. 116.

annual festival at Tanésar. He endeavoured at first by all means to bring about an amicable settlement; but finding all was in vain, he determined to allow them to fight it out, and looked on at the conflict in which they immediately engaged. At length one party prevailed, and Akber, to prevent the slaughter that would have followed, ordered his guards to check the victors, and thus put an end to the battle.*

CHAP. I.

Foreign affairs.

The Rájpúts.

During his struggle with the military aristocracy, Akber was fighting for his crown no less than in his contests with the successors of Shír Sháh; but by the time he had completed his twenty-fifth year he had crushed his adversaries by his vigour, or attached them by his clemency, and had time to turn his thoughts to foreign countries. The first which attracted his attention was that of the Rájpút princes. Bahára Mal, the rája of Ambér (now Jeipúr) was always on friendly terms with him, and had, at an early period, given his daughter in marriage to Akber; both he and his son, Bhagwán Dás, being at the same time admitted to a high rank in the imperial army.

A.D. 1567-8, A.H. 975.

Soon after the fall of Behrám (A.D. 1561, A.H. 969) he had sent a force against Márwár, and by the capture of the strong fort of Mírta had made an impression on that country which he was unable to follow up. He now turned his arms against the rána of Chitór (or Oudipúr). U'di Sing, the reigning rána, was the son of Báber's competitor,

* Akbernámeh.

Rána Sanga, but was a man of a feeble character. On the approach of Akber, he withdrew from Chitór, and retreated into the hilly and woody country north of Guzerát. His absence did not facilitate the capture of the fortress. There was still a strong garrison under Jei Mal, a chief of great courage and ability; and the place, though twice taken before, was still regarded by the Ráj-púts of Méwár as a sort of sanctuary of their monarchy. Akber carried on his approaches with caution and regularity. His trenches are minutely described by Ferishta, and closely resemble those of modern Europe. They were zigzags, protected by gabions and by earth thrown from the trench. The object, however, was not to establish a breaching battery, but to get near enough for sinking mines. This was done in two places; and the troops being prepared for the occasion, fire was set to the train. The explosion was the signal for the storming party to rush forward; but it had only taken effect in one of the mines; and while the soldiers were climbing up the breach, the second mine exploded, destroyed many of both parties, and struck such a panic as to occasion the immediate flight of the assailants.

The operations of the siege had now to be recommenced; but Akber, one night, in visiting the trenches, perceived Jei Mal on the works, where he was superintending some repairs by torch-light; he immediately singled him out, and was so fortunate as to shoot him through the head with his own hand. The garrison lost heart on the death of their gallant leader; and, with their usual infatuation, abandoned the breaches and withdrew to the interior of the fort, where they devoted themselves with the accustomed solemnities. The women were committed to the flames with the body of Jei Mal, and the men ran out to meet death from the Mussulmans, who had mounted the ramparts unopposed. Eight thousand men were killed on this occasion, by the Rájpút account; and the Mahometan writers make the number still greater.* The rána, notwithstanding the loss of his capital, remained independent in his fastnesses. Nine years afterwards his son and successor, Rána Pertáb, was deprived of his strongholds of Komulnér and Gogunda (probably in A.D. 1578, A.H. 986†), and was compelled for a time to fly towards the Indus. But, unlike his father, he was an active, high-spirited prince; and his perseverance was rewarded by success: before the death of Akber he recovered a great portion of the open part of his dominions, and founded the new capital called Oudipúr, which is still occupied by his descendants.‡ His house, alone, of the Rájpút royal families has rejected all matrimonial connections

A. D. 1568, March; A. H. 975, Shabán.

* One body of 2000 men escaped by an extraordinary stratagem: they bound the hands of their own women and children, and marched with them through the troops who had stormed the place, as if they had been a detachment of the besiegers in charge of prisoners.

† Ferishta. Muntakhab ul Towárikh.

‡ Tod's Rajasthan, vol. i. p. 332, &c.

BOOK IX.

with the kings of Delhi; and has even renounced all affinity with the other rájas, looking on them as contaminated by their intercourse with an alien race.

Such connections were zealously promoted by Akber, and were long kept up by his successors. He himself had two Rájpút queens, of the houses of Jeipúr and Márwár; and his eldest son was married to another princess of Jeipúr. The bride, on these occasions, acquired a natural influence over her husband; her issue had equal claims to the throne with those born of a Mahometan mother; and the connection was on a footing of so much equality, that from being looked on with repugnance as a loss of cast, it soon came to be coveted as an honourable alliance with the family of the sovereign.

In the course of the next year Akber took the strong hill forts of Rintimbór and Cálinjer: he went in person against the former place. On a subsequent occasion, being near the frontier of Jódpúr, Máldéo, the old rája of Jódpur, sent his
A. D. 1570, A. H. 978. second son to meet him.* This Akber resented, as an imperfect substitute for his own appearance; and afterwards, assuming a superiority to which he was not entitled, made a formal grant of Jódpúr to
A. D. 1572, A. H. 980. Rái Sing of Bíkanír, a junior member of the same family. Rái Sing, however, did not obtain possession; and, on the death of Máldéo, his son

* Ferishta.

submitted, and was afterwards treated with the greatest favour and distinction by the emperor.*

Conquest of Guzerát.

Akber's attention was soon after drawn to an enterprise of greater magnitude, involving the re-annexation of Guzerát to the empire. That kingdom had passed, on the death of Bahádur Sháh, to his nephew, Mahmúd II.; and on the death of the latter king, *his* favourite, Etimád Khán, who had been a Hindú slave, carried on the government in the name of a boy whom he pretended to be a son of Mahmúd, and who bore the title of Mozaffer III. The usurpation was opposed by another chief named Chengíz Khán; and it was with this last person that the Mírzas, whose revolt was mentioned in A.D. 1566, took refuge on their flight. Their extravagant pretensions soon drove them into a quarrel with their protector; and, after some partial success, they were expelled from Guzerát, and made an attempt to seize on Málwa, not long after the taking of Chitór, in A.D. 1568. Akber forthwith sent an army against them; but its services were not required; for Chengíz Khán had in the mean time been assassinated, and the Mírzas returned to Guzerát to take advantage of the confusions which followed. Those confusions continued to rage without intermission till the year 1572, when Akber was solicited by Etimád Khán to put an end to the distractions of Guzerát by taking the kingdom into his own possession. He marched from Delhi in September, 1572, and soon

A. D. 1572, September; A. H. 980, Jamádi ul awal.

* Tod's Rajasthan, vol. ii. p. 34.

reached Patan, between which place and Ahmedábád he was met by the pageant king Mozaffer, who formally transferred his crown to the emperor of Delhi. Some time was spent in reducing refractory chiefs; in endeavours to seize the Mírzas, or, at least, to disperse their troops; and in the siege of Surat, which was carried on by the king in person. Before the place was invested, the principal mírzas quitted it with a light detachment, and endeavoured to join their main body in the north of Guzerát. Akber made a sudden and rapid movement to intercept them, and succeeded in overtaking them before they had attained their object. He had advanced with such inconsiderate haste that he found himself in front of his enemy, who were 1000 strong, with a party which, after waiting to allow stragglers to come up, amounted only to 156 men. With this handful he commenced the attack, but was repulsed, and compelled to take his stand in some lanes formed by strong hedges of cactus, where not more than three horsemen could advance abreast. He was here hard pressed, and once was separated from his men, and nearly overpowered. But in his small band were several chiefs of note, and among the rest Rája Bhagwán Sing, of Jeipúr, with his nephew and adopted son, Rája Mán Sing; and it was to the exertions of these two that Akber owed his personal deliverance, and the ultimate success of the day. The Mírzas, however, effected their junction with their troops. They afterwards dispersed, met with different adventures, and came to various ends. One was cut off in Guzerát; the principal ones made their way to the north of India; and, after suffering a defeat from Rája Rái Sing near Nágór, revisited their original seat of Sambal; and when driven thence, they plundered in the Panjáb, and again pursued their flight towards the Indus, until they fell into the hands of the king's officers and were put to death. One only of the Mírzas, named Husén, fled from Guzerát into the hills near Cándésh, and remained unnoticed; while Akber returned to Agra, having once more annexed Guzerát to his crown.

A. D. 1573, June 4; A. H. 981, Safar 2.

He had not been a month at his capital, when he learned that Mírza Husén had again entered Guzerát, had been joined by one of the principal officers of the former king, and had already reduced the royal troops of the province to a defensive position, which they found some difficulty in maintaining. The rains had also set in, so that the march of a regular army was impossible; but Akber, with the activity, and perhaps temerity, that characterised him, at once determined to retrieve his affairs in person. He sent off 2000 horse to make the best of their way to Patan, and soon after followed, himself, with 300 persons (chiefly men of rank) on camels. He performed the journey of more than 450 miles with such celerity that, in spite of the season, he had assembled his troops, and faced his enemy at the head of 3000 men, on the ninth day from leaving

BOOK IX.

Agra. His force was still very unequal to that of the rebels; but they were astonished at the sudden apparition of the emperor, and were, moreover, engaged in a siege, and exposed to a sally from the garrison. Akber, therefore, though again exposed to imminent personal hazard from his own thoughtless impetuosity, was at last successful. Both the insurgents were killed; and tranquillity being completely restored, he again returned to Agra.*

Conquest of Bengal.

Akber's next great enterprise was the conquest of Bengal. Part of Behár had been occupied after the defeat of Shír Sháh II. in A.D. 1560; the rest of the province, with all the country to the east of it, was still to be subdued. Bengal had revolted from Sultán A'dili before the return of Humáyun, and had remained under different Afghán kings till now. It was held by Dáúd, a weak and debauched prince, who had been nearly supplanted by his vizír, and was engaged in a civil war occasioned by his execution of this dangerous minister.

* Before this battle, while Akber was arming, he saw a stripling (the son of one of the Rájpút rájas) labouring under the weight of a suit of mail, out of all proportion to his strength. He immediately exchanged it for a lighter suit of his own; and seeing another rája unprovided, he told him to put on the heavy armour which had remained unoccupied. This rája was a rival of the father of the young Rájpút, who was so indignant at the use made of his armour, that he tore off that given him by the king, and declared that he should go into the action without any armour at all. Akber took no notice of this disrespect but to say, that he could not allow his chiefs to be more exposed than himself, and that he would also go unarmed into the battle. (*Akbernámeh.*)

CHAP. I.

Akber had profited by these dissensions to obtain a promise of tribute from Dáúd: a temporary prospect of security had led that unsteady prince to reassert his independence, and the king thought the occasion favourable for going against him in person. He left Agra in the height of the rainy season, availing himself of the Jamna and Ganges for the transport of his stores and part of his army. He scarcely met with any opposition during his advance into Behár. Dáúd Khán retired to Bengal Proper; and Akber left his lieutenants to pursue the conquest, and returned himself to Agra.

A. D. 1575, A. H. 983.

The reduction of Bengal did not prove so easy a task as was expected. Although Dáúd at first withdrew to Orissa *, he afterwards twice encountered and routed the royal troops; and when at length defeated himself, and driven to the shores of the Bay of Bengal, he was strong enough to make terms, and to retain the province of Orissa for himself. One of the most distinguished of the commanders in this war was Rája Tódar Mal, so celebrated as Akber's minister of finance. He and the other commanders were withdrawn after the peace, and an officer of high rank was left as governor of Bengal. He died from the influence of the climate of Gour, or Lacnouti, the ancient capital, to which he had returned after it had been for some time deserted: and his successor had scarcely taken charge, when Dáúd renewed

* Orissa is applied here to the small portion of the country so called that formed the Mahometan province.

BOOK IX.

the war and overran Bengal, compelling the king's troops to concentrate and wait for assistance from Behár. A battle at length took place, and terminated in the defeat and death of Dáúd. Soon after, the fort of Rohtás, in Behár, which had held out till now, was compelled, by a long blockade, to surrender to a force employed for the purpose.

A. D. 1576, A. H. 984.

Bengal and Behár were now reannexed to the empire; and the remains of the Afghán monarchy in Hindostan were thus completely extinguished.

State of that province.

But the situation of those provinces was unfavourable to their permanent tranquillity: the hilly and woody tract on the south, the vast mountains and forests on the north, the marshes and jungles towards the sea, still afforded a safe retreat for the turbulent; and there was no want of materials to spread disaffection. Bengal had not before been subjugated by the Moguls, and was filled with Afghán settlers, whose numbers had been greatly increased by the retreat of such of their nation as refused to enter the service of the house of Tamerlane after its conquest of Upper Hindostan. The Mogul chiefs had profited by the unsettled state of the country: they seized on the jágírs of the Afgháns for their own benefit, and accounted for the rest of the royal revenue as expended on military operations.

Mutiny of the troops in Bengal and Behár.

The conquest was completed about the time of Akber's great financial reform, and the governor was required to remit revenue to the treasury; while all jágírs were strictly inquired into, and musters

CHAP. I.

of the troops for which each was held were rigorously exacted. The new conquerors were too conscious of their strength to submit to these regulations.* They revolted first in Bengal, and soon afterwards in Behár; when Akber found himself completely dispossessed of the fruits of his victory, and a formidable army of 30,000 men in the field to oppose him. After much ill success on the part of the king's troops, Rája Tódar Mal was sent to recover the province. He was at first successful, partly owing to his influence with the Hindú zemíndárs; but some harsh pecuniary demands on the part of the vizír at Delhi led to numerous desertions, even among the chiefs unconnected with the rebels, and it was not till the end of the third year from the breaking out of the rebellion that it was finally put an end to by Azíz, or A'zim Khán, who had succeeded Tódar Mal, and seems to have bought off many chiefs, and continued their lands to many of the troops (Afgháns as well as Moguls), who had heretofore enjoyed them.†

A. D. 1579, A. H. 987.

Insurrection of the Afgháns in Bengal.

The old Afghán adherents of Dáúd Khán had not been idle during these dissensions among the Moguls. They assembled soon after the rebellion broke out under a chief called Kuttu, and before long made themselves masters of Orissa and of all the country up to the river Damóder, near Bardwán. Azíz, having left the province after the rebellion was subdued, Rája Mán Sing was sent from

* Stewart's History of Bengal. Muntakhab al Tawárikh.

† Stewart's History of Bengal.

Cábul to conduct this new war. He entered the country held by the Afgháns, and cantoned for the rains near the present site of Calcutta. A large detachment of his was afterwards defeated by the enemy, and his son, who commanded it, taken prisoner; so that his affairs wore an unfavourable aspect; when Kuttu luckily died (1590), and I'sa, a prudent and moderate chief, became guardian to his sons. With this chief an agreement was soon concluded by Mán Sing, allowing the sons of Kuttu to retain Orissa as dependents or subjects of the emperor. After two years, I'sa died. His successor incurred general odium, by seizing on the revenues of the great temple of Jaganáth. Akber took advantage of this mistake to send Mán Sing again with an army, who defeated the Afgháns on the borders of Bengal, drove them to Cattak, and, by concessions of jágírs, added to more rigorous measures, finally reduced them to submission.

Final settlement of the province after fifteen years of disturbance.

Their last struggle was in 1592; and thenceforth (although 'Osmán, one of Kuttu's sons, rebelled again in A. D. 1600) the pretensions of the Afgháns to the possession of the province may be considered as quite extinguished.

Revolt of Prince Hakím.

While his officers were employed in the settlement of Bengal, Akber's own attention was drawn to a distant part of his dominions. His brother, Mírza Hakím, who had long been undisturbed in Cábul, was led, by a wish for further aggrandizement, again to invade the Panjáb. Rája Mán Sing, the governor, was compelled to retire before him, and to take refuge in Láhór; and Akber found it necessary to proceed, himself, with an army to raise the siege and deliver the province. Mírza Hakím retreated before him; and the emperor, whose situation no longer required his allowing such attacks to pass with impunity, followed up his success, crossed the Indus, and, after a feeble opposition on the part of his brother, took possession of Cábul. Mírza Hakím fled to the mountains. He afterwards made his submission, and Akber generously restored him to his government. He thenceforth, probably, remained in real subordination to his brother.

A. D. 1581, February; A. H. 989, Moharram.

Reduction of Cábul.

After this settlement, Akber returned to Agra, leaving Rája Bhagwán Dás of Jeipúr governor of the Panjáb. On his way he founded the fort which still stands at the principal ferry of the Indus, and gave it the name of Attok Benáris.

Insurrection in Guzerát.

After the abdication of Mozaffer Sháh of Guzerát, he accompanied the army to Agra, and was kept for some time about the court. He had latterly been allowed to reside at a jágír, which had been given to him, and was no longer looked on with suspicion (from 1573 to 1581). In this case, as in many others, Akber paid dear for his magnanimity. New intrigues arose in Guzerát, and Mozaffer was invited, by Shír Khán Fuládi, one of the principal actors in the former troubles, to fly from his residence in Hindostan, and put himself at the head of his old kingdom. An insurrection ensued, which reached to such a height

A. D. 1581, A. H. 989.

BOOK IX.

that the king's troops were obliged to withdraw to Patan, in the north of Guzerát, while Mozaffer Sháh occupied Ahmedábád, Baróch, and almost the whole of the province. Mírza Khán (the son of Behrám Khán) was sent to quell this rebellion. He defeated Mozaffer, and recovered the continental part of Guzerát; but Mozaffer retired among the almost independent chieftains of the peninsula, repelled the attacks of Mírza Khán, and made various attempts, at different periods, to recover his dominions. His efforts were all unsuccessful; but the endeavours of the Moguls to penetrate his retreat in the peninsula were attended with as little effect; and no result was produced for a long period, except alternate victories and heavy loss on both sides.

A. D. 1584, January; A. H. 992, Moharram.

On one occasion, indeed, in A. D. 1589, Azíz made his way to the sea coast on the south, and fought a great battle. The victory was doubtful, but was followed by the retreat of the Moguls; and it was not till four years after this period, and twelve after his rebellion (in A. D. 1593), that Mozaffer Sháh was taken, on an incursion into the settled part of the province, and cut his throat with a razor while on his way to the court at Agra.

CHAP. II.

FROM 1586 TO THE DEATH OF AKBER.

CHAP. II.

Akber interferes in the disputes of the Deckan.

After Mozaffer had been driven into the peninsula, Akber began to take part in the disputes of the Deckan (in A. D. 1586). His first attempts failed, as will hereafter be related; and before long he was fully occupied by the affairs of his own northern dominions. In the year 1585 his brother, Mírza Hakím, died; and, although he had no difficulty in taking the territories held by that prince into his immediate possession, yet he heard, about the same time, that Mírzá Solimán had been driven out of Badakhshán by Abdullah, the Khán of the Uzbeks; and it was probably apprehension of the further progress of that formidable neighbour which chiefly induced him to go in person to Cábul. Abdullah Khán, however, was contented with Badakhshán; and as Akber made no attempt to recover that possession of his family, the peace remained undisturbed. The emperor was now in the neighbourhood of the northern mountains, a great portion of which was comprised within his dominions; and he was engaged by this circumstance in wars of a new description, attended with greater difficulties than any he had yet encountered.

Akber moves to Attok on the Indus.

Conquest of Cashmír.

The first was the conquest of Cashmír. That celebrated kingdom is an extensive plain, situated

BOOK IX.

in the heart of the Hémaláya mountains, and more than half way up their height. Placed, by its elevation, above the reach of the heat of Hindostan, and sheltered by the surrounding mountains from the blasts of the higher regions, it enjoys a delicious climate, and exhibits, in the midst of snowy summits, a scene of continual verdure, and almost of perpetual spring. Trees belonging to different climates are scattered over its surface, while fruits of various kinds and flowers of innumerable descriptions are poured forth with spontaneous profusion over the hills and plains. The level country is watered by rills, which issue from the valleys or fall in cascades down the mountains, and collect in different places, especially in two lakes, whose varied banks and floating gardens are the great boast of the valley.

This terrestrial paradise can only be approached by difficult and dangerous passes. The road, though a steep ascent on the whole, often rises and descends over rocky ridges; sometimes winds through long and close defiles; and sometimes runs along the face of precipices overhanging deep and rapid rivers. The higher part of the mountain, from whence the descent into Cashmír commences, is at one season further obstructed, and in some places rendered impassable, by snow.

Cashmír had been ruled by a long succession of Hindú, and sometimes, perhaps, of Tartar princes, from a very remote period till the beginning of the fourteenth century, when it fell into the hands of a

Mahometan adventurer, and was held by princes of the same religion till the time of Akber's invasion.* The hopes of that enterprising monarch were excited by distractions which prevailed among the reigning family; and while at Attok, in A.D. 1586, he sent a detachment, under Sháh Rókh Mírza, the son of Mírza Solimán (who had entered his service when driven out of Badakhshán), and his own brother-in-law, Rája Bhagwán Dás of Jeipúr, to take possession of the prize thus exposed to hazard by the contention of its owners. A. D. 1586, A. H. 994.

The obstacles already mentioned, especially the snow, retarded the progress of the army; and although it, at last, penetrated through a pass which had not been guarded, yet its supplies had been exhausted in these unproductive and inaccessible mountains, and the remaining difficulties seemed so considerable that the two chiefs entered into a treaty with the ruling power of Cashmír, by which the sovereignty of Akber was acknowledged, but his practical interference with the province forbidden. The emperor disapproved of this engage-

* The History of Cashmír called the "Raj Taringi" is remarkable, as the only specimen of that department of literature in the Shanscrit language. It is executed by four different hands; the first of whom wrote in A. D. 1148, but quotes the works of earlier historians with a precision that gives confidence in his accuracy. The early part, as in all history, is fabulous, but it gradually approaches to consistency in facts and dates until about A. D. 600, from which period the chronology is perfectly accurate. (Wilson's History of Cashmír, *Transactions of the Asiatic Society*, vol. xv. pp. 3. 85.)

BOOK IX.

ment; and next year sent another army, whose efforts were attended with more success. The dissensions which prevailed in Cashmír extended to the troops stationed to defend the pass: part came over to the Moguls; the rest quitted their post and retired to the capital. The barrier once surmounted, Cashmír lay at the mercy of the invaders. The king submitted, was enrolled among the nobles of Delhi, and was assigned a large jágír in Behár. Akber afterwards made a journey to Cashmír to enjoy the pleasures of his new conquest. He only repeated his visit twice during the rest of his reign; but Cashmír became the favourite summer retreat of his successors, and still maintains its celebrity as the most delicious spot in Asia, or in the world.

Wars with the north-eastern Afgháns.

Though Akber's next operations were not unprovoked like those against Cashmír, they were opposed with much greater obstinacy, and terminated with less success. They were directed against the north-eastern tribes of the Afgháns, who inhabit the hilly countries round the plain of Pesháwer.

Description of those tribes and of their country.

The plain is of great extent and prodigious fertility, combining the productive soil of India with many of the advantages of the temperate countries in the west. It is bounded on the north by the great chain of Hindú Cush; on the west by the high range of Sólimán; and on the south by a lower range, called the hills of Kheiber, which extends from that of Sólimán to the Indus. This tract forms about one tenth of the proper country of the Afgháns. Its inhabitants are now called Berduránis, and are distinguished from the other Afgháns by some peculiarities of dialect and manners.

The northern part belongs to the Eusofzeis, who are by much the most considerable of these north-eastern tribes, and who afford a good specimen of the rest. Their territory includes the northern part of the plain of Pesháwer, and stretches up the mountains to the snowy ridge of Hindú Cush, embracing some valleys of thirty or forty miles in length, and corresponding breadth, from each of which other valleys run up on both sides; all rivalling Cashmír in climate and beauty, and all ending in narrow glens, hemmed in by high precipices or lost in woods and forests. Such a country is full of intricacy and obstruction to an invading army, but affords easy communications to the natives, who know the passes from one valley to another, and who are used to make their way even when there is no path to assist them. The original population was Indian, consisting, probably, of descendants of the ancient Paropamisadæ.* It had, at a comparatively recent period, been conquered and reduced to a sort of villanage by certain Afghán tribes; and they, in their turn, were dispossessed, about a century before this period, by the Eusofzeis, a tribe from near Candahár, which had just suffered a similar expulsion from its native seats. With such possessions, and with their numerous

* See vol. i. p. 450.

BOOK IX.

vassals, the Eusofzeis added the pride of wealth to the independence natural to mountaineers; and their self-importance was increased by their democratic constitution. Though each of their clans had a hereditary chief, he had no authority in time of peace, except to consult the people and to make known their wishes to the other clans. Internal affairs were conducted by the inhabitants of each village; causes were tried by a sort of jury, and meetings for one or other purpose were constantly held in the public apartment of the village, which served also as a place of relaxation for the inhabitants, and of entertainment to guests or passing strangers. The land was equally divided; and equality was maintained by new distributions of it from time to time. The Indian vassals were well treated, but they had no share in the government; and the conquerors were not more distinguished by their fair complexions than the superiority apparent in their demeanour.

The other tribes inhabiting the plains and the lower hills to the south had been longer settled there, and had had more intercourse with the Mahometans of India; but some of those in the Sólimáni mountains had a still more rugged country and less civilised manners than the Eusofzeis. The emperor Báber had endeavoured to bring the north-eastern tribes under his dominion, and partially succeeded with some. He failed entirely with the Eusofzeis, though he employed the means of conciliation as well as destructive inroads into the accessible part of their country.

CHAP. II.

Sect of the Roushenías.

The present quarrel originated in a fanatical spirit, which had sprung up, many years before, among this portion of the Afgháns. A person, named Báyazíd, had then assumed the character of a prophet; had set aside the Korán, and taught that nothing existed except God, who filled all space, and was the substance of all forms. The Divinity despised all worship and rejected all mortifications; but he exacted implicit obedience to his prophet, who was the most perfect manifestation of himself. The believers were authorised to seize on the lands and property of infidels, and were promised, in time, the dominion of the whole earth. Báyazíd soon formed a numerous sect (which took the name of Roushenía, or enlightened), and established his authority in the hills of Sólimán and Kheiber, with an influence over the neighbouring tribes. He was so long successful, that the government was obliged to make an exertion to put him down. His own presumption and the blind confidence of his followers led him to meet the royal troops in the plain. He was defeated with great slaughter, and died soon after of fatigue and vexation.* His sons dug up his bones, and bore them in an ark, at the head of their column; but they ceased to be formidable beyond their hills till about A. D. 1585, when one of the youngest, named Jelála, assumed the command, and exercised it with such vigour,

* Dr. Leyden's Account of the Raushenía Sect, *Asiatic Researches*, vol. ii. p. 363.

BOOK IX.

that the ordinary government of Cábul was found incompetent to resist him. When prince Hakím died, and Cábul came directly under Akber, the government was given to Rája Mán Sing, whose talents and connection with the emperor were supported by the forces which he could draw from his hereditary dominions. Even these advantages did not prove effectual; and one of the professed objects of Akber's expedition to the Indus was to settle the Afgháns. With this view he sent successive detachments from his camp on the east bank of the Indus; and commenced his operations by an attack on the Eusofzeis, although they had long before quarrelled with the Roushenías, and renounced the tenets of the sect.

Destruction of the invading army by the Eusofzeis.

The chief commanders in the force detached were Zein Khán, the emperor's foster-brother, and Rája Bír Bal, his greatest personal favourite. So great was the importance attached to this expedition, that Abul Fazl relates that he himself drew lots with Bír Bal who should command one of the divisions, and was much mortified by being disappointed in this opportunity of distinguishing himself: his brother Feizi accompanied the force.* The open country was soon overrun and laid waste; but on Rája Bír Bal's advancing up one of the valleys, he found himself, by degrees, involved among defiles, where there was no outlet, and was at last obliged to give up the enterprise, and retrace

A. D. 1586, January; A. H. 994, Safar.

* Akbernámeh.

his steps to the plain. Zein Khán showed more perseverance: he made his way through many rugged and dangerous mountains, and even built a redoubt in a place convenient for controlling the neighbourhood; but his troops were by this time so much exhausted by fatigue, and so much harassed by the increasing numbers and audacity of their enemies, that he was compelled to form a junction with Bír Bal; and both combined would have been unable to pursue their operations if they had not received further reinforcements from Akber.

They now resumed their plan of invasion. Bír Bal was on bad terms with Zein Khán, and it was contrary to the strongest remonstrances of the latter that they determined to risk their whole force in a desperate attack on the Afgháns. The resolution taken, they advanced into the mountains. They soon came to a strong pass, which Bír Bal succeeded in ascending; but on reaching the top, after a day of fatigue, he was set on by the Afgháns, with such effect, that his men dispersed, and made their way, as they best could, to the plain. Zein Khán, who had remained at the foot of the pass was attacked at the same time, and defended himself with difficulty, during the night and part of the next day, when both chiefs were at last enabled to come to a halt, and to collect their scattered forces. Zein Khán recommended that they should endeavour to capitulate with the enemy; but Bír Bal could not be prevailed on to accede to any of his suggestions; and, having received information that the Afgháns intended to complete the ruin of the army by a night attack, he marched off his troops without consulting Zein Khán, and endeavoured to make his way through a defile, which would have afforded him the means of retreating to the open country. The intelligence was probably given for the purpose of drawing him into an ambuscade, for he had no sooner reached the gorge at the head of the pass, than he was assailed on all sides by the Afgháns, who overwhelmed him with showers of stones and arrows, and, rushing down the sides of the hills, fell, sword in hand, on his astonished soldiers. All attempts to preserve order on his part were vain; men, horses, and elephants were huddled together in their flight down the defile; and Bír Bal himself, with several other chiefs of note, were slain in the rout and slaughter which ensued. Nor was Zein Khán more fortunate in his position on the plain: for, although during the day he kept up an orderly retreat, amidst swarms of archers, matchlock men, and slingers; yet, after a short respite which he was allowed in the evening, the alarm of "The Afgháns!" was again raised, and his troops fled in disorder, during the darkness of the night, losing many men killed, and more prisoners, while he, himself, escaped on foot, and made his way with difficulty to Attok.*

* Akbernámeh. Muntakhab ul Tawárikh. Kháfi Khán. Abul Fazl must have been minutely informed of the real his-

The news of this disaster spread alarm in the emperor's camp. One of his sons, Prince Morád, under the guidance of Rája Tódar Mal, was ordered out with a force to check the approach of the Afgháns. After the first apprehension had subsided, the prince was recalled, and the force left under the command of Tódar Mal and Rája Mán Sing.

Akber refused to see Zein Khán, and was long inconsolable for the death of Bír Bal. As the rája's body was never found, a report gained currency that he was still alive among the prisoners: and it was so much encouraged by Akber, that, a long time afterwards, an impostor appeared in his name; and as this second Bír Bal died before he reached the court, Akber again wore mourning as for his friend. Bír Bal's favour was owing to his companionable qualities, no less than to his solid merit. He was a man of very lively conversa-

---

tory of this transaction; but his anxiety to soften the disgrace of Akber's arms, and to refrain from any thing that may reflect on Bír Bal, was so great, that his account is confused and contradictory, and I have been obliged to supply his deficiencies from the "Muntakhab ul Tawárikh." As a proof of the defects I have ascribed to him, I may mention that, although he gives a full and even eloquent description of the total destruction of the army, he concludes by stating the loss at 500 men. Kháfi Khán, with equal inaccuracy, asserts that of 40,000 or 50,000 horse and foot, *not a single person* escaped alive. The defeat seems to have taken place in the mountains of Swát, and the names given to the passes are Karah, or Karah-Korah, and Bilandzei.

BOOK IX.

tion, and many of his witty sayings are still current in India.*

The Eusofzeis made no attempt to pursue their advantages. Tódar Mal and Mán Sing took up and fortified positions in different parts of the country, and prevented the Eusofzeis from cultivating their portion of the plain. By these means, according to Abul Fazl, they were reduced to unqualified submission; and, in reality, some temporary agreement or tacit understanding was brought about, so as to leave Mán Sing at liberty to act against the Roushenías, under Jelála, in the southern and western hills.

A. D. 1586, A. H. 995.

Accordingly, in the course of the same summer, he marched against them; and, after being exposed to considerable hazard, he succeeded in gaining a partial success. The Roushenías, however, stood their ground, and the ascendancy of the

A. D. 1587, A. H. 995.

government was not restored till the next year, when a combined attack was made by Mán Sing, from Cábul, and a force detached by Akber, to cross the Indus to the south of the salt range, and come in on the enemy from their rear. Jelála was at that time completely defeated; he, however, almost immediately renewed his operations, which

From A. D. 1587, to A. D. 1600.

were kept up for many years, and were sometimes aided by contests between the government and the Eusofzeis, which produced no permanent results. During this time, it was the policy of the Moguls

* Chiefly from the Muntakhab ul Tawárikh.

to prevent the cultivation of the fertile plains and valleys; so that Jelála was often compelled, by want of supplies, to leave the strong countries he occupied, and expose himself to the risk of battles on more equal ground. He was several times obliged to fly to the mountains of the Cáfirs, and once to the court of Abdúllah, the Khán of the Uzbeks: still he always returned and renewed his attacks; and in A.D. 1600, he was in sufficient strength to obtain possession of the city of Ghazni.

This was the last of Jelála's exploits. He was soon driven out of the city; and, being repulsed and wounded in an attempt which he afterwards made to recover it, he was pursued on his retreat, and was overtaken and killed before he could make his way to a place of safety.

The religious war was continued by his successors, during the two next reigns (of Jehángír and Sháh Jehán); and when, at last, the enthusiasm of the Roushenías wore out, the free spirit of the Afgháns, which had owed nothing to its success, survived its extinction: the north-eastern tribes were never more formidable than in the reign of Aurangzíb; and the Eusofzeis have resisted repeated attacks from the Mogul emperors, and afterwards from the kings of Persia and Cábul, and retain their turbulent independence undiminished to the present day.*

Imperfect settlement at the end of fifteen years.

* Abul Fazl's account of these wars is a curious specimen of his adulation and his inconsistency. Immediately after Bír Bal's calamity (that is, in the first year of the war), he says:

BOOK IX.

The nature of the war with Jelála had not, latterly, been such as to prevent Akber's employing his troops in the adjoining countries. It was some years before the death of that leader, that he made the important acquisitions of Sind and Candahár.

Conquest of Sind.

The province of Sind had passed from the Arghúns * into another family of military adventurers, and Akber took advantage of some dissensions which afterwards took place among these new usurpers, to endeavour to recover that old possession of the kings of Delhi. He sent an army from Láhór, where he was himself at the time, to enter Sind from the north, and lay siege to the fort of Sehwán, the key to Lower Sind, and a place of great importance to the security of the whole province.

A. D. 1591, A. H. 999.

The success of this attempt was prevented by the chief of Sind, who drew near with his army,

"The highlands were soon cleared of the rubbish of rebellion. Many were killed, and a large number took refuge in I'rán and Túran (Persia and Tartary); and thus the countries of Bájaur, Swád, and Tírah, which are rarely to be equalled in the world for their climate and fertility, and the plenty of their fruits, were cleansed of these wicked wretches." Yet this alleged conclusion of the war does not prevent Abul Fazl's relating the various events which took place during the course of it in the remaining fifteen years that are included in his history. He even accounts for Akber's fourteen years' stay in the Panjáb, by "his being at one time engaged in suppressing the Tájiks (Roushenias), and at another in reducing the inhabitants of the northern hills. (*Chalmers's MS. Translations of the Akbernámeh.*)

* See pp. 141. 685, 686.

and intrenched himself in such a situation that Akber's general could neither attack him nor carry on the siege while he was so near.

This difficulty was surmounted by the sagacity of the emperor himself. He sent another detachment to enter Sind by the way of Amercót; and, by thus distracting the attention of the chief, deprived him of the advantages of his position, and before long, reduced him to give up the province. He received very favourable terms, and was appointed by Akber, according to that monarch's practice, to a high rank among the nobles of the empire.

A. D. 1592, A. H. 1000.

It is mentioned in the "Akbernámeh" that the chief of Sind employed Portuguese soldiers in this war, and had also 200 natives dressed as Europeans. These were, therefore, the first *Sepoys* in India.

The same chief is also said to have had a fort defended by an Arab garrison: the first instance in which I have observed any mention of that description of mercenaries, afterwards so much esteemed.

Recovery of Candahár.

After the treacherous seizure of Candahár by Humáyun, the king of Persia made several attempts to recover possession. He had no success until the beginning of Akber's reign, when the divided state of the monarchy enabled him to effect his purpose. Similar disorders in the early part of the reign of Sháh Abbás gave a corresponding advantage to Akber. The Persian chiefs fell out

BOOK IX.

among themselves; one of them fled to India; and all parties ultimately turned their eyes to the same quarter; so that, at length, both the town and territory fell, without a blow, into the hands of the Mogul prince.

A. D. 1594, A. H. 1003.

These proceedings led to no quarrel with Persia: Sháh Abbás was fully employed at home, and, being desirous of Akber's assistance against the Uzbeks, he soon after renewed the friendly intercourse which had long been suspended between the courts, and patiently waited his opportunity of recovering Candahár; which did not present itself till after the death of Akber.

Complete settlement of Hindostan.

The acquisition of Candahár placed Akber in complete possession of his hereditary kingdom beyond the Indus (the war with the north-eastern Afgháns being now confined to the mountains): and nearly at the same time he had completed the conquest of Hindostan Proper. Sind had fallen in 1592; the last attempt at rebellion in Cashmír was quashed about the same time; the reduction of Bengal was completed by the submission of Orissa; and all disturbances in Guzerát terminated by the death of Mozaffer in 1593; so that the whole of Hindostan to the Nerbadda was more under Akber's authority than it had been under any former king. The rána of Oudipúr, indeed, continued unsubdued; but the other Rájpút chiefs were changed from jealous tributaries to active and attached adherents.

Expedition to the Deckan.

The next object for Akber was to extend his

CHAP. II.

dominions over the Deckan. As early as A.D. 1586 he had taken up the cause of Burhán, a brother of Murtezza Nizám Sháh, the fourth king of Ahmednagar, who claimed to administer the government on the ground of the mental derangement of its actual possessor. An expedition sent by Akber from Málwa to support this claim had failed, and Burhán remained for some years under Akber's protection. At a later period (A.D. 1592), after his brother's death, Burhán acquired possession of his hereditary kingdom without any aid from Akber; but he found it divided by internal faction, and engaged in war with his neighbour the king of Bíjapúr. All these distractions were increased on the death of Burhán. That event happened after a short reign; and in A.D. 1595 there were no less than four parties in the field, each supporting a separate claimant. The chief of the party that was in possession of the capital had recourse to the aid of the Moguls; and, at his invitation, Prince Morád entered the Deckan from Guzerát, and Mírza Khán, the Kháni Khánán, from Málwa, the two armies forming a junction within a short distance of Ahmednagar. But, in the mean time, the chief by whom they were called in had been obliged to leave the capital, and it was now in the hands of Chánd Sultána, or Chánd Bíbí, one of the most distinguished women that have ever appeared in India. This princess was acting as regent for her infant nephew, Bahádur Nizám Sháh, and she no sooner was aware of the approach of the Mo-

A. D. 1595, about Nov.; A. H. 1004, about the end of Rabi ul Akhir. Chánd Sultána.

BOOK IX.

guls than she applied herself to conciliate the king of Bíjapúr, her relation, and at the same time to reconcile the heads of the other internal parties; that all might, for a time at least, unite to resist the power whose ambition threatened equal danger to them all. So successful was her appeal, that one of the chiefs, Nehang, an Abyssinian, immediately set out to join her, and cut his way into Ahmednagar while the Moguls were in the act of investing the place: the other two likewise laid aside their private animosities, and joined the army of Bíjapúr, then marching against the Moguls.

Her defence of Ahmednagar.

These preparations increased the eagerness of Prince Morád. He pressed on the siege, and had already run two mines under the works, when they were discovered and rendered useless by the countermines of the besieged, Chánd Bíbí herself superintending the workmen, and exposing herself to the same dangers as the rest. The third mine was fired before the means taken to render it ineffectual were completed: the counterminers were blown up, a wide breach was made in the wall, and such a sudden terror was struck among those who defended it, that they were on the point of deserting their posts and leaving the road open to the storming party which was advancing. But they were soon recalled by Chánd Bíbí, who flew to the breach in full armour, with a veil over her face and a naked sword in her hand; and having thus checked the first assault of the Moguls, she continued her exertions till every power within the place was called forth against them: matchlock-balls and arrows poured on them from the works; guns were brought to bear upon the breach; rockets, gunpowder, and other combustibles were thrown among the crowd in the ditch; and the garrison in front opposed so steady a resistance, that, after an obstinate and bloody contest, which lasted till evening, the Moguls were obliged to draw off their troops and postpone the renewal of the assault till the next day. But the garrison and inhabitants had been raised to enthusiasm by the example of the regent; and, as her activity and energy were not slackened during the night, the Moguls found, when the day dawned, that the breach had been built up to such a height as to render it impossible to mount it without new mines. Meanwhile the confederates drew near; and, though the Moguls were still superior in the field, they were unwilling to risk all on the chance of a battle. Chánd Bíbí, on the other hand, was well aware of the precarious duration of a combination like the present; and both parties were well satisfied to come to terms, the king of Ahmednagar surrendering to the emperor his claims on Berár, of which he had recently made a conquest.*

Peace agreed on. A. H. 1004, Rajab; A. D. 1596, about February.

* Chánd Bíbí is the favourite heroine of the Deckan, and is the subject of many fabulous stories. Even Kháfi Khán mentions her having fired silver balls into the Mogul camp; and the common tradition at Ahmednagar is, that when her shot was expended, she loaded her guns successively with copper, with silver, and with gold coin, and that it was not till she had begun to fire away jewels, that she consented to make peace.

BOOK IX.

War renewed, and extended to the whole of the Deckan.

The Moguls had not long withdrawn, when fresh dissensions broke out in Ahmednagar. One Mohammed Khán, whom Chánd Bíbí had appointed péshwa*, or prime minister, plotted against her authority, and finally applied for aid to Prince Morád. The prince was already engaged in a dispute with the Deckan princes about the boundaries of Berár; both parties had once more recourse to hostilities, and before the expiration of a year from the peace they again met each other in the field in greater force than before.

The king of Cándésh, who acknowledged himself Akber's subject, appeared on his side on this occasion, while the king of Golcónda had now joined his forces to those of Bíjapúr and Ahmednagar. The battle took place on the river Godáveri: though maintained with great fury for two days, its result was indecisive. The Moguls claimed the victory, but made no attempt to advance; and their ill success, together with the disagreement between Prince Morád and the Kháni Khánán, induced Akber to recall them both. Abul Fazl (the author), who was his prime minister, and had been lately in temporary disgrace, was sent to remove the prince; and, if necessary, to take the command of the army. His representations convinced Akber that his own presence was required: he

A. D. 1596, December, or Jan. 1597.

Akber goes in person to the Deckan.

* The title of péshwa (*i. e.* leader) had been used under the Bahmani sovereigns. It has since become famous as that under which the Bramin ministers of the rája of Sátára so long governed the Maratta empire.

CHAP. II.

therefore left the Panjáb towards the end of 1598 (after a residence of fourteen years in the countries near the Indus); and before the middle of 1599 he arrived on the river Nerbadda. The strong fortress of Doulatábád had been taken before he appeared; several other hill forts fell about the same time; and as soon as the royal army reached Burhánpúr, on the Tapti, a force was sent forward under his son, Prince Dániál, and the Kháni Khánán, to lay siege to Ahmednagar. Chánd Bíbí's government was now in a more disturbed state than ever. Nehang, the Abyssinian chief, who had joined her in Ahmednagar at the beginning of the former siege, was now besieging her. He drew off on the approach of the Moguls; but the intestine disturbances still rendered a defence hopeless; and Chánd Bíbí was negotiating a peace with the Moguls, when the soldiery, instigated by her factious opponents, burst into the female apartments and put her to death. Their treason brought its own reward: in a few days the breach was practicable; the storm took place; the Moguls gave no quarter to the fighting men; and the young king, who fell into their hands, was sent prisoner to the hill fort of Gwálíór. But the fall of the capital did not produce the submission of the kingdom. Another pageant king was set up, and the dynasty was not finally extinguished till the reign of Sháh Jehán, in A. D. 1637.

Death of Chánd Sultána.

Taking of Ahmednagar.

A. D. 1600, about July; A. H. 1009, Safar.

Before the siege of Ahmednagar, a disagreement had taken place between Akber and his vassal,

Conquest of Cándésh.

Akber re-

BOOK IX.

turns to Hindostan.

the former king of Cándésh, which induced the emperor to annex that country to his immediate dominions. The military operations which ensued occupied Akber for nearly a year, and it was not till some months after the storm of Ahmednagar that the reduction of the province was completed by the fall of Asírghar, when Akber appointed Prince Dániál viceroy of Cándésh and Berár, with the Kháni Khánán for his adviser; and marched, himself, to Agra, leaving the command in the Deckan and the prosecution of the conquest of Ahmednagar to Abul Fazl.

Spring of A. D. 1601, end of A. H. 1009. Refractory conduct of his eldest son, Selím.

Before his departure Akber had received embassies and presents from the kings of Bíjapúr and Golcónda, and had married his son Dániál to the daughter of the former prince.* Akber's return to Hindostan was rendered necessary by the refractory conduct of his eldest son Selím.† The prince, who was now turned of thirty, does not appear to have been deficient in natural abilities; but his temper had been exasperated, and his understanding impaired, by the excessive use of wine and opium.‡ He had always looked on Abul

* The account of the operations in the Deckan is from the "Akbernámeh," and Ferishta, especially his "History of Ahmednagar," vol. iii.

† Afterwards the Emperor Jehángír.

‡ His own account is, that in his youth he used to drink at least twenty cups of wine a day, each cup containing half a sír (six ounces, *i. e.* nearly half a pint); and that if he was a single hour without his beverage, his hands began to shake, and he was unable to sit at rest. After he came to the throne, he

Fazl as his mortal enemy; and the temporary disgrace of that minister, and his subsequent removal to the Deckan, were concessions made by Akber to the complaints and jealousy of his son. On his own departure for the Deckan, Akber declared Selím his successor, appointed him viceroy of Ajmír, and committed to him the conduct of the war with the rána of Oudipúr, sending Rája Mán Sing to assist him with his arms and counsels. After much loss of time Selím set forth on this duty, and had made some progress in the fulfilment of it, when intelligence arrived of the revolt under Osmán in Bengal, of which province Mán Sing was the viceroy. He immediately set off for his government; and Selím, now free from all control, and seeing the emperor's whole force employed in other quarters, was tempted to seize on the provinces of Hindostan for himself. He marched to Agra; and, as the governor of that city contrived to elude his demands for its surrender, he proceeded to Allahábád, and took possession of the

A. D. 1600, about Nov.; A. H. 1009, Shábán.

---

says, he drank only five cups (*i. e.* little more than a quart), and only took it after nightfall. It does not appear how long he adhered to this sobriety. (*Price's Jehángír*, pp. 6, 7.) Drinking seems to have been the vice of the age among the Mahometan kings and great men: Báber and Humáyun both drank hard: the princes of Túrk dynasties seem all to have had the same propensity; and even the Sófis of Persia, so lately elevated by the sanctity of their family, not only drank to excess in private, but made their piles of cups and flagons of gold and jewels compose a great part of the splendour of their court.

BOOK IX.

surrounding countries of Oud and Behár. He at the same time seized on the local treasure, amounting to thirty lacs of rupees (300,000*l.*) and assumed the title of king.

However much Akber may have been afflicted by this conduct, he determined not to drive his son to extremities. He wrote a temperate letter, warning him of the consequences of his conduct, and assuring him of his own undiminished affection, if he would in time return to the path of his duty. As these remonstrances were soon followed by Akber's return to Agra, Selím replied in the most submissive terms, and actually marched as far as Etáyah with the professed intention of waiting on his father. Whether he in reality intended his approach to be hostile, or entertained apprehensions for his own safety, he spared no efforts to raise troops, and had assembled such a body that Akber sent to desire him to advance slightly attended, or else to return to Allahábád. Selím chose the latter course. It is not improbable that this retreat was procured by negotiation; for it was soon followed by a grant of Bengal and Orissa by Akber to his son, and by renewed professions of fidelity and devotion on the part of the latter. During this deceitful calm, the prince had an opportunity, which he did not let slip, of revenging his own supposed injuries, while he inflicted the severest blow on the feelings of his father. Abul Fazl had at this time been recalled from the Deckan, and was advancing with a small escort towards Gwáliór,

Murder of Abul Fazl.

when he fell into an ambuscade laid for him by Narsing Deó, rája of O'rcha in Bundélcand, at the instigation of Prince Selím; and although he defended himself with great gallantry, he was cut off with most of his attendants, and his head sent to the prince.* Akber was deeply affected by the intelligence of this event. He shed abundance of tears, and passed two days and nights without food or sleep. He immediately sent a force against Narsing Deó, with orders to seize his family, ravage his country, and exercise such severities as on other occasions he never permitted. He does not seem to have known of his son's share in the crime: so far from interrupting his intercourse with him, he sent Selíma Sultána, one of his wives, who had adopted Selím after his own mother's death, to endeavour to soothe his mind and bring about an entire reconciliation.

A. D. 1602, A. H. 1011.

Reconciliation of Akber with Selím.

This embassy was attended with the desired effect. Selím soon after repaired to court and made his submission. Akber received him with his usual kindness, and conferred on him the privilege of using the royal ornaments. Selím was

A. D. 1603, A. H. 1012.

* Selím, in his Memoirs, written after he was emperor, acknowledges the murder, and defends it on the ground that Abul Fazl had persuaded Akber to renounce the Korán, and to deny the divine mission of Mahomet. On the same ground he justifies his own rebellion against his father. (*Price's Memoirs of Jehángír*, p. 33.) One of his first acts after his accession was to promote the murderer, Narsing Deó (who had escaped the unrelenting pursuit of Akber), to a high station, and he always continued to treat him with favour and confidence.

BOOK IX.

Continued misconduct of Selím.

soon after again dispatched with a force against the rána of Oudipúr; but he protracted his march on various pretences, and showed so little disposition to involve himself in a permanent contest of that nature, that Akber, desirous to avoid a rupture at all costs, sent him leave to return to his almost independent residence of Allahábad. Here he gave himself up more than ever to debauchery. He had always entertained a peculiar dislike for his eldest son, Prince Khusru, whose own levity and violence seem to have given him reason for his displeasure. Some circumstance in their disputes at this time so affected Khusru's mother (the sister of Rája Mán Sing) that she swallowed poison, and thus added a fresh sting to the already inflamed mind of her husband. Selím's irascibility now became so great that his attendants were afraid to approach him; and he was guilty of cruelties which had been so long disused that they excited horror among all who heard of them, and which were peculiarly repugnant to the humane nature of Akber.*

The emperor was much perplexed as to the course to pursue, and determined to try the effect of a personal interview with his son. He therefore set off for Allahábád, and had advanced one or two

* On one occasion Selím ordered an offender to be flayed alive, and Akber could not conceal his disgust when he heard of it, but said he wondered how the son of a man who could not see a dead beast flayed without pain could be guilty of such cruelty to a human being.

marches, when he heard of the alarming illness of his own mother, and returned just in time to receive her last breath.

On hearing of this journey, and the cause of its suspension, Selím perhaps animated by some sense of duty or natural affection, or perhaps conceiving that his interests would be best served by his presence at court, determined to repair to Agra, and to submit in good earnest to his father.

He is placed under restraint, and soon after released.

On reaching Agra he was kindly received, but was for a short time placed under restraint; and either to lessen the disgrace of his confinement, or to prevent his indulging in his usual excesses, he was put under the care of a physician. Before long he was restored to freedom and to favour. Still the violence of his temper does not appear to have abated; and his jealousy of his son Khusru led to such a disorderly scene at an elephant fight in Akber's presence, that he was in imminent danger of again incurring the public displeasure of the emperor. Khusru took up the quarrel with as much vehemence as his father, and did all he could to exasperate Akber against him. It is even probable that Khusru had, long ere this, entertained views of supplanting his father in the succession; and Selím, in his Memoirs, appears to have been convinced that Akber at one time had serious thoughts of such a supersession *; but the real favourite with Akber, as well as with Selím himself, was

His quarrels with his own son, Khusru.

* Price's Memoirs of Jehángír, p. 33.

BOOK IX.

Khurram *, the third and youngest son of the latter; and their preference of that prince was among the principal causes of the discontent of his elder brother.

Death of Dániál, Akber's third son.

Akber had, some years before, lost his second son, Morád: he now received accounts of the death of his third son, Dániál, who fell a victim to intemperance in the thirtieth year of his age. His health having already received a severe shock from his excess, he was obliged to pledge his word to his father to leave off the use of wine, and was so surrounded by people of the emperor's, that he was unable to gratify his propensity, which had become irresistible. His resource was to have liquor secretly conveyed to him in the barrel of a fowling piece; and having thus again free access to indulgence, he soon brought his life to a close. This calamity was felt by Akber in the degree that was to be expected from the strength of his attachments; and it is probable that his domestic afflictions, and the loss of his intimate friends, began to prey upon his spirits and undermine his health.

Sickness of Akber.

He appears to have been for some time ill †, when, in the middle of September, 1605, his complaint came on with additional violence, accompanied by total loss of appetite; and it became apparent, before long, that there were little hopes of his recovery. For the last ten days he was confined to his bed; and although he appears to have

* Afterwards Sháh Jehán.

† Price's Memoirs of Jehángír, p. 70.

retained his faculties to the last, he was no longer capable of taking part in business. From this time all eyes were directed to the succession, and the court became an arena for the struggles of the contending parties. Selím was the acknowledged heir, and the only remaining son of the emperor; but his rebellion had weakened his reputation, and he was now in a sort of disgrace, removed from his troops, and from all those over whom he was accustomed to exercise authority. On the other hand, Rája Mán Sing was maternal uncle to Khusru, who was moreover married to the daughter of Azíz, the Khán i A'zim, the first of Akber's generals; and those great personages, foreseeing an increase to their own power in the succession of their young relation, took immediate measures for securing the palace, which forms also the citadel of Agra, and made all dispositions for placing Khusru on the throne. Selím was now justly alarmed for his personal safety, and forebore visiting the palace on pretence of illness. His son, Prince Khurram, though only a boy, disregarded both his father's injunctions and his own danger, and declared that he would never quit his grandfather while he continued to live. Akber was distressed by his son's absence, of which he surmised the cause. He repeatedly expressed his anxiety to see him, and again pronounced him the lawful successor to the kingdom, while he expressed his desire that Khusru should be provided for by a grant of the province of Bengal. These declarations, together with the

Intrigues regarding the succession.

Unsuccessful combination to set aside Selím.

BOOK IX.

exertions of some of the most respectable nobles, who still adhered to Selím, had a great effect in drawing off the inferior chiefs who had attached themselves to the opposite party; and Azíz soon perceived that he was likely to be deserted if he persevered, and took the prudent course of opening a private negotiation with Selím. Mán Sing, whose influence depended on the loyalty of his followers to himself and not to the emperor, was not exposed to the same danger; but finding himself left alone, and having received flattering overtures from Selím, he also at length promised his support to the heir apparent, who now repaired to the palace, and was affectionately received by the dying monarch. The last moments of Akber are only recorded by his successor. He says that, at this interview, Akber desired him to bring all his omrahs into the chamber where he was lying; "for" said he, "I cannot bear that any misunderstanding should subsist between you and those who have, for so many years, shared in my toils and been the companions of my glory." When they were assembled he delivered a suitable address to them; and, after wistfully regarding them all round, he desired them to forgive any offences of which he might have been guilty towards any of them. Selím now threw himself at his feet, and burst into a passion of tears; but Akber pointed to his favourite scymitar, and made signs to his son to bind it on in his presence. He seems afterwards to have recovered from this exhaustion: he addressed himself to Selím, and

Death of Akber. A. D. 1605, A. H. 1014. Oct. 13.

earnestly conjured him to look to the comfort of the ladies of his family, and not to forget or forsake his old friends and dependents. After this he permitted one of the chief mullahs, who was a personal friend of Selím's, to be brought to him, and in his presence he repeated the Mahometan confession of faith, and died in all the forms of a good Mussulman.*

His character.

Akber is described as a strongly built and handsome man, with an agreeable expression of countenance, and very captivating manners.† He was endowed with great personal strength and activity. In his youth he indulged in wine and good living, but early became sober and abstemious, refraining from animal food on particular days, making altogether nearly a fourth part of the year. He was

* Akber was buried near Agra. His tomb is thus described by Bishop Heber. The central building "is a sort of solid pyramid, surrounded externally with cloisters, galleries, and domes, diminishing gradually on ascending it, till it ends in a square platform of white marble surrounded by the most elaborate lattice-work of the same material, in the centre of which is a small altar tomb, also of white marble, carved with a delicacy and beauty which do full justice to the material, and to the graceful forms of the Arabic characters which form its chief ornament." (*Bishop Heber's Narrative*, vol. i. p. 587.) This immense pile served as quarters to an European regiment of dragoons for a year or two after the first conquest of that territory by the British.

† Price's Memoirs of Jehángír, p. 45. The following is the account given of him by the Portuguese Jesuits who went to visit him from Goa. He was about "fifty years old, white like an European, and of sagacious intellect. He received them with singular affability, &c. (*Murray's Discoveries in Asia*, vol. ii. p. 89.)

always satisfied with very little sleep, and frequently spent whole nights in those philosophical discussions of which he was so fond. Although so constantly engaged in wars, and although he made greater improvements in civil government than any other king of India; yet, by his judicious distribution of his time, and by his talents for the dispatch of business, he always enjoyed abundant leisure for study and amusement. He was fond of witnessing fights of animals, and all exercises of strength and skill; but his greatest pleasure was in hunting, especially in cases like the destruction of tigers, or the capture of herds of wild elephants, which gave a scope to his enjoyment of adventure and exertion. He sometimes also underwent fatigue for the mere pleasure of the exercise, as when he rode from Ajmír to Agra (220 miles) in two successive days, and in many similar journeys on horseback, besides walks on foot of thirty or forty miles in a day. His history is filled with instances of romantic courage, and he seems to have been stimulated by a sort of instinctive love of danger as often as by any rational motive. Yet he showed no fondness for war: he was always ready to take the field and to remain there, exerting all his talents and energy, while his presence was required; but when the fate of a war was once decided, he returned to the general government of his empire, and left it to his lieutenants to carry on the remaining military operations. These were, in some cases, very long protracted; but his conquests, when concluded, were complete; and no part of India, except that near the capital, can be said to have been thoroughly subdued until his time. He was not free from ambition; but as the countries he invaded had been formerly subject to Delhi, he would have incurred more blame than praise among his contemporaries if he had forborne from attempting to recover them.

CHAP. III.

INTERNAL POLICY.

BOOK IX.

His internal policy, religious and civil.

His general toleration and impartiality.

But it is to his internal policy that Akber owes his place in that highest order of princes, whose reigns have been a blessing to mankind; and that policy shows itself in different shapes, as it affects religion or civil government. Akber's tolerant spirit was displayed early in his reign, and appears to have been entirely independent of any doubts on the divine origin of the Mahometan faith. It led him however to listen, without prejudice, to the doctrines of other religions, and involved him in enmity with the bigoted members of his own; and must thus have contributed to shake his early belief, and to dispose him to question the infallible authority of the Koran. The political advantages of a new religion, which should take in all classes of his subjects, could not fail, moreover, to occur to him.

Progress of his religious opinions.

In the first part of his reign, he was assiduous in visiting sacred places, and in attendance on holy men: even in the twenty-first year of his reign, he spoke seriously of performing the pilgrimage to Mecca; and it was not till the twenty-fourth year (A.D. 1579), that he made open profession of his latitudinarian opinions.

It is not impossible that some even of the holy persons whom he visited may have held the free notions common with particular sects of Mahometan ascetics; but the blame of corrupting Akber's orthodoxy is thrown by all Mussulman writers on Feizi and his brother Abul Fazl. These eminent persons were the sons of a learned man named Mobárik, who was probably a native of Nágór, and who, at one time, taught a college or school of law and divinity at Agra. He was at first a Sunni, but turned Shía; and afterwards took to reading the philosophical works of the ancients, and became a freethinker, or, according to his enemies, an atheist. So great a persecution was raised against him on this account, that he was constrained to give up his school, and fly with his family from Agra. His sons conformed, in all respects, to the Mahometan religion; though it is probable that they never were deeply imbued with attachment to the sect.

Feizi.

His translations from the Shanscrit.

Feizi was the first Mussulman that applied himself to a diligent study of Hindú literature and science. It does not appear whether his attention was directed to these researches by Akber, or whether he undertook them of his own accord. It was, however, by the aid and under the direction of the emperor that he conducted a systematic inquiry into every branch of the knowledge of the Bramins. Besides Shanscrit works in poetry * and

* He translated the "Nala and Damyanta," an episode of the "Mahá Bhárat." (See Vol. I. p. 299.) Feizi was likewise author of a great deal of original poetry, and of other works, in Persian. He seems to have been more studious and less a man of the world than Abul Fazl.

BOOK IX.

philosophy, he made a version of the "Bíja Ganita" and "Lílawatí" of Bháscara Achárya, the best Hebrew books on algebra and arithmetic.

He superintends translations from that and other languages.

He likewise superintended translations made from the Shanscrit by other learned men, including one, at least, of the Védas, the two great historical and heroic poems the "Mahá Bhárat" and "Rámáyana," and the "History of Cashmír," the only specimen of that sort of composition in Shanscrit prose.*

Akber's acquisitions of this nature were not confined to Shanscrit. He prevailed on a Christian priest, whom Abul Fazl calls Padre Farábatún, and describes as learned in science and history, to come from Goa, and undertake the education of a few youths destined to be employed in translating the productions of Greek literature into Persian. Feizi himself was directed to make a correct version of the Evangelists. †

Abul Fazl.

Feizi was first presented to Akber in the twelfth

* Muntukhab ul Tawárikh.

† The taste for literature and accomplishments seems to have been much diffused in Akber's court: Azíz (or Kháni A'zim) was a man of great learning; Mírza Khán (Khán Khánan), son of Behrám Khán, and the second of Akber's generals, made the excellent Persian translation now extant of Báber's "Memoirs," from the Turkish. Among the distinguished men of this time, all historians mention Tánsén, a celebrated composer, whose music is still much admired. Even Zein Khán (so often mentioned as an able and active general) is said to have played well on several instruments. Akber encouraged schools, at which Hindú as well as Mahometan learning was taught, and "every one was educated according to his circumstances and particular views in life." (*Akbernámeh.*)

year of his reign, and introduced Abul Fazl six years later, in A. D. 1574.

CHAP. III.

Akber's attachment to those brothers.

Those brothers soon became the intimate friends and inseparable companions of their sovereign. They not only were the confidants of all his new opinions in religion, and his advisers in his patronage of literature, both in foreign countries and in his own, but were consulted and employed in the most important affairs of government. Feizi was sent on a special embassy to the kings of the Deckan previous to the invasion of that country; and Abul Fazl lived to attain the highest military rank, and to hold the office of prime minister. Akber's distress at the loss of Abul Fazl has been mentioned, and the account of his behaviour at the death of Feizi is the more to be relied on as it is given by an enemy. It was midnight when the news was brought to him that Feizi was dying; on which he hastened to his apartment, but found him already nearly insensible: he raised his head, and called out to him, with a familiar term of endearment, "Shékhjí! I have brought Ali the physician to you; why do not you speak?" Finding that he received no answer, he threw his turban on the ground and burst into the strongest expressions of sorrow. When he had recovered his composure, he went to Abul Fazl, who had withdrawn from the scene of death, and remained for some time endeavouring to console him, before he returned to his palace.*

* Muntakhab ul Tawárikh. The same author, whose name

BOOK IX.

Akber's religious and philosophical conferences.

Along with Feizi and Abul Fazl, there were many other learned men of all religions about the court; and it was the delight of Akber to assemble them, and sit for whole nights assisting at their philosophical discussions. His regular meetings were on Friday; but he often sent for single Bramins or Mahometan Súfis on other occasions, and entered into long inquiries regarding the tenets of their different schools. *

Some specimens of the discussions at those meetings (probably imaginary ones) are given in the "Dabistán," a learned Persian work on the various religions of Asia.

---

was Abdul Kádir, relates that Feizi continued to blaspheme in his dying moments, and that at last he barked like a dog, while his face became disfigured and his lips black, as if he already bore the impress of the damnation that awaited him. Abdul Kádir inserts in his book a letter in his favour from Feizi to Akber, and defends himself from the charge of ingratitude in defaming his benefactor after his death, by saying that it was a paramount duty he owed to God and to religion. The letter shows Feizi's zeal for his friends in a strong point of view. It expatiates on the services of the bearer, and his ill luck in their not having attracted notice; speaks of him in the warmest terms as an intimate acquaintance of thirty-seven years' standing, a true and faithful friend, and a person of many virtues and accomplishments; and ends by strongly recommending him to the emperor. Though Abdul Kádir had quarrelled with Feizi and Abul Fazl on points of religion, this dispute does not seem to have led to his disgrace with Akber; for he mentions that he was employed by that monarch to make a catalogue of Feizi's library after his death, and that it consisted of 4060 books, carefully corrected and well bound, on poetry and literature, moral and physical science, and theology.

* Akbernámeh. Muntakhab ul Tawárikh.

The fullest is a dialogue between a Bramin, a Mussulman, a worshipper of fire, a Jew, a Christian, and a philosopher.* The representative of each religion brings forth his arguments; which are successively condemned, some on account of the vicious character of their founders, and all for the absurdity of their doctrines, and the want of proof of their alleged miracles. The philosopher winds up the discourse by recommending a system which shall have no ground but reason and virtue. An account of a real debate of this kind is given in the "Akbernámeh." It was carried on before an assembly of the learned of all religions, between Padre *Redíf*, a Christian priest, and a body of Mahometan mullahs: a decided advantage, both in temper and argument, is given to the Christian. It was concluded by Akber's reproving the mullahs for their violence, and expressing his own opinion that God could only be adequately worshipped by following reason, and not yielding implicit faith to any alleged revelation.†

* Translated by Colonel Kennedy, *Transactions of the Bombay Literary Society*, vol. ii. p. 247, &c.

† A circumstance is related regarding this meeting, of which the Christians and Mahometans give different accounts; and, what is rather unusual in controversies, each tells the story in the way least favourable to his own faith. The disputants having split on the divinity of their respective scriptures, the Christian, according to Abul Fazl, offered to walk into a flaming furnace, bearing the Bible, if the Mahometan would show a similar confidence in the protection of the Korán. To this, he says, the Mussulmans only answered by reproaches. The missionaries, on the other hand, say the proposal came from the

BOOK IX.

Religious system of Akber.

The religion of Akber himself may be inferred from what has been said. It seems to have been pure deism; in addition to which some ceremonies were permitted in consideration of human infirmity. It maintained that we ought to reverence God according to the knowledge of him derived from our own reason, by which his unity and benevolence are sufficiently established; that we ought to serve him, and to seek for our future happiness by subduing our bad passions, and practising such virtues as are beneficial to mankind; but that we should not adopt a creed, or practise a ritual, on the authority of *any* MAN, as all were liable to vice and error like ourselves. If it were absolutely necessary for men to have some visible object of adoration, by means of which they might raise their soul to the Divinity, Akber recommended that the sun, the

---

Mussulmans, and was rejected by them, contrary to the wish of Akber. (Murray's *Asiatic Discoveries*, vol. ii. p. 91.) The probability is, that Akber may have taken this way of amusing himself with the extravagance of both parties. It does not appear that he had any design to turn the Christians at least into derision. The missionaries, provoked at the disappointment of their sanguine hopes of converting the emperor, appear at length to have suspected that he had no object in encouraging them, except to gratify his taste with their pictures and images, and to swell the pomp of his court by their attendance (Ibid. vol. ii. p. 91.); but, besides his intense curiosity about the religious opinions of all sects, both Abul Fazl and Abdul Kádir represent him as entertaining a real respect for Christianity. The latter author says that he made his son Morád be instructed in the Gospel, and that those lessons were not begun according to the usual form, "In the name of God," but, "In the name of Jesus Christ."

planets, or fire, should be the symbols. He had no priests, no public worship, and no restrictions about food, except a recommendation of abstinence, as tending to exalt the mind. His only observances were salutations to the sun, prayers at midnight and day-break, and meditations at noon on the sun. He professed to sanction this sort of devotion, from regard to the prejudices of the people, and not from his own belief in their efficacy. It is, indeed, related by Abul Fazl, that, being once entreated to pray for rain, he refused, observing that God knew our wants and wishes better than we did ourselves, and did not require to be reminded, to exert his power for our benefit. But as Akber *practised* all his ceremonies, as well as permitted them, it may be doubted whether they had not gained some hold on his imagination. He seems to have been by nature devout, and, with all his scepticism, to have inclined even to superstitions that promised him a closer connection with the Deity than was afforded by the religion which his reason approved. To this feeling we may ascribe, among other instances, the awe and veneration with which he adored the images of Jesus Christ and the Virgin, when they were shown to him by the missionaries.*

Notwithstanding the adulation of his courtiers, and some expressions in the formulæ of his own religion, Akber never seems to have entertained the least intention of laying claims to supernatural

* Murray, vol. ii. p. 89.

BOOK IX.

illumination. His fundamental doctrine was, that there were no prophets; his appeal on all occasions was to human reason; and his right to interfere at all with religion was grounded on his duty as civil magistrate.* He took the precaution, on promulgating his innovations, to obtain the legal opinions of the principal Mahometan lawyers, that the king was the head of the church, and had a right to govern it according to his own judgment†, and to decide all disputes among its members; and, in in his new confession of faith, it was declared that "There was no God but God, and that Akber was *his calif.*"

A. D. 1579, A. H. 987, in Rejib.

In the propagation of his opinions, Akber confined himself to persuasion, and made little progress except among the people about his court and a few learned men; but his measures were much stronger in abrogating the obligations of the Mussulman religion, which, till now, had been enforced by law. Prayers, fasts, alms, pilgrimages, and public worship were left optional: the prohibition of unclean animals, that of the moderate use of wine, and that of gaming with dice, were taken off; and circumcision was not permitted until the age of twelve, when the person to undergo it could judge of the propriety of the rite. ‡

* Some of his practices, as breathing on his disciples, &c., which have been mentioned as implying pretensions to miraculous powers, are the common forms used by spiritual instructors throughout India.

† Muntakhab ul Tawárikh.

‡ Colonel Kennedy adds that the marriage of more than one wife was forbidden.

His discouragement of the Mahometan peculiarities.

Some of the other measures adopted seemed to go beyond indifference, and to show a wish to discountenance the Mahometan religion. The æra of the Hijra and the Arabian months were changed for a solar year, dating from the vernal equinox nearest the king's accession, and divided into months named after those of ancient Persia. The study of the Arabic language was discouraged: Arabian names (as Mohammed, Ali, &c.) were disused. The ordinary salutation of Salám alékum! (Peace be unto you!) was changed into Alláho Akber! (God is most great!); to which the answer was, Jillí Jelálihú! (May his brightness shine forth!).* Even wearing the beard, a practice enjoined by the Korán, was so offensive to Akber, that he would scarcely admit a person to his presence who conformed to it. This last prohibition gave peculiar disgust to the Mahometans, as did a regulation introducing on certain occasions the Persian custom of prostration (or kissing the ground, as it was called) before the king; a mark of respect regarded by the Mahometans as exclusively appropriated to the Deity.

His restrictions on the Hindú superstition.

As the Hindús had not been supported by the government, Akber had less occasion to interfere with them; and, indeed, from the tolerant and inoffensive character of their religion, he seems to have had little inclination. He however forbade trials by ordeal, and marriages before the age of

* These phrases include the emperor's name, Jelál u dín Akber.

BOOK IX.

puberty, and the slaughter of animals for sacrifice. He also permitted widows to marry a second time, contrary to the Hindú law*: above all, he positively prohibited the burning of Hindú widows against their will, and took effectual precautions to ascertain that their resolution was free and uninfluenced. On one occasion, hearing that the rája of Jódpúr was about to force his son's widow to the pile, he mounted his horse and rode post to the spot to prevent the intended sacrifice.†

His general indulgence to Hindús.

His most important measures connected with the Hindús were of a purely favourable nature, but had been adopted many years before his innovations in religion. His employment of them equally with Mahometans began with his assumption of the government. In the seventh year of his reign he abolished the jezía or capitation tax on infidels; an odious impost which served to keep up animosity between people of the predominant faith and those under them. About the same time he abolished all taxes on pilgrims; observing that, "although the tax fell on a vain superstition, yet, as all modes of worship were designed for one great Being, it was wrong to throw an obstacle in the way of the devout, and to cut them off from their mode of intercourse with their Maker."‡

Another humane edict, issued still earlier (A. D. 1561), though not limited to any one class, was, in practice, mainly beneficial to the Hindús: it was

* Colonel Kennedy, *Bombay Transactions*, vol. ii. p. 261.

† Akbernámeh.

‡ Chalmers's MS. translation of the "Akbernámeh."

CHAP. III.

a prohibition against making slaves of persons taken in war. It appears that in the previous disturbances this abuse had been carried to such a height, that not only was it practised towards the wives and children of garrisons who stood a storm, but even peaceable inhabitants of a hostile country were seized and sold for slaves. All this was positively prohibited.

Discontents among the Mussulmans.

Although Akber's religious innovations were not all introduced at once, and although some of those found to be particularly obnoxious to censure were cancelled or confined to the palace, yet they did not fail to excite great discontent among the stricter Mussulmans, and especially among the mullahs, whose disgust was increased by some changes affecting lands granted for religious purposes, which took place in the course of the general revenue reform. The complaints of these classes are zealously set forth by an author already often referred to *, who accuses Akber of systematic depression of the Mussulman religion, and even of persecution of such persons as distinguished themselves by adhering to it. It is not improbable that he showed some prejudice against those who were active in opposing him; and he certainly restricted his patronage to the more compliant; but in all the instances of harsh language and conduct to individuals, brought forward by this writer, Akber seems to have been justified by par-

* Abdul Kádir, the writer of the "Muntakhab ul Tawáríkh."

BOOK IX.

ticular acts of disrespect or factious conduct. The cases in question are not confined to mullahs. One of his principal courtiers was ordered out of the royal apartment for attacking his proceedings, and asking what he imagined orthodox princes of other countries would say of them? and another, who applied the epithet "hellish" to the king's advisers, was told that such language deserved to be answered by a blow. The most considerable of these malecontents was Azíz (the Khán i A'zim), who was Akber's foster-brother, and one of his best generals. This nobleman having been long absent in the government of Guzerát, his mother prevailed on Akber to invite him to come to court. Azíz excused himself; and it appeared that his real objection was to shaving his beard and performing the prostration. Akber, on this, wrote him a good-humoured remonstrance; but, Azíz persevering, he sent him a positive order to come to the capital. Azíz, on this, threw up his government; and after writing an insolent and reproachful letter to Akber, in which he asked him if he had received a book* from heaven, or if he could work miracles like Mahomet, that he presumed to introduce a new religion, warned him that he was on the way to eternal perdition, and concluded with a prayer to God to bring him back into the path of salvation. After this explosion of zeal he embarked for Mecca

* The Korán, the Old and New Testament, and the Psalms of David, are called *books* by way of excellence, and their followers, "People of the Book."

without leave or notice. In a short time, however, he found his situation irksome in that country, and returned to India, where he made his submission, and was restored at once to his former place in the emperor's favour and confidence.

Limited progress of his own religion

But although this sort of opposition was surmounted, Akber's religion was too spiritual and abstracted to be successful with the bulk of mankind. It seems never to have gone beyond a few philosophers and some interested priests and courtiers; and, on Akber's death, it expired of itself, and the Mussulman forms were quietly and almost silently restored by Jehángír. The solar year was retained for some time longer, on account of its intrinsic advantages. A liberal spirit of inquiry, however, survived the system to which it owed its rise; and if extrinsic causes had not interrupted its progress, it might have ripened into some great reform of the existing superstitions.

Akber cannot claim the merit of originality for his doctrines. The learned Hindús had always maintained the real unity of God, and had respected, without believing, the mythological part of their creed. The Cabír Pantis, a Hindú sect which sprung up nearly a century before Akber, had come still nearer to his views; and from them he appears to have borrowed some of the arbitrary parts of his religious rules: still he excelled all his predecessors in his conception of the Divine nature; and the general freedom which he allowed to private judgment was a much more generous effort

BOOK IX.

in a powerful monarch than in a recluse reformer, himself likely to be an object of persecution.*

His civil government — Revenue system.

Akber's revenue system, though so celebrated for the benefits it conferred on India, presented no new invention. It only carried the previous system into effect with greater precision and correctness: it was, in fact, only a continuation of a plan commenced by Shír Sháh, whose short reign did not admit of his extending it to all parts of his kingdom.

The objects of it were — 1. To obtain a correct measurement of the land. 2. To ascertain the amount of the produce of each bígah† of land, and to fix the proportion of that amount that each ought to pay to the government. 3. To settle an equivalent for the proportion so fixed, in money.

1. For the first purpose Akber established an uniform standard to supersede the various measures formerly employed even by public officers. He also improved the instruments of mensuration, and he then deputed persons to make a complete measurement of all the lands capable of cultivation within the empire.

* In comparing Akber's attempt to found a system of pure deism with similar experiments by modern governments, we must remember the incurable defects of all the religions with which he was acquainted, and must distinguish between the merit of a man who takes the lead of his generation, and that of another who follows the crowd even in its errors and extravagances.

† An Indian land measure, considerably more than half an acre.

CHAP. III.

2. The assessment was not so simple as the measurement. The land was divided into three classes, according to its fertility; the amount of each sort of produce that a bígah of each class would yield was ascertained: the average of the three was assumed as the produce of a bígah, and one third of that produce formed the government demand.* But this assessment seems to have been only designed to fix a maximum; for every cultivator who thought the amount claimed too high, might insist on an actual measurement and division of the crop.

As lands of equal fertility might be differently circumstanced in other respects, the following classification was formed for modifying that first men-

* Thus, assuming the produce of a bígah of wheat, in mans (a measure of something less than forty pounds),—

	mans.	sérs.
Class 1. would yield - -	18	
Class 2. - - - -	12	
Class 3. - - - -	8	35
Aggregate - -	38	35

which, divided by 3, gives the average — 12 mans 38⅓ sérs; and that again divided by 3 gives the king's demand on each bígah — 4 mans 12½ sérs.

If the produce of a bígah of cotton be assumed,—

	mans.	sers.
Class 1. will yield - - -	10	
Class 2. - - - -	7	20
Class 3. - - - -	5	
Aggregate - - - -	22	20
Average of the three classes -	7	20
King's demand (one third of the average) - - - -	2	20

BOOK IX.

tioned:—1. Land which never required a fallow paid the full demand every harvest. 2. Land which required fallows only paid when under cultivation. 3. Land which had suffered from inundation, &c., or which had been three years out of cultivation and required some expense to reclaim it, paid only two fifths for the first year, but went on increasing till the fifth year, when it paid the full demand. 4. Land which had been more than five years out of cultivation enjoyed still more favourable terms for the first four years.

It is not explained in the "A'yeni Akberi" how the comparative fertility of fields was ascertained. It is probable that the three classes were formed for each village, in consultation with the inhabitants, and the process would be greatly facilitated by another classification made by the villagers for their own use, which seems to have subsisted from time immemorial. By that distribution, all the land of every village is divided into a great many classes, according to its qualities; as black mould, red mould, gravelly, sandy, black mould mixed with stones, &c. Other circumstances are also considered, such as command of water, vicinity to the village, &c.; and great pains are taken so to apportion the different descriptions among the cultivators as to give equal advantages to all.

3. The quantity of produce due to the government being settled, it was next to be commuted for a money payment. For this purpose, statements of prices current for the nineteen years preceding the

survey were called for from every town and village; and the produce was turned into money according to the average of the rates shown in those statements. The commutation was occasionally reconsidered, with reference to the actual market prices; and every husbandman was allowed to pay in kind if he thought the money rate was fixed too high.

All these settlements were at first made annually; but their continual recurrence being found to be vexatious, the settlement was afterwards made for ten years, on an average of the payments of the preceding ten.

The prolongation of the term mitigated another evil inherent in the system; for, as the assessment varied with the sort of cultivation, it had all the effect of a tithe in indisposing the husbandman to cultivate a richer description of produce, which, though it might yield a greater profit, would have a higher tax to pay at the next settlement.

The above measurements and classifications were all carefully recorded; the distribution of land, and increase or diminution of revenue, were all yearly entered into the village registers agreeably to them; and they still continue in use, even in parts of India which had not been conquered in Akber's time, and where their own merits have since introduced them.

At the same time when Akber made these improvements respecting the land tax, he abolished a vast number of vexatious taxes and fees to officers.

He also made a new revenue division of the country into portions, each yielding a crór (*i. e.*

BOOK IX.

10,000,000) of dáms, equal to 250,000 rupees, or 25,000*l.*; the collector of each of which was called the cróri. This arrangement did not last, and the ancient Hindú division is again universally established.

The result of these measures was, to reduce the amount of the public demand considerably, but to diminish the defalcation in realising it; so that the profit to the state remained nearly the same, while the pressure on individuals was much lessened. Abul Fazl even asserts that the assessment was lighter than that of Shír Sháh, although *he* professed to take only one fourth of the produce, while Akber took one third.

Akber's instructions to his revenue officers have come down to us, and show his anxiety for the liberal administration of his system, and for the ease and comfort of his subjects. Some particulars of his mode of management also appear in those instructions. There is no farming of any branch of the revenue, and the collectors are enjoined, in their agreements and collections, to deal directly with individual cultivators, and not to depend implicitly on the headman and accountant of the village.*

On the whole, this great reform, much as it promoted the happiness of the existing generation, contained no principle of progressive improvement, and held out no hopes to the rural population by opening paths by which it might spread into other occupations, or rise by individual exertions

* Gladwin's A'yeni Akberi, vol. i. pp. 303—312.

within its own. No mode of administration, indeed, could effect these objects as long as the subdivision of land by inheritance checked all extensive improvement in husbandry, at the same time that it attached to the soil those members of each family who might have betaken themselves to commerce, or other pursuits, such as would have increased the value of raw produce, and raised the price of agricultural labour, by diminishing the competition for that species of employment.

Tódar Mal.

The author of the reform was Rája Tódar Mal, by whose name it is still called everywhere. The military services of this minister have already been mentioned. Abul Fazl describes him as entirely devoid of avarice, and quite sincere, but of a malicious and vindictive temper, and so observant of the fasts and other superstitions of the Hindú religion, as to draw down on him reproof even from Akber.*

Though we have not a particular explanation of Akber's system in other departments, as we have in that of revenue, a general notion of it may be made out from his instructions to his officers.†

Subahs, or governments, and

The empire was divided into fifteen subahs or provinces.‡ The chief officer in each was the

* Chalmers's MS. translation of the "Akbernámeh."

† Gladwin's A'yeni Akberi, vol. i. pp. 29—303.

‡ Twelve of these were in Hindostan and three in the Deckan: these last were increased, after the conquest of Bíjapúr and Golcónda, to six. The title of sipáh sálár was changed after Akber's time to subahdár, and an additional officer was introduced under the title of díwán, for the purpose of superintending the finances of the province. He was subordinate to the subahdár, but was appointed by the king.

BOOK IX.

viceroy (sipáh sálár), who had the complete control, civil and military, subject to the instructions of the king.

their establishments, —military, judicial, and police.

Under him were the revenue functionaries above mentioned, and also the military commanders of districts (foujdárs), whose authority extended over the local soldiery or militia, and over all military establishments and lands assigned to military purposes, as well as over the regular troops within their jurisdiction; and whose duty it was to suppress all disorders that required force within the same limits.

Justice was administered by a court composed of an officer named mír adel (lord justice), and a cázi. The latter conducted the trial and stated the law; the other passed judgment, and seems to have been the superior authority; the distinction probably arising from the modifications introduced by the will of the prince and the customs of the country into the strict Mahometan law, of which the cázi was the organ.

The police of considerable towns was under an officer called the cótwál; in smaller places it was under the revenue officer; and in villages, of course, under the internal authorities.

The tone of instructions to all these functionaries is just and benevolent, though by no means exempt from the vagueness and puerility that is natural to Asiatic writings of this sort.

Those to the cótwál keep up the prying and meddling character of the police under a despotism: they prohibit forestalling and regrating, &c.; and, in the midst of some very sensible directions, there is an order that any one who drinks out of the cup of the common executioner shall lose his hand; a law worthy of Menu, and the more surprising as the spirit of all the rules for administering justice is liberal and humane. A letter of instructions to the governor of Guzerát, preserved in a separate history of that province, restricts his punishments to putting in irons, whipping, and death; enjoining him to be sparing in capital punishments, and, unless in cases of dangerous sedition, to inflict none until he has sent the proceedings to court and received the emperor's confirmation. Capital punishment is not to be accompanied with mutilation or other cruelty.*

Reform and new model of the army.

Amidst the reforms of other departments, Akber did not forget his army. If it had cost a long and dangerous struggle to bring that body to submit to orders, it scarcely required a less exertion, at a later period, to introduce economy and efficiency into the management of it.

It had been usual to grant lands and assignments on the revenue, and leave the holder to realise them without check; while musters were irregular and deceptive, being often made up by servants and camp followers mounted for the day on borrowed horses.

Akber put a stop to the first of these abuses, by paying the troops in cash from the treasury whenever it was practicable; and establishing checks on

* Bird's History of Guzerát, p. 391.

jagírs, where such existed. The other was cured by rendering musters necessary before pay, by describing every man's features and person on the roll, and branding every horse with the king's mark that ever had been numbered in his service. Camels, oxen, carts, and all things necessary for the movement of troops, were also mustered and paid at fixed rates.

But even in its highest state of perfection the army was not very well organised. It was not divided into bodies, each of a certain number, and with a fixed proportion of officers: the system was, for the king to name officers as he thought necessary, who were called mansabdárs, and who were divided into classes, of commanders of 10,000, commanders of 5000, &c., down to commanders of 10. These numbers, in all but the lowest classes, were merely nominal, and were adopted to fix the rank and pay of the holders. Each entertained whatever number he was specially authorised to keep (sometimes not a tenth of his nominal command), and that number was mustered, and paid from the treasury. Their united quotas made up the army; and when a force went on service, the king appointed the commander, and some of the chief officers, below whom there was, probably, no chain of subordination, except what arose from each man's authority over his own quota. None but the king's sons held a rank above the command of 5000; and of the latter class there were only thirty persons, including princes of the blood and

Rájpút rájas. The whole number, down to commanders of 200, was not 450.*

Each mansabdár was required to keep half as many infantry as horsemen; and of the infantry, a fourth were required to be matchlockmen: the rest might be archers.

Besides these troops under mansabdárs, there was a considerable body of the best description of horsemen, who took service individually, and were called ahdis (*i.e.* single men, or individuals). Their pay depended on their merits; it was always much higher than that of a common horseman. These last, if from beyond the Indus, received 25 rupees a month; and if Indian, 20. The matchlockmen received 6 rupees at most, and the archers as low as 2½.

The mansabdárs were very liberally paid †, but no part of their emoluments or commands were hereditary. On a chief's death, the king conferred some rank — generally a moderate one at first — on his son, and added a pension if the father's merits entitled him to it.

* These numbers are from the list in the "A'yeni Akberi;" it is uncertain to which period of the reign it refers. The extremely small number of officers is explained by the absence of discipline and of instruction in tactics, as well as by the character of the horsemen, who were a sort of gentlemen, and more intelligent than ordinary troopers in a regular army.

† The sums in the tables in the "A'yeni Akberi" cannot relate to personal allowances alone; but see Bernier, vol. i. p. 289. He mentions that his patron, Dánishmand Khán, had the rank of 5000, with the real command of 500 horse, and had near 5000 *crowns* of pay per mensem.

BOOK IX.

We have no means of guessing the number of the troops. In later times, Aurangzíb was conjectured to have had 200,000 effective cavalry *, besides artillery and undisciplined infantry. It is not likely that Akber had as many. Abul Fazl says the local militia of the provinces amounted to 4,400,000; but this is probably an exaggerated account of those bound by their tenure to give a limited service in certain cases: probably few could be called on for more than a day or two to beat the woods for a hunting party; and many, no doubt, belonged to hill rájas and tribes who never served at all.

Fortifications and public works.

Besides the fort of Attok, already mentioned, many military works were erected by Akber. The walls and citadels of Agra and Allahábád much surpass the rest: they are lofty curtains and towers of cut stone, with deep ditches, and ornamented, in the Indian way, with turrets, domes, and battlements; each of the gateways being a stately edifice that would make a suitable entrance to a royal palace. He also built and fortified the town of Fattehpúr Síkri, which was his principal residence, and which, though now deserted, is one of the most splendid specimens that remain of the former grandeur of India. †

* Bernier.

† Bishop Heber describes its commanding situation on a hill, the noble flight of steps which ascends to the portal tower, the extent and rich carving of the palace; above all, the mosque, with the majestic proportions and beautiful architecture of the

CHAP. III.

Household and court.

The same methodical system was carried through all branches of Akber's service. The "A'yeni Akberi" (Regulations of Akber) by A'bul Fazl, from which the above account of the civil and military arrangements is mostly taken, contains a minute description of the establishment and regulations of every department, from the Mint and the Treasury down to the fruit, perfumery, and flower offices, the kitchen, and the kennel. The whole presents an astonishing picture of magnificence and good order; where unwieldy numbers are managed without disturbance, and economy is attended to in the midst of profusion.

The extent of these establishments appears from the work just mentioned, and the contemporary historians *; but the *effect* can be best judged of

---

quadrangle and cloisters, of which it forms one side. (Vol. i. p. 596.) The same judicious observer gives an account of the buildings within Agra. The principal are, "a beautiful mosque of white marble, carved with exquisite simplicity and elegance;" and the palace, built mostly of the same material, and containing some noble rooms. The great hall is "a splendid edifice, supported by pillars and arches of white marble, more nobly simple than that of Delhi. The ornaments, carving, and mosaic of the smaller apartments are equal or superior to any thing which is described as found in the Alhambra." (Vol. i. p. 587.) Among Akber's principal works must be mentioned the tomb of Humáyun at Delhi, a great and solid edifice erected on a terrace raised above the surrounding country, and surmounted by a vast dome of white marble.

* Akber had never less than 5000 elephants and 12,000 stable horse, besides vast hunting and hawking establishments, &c. &c. (*Ferishta*, vol. ii. p. 281.)

BOOK IX.

by the descriptions of the Europeans, who saw them in Akber's own time, or under the reign of his immediate successor, Jehángír.

His camp equipage consisted of tents and portable houses, in an inclosure formed by a high wall of canvass skreens, and containing great halls for public receptions, apartments for feasting, galleries for exercise, and chambers for retirement; all framed of the most costly materials, and adapted to the most luxurious enjoyment.

The inclosure was 1530 yards square. The tents and wall were of various colours and patterns within, but all red on the outside, and crowned with gilded globes and pinnacles, forming a sort of castle in the midst of the camp. The camp itself showed like a beautiful city of tents of many colours, disposed in streets without the least disorder, covering a space of about five miles across, and affording a glorious spectacle when seen at once from a height.*

The greatest displays of his grandeur were at the annual feasts of the vernal equinox, and the king's birthday. They lasted for several days, during which there was a general fair and many processions and other pompous shows. The king's usual place was in a rich tent, in the midst of awnings to keep off the sun. At least two acres were thus spread with silk and gold carpets and hangings, as rich as velvet, embroidered with gold, pearl,

* Sir Thomas Roe, in "Churchill's Voyages." Terry's Voyage, p. 398.

and precious stones, could make them.* The nobility had similar pavilions, where they received visits from each other, and sometimes from the king; dresses, jewels, horses, and elephants were bestowed on the nobility; the king was weighed in golden scales against silver, gold, perfumes, and other substances, in succession, which were distributed among the spectators. Almonds and other fruits, of gold and silver, were scattered by the king's own hand, and eagerly caught up by the courtiers, though of little intrinsic value. On the great day of each festival, the king was seated on his throne, in a marble palace, surrounded by nobles wearing high heron plumes and "sparkling with diamonds like the firmament."† Many hundred elephants passed before him in companies, all most richly adorned, and the leading elephant of each company with gold plates on its head and breast, set with rubies and emeralds.‡

Trains of caparisoned horses followed; and after them, rhinoceroses, lions, tigers and panthers, hunting leopards, hounds, and hawks§; the whole concluding with an innumerable host of cavalry glittering with cloth of gold.

In the midst of all this splendour, Akber appeared with as much simplicity as dignity. He is thus described by two European eye-witnesses,

* Hawkins, in "Purchas's Pilgrims," vol. i.

† Sir T. Roe says, "I own I never saw such inestimable wealth."

‡ Sir T. Roe.

§ Bernier, vol. i. p. 42.

BOOK IX.

with some parts of whose account I shall close his history.* After remarking that he had less show or state than other Asiatic princes, and that he stood or sat *below the throne* to administer justice, they say, that "he is affable and majestical, merciful, and severe;" that he is skilful in mechanical arts, as "making guns, casting ordnance, &c.; of sparing diet, sleeps but three hours a day, curiously industrious, affable to the vulgar, seeming to grace them and their presents with more respective ceremonies than the grandees; loved and feared of his own, terrible to his enemies."†

* Purchas, vol. v. p. 516.

† The principal authorities for this account of Akber's reign are, Ferishta, the "Akbernámeh" by Abul Fazl, the "Muntakhab ul Tawárikh," Kháfi Khán, and the "Kholásat ul Tawárikh." Abul Fazl, in this reign, shows all his usual merits, and more than his usual defects. (See p. 126.) Every event that had a tendency to take from the goodness, wisdom, or power of Akber, is passed over or misstated; and a uniform strain of panegyric and triumph is kept up, which disgusts the reader with the author, and almost with the hero. Amidst these unmeaning flourishes, the real merits of Akber disappear, and it is from other authors that we learn the motives of his actions, the difficulties he had to contend with, and the resources by which they were surmounted. The gross flattery of a book written by one so well acquainted with Akber's disposition, and submitted, it appears, to his own inspection, leaves an impression of the vanity of that prince, which is almost the only blot on his otherwise admirable character. The "Akbernámeh" was brought down by Abul Fazl nearly to the time of his own death, in the forty-seventh year of the reign, and was continued for the remaining period of upwards of three years by a person named Enáyet Ullah, or Mohammed Sália. I could never have availed myself of this work without the aid of a manuscript

translation of Lieutenant Chalmers of the Madras army, in the possession of the Royal Asiatic Society. The "Muntakhab ul Tawárikh" was finished in the end of the fortieth year of the reign. It is written by Abdul Kádir of Badáyun, and is a history of the Mahometan kings of India. The facts are chiefly taken from the "Tabakáti Akberi" down to the thirty-seventh year of Akber's reign, when that book ends. The whole of that reign, however, has many additions from the author's own knowledge, and takes its colour from his prejudices. Abdul Kádir was a learned man employed by Akber to make translations from Shanscrit; but, being a bigoted Mussulman, he quarrelled with Abul Fazl and Feizi, and has filled his book with invectives against their irreligion and that of Akber (see page 283. note). He has also recorded many other grievances complained of at that time, and has disclosed those parts of the picture which were thrown into the shade by Abul Fazl. The impression of Akber left by this almost hostile narrative is much more favourable than that made by his panegyrist. Kháfi Khán and the author of the "Kholásat ul Tawárikh" are later compilers. The "Tabakáti Akberi," written by Nizám u dín Hervi, is a history of the Mahometan kings down to the thirty-seventh of Akber, and is said to be a work of great merit; but, although I have access to a copy, I am unable to avail myself of it, for want of the assistance I require to make out the character. Besides the original of Khafi Khan, I am indebted to the kindness of Major A. Gordon of the Madras establishment, for the use of a manuscript translation made by him of the work of that historian down to near the end of Jehángír's reign. It is much to be regretted that this excellent translation has not been carried on to the end of the history, which comes down to recent times, and affords the only full and connected account of the whole period which it embraces.

BOOK X.

JEHÁNGÍR — SHÁH JEHÁN.

CHAP. I.

JEHÁNGÍR.

BOOK X.

A. D. 1605, October; A. H. 1014, Jemádi ul ákhir.

SELÍM took possession of the government immediately on his father's death, and assumed the title of Jehángír (Conqueror of the World).

State of India at the accession of Jehángír.

He found the whole of his dominions on the north of the Nerbadda in a state of as great tranquillity as could be expected in so extensive an empire. The rebellion of Osmán continued in Bengal, but was confined to part of that province. The contest with the rána of Oudipúr was a foreign war, and the success, though not complete, was on the side of the emperor.

Affairs wore a worse aspect in the Deckan, where the Nizám Sháhi government of Ahmednagar seemed to be recovering from the loss of its capital, and more likely to regain some of the territory it had been deprived of than to be completely subverted by the arms of the Moguls.

Moderate measures at the com-

Jehángír's first measures were of a much more benevolent and judicious character than might

mencement of his reign.

have been expected of him. He confirmed most of his father's old officers in their stations; and issued edicts, remitting some vexatious duties which had survived Akber's reforms, forbidding the bales of merchants to be opened by persons in authority without their free consent, directing that no soldiers or servants of the state should quarter themselves on private houses, abolishing the punishments of cutting off ears and noses, and introducing other salutary regulations. Notwithstanding his own notorious habits, he strictly forbade the use of wine, and regulated that of opium; subjecting all offenders against his rules to severe punishment.

He restored the Mahometan confession of faith on his coin, together with most of the forms of that religion. He, however, kept up some of Akber's rules regarding abstinence from meat on particular days. He observed some of his superstitious devotions; he exacted the ceremony of prostration from all who approached him; and although, in his writings, he affects the devout style usual to all Mussulmans, he never acquired, and probably did not seriously pretend to, the character of a religious man. The general impression is, that, though more superstitious, he was less devout, than Akber, and had little feeling of religion even when abstracted from all peculiar tenets.

Among his earliest measures was one for affording easy access to complaints, on which he valued himself at least as highly as the efficacy of the invention deserved: a chain was hung from a part of

BOOK X.

the wall of the citadel, accessible, without difficulty, to all descriptions of people; it communicated with a clustre of golden bells within the emperor's own apartment, and he was immediately apprised, by the sound of the appearance of a suitor, and thus rendered independent of any officers inclined to keep back information.

Flight of Prince Khusru.

The hatred which had so long subsisted between the new emperor and his eldest son was not likely to have been diminished by the events which preceded the accession. Khusru had ever since remained in a state of sullenness and dejection; and it is by no means probable that Jehángír's treatment of him was such as would be likely to soothe his feelings. His behaviour does not appear to have given rise to any suspicion, until upwards of four months after the accession; when Jehángír was awaked, at midnight, with the intelligence that his son had fled, with a few attendants, and taken the road to Delhi. He immediately dispatched a light force in pursuit of him, and followed himself, in the morning, with all the troops he could collect.

A. D. 1606, March; A. H. 1014, Zi Haj 8.

His rebellion.

Khusru was joined, soon after leaving Agra, by a body of 300 horse, whom he met on their march to the capital. He proceeded by Delhi, subsisting his troops by plunder, and by the time he reached the Panjáb, had collected a body of upwards of 10,000 men. The city of Láhór was betrayed to him, and he was making an ineffectual attempt to reduce the citadel, when he was disturbed by the approach of his father's advanced guard. When this was announced to him, he drew his force out of Láhór, and attacked the royal troops; but, although he had the advantage of engaging a detachment, he was unable to offer a successful opposition. He was totally defeated, and, having fled in the direction of Cábul, he was run aground in a boat as he was passing the Hydaspes, and was seized and brought in chains before his father. The whole rebellion did not last above a month.

Quashed.

Barbarous punishment of the rebels.

Khusru's principal advisers, and many of his common followers, fell into the hands of the emperor, and afforded him an opportunity of displaying all the ferocity of his character. He ordered 700 of the prisoners to be impaled in a line leading from the gate of Láhór; and he expatiates, in his Memoirs, on the long duration of their frightful agonies.* To complete his barbarity, he made his son Khusru be carried along the line on an elephant, while a mace-bearer called out to him, with mock solemnity, to receive the salutations of his servants.† The unhappy Khusru passed three days, in tears and groans, without tasting food‡; and remained for long after a prey to the deepest melancholy.

Imprisonment of Khusru.

Prince Parvíz, the emperor's second son, had

* Price's Memoirs of Jehángír, p. 88.

† Kháfi Khán.

‡ Memoirs of Jehángír, p. 89. The general account of the rebellion is from Jehangír's Memoirs, Kháfi Khán, and Gladwin.

BOOK X.

been sent, under the guidance of Asof Khán, against the rána of Oudipúr, very soon after the accession: he was recalled on the flight of Khusru, but in that short interval he had effected an accommodation with the rána, and now joined his father's camp.

A. D. 1606, March; A. H. 1015, Zí Haj.

In the spring of the next year, Jehángír went to Cábul; and, when at that city, he showed some favour to Khusru, ordering his chains to be taken off, and allowing him to walk in a garden within the upper citadel. If he had any disposition to carry his forgiveness further, it was checked by a conspiracy, which was detected some time after, to release Khusru and to assassinate the emperor.

A. D. 1607, A. H. 1016. Wars in Méwár and in the Deckan.

On his return to Agra, Jehángír sent an army, under Mohábat Khán, against the rána of Oudipúr, with whom the war had been renewed; and another, under the Khán Khánán, to effect a settlement of the Deckan. Prince Parvíz was afterwards made nominal commander of the latter force: he was too young to exercise any real authority.

Insurrection of a pretended Khusru. A. D. 1007, to 1661, A. H. 1017, to 1019.

The only event of importance in the following years was an insurrection at Patna by a man of the lowest order, who assumed the character of Khusru, and, seizing on the city in consequence of the supineness of the local officers, drew together so many followers, that he engaged the governor of the province in the field, and some time elapsed before he was driven back into Patna, made prisoner, and put to death.

Ill success of the war

In the end of the year 1610, affairs in the

Deckan assumed a serious aspect. After the taking of Ahmednagar, the conduct of the government of the new king fell into the hands of an Abyssinian named Malik Amber. This minister founded a new capital on the site of the present Aurangábád; and maintained, for a long series of years, the apparently sinking fortunes of the Nizám Sháhi government. His talents were not confined to war: he introduced a new revenue system into the Deckan, perhaps in imitation of Tódar Mal; and it has given his name an universal celebrity in the Deckan equal to that enjoyed in Hindostan by the other great financier.* Malik Āmber profited by some dissensions which fell out between the Kháni Khánán and the other generals; and prosecuted his advantages with such success that he repeatedly defeated the Mogul troops, retook Ahmednagar, and compelled the Kháni Khánán himself to retire to Burhánpúr. In these circumstances, Jehángír recalled his general, and conferred the command on Khán Jehán.

in the Deckan. Malik Amber.

He recovers Ahmednagar.

It was in the sixth year of his reign that Jéhangír contracted a marriage with the celebrated Núr Jehán, an event which influenced all the succeeding transactions of his life.

A. D. 1611, A. H. 1020. Marriage of the emperor with Núr Jehán.

The grandfather of this lady was a native of Teherán, in Persia, and held a high civil office under the government of that country. His son, Mírza Gheiás, was reduced to poverty, and deter-

Her history.

* Grant's History of the Marrattas, vol. i. p. 95.

BOOK X.

mined to seek for a maintenance by emigrating, with his wife, and a family consisting of two sons and a daughter, to India. He was pursued by misfortune even in this attempt; and by the time the caravan with which he travelled reached Candahár, he was reduced to circumstances of great distress. Immediately on his arrival in that city his wife was delivered of Núr Jehán; and into so abject a condition had they fallen, that the parents were unable to provide for the conveyance of their infant, or to maintain the mother so as to admit of her giving it support. The future empress was therefore exposed on the road by which the caravan was next morning to proceed. She was observed by a principal merchant of the party, who felt compassion for her situation, and was struck with her beauty: he took her up, and resolved to educate her as his own.

As a woman in a situation to act as a nurse was not easy to be found in a caravan, it is a matter of no surprise that her own mother should have been the person employed in that capacity; and the merchant's attention being thus drawn to the distresses of the family, he relieved their immediate wants; and perceiving the father and his eldest son to be men much above their present condition, he employed them in matters connected with his business, and became much interested in their fate. By his means they were introduced to Akber; and, being placed in some subordinate employments, they soon rose by their own abilities.

In the mean time Núr Jehán grew up, and began to excite admiration by her beauty and elegance. She often accompanied her mother, who had free access to the harem of Akber, and there attracted the notice of Jehángír, then Prince Selím. His behaviour gave so much uneasiness to her mother, as to induce her to speak of it to the princess whom she was visiting. Through her, the case was laid before Akber, who remonstrated with his son; and, at the same time, recommended that Núr Jehán should be married, and removed from the prince's sight. She was bestowed on Shír Afgan Khán, a young Persian lately come into the service, and to him Akber gave a jágír in Bengal.

But these means were not sufficient to efface the impression made on Jehángír; and, after he had been about a year on the throne, he took the opportunity of his foster-brother Kutb u dín's going as viceroy of Bengal to charge him to procure for him the possession of the object of his passion.

It was probably expected that all opposition from the husband would be prevented by influence and promises; but Shír Afgan had a higher sense of honour, and no sooner suspected the designs that were entertained, than he resigned his command, and left off wearing arms, as a sign that he was no longer in the king's service.

The further progress of the affair does not appear: it must have been such as to alarm Shír

BOOK X.

Afgan; for the viceroy having taken occasion to visit the part of the province where he resided, and having sent to invite his attendance, he went to pay his visit with a dagger concealed in his dress. An interview begun in such a spirit might be expected to close in blood. Shír Afgan, insulted by the proposals, and enraged at the threats of the viceroy, took his revenge with his dagger, and was himself immediately dispatched by the attendants.

The murder of the viceroy, which was ascribed to a treasonable conspiracy, gave a colour to all proceedings against the family of the assassin. Núr Jehán was seized, and sent as a prisoner to Delhi. Jehángír soon after offered her marriage, and applied all his address to soothe and conciliate her; but Núr Jehán was a high-spirited as well as an artful woman, and it is not improbable that she was sincere in her rejection of all overtures from one whom she looked on as the murderer of her husband. Her repugnance was so strongly displayed as to disgust Jehángír. He at length placed her among the attendants on his mother, and appeared to have entirely dismissed her from his thoughts.

His passion, however, was afterwards revived; and reflection having led his mistress to think more favourably of his offers, their marriage was celebrated with great pomp; and Núr Jehán was raised to honours such as had never before been enjoyed

Her influence.

by the consort of any king in India.* From this period her ascendency knew no bounds: her father was made prime minister; her brother was placed in a high station. The emperor took no step without consulting her; and, on every affair in which she took an interest, her will was law. Though her sway produced bad consequences in the end, it was beneficial on the whole. Her father was a wise and upright minister; and it must have been, in part at least, owing to her influence that so great an improvement took place in the conduct of Jehángír after the first few years of his reign. He was still capricious and tyrannical, but he was no longer guilty of such barbarous cruelties as before; and although he still carried his excess in wine to the lowest stage of inebriety, yet it was at night, and in his private apartments. In the occupations which kept him all day before the eyes of his subjects, he seems to have supported his character with sufficient dignity, and without any breaches of decorum. Núr Jehán's capacity was not less remarkable than her grace and beauty; it was exerted in matters proper to her sex as well as in state affairs. The magnificence of the emperor's court was increased by her taste, and the expense was diminished by her good arrangement. She contrived improvements in the furniture of apartments; introduced female dresses more becoming than any in use before her time; and it is a ques-

* Among other marks of sovereignty, her name was put on the coin along with the emperor's.

BOOK X.

tion in India whether it is to her or her mother that they owe the invention of ottar of roses.* One of the accomplishments by which she captivated Jehángír is said to have been her facility in composing extemporary verses.

A. D. 1612, A. H. 1021.

It was not long after the time of this marriage that the disturbances in Bengal were put an end to by the defeat and death of Osmán. The satisfaction derived from this event was more than counterbalanced by the ill success of the war in the Deckan.

Combined attack on Ahmednagar.

Jehángír had determined to make up for the languor of his former operations by a combined attack from all the neighbouring provinces. Abdullah Khán, viceroy of Guzerát, was to invade Malik Amber's territory from that province at the same moment that the armies under Prince Parvíz and Khán Jehán Lódi, reinforced by Rája Mán Sing, were to advance from Cándésh and Berár.

Defeated by Malik Amber.

But this well-concerted plan entirely failed in the execution. Abdullah Khán advanced prematurely from Guzerát, and Malik Amber did not lose a moment in profiting by his mistake. His mode of war was much the same as that of the modern Marattas. Owing to the neighbourhood of the European ports, his artillery was superior to that of the emperor, and afforded a rallying point

* Great improvements must have taken place in later times; for Kháfi Khán mentions that the same quantity of ottar (one tóla), which he remembers selling in the beginning of Aurangzíb's reign for eighty rupees, was to be had, when he wrote, for seven or eight.

on which he could always collect his army; but his active means of offence were his light cavalry. He intercepted the supplies and harassed the march of the Moguls; he hovered round their army when halted; alarmed them with false attacks; and often made real incursions into different parts of the encampment, carrying off much booty, and keeping up continual disorder and trepidation. Abdullah Khán was so completely worn out by this sort of warfare, that he soon determined to retire. The consequences of a retreat before such an enemy were easy to be foreseen: all his evils multiplied upon him from the day that it commenced; his rear-guard was cut to pieces; and his march had nearly become a flight before he found refuge in the hills and jungles of Báglána, whence he proceeded without molestation into Guzerát. The other armies had by this time taken the field; but seeing Malik Amber, on his return, flushed with success over their colleague, they thought it prudent to avoid a similar calamity, and concentrated at Burhánpúr.

A. D 1612, A. H. 1021.

War with Méwár.

Jehángír's arms were attended with better fortune in his war with the rána of Oudipúr; and his success was the more welcome, as the fruit of the abilities of his favourite son. Mohábat Khán, when first sent on that service, had gained a victory over the rána, but was unable to do any thing decisive from the strength of the country into which he, as usual, retreated. The same fortune attended Abdullah Khán, afterwards appointed to succeed

BOOK X.

Mohábat; but Prince Khurram (Sháh Jehán)*, who was now sent with an army of 20,000 men, evinced so much spirit in his attacks on the Rájpút troops, and so much perseverance in bearing up against the strength of the country and the unhealthiness of the climate, that the rána was at last induced to sue for peace; and his offer being readily accepted, he waited on Sháh Jehán in person, made offerings in token of submission, and sent his son to accompany the prince to Delhi.

Victories and moderation of Sháh Jehán (Prince Khurram).

Sháh Jehán, on this occasion, did not forget the policy of Akber. The moment the rána's homage was paid, he raised him in his arms, seated him by his side, and treated him with every form of respect and attention. All the country conquered from him since the invasion of Akber was restored;

The rána submits on honourable terms.

and his son, after an honourable reception from Jehángír, was raised to a high rank among the military chiefs of the empire.

A. D. 1614, A. H. 1023.

The merit of this campaign belonged exclusively to Sháh Jehán; for Azíz, who had been sent to assist him, had behaved to him with so much arrogance, that Jehángír was soon obliged to remove him, and commit him for a time to confinement.

Influence of Sháh Jehán.

This exploit raised Sháh Jehán's credit to the highest pitch; and, as he had lately married the

* The name of this prince was Khurram, and he bore no other at the commencement of his father's reign; but as he received the title of Sháh Jehán long before his own accession, it will prevent confusion to give him that name from the first.

niece of Núr Jehán, he was supported by her powerful influence, and was generally looked on as the chosen successor to the empire.

Supported by Núr Jehán.

Insurrection in Cábul quelled.

During these events, Rája Mán Sing died in the Deckan. A rebellion of the Roushenías, which broke out in 1611, and in which the city of Cábul had been exposed to danger, was now terminated by the death of Ahdád, the grandson and spiritual successor of Báyazíd. Abdullah Khán, viceroy of Guzerát, having incurred the king's displeasure, by oppressions in the province, and by the indignity with which he treated the royal newswriter, was ordered to be seized and sent to the capital. He anticipated the order by setting off on foot, with his troops and attendants following at a great distance. He came to court barefooted and in chains, and threw himself at the king's feet; but was pardoned, and not long after restored to favour at the intercession of Sháh Jehán.

Embassy of Sir T. Roe.

It was not long after the return of Sháh Jehán that Sir T. Roe arrived at the court, as ambassador from King James I.* His accounts enable us to judge of the state of India under Jehángír.

His account of the empire, court, and character of Jehángír.

The sea-ports and the customs were full of gross abuses, the governor seizing on goods at arbitrary prices. Even Roe, though otherwise treated with hospitality and respect, had his baggage searched

* He arrived at Ajmír on December 23. 1615, accompanied the king to Mándu and Guzerát, and left him in the end of 1618.

BOOK X.

and some articles taken by the governor.* His journey from Surat, by Burhánpúr and Chitór, to Ajmír, lay through the Deckan, where war was raging, and the rána's country where it had just ceased; yet he met with no obstruction or alarm, except from mountaineers, who then, as now, rendered the roads unsafe in times of trouble.

The Deckan bore strong marks of devastation and neglect. Burhánpúr, which had before, as it has since, been a fine city, contained only four or five good houses amidst a collection of mud huts; and the court of Parvíz, held in that town, had no pretensions to splendour.

In other places he was struck with the decay and desertion of some towns, contrasted with the prosperity of others. The former were, in some instances at least, deserted capitals†; and their decline affords no argument against the general prosperity.

The administration of the country had rapidly

* It must, however, be observed, that this governor, Zúlfikár Khán, was very inimical to the English, and had lately concluded an agreement with the Portuguese, by which he engaged to exclude English vessels from his ports. The agreement was not ratified by the emperor; and Zúlfikár was constrained, by his duty to his own government, to maintain outward appearances towards a foreign ambassador. (Orme, vol. iii. p. 361, &c.)

† Such were Mándu and Tódah, of both of which he speaks in the highest terms of admiration. Mándu, the former capital of Málwa, is still generally known; but Tódah (the capital of a Rájpút prince in the province of Ajmir) enjoys no such celebrity.

declined since Akber's time. The governments were farmed, and the governors exacters and tyrannical.

Though a judicious and sober writer, Roe is profuse in his praise of the magnificence of the court; and he speaks in high terms of the courtesy of the nobility, and of the order and elegance of the entertainments they gave to him. His reception, indeed, was in all respects most hospitable, though the very moderate scale of his presents and retinue was not likely to conciliate a welcome where state was so generally maintained. He was excused all humiliating ceremonials, was allowed to take the highest place in the court on public occasions, and was continually admitted into familiar intercourse with the emperor himself.

The scenes he witnessed at his private interviews form a curious contrast to the grandeur with which the Mogul was surrounded. He sat on a low throne all covered with diamonds, pearls, and rubies; and had a great display of gold plate, vases, and goblets, set with jewels. The party was free from all restraint, scarcely one of them remaining sober except Sir Thomas and a few other grave personages, who were cautious in their indulgence. Jehángír himself never left off till he dropped asleep, when the lights were extinguished and the company withdrew. On these occasions he was overflowing with kindness, which increased with the effects of the wine; and once, after talking

BOOK X.

with great liberality of all religions, "he fell to weeping, and to various passions, which kept them to midnight."

But he did not retain these sociable feelings in the morning. On one occasion, when a courtier indiscreetly alluded in public to a debauch of the night before, Jehángír affected surprise, inquired what other persons had shared in this breach of the law, and ordered those named to be so severely bastinadoed that one of them died. He always observed great strictness in public, and never admitted a person into his presence who, from his breath or otherwise, gave any signs of having been drinking wine. His reserve, however, was of little use: like great men at present, he was surrounded by newswriters; and his most secret proceedings, and even the most minute actions of his life, were known to every man in the capital within a few hours after they took place.

Notwithstanding the case above mentioned, and some other instances of inhumanity, Roe seems to consider Jehángír as neither wanting in good feelings nor good sense; although his claim to the latter quality is impaired by some weaknesses which Sir Thomas himself relates. In one case he seized on a convoy coming to the ambassador from Surat, and consisting of presents intended for himself and his court, together with the property of some merchants who took advantage of the escort: he rummaged the packages himself with childish curiosity; and had recourse to the meanest apologies to appease and cajole Roe, who was much provoked at this disregard of common honesty.

Though Roe speaks highly in some respects of particular great men, he represents the class as unprincipled, and all open to corruption. The treaty he had to negotiate hung on for upwards of two years, until he bribed Asof Khán with a valuable pearl; after which all went on well and smoothly. Both Roe and other contemporary travellers represent the military spirit as already much declined, and speak of the Rájpúts and Patáns as the only brave soldiers to be found.*

The manual arts were in a high state, and were not confined to those peculiar to the country. One of Sir T. Roe's presents was a coach, and within a very short period several others were constructed, very superior in materials, and fully equal in workmanship. Sir Thomas also gave a picture to the Mogul, and was soon after presented with several copies, among which he had great difficulty in distinguishing the original.† There was a great influx of Europeans, and considerable encouragement to their religion. Jehángír had figures of Christ and the Virgin at the head of his rosary; and two of his nephews embraced Christianity, with his full approbation.‡

* Roe. Terry. Hawkins.

† Among the articles he recommends for presents, are historical paintings, night-pieces, and landscapes: "but good, for they understand them as well as we."

‡ Roe. Hawkins. Terry. Coryat.

BOOK X.

The language of the court was Persian, but all classes spoke Hindostáni; and Hawkins, who only knew Turkish, found the emperor himself and the Kháni Khánán well versed in that tongue.

Prince Khusru.

No subject seems to have excited more interest, both in the ambassador and the court, than the fate of Prince Khusru. All his bad qualities were forgotten in his misfortunes; he was supposed to be endowed with every virtue; the greatest joy prevailed when any sign appeared of his restoration to favour, and corresponding indignation when he fell into the power of his enemies. Even the king was supposed to be attached to him, though wrought on by the influence of Sháh Jehán and the arts of Asof Khán and Núr Jehán.* Khusru's exclusion was not the more popular for its being in favour of Sháh Jehán; who, according to Sir T. Roe, was "flattered by some, envied by others, loved by none." Roe himself represents him as a bigot and a tyrant; but as his conduct shows nothing but ability and correctness, it is probable that he owed his unpopularity to his cold and haughty manners; the ambassador himself remarking, that he never saw so settled a countenance, or any man keep so constant a gravity, never smiling,

Unpopularity of Sháh Jehán.

* Sir T. Roe once met Khusru, while moving in loose custody, along with the army. He stopped under the shade of a tree during the heat, and sent for Sir Thomas, who was near. His person was comely, his countenance cheerful, and his beard was grown down to his girdle. He knew nothing of what was passing, and had not heard either of the English or their ambassador.

nor by his looks showing any respect or distinction of persons, but entire pride and contempt for all. Yet the prince could not at that time have been older than twenty-five.

Prince Parvíz.

Sháh Jehán might have expected to find a formidable rival in Parvíz, his elder brother; but that prince, though sometimes an object of jealousy to him, could offer no really formidable opposition to the superior abilities of Sháh Jehán, supported by the influence of the empress.

Sháh Jehán declared heir apparent.

A final blow was given to any hopes that Parvíz may have entertained, by the elevation of his brother to the title of king *, on his undertaking a great expedition against the Deckan. He was invested with ample powers on this occasion; and Jehángír himself moved to Mándu, to be at hand to support him in case of need.

Sent to settle the Deckan.

The emperor moves to Mándu.

A. D. 1616, October; A. H. 1025, Zi Káda.

Sir T. Roe's description of his march.

Roe accompanied the emperor on his march; and his account of the movement of the army forms a striking contrast to the good order and discipline he had hitherto admired. The court and camp, while halted, were as regular as ever; but the demand for carriage cattle created a general scramble and confusion. The Persian ambassador and Roe were left for some days at Ajmír, from the want of conveyance for their baggage; and the tents of the soldiers and followers were set fire to, to compel them to proceed, though ill provided. When actually in motion, the same want

* From this time some writers call him Sháh Khurram, and others Sháh Jehán.

of arrangement was felt: sometimes there was a deficiency of water; and sometimes, in long and difficult marches through woods and mountains, the road was scattered with coaches, carts, and camels, unable to proceed to the stage.*

Complete success of Sháh Jehán.

The state of affairs in the Deckan was very favourable to Sháh Jehán. The ascendency of a private person, like Malik Amber, led to jealousy among his confederates, and even his own officers. In consequence of these dissensions, he had suffered a defeat, which produced still further discouragement among the allies; so that when Sháh Jehán entered the Deckan, he found little difficulty in detaching the king of Bíjapúr from the confederacy; and Amber, seeing himself entirely deserted, was likewise compelled to make submission on the part of his nominal sovereign, Nizám Sháh; and to restore the fort of Ahmednagar and all the other territory which he had re-conquered from the Moguls.

A. D. 1617, March; A. H. 1026, Rabi ul awal.

After this glorious termination of the war, Sháh Jehán returned to Mándu, and joined his father, within a twelvemonth of the time when they had marched from Ajmír.

A. D. 1617, September; A. H. 1026, Shawál.

Residence of the emperor and Sháh Jehán in Guzerát.

Jehángír took this occasion to visit the province of Guzerát; he remained there for near a year, and added the viceroyalty of that province to the governments previously held by Sháh Jehán.

* "In following the Mogul's court," says Roe, "I encountered all the inconveniences that men are subject to under an ill government and an intemperate climate."

CHAP. I.

A. H. 1027, Ramzan.

He quitted Guzerát in September 1618; and the next two years are marked by no events, except an insurrection in the Panjáb; the capture of the fort of Kángra or Nagarcót, under the mountains; and a journey of the emperor to Cashmír.

Renewal of the disturbances in the Deckan. A. D. 1621, A. H. 1030.

While in that valley, he received intelligence of a renewal of the war in the Deckan. It seems to have been begun, without provocation, by Malik Amber, who probably was tempted by some negligence on the other side, for he had little difficulty in taking possession of the open country, and driving the Mogul commanders into Burhánpúr, from whence they sent most earnest entreaties for help from Jehángír. Sháh Jehán was again ordered to march with a powerful army; and great treasures were collected to supply him after he reached the frontier. From some rising distrust in his mind, he refused to march, unless his brother, prince Khusru, were made over to his custody, and allowed to go with him to the Deckan. Being gratified in this respect, he entered on the service with his usual ability. Before he reached Málwa, a detachment of Malik Amber's had crossed the Nerbadda, and burned the suburbs of Mándu; but they were driven back as the prince advanced; and he, in turn, crossed the Nerbadda, and began offensive operations. Malik Amber had recourse to his usual mode of war, cut off supplies and detachments, hung upon the line of march, and attempted, by long and rapid marches, to surprise the camp. He found Sháh Jehán always on his

Sháh Jehán marches to quell them.

BOOK X.

guard; was at last compelled to risk the fate of the campaign in a general action, and was defeated with considerable loss.

His success in the field.

But although Sháh Jehán had a clear superiority in the field, he still found a serious obstruction in the exhausted state of the country. It was therefore with great satisfaction that he received overtures from Amber, offering a further cession, and agreeing to pay a sum of money.

He comes to terms with Malik Amber.

Dangerous illness of the emperor.

Not long after this success, Jehángír was seized with a violent attack of asthma, a complaint from which he suffered severely during the rest of his life. He was for some time in such imminent danger, as to lead to expectations of an immediate vacancy of the throne.

Measures of Parvíz and Sháh Jehán.

A. D. 1621, about Sept. A. H. 1030.

Suspicious death of Khusru.

Parvíz hastened to court, but was sent back to his government with a reprimand; and though Sháh Jehán had not time to take such a step before he heard of his father's recovery, yet the sudden death of prince Khusru, which happened at this juncture, was so opportune, that it brought the strongest suspicions of violence against the rival to whose custody he had been intrusted. We ought not, however, too readily to believe that a life not sullied by any other crime could be stained by one of so deep a dye.

Alienation of the empress from Sháh Jehán.

This event, which seemed to complete the security of Sháh Jehán's succession, was, in reality, the cause of a series of dangers and disasters that nearly ended in his ruin. Up to this period, his own influence had been strengthened by the all-

CHAP. I.

powerful support of Núr Jehán ; but, about the time of his departure for the Deckan, that princess had affianced her daughter by Shír Afgan to Prince Shehriár, the youngest son of Jehángir * ; a connection of itself sufficient to undermine her exclusive attachment to the party of her more distant relative. But her views were further changed by a consideration of the impossibility of her gaining an ascendency, such as she now possessed, over an active and intelligent prince like Sháh Jehán. During her father's lifetime, she had been kept within bounds of moderation by his prudent counsels : after his death, which happened about this time, she exercised her dominion over the emperor without the least control ; her brother, Asof Khán (to whose daughter Sháh Jehán was married) being a mere instrument of her will. Unwilling to relinquish such unlimited power, she determined by all means to oppose the succession of Sháh Jehán ; and, warned by the death of Khusru, and the danger of Jehángír, she saw that she had not a moment to lose in cutting off the resources which might at any time enable the prince to overcome her opposition.

Candahár taken by the Persians. A. D. 1621, A. H. 1031. Sháh Jehán ordered to retake it.

An opportunity was not long wanting of pursuing this design. Candahár having been taken by the Persians, it was pointed out as an enterprise worthy of the conqueror of the Deckan, to recover that ancient possession. Sháh Jehán at first gave

* Kháfi Khán.

BOOK X.

in to the project, and advanced as far as Mándu, on his way to the north; but, perceiving, before long, that the object was to remove him from the country where his influence was established, and engage him in a remote and difficult command, he put off his further march, on pretext of the season and the state of his troops, and began to stipulate for some securities to be given to him before he should venture to move out of India. These demands were represented to Jehángír as arising from a project of independence; and Sháh Jehán was directed, in reply, to send the greater part of his army to the capital, in order that it might accompany Shehriár, to whom the recovery of Candahár was to be committed. Orders were also sent direct to the principal officers, to leave Sháh Jehán's camp and repair to that of Shehriár. This drew a remonstrance from Sháh Jehán, who now desired to be allowed to wait on his father, while the other as peremptorily ordered him to return to the Deckan. The jagírs which Sháh Jehán held in Hindostan were transferred to Shehriár during these discussions; and Sháh Jehán, who had not been consulted in the arrangement, was desired to select an equivalent in the Deckan and Guzerát. As things drew towards a crisis, Núr Jehán, distrusting both the military talents of her brother and his zeal in her present cause, cast her eyes on Mohábat Khán, the most rising general of the time, but hitherto the particular enemy of Asof Khán. He was accordingly summoned to court from his govern-

His reluctance to leave India.

The enterprise committed to Prince Shehriár; To whom most of Sháh Jehán's troops are transferred.

Mohabát Khán called to court by the empress.

ment of Cábul, and was treated with every mark of favour and confidence.

A. D. 1622, about Oct.; A. H. 1031.

Jehángír, who had been again in Cashmír, returned on the commencement of these discussions, and fixed his court at Lahór, to be at hand in case his presence should be required.

Increased distrust between the emperor and Sháh Jehán.

In the mean time messages passed between Sháh Jehán and the emperor, but with so little effect in producing a reconciliation, that Jehángír put several persons to death on suspicion of a plot with his son; and Sháh Jehán, finding that his fate was sealed, marched from Mándu with his army towards Agra; Jehángír, on this, marched from Lahór, and, passing through the capital, arrived within twenty miles of the rebel army lying at Belóchpúr, forty miles south of Delhi. Sháh Jehán retired into the neighbouring hills of Mewát, and disposed his troops so as to shut the passes against a force which the emperor detached in quest of him. A partial and indecisive action took place, and is said to have been followed by negotiations. The result was, that Sháh Jehán determined to retire, and set out on his march for Mándu.

Rebellion of Sháh Jehán.

Advance of the emperor.

A. D. 1623, February; A. H. 1032.

Retreat of Sháh Jehán.

Its consequences.

It does not appear what induced him to adopt this step: it was attended with all the consequences usual with attempts to recede in civil wars. Jehángír advanced in person to Ajmír, and sent on a strong force, under Prince Parvíz and Mohábat Khán, to follow up the retiring rebels. Rustam Khán, whom Sháh Jehán had left to defend the hills on the Chambal, deserted to the enemy; the

BOOK X.

province of Guzerát expelled his governor, and he was himself compelled, by the advance of the imperial army, to cross the Nerbadda and retire to Burhánpúr. Nor was he long permitted to remain there in tranquillity; for Mohábat Khán, having blinded him by some delusive negotiations, crossed the Nerbadda, and was joined by the Kháni Khánán, who till this time had been attached to Sháh Jehán. The rains were at their height when Sháh

Sháh Jehán retreats into Télingána.

Jehán commenced his retreat into Télingána, and a great part of his forces had deserted him before he directed his course to Masulipatam, with the

Makes his way to Bengal.

A. D. 1624, A. H. 1033.

intention of making his way to Bengal. He accomplished this long and arduous march by the early part of the succeeding year, and met with no opposition in Bengal, until he reached Ráj Mahal, where the governor of the province engaged him,

Obtains possession of Bengal and Behár.

and was defeated in a pitched battle. By this victory Sháh Jehán obtained possession of Bengal, and was enabled to seize on Behár, and to send on a detachment under Bhím Sing, the brother of the rána of Oudipúr, to endeavour to secure the fort of Allahábád.

He is pursued by Prince Parvíz and Mohábat Khán.

In the mean time prince Parvíz and Mohábat Khán, after chasing Sháh Jehán from the Deckan, had cantoned for the rainy season at Burhánpúr. On hearing of his arrival and rapid progress in Bengal, they put themselves in motion in the direction of Allahábád. Sháh Jehán crossed the Ganges to meet them; but the people of the country, who were not inclined to enter on opposition to the emperor, refused to bring in supplies to his camp, or to assist in keeping up his communications by means of the boats on the Ganges. The discouragement and privations which were the consequence of this state of things, led to the desertion of the new levies which Sháh Jehán had raised in Bengal; and when, at last, he came to an action with his opponents, he was easily overpowered, his army dispersed, and himself constrained once more to seek for refuge in the Deckan. Affairs in that quarter were favourable to his views. During his first flight to the Deckan the king of Bíjapur and Malik Amber had both remained steady to their engagement with Jehángír; and the king of Golcónda had shown no disposition to assist him during his retreat through Télingána. Since that time the Moguls had taken part on the side of the king of Bíjapúr in a dispute between him and Malik Amber, and the latter chief retaliated by invading the Mogul dominions, and carrying his ravages to the neighbourhood of Burhánpúr. He was therefore prepared to receive Sháh Jehán with open arms; and wrote to press him to undertake the siege of Burhánpúr. Sháh Jehán complied, and commenced his operations. The place made an obstinate defence; and, in the end, the return of Parvíz and Mohábat to the Nerbadda obliged him to raise the siege and attend to his own safety. His adherents now deserted him in greater numbers than before; and, being dispirited by ill health as well as adverse fortune,

Is defeated, and flies to the Deckan.

State of the Deckan.

Sháh Jehán unites with Malik Amber.

Pressed by Parvíz and Mohábat Khán.

BOOK X.

Deserted by his army.

he wrote to beg his father's forgiveness, and to express his readiness to submit to his commands. Jehángír directed him to give up the forts of Rótás in Behár, and Asírghar in the Deckan, both of which were still in his possession, and to send two of his sons, Dárá Shekó and Aurangzíb, to court, as hostages for his good behaviour. These demands were complied with; but we are prevented judging of the treatment designed for Sháh Jehán by an event which, for a time, threw the whole empire into confusion.

Offers his submission to the emperor. A. D. 1625, A. H. 1034.

After the first retreat of Sháh Jehán to the Deckan, Jehángir returned from Ajmír to Delhi; and believing all serious danger to his government to be at an end, he went on his usual expedition to Cashmír, and repeated it in the following year. On the third year he was induced, by a new revolt of the Roushenías, to change his destination for Cábul; and although he soon heard of the suppression of the rebellion, and received the head of Ahmed, the son of Ahdád, who was the leader of it, he made no change in his determination.

The emperor marches against the Roushenías in Cábul.

Persecution of Mohábat Khán by the empress.

But he was not destined to accomplish this journey in tranquillity; for no sooner was Sháh Jehán reduced to submission than the domineering spirit of Núr Jehán proceeded to raise up new enemies. Mohábat Khán was the son of Ghór Bég, a native of Cábul.* He had attained the rank of a commander of 500 under Akber, and

His history.

* Memoirs of Jehángír, p. 30.

CHAP. I.

was raised to the highest dignities and employments by Jehángír. He had long enjoyed a high place in the opinion of the people *, and might now be considered as the most eminent of all the emperor's subjects. This circumstance alone might have been sufficient to excite the jealousy of Núr Jehán. It is probable, however, that she also distrusted Mohábat for his old enmity to her brother, and his recent connection with Parvíz.

He is summoned to court.

Whatever might be the motive, he was now summoned to court to answer charges of oppression and embezzlement during the time of his occupation of Bengal. He at first made excuses for not attending, and was supported by Parvíz; but, finding that his appearance was insisted on, he set out on his journey, accompanied by a body of 5000 Rájpúts whom he had contrived to attach to his service.

Brutal treatment of his son-in-law by the emperor.

Before his arrival, he betrothed his daughter to a young nobleman, named Berkhordár, without first asking the emperor's leave, as was usual with persons of his high rank. Jehángír was enraged at this apparent defiance: he sent for Berkhordár, and, in one of those fits of brutality which still broke out, he ordered him to be stripped naked and beaten with thorns in his own presence; and then seized on the dowry he had received from Mohábat, and sequestrated all his other property.

* Sir T. Roe, in A.D. 1616, says of him, that he is a noble and generous man, well beloved by all men, and the king's only favourite, but cares not for the prince (Sháh Jehán).

BOOK X.

When Mohábat himself approached the camp, he was informed that he would not be admitted to the emperor's presence; and, perceiving that his ruin was predetermined, he resolved not to wait till he should be separated from his troops, but to strike a blow, the very audacity of which should go far to insure its success.

Mohábat seizes on the emperor's person. A. D. 1626, March; A. H. 1035, Jemádi 2.

Jehángír was at this time encamped on the Hydaspes; and was preparing to cross it, by a bridge of boats, on his way to Cábul. He sent the army across the river in the first instance, intending to follow at his leisure when the crowd and confusion should be over. The whole of the troops had passed, and the emperor remained with his personal guards and attendants, when Mohábat, getting his men under arms a little before day-break, sent a detachment of 2000 men to seize the bridge, and moved, himself, with all speed, to the spot where the emperor was encamped. The place was quickly surrounded by his troops; while he himself, at the head of a chosen body of 200 men, pushed straight for the emperor's tent. The attendants were overthrown and dispersed before they were aware of the nature of the attack; and Jehángír, who was not quite recovered from the effects of his last night's debauch, was awakened by the rush of armed men around his bed: he started up, seized his sword, and, after staring wildly round, he perceived what had befallen him, and exclaimed, "Ah! Mohábat Khán! traitor! what is this?" Mohábat Khán replied by prostrating himself on the ground, and lamenting that the persecution of his enemies had forced him to have recourse to violence to obtain access to his master. Jehángír at first could scarcely restrain his indignation; but, observing, amidst all Mohábat's humility, that he was not disposed to be trifled with, he gradually accommodated himself to his circumstances, and endeavoured to conciliate his captor. Mohábat now suggested to him that, as it was near his usual time of mounting, it was desirable that he should show himself in public to remove alarm, and check the misrepresentations of the ill disposed. Jehángír assented, and endeavoured to withdraw, on pretence of dressing, to his female apartments, where he hoped to have an opportunity of consulting with Núr Jehán: being prevented from executing this design, he prepared himself where he was, and at first mounted a horse of his own in the midst of the Rájpúts, who received him with respectful obeisances; but Mohábat, reflecting that he would be in safer custody, as well as more conspicuous, on an elephant whose driver could be depended on, urged him to adopt that mode of conveyance, and placed him on one of those animals with two armed Rájpúts by his side. At this moment, the chief elephant driver, attempting to force his way through the Rájpúts, and to seat the emperor on an elephant of his own, was dispatched on a sign from Mohábat. One of Jehángír's personal attendants who reached the elephant, not without a wound, was allowed to mount with his master, and

BOOK X.

the same permission was given to the servant who was intrusted with the bottle and goblet, so essential to Jehángír's existence.

These examples of the consequences of resisance had their full effect on the emperor; and he proceeded very tractably to the tents of Mohábat Khán.

Spirited conduct of Núr Jehán.

Meanwhile, Núr Jehán, though dismayed at this unexpected calamity, did not lose her presence of mind. When she found all access cut off to the emperor, she immediately put on a disguise, and set out for the bridge in a litter of the most ordinary description. As the guards were ordered to let every one pass, but permit no one to return, she crossed the river without obstruction, and was soon safe in the midst of the royal camp. She immediately sent for her brother and the principal chiefs, and bitterly reproached them with their cowardice and neglect, in allowing their sovereign to be made a prisoner before their eyes. She did not confine herself to invectives, but made immediate preparations to rescue her husband by force; and although Jehángír, probably in real apprehension of what might happen to himself in the confusion, sent a messenger with his signet to entreat that no attack might be made, she treated the message as a trick of Mohábat's, and only suspended her proceedings until she could ascertain the real position of the enemy's camp, and the part of it inhabited by the emperor. During the night, a nobleman named Fedái Khán made an attempt to carry off Jehángír by swimming the river at the head of a small body of horse: his approach was discovered, and it was with difficulty he effected his escape, after losing several of his companions killed and drowned in the river.

She attacks Mohábat's camp.

Next morning, the whole army moved down to the attack. It was headed by Núr Jehán herself, who appeared on the howdah of a high elephant, with a bow and two quivers of arrows. The bridge had been burned by the Rájpúts, and the army began to cross by a ford which they had discovered lower down the river. It was a narrow shoal, between deep water, and full of dangerous pools; so that the passage was not effected without the utmost disorder; many were obliged to swim, and all landed with their powder wetted, weighed down with their drenched clothes and armour, and obliged to engage hand to hand before they could make good their footing on the beach. Núr Jehán was among the foremost, on her elephant, with her brother and some of the principal chiefs around her: she with difficulty effected a landing, but found it impossible to make any impression on the enemy. The Rájpúts had the advantage of the ground; they poured down showers of balls, arrows, and rockets on the troops in the ford; and, rushing down on those who were landing, drove them back into the water sword in hand.

A scene of universal tumult and confusion ensued: the ford was choked with horses and elephants; some fell and were trampled under foot;

BOOK X.

others sunk in the pools, and were unable to regain the shoal; and numbers plunged into the river, and ran the chance of making good their passage, or being swept away by the stream. The most furious assault was directed on Núr Jehán: her elephant was surrounded by a crowd of Rájpúts; her guards were overpowered and cut down at its feet; balls and arrows fell thick round her howdah; and one of the latter wounded the infant daughter of Shehriár, who was seated in her lap.

Is repulsed with heavy loss.

At length her driver was killed; and her elephant, having received a cut on the proboscis, dashed into the river, and soon sunk in deep water, and was carried down by the stream: after several plunges, he swam out and reached the shore, when Núr Jehán was surrounded by her women, who came shrieking and lamenting, and found her howdah stained with blood, and herself busied in extracting the arrow, and binding up the wound of the infant. Fedái Khán had made another attempt, during the confusion of the battle, to enter the enemy's camp at an unsuspected point, and had penetrated so far that his balls and arrows fell within the tent where Jehángír was seated; but the general repulse forced him also to retire. He effected his retreat, wounded, and with the loss of many of his men, and immediately retired to the neighbouring fort of Rohtás, of which he was the governor.

She joins the emperor in his confinement.

Núr Jehán now saw that there was no hope of rescuing her husband by force; and she determined to join him in his captivity, and trust to fortune and her own arts for effecting his deliverance.

Insecurity of Mohábat's power.

Mohábat Khán, after his success at the Hydaspes, advanced to Attok, where Asof Khán had retired. His authority was now so well established that it was recognised by most of the army; and Asof Khán, and such leaders as attempted to hold out, were obliged in the end to give themselves up as prisoners. But the security and even the extent of Mohábat's power was far from being so great as it appeared; his haughty and violent behaviour to those who had been opposed to him took deep root in their breasts. The ascendency of the Rájpúts was offensive to the other troops; and, as the provinces were still faithful to the emperor, and two of his sons at large, Mohábat was obliged to use great management in his treatment of his prisoner, and to effect his objects by persuasion rather than by force or fear. Jehángír, tutored by Núr Jehán, took full advantage of the circumstances in which he was placed: he affected to enter into Mohábat's views with his usual facility; expressed himself pleased to be delivered from the thraldom in which he had been kept by Asof Khán; and even carried his duplicity so far as to warn Mohábat that he must not think Núr Jehán was as well disposed to him as he was himself; and to put him on his guard against little plots that were occasionally formed for thwarting his measures. Mohábat was completely blinded by these artifices; and thinking himself sure of

Artifices of the emperor.

the emperor, he gave less heed to the designs of others.

During these proceedings the army advanced to Cábul; the neighbourhood of the Afgháns made it necessary to increase the king's guard, and Núr Jehán seized the opportunity of getting persons in her interest to offer their services in such a way as to avoid suspicion. Jehángír was allowed, at this time, to go out to shoot on an elephant, always surrounded by Rájpúts, and with one in particular, who stuck to him like his shadow, and never for a moment let him out of his sight. On one of these occasions an affray took place between the Rájpúts with the emperor and some of the Ahdis, a select body of single horsemen, whose duty it was to attend on His Majesty. The largest part of the escort being composed of Rájpúts, the Ahdis were overpowered and several of them killed; and on their complaining to Mohábat, he said he would be happy to punish the offence if they could bring it home to any individuals. The Ahdis, incensed at this evasion, fell with their whole force on a body of Rájpúts, killed many, and drove others into the hills, where they were made slaves by the Hazárehs. Mohábat himself was exposed to so much danger in this disturbance that he was forced to take refuge in the king's tent. Next day the ringleaders were punished; but a portion of the army was left in open enmity with the Rájpúts, whose numbers were also diminished; and the Afgháns of the neighbourhood showed every disposition to

Quarrel between the Rájpúts and the king's troops.

take part with the emperor. Núr Jehán could therefore pursue her schemes with less obstruction and less fear of detection. She employed agents to enlist fit men in scattered points at a distance, whence some were to straggle into camp as if in quest of service, while the others were to remain at their positions, and await her further orders. She next made Jehángír suggest a muster of the troops of all the jágírdárs; and when she was summoned to produce her contingent, she affected to be indignant at being put on a level with an ordinary subject, and said she would take care that her muster should not turn out to her discredit. Accordingly she dressed out her old troops so as to make the smallness of their number conspicuous, entertained new levies as if to complete her contingent, and at the same time directed her recruits in the country to repair by twos and threes to the army. All this could not be done without some alarm to Mohábat Khán; but he was no longer able to crush opposition by force, and he suffered himself to be persuaded by Jehángír to avoid personal risk by forbearing to accompany him to the muster of Núr Jehán's contingent. Jehángír advanced alone to the review; and he had no sooner got to the centre of the line, than the troops closed in on him, cut off the Rájpút horse by whom he was guarded; and, being speedily joined by their confederates, rendered it impossible to make any attempt to seize his person. Mohábat Khán perceived that his power was irretrievably lost; and

Plots and preparations of Núr Jehán.

Rescue of Jehángír.

BOOK X.

immediately withdrew to a distance with his troops, and entered on negotiation to procure his pardon and assurances of safety.

Terms granted to Mohábat Khán.

Jehángír was now restored to liberty, and Núr Jehán to power. She had relinquished none of her designs during the period of her adversity; and as she was obliged to make terms with Mohábat, to procure the release of her brother, who was his prisoner, she determined to connect the pardon of one enemy with the destruction of another; and made it a condition of the emperor's reconciliation with Mohábat, that he should immediately have the use of his services against Sháh Jehán. That prince, after his own submission and the misfortune of his father, had come from the Deckan to Ajmír with only 1000 men, in the hopes that his army might increase as he advanced; but Rája Kishen Sing, his principal adherent, dying at that place, instead of an accession, he suffered the loss of half his numbers, and was obliged, as the only means of securing his personal safety, to fly across the desert to Sind. He was then in the lowest state of depression, and would have retired to Persia if he had not been prevented by ill health. From this time his fortunes began to brighten: he heard of the death of Parvíz at Burhánpúr, and learned also that Mohábat, instead of pursuing him, was now himself pursued by an army of the emperor, with whom he had again come to a rupture.

He is sent against Sháh Jehán.

He breaks with the emperor,

Encouraged by these circumstances, he set off, through Guzerát, for the Deckan, where he was soon joined by Mohábat, with such part of his force as still remained.*

CHAP. I.

and joins Sháh Jehán.

Jehángír, soon after his deliverance, marched back from Cábul to Láhór. Some time was spent in restoring every branch of the government to its old footing; and when all had been satisfactorily arranged, the emperor set off on his annual visit to Cashmír.

Sickness

Some time after his arrival in that valley, Shehriár was seized with so violent an illness that he was obliged to leave Cashmír for the warmer climate of Láhór. Not long after his departure, Jehángír was himself taken ill with a severe return of his asthma; and it soon became evident that his life was in great danger. An attempt was made to remove him to Láhór; his complaint was increased by the motion and passage of the mountains; and before he had got over a third of his journey he had a severe attack, and died soon after reaching his tent, in the sixtieth year of his age.

and death of Jehángír. A. D. 1627. Oct. 28.; A. H. 1037. Safar 28.

Several of the great men of the time of Akber died shortly before Jehángír. Azíz died before the usurpation of Mohábat; Malik Amber, during its continuance; and Mírza Khán (the Kháni Khánán), shortly after it was suppressed.

* Gladwin's Jehángír. Kháfi Khán makes an intermediate reconciliation between Mohábat and Jehángír, and another visit of Mohábat to court, followed by a fresh revolt: but these rapid changes appear inexplicable; and it is not easy to believe that if Mohábat had been in Núr Jehán's hands, having no longer her brother for a hostage, he would again have been allowed to retire in safety.

BOOK X.

Among the occurrences of Jehángír's reign may be mentioned an edict against the use of tobacco, which was then a novelty. It would be curious, as marking the epoch of the introduction of a practice now universal in Asia, if the name of tambácu, by which it is known in most eastern countries, were not of itself sufficient to show its American origin.*

* Where no other authority is quoted for facts in this reign, they are taken from Kháfi Khan, from Gladwin's "Reign of Jehángír," or from the autobiographical Memoirs of the emperor. Kháfi Khán's history is compiled from various accounts written and oral. Mr. Gladwin's is evidently all drawn from written histories, but he only quotes the "Maásiri Jehángíri," and the Memoirs of the emperor, of which last he possessed a much more complete copy than that translated by Major Price. The Memoirs themselves contain a great deal of information regarding particular periods and the characters of individuals; and though written in a rambling and inaccurate manner, are not without signs of talent. A large portion of them is composed of stories of magical performances; some, though greatly exaggerated, are obviously tricks of ventriloquism and legerdemain, but all regarded by the emperor as in some degree the result of supernatural power. Those fables would lead to a lower estimate of his intelligence, if we did not remember the demonology of his contemporary in England.

CHAP. II.

SHÁH JEHÁN, TILL 1657.

CHAP. II.

Asof Khán takes part with Sháh Jehán.

The influence of Núr Jehán expired with her husband; and the fruit of all her long intrigues was lost in a moment. Her favourite, Shehriár, was absent, and Asof Khán, who was all along determined to support Sháh Jehán, immediately sent off a messenger to summon him from the Deckan. In the mean time, to sanction his own measures by the appearance of legal authority, he released Prince Dáwar, the son of Khusru, from prison, and proclaimed him king.* Núr Jehán, endeavouring to support the cause of Shehriár, was placed under a temporary restraint by her brother; and from that time, although she survived for many years, her name is never again mentioned in history.†

Imprisons the empress.

Defeats Shehriár, who is put to death.

Asof Khán then continued his march to Láhór. Shehriár, who was already in that city, seized the royal treasure, bought over the troops, and, forming a coalition with two sons of his uncle, the late

* Kháfi Khán.

† She died in A.D. 1646, A.H. 1055. She was treated with respect and allowed a stipend of 250,000*l.* a year. She wore no colour but white after Jehángír's death, abstained from all entertainments, and appeared to devote her life to the memory of her husband: she was buried in a tomb she had herself erected close to that of Jehángír at Láhór. (*Kháfi Khán.*)

BOOK X.

Prince Dániál, marched out to oppose Asof Khán. The battle ended in his defeat: he fled into the citadel, was given up by his adherents, and he was afterwards put to death with the sons of Dániál, by orders from Sháh Jehán.*

Sháh Jehán arrives from the Deckan, and is proclaimed at Agra. A. D. 1628, Jan. 26.; A. H. 1037, Jamádi al A'khir 7.

The new emperor lost no time in obeying the summons of Asof Khán. He left the Deckan accompanied by Mohábat, and on his arrival at Agra caused his accession to be proclaimed, and took formal possession of the throne.†

The highest honours were conferred on Asof Khán and Mohábat, and great promotions and distributions of money were made to the friends and adherents of the emperor. Among his first acts were, to abolish the ceremony of prostration; to restore the Mahometan lunar year in ordinary correspondence; and to make some other slight changes favourable to the Mussulman religion.

When firmly established in his government, Sháh Jehán seems to have indemnified himself for his late fatigues and privations, by giving a loose to his passion for magnificent buildings and expensive entertainments. He erected palaces in his principal cities; and, on the first anniversary of his accession, he had a suite of tents prepared in Cashmír, which, if we are to believe his historian‡, it

* Kháfi Khán.

† Dáwar Shekó (also called Boláki), who had been set up for king by Asof Khán, found means to escape to Persia, where he was afterwards seen by the Holstein ambassadors in 1633. (Olearius, *Ambassadors' Travels*, p. 190.)

‡ Kháfi Khán.

took two months to pitch. He introduced new forms of lavish expenditure on that occasion ; for, besides the usual ceremony of being weighed against precious substances, he had vessels filled with jewels waved round his head, or poured over his person (according to the superstition that such offerings would avert misfortunes) ; and all the wealth so devoted was immediately scattered among the bystanders, or given away in presents. The whole expense of the festival, including gifts of money, jewels, rich dresses and arms, elephants and horses, amounted, by the account of the same historian, to 1,600,000*l.* sterling.

Local disturbances.

He was disturbed in these enjoyments by an irruption of the Uzbeks in Cábul : they ravaged the country and besieged the capital, but retired on the approach of a light force, followed up by an army under Mohábat Khán. To this invasion succeeded the revolt of Narsing Deó, the murderer of Abul Fazl. He opposed a long resistance in Bundélcand, before he was brought to submit.*

Mohábat had only reached Sirhind on his way to Cábul, when the intelligence of the retreat of the Uzbeks was received. He was immediately recalled to the capital, and directed to prepare for a march into the Deckan.

History of Khán Jehán Lódi.

Khán Jehán Lódi was an Afghán of low birth, but with all the pride and unruliness of his nation in India. He had held great military charges in

* Kháfi Khán.

BOOK X.

the reign of Jehángír, and commanded in the Deckan under Parvíz at the time of that prince's death. Being left with undivided authority, he thought it for his advantage, perhaps for that of the state, to make peace with the son of Malik Amber, now at the head of the Nizám Sháhi government. He gave up what still remained to the Moguls of Sháh Jehán's conquests, and entered into a close intimacy with his late enemies.

When Sháh Jehán set out to assume the throne, he refused to join him, marched into Málwa, laid siege to Mándu, and seemed to be aiming at independence. He returned to obedience when Sháh Jehán's accession was secure; and it was thought prudent, at first, to confirm him in his government, and afterwards to be content with removing him to that of Málwa, while the Deckan was given to Mohábat Khán.

Having co-operated in the reduction of Rája Narsing Deó, he was invited to court, and treated with great attention; but, before he had been long there, he received intimations from some of his friends that the emperor harboured designs against him, and was only waiting an opportunity to find him off his guard. These suggestions, whether true or false, made an impression on his jealous nature. He refused to attend on the king, assembled his troops round the palace he inhabited, and stood prepared to defend himself against any attempt that might be made on him. Negotiations then took place, and were so successful that all differences appeared to be removed, when some new circumstance excited Khán Jehán's distrust, and decided him to run all risks rather than remain within the power of men on whose faith he could not rely. One night, soon after dark, he assembled all his troops, placed his women in the centre on elephants, and marched openly out of Agra with his kettle-drums beating, at the head of 2000 veteran Afgháns, and accompanied by twelve of his own sons. He was pursued within two hours by a strong body of the royal troops, who overtook him at the river Chambal. He had scarcely time to send his family across the river, when he was obliged to cover their retreat by engaging the very superior force that was in pursuit of him. The severest part of the action was between the Afgháns and a body of Rájpúts, who dismounted and charged with pikes, according to their national custom. Rája Pírti Sing Ráhtór and Khán Jehán were engaged hand to hand, and separated with mutual wounds. After a long resistance, Khán Jehán plunged into the stream, and effected his passage with the loss of a few men drowned, besides those he had lost in the action. The royal troops did not, at first, venture to follow him; and when they had been joined by reinforcements, and were emboldened to renew the pursuit, Khán Jehán had got so much the start of them, that he was able to make his way through Bundélcand into the wild and woody country of Góndwána, from whence he

His flight from Agra.

BOOK X.

soon opened a communication with his old ally, the king of Ahmednagar.

His proceedings in the Deckan.

The emperor marches against him.

The affair now assumed so serious an aspect that Sháh Jehán thought it necessary to take the field in person, and moved into the Deckan at the head of a great armament.

A. D. 1629, October; A. H. 1039, Rabi ul Awal.

He halted, himself, at Burhánpúr, and sent on three detachments, or rather armies*, into the hostile territory.

State of the Deckan.

The three Deckan monarchies had, at this time, recovered their ancient limits, and (except the fort of Ahmednagar, which still held out in disregard of Khán Jehán's cession) the Moguls were reduced to the eastern half of Cándésh and an adjoining portion of Berár. The greatest of the Deckan kingdoms was that of Ahmednagar, which was contiguous to the Mogul territory. Mortezza Nizám Sháh (the king set up by Malik Amber) was well inclined to act for himself on the death of that minister; but he would, perhaps, have remained a pageant, if the sons of Malik Amber had possessed talents equal to their father's. The fact was far otherwise; and Mortezza soon displaced and imprisoned Fatteh Khán, the eldest of them, and afterwards conducted the administration himself. He did so with so little ability, that his kingdom became a scene of faction, affording every advantage to his foreign enemies.†

I'brahim A'dil Sháh of Bíjapúr, who died about

* The native historian estimates them at 50,000 men *each*.

† Grant Duff. Kháfi Khán.

CHAP. II.

the same time with Amber, and left his country in a much more prosperous condition to his son, Mohammed A'dil Sháh; and Abdullah Kutb Sháh of Golcónda, who was probably aggrandising himself at the expense of his Hindú neighbours in Télingána, took no part in the quarrels of the Mahometan kings.

Khán Jehán driven out of Ahmednagar.

By the time Sháh Jehán reached Burhánpúr, Khán Jehán had moved from Góndwána into the country under Ahmednagar. The Mogul armies, in consequence, marched into that territory, and were assisted by a simultaneous movement from the side of Guzerát. Khán Jehán, after some unavailing attempts by himself and his allies to make head against this disproportioned force, retired to the southward, and eluded the Mogul detachments by moving from place to place. At length A'zim Khán, the most active of Sháh Jehán's officers, by a succession of forced marches, succeeded in surprising him, took his baggage, and forced him to seek shelter by retiring among the hills and woods, where the whole of the enemy's force could not be brought to bear on him. He then kept retreating; sometimes checking his pursuers by defending favourable positions, and sometimes escaping from them by long and unexpected marches. In this manner he reached Bíjapúr. He expected to persuade the king to take his part; but he found Mohammed A'dil Sháh entirely disinclined to enter on such a contest, and was obliged once more to return to the territories of the king of Ahmed-

Pursued by A'zim Khán.

Fails in obtaining an asylum at Bíjapúr.

BOOK X.

His ally, the king of Ahmednagar, defeated.

nagar. Mortezza Nizám Sháh had himself been hard pressed during this interval, and two of the greatest of the Hindú chiefs under him had gone over to the enemy. He had still sufficient confidence to try the effect of a decisive battle. He assembled his army at Doulatábád, and took post in strong ground among the neighbouring passes: this advantage did not compensate for the superior numbers of his enemies; he was defeated, and obliged to seek protection in his forts and in desultory warfare.

Khán Jehán flies from the Deckan.

Meanwhile Khán Jehán, overwhelmed by the defeat of his allies, the destruction of their country, and the additional calamities of famine and pestilence with which it was now visited, determined to quit the scene, and to take refuge (as was supposed) with the Afgháns near Péshâwer, where all the north-eastern tribes were at that time up in arms. If such was his intention, he was unable to accomplish it: after passing the Nerbadda near the frontier of Guzerát, he crossed all Málwa towards Bundélcand, where he hoped to be able to revive the spirit of insurrection; but the rája of that country turned against him, and cut off his rear-guard under his long-tried and attached friend Deria Khán; and, being overtaken by the Moguls, he sent off his wounded and made a stand with the remains of his force, now reduced to 400 Afgháns. His resistance, though long and desperate, was vain his party was destroyed or dispersed, and he was obliged to fly with a few devoted adherents. He endeavoured to force his way into the hill fort of Cálinjer, was repulsed with the loss of his son, and was at last overtaken at a pool where he had stopped from exhaustion; and, after defending himself with his usual gallantry, and receiving many wounds, was struck through with a pike by a Rájpút, and his head was sent as a most acceptable present to the Mogul emperor.*

Is cut off in Bundélcand.

A. D. 1630, A. H. 1040.

The war with Nizám Sháh was not concluded by the removal of its original cause. At this time a destructive famine desolated the Deckan. It began from a failure of the periodical rains in A. D. 1629, and was raised to a frightful pitch by a recurrence of the same misfortune in 1630. Thousands of people emigrated, and many perished before they reached more favoured provinces; vast numbers died at home; whole districts were depopulated; and some had not recovered at the end of forty years.† The famine was accompanied by a total failure of forage, and by the death of all the cattle; and the miseries of the people were completed by a pestilence such as is usually the consequence of the other calamities. In the midst of these horrors, A'zim Khán carried on his operations against Mortezza Nizám Sháh; and that prince, ascribing all his disasters to the misconduct of his minister, removed him from his office, and conferred it on Fatteh Khán, son of Malik Amber, whom he released from prison for the purpose.

Continuance of the war with Ahmednagar.

Famine and pestilence in the Deckan.

The prospect of the ruin of the Nizám Sháh,

The king of Bíjapúr

* Grant Duff. Kháfi Khán.

† Kháfi Khán.

joins the king of Ahmednagar.

which now seemed at hand, alarmed Mohammed A'dil Sháh, who, though pleased, at first, with the humiliation of his hereditary enemy, was not insensible of the danger certain to result to himself from the entire subversion of the neighbouring monarchy. He therefore brought a seasonable relief to the weaker party, by declaring war with the Moguls. But his assistance came too late to preserve Mortezza Nizám Sháh from the consequences of his own imprudence: Fatteh Khán, more mindful of former injuries than recent favours, and ambitious of recovering the authority once possessed by his father, applied all the power which had been confided to him to the destruction of the donor; and, aided by the weakness and unpopularity of Mortezza himself, was soon strong enough to put that prince and his chief adherents to death, and to take the government into his own hands. At the same time, he sent to offer submission, and a large contribution to the Moguls, and placed an infant on the throne, with an open profession that he was to hold his dignity in subordination to Sháh Jehán.

Murder of the king of Ahmednagar by his minister, Fatteh Khán.

who submits to Sháh Jehán.

War with Bíjapúr continues. Tergiversation of Fattéh Khán.

His terms were immediately accepted, and Sháh Jehán turned his whole force against Bíjapúr. Fatteh Khán, however, evaded the fulfilment of his promises, was again attacked by the Moguls, and once more joined his cause with that of A'dil Sháh. He was afterwards reconciled to the Moguls; and various similar changes took place in the progress of the war, from his perfidious and shifting policy.

CHAP. II.

Siege of Bíjapúr.

During one of those vicissitudes, the king of Bíjapúr was borne down by the superior force of his enemies, and was constrained to take refuge in his capital, where he was besieged by a great army under the command of Asof Khán. In this desperate situation, he must have shared the fate of his former rival, if he had not found resources in his own abilities and address. While he used every exertion to defend his town, and to harass the assailants, he amused Asof Khán, and delayed his operations by a variety of well-contrived artifices: sometimes he entered on negotiations himself, and held out hopes of his immediately yielding to Sháh Jehán's demand, without the risk of further hostilities; at other times, he engaged Asof Khán in intrigues with chieftains who pretended to make bargains for their defection, and sometimes led him into disasters by feigned offers from individuals to desert their posts when attacked, or to admit his troops by night into parts of the fortifications intrusted to their charge. During all this time, disease and famine were playing their parts in the camp of Asof Khán; and he at last found himself under the necessity of raising the siege, and revenged himself by cruelly ravaging the unexhausted parts of the kingdom.*

Failure of the siege.

The emperor re-

It was about the time of this failure, that Sháh

* Grant Duff. Kháfi Khán.

BOOK X.

turns to Delhi.

A. D. 1632, March; A. H. 1041, Rámzán.

Jehán returned to his capital, leaving Mohábat Khán in the supreme government of the Deckan.* The operations carried on under that general led, at length, to Fatteh Khán's being shut up in the fort of Doulatábád, where he defended himself, with occasional assistance from the king of Bíjapúr; and the fate of the Nizám Sháhi monarchy seemed to rest on the result of the struggle. It was decided by a general action, in which the combined force of the Deckanis was defeated in an attempt to raise the siege, and Fatteh Khán soon after surrendered and entered into the Mogul service, while the king whom he had set up was sent off a prisoner to Guáliór.†

A. D. 1633, February; A. H. 1042.

Ill success of the operations in the Deckan.

The king of Bíjapúr, being now left alone, made overtures of negotiation which were not favourably received; he then continued to defend himself; and all the efforts of Mohábat Khán were ineffectual to subdue him. An important point of the war was the siege of Perinda, on his failure in which, Mohábat Khán was obliged to fall back on Burhánpúr and desist from aggressive operations.‡ He had before been put under the nominal command of the emperor's second son, Shújá, who was a boy; and he was now recalled to court, and the Deckan was divided into two commands, under Kháni Dourán and Kháni Zeman.

A. D. 1634.

These officers were less successful than their

* Kháfi Khán. † Grant Duff.

‡ Grant Duff. There is a considerable difference between his dates and those of Kháfi Khán at this period.

predecessor. Mohammed A'dil Sháh continued to hold out, and the Nizám Sháh monarchy, which seemed to have come to an end on the surrender of Fatteh Khán, was revived by a chief whose family were afterwards to act an important part as the founders of the Maratta nation. This was Sháhjí Bosla, who had risen to considerable rank in the time of Malik Amber, and had distinguished himself as a partisan during the late wars. After the fall of Doulatábád, he drew off to the rugged country in the west of the Deckan; and, some time after, was so strong as to set up a new pretender to the throne of Ahmednagar; and, in time, to get possession of all the districts of that kingdom from the sea to the capital.*

Sháhjí Bosla attempts to restore the king of Ahmednagar.

The Deckan, therefore, was as far as ever from being subdued; and Sháh Jehán perceived the necessity of returning in person to that country, to make another effort to reduce it.

He marched from Agra towards the end of 1635†, and, on arriving in the Deckan, he adopted his former plan of breaking his army into divisions, and sent them, in the first instance, to recover the kingdom of Ahmednagar. When they had driven Sháhjí from the open country, and reduced many of his principal forts, Sháh Jehán turned his whole force on Bíjapúr, took several strong places, and constrained Mohammed A'dil Sháh once more to shut himself up in his capital. The talents which

The emperor returns to the Deckan. A. D. 1635, November; A. H. 1045, Jamádi ul awal.

Failure of another attempt on Bíjapúr.

* Grant Duff. Kháfi Khán.

† Kháfi Khán.

BOOK X.

had delivered him during the former siege did not desert him on this occasion. He laid waste the country for twenty miles round Bíjapúr, destroying every particle of food or forage; filled up the wells, drained off the reservoirs, and rendered it impossible for any army to support itself during an attack on the city.

The Moguls were therefore reduced to the plunder of his territories, and met with frequent losses from the spirit and activity of his detachments. Both parties, ere long, were wearied with this sort of warfare; and A'dil Sháh, making the first overture, peace was concluded, on terms much more favourable than he could have expected. He consented to an annual payment of 200,000*l.* a year to Sháh Jehán; but he was to receive, in return, a share of the Nizám Sháhi dominions, which much extended his territory on the north and east.

Peace with Bíjapúr. A. D. 1636, A. H. 1046.

Shálijí held out for some time longer: at length he also submitted, gave up his pretended king, and entered into the service of the king of Bíjapúr with the consent of Sháh Jehán.

Submission of Sháhjí Bosla.

At an early period of this invasion, Sháh Jehán had overawed the king of Golcónda, and had forced him to desist from reciting the name of the king of Persia in the public prayers, and to agree to pay a regular tribute.*

The emperor exacts a tribute from Golcónda.

These transactions being concluded, Sháh Jehán returned to his capital, and the kingdom of Ahmednagar was at length extinguished for ever.

Returns to Delhi. A. D. 1637, A. H. 1046.

* Grant Duff. Kháfi Khán.

While Sháh Jehán's attention was principally engaged with the Deckan, some events of less moment were taking place in other quarters. The Portuguese fort of Húgli, not far from Calcutta, was taken, after a siege, by the governor of Bengal (1631.) There were revolts of the Bundélas, in the first of which the son of Narsing Deó was killed. One portion of the troops on the eastern frontier completed the settlement of Little Tibet (1634 and 1636); another was defeated and almost destroyed in an attempt to conquer Srínagar (1634); and a third, which invaded the petty state of Cúch Behár from Bengal, was compelled, by the unhealthiness of the climate, to relinquish the country after they were in possession (1637).

Local disturbances and successes in Hindostan.

The most important occurrence of these times was the acquisition of Candahár, the governor of which, Ali Merdán Khán, found himself exposed to so much danger from the tyranny of his sovereign, the king of Persia, that he gave up the place to Sháh Jehán, and himself took refuge at Delhi. He was received with great honour, and was afterwards, at different times, made governor of Cashmír and Cábul, and employed on various wars and other duties. He excited universal admiration at the court by the skill and judgment of his public works, of which the canal which bears his name at Delhi still affords a proof, and by the taste and elegance he displayed on all occasions of show and festivity.

Recovery of Candahár.

Ali Merdán Khán.

A. D. 1637, A. H. 1047.

His military talents were first tried in an invasion

Invasion of Balkh.

BOOK X.

of Balkh and Badakhshán. Those provinces had remained in the hands of the Uzbeks since they were lost by Mírza Sóliman, and were now held by Nazar Mohammed, the younger brother of Imám Kúli, sovereign of all the territory beyond the Oxus, from the Caspian Sea to Mount Imaus.

The revolt of Nazar Mohammed's son, Abdul Azíz, encouraged by his powerful uncle, tempted Sháh Jehán, who had enjoyed several years of

A. D. 1644, A. H. 1054

repose, to assert the dormant rights of his family: Ali Merdán penetrated the range of Hindú Cush and ravaged Badakhshán; but the advance of the winter, and the fear of being cut off from the southern countries, compelled him to retreat without having gained any solid advantage. Next year, the enterprise was attempted by Rája Jagat Sing *, whose chief strength lay in a body of 14,000 Rájpúts, raised in his own country, but paid by the emperor.

Services of the Rájpúts in the mountains of Hindú Cush.

The spirit of the Rájpúts never shone more brilliantly than in this unusual duty: they stormed mountain passes, made forced marches over snow, constructed redoubts by their own labour, the rája himself taking an axe like the rest, and bore up against the tempests of that frozen region as firmly as against the fierce and repeated attacks of the Uzbeks.

But, with all these exertions, the enterprise now appeared so arduous that Sháh Jehán himself re-

* Probably the rája of Cóta.

solved to move to Cábul, and to send on his son, Prince Morád, under the guidance of Ali Merdán Khán, with a large army, into Balkh.* This expedition was completely successful: Morád was joined by some of Nazar Mohammed's sons, and afterwards received the submission of that chief; but, just as he had taken possession of the capital, a new rupture took place (with some suspicion of bad faith on the part of the Moguls). Nazar Mohammed, now divested of his defensible places, was obliged to fly to Persia; and his dominions were annexed, by proclamation, to those of Sháh Jehán. But this conquest was not long left undisturbed: Abdul Azíz collected a force beyond the Oxus, and sent numerous bands of plunderers to lay waste the newly conquered territory. Sháh Jehán had, by this time, returned to Delhi; and Morád, tired of the service, and impatient of the control of Ali Merdán, had left his province without leave, and was sent away from court in disgrace. The charge of restoring order was therefore imposed on Prince Aurangzíb, while the king himself again repaired to Cábul to support him. Aurangzíb at first obtained a great victory over the Uzbeks; its effects, however, were by no means decisive, for Abdul Azíz crossed the Oxus in person, and so harrassed the Moguls, that Aurangzíb, after some partial successes, was obliged to seek protection from the walls of Balkh itself.

A. D. 1645, A. H. 1055.

Sháh Jehán moves to Cábul.

Balkh reduced by Prince Morád and Ali Merdán Khán.

A. D. 1646, July; A. H. 1056, Jamádi al A'khir.

Overrun by the Uzbeks from beyond the Oxus.

Aurangzíb sent against them.

A. D. 1647, A. H. 1057.

Is besieged in Balkh.

* Kháfi Khán says 50,000 cavalry and 10,000 foot.

BOOK X.

Sháh Jehán abandons his conquest.

About this time, Nazar Mohammed, having failed to obtain aid in Persia, threw himself on the clemency of Sháh Jehán; and the latter prince, perceiving how little his prospects were advanced by such an expenditure of blood and treasure, came to the prudent resolution of withdrawing from the contest: and that he might do so with the less humiliation, he transferred his rights to Nazar Mohammed, then a suppliant at his court. Aurangzíb was accordingly directed to make over the places that remained in his possession; and he began his retreat from Balkh under continual attacks from the Uzbeks of Abdul Azíz's party. When he reached the passes of Hindú Cush, the persecution was taken up, for the sake of plunder, by the mountaineers of the Hazáreh tribes, and, to complete his misfortunes, the winter set in with violence; and though the prince himself reached Cábul with a light detachment, yet the main body of his army was intercepted by the snow, and suffered so much in this helpless condition from the unremitting assaults of the Hazárehs, that they were glad to escape in separate bodies with the loss of all their baggage and almost all their horses.*

Disastrous retreat of Aurangzíb.

About the end of A. D. 1647, A. H. 1057.

Candahár retaken by the Persians.

The tranquillity purchased by the relinquishment of Balkh was first disturbed by an attack on Candahár by the Persians. During the weak and tyrannical reign of Sháh Safi, and the minority of his son, Sháh Abbás II., the Moguls had been

* Kháfi Khán.

allowed to enjoy the fruits of Ali Merdán's desertion unmolested; but as Abbás advanced towards manhood, his ministers induced him to assert the dignity of his monarchy by restoring it to its ancient limits. He assembled a large army, and marched against Candahár. He showed much judgment in beginning the siege in winter, when the communication between India and Cábul was cut off by the snow, while his own operations went on unobstructed in the mild climate of Candahár. The consequence was, that, although Aurangzíb and the vizír Saád Ullah Khán were ordered off in all haste from the Panjáb, and although they made their way with great exertions through the mountains, they arrived too late to save Candahár, which had been taken after a siege of two months and a half. The exhausted condition of the army after their winter march compelled Aurangzíb and Saád Ullah to halt and refit at Cábul; while the king of Persia withdrew to Herát, leaving a strong garrison in Candahár.*

A. D. 1648, A. H. 1058.

The Indian army came before that city in May, 1649. They immediately opened their batteries, and the contest was actively conducted on both sides, with springing of mines, assaults by the besiegers, and sallies by the garrison. These operations were not interrupted by the approach of an army sent by Sháh Abbás to raise the siege. Aurangzíb was contented with sending a detachment

Aurangzíb sent to recover it.

A. H. 1059, Jamádi al Awal.

* Kháfi Khán.

BOOK X.

to oppose the attack, and remained, himself, in his lines before the city. The force he had employed was sufficient to repel the Persians, but it could not prevent their destroying the forage and cutting off the supplies of the besiegers; and as the governor defended his town with as much skill as obstinacy, Aurangzíb was at length constrained to raise the siege, and commence his retreat to Cábul above four months after he had opened his batteries.* Sháh Jehán, who had followed Aurangzíb to Cábul, marched from that city before the prince's return, and was not overtaken by him until he had reached Láhór.

A. D. 1649, about Sept.; A. H. 1059, Rámzán. Fails in the siege of Candahár.

A. D. 1651, A. H. 1 60.

The next year passed in inaction, to which the king's usual visit to Cashmír forms no exception. The time he spent in that delicious retirement was devoted to feasts and dances, to gardens, excursions by land and water, and other pleasures congenial to the climate and scenery.

Second attempt on Candahár under Aurangzíb.

A. D. 1652, A. H. 1061.

In the year next succeeding, Aurangzíb and the vizír, Saád Ullah, were again dispatched to Candahár, with a numerous and well-equipped army and ample provision of tools and workmen to conduct all the operations of a siege.†

These great preparations were as unavailing as before; and Aurangzíb, after exhausting every resource supplied by the skill and courage of Saád

* Kháfi Khán.

† It is worthy of remark, that, with so great a force assembled on purpose for a siege, there were only eight battering guns, and twenty smaller pieces of ordnance.

Ullah and the bravery of the Rájpúts, was compelled to return to Cábul, and was sent to be viceroy of the Deckan.

CHAP. II.

Its failure.

Sháh Jehán was not discouraged by his repeated failures, and next year prepared for a still greater effort than had yet been put forth.

Great expedition under Prince Dárá Shekó.

His eldest son Dárá Shekó, though treated as superior in station to the rest, was kept at court, and looked with envy on the opportunities of distinction enjoyed by his brothers, especially Aurangzíb, of whom he seems to have entertained a sort of instinctive jealousy. Urged by these feelings, he entreated Sháh Jehán to allow him to try his skill and fortune at the siege of Candahár, and was put at the head of an army much exceeding that formerly employed. It assembled at Láhór in the winter of 1652, and commenced its march in the spring of the next year, Sháh Jehán himself following as usual to Cábul.

A. D. 1653,
A. H. 1063.

Siege of Candahár.

Dárá opened his trenches, as Aurangzíb had done before him, on a day and hour fixed by the astrologers, and ordered by the emperor before the army set out on its march. He began the siege on a scale proportioned to his armament. He mounted a battery of ten guns on a high and solid mound of earth, raised for the purpose of enabling him to command the town; and he pushed his operations with his characteristic impetuosity, increased, in this instance, by rivalry with his brother. He assembled his chiefs, and besought them to support his honour, declaring

BOOK X.

his intention never to quit the place till it was taken; he urged on the mines, directed the approaches, and the besieged having brought their guns to bear on his own tent, he maintained his position until their fire could be silenced by that of his artillery. But, after the failure of several attempts to storm, and the disappointment of near prospects of success, his mind appears to have given way to the dread of defeat and humiliation; he entreated his officers not to reduce him to a level with the twice-beaten Aurangzíb; and he had recourse to magicians and other impostors, who promised to put him in possession of the place by supernatural means. Such expedients portended an unfavourable issue; and accordingly, after a last desperate assault, which commenced before daybreak, and in which his troops had at one time gained the summit of the rampart, he was compelled to renounce all hope, and to raise the siege, after having lost the flower of his army in the prosecution of it. He was harassed on his retreat both by the Persians and Afgháns; and it was not without additional losses that he made his way to Cábul, whence he pursued his march to Láhór.

A. D. 1653, September; A. H. 1063, Shawál 9.

Failure and retreat of Dárá Shekó.

A. D. 1653, November; A. H. 1064, Moharram.

Thus terminated the last attempt of the Moguls to recover Candahár, of which they had held but a precarious possession from the first conquest of it by Báber.

End of A. D. 1653 to 1655, A. H. 1064 and 1065.

It was followed by nearly two years of undisturbed tranquillity. During that time Sháh Jehán, having completed a revenue survey of his possessions in the Deckan, which is said to have occupied him for nearly twenty years *, gave orders for the adoption of the system of assessment and collection introduced by Tódar Mal.†

Death of the vizír, Saád Ullah Khán.

The same period is marked by the death of the vizír, Saád Ullah Khán, the most able and upright minister that ever appeared in India. He makes a conspicuous figure in all the transactions of Sháh Jehán, and is constantly referred to as a model in the correspondence of Aurangzíb during the long reign of that monarch. Kháfi Khán says that his descendants, in *his* time, were still distinguished for their virtues and intelligence, near a century after the death of their ancestor; and contrasts the respectability of their conduct with the effeminacy and frivolity of the other nobles of that æra.

Renewal of the war in the Deckan under Aurangzíb.

The next year was destined to put an end to this state of repose, and to light up a conflagration which was never effectually suppressed, and was not extinguished until it had consumed the empire.

Since the last pacification, Abdullah Kutb Sháh had paid his tribute regularly, and had shown a desire to secure the favour of Sháh Jehán, who but for a particular concurrence of circumstances, would probably never have wished to molest him.

Intrigues of Aurangzíb at Golcónda. Mír Jumla.

The prime minister of Abdullah was a person named Mír Jumla. He had formerly been a diamond merchant, and had been known and respected throughout the Deckan for his wealth and abilities

* Grant Duff's "History of the Marattas, vol. i. p. 126."

† Kháfi Khán.

BOOK X.

long before he attained his present high station. His son, Mohammed Amín, a dissolute and violent young man, had drawn on himself the resentment of Abdullah Kutb Sháh, and had involved his father in a dispute with the court. Mír Jumla was absent in command of an army in the eastern part of the kingdom of Golcónda; and, finding himself unable to obtain such concessions as he desired from his own sovereign, determined to throw himself on the protection of the Mogul. He applied to Aurangzíb, to whom, as well as to the emperor, he was already known. Such an opportunity of interference afforded an irresistible temptation to a man of Aurangzíb's intriguing dispósition, and he strongly recommended the case of Mír Jumla to his father's favour. Sháh Jehán, influenced by this advice, dispatched a haughty mandate to Abdullah Sháh to redress the complaints of his minister; but Abdullah was further irritated by this encroachment on his independence, and committed Amín to prison, while he sequestrated the property of Mír Jumla. Sháh Jehán, now provoked in his turn, sent orders to his son to carry his demands into effect by force of arms; and Aurangzib, who had been waiting impatiently for this result, entered with alacrity on the duty, and executed it in a manner entirely suitable to his wily nature.

Treacherous attack on Heiderábád by Aurangzíb.

Without any further manifestation of hostility, he sent out a chosen force, under pretence of escorting his son, Sultán Mohammed, to Bengal, for the purpose of celebrating his nuptials with the

A. D. 1650. January; A. H. 1066. Rabi al awal.

daughter of his own brother, Prince Shujá, who was viceroy of that province. The road from Aurangábád to Bengal made a circuit by Masulipatam, so as to avoid the forests of Góndwána, and thus naturally brought the prince within a short distance of Heiderábád, the capital of Golcónda. Abdullah Sháh was preparing an entertainment for his reception, when he suddenly advanced as an enemy, and took the king so completely by surprise that he had only time to fly to the hill fort of Golcónda, six or eight miles from the city; while Heiderábád fell into the hands of the Moguls, and was plundered and half burned before the troops could be brought into order. Aurangzíb had, before this, found a pretence for assembling an army on the nearest point of his province; and being joined by fresh troops from Málwa, he had ample means of sending on reinforcements to Golcónda. Mír Jumla also in time drew near, and was ready to turn his master's arms against himself. Abdullah Sháh, on his first flight to the hill fort, had released Mohammed Amín, and given up the sequestrated property; and he did all in his power to negotiate a reasonable accommodation; while at the same time he spared no effort to procure aid from Bíjapúr: no aid came, and the Moguls were inexorable; and, after several attempts to raise the siege by force, he was at last under the necessity of accepting the severe terms imposed on him; to agree to give his daughter in marriage to Sultán Mohammed, with a

BOOK X.

dowry in territory and money; to pay a crore of rupees (1,000,000*l.* sterling) as the first instalment of a yearly tribute; and promised to make up the arrears of past payments within two years.

Submission of the king of Golcónda.

Sháh Jehán would have been content with easier terms, and did in fact make a great remission in the pecuniary part of those agreed on; but the rest were executed, and the Mogul prince returned to Aurangábád. Mír Jumla remained in the Mogul service, became the chosen counsellor of Aurangzíb, and was afterwards one of the most useful instruments of his ambitious designs.

A.D. 1656, May; A.H. 1066.

Unprovoked war with Bíjapúr.

Aurangzíb had scarcely reaped the fruits of his success in Golcónda before an opportunity was afforded him of gaining similar advantages over the neighbouring kingdom. The peace with Bíjapúr had remained unbroken since the last treaty. Mohammed A'dil Sháh had successfully cultivated the friendship of Sháh Jehán, but had excited the personal enmity of Aurangzíb by a close connection with Dárá Shekó. On his death, which took place in November, 1656 *, he was succeeded by his son, Ali, a youth of nineteen; and Sháh Jehán, was tempted, by the persuasion of his younger son, to deny that the minor was the real issue of the late king, and to assert his own right to decide on the succession to his tributary. Though the force of the kingdom of Bíjapúr was still undiminished, it was in no state of preparation for

* Grant Duff. It corresponds to Moharram 1067.

war; and a large portion of its army was employed at a distance in wars with the Hindú petty princes of Carnáta. Aurangzíb, therefore, met with little difficulty in his invasion of the territory; and a fortunate accident having thrown the strong frontier fort of Bidr into his hands, he advanced without further obstruction to the capital.* The suddenness of the attack had prevented the mode of defence by destroying the country, so successfully practised on former occasions. No resource, therefore, was left to the new king, but to sue for peace on the most unfavourable terms. Even those were peremptorily rejected by Aurangzíb; and he would probably ere long have obtained possession both of the capital and the country, if he had not been called off by a matter that touched him more nearly than the conquest of any foreign kingdom.

A. D. 1657, March; A. H. 1067.

* Grant Duff.

CHAP. III.

FROM 1657 TO THE DEPOSAL OF SHÁH JEHÁN.

BOOK X.

Dangerous illness of the emperor.

THE emperor had been seized with an illness of so serious a nature, that it not only threatened an immediate transfer of the crown to Dárá Shekó, but invested him at the moment with the administration of his father's government. This state of affairs, involving all Aurangzíb's prospects of aggrandizement and even of safety, turned hs exertions towards the seat of the monarchy, and for a long time withdrew his attention from the affairs of the Deckan.

Characters and pretensions of his sons.

Sháh Jehán had four sons, all of an age to render them impatient of a subordinate station. Dárá Shekó was in his forty-second year; Shujá was forty; and Aurangzíb thirty-eight. Even Morád, the youngest, had long been employed in great commands.* Dárá Shekó was a frank and high-spirited prince, dignified in his manners, generous in his expense, liberal in his opinions, open in his enmities; but impetuous, impatient of opposition, and despising the ordinary rules of prudence as signs of weakness and artifice. His overbearing temper made him many enemies; while his habitual indiscretion lessened the number as well as the con-

Dárà Shekó.

* Gladwin's History of Jehángír.

Shujá. Aurangzíb.

fidence of his adherents. Shujá was not destitute of abilities, but given up to wine and pleasure. Aurangzíb was a perfect contrast to Dárá Shekó. He was a man of a mild temper and a cold heart; cautious, artful, designing; a perfect master of dissimulation; acute and sagacious, though not extended in his views; and ever on the watch to gain friends and to propitiate enemies. To these less brilliant qualities he joined great courage, and skill in military exercises; a handsome, though not athletic form; affable and gracious manners; and lively agreeable conversation. He was so great a dissembler in other matters, that he has been supposed a hypocrite in religion. But, although religion was a great instrument of his policy, he was, beyond doubt, a sincere and bigoted Mussulman. He had been brought up by men of known sanctity, and had himself shown an early turn for devotion; he at one time professed an intention of renouncing the world, and taking the habit of a fakír; and throughout his whole life he evinced a real attachment to his faith in many things indifferent to his interest, and some most seriously opposed to it. His zeal was shown in prayers and reading the Korán, in pious discourses, in abstemiousness (which he affected to carry so far as to subsist on the earnings of his manual labour), in humility of deportment, patience under provocation, and resignation in misfortunes; but, above all, in constant and earnest endeavours to promote his own faith and to discourage idolatry and infidelity. But neither religion nor morality stood for a moment in his way when they interfered with his ambition; and, though full of scruples at other times, he would stick at no crime that was requisite for the gratification of that passion.

His political use of religion arose from a correct view of the feelings of the time. Akber's innovations had shocked most Mahometans, who, besides the usual dislike of the vulgar to toleration, felt that a direct attack was made on their own faith. Jehángír's restoration of the old ritual was too cold to give full satisfaction; and, though Sháh Jehán was a more zealous Mussulman, Dárá openly professed the tenets of Akber, and had written a book to reconcile the Hindu and Mahometan doctrines. No topic, therefore, could be selected more likely to make that prince unpopular than his infidelity, and in no light could the really religious Aurangzíb be so favourably opposed to him as in that of the champion of Islám. In this character he had also an advantage over Shujá, who was looked on with aversion by the orthodox Mahometans from his attachment to the Persian sect of the Shías.

Morád.

Morád was brave and generous, but dull in intellect, and vulgar in his pursuits. He was abundantly presumptuous and self-willed; but his object never was more exalted than the indulgence of his humours, and the enjoyment of sensual pleasures.*

* The characters of the princes are taken from Bernier, modified by the facts in Kháfi Khán, and by some passages in Aurangzíb's letters. The following is given by that monarch

Daughters of Sháh Jehán.

Sháh Jehán had, by the same mother as his sons*, two daughters. To the eldest, Pádsháh Bégam, he was devotedly attached. She was endowed with beauty and talents, and was a great support to the interest of Dárá Shekó. Roushanárá, the second daughter, had fewer personal attractions and less influence; but her talent for intrigue, and her knowledge of the secrets of the harem, enabled her to be of the greatest assistance to her favourite brother, Aurangzíb.

Dárá administers the government under the emperor.

It was from this princess that Aurangzíb obtained the intelligence on which he now acted. Though Sháh Jehán had only attained his sixty-seventh year, the habits of indolence and pleasure in which he had indulged seem to have latterly diminished his attention to business, and allowed a greater share of influence to Dárá Shekó, on whom, as heir apparent, he devolved such of his duties as he did not himself perform. Things were in this state when the emperor was seized with a sudden

as Sháh Jehán's opinion of his four sons. Dárá (he said) had talents for command, and the dignity becoming the royal office, but was intolerant to all who had any pretensions to eminence; whence he was "bad to the good, and good to the bad." Shujá was a mere drunkard; and Morád, a glutton and a sensualist. Aurangzíb excelled both in action and counsel, was well fitted to undertake the burden of public affairs, but full of subtle suspicions, and never likely to find any one whom he could trust. (*Letter from Aurangzíb to his son, in the "Dastúr al Amal A'gáhi."*)

* Gladwin's History of Jehángír.

disorder in his kidneys, together with a suppression of urine, which entirely incapacitated him from business, and soon brought him to the brink of the grave.* During this crisis Dárá stopped all correspondence, and detained all travellers likely to spread the news of the king's danger throughout the provinces. He could not, however, long elude the vigilance of his brothers. Aurangzíb in particular was minutely informed of all his proceedings during the whole of the struggle which followed.

A. D. 1657, October; A. H. 1067, Zí Haj 7.

Rebellion of Shujá,

The first to act on the emergency was Prince Shujá, the viceroy of Bengal. He assembled the troops of his province, and immediately marched into Behár on his way to the capital.

and of Morád.

Prince Morád, viceroy of Guzerát, soon followed his example: he seized on all the money in the district treasuries, and laid siege to Surat, where there was a governor independent of his authority, and where he thought there was a considerable sum in deposit.

Cautious measures of Aurangzíb.

Aurangzíb conducted himself with more caution. He did not assume the royal title, as Shujá and Morád had done; and although he instantly moved to his northern frontier, and urged on the preparation of his army, he made no open declaration till orders came from Dárá, in the emperor's name, to direct Mír Jumla and the other military commanders to quit his standard. Mír Jumla, after

His collusion with Mír Jumla.

* Kháfi Khán.

he joined the Moguls, had been summoned to the capital, aud had for a time been intrusted with the highest offices in the state. He had afterwards been sent back to the Deckan; but his family was still at Agra, and the fear of the consequences to them made him hesitate to oppose an order of the emperor. But his embarrassment was removed by a stratagem suggested by Aurangzíb.

According to a concerted plan he sent for Mír Jumla to his court; and when that commander, after some affected delays and alarms, presented himself, he ordered him to be made prisoner and confined in the fort of Doulatábád, while his principal officers, secretly influenced by their commander, continued to serve with Aurangzíb. Even when he had thrown off the mask he still proceeded with his usual policy. He left Dárá and Shujá to weaken each other for his profit, and applied all his art to gain Morád, whom he might hope to render an instrument in his own hands. He wrote to him with the most vehement professions of attachment, congratulating him on his accession to the crown, and declaring his own intention of renouncing the world and indulging his love of devotion in retirement at Mecca. He nevertheless offered his zealous services against the irreligious Dárá, and advised that, as their father was still alive, they should present themselves before him, when, if received with favour, they should secure him from undue influence, while they interceded for the pardon of their erring brother; meanwhile

He marches to join Morád.

BOOK X.

they should unite their forces and proceed to engage the infidel Jeswant Sing, who, it was understood, had been sent against them.* It seems incredible that Morád should have been deceived by so improbable a profession, but the coarseness of the artifice was disguised by the masterly execution; and the assiduous flatteries of Aurangzíb found a willing auditor in his brother, naturally unsuspicious, and dazzled by the prospect of assistance so necessary to the support of his feeble cause.

Defensive measures of Dárá.

Before this period Dárá had taken measures to resist the threatened attacks of his rivals. He sent Rája Jeswant Sing into Málwa to watch Morád and Aurangzíb; and to act against them, with his whole army, or by dividing it, as circumstances might suggest. At the same time he himself advanced to Agra, and dispatched an army under the command of his own son, Sólimán Shekó, assisted by Rája Jei Sing, to oppose the approach of Shujá.

A. D. 1657, November; A. H. 1068, Rebi al Awal 4.

Sháh Jehán reassumes the government.

By this time Sháh Jehán was sufficiently recovered to resume the general control of the government; but his confidence in Dárá was only increased by the misconduct of the other princes. He wrote to Shujá, commanding him in positive terms to return to his government. Shujá pretended to consider these orders as dictated by Dárá Shekó, and probably still looked on the emperor's recovery as doubtful. He continued to move on until he met

Shujà continues to advance on Agra.

* Kháfi Khán.

Sóliman Shekó in the neighbourhood of Benáres. A battle then took place, and Shujá, though his army was not dispersed, was defeated, and compelled to return into Bengal.

Is defeated by Sólimán, son of Dárá, and returns to Bengal.

Meanwhile Aurangzíb quitted Burhánpúr* and marched into Málwa. He there formed a junction with Morád; and the combined armies marched to attack Rája Jeswant Sing, who was encamped near Ujén. The rája drew up his army on the bank of the river Sípra, which at that season was nearly dry, but still presented a formidable obstruction from the rocky nature of its bed.

A. D. 1658, end of March; A. H. 1068, Jamádi al A'khir 25.

A. D. 1658, April; A. H. 1068, Rajab.

The battle was bravely contested by the Rájpúts, who were ill supported by the rest of the troops. It was chiefly decided by the gallantry of Morád: Jeswant Sing retired in disorder to his own country, and the rest of the army dispersed.† On rewarding his chiefs after this battle, Aurangzíb sent them all to return their thanks to Morád, as if he alone were the fountain of all honour. On the first junction he had taken an oath to adhere to that prince, and renewed all his promises with every appearance of warmth and sincerity; and throughout the whole campaign, although his abilities gave him the real control of all operations, he continued his professions of devotion and humility, always acknowledging Morád as his superior, and treating

Aurangzíb and Morád defeat the imperial army under Jeswant Sing at Ujén.

* Kháfi Khan.

† Kháfi Khán. Bernier. Bernier, who soon after joined the emperor's army, accuses Kásim Khán, who commanded along with Jeswant Sing, of disaffection.

BOOK X.

A. D. 1658, May; A. H. 1068, from Rejab 27. to Shábán. 25.

him on all occasions with the utmost respect and attention.* After this victory the princes advanced by slow marches to the Chambal, near Gwáliór.†

Some dispositions made by Dárá Shekó for the defence of that river were rendered ineffectual by the manœuvres of Aurangzíb, and the army crossed without opposition.

Sháh Jehán's anxiety for an accommodation.

Before Jeswant Sing's defeat, Sháh Jehán, unable to bear the heat of the season, had set out on his way to Delhi. The news of that misfortune recalled him, much against his will, to Agra. He found that during his absence Dárá had thrown Amín, the son of Mír Jumla, into confinement; but, as he disapproved of the proceeding, it was immediately countermanded by the prince himself. Sháh Jehán, at this time, notwithstanding his feeble health, had ordered his tents to be prepared, and intended to take the field in person. His hope was, that he should be able to bring about an adjustment by his presence and authority, and to avoid a war which could not but bring many dangers and calamities on himself and all the parties engaged. He was dissuaded from this resolution by his brother-in-law, Sháista Khán. If it had been pursued, it would have had no effect on the princes, whatever it might on the armies; for all were now too far engaged to recede, or to trust their future safety to any thing so precarious as the life of Sháh Jehán. Dárá likewise looked with an ill eye on

* Kháfi Khán. Bernier.

† Kháfi Khán.

an accommodation that must have removed him from almost unlimited power, and restored the administration to its ordinary train under the immediate control of the emperor. Urged on by this consideration, and confident in his superior numbers, he refused even to wait for Sólimán, then on his march from Benáres with the most efficient part of the army. Contrary to the earnest injunctions of Sháh Jehán, he marched out at the head of an army which seemed irresistible from its numbers and equipment, but was rendered weak, in reality, by the arrogance of the commander, the disaffection of the chiefs, and the absence of the flower of the fighting men.*

Dárá marches from Agra to oppose his brothers, against the wish of Sháh Jehán.

On the 6th of Ramzán, 1068, the two armies approached each other at Samaghar, one march from Agra: they drew up face to face on the next day, but did not join battle until the succeeding morning.

A. D. 1658, beginning of June.

The action began by a charge of a body of Dárá's cavalry, under Rustam Khán. It was unable to penetrate a row of guns chained together in front of Aurangzíb's line. A second and more powerful charge, headed by Dárá himself, was equally unsuccessful; but his attack was renewed and kept up without intermission on the centre,

Is totally defeated.

* Kháfi Khán says the army consisted at Agra of upwards 70,000 horse, with innumerable elephants and guns. Bernier, though generally distrustful of native numbers, thinks it may have been 100,000 horse, 20,000 foot, and 80 pieces of artillery. He reckons Aurangzíb's and Morád's army at 30,000 or 35 000 horse.

where Aurangzíb was stationed, In the mean time Morád was attacked by 3000 Uzbeks, who poured in flights of arrows on him, with such rapidity that it was with difficulty he could bear up against them. His elephant gave way before the storm, and would have run off the field if Morád had not ordered its feet to be chained; thus cutting off the power of retreat for himself. This sharp contest with the Uzbeks was succeeded by a much more formidable attack. A large body of Rájpúts rushed on the prince with an impetuosity that nothing could resist. Rám Sing, their rája, in a saffron robe, and with a chaplet of pearls on his head, ran up to Morád's elephant, and hurled his pike at the prince, while he shouted to the driver to make the elephant kneel down. Morád received the pike on his shield, and nearly at the same moment laid the rája dead with an arrow.* His death only exasperated the Rájpúts, who fought with desperate fury, and fell in heaps round the prince's elephant. At this time Aurangzíb was about to move to his brother's assistance, but he had soon full employment where he was; for Dárá, having at length broken through the line of guns, charged his centre at full speed, and carried all before him, by the united force of velocity and numbers.

* Kháfi Khán. Bernier. Colonel Tod (vol. ii. p. 481.) ascribes this attack to Rája Chitar Sál of Bundi, who was a distinguished commander in the reign of Sháh Jehán, and was likewise killed in this battle.

Aurangzíb alone remained unshaken: he presented his elephant wherever there was the greatest danger, and called aloud to his troops that "God was with them, and that they had no other refuge or retreat."* In the height of this contest Rája Rúp Sing leaped from his horse, and running up to Aurangzíb's elephant, began to cut away the girths with his sword. Aurangzíb was struck with his audacity, and even in that moment of alarm called out to his men to spare him; but before his voice could be heard the rája had fallen, almost cut to pieces. At this critical juncture Morád, having at length repelled the Rájpúts, was able to turn his attention to the centre; and Dárá, who found his right thereby exposed, was obliged to abate the vigour of his front attack. His numbers, however, might in the end have prevailed; but as he was pressing forward on his elephant, conspicuous to all his troops, whom he was encouraging by his voice, and by waving his hand to them to advance, a rocket from the enemy struck the elephant, and rendered it so ungovernable that Dárá had no choice but to throw himself from its back and to mount a horse with all expedition. His disappearance struck a sudden alarm among the distant troops; and an attendant being carried off by a shot at his side, while fastening on his quiver after he mounted, those immediately round him were also thrown into confusion: the panic spread, and its

* Bernier has preserved his words in the original Hindostani.

BOOK X.

effects were soon felt throughout the whole army. The death of an Asiatic leader is often the loss of the battle: in a civil war it is the annihilation of the cause. Success seemed now useless, and every man's thoughts were turned to safety. Even the part of the line which was not engaged began to waver, while the princes pressed forward amidst the disorder of the centre, and compelled the troops opposed to them, and even Dárá himself, to take to flight.

The victory was no sooner decided than Aurangzíb threw himself on his knees and returned his thanks to Divine Providence for the mercy it had vouchsafed to him. His next care was to salute his brother, and congratulate him on the acquisition of a kingdom. He found Morád's howdah bristled with arrows, and himself wounded in several places; and, after expressing the greatest joy at *his* victory, he began to wipe the blood from his face, and to show the most affectionate attention to his sufferings.*

Dárá flies to Delhi.

While this was passing on the field, the unfortunate Dárá pursued his flight towards the city: he arrived in the evening with 2000 horse, many of them wounded; all he now had of the great force with which he had so lately marched out.

He was ashamed to present himself before his father, to the disregard of whose opinion he owed

* Morád's howdah was preserved as a curiosity to the time of Ferókhsír, when it was seen by Kháfi Khán, who says it was stuck as full of arrows as a porcupine is of quills.

his ruin; and after securing some valuables at his own palace, he continued his flight towards Delhi, accompanied by his wife and two of his children. He had already reached the third regular stage from Agra, before he was overtaken by 5000 horse, sent by Sháh Jehán to his assistance.*

Aurangzíb enters Agra.

A. D. 1658, June; A. H. 1068, Rámzán 10.

Sháh Jehán adheres to the cause of Dárá.

Aurangzíb marched to Agra three days after the battle. He encamped before the walls, and took immediate possession of the city. Some more days elapsed before he interfered with the interior of the royal residence. He employed the interval in humble messages to his father, pleading the necessity of his case, and protesting his inviolable

* In the account of the battle I have taken some circumstances from Bernier, but have preferred the general narrative of Kháfi Khán, who, besides his access to verbal and written evidence, refers to his own father, who was present in the action. Bernier lived nearer the time, and is an excellent writer; but his acquaintance both with men and books must have been limited, and his means of judging Indians imperfect; his relation, besides, is mixed with some anecdotes which look like popular inventions. Dárá's descent from his elephant (for instance) is ascribed to the insidious advice of a traitor in the moment of victory; while Kháfi Khán says he was obliged to get down in such precipitation, that he left his slippers, and mounted his horse with bare feet and without arms. Bernier afterwards relates a plot of Sháh Jehán to seize Aurangzíb, and a counter plot of the latter, which ended in the seizure of Sháh Jehán; but the story is improbable in itself, and is not alluded to by Kháfi Khán. It is necessary throughout to look closely into the accounts which favour Aurangzíb; for though Bernier himself is captivated with the open character of Dárá, his master was a personal enemy of that prince, against whom Kháfi Khán also has a strong prejudice; and both wrote after Aurangzíb had been successful, and was cried up as the Mussulman hero and the greatest of emperors.

BOOK X.

respect and duty: it is probable, indeed, that he was sincerely desirous of conciliating his father, and would have preferred carrying on the government in his name; but he found it impossible to gain his confidence or to shake his attachment to Dárá; and at length sent his own son, Mohammed Sultán, to take complete possession of the citadel, and to prevent all communications between the

Rámzán 17. Is confined in his palace.

emperor and every one beyond its walls. Sháh Jehán was still treated with the highest respect; but, although he lived for seven years longer, his reign ends at this period. It seems unaccountable that so able a prince should have thus been dethroned without any of his old servants attempting to stir in his favour: the truth is, that his habits of indulgence had impaired his energy; and as he had long ceased to head his armies, the troops turned their eyes to the princes who led them in the field, and who had the immediate distribution of their honours and rewards. To this must be added the peculiar abilities of Aurangzíb; who was more successful in defeating conspiracies and managing factions than in any other branch of government, though he was good in all.

Aurangzíb imprisons Morád, and openly assumes the government.

Having now no further use for Morád, Aurangzíb dismissed him from his pretended sovereignty, without even the ceremony of a quarrel or a complaint. He kept up the delusion of that simple prince by submissive behaviour and constant presents and attentions, till they had marched from Agra in pursuit of Dárá; when he one day in-

CHAP. III.

vited Morád to supper, and so far waved his own scruples as to allow the free use of the goblet; of which Morád so fully availed himself that he was soon in a state of helpless intoxication. On this he was stripped of his arms without resistance, was cast into chains, and sent off on an elephant to Selímghar, part of the citadel of Delhi; while three other elephants were dispatched, under similar escorts, in different directions, to mislead people as to his place of confinement. He was afterwards removed to Gwáliór, the great state prison of those days. Aurangzíb then continued his march to Delhi, where he caused himself to be proclaimed emperor.* He did not put his name on the coin, and was not crowned until the first anniversary of his accession; a circumstance which has introduced some confusion into the dates of his reign.

A.D. 1658, Aug. 20.; A.H. 1068, Zí Cáad 1.

High prosperity of India under Sháh Jehán.

The reign of Sháh Jehán, thus harshly closed, was perhaps the most prosperous ever known in India. Though sometimes engaged in foreign wars, his own dominions enjoyed almost uninterrupted tranquillity, together with a larger share of good government than often falls to the lot of Asiatic nations.

Notwithstanding Sháh Jehán's love of ease and pleasure, and the time spent in his visits to Cashmír and the erection of those celebrated structures in which he took so much delight, he never remitted his vigilance over his internal government;

* Kháfi Khán.

BOOK X.

and by this, and the judicious choice of his ministers, he prevented any relaxation in the system, and even introduced important improvements,—such as his survey of the Deckan.

Kháfi Khán, the best historian of those times, gives his opinion, that, although Akber was pre-eminent as a conqueror and a lawgiver, yet, for the order and arrangement of his territory and finances, and the good administration of every department of the state, no prince ever reigned in India that could be compared to Sháh Jehán.

Whatever might be the relative excellence of his government, we must not suppose that it was exempt from the evils inherent in a despotism: we may assume some degree of fraudulent exaction in the officers of revenue, and of corruption in those of justice; and we have the testimony of European travellers to acts of extortion by custom-house officers, and of arbitrary power by governors of provinces; but, after all deductions on these accounts, there will remain enough to convince us that the state of India under Sháh Jehán was one of great ease and prosperity.*

* Tavernier, who had repeatedly visited most parts of India, says that Sháh Jehán "reigned not so much as a king over his subjects, but rather as a father over his family and children," and goes on to commend the strictness of his civil government, and to speak in high terms of the security enjoyed under it. (Page 108. of the English translation of 1678.) Pietro Della Valle, who wrote in the last years of Jehángír (1623), when things were in a worse state than under his son, gives the following account:—"Hence, generally, all live much after a

The erection of such a capital as Delhi proves great private as well as public wealth. Mandesloe describes Agra as at least twice as large as Isfahán (then in its greatest glory); with fine streets, good shops, and numerous baths and caravanserais. Nor was this prosperity confined to royal residences; all travellers speak with admiration of the grandeur of the cities, even in remote provinces, and of the fertile and productive countries in which they stood.*

Those who look on India in its present state may be inclined to suspect the native writers of exaggerating its former prosperity; but the deserted cities, ruined palaces, and choked up aqueducts which we still see, with the great reservoirs and embankments in the midst of jungles, and the decayed causeways, wells, and caravanserais of the royal roads, concur with the evidence of contemporary travellers in convincing us that those historians had good grounds for their commendation.

The whole continent of India, however, was far from being in a uniform state: vast tracts were still covered with forests; and the mountainous

---

genteel way; and they do it securely as well, because the king does not persecute his subjects with false accusations, nor deprive them of any thing when he sees them live splendidly, and with the appearance of riches (as is often done in other Mahometan countries), as because the Indians are inclined to those vanities, &c. &c." (Page 22. English translation of 1665.)

* Mandesloe, for Guzerát; Graaf and Bruton (in Murray's *Asiatic Discovery*), for Bengal, Behár, and Orissa; and Tavernier, for most parts of the empire.

BOOK X.

ranges often harboured wild and predatory inhabitants. Even in the best cleared parts, there were sometimes revolts of subject rájas, as in Bundélcand, during the present reign; but in that case the disturbance was confined to a district of less extent than the Tyrol, while populous provinces as large as France or England were scarcely aware of its existence.

But, after all allowances, the state of the people must have been worse than in an indifferently governed country in *modern* Europe. On the one side, there are the absence of slavery and polygamy, less personal oppression by the great, and less fear of scarcity and consequent disease; while on the other there is nothing to oppose but lighter taxation and freedom from a meddling and complicated system of law and regulation. A fairer object of comparison would be the Roman Empire, under such a prince as Severus: we should there find the same general tranquillity and good government, with similar examples of disturbance and oppression; the same enjoyment of physical happiness, with the same absence of that spirit which would tend to increase the present felicity, and which might afford some security for its duration beyond the life of the reigning monarch. The institutions, traditions, and opinions which remained from better times, must, even in this case, have given a superiority to the European empire.

Magnificence of Sháh Jehán.

Sháh Jehán was the most magnificent prince that ever appeared in India. His retinue, his state establishments, his largesses, and all the pomp of his court, were much increased beyond the excess they had attained to under his predecessors. His expenses in these departments can only be palliated by the fact that they neither occasioned any increase to his exactions nor any embarrassment to his finances. The most striking instance of his pomp and prodigality was his construction of the famous peacock throne. It took its name from a peacock with its tail spread (represented in its natural colours in sapphires, emeralds, rubies, and other appropriate jewels), which formed the chief ornament of a mass of diamonds and precious stones that dazzled every beholder. Tavernier, a jeweller by profession, reports, without apparent distrust, the common belief, that it cost 160,500,000 livres, nearly six millions and a half sterling.

His buildings.

But his greatest splendour was shown in his buildings. He founded a new city at Delhi, built on a regular plan, and far surpassing the old one in magnificence: three wide streets (one of great length, ornamented by a canal and rows of trees, and composed of houses rising over a line of shops under arcades), led to a spacious esplanade, in the centre of which, and on the Jamna, stood the fortified palace; the spacious courts, marble halls, and golden domes of which have so often been the subject of enthusiastic description. The great mosque of the same city is a work of extraordinary elegance and grandeur.

The Táj Mahal.

But of all the structures erected by Sháh Jehán,

BOOK X.

there is none that bears any comparison with the Táj Mahal at Agra, a mausoleum of white marble decorated with mosaics, which, for the richness of the material, the chasteness of the design, and the effect at once brilliant and solemn, is not surpassed by any other edifice, either in Europe or Asia.*

* Táj Mahal is a corruption of Mumtáz Mahal, the name of Sháh Jehán's queen, whose sepulchre it forms. It stands on a marble terrace over the Jamna, is flanked at a moderate distance by two mosques, and is surrounded by extensive gardens. The building itself, on the outside, is of white marble, with a high cupola and four minarets. In the centre of the inside is a lofty hall of a circular form under a dome, in the middle of which is the tomb, inclosed within an open screen of elaborate tracery formed of marble and mosaics. The walls are of white marble, with borders of a running pattern of flowers in mosaic. The graceful flow, the harmonious colours, and, above all, the sparing use of this rich ornament, with the mild lustre of the marble on which it is displayed, form the peculiar charm of the building, and distinguish it from any other in the world. The materials are lapis lazuli, jasper, heliotrope or blood stone, a sort of golden stone (not well understood), with calcedony and other agates, cornelians, jade, and various stones of the same description. "A single flower in the screen," says Mr. Voysey, (*Asiatic Researches*, vol. v. p. 434.) "contains a hundred stones, each cut to the exact shape necessary, and highly polished;" and "yet," says Bishop Heber, "though every thing is finished like an ornament for a drawing-room chimney-piece, the general effect produced is rather solemn and impressive than gaudy." In the minute beauties of execution, however, these flowers are by no means equal to those on tables and other small works in "Pietra Dura" at Florence. It is the taste displayed in the outline and application of this ornament, combined with the lightness and simplicity of the building, which gives it so prodigious an advantage over the gloomy panels of the chapel of the Medici. The mosaics of the Táj are said, with great probability, to be the workmanship of Italians. It is singular that

CHAP. III.

His economy.

All these vast undertakings were managed with so much economy that, after defraying the expenses of his great expeditions to Candahár, his wars in Balkh, and other heavy charges, and maintaining a regular army of 200,000 horse, Sháh Jehán left a treasure, which some reckon at near six, and some at twenty-four millions sterling, in coin, besides his vast accumulations in wrought gold and silver, and in jewels.*

His personal character.

Notwithstanding the unamiable character given of him in his youth, the personal conduct of Sháh Jehán seems to have been blameless when on the throne. His treatment of his people was beneficent and paternal, and his liberal sentiments towards those around him cannot be better shown than by the confidence which (unlike most Eastern princes) he so generously reposed in his sons.

Sháh Jehán had reigned thirty years; he was sixty-seven years old when he was deposed, and seventy-four when he died.

---

artists of that nation should receive lessons of taste from the Indians.

* Bernier says under 6,000,000*l.* (vol. i. p. 305.). Kháfi Khán says 24,000,000*l.*, and he is not likely to exaggerate, for he makes Sháh Jehán's revenue 23,000,000*l.* (only 1,000,000*l.* more than that now collected in the British portion of India), while it is generally reckoned to have been 32,000,000*l.*, and is admitted by Bernier, when depreciating it, to be greater than that of Persia and Turkey put together (vol. i. p. 303.).

BOOK XI.

AURANGZÍB (OR ÁLAMGÍR*).

CHAP. I.

FROM 1658 TO 1662.

BOOK XI.

Sólimán deserted by Jei Sing and Dilír Khán.

Though Aurangzíb's main object was the pursuit of Dárá, he did not fail to attend to the motions of Sólimán, who was marching to his father's aid at the time of the fatal battle. He was a young man of twenty-five, and was assisted in his command by Rája Jei Sing, and accompanied by another general named Dilír Khán. Jei Sing, like the other Rájpút princes, had adhered to Dárá, as well on account of his lawful claims as of his liberal principles in religion; but though he had acted with decision against Shujá, the case was different with Aurangzíb. His inclinations probably favoured that prince, with whom he had served in Balkh, and his interest counselled him against opposition to the actual pos-

* Aurangzíb, on his accession, took the title of A'lamgír, by which he is designated in Indian history and in all regular documents. Europeans, however, as well as some of his own countrymen, still call him Aurangzíb (properly pronounced Ourangzíb).

sessor of the throne. He determined to abandon Sóliman; Dilír Khán took the same resolution; and their defection was aggravated rather than palliated by the paltry pretexts they employed to excuse it. Sólimán, thus deprived of the strength of his army, formed a design of avoiding Aurangzíb by keeping close to the mountains, and thus making his way to join his father at Láhór. Aurangzíb frustrated his project by sending a detachment to Hardwár to intercept him; and this disappointment occasioned the desertion of most of his remaining troops. He next sought refuge in Sirinagar; but the rája refused him an asylum unless he would send away the 500 horse that still adhered to him. After a vain attempt to return to the fort of Allahábád, in which his small band was reduced to 200, he agreed to the rája of Sirinagar's terms, entered his fort with five or six attendants, and, though treated with civility, soon found that he was, in reality, in a sort of confinement.

Flies to Sirinagar, and is made prisoner by the rája.

Aurangzíb marches from Delhi in pursuit of Dárá.

A. D. 1658, July 28.; A. H. 1068, Zí Cáda 7.

Aurangzíb did not wait till the conclusion of these operations. After settling his affairs at Delhi, he continued his march against Dárá. That unfortunate prince, at the commencement of his flight, had halted for a few days at Delhi, where he obtained some treasure, and collected some thousand troops: he then marched rapidly to Láhór, and, finding a large sum of money in the royal treasury, began to raise an army. Before he had made much progress he heard of the advance of Aurangzíb, and soon after, of the near approach of

BOOK XI.

a light detachment sent on in pursuit of him. Sháh Jehán had written to Mohábat Khán (son of the great general), who was viceroy of Cábul; and it is probable that Dárá had been expecting encouragement from him. Besides the troops of the province, Cábul would have afforded a ready refuge, in case of need, among the Afghán tribes, and an easy exit to the territories of the Uzbeks or the Persians; but these views, if entertained, were disconcerted by the prompt measures of Aurangzíb; and Dárá, unable to resist the force that threatened him, left Láhór with 3000 or 4000 horse, and took the road of Multán on his way to Sind.

Dárá flies from Láhór.

Aurangzíb returns to Delhi.

On this, Aurangzíb, who had already crossed the Satlaj, altered his course for Multán. Before he reached that city, he heard that Dárá had proceeded on his flight, and at the same time received intelligence of the advance of his brother Shujá from Bengal. He therefore gave up his march to the westward, and returned without delay to Delhi.

A.D. 1658, from Sept. 30. to Nov. 21.; A.H. 1069, from Moharram 12. to Rabi al Awal 4.

Marches against Shujá, who is advancing from Bengal.

Meanwhile, Shujá had advanced to Benáres with 25,000 horse and a numerous train of artillery; and Aurangzíb, after some stay at Delhi, set out to arrest his progress. They met at Cajwa, half way between Allahábád and Etáya. Shujá was advantageously posted; and, though both drew up their armies, neither was anxious to begin the attack. On the third or fourth day, Aurangzíb was forming his line before daybreak, according to his usual practice, when he was surprised by a prodigious uproar that suddenly arose in his rear. This was

A.D. 1659, Jan. 3.; A.H. 1069. Rabi Second 17.

Treacherous attack on his bag-

occasioned by Rája Jeswant Sing, who, though now serving in his camp, had treacherously attacked his baggage. CHAP. I. gage by Jeswant Sing.

The rája had submitted when Dárá's case became hopeless: he had not been received with the confidence or distinction he expected, and had entered on a correspondence with Shujá, promising to fall upon the baggage at a particular hour, when the prince's army was also to attack in front. Had the co-operation been complete, it must have been entirely successful; for, although Shujá was not at his post in time, it had nearly occasioned the dispersion of his rival's army. The tumult created by the unexpected onset, combined with the darkness and their ignorance of the cause, spread the greatest confusion among the troops who were forming; some left the field, others flew to protect their baggage, and a few went over to the enemy. In the midst of this perturbation, Aurangzíb dismounted and seated himself on a portable throne, from which he issued his directions with a serene and cheerful countenance, sent a party to repel the attack, and took measures for checking the disorder which had already spread so far. In the mean time, Jeswant found that he was not supported; and, expecting to have the whole army turned upon him, was glad to recall his troops from plunder, and to retire to a place out of reach, where he could await in safety the event of the approaching contest.

By this time the sun had risen, and Shujá was

BOOK XI.

seen advancing to the attack. The battle began by a cannonade, soon followed by a close action: Aurangzíb's right was forced back, and his centre, where he was himself, was hard pressed. He was often in imminent danger; and his elephant was charged by another of greater strength, and would have been borne to the ground if the opposite driver had not been shot by one of the king's guards. But he still continued to press upon the enemy's centre, until they at length gave way and fled from the field, leaving 114 pieces of cannon and many elephants to the victor.

Defeat of Shujá.

Aurangzíb sent his son, Prince Mohammed Sultán, in pursuit of Shujá from the field of battle, and some days after dispatched a regular army to support the prince, under the command of Mír Júmla, who, having been released from his mock imprisonment, had joined the army a day or two before the engagement, and acted as second in command on that occasion. Having made these dispositions, he returned to Agra.

A.D. 1659, Jan. 15.; A.H. 1069, Jamádi al Awal 1.

Jeswant Sing threatens Agra and flies to Márwár.

That city, the most vulnerable point of his possessions, had just been exposed to considerable alarm and danger. Jeswant Sing, as soon as he perceived the victory to incline to his enemies, commenced his retreat towards his own country, and unexpectedly presented himself at Agra before the result of the battle was accurately known. He had it in his power to have made an effort for delivering and restoring Sháh Jehán; and it is probable the popular feeling was already strongly inclined in that direction; for Sháista Khán, who was governor, had given himself up to despair, and was on the point of swallowing poison.* He was relieved by the departure of Jeswant; who, considering how much he might lose by pushing things to extremities, pursued his march, and was soon safe among the hills and sands of Jódpúr.

A. D. 1659, Feb. 2.; A.H. 1069, Jamádi al Awal 17.

Aurangzíb, on reaching Agra, dispatched a force of 10,000 men in pursuit of him; and about the same time he received a report from Prince Sultán that the fort of Allahábád had been given up by Shujá's governor, and that Shujá himself had retired to Bengal.

Dárá Shekó appears in Guzerát, and is acknowledged in that province.

These successes were more than counterbalanced by the intelligence he received of the proceedings of Dárá Shekó. By the last accounts, that prince had deposited his baggage at Bakkar on the Indus; and, being forced by the desertion of his men and the death of his carriage cattle to relinquish his design on Sind, he had no means of escaping the detachment in pursuit of him, but by endeavouring to cross the desert to Cach. It now appeared that he had made little stay in that district, that he had entered Guzerát, and had been joined by the governor, Sháh Nawáz Khán (one of whose daughters was married to Morád, and another to Aurangzíb himself), and by *his* powerful assistance had occupied the whole province, including Surat and Baróch. He had opened a negotiation with the kings

* Bernier.

BOOK XI.

He sets out to join Jeswant Sing. Jeswant Sing is won over by Aurangzíb.

of the Deckan; but had turned his immediate attention to a march to Hindostan, and a junction with Jeswant Sing. Amidst the surprise occasioned by this rapid change of circumstances, Aurangzíb did not fail to perceive the increased importance of the Rájpút prince, whose territories extended from Guzerát to Ajmír; and as he never allowed his passions to interfere with his interests, he forgot the perfidy and outrage with which he had just been treated, and set all his usual arts to work to win over his rebellious dependent. He wrote a complimentary letter with his own hand, conceding the rank and titles, his previous refusal of which was the ground of Jeswant's discontent; and at the same time he called in the aid of Jei Sing, to convince his brother rája of the confidence that might be placed in the king's good will, and of the ruin that awaited all who joined the hopeless cause of his rival. These arguments and concessions had their weight with Jeswant; and although Dárá had marched from Ahmedábád, and was arrived within fifty miles of Jódpúr, he sent to apprise him that he felt himself unable to contend alone with the power of Aurangzíb, and could not undertake to join him unless some other of the great Rájpút princes could be prevailed on to embark in the same cause. After repeated attempts to bring back Jeswant to his former views and promises, Dárá was obliged to renounce all hopes of his assistance, and to move with his own forces into the adjoining province of Ajmír. He had

A. D. 1659, Feb. 14.; A. H. 1069. Jamádi al Awal 1.

Abandons Dárá.

assembled an army of 20,000 men in little more than a month after his arrival in Guzerát, and had left that province with a considerable increase of numbers, and with the addition of thirty or forty guns. With this force he took up and fortified a commanding position on the hills near Ajmír.

Dárá is attacked and defeated by Aurangzíb.

Aurangzíb, who marched from Agra as soon as he heard of the proceedings in Guzerát, was now at Jeipúr, and soon arrived in front of Dárá's position. After cannonading for three days with loss to his own army, he ordered a general assault. It was obstinately resisted for many hours, till the death of Sháh Nawáz, who fell just as a party of Aurangzíb's troops had mounted the rampart, so disheartened Dárá, that he fled with precipitation, and his troops dispersed in all directions. Even the body of horse that adhered to his person gradually straggled and fell off, and some even plundered the treasure which he was endeavouring to save from the wreck of his resources.

Disasters of his flight to Guzerát.

He reached the neighbourhood of Ahmedábád after eight days and nights of almost incessant marching, rendered nearly intolerable by the heat and dust of a scorching season. To this were latterly added the merciless attacks of the Cólís in the hills, who hung upon his devoted band, and stripped or massacred every man who fell into the rear. It was in the midst of these calamities that Dárá was met by the celebrated traveller Bernier, who was on his way to Delhi unconscious of what had just been passing. As Dárá's wife was

He is met by Bernier.

wounded, and he had no physician, he obliged Bernier to turn back with him, and they remained together for three days. On the fourth they were within a march of Ahmedábad, where they counted on a secure refuge and on some repose after all their sufferings. They slept that night in a caravanserai, which afforded them protection from the attacks of the Cólís, but was so confined that Bernier was only separated by a canvass screen from the princesses of Dárá's family. About daybreak, when they were preparing for what they thought the last of their distressing marches, news was brought to Dárá that the gates of Ahmedábád were shut against him, and that if he had any regard for his own safety, he would instantly remove from the neighbourhood. These tidings were first made known to Bernier by the cries and lamentations of the women, and soon after Dárá came forth half dead with consternation. The bystanders received him with a blank silence, and Bernier could not refrain from tears when he saw him addressing himself to each of them, down to the meanest soldier, conscious that he was deserted by all the world, and distracted with the thoughts of what would become of himself and his family. Bernier saw him depart with the most melancholy forebodings. He was accompanied by four or five horsemen and two elephants; with these he made his way to Cach, and was there joined by about fifty horse and two hundred matchlockmen, who had accompanied one of his faithful adherents from

Ahmedábád shuts its gates on him.

He flies towards Sind.

Guzerát. The chief of Cach, who had been hearty in his cause when he first entered Guzerát, now received him coldly. He pursued his march towards Candahár, and reached the small territory of Jún, or Juín, on the eastern frontier of Sind. The chief of the place, who seems to have been an Afghán, was under great obligations to Dárá, and received him with every demonstration of attachment, while his only thought was how to betray him to his enemies. Dárá's wife (the daughter of his uncle, Parvíz) died at this place of her fatigues and sufferings; and the prince, with a disregard of circumstances that looks like infatuation, sent a portion of his small escort, with two of his most confidential servants, to attend her remains to Láhór. When the period of mourning permitted he set out on prosecution of his journey to the Indus. The chief of Jún accompanied him for one march, and then returned on some pretext, leaving his brother and a body of troops, as if to attend the prince to the frontier. No sooner was he gone than his brother fell suddenly on Dárá, made him and his son Sepehr Shekó prisoners, and sent to all the king's officers to announce his capture.

He is betrayed by the chief of Jún, and delivered up to Aurangzíb.

The news reached Aurangzíb while he was celebrating the first anniversary of his accession. He concealed the intelligence until it was confirmed beyond doubt, when he ordered public rejoicings, and directed the feast of the accession to be prolonged. It had scarcely expired, when his prisoners arived at the capital. Dárá, by special

It began A. D. 1659, June 6.; A. H. 1069, Rámzán 24.

He is brought to Delhi.

BOOK XI.

A.D. 1659, July 26.; A.H. 1069. Zí Cáad 15.

Sympathy of the people.

orders, was brought in loaded with chains, on a sorry elephant, without housings, and was thus conducted up the most populous streets of the city. The sight awakened a general feeling of compassion and indignation; and Bernier thought an insurrection so probable, that he went into the street armed and prepared for any exigency that might arise; but the sympathy of the people was only shown in tears and groans. Dárá was exposed through all the principal places, and then led off to a prison in old Delhi. The inhabitants were less patient on the next day, when the chief of Jún was recognised on his way to court. A mob immediately assembled, who first assailed him with reproaches and curses; and, growing warmer as their numbers increased, began to throw mud; then tiles and stones; and, at last got to such a pitch of fury, that several lives were lost, and the chief himself would have been torn to pieces if he had not been rescued by the police.

He is put to death.

Next day the leader of the riot was put to death A few days after this tumult, a mock consultation was held with some of the king's counsellors and some learned lawyers, at which Dárá was pronounced worthy of death, as an apostate from the Mahometan religion. Aurangzíb, with seeming reluctance, gave his orders conformably to this opinion, and a personal enemy was selected to carry the sentence into effect. Dárá was, with his son, preparing some lentils, the only food they would touch, for fear of poison, when he saw the executioners, and at once guessed his fate: he snatched up a small knife which he had just been using, and defended himself manfully, until oppressed by numbers. His body was exhibited to the populace on an elephant; his head was cut off and carried to Aurangzíb, who ordered it to be placed on a platter, and to be wiped and washed in his presence. When he had satisfied himself that it was the real head of Dárá, he began to weep, and, with many expressions of sorrow, directed it to be interred in the tomb of Humáyún. Sepehr Shekó was sent away, in confinement, to Gwálíór.*

Operations against Shujá by Prince Sultán and Mír Jumla.

During these transactions, prince Sultán and Mír Jumla were carrying on their operations against Shujá. That prince, on retiring towards Bengal, had taken up a position at Móngír, and had thrown up a strong intrenchment between the hills and

* Almost all the account of Dárá's proceedings is taken from Kháfi Khán. I have seldom used Bernier's delightful narrative, except when he was an eye-witness; for, although he does not differ in the main from the native historian, he introduces many particulars not probable in themselves, and not alluded to by the other. It is true that he must have received his accounts from persons engaged in the transactions, and *that* almost immediately after they had occurred; but such fresh materials have their disadvantages as well as their advantages. Before the subjects have been discussed and examined, each man knows but a fragment of the whole, and to it he adapts the reports he hears from others: the beaten party have always some act of treachery, or some extraordinary accident, with which to excuse their defeat; and all men take a pleasure in discovering secret histories and latent motives, which are soon forgotten unless confirmed by further testimony.

BOOK XI.

the Ganges; but Mír Jumla turned his left flank by a march through the hills, and compelled him to fall back on Ráj Mahal, where, during his long government of Bengal, he had established a sort of capital. The rainy season now set in, which, in that country, puts an end to every sort of movement by land, and Mír Jumla cantoned at some distance from Ráj Mahal. An important event to both parties had taken place before this pause. Prince Sultán had long been discontented with playing the part of a pageant under the authority of Mír Jumla; and his impatience became so ungovernable, that, although he was the eldest son and recognised heir of Aurangzíb, he entered into a correspondence with Shujá, and finally deserted to his camp. Shujá received him with honour, and gave him his daughter in marriage; but, either from disappointed expectations or natural levity of temper, Sultán became as much dissatisfied in his new situation as he had been before; and after taking an active part in the hostilities which recommenced after the rainy season, he again deserted his party, and returned to Mír Jumla's camp.

Prince Sultán goes over to Shujá. A.D. 1659, June; A.H. 1069, Rámzán.

Returns to his allegiance; A.D. 1660, Jan. 27.; A.H. 1070, Jamádi u Sáni 6.;

Aurangzíb, who had at one time determined on a journey to Bengal, had given it up before this news reached him. He showed himself little affected by his son's behaviour: he ordered him to be committed to prison, and kept him in confinement for many years.

and is imprisoned by his father.

From this time Shujá's affairs went progressively

to decay. After a series of unsuccessful struggles, he was compelled to retreat to Dacca; and, Mír Jumla continuing to press him with vigour, he quitted his army, fled with a few attendants, and took refuge with the rája of Aracán. His subsequent story is uncertain. It would appear that the rája took some unfair steps to prevent his leaving Aracán, and that Shujá entered into a plot with the Mussulmans of the country to overturn the rája's government: this much is certain, that Shujá and all his family were cut off, and, though there were many rumours regarding them, were never heard of more.

CHAP. I.

Shujá flies to Aracán. A. D. 1660. April or May; A. H. 1070, Shábán or Rámzán.

Uncertainty regarding his fate.

His ignorance of Shujá's fate left Aurangzíb in some uneasiness for a time; but that, and all his other grounds of anxiety, were removed before the end of the next year. He had attempted, by means of threats, and afterwards by force, to compel the rája of Sirinagar to give up Sóliman Shekó. The rája (whether from avarice, or policy, or sense of honour) withstood all his demands, until he had recourse to Jei Sing, his zealous agent in all negotiations with Hindús. By that chief's persuasion, the rája was, at length, induced to make over Sólimán to the imperial officers, and by them he was conveyed to Delhi.*

Sólimán given up by the rája of Sirinagar. A. D. 1661, Jan. 3.; A. H. 1071, Jamádi al Awal 11.

He was paraded through the city on an elephant, and then brought before the emperor. The chains were taken off his legs, but his hands were still

* Kháfi Khán.

BOOK XI.

secured in gilded fetters. His appearance affected many of the courtiers to tears. Even Aurangzíb put on an appearance of compassion; and when he entreated that, rather than have his strength and reason undermined by drugs (as was thought to be often the fate of captive princes), he might be put to death at once, the emperor addressed him in the mildest accents, and assured him of safety and good treatment.* It was not believed that he kept his word, for Sólimán, his brother Sepehr Shekó, and the young son of Morád, all died in Gwálior within a short space†; while the emperor's own son, Sultán, who was confined in the same fort, lived several years, and was partially restored to freedom.

Morád murdered in his prison.

The atrocious murder of Morád, which took place a few months after Sólimán's imprisonment, justifies the worst suspicions. That unfortunate prince had endeavoured to escape by means of a rope let down from the battlements; but the wailing of a Hindú concubine, of whom he was taking leave, drew the attention of the guard, and led to the discovery of his design. Aurangzíb felt that his own security was incomplete while his brother lived; and, as he had not even the shadow of an offence to allege against him, he instigated the son of a man who had been arbitrarily put to death by the prince while viceroy of Guzerát to complain of him as a murderer; when, after the ceremony of a

* Bernier; who was present at the interview.

† Ibid.

trial, and a legal sentence, the unhappy Morád was executed in his prison.*

CHAP. I.

A. D. 1661, November; A. H. 1072, Rabi u Sáni.

Some time before this period Aurangzíb sent a force against the rája of Bikanír, who had deserted him in the Deckan, and still held out against him. He was reduced to submission by this expedition.

Expedition of Mír Jumla to Assám.

When the quiet of Bengal had been restored by the successes of Mír Jumla, it seems to have been an object with Aurangzíb to find employment for that powerful minister. To that end he engaged him in the conquest of Assám, a rich country lying along the river Baramputer, and shut in on both sides by woody mountains. Mír Jumla marched from Dacca, up the river, conquered the petty principality of Cúch Behár, overran the plain of Assám, and took possession of Ghérgong, the capital. He announced his success with great exultation to the emperor, and boasted of his intention of pursuing his conquests, and opening the way to China. Soon after this the rainy season set in; the whole plain was flooded; the cavalry could not march nor even forage; the natives assembled on all sides, cut off supplies and stragglers, and distressed the camp; and as the rains subsided, a pestilential disorder broke out among the troops; so that when the season opened, Mír Jumla, although he had received reinforcements, was obliged to renounce his magnificent projects, and even required the exertion of his known talents to obtain

A. D. 1652, March 12.; A. H. 1072, Shábán 6.

* Kháfi Khán. Bernier.

BOOK XI.

A.D. 1663, Jan. 6.; A.H. 1073, Jamádi Second 6.

Death of Mír Jumla.

A.D. 1663, March 31., A.H. 1073, Rámzán 2.

such contributions and cessions from the rája as might save his honour from the appearance of a defeat. When he had accomplished this object he withdrew his army; but died before he reached Dacca, worn out with the fatigues and sufferings which, though at a very advanced age, he had encountered equally with the humblest soldier.* The emperor immediately raised his son Mohammed Amín to the high rank and honours which had been possessed by the deceased.

Dangerous illness of Aurangzíb.

The death of this powerful subject seemed to relieve Aurangzíb from every ground for jealousy or apprehension; but he had recently received a severe warning of the precarious terms on which he still held his life and empire. Soon after the fifth anniversary of his accession he was seized with a violent illness, which at first threatened his immediate death, and afterwards left him in a state of extreme bodily weakness, and almost entirely deprived of the use of speech. This unexpected calamity shook his newly established government to its foundations.

Intrigues and agitation.

Reports were current that Rája Jeswant was in full march to release Sháh Jehán, and that Mohábat Khán was coming from Cábul with the same intention. The partisans of the deposed monarch began to intrigue at the capital; while two parties were formed among the emperor's own adherents; one anxious to secure the succession to his second son, Moazzim; and the other, to

* Kháfi Khán. Bernier.

raise his third son, Akber, to the throne. These dangers were averted by the constancy and force of mind of Aurangzíb himself. On the fifth day of his illness, though scarcely rescued from the jaws of death, he caused himself to be raised up, and received the homage of his principal courtiers; and on a subsequent day, when his having a fainting fit had led to a general report that he was dead, he summoned two or three of the greatest nobles to his bed side; and although not yet recovered from the paralysis which had affected his tongue, he wrote an order, in their presence, to his sister Roushanárá to send his great seal, which had been entrusted to her, and placed it near himself, that no use might be made of it without his special orders. The respect and admiration inspired by his conduct on these occasions had as much effect in suppressing disturbances as the prospect they afforded of his recovery.*

Firmness and self-possession of Aurangzíb.

As soon as he was able to travel he set off for Cashmír, where he hoped to regain his strength sooner than at any place in the plains.†

His recovery. A.D. 1662, Dec. 6.

While Aurangzíb was seeking repose in the north, a scene was opening in the Deckan with which his thoughts were soon to be fully employed.

Disturbances in the Deckan.

The Maratta race, it will be remembered, inhabits the country lying between the range of mountains which stretches along the south of the

Description of the Maratta country.

* Bernier. Kháfi Khán merely mentions a dangerous illness.

† Bernier.

BOOK XI.

Nerbadda, parallel to the Vindya chain; and a line drawn from Goa, on the sea coast, through Bidr to Chánda, on the Warda. That river is its boundary on the east, as the sea is on the west.

The great feature of the country is the range of Siádri, more commonly called the Gháts, which runs along the western part of it, thirty or forty miles from the sea; and, though only from 3000 to 5000 feet high, is made very remarkable by its own peculiarities, and by the difference between the tracts which it divides. On the west it rises abruptly nearly from the level of the sea, and, on that side, presents an almost inaccessible barrier; but, on the east, it supports a table land 1500 or 2000 feet high, extending eastward with a gradual slope, far beyond the Maratta limits, to the Bay of Bengal.

The strip of land between the Gháts and the sea is called the Cóncan, and is, in general, very rugged. Towards the coast are small rich plains producing rice; the rest is almost impervious from rocks and forests, cut by numerous torrents, which change, when near the sea, into muddy creeks, among thickets of mangrove.* The summits of the ridge itself are bare rocks; its sides are thickly covered with tall trees mixed with underwood. The forest spreads over the contiguous part of the table land to the east, a tract broken by deep

* The native legends relate that the sea once washed the foot of the Gháts, and that the Concan was rescued from it by a miracle of one of the gods.

winding valleys and ravines, forming fit haunts for the wild beasts with which the range is peopled. Fifteen or twenty miles from the ridge, the valleys become wide and fertile, and, by degrees, are lost in open plains, which stretch away to the eastward, covered with cultivation, but bare of trees, and rarely crossed by ranges of moderate hills. The great chain of the Gháts receives the whole fury of the south-west monsoon, the force of which is thus broken before it reaches the plains. For several months the high points are wrapped in clouds, and beaten by rains and tempests. The moisture soon runs off from the upper tracts, but renders the Cóncan damp and insalubrious throughout the year.

The greatest of the inferior branches of hills which run east from the Gháts, is that called the range of Chándór, from one of the forts constructed on its summits. It separates the low basin of the Tápti from that of the Godáveri, on the table land. The basin of the Tápti is composed of Candésh and Berár, fertile plains, only separated from Guzerát by the forest tract of Báglána, and differing, in many respects, from the high country, which is more peculiarly that of the Marattas.

The whole of the Gháts and neighbouring mountains often terminate towards the top in a wall of smooth rock, the highest points of which, as well as detached portions on insulated hills, form natural fortresses, where the only labour required is to get access to the level space, which generally lies on the summit. Various princes, at different times, have profited by these positions. They have cut flights of steps or winding roads up the rocks, fortified the entrance with a succession of gateways, and erected towers to command the approaches; and thus studded the whole of the region about the Gháts and their branches with forts, which, but for frequent experience, would be deemed impregnable.

Account of the nation.

Though the Marattas had never appeared in history as a nation, they had as strongly marked a character as if they had always formed a united commonwealth. Though more like to the lower orders in Hindostan than to their southern neighbours in Cánara and Télingána, they could never, for a moment, be confounded with either.

They are small sturdy men, well made, though not handsome. They are all active, laborious, hardy, and persevering. If they have none of the pride and dignity of the Rájpúts, they have none of their indolence or their want of worldly wisdom. A Rájpút warrior, as long as he does not dishonour his race, seems almost indifferent to the result of any contest he is engaged in. A Maratta thinks of nothing *but* the result, and cares little for the means, if he can attain his object. For this purpose he will strain his wits, renounce his pleasures, and hazard his person; but he has not a conception of sacrificing his life, or even his interest, for a point of honour. This difference of sentiment affects the outward appearance of the two nations: there is something noble in the carriage even of an ordinary Rájpút; and something vulgar in that of the most distinguished Maratta.

The Rájpút is the most worthy antagonist; the Maratta the most formidable enemy; for he will not fail in boldness and enterprise when they are indispensable, and will always support them, or supply their place by stratagem, activity, and perseverance. All this applies chiefly to the soldiery, to whom more bad qualities might fairly be ascribed. The mere husbandmen are sober, frugal, and industrious; and, though they have a dash of the national cunning, are neither turbulent nor insincere.

Their chiefs, in those days, were men of families who had for generations filled the old Hindú offices of heads of villages or functionaries of districts *, and had often been employed as partisans under the governments of Ahmednagar and Bíjapúr. They were all Súdras, of the same cast with their people; though some tried to raise their consequence by claiming an infusion of Rájpút blood.

The early Mahometan writers do not seem to have been aware of the existence of the Marattas. We can perceive, by the surnames of some chiefs whom they mention, that they must have belonged to that race; but the word Maratta first occurs in Ferishta, in the transactions of the year A.D. 1485; and is not then applied in a general sense. It has

* Patéls, désmukhs, déspándís, &c. &c. See Vol. I. pp. 120. and 485.

BOOK XI.

been mentioned that, in the middle of the sixteenth century, the king of Bíjapúr adopted the Maratta language, instead of Persian, for his financial papers; and, as he was substituting natives of the Deckan for foreigners in his armies, he enlisted a considerable number of Marattas among them. They were at first chiefly employed in the lowest military capacity, that of garrisoning forts: by degrees their aptitude for service as light cavalry was discovered, and they began to obtain military rank under the governments of Bíjapúr and Ahmednagar: while individuals were also engaged in the service of the Kutb Sháh, king of Golcónda. Still they are very little mentioned by the Mussulman writers, until the beginning of the seventeenth century. In the time of Malik Amber they emerge into notice, and thenceforward occupy a conspicuous part in the history of the Deckan.*

Rise of the Bólsa family.

Among the officers of Malik Amber was a person named Málojí, of a respectable, though not a considerable, family, the surname of which was Bósla. He served with a few men mounted on his own horses, and was especially dependent on the protection of Jádu Ráo.

If any Maratta had a claim to Rájpút descent, it was the family of Jádu. The name is that of one of the Rájpút tribes: it was borne at the first Mahometan invasion by the rája of Deógíri, the greatest prince in the Deckan; and it is not im-

* Grant Duff, vol. i. p. 73—96.

probable that the protector of Málojí (who was désmukh of a district not far from Deógíri, may have been descended from that stock. Whatever was his origin, Lúkjí Jádu Ráo had attained to a command of 10,000 men, under Malik Amber, and was a person of such consequence, that his desertion to Sháh Jehán turned the fate of a war against his former master.

It was long before this defection that Málojí Bósla attended a great Hindú festival at the house of Jádu, accompanied by his son, Shájí, a boy of five years old. During the merriment natural to such an occasion Jádu Ráo took young Sháhjí and his own daughter, a girl of three years old, on his knees, and said, laughing, "that they were a fine couple, and ought to be man and wife." To his surprise, Málojí instantly started up, and called on the company to witness that the daughter of Jádu was affianced to his son. It did not require the pride of birth to raise Jádu's indignation at the advantage taken of him; and the consequence was, a rupture between him and his dependant. But Málojí was by this time on the road to fortune: he acquired a considerable sum of money, increased his party, and, being an active partisan, rose at last to a command of 5000 horse in the service of Ahmednagar, and to the possession of a large jágír, of which the chief place was Púna. He had still kept up his son's claim to the daughter of Jádu Ráo, which, in his present prosperity, was no longer looked on as so unreasonable; and Jádu Ráo at last consenting, his daughter was regularly married to Sháhjí. One of the fruits of this union was Sévají, the founder of the Maratta empire.*

Sháhji Bósla.

Sháhjí has already been mentioned as a great actor in the last events of the kingdom of Ahmednagar.† He then entered the service of Bíjapúr, and was continued in his jágír, which had fallen to that state in the partition of the Ahmednagar territory. He was afterwards employed on conquests to the southward, and obtained a much more considerable jágír in the Mysore country, including the towns of Síra and Bangalór.

Sévaji Bósla.

As all Maratta chiefs were wholly illiterate, their affairs were managed by Bramins, who formed a numerous class of men of business, even under the Mahometans. A person of that cast, therefore, whose name was Dádají Cóndu, was left in charge of the jágír at Púna, and to him was committed the care of the chief's second son, Sévají; the elder accompanying his father to the Mysore. The education of a young Maratta consisted in horsemanship, hunting, and military exercises; and, as Púna is situated at the junction of the hilly country with the plains, Sévají's principal associates were the soldiery belonging to his father's horse, or the plundering highlanders of the neighbouring Gháts. From such companions he imbibed an early love of adventure, which was increased by his fondness for listening to the ballads of his country. By the

* He was born in May, 1627 (Grant Duff, vol. i. p. 122.).

† A. D. 1636. See p. 363.

time he was sixteen he began to be beyond the control of Dádají, by whom he had been admitted to a share in the management of the jágír; and though he was generally popular for his conciliating manners, he was already suspected of sharing in several extensive gang robberies committed in the Cóncan. Those practices and his hunting excursions made him familiar with every path and defile throughout the Gháts; and he was, before, well acquainted with their wild inhabitants. Those in the parts of the range north of Púna were Bhíls and Cólís *, and those to the south, Rámúsís; but immediately to the west of Púna were Marattas, who had long braved the dangers and hardships of that uncultivated region, and who were called Máwalis, from the appellation of the valleys where they resided. It was from among these last that Sévají chose his earliest adherents; and, as he was remarkably quick and observing, he soon perceived a way of employing them on higher objects than he had yet been engaged with.

His robberies.

His adherents.

The hill forts belonging to Bíjapúr were generally much neglected; being remote and unhealthy, they were sometimes occupied by a single Mahometan officer, with a small garrison of ill-paid local troops; at other times they were left in charge of the nearest désmúkh, or other revenue officer. Among those in the last predicament was Tórna, a strong fort, twenty miles south west of Púna.

He surprises a hill fort.

* Hill tribes. See Vol. I. p. 374.

BOOK XI.

A.D. 1646.

Of this place Sévají contrived to get possession*, and succeeded, by a proper application of arguments and money, in convincing the court of Bíjapúr that it was better in his hands than in those of the désmúkh. But on his afterwards fortifying a neighbouring hill, the attention of the government was seriously drawn to him, and remonstrances were addressed to Sháhjí on his son's proceedings. Sháhjí made the best excuse he could, and wrote in strong terms to Dádají and Sévají to forbid their attempting any further encroachments. The Bramin used all his endeavours to persuade his young chief to attend to these injunctions; but he did not long survive the receipt of them, and Sévají, when freed from his control, pursued his enterprises with more audacity than before. He withheld the revenue of the jágír which was due to Sháhjí; and as there were two forts within it (Chákan and Súpa), held by officers immediately under his father, he gained over the first and surprised the second; and being now master within his own jágír, he proceeded to more extensive undertakings. He bribed the Mahometan governor to surrender Condána, or Singhar, a stong hill fort near Púna: and, by taking advantage of a dispute between two Bramin brothers, friends of his own, who were contesting the command of the still stronger hill fort of Purandar, he introduced a body of Máwalis into the place, and treacherously took possession of it for himself.†

He usurps his father's jágír.

Obtains possession of several forts.

A.D. 1647.

* Grant Duff, vol. i. p. 131.

† Grant Duff.

As all these acquisitions were made without bloodshed, and without disturbing the neighbouring districts, they called forth no exertion on the part of the king of Bíjapúr, who was at this time occupied with conquests to the southward, and with the magnificent buildings which he was erecting at his capital.*

Revolts against the government of Bíjapúr. A. D. 1648.

But the time was come when Sévají's own views required that he should throw off the mask.† The signal of open rebellion was the plunder of a convoy of royal treasure in the Cóncan; and before the court recovered its surprise at this outrage, it heard that five of the principal hill forts in the Gháts had fallen into the hands of Sévají. Almost immediately after this, a Bramin officer of his surprised and made prisoner the Mahometan governor of the northern Cóncan, and not only took possession of Calián, where he resided, but occupied the whole of his province, and compelled him to give orders for the surrender of all his forts. Sévají was transported with this success. He received the governor with respect, and dismissed him with

Takes possession of the northern Concan.

* "Thus did Sévají obtain possession of the tract between Chacun and the Neera, and the manner in which he established himself, watching and crouching like the wily tiger of his own mountain valleys, until he had stolen into a situation from whence he could at once spring on his prey, accounts both for the difficulty found in tracing his early rise, and the astonishing rapidity with which he extended his power, when his progress had attracted notice, and longer concealment was impossible." (Grant Duff; of whose clear and animated account of Sévají that inserted in the text is a mere abstract.)

† Grant Duff.

BOOK XI.

His attachment to the Hindú religion.

honour. His first care in his conquest was, to restore Hindú endowments, and revive old institutions. He had been brought up in a strong Hindú feeling, which, perhaps, was, at first, as much national as religious; and out of this sprung up a rooted hatred to the Mussulmans, and an increasing attachment to his own superstitions. This inclination fell so well in with his policy, that he began to affect peculiar piety, and to lay claim to prophetic dreams, and other manifestations of the favour of the gods.

The government of Bíjapúr seize Sháhjí as a hostage for his son.

The court of Bíjapúr, when at length awakened to Sévají's designs, was still misled by the belief that he was instigated by his father. They therefore dissembled their displeasure until they had an opportunity of making Sháhjí prisoner. His seizure was effected under pretence of a friendly entertainment by a chief of the family of Górpara, on whom Sévají afterwards most amply revenged his
A. D. 1649. treachery.* Sháhjí's assurances that he was innocent of his son's transgressions received little credit from the court of Bíjapúr; and, after being allowed a reasonable time to put a stop to the insurrection, he was thrown into a dungeon, and told that the entrance would be built up after a certain period, unless Sévají should make his submission in the interval. Sévají was seriously alarmed by this threat; but reflection convinced him that submission was not the way to gain safety from so

* Grant Duff.

treacherous an enemy. He held out as before, and made overtures to Sháh Jehán, whose territories he had carefully abstained from injuring. The emperor received his application favourably, took him into his service, and appointed him to the rank of a commander of 5000. It was probably owing to *his* powerful interposition that Sháhjí was released from his dungeon, although he remained for four years a prisoner at large in Bíjapúr. Tranquillity prevailed during this interval, Sévají being restrained by fears for his father, and the government of Bíjapúr by the apprehension that Sévají might call in the Moguls.

A. D. 1649 to 1653.

Sháhjí released.

At the end of that time the disorders in Carnáta rendered Sháhjí's presence necessary to the interests of the government. His own jágír had been overrun, and his eldest son killed, while all the surrounding country was in arms, and threatened the speedy expulsion of the Bíjapúr authorities.

Renewal of Sévají's encroachments.

No sooner was his father released and the attention of the Bíjapúr government turned to the affairs of Carnáta, than Sévají began with fresh activity to renew his plans of aggrandizement. The whole of the hilly country south of Púna, from the Gháts inclusive to the upper Kishna, was in the hands of a Hindú rája, whom Sévají could never prevail on to join in his rebellion. He now procured his assassination, and profited by the consternation which ensued to seize on his territory. After this atrocity he surprised some hill forts and built others,

BOOK XI.

and went on extending his authority until Prince Aurangzíb was sent down to the Deckan in 1655. Sévají at first addressed the prince as a servant of the Mogul government, and obtained a confirmation of his possessions from the imperial authority. But when he found Aurangzíb engaged in war with the king of Golcónda, and fancied he saw the prospect of long troubles, he determined to profit by the confusion at the expense of all the combatants, and for the first time invaded the Mogul territories. He surprised the town of Junér, and carried off a large booty; and afterwards attempted the same operation at Ahmednagar, where he met with only partial success. The rapid conquests of Aurangzíb disappointed all his hopes; and, during the prince's operations against Bíjapúr, he endeavoured, by every sort of excuse and promise, to obtain forgiveness for his rash attack. When the sickness of Sháh Jehán called off Aurangzíb to Delhi, Sévají continued to profess his devotion, and offered his zealous services, provided attention were paid to some claims he pretended to possess within the Mogul territory. The prince readily granted him forgiveness on his engaging to send a body of horse to the army, but endeavoured to reserve the question of his claims for future inquiry; and Sévají, who was as artful as himself, in like manner suspended the dispatch of his horse, and confined his services to promises and professions.

Plunders the Mogul provinces.

Obtains forgiveness from Aurangzíb. A.D. 1658.

He now renewed his attacks on Bíjapúr (where the king had been succeeded by his son, a minor);

Afzal Khán sent against him from Bíjapúr.

and the regency, at length aware of the danger of neglecting his advances to power, dispatched a large army against him. The commander was Afzal Khán, who to the usual arrogance of a Mahometan noble joined an especial contempt for his present enemy. But that enemy knew well how to turn his presumption to account: he affected to be awed by the reputation of Afzal Khán, and to give up all hopes of resisting his arms. He sent humble offers of submission to the khán, who deputed a Bramin high in his confidence to complete the negotiation. This man Sévají won over, and by his assistance Afzal Khán was easily persuaded that Sévají was in a state of great alarm, and was only prevented surrendering by his apprehension of the consequences. During these negotiations Afzal advanced through intricate and woody valleys to the neighbourhood of the hill fort of Partábghar, where Sévají was residing, and the Maratta consented to receive his assurances of forgiveness at a personal interview, if the khán would concede so much to his fears as to come unattended for the purpose of meeting him. Afzal Khán on this quitted his army, and went forward with an escort, which he was afterwards persuaded to leave behind and advance with a single attendant. He was dressed in a thin muslin robe, and carried a straight sword, more for state than any expectation of being required to use it. During this time Sévají was seen slowly descending from the fort: he advanced with a timid and hesitating air, accompanied by

BOOK XI.

one attendant, and to all appearance entirely unarmed; but under his cotton tunic he wore a shirt of chain armour, and besides a concealed dagger, he was armed with sharp hooks of steel, which are fastened on the fingers, but lie concealed in the closed hand, and are known by the descriptive name of "tiger's claws." The khán looked with contempt on the diminutive figure which came crouching on to perform the usual ceremonies of meeting; but at the moment of the embrace, Sévají struck his claws into his unsuspecting adversary, and, before he could recover from his astonishment, dispatched him with his dagger. He had, before this, drawn his troops from all quarters by secret paths into the woods round Afzal's army; and, on a signal from the fort, they rushed at once on the Mussulmans, who were reposing in insolent security, and slaughtered and dispersed them almost without resistance.* As soon as the victory was secure, Sévají issued orders to spare the fugitives: vast numbers fell into the hands of the conqueror, after wandering in the woods until subdued by hunger. They were all treated with humanity: many of them who were Marattas entered into Sévají's service, and a chief of that nation, who refused to forfeit his allegiance, was dismissed with presents. During his whole career, Sévají, though he inflicted death and torture to force confessions of concealed treasure, was never personally guilty of any *useless* cruelty.

Is assassinated by Sévají,

and his army dispersed.

A.D. 1659, October.

* Grant Duff.

CHAP. I.

This victory gave a fresh impulse to Sévají's progress. He overran all the country near the Gháts, and took possession of all the hill forts, and was going on to complete the reduction of the Concan, when he was recalled by the march from Bíjapúr of an army much more formidable than the first. He threw part of his troops into forts, and employed the rest to cut off the enemy's supplies*; but he allowed himself to be shut up in the almost inaccessible fort of Panála, and would have been compelled to surrender after a siege of four months, if he had not contrived, with his usual mixture of boldness and dexterity, to quit the place during a dark night, after he had amused the besiegers with the prospect of a capitulation. His escape was ascribed at Bíjapúr to treachery in their general, Sídí Jóhar, an Abyssinian, whose indignation was excited by this calumny, and added to the elements of discord already abundant at Bíjapúr.

Another army sent from Bíjapúr.

A. D. 1660, May.

The king now took the field in person, and brought such a force along with him as Sévají was unable to resist. His operations during the whole of this invasion were desultory and ill-directed; and before the end of a year he found himself stripped of almost all his conquests. The king of Bíjapúr's affairs now obliged him to turn his attention to Carnáta, where his presence was further required by the revolt of Sídí Jóhar. He was employed in that country for two whole years, during

The king of Bíjapúr takes the field.

A. D. 1661 January.

Recovers most of Sévají's conquests.

A. D. 1662.

* Grant Duff.

BOOK XI.

which Sévají recovered and increased his territories.

Sévají makes a very favourable peace.

Extent of his territory.

At the end of that time a peace was mediated by Sháhjí; and Sévají remained in possession of a territory including upwards of 250 miles of the country on the sea (being the part of the Concan between Goa and Calián), while above the Gháts its length was more than 150 miles from the north of Púna to the south of Mirich on the Kishna. Its breadth, from east to west, was, at the widest part, 100 miles. In this small territory the hardiness

A. D. 1662.

and predatory habits of his soldiers enabled him to maintain an army of 7000 horse and 50,000 foot.*

* Grant Duff.

CHAP. II.

FROM 1662 TO 1681.

CHAP. II.

Sévají's rupture with the Moguls. About the end of A. D. 1662, A. H. 1073.

It was about this period that Aurangzíb was attacked by the violent sickness which exposed his life to so much danger.* He had previously appointed his maternal uncle, Sháista Khán, to the viceroyalty of the Deckan, and that officer was now residing at Aurangábád.

It does not appear what led to an open rupture between Sévají and the Moguls; but soon after the peace with Bíjapúr we find Sévají's horse ravaging their country nearly to Aurangábád, and himself taking their forts in the neighbourhood of Junér.

Sháista Khán marches against him. Occupies Púna.

To put an end to these aggressions, Sháista Khán marched from Aurangábád, drove Sévají's army out of the field, took the fort of Chákan, and finally took up his ground at Púna, within twelve miles of Singhar, the hill fort into which Sévají had retired. At Púna, Sháista occupied the house in which Sévají had passed his early days; and it was probably the local knowledge thus acquired that suggested a plan for chastising the intruder. The khán had taken every precaution to guard against the advance of troops, and also against the admis-

Night exploit of Sévají.

* See p. 416.

BOOK XI.

sion of Marattas individually into the town; and in these circumstances, and with his troops cantoned around him, he thought himself as secure as if he were in a peaceful country. But Sévají, who was well aware of all that was passing, left Singhar one evening after dark, and, posting small bodies of infantry on the road to support him, went on with twenty-five Máwalís to the town. He gained admission by joining a marriage procession, with the conductor of which he had a previous concert. Being now within the line of guards, he proceeded direct to the house, and entered by a back door before any person within had a suspicion of danger. So completely was Sháista Khán surprised, that he had barely time to escape from his bedchamber, and received a blow from a sword which cut off two of his fingers as he was letting himself down from a window into the court below. His son and most of his attendants were cut to pieces in a moment. Sévají's retreat was as rapid as his attack: he was joined by his parties on the road as he retired, and ascended to Singhar amidst a blaze of torches, which made his triumph visible from every part of the Mogul camp. This exploit, so congenial to the disposition of his countrymen, is the one of all his actions of which the Marattas still speak with the greatest exultation. It was attended with consequences that could scarcely have been foreseen; for Sháista Khán imputed his danger to treachery on the part of Rája Jeswant Sing, who had, not long before, been sent to reinforce him; and the dissensions of the leaders crippled the army, until Aurangzíb removed Sháista Khán to the government of Bengal, and sent his son, Prince Moazzim, to command, with the assistance of Jeswant Sing. Before the prince's arrival, Jeswant had withdrawn to Aurangábád, after an attempt to reduce Singhar; and Sévají was preparing to take a full retaliation for the attack he had been exposed to. During his operations in the mountains, his chief force was in his infantry; but the Marattas had been distinguished in the Bíjapúr armies for their services as light cavalry, and it was in this shape that Sévají now resolved to employ them. After gaining intelligence of the state of affairs where he was going, and deceiving his enemies by various feigned movements, he suddenly set off with 4000 horse, and came at once on the rich and defenceless city of Surat, in a part of the country which was thought to be beyond the reach of his arms. He plundered it at leisure for six days; and though beaten off from the English and Dutch factories, where some of the native merchants had also taken refuge, he carried off an ample booty, and lodged it in safety in his fort of Réri, or Ráighar, in the Concan.

Prince Moazzim sent against him.

Sévají plunders Surat.

A. D. 1664, Jan. 5.; A. H. 1074, Jamádi Second 15.

It was soon after this expedition that Sévají heard of the death of Sháhjí. Although of a great age, he was killed by a fall in hunting. He had restored his jágír to perfect order, and had extended his conquests to the southward (under the name of the king of Bíjapúr), until they compre-

Death of Sháhjí.

His possessions in the south of India.

BOOK XI.

hended the country near Madras and the principality of Tanjore.

Maritime exploits of Sévají.

Sévají was now again at war with Bíjapúr, and chiefly carried on his operations in the Concan, where he had established his capital at Ráighar. He collected a fleet, took many Mogul ships, and on one occasion embarked with a force of 4000 men on 87 vessels, and, landing at a remote point in the province of Canara, sacked Barcelór, a wealthy sea-port belonging to Bíjapúr, and plundered all the adjoining tract, where there was not the slightest apprehension of a visit from such an enemy. Nor did he, during these employments, leave the country quiet above the Gháts: he sent troops to ravage the territory of Bíjapúr, and led, in person, a destructive inroad into the Mogul dominions. This injury did not exasperate Aurangzíb so much as the capture of some vessels conveying pilgrims to Mecca, and the violation of Surat, which derives a sort of sanctity from being the place of embarkation for those devotees. Sévají had added another provocation to these offences: soon after his father's death, he had assumed the title of rája, and began to coin money, one of the most decisive marks of independent sovereignty. A large army was therefore sent to the Deckan, at the head of which was Rája Jei Sing, the constant engine in all difficult affairs with Hindús; but the emperor's suspicious temper made him still adhere to the system of divided authority, and Dilír Khán was associated on equal terms in the command. These appoint-

A. D. 1665, February.

Sévají assumes sovereignty.

Rája Jei Sing sent against him.

ments superseded Jeswant Sing and Prince Móazzim, who returned to Delhi. As Aurangzíb anticipated little opposition from Sévají, Jei Sing had orders, as soon as he should have reduced the Maratta, to employ his arms in the conquest of Bíjapúr.

Submission of Sévají.

A. D. 1665.

These chiefs crossed the Nerbadda in February, and advanced unopposed to Púna, when Jei Sing undertook the siege of Singhar, and Dilír Khán that of Purandar. Both places held out; but Sévají seems himself to have despaired of successful resistance; and he may, perhaps, have looked to some recompence for the temporary sacrifice of his pride, in the advantages he might gain by cooperating with the Moguls against Bíjapúr. He opened a negotiation with Jei Sing; and, after receiving assurances, not only of safety, but of favour, from the emperor, he privately withdrew himself from his own army, and went, with a few attendants, to the rája's camp. He was received with great distinction, and on his part made the humblest professions of fidelity. An agreement was concluded, by which Sévají was to give up twenty out of the thirty-two forts he possessed, together with the territory attached to them. The remaining twelve forts, with their territory and all his other possessions, he was to hold as a jágír from the Mogul emperor, in whose service his son Sambají, a boy of five years old, was to receive the rank of a commander of 5000. In addition to these advantages, Sévají was to be entitled to a sort of

BOOK XI.

per centage on the revenue of each district under Bíjapúr; and this grant was the foundation of the ill-defined claims of the Marattas, which afforded them such constant pretexts for encroachment on foreign territories in later times. These terms, except the last (which was not noticed), were distinctly confirmed in a letter from Aurangzíb to Sévají. He now joined the imperial army with 2000 horse and 8000 infantry; and the whole body commenced its march on an invasion of Bíjapúr.

He co-operates with Jei Sing against Bíjapúr.

The Marattas distinguished themselves in this campaign, and Sévají was gratified by two letters from Aurangzíb; one complimenting him on his services, and the other containing great but general promises of advancement, and inviting him to court, with a promise that he should be allowed to return to the Deckan. Won by these attentions, and by the cordiality with which he was treated by Jei Sing, Sévají made over his jágír to three of his chief dependents, and set off for Delhi, accompanied by his son Sambají, and escorted by 500 chosen horse and 1000 Máwalis.

Goes to Delhi.

Haughty reception by Aurangzíb.

Aurangzíb had now an opportunity of uniting Sévají's interests to his own by liberal treatment, and of turning a formidable enemy into a zealous servant, as had been done before with so many other Hindú princes: but his views in politics were as narrow as in religion; and, although he could easily suppress his feelings to gain any immediate advantage, he was incapable of laying aside his prejudices, or making such full and free concessions, as might secure permanent attachment. Moreover, he despised as well as disliked Sévají: he felt the insults offered to his religion and his dignity the more, because they came from so ignoble a hand; and he so far mistook the person he had to deal with as to think he would be most easily managed by making him sensible of his own insignificance.

Accordingly, when Sévají was about to enter Delhi, an officer of inferior rank was sent, on the emperor's part, along with Rám Sing, the son of Jei Sing, who went out to meet him; and his reception, when he came to court, was conducted in the same spirit. Sévají performed his obeisance, and presented his offerings, in the most respectful manner, and probably intended to have made his way, as usual, by suppleness and humility; but when he found he was received without notice, and placed, undistinguished, among the officers of the third rank*, he was unable any longer to control his feelings of shame and indignation; he changed colour, and, stepping back behind the line of courtiers, sank to the ground in a swoon. When he came to himself, he reproached Rám Sing with the breach of his father's promises, and called on the government to take his life, as it had already deprived him of his honour. He then retired, without taking leave, or receiving the honorary dress usual on such occasions.† Aurangzíb was

* Commanders of 5000, the station which had been promised to his infant son.

† Kháfi Khán.

BOOK XI.

not prepared for this decided conduct; he ordered Sévají's motions to be watched, while he professed to wait for a report from Jei Sing as to the promises he had really made to him.

From this time, Sévají's whole thoughts were turned to the means of making his escape, which was soon rendered more difficult by guards being posted round his residence. He applied for leave to send back his escort, with whom he said the climate of Delhi did not agree; and, as this arrangement seemed to leave him more than ever in the power of the government, it was willingly agreed to. He next took to his bed on pretence of sickness, gained over some of the Hindú physicians who were allowed to attend him, and by their means established a communication with his friends without. He also made a practice of sending presents of sweetmeats and provisions to be distributed among fakírs and other holy men, Mahometan as well as Hindú; and thus accustomed his guards to the passage of the large baskets and hampers in which those donations were conveyed.

Sévají escapes from confinement.

At length, one evening, when he had concerted his measures with those without, he concealed himself in one of the hampers, and his son in another, and was carried out unquestioned through the midst of the sentinels. His bed was occupied by a servant; and a long time elapsed before his escape was suspected. In the mean time, he repaired to an obscure spot, where he had a horse posted, mounted it with his son behind him, and made the best of his way to Mattra. At this place were some of his chosen companions in assumed characters; and he himself put on the dress of a Hindú religious mendicant, shaving off his hair and whiskers, and rubbing over his face with ashes. In this disguise he pursued his journey by the least suspected roads, to the Deckan, leaving his son at Mattra in charge of a Maratta Bramin.

Arrives at Ráighar.

It must have required much address to elude his pursuers, who had a long time to be prepared for him before he made good his retreat to Ráighar. He reached that place on his return, nine months after his departure for Delhi.*

A. D. 1666, December.

Death of Sháh Jehán.

A. D. 1666, December; A. H. 1076, Rejeb.

Soon after Sévají's flight died Sháh Jehán. Though always confined to the citadel of Agra, he had been treated with great respect, and allowed an ample establishment and complete authority within the palace. He carried this control so far as to prevent the removal of Dárá's daughter, whom Aurangzíb wished to marry to a son of his own; and also to withhold some valuable crown jewels which the emperor was anxious to possess: on these subjects, several letters of remonstrance and expostulation passed between him and his son.

Prosperous state of Aurangzíb's empire.

This was the most prosperous period of the reign of Aurangzíb. Every part of his own dominions was in the enjoyment of perfect tranquillity. His governor of Cashmír had just brought Little Tibet

* The English factors at Carwar, in the Concan, write, September 29th, "*If it be true* that Sévají has escaped, Aurangzíb will quickly hear of him to his sorrow."

BOOK XI.

under his authority; and his viceroy of Bengal made an acquisition of more real value in the fine country of Chittagong, on the eastern shore of the Bay of Bengal.

He had also received marks of respect from most of the neighbouring powers. The sheríf of Mecca, and several other princes of Arabia, sent embassies; as did the king of Abyssinia, and the khán of the Uzbeks. The most important came from the king of Persia, and was returned by an embassy of unusual splendour. But this last interchange of missions did not lead to permanent friendship; for some questions of etiquette arose between the monarchs, which led to so much irritation on the part of Sháh Abbás II., that he assembled an army in the neighbourhood of Candahár; and Aurangzíb was thinking seriously of moving in person against him, when he heard of the sháh's death, and the discontinuance of all his preparations.

Failure of Jei Sing's attack on Bíjapúr.

The only exception to the general prosperity of the empire was the ill success of its army in the territory of Bíjapúr. Jei Sing's operations in that country had at first gone on to his wish; but as soon as he had formed the siege of the capital, the old plan of defence was adopted against him: the surrounding country was reduced to a desert, and all his supplies were cut off by plundering horse. The king of Golcónda also secretly assisted his neighbour; and Jei Sing, perceiving that he had no chance of success, retreated, not without loss and difficulty, to Aurangábád. He was removed after this failure, and died on his way to Delhi. Prince Móazzim was sent to replace him, with Jeswant Sing to assist: Dilír Khán, who was unacceptable to the prince as well as to the rája, was left as an additional check on both.

His death.

Return of Prince Móazzim and Jeswant Sing.

A. D. 1667, A. H. 1077.

Progress of Sévají.

Jei Sing's misfortune was of the utmost importance to Sévají. During his struggle and retreat he had withdrawn all his troops from the country near the Ghâts, had evacuated many forts, and left others with scarcely any garrisons. Many of these were occupied by Sévají's officers before he himself reached the Deckan; and his own arrival was speedily followed by still more extensive acquisitions.

He makes peace with the emperor.

The change in the Mogul commanders was yet more to Sévají's advantage. Jeswant Sing had a great ascendency over Prince Móazzim, and was much better disposed to the Hindús than to the government which he served; and it was, moreover, believed that he was not inaccessible to the influence of money. By these means combined, Sévají enlisted him on his side; and, through his and the prince's aid, obtained a peace with Aurangzíb on terms exceeding his most sanguine hopes. A considerable portion of territory was restored to him, and a new jágír granted to him in Berár. His title of rája was acknowledged, and all his former offences seemed to be buried in oblivion.

Levies tribute on Bíjapúr

Thus delivered from his most powerful enemy, Sévají turned his arms against Bíjapúr and Gol-

BOOK XI.

and Golcónda.

cónda; and those states, weak within, and threatened by the Moguls, were unwilling to enter on a new contest with their formidable neighbour, and averted the evil by the humiliating expedient of agreeing to an annual tribute.

His internal arrangements.

A. D. 1668 and 1669, A. H. 1078 and 1079.

A long period of tranquillity which followed was employed by Sévají in giving a regular form to his government; and none of his military successes raise so high an idea of his talents as the spirit of his domestic administration. Instead of the rules of a captain of banditti, we are surprised to find a system more strict and methodical than that of the Moguls. The army, both horse and foot, was formed into uniform divisions, commanded by a regular chain of officers, from heads of ten, of fifty, &c. &c., up to heads of 5000, above which there was no authority except that of the general appointed to command a particular army; and these officers were not feudal chiefs, but servants of the government, placed over soldiers mustered and paid by *its* agents. Both troops and officers received high pay, but were obliged to give up their plunder of every description to the state. The most minute attention to economy pervaded every department of Sévají's service.

His civil government was equally regular, and very vigorous, both towards its own officers and the heads of villages; and this, in checking oppression of the cultivators, no less than frauds against the state. His civil officers were all Bramins, and those of the highest rank were often employed in military commands also. CHAP. II.

Schemes of Aurangzíb to entrap Sévají.

The real motive of Aurangzíb's concessions was the hope of getting Sévají again into his power, without the expense and damage of a protracted war with him. He pursued his object with his usual patience, enjoining Prince Móazzim and Jeswant Sing to keep up a constant intercourse with Sévají, and let slip no opportunity of making him their prisoner. They were even directed to feign disaffection to his own government, and to show a disposition for a secret and separate alliance with the Marattas.* But Sévají turned all the em- A. D. 1670, A. H. 1080.

* Grant Duff. He, however, doubts whether Móazzim ever gave in at all to the emperor's design, and whether he ever attempted to deceive Sévají by a show of disaffection; but it seems probable that he must, to a certain extent, have conformed to his instructions; and that it was his consequent proceedings that gave rise to the story first told by Catrou (or Manucci), of a mock rebellion of Prince Móazzim, got up by his father's desire, for the double purpose of finding out his secret enemies and of discrediting his son, in case that prince should ever be disposed to rebel in earnest. According to this account, Prince Móazzim openly declared against his father, and was joined by Jei Sing and all the rest of the army, except Dilír Khán, and had actually marched to the river Chambal (towards Agra), before he professed to renounce his design. The only use (it says) made by Aurangzíb of the knowledge obtained at so great a hazard was, to secure himself against one of his enemies by poisoning Jei Sing. But Jei Sing had been removed from the Deckan before the prince's arrival, and was dead before the date of the pretended insurrection. This last inconsistency was discovered by Orme, who does not doubt the rest of the story; but the absurdity of the whole is laid open in a few words by Grant Duff (vol. i. p. 221.). It is not the

BOOK XI.

peror's plans against himself: he conciliated Móazzim and Jeswant by bribes and presents, and made them his instruments in deceiving Aurangzíb. That monarch was too sagacious not to discover in time the failure of his scheme; and when he had ascertained it beyond doubt, he gave orders for an open attempt to seize Sévají, which of course involved a renewal of the war.

Aurangzíb breaks the peace.

Sévají surprises Singhar.

The first blow struck by Sévají was the recovery of Singhar, near Púna. The Moguls were as sensible as he was of the importance of this place, and maintained in it a strong garrison of Rájpúts, under an experienced officer. Yet it was surprised by 1000 Máwalis, under Sévají's great friend and confidant, Tánají Málúsri, who contrived to climb up that apparently inaccessible rock in the night-time, and to escalade the walls, before they were discovered by the guards. They, however, met with an obstinate resistance; and it was not without the loss of their leader, and a large proportion of their number, that they at length

only occasion in which the wily character of Aurangzíb has led to his being suspected of deep schemes and intrigues in which he never was engaged. Dow substitutes Jeswant Sing for Jei Sing, and makes Móazzim's rebellion a real one, which, he says, was only frustrated by a succession of skilful operations on the part of Dilír Khán, after Aurangzíb himself had been obliged to take the field. He seems to draw his account from the "Bondéla Memoirs," afterwards translated by Scott (*Deckan*, vol. ii. p. 24.); but he goes beyond his authority in some things, and omits the Bondéla's statement (doubtless an erroneous one) that Sévají actually joined the prince.

overpowered the garrison. Sévají was so much impressed with the difficulty and importance of the undertaking, that he conferred a silver bracelet on every individual of the survivors.

Ravages the Mogul territory.

He failed in some attacks on other forts, but reduced a much greater number, and occupied much territory: he also again plundered Surat, carried his ravages over Cándésh, and, for the first time, levied the *chout*, afterwards so celebrated in Maratta history. It was a permanent contribution of one fourth of the revenue, and exempted the districts that agreed to it from plunder as long as it was regularly paid. Sévají also equipped a powerful fleet, and renewed his attacks on his old enemies, the Abyssinians of Jinjera, who held a small principality as admirals to the king of Bíjapúr. This attack was injudicious; for it led to the Abyssinians placing themselves under the Moguls, and thus increasing the power of Sévají's only formidable enemy.

A. D. 1670, December; A. H. 1081.

Chout.

The rapidity of Sévají's progress was owing to the inadequacy of the force under Móazzim, whom Aurangzíb long refused to reinforce from distrust: and when, at last, he was convinced of the necessity of having more troops in the Deckan, he sent down an army of 40,000 men, under Mohábat Khán, and quite independent of the prince's authority. Nor was he by any means entirely satisfied even with this new commander: shortly before his march from Delhi he took offence at some of his proceedings, and ordered one of the

A. D. 1671, A. H. 1081.

BOOK XI.

ministers to remonstrate with him in private. The arrival of his army was attended with no corresponding result. Móazzim remained inactive at Aurangábád; and Mohábat Khán, after undertaking some sieges, was obliged to suspend his proceedings by the approach of the rainy season.

Defeats the Moguls in a field action.

When he again began operations, Sévají sent an army to raise a siege in which Mohábat was engaged, and the latter, in an injudicious attempt to cover the siege, exposed a body of 20,000 men to

A. D. 1672, A. H. 1082.

a total defeat by the Marattas.* This was the first field action won by Sévají's troops, and the first instance of success in a fair conflict with the Moguls.

Khán Jehán made viceroy of the Deckan.

It seems to have made a strong impression on the beaten party: they immediately concentrated their forces on Aurangábád, and both Móazzim and Mohábat were soon after recalled; Khán Jéhan, the viceroy of Guzerát, was sent to take their place; Aurangzíb's exertions were re-

Suspension of active operations in the Deckan.

quired in another quarter, and the war languished for a period of several years.

Aurangzíb occupied by a war with the north-eastern Afghâns.

What drew off Aurangzíb's attention was, the increasing importance of a war which had for some time been going on with the north-eastern Afgháns. It was always a matter of difficulty to remain at peace with those tribes; but, as the communication with Cábul and other western countries lay

* There are doubts about this battle, which some say was with a detachment of Dilír Khán's, and others, of Mohábat's. The obscurity arises from the same cause as the defeat, — the divided command of the Mogul army.

through their lands, it was necessary to find some means of keeping them quiet; and as the tribes upon the road were also the most open to attack, it was generally managed, between threats and pensions, to retain them in a certain degree of submission to the royal government. The more powerful tribes were let alone, and remained quiet within their own limits. But, from the numerous small communities, and the weakness of the internal government even in the large ones, there must often have been acts of aggression by individuals, which required forbearance on the part of the royal officers. As Aurangzíb was very jealous of his authority, and as he knew nothing of the structure of society among the Afgháns, it is not unlikely that he suspected the chiefs of countenancing these irregularities underhand; but, from whatever cause it proceeded, he fell out with the whole of the tribes, even including the Eusofzeis. This was the state of things in A. D. 1667, when Amín Khán, the son of the celebrated Mír Jumla, and the successor to his rank and title, was appointed governor of Cábul, and gained such success as for a time prevented the disturbances increasing, although they never were entirely suspended. But, in A.D. 1670, the Afgháns regained their superiority, defeated Amín Khán in a great battle, and totally destroyed his army: even his women and children fell into their hands, and were obliged to be redeemed by the payment of a ransom.

BOOK XI.

The Afgháns, about the same time, set up a king, and coined money in his name.*

A. D. 1673, about Jan.; A. H. 1083, Rámzán.

The emperor at last determined to conduct the war in person. He marched to Hasan Abdál, and sent on his son, Prince Sultán, whom he had now released and intrusted with the command of an army. He probably was prevented going himself by the fear of committing his dignity in a strong country, where great blows could not be struck, and where great reverses might be sustained.

From A. D. 1673, January, to A. D. 1675, October; A. H. 1083, Rámzán, to A. H. 1086, Jamádi 2., or thereabouts.

This war occupied Aurangzíb for more than two years†, and was carried on through his lieutenants after his own return to Delhi, until the increased disturbances in India, and the hopelessness of success, at length compelled him to be contented with a very imperfect settlement. But although the contest was of such importance at the time, it had no permanent influence on the history of India; and the events of it, though varied and interesting, may be imagined from those already related under the reign of Akber.‡

* The Indian writers seem to consider this person as an Afghán chief; but such a nomination is equally inconsistent with the feelings and institutions of that people; and (although the authority is, no doubt, inferior) I am inclined to believe, with the Europeans, that the pretended king was an impostor, who was passed off for Shújá, whom the Afgháns represented to have taken refuge among them, and whose pretensions to the throne of India would furnish good means of annoying Aurangzíb.

† Kháfi Khán.

‡ This war derives additional interest from the picture of it preserved by one of the principal actors. Khúsh Khál, the khán

CHAP. II.

A. D. 1676, A. H. 1087.

Aurangzíb returns to Delhi.

Insurrection of the Satnarámi religionists.

The emperor had scarcely resurned from this unsuccessful expedition when an extraordinary insurrection broke out near the capital. A sect of Hindú devotees, called Satnarámis, were settled near the town of Nárnól: they were principally engaged in trade and agriculture; and, though generally peaceable, carried arms, and were always ready to use them in their own defence. One of their body, having been mobbed and beaten by the comrades of a soldier of the police, with whom he had quarrelled, collected some of his brethren to retaliate on the police. Lives were lost, and the affray increased till several thousand Satnarámis were assembled; and the chief authority of the place having taken part against them, they defeated a band of troops, regular and local, which he had got together; and finally took possession of the town of Nárnól. An inadequate force sent against them from Delhi was defeated, and served only to add to their reputation; a repetition of the same circumstance raised the wonder of the country; and, joined to their religious character, soon led to a belief that they were possessed of magical powers: swords would not cut, nor bullets pierce them; while their enchanted weapons dealt death at every

of the tribe of Khatak, was a voluminous author, and has left several poems, written at this time, for the purpose of exciting the national enthusiasm of his countrymen. They are remarkable for their high and ardent tone, and for their spirit of patriotism and independence, so unlike the usual character of Asiatics.

BOOK XI.

blow. The belief that they were invincible nearly made them so in reality. Many of the zemíndárs of the neighbourhood took part with them; no troops could be got to face them; and as they approached Delhi, Aurangzíb ordered his tents to be prepared to take the field, and with his own hand wrote extracts from the Korán, to be fastened to the standards, as a protection against enchantment. The absolute necessity of resistance, and the exertions of some chiefs both Mussulman and Hindú, at last prevailed on the royal troops to make a stand, when the insurgents were defeated and dispersed with great loss. But the previous success had tempted many of the Hindú population to take up arms, and had thrown the whole provinces of Ajmír and Agra into such confusion that Aurangzíb thought his own presence necessary to restore order.*

Aurangzíb's bigotry.

These disturbances had irritated his temper, already ruffled by his failure beyond the Indus; and led him, while he was still in Delhi, to take the last step in a long course of bigotry and impolicy, by reviving the jeziá or capitation tax on Hindús.

At the second anniversary of his accession (A. D. 1659), he forbade the solar æra, as an invention of fire worshippers, and directed the Mahometan lunar year to be used on all occasions; and in this resolution he persevered, notwithstanding long-continued remonstrances from his official

* Kháfi Khán.

people, on the disadvantage of a calendar that did not agree with the seasons.*

CHAP. II.

His vexatious treatment of the Hindús.

At the same time he appointed a mullah, with a party of horse attached to him, to suppress all drinking and gambling houses, and to check all ostentatious display of idol worship.† Not long afterwards, he abolished all taxes not expressly authorised by the Mahometan law, and all duties on goods sold at the great Hindú fairs, which he considered as polluted by their original connection with idolatry. His remissions, as far as they were carried into effect, were productive of great inequality; the unauthorised taxes being chiefly those that fell on bankers, great traders, and other inhabitants of towns, whom the new rule would have left nearly exempt from contribution. The land revenue remained as before; and the customs and road duties, which were by much the most vexatious of all, were rather increased than diminished.‡

But, in fact, the alteration produced a heavy loss to the state, without affording any relief to the subject; except in a few cases where the exaction was likely to attract notice, the revenue officers and jágírdárs confined the remission to their accounts with the government, and levied the taxes without diminution on those under their authority. Some years later he forbade fairs on Hindú festivals

* Kháfi Khán. † Ibid. ‡ Ibid.

BOOK XI.

altogether; and about the same time he issued an edict against music, dancing, and buffoons, and discharged all the singers and musicians attached to the palace. He likewise forbade astrology, and dismissed the astrologers previously attached to the court. He also discountenanced poets, who used to be honoured and pensioned; and abolished the office and salary of royal poet. It is even distinctly related that he prohibited the composition and recitation of poetry *; but this extreme austerity must have been of very short duration, for his own notes and letters are filled with poetical quotations, and sometimes with extemporary verses made by himself. His prohibition of history was more permanent; he not only discontinued the regular annals of the empire, which had before been kept by a royal historiographer, but so effectually put a stop to all record of his transactions, that from the eleventh year of his reign, the course of events can only be traced through the means of letters on business and of notes taken clandestinely by private individuals. A few years later he took off one half of the customs paid by Mahometans, while he left those of Hindús undiminished. Among other minute reforms, he made further changes in the mode of saluting him; and discontinued his public appearance at the window of his palace, for fear of affording an opportunity for the ceremony of adoration. Though few of these alterations bore di-

* Ḳháfi Khán.

rectly on the Hindús, they all tended to stir up a scrupulous and captious spirit, and to mark the line between the followers of the two religions which it had been the policy of former monarchs to efface.

His present measures were far more decidedly intolerant; for, although he began with an equitable edict, by which all claims on the government were to be received in the courts, and tried according to the Mahometan law, yet, at the same time, a circular order was sent to all governors and persons in authority to entertain no more Hindús, but to confer all the offices immediately under them on Mahometans only.

It was found quite impracticable to comply with this order; and, in fact, most of the above edicts remained a dead letter, and had no other effect but to excite alarm and disaffection.

He revives the jezía, or poll tax on infidels.

But no such laxity appeared in the levy of the jezía. The poll tax so called was imposed, during the early conquests, on all infidels who submitted to the Mahometan rule, and was the test by which they were distinguished from those who remained in a state of hostility. The revival of it excited the utmost discontent among the Hindús. Those at Delhi and the neighbourhood assembled in crowds, and besieged the king's palace with their complaints and clamours. No attention was paid to these remonstrances. On the next Friday, when the king was going in procession to the mosque, he found the streets completely choked

BOOK XI.

by the crowd of suppliants. He waited some time in hopes that a passage might be opened by fair means; but as the mob continued to hold their ground, he ordered his retinue to force their way through; and many persons were trampled under foot by the horses and elephants. This harsh conduct was successful in striking terror, and the tax was submitted to without further demur.

A. D. 1677, A. H. 1088. General disaffection of the Hindús.

The effects of these fanatical proceedings were not long in showing themselves. At the beginning of this reign, the Hindús served the state as zealously as the Mussulmans; and that, even when employed against people of their own religion; but their attachment declined as they had experience of the new system; discontent spread among the inhabitants of the emperor's own dominions; the Rájpúts began to be disaffected; and every Hindú in the Deckan became at heart a partisan of the Marattas.*

* Kháfi Khán. The general sentiment of the time is well shown in a letter to Aurangzíb, commonly ascribed to Jeswant Sing. It cannot be his work; for it is the letter of an open enemy, whose dominions are about to be invaded; and Jeswant Sing was serving against the Afgháns when the jezía was imposed, and continued beyond the Indus till his death: it must, besides, have been written at a later period, after the decline of the empire had become apparent. It is also assigned to Ráj Sing, rána of Oudipúr, as well as to a rája named Subah Sing; and the Marattas claim it for Sévají (Grant Duff, vol. i. p. 219.). It is not improbable that it is the work of some private Hindú politician, who chose this way of publishing a sort of manifesto against the government. It is not destitute of ability. It maintains the principles of toleration, which are violated by the jezía;

These religious animosities were kindled into a flame by an event which took place a few months after the imposition of the jezía. Rája Jeswant Sing died at Cábul, leaving a widow and two infant sons. The widow immediately set out for India without leave or passports; and, on her being stopped at the Indus, her escort made an attempt to force the guard at Attok, and afterwards did effect their passage by some neglected ford. This violence afforded a pretext for Aurangzíb to get the children into his power. He refused them admission into Delhi, and surrounded their encampment with his troops.

Oppressive measures against the widow and children of Rája Jeswant Sing.

But on this occasion the Rájpúts united considerable address to their accustomed courage. Their leader, Durga Dás, obtained leave to send off part of the escort with their women and children to their own country: along with this party he despatched the ráni and her infants in disguise, while he substituted two children of the same age for the young princes, and employed one of her female attendants to personate the ráni; all which was rendered more easy by the privacy of the

They escape from Delhi.

exalts the liberality of the former princes of the house of Teimúr; and contrasts the flourishing state of the empire in their time with that of the present reign; when men of all classes and religions are discontented, the revenue gone to ruin, the people oppressed and yet the treasury empty, the police neglected, the cities insecure, and the forts falling into decay. [A translation of this letter is given in "Orme's Fragments," p. 252. A closer translation, with the Persian, was published by Mr. Weston, in 1803.]

BOOK XI.

women's apartments. In spite of these precautions many hours had not elapsed before Aurangzíb's suspicions were awakened, and he sent orders that the ráni and her children should be brought into the citadel. His fears for their actual escape were for the time removed by the obstinacy of the Rájpúts, who refused to give up the widow and children of their rája, and declared themselves ready to die in their defence. His attention was now occupied in overcoming their resistance: troops were sent against them, whom they gallantly repulsed; at length, after the loss of the greater part of their number, the supposed ráni and her family were seized, while Durga Dás and the survivors dispersed for the time; and, again assembling at a distance, retired to their own country. Their protracted defence had given time for the ráni to effect her escape. She arrived in safety in Jódpúr, and her eldest son, Ajít Sing, lived to enjoy a long reign over Márwár, and to be a formidable enemy to Aurangzíb for all the rest of that monarch's life. His identity, however, was long exposed to question; for Aurangzíb, with his usual adroitness, received the supposititious children as the undoubted issue of Rája Jeswant Sing, directed them to be honourably treated, and afterwards employed their pretensions in aid of his attacks on Jódpúr.

Combination of the Rájpúts.

This outrage towards the family of one of their body, combined with the imposition of the jeziá, disposed the Rájpúts to unite in their own defence. Rája Rám Sing of Jeipúr or Ambér, whose family was connected with that of the emperor by so many intermarriages and the distinguished services of several generations, retained his attachment even at the present crisis; but Ráj Sing, rána of Oudipúr or Méwár, entered heartily into the cause of the children of Jeswant Sing, and at the same time peremptorily refused to agree to the jezía. The whole of the western part of Rajpútána being now opposed to him, Aurangzíb assembled an army and marched to Ajmír.* From that place he sent on detachments to ravage Márwár; and, with his main army, he made so great an impresssion on the rána as to reduce him to send in overtures of submission. He was allowed very favourable terms: a small cession of territory being accepted in lieu of the jeziá, and no other sacrifice demanded but a promise not to assist Jódpúr.

The emperor marches against them.

A. D. 1679, January; A. H. 1089, Zí Haj.

Grants favourable terms to the rána of Méwár.

This arrangement concluded, the emperor returned to Delhi, having been absent less than eight months.† He had scarcely reached his capital, when he learned that the rána had broken the treaty (probably by giving secret assistance to Jódpúr,), and before many months were over he again set out for Ajmír. On this occasion, he put forth his utmost strength and applied all his energy to the speedy suppression of the combination against him. He summoned Prince Móazzim from the Deckan and Prince A'zim from Bengal; and at a later period he ordered the viceroy of

The rána breaks the peace.

A. D. 1679, July; A. H. 1090, Rajab.

* Kháfi Khán.

† Ibid.

Guzerát to invade the Rájpút territory from that quarter also. But the principal attack was made by his own army, which was sent under Prince Akber (assisted by Tohavvar Khán) direct to Oudipúr, while the rána, intimidated by the forces which threatened him on all sides, abandoned his capital, and took refuge in the Aravelli mountains. He was pursued into his retreat by Akber, who left a detachment behind him to ravage the open plains. Prince Móazzim had by this time reached U'jén, and was ordered to adopt the same course; and Prince A'zim, on his arrival, was directed against the Jódpúr territory and the adjoining part of the rána's. Their orders were, to employ part of their troops to cut off all supplies from the fugitives in the hills; and with the rest to lay waste the country, burn and destroy the villages, cut down the fruit trees, and carry off the women and children; so as to make the enemy feel all the evils of war in their utmost severity.

Devastation of the Rájpút territory.

Permanent alienation of the Rájpúts.

It is consistent with Aurangzíb's character to suppose that these inhuman orders were dictated by an unfeeling policy alone; but his religious prejudices and his hatred of opposition make it probable that anger and revenge also had an influence even on his calculating temper. Whatever were the motives, the effect was to complete for ever the alienation of the Rájpúts. They were afterwards often at peace with Aurangzíb's successors, and they sometimes even furnished their contingents, and professed their allegiance; but their service was yielded with constraint and distrust, very unlike the zealous attachment which formerly made them the prop of the monarchy.

During all this time, the Rájpúts kept a body of 25,000 horse, chiefly Ráhtórs of Jódpúr, in the field, with which, aided by their infantry in the hills, they occasioned much distress and some danger to their adversaries: they cut off convoys, attacked detachments, defended favourable positions, and sometimes gained important advantages by surprises and night attacks. But Durga Dás, who still acted a prominent part in their councils, did not trust to force alone for the deliverance of his country. He endeavoured to open a negotiation with Prince Móazzim, and to draw him off from his allegiance by offers to support him in possessing himself of the crown. These prospects seem, for a time, to have had some charms even for Móazzim, a prince of mature years, and next in succession to the throne; but on his rejection of them, they were eagerly embraced by Prince Akber, the youngest of the brothers, who was then only twenty-three, and who, in his boyhood, had been considered as the chosen heir of his father.* He at once entered into Durga Dás's views; and although Prince Móazzim warned the emperor of the plots which were going on, yet Aurangzíb was attached to Akber, whose youth, he thought, prevented his being dangerous, and at the same time,

Prince Akber joins the Rájpúts with his army.

* Bernier, vol. i. p. 193.

BOOK XI.

he entertained the greatest jealousy of Móazzim himself. He therefore set down his information to envy, or some worse motive, and took no step to guard against Akber's infidelity, until he heard that Durga Dás was encamped beside him, and that he had assumed the title and all the functions of a king. Tohavvar Khán became his prime minister; Majáhid Khán, another great nobleman, also accepted of an office; and the rest of the army, destitute of a leader, continued submissive to the authority which they had been accustomed to obey.

Is proclaimed emperor.

Marches against Aurangzíb.

Aurangzíb had sent all his troops on different detachments; and had scarcely 1000 men with him at Ajmír, when he heard that Akber was in full march against him. He instantly called in Móazzim, with as many of his troops as he could assemble; but they produced nothing capable of opposing Akber, now at the head of 70,000 men.

Dangerous situation of the emperor.

Aurangzíb's situation seemed hopeless; and, to render it still more desperate, he gave way to his old suspicions of Móazzim, and ordered his guns to be pointed on that prince's division. But he did not lose his penetration even in this perplexity: conjecturing that the bulk of Akber's army had been surprised into revolt, rather than led to it by any real disaffection, he sent an officer of ability, who was brother to Majáhid Khán, with a small body of horse, to get as near as he could to the enemy, and try to open a communication with his brother. Majáhid, who had never sincerely united with Akber, took the first opportunity of coming

His presence of mind.

CHAP. II.

over to his brother. His example was followed by other chiefs; and the general inclination was so evident, that Tohavvar Khán, when next day sent out with the advanced guard, came forward as if to engage with that opposed to him, and at once passed over to the emperor's side.

Defection of Akber's army.

It is not clear whether there was a real or affected suspicion that he came over with treacherous intentions; or whether, which is extremely improbable, he really did entertain such designs; but a report was set on foot, that he intended to assassinate the emperor, and, on his refusing to give up his arms, force was used, and he was cut down close to the royal pavilion.

Akber flies to the Marattas.

Meanwhile, his desertion, and that of so many other men of all ranks, struck the Rájpúts with dismay; and, finding themselves left to oppose the whole Mussulman army, they thought it necessary at last to attend to their own safety; only Durga Dás remaining, with 3000 horse, to protect Prince Akber on his retreat. That prince was left with scarcely a single Mahometan soldier; and all he could expect from the Rájpúts was to be allowed to share in their privations. He therefore resolved to seek an asylum with the Marattas; and, eluding pursuit by a march through the hills into Guzerát, he made his way to the Concan, and arrived in safety, still escorted by Durga Dás, with 500 Rájpúts.*

A. D. 1681, June 1.

* Letters from Bombay, quoted in Orme's "Fragments," p. 267.

Protracted war with the Rájpúts.

But the war with Mewár and Jódpúr, though it had returned into its old channel, continued unabated. The Moguls went on with their ravages: the Rájpúts retaliated by similar inroads into Málwa; and having, at length, caught the spirit of intolerance from their persecutors, they plundered the mosques, burned the Korán, and insulted the mullahs. The chief sufferer by this system of hostility was the rána of Oudipúr, whose fertile territory lay nearest the Moguls, and was occupied by their troops; while the remote and barren tracts under Jódpúr were less exposed to such an impression. Aurangzíb himself was desirous of putting an end to a struggle which withdrew him from more important affairs; and, by his contrivance, the rána was induced to make overtures, which were immediately and favourably received. The jezía was passed over in silence, the small cession formerly made in lieu of that impost was now given as a penalty for having assisted Akber; but all the other articles were favourable to the rána, whose honour was saved by a clause promising the restoration of Ajít Sing's country to him when he should come of age.* This treaty allowed Aurangzíb to draw off his army, without discredit, to the Deckan, where its presence could no longer be dispensed with; but it did little towards the real restoration of tranquillity. The western Rájpúts were still in arms; the war with

* Orme's Fragments, p. 106. Tod's Rajasthan, vol. i. p. 388.

the rána was renewed at no distant period, and the whole of the Rájpút states, except Jeipúr and the little principalities towards the east, continued in a state of open hostility till the end of Aurangzíb's reign. The capitals remained in the hands of the Moguls; but, though the dissensions among the Rájpúts prevented their making solid acquisitions, they still severely harassed the troops in their own country, and often laid waste the neighbouring provinces.*

* Tod's Rajasthan, vol. ii. p. 69, &c. Colonel Tod's account of the transactions subsequent to the treaty is probably rectified from the Mahometan newspapers (akhbárs) of the day, which he mentions were in his possession. It is certainly quite unlike the Rájpút legends; being distinct and consistent, and constantly referring to dates, which coincide with those of events related by other authors.

CHAP. III.

FROM 1681 TO 1698.

BOOK XI.

Affairs of the Deckan resumed.

The continuance of this warfare did not prevent Aurangzíb from turning all the resources he could command to the settlement of the Deckan, where many changes of moment had taken place while he was engaged in other quarters. When his forces were first drawn off for the war with the Afgháns (A. D. 1672), Khán Jehán, his general in the Deckan, found himself too weak to prosecute active hostilities against the Marattas; and would probably have been unable to defend his own province, if their leader had been disposed to attack it.

Sévají's conquests from Bíjapúr.

But while things were in this position, the king of Bíjapúr died, and the state of discord into which his country fell offered greater temptations to Sévají than were presented by any attack on the Moguls. The part of Bíjapúr which most attracted him on this occasion, was that on the sea, with the adjoining Ghats; and in the course of the years 1673 and 1674 A. D., after a succession of battles and sieges, he made himself master of the whole of the southern Concan (except the points held by the English, Abyssinians, and Portuguese), and of a tract above the Gháts, extending further to the east than the upper course of the Kishna.

Is crowned at Ráighar with addi-

Though Sévají had long borne the privileges of sovereignty,

he conceived it suitable to the undertakings he had now in view to assume the exercise of them with greater solemnity than before. He was therefore again inaugurated at Ráighar with all the ceremonies of a Mogul coronation, including his being weighed in gold and distributing rich presents to all around him. At the same time he changed the titles of his principal officers from Persian to Shanscrit; and while he thenceforth assumed all the pomp of a Mahometan prince, he redoubled his attention to the duties of his religion, and affected greater scrupulosity than ever in food and other things connected with cast.*

tional solemnity.

Makes an incursion into the Mogul territory,

The long period for which Sévají had been employed in his conquests encouraged the Moguls to make an incursion into his possessions soon after this ceremony; but they had reason to repent their temerity. Sévají, without moving in person sent detachments into the Imperial territory, and these bands took two forts, plundered the country to the heart of Candésh and Berár, and even penetrated into Guzerát as far as Baróch, where for the first time they crossed the river Nerbadda. These incursions took place in 1675; and as he hoped they might induce the Moguls to refrain from disturbing him again, they left Sévají at liberty to execute a design that had long occupied

and first crosses the Nerbadda.

* Mr. Oxenden, who was envoy from Bombay to Sévají, was present at his coronation, and describes it as much more splendid than would have been expected among early Marattas. It took place on the 6th of June, 1674.

BOOK XI.

Sévají's expedition to the south of India.

his thoughts. This was the recovery of his father's jágír, and a further extension of his conquests in the south of India. The jágír had hitherto remained in the hands of his younger brother, Véncají, who held it under the nominal supremacy of the government of Bíjapúr. Sévají was therefore now at liberty either to claim it as heir, or to conquer it as an enemy; and his views were particularly directed to it from his having lately been joined by Ragunát Náráin, the Bramin who had formerly managed it on the part of Sháhji, and had afterwards been minister to Véncají until a recent quarrel. This man was useful to Sévají both from his knowledge and connections. But as he could not safely set out on so remote an expedition without leaving a friend in his rear, he took advantage of the jealousy of Bíjapúr and fears of the Moguls entertained by the king of Golcónda, and proposed an alliance to him against their common enemies. His overtures being encouraged, he marched for Golcónda with an army of 30,000 horse and 40,000 infantry. He halted for some time at Golcónda to make a definitive settlement of his alliance; when it was agreed that he was to share with the king whatever conquests he made beyond his father's jágír, and that the king was to supply him with a sum of money and a train of artillery, reserving all his other forces to keep the armies of Bíjapúr and the Moguls in check. Having thus secured his rear, Sévají crossed the Kishna at Carnúl, proceeded through

Towards the end of A. D. 1676.

A. D. 1677, March.

Cadapa, and passing close to Madras*, presented himself before Jinjí (Gingee) 600 miles from his own territories. Jinjí was a strong and important hill fort belonging to Bíjapúr, but was given up in consequence of a previous understanding with the commander. The heavy part of his army, which he had left behind, next laid siege to, and ultimately took, Vellór; while Sévají had a personal interview with his brother, and endeavoured to persuade him to give him a share of their father's possessions. Having failed in this negotiation, he took A'rní, and various other forts, and forcibly occupied the whole of Sháhjí's jágír in the Mysore. While thus employed, he heard of the invasion of Golcónda by the Moguls and the government of Bíjapúr; on which he marched off to the north, leaving his conquests in charge of his half-brother, Santají, who had joined him on his first arrival. As soon as Sévají was out of reach, Véncají made an attempt to recover his possessions; and the dispute terminated in a compromise, by which Véncají was to retain the jágír, but pay half the revenue to Sévají who was to keep to himself the places which *he* had conquered from Bíjapúr. The king of Golcónda had by this time come to a settlement with the Moguls; and Sévají, after conquering the districts of Belári and Adóni on his way, passed on to Ráighar, which he reached after an absence of eighteen months.

He takes Jinjí, and Vellór, and recovers all his father's jágír in Mysore.

About the middle of A. D. 1678.

* First week of May, 1677. Wilks's Mysore, from the "Madras Records."

BOOK XI.

The Moguls, under Dilír Khán, invade Golcónda.

The invasion of Golcónda was owing to a change in the policy of the Moguls. Khán Jehán had been removed, and succeeded by Dilír Khán, perhaps the best of Aurangzíb's officers. His force was still small; but a considerable portion of his troops were Patáns, like himself, and he made up for all deficiencies by his own vigour and activity. The king of Bíjapúr was still a minor, and various revolutions had taken place among his ministers and guardians. Dilír formed a union with one of them, and made the above mentioned attack on Golcónda. The regent of Bíjapúr, who acted with him on that occasion, died soon after; and Dilír, by supporting the claims of an Abyssinian, named Masáúd, to succeed him, acquired a perfect ascendancy in the councils of Bíjapúr. But Aurangzíb, not satisfied with these advantages, sent down prince Móazzim, as viceroy, to advance further demands, which Dilír, as general, was to enforce. In execution of this plan, Dilír renewed the war with Bíjapúr, and laid siege to the capital. The regent, in despair, had recourse to Sévají, who, not finding himself strong enough to attack the besieging army, invaded and laid waste the Mogul territory with more than ordinary severity. He was nearly cut off on his retreat, or rather flight, from one of those inroads; but, almost immediately afterwards, appeared in greater strength than ever, and took several forts from the Moguls. But Dilír Khán still persevered in the siege, and the regent, reduced to extremity, entreated Sévají

Lay siege to Bíjapúr. A. D. 1679.

to come to his assistance before it was too late. Sévají had set off for this purpose, when he was surprised by the intelligence that his son, Sambají, had deserted to the Moguls. This young man, who had none of his father's qualities, except his courage, had given himself up to debauchery; and having attempted to violate the wife of a Bramin, was imprisoned, by Sévají, in one of his hill forts. He now escaped from his place of confinement, and fled to Dilír, who received him with open arms, intending to make use of him among the Marattas as a counterpoise to his father. The embarrassment this occasioned to Sévají was only temporary, for Aurangzíb, disapproving of Dilír's views, ordered Sambají to be sent prisoner to his own camp; and Dilír, whose honour was pledged for his safety, connived at his return to his father. Meanwhile, the defence of Bíjapúr had surpassed expectation: Sévají, as soon as he recovered from his first surprise, had renewed his exertions; and Dilír Khán, finding his supplies cut off, was obliged to raise the siege. The price of Sévají's alliance was a cession of the territory between the Tumbadra and Kishna, and of all the king's rights over the jágír of Sháhjí. This last acquisition gave him the right, as his success did the power, of exercising a more effectual control over his brother; and Véncají's mortification at the change had led him to the thoughts of renouncing worldly affairs; when all Sévají's designs were cut short by an

Sévají's son, Sambají, deserts to the Moguls.

He returns to his father.

Siege of Bíjapúr raised.

BOOK XI.

illness which carried him off on the 5th of April, 1680, in the fifty-third year of his age.

Death of Sévaji. His character.

Though the son of a powerful chief, he had begun life as a daring and artful captain of banditti, had ripened into a skilful general and an able statesman, and left a character which has never since been equalled or approached by any of his countrymen. The distracted state of the neighbouring countries presented openings by which an inferior leader might have profited; but it required a genius like his to avail himself as he did of the mistakes of Aurangzíb, by kindling a zeal for religion, and, through that, a national spirit among the Marattas. It was by these feelings that his government was upheld after it passed into feeble hands, and was kept together, in spite of numerous internal disorders, until it had established its supremacy over the greater part of India. Though a predatory war, such as he conducted, must necessarily inflict extensive misery, his enemies bear witness to his anxiety to mitigate the evils of it by humane regulations, which were strictly enforced. His devotion latterly degenerated into extravagances of superstition and austerity, but seems never to have obscured his talents or soured his temper.

Unsuccessful attempt to set aside Sambají.

When Sambají returned from the Mogul camp, he was again placed in confinement at Panálla, and was there when his father died. This circumstance, and some expressions of uneasiness which had fallen from Sévají regarding the future conduct of his eldest son, afforded a pretext for alleging that he designed the succession for the second, Rája Rám, a boy of ten years old. The intrigues of this young prince's mother gained acceptance to the story; and the Bramin ministers, who dreaded Sambají's violence, and looked with pleasure to a long minority, affected to receive it as authentic, and sent orders for the close arrest of Sambají, concealing Sevají's death till that object should be accomplished.

He is acknowledged rája.

But Sambají, who was a prisoner at large within Panálla, contrived to get possession of the secret, and announced his own accession to the garrison, who immediately acknowledged his authority. He did not at first venture out of his strong hold, but the public opinion was favourable to his right; the Bramin ministers fell out among themselves; a force that was sent to besiege him was gained over to his interest; and he at length made his entry into Ráighar as undisputed sovereign (June, 1680).

Sambají's cruelty.

His prudence, up to this time, had gone far to remove the prejudice entertained against him; but the favourable impression was effaced by his cruelties after his accession. He put the widow of Sévají to a painful and lingering death; he imprisoned her son, Rája Rám; threw the Bramin ministers, who had been most active against him, into irons; and beheaded such of his other enemies as were not protected by the sanctity of their class. The same prevalence of passion over policy ap-

BOOK XI.

peared in his foreign proceedings. Sévají had always been in a state of hostility with the Abyssinians of Jinjera, and had occasionally made great efforts to reduce them. Sambají's first operations were against these people; and, as they were near neighbours to his capital, he took a personal interest in the war, and for a long time gave up his whole thoughts to subduing them, as if he had had no other enemy in the world. He was not diverted from this pursuit even by the arrival of Prince Akber in his camp (June, 1681). He received the prince with honour, and acknowledged him as emperor, yet showed no intention of rendering his pretensions useful by supporting them against Aurangzíb. The arrival of Akber suggested to the party still secretly opposed to Sambají the possibility of obtaining his sanction to the claim of Rája Rám. Their plot was soon discovered; many of their leaders were trampled to death by elephants; and among the sufferers was one of the chief Bramin ministers, whose eminent services to Sévají seemed to protect him from capital punishment almost as much as his sacred order.

His obstinacy in besieging Jinjera.

Joined by Prince Akber.

Plots against his authority.

Executions.

Gives himself up to a favourite, Calúsha.

The disaffection to Sambají's government produced by these executions was increased by other causes. He neglected or persecuted his father's ministers, while he threw his own affairs, without reserve, into the hands of Calúsha, a Bramin from Hindostan, who had gained his favour by encouraging his vices, as well as by his insinuating manners and superficial accomplishments.

With the aid of this counsellor, he eagerly prosecuted his operations against Jinjera (A. D. 1682). He endeavoured to construct a mound to connect the island with the main land, and he afterwards attempted an assault by means of boats. All his exertions were in vain; and when he was constrained to raise the siege, the Abyssinians increased his mortification by sallying out and plundering his villages. They soon after injured him still more sensibly by entirely defeating his fleet at sea. Exasperated by these affronts, he charged the Europeans settled on the coast with having contributed to produce them: he began hostilities in person against the Portuguese, with whom Sévají had also been at war, and nearly proceeded to the same extremity with the English, although they had hitherto always been treated as friends. These petty operations were interrupted by attacks from the Moguls, the precursors of the appearance of Aurangzíb. Sambají's chiefs had not been entirely inactive in the Deckan during his own occupation with the Abyssinians; but great relaxation had been introduced into discipline; and it was increased, along with all other disorders, by the habits to which the rája had given himself up. His whole time was spent in idleness and debauchery: the vast treasures left by Sévají were soon dissipated; and, although Calúsha added to the general disaffection by increasing the land revenue, the income of the state was inadequate to its expenditure. The troops, left long in arrears, appropriated the plun-

Fails at Jinjera.

Decline of his affairs in the Deckan.

BOOK XI.

der taken on expeditions to their own use, and degenerated from the comparatively regular bands of Sévají into the hordes of rapacious and destructive freebooters which they have ever since remained.

A. D. 1683. Aurangzíb arrives in the Deckan.

By this time Aurangzíb had made his treaty with the rána of Oudipúr; and, after leaving a detachment to ravage the Jódpúr territory, moved with the whole force of his empire to the conquest of the Deckan.

His views.

It would appear to have been sound policy for Aurangzíb to have combined with the kings of Bíjapúr and Golcónda in putting down Sambají, and restoring the tranquillity of the Deckan; but he, perhaps, thought that those monarchs were more jealous of him than of the Marattas, and would not sincerely unite with him, so that Sambají would never want a retreat while they had dominions in which to harbour him. It is at least as probable that the acquisition of the kingdoms of Bíjapúr and Golcónda was Aurangzíb's primary object, and that he judged the reduction of Sambají to be a necessary consequence of success in his other more important undertaking. He had seen with pleasure the wars of those kings with each other, and with the Marattas; had fomented their internal disorders; and seemed so far blinded as to think that every thing that threw the Deckan into confusion must turn to his advantage.

A. D. 1683.

His first advance was to Burhánpúr, where he made a long halt, as he afterwards did at Aurangábád. He was occupied during those periods on political and financial arrangements; and, by a sort of infatuation, he took this occasion to enforce the strict exaction of the jezía, which the common sense of his officers had led them to avoid.

His first operations.

Before he had left Burhánpur, he sent Prince A'zim with a considerable force to reduce the hill forts near the junction of the Chandór range with the Gháts, and Prince Móazzim, with a still larger one, to overrun the Concan, and penetrate to the south of Sambají's country, and the borders of that of Bíjapúr. It is as difficult to see any general design in the employment of these armies as to understand the principles on which their operations were conducted. The strong fort of Sálér was given up by previous concert to Prince A'zim, and this petty intrigue may have tempted Aurangzíb to detach a force to this unconnected point; but to send a large army of cavalry * among the rocks and thickets of the Concan, where there were no roads, no forage, and no field for the employment of horse, shows a want of judgment that it is quite impossible to explain. Móazzim marched the whole length of the Concan unopposed; yet, by the time he got to the neighbourhood of Goa, he had lost almost the whole of his horses and cattle, and even his men began to suffer from scarcity. The pressure was increased by Sambají, who stopped up the Gháts, while his cruizers cut off

A. D. 1684.

Destruction of Prince Móazzim's army in the Concan.

* Orme says 40,000.

BOOK XI.

the vessels that were sent with supplies by sea; and Móazzim thought himself fortunate when he was able to emerge into the country above the Gháts with the remains of his dismounted army. He was pursued by the effects of an unwholesome climate and unusual food, and lost a great portion of his men by an epidemic which broke out at Wálwa, near Mirich, on the Kishna, where he encamped for the period of the rains.

Invasion of Bíjapúr.

When the season opened he was directed to enter the territory of Bíjapúr from the south-west, so as to co-operate with Prince A'zim, who, after failing in his expedition against the forts, was dispatched with a powerful army to invade Bíjapúr; while Aurangzíb himself advanced to Ahmednagar, leaving a reserve under Khán Jehán at Aurangábád.

A. D. 1685.

Sambají ravages the country in the emperor's rear.

This movement gave Sambají an opportunity to retaliate the invasion of his country. He gradually assembled a body of horse in the north of the Concan, behind the right flank of Aurangzíb's armies, which from thence moved rapidly along their rear, sacked and burned the great city of Burhánpúr, and then drew off again to the Concan, leaving all the country through which it had passed in a blaze. So secret as well as rapid were the movements of this body, that Khán Jehán, marching on a point where he thought to intercept it, found himself entirely off the line of its retreat.

Meanwhile Prince A'zim had taken Sólapúr, and was advancing towards Bíjapúr; but he found himself unable to cope with the army that was sent out to oppose him, and was compelled to retreat beyond the Bíma; while Móazzim, too weak to attempt any movement by himself, was obliged to wait for reinforcements, by which he was escorted to Ahmednagar with the wreck of his fine army.

Failure of the invasion of Bíjapúr.

After these failures Aurangzíb advanced in person to Sólapúr, and sent on Prince A'zim with his army reinforced: although the distance was so short, the Bíjapúr troops cut off the prince's supplies, and would have destroyed his army, if a large convoy of grain had not been skilfully conducted into his camp by Ghází u dín.* The impression he made was still small, until Aurangzíb, at a later period, moved on to the siege in person. A. D. 1686.

Sambají plunders Baróch.

It was in the present stage of the war that the Marattas, seeing the Moguls drawn off to the south, made another bold inroad into the territory in their rear, plundered the city of Baróch, and retreated after ravaging the adjoining part of Guzerát. It is not clear whether Sambají sent out this expedition from motives of his own, or in concert with the Deckan kings. He had about this time entered into a defensive alliance with the king of Golcónda; and on this fact becoming known to Aurangzíb, he did not allow his attention to be drawn off to Sambají, but immediately made it a ground of quarrel with Golcónda, and sent an army to invade that kingdom. From his usual

* The ancestor of the present Nizám.

BOOK XI.

Aurangzíb invades Golcónda.

distrust of powerful armies and great commanders, the force he sent was insufficient; and ere long he was constrained to send his son, Prince Móazzim, with a large body of troops, to support the first army, and take the command of the whole. The government of Golcónda was in a very different state from the distracted condition of Bíjapúr. The king, Abul Hasan, though indolent and voluptuous, was popular; and his government and finances were ably conducted by Madna Pant, a Bramin, to whom he wisely gave his full confidence. But the exclusive employment of this minister was odious to the Mussulmans, and especially to I'bráhím Khán, the commander-in-chief, into whose hands the power would probably have fallen under any different arrangement. When Móazzim drew near, this man deserted to him with the greater part of his army. Madna Pant was murdered in a simultaneous tumult in the city; the king fled to the hill fort of Golcónda, and Heiderábád was seized and plundered for three successive days. Móazzim did his best to check this breach of discipline; and it gave the utmost displeasure to the emperor, not so much from humanity, or even policy, as on account of the quantity of treasure lost to the crown, which he violently suspected that Móazzim had embezzled for his own ambitious purposes, as he himself had done on a similar occasion under Sháh Jehán. Having thus effectually crippled the king of Golcónda, he granted him peace for a great pecuniary payment, and turned his whole forces to the reduction of Bíjapúr.

Makes peace with the king.

Aurangzíb, in person, moves against Bíjapúr.

The army of that monarchy appears at this time to have melted away; for, although the walls of the city are six miles in circumference, Aurangzíb was able to invest it completely, while he employed a portion of his army on a regular attack and breach. So well was the blockade kept up, that by the time the breach was practicable the town was distressed for provisions; and as the garrison, though small, was composed of Patáns, it was thought prudent to give them favourable terms: Aurangzíb entered the place on a portable throne through the breach, the young king was made prisoner, and Bíjapúr, ceasing to be a capital, was soon reduced to the deserted condition in which it now stands.*

Takes the capital, and destroys the monarchy. A. D. 1686, Oct. 15.

* "The walls, which are of hewn stone, and very lofty, are to this day entire, and, being surmounted by the cupolas and minarets of public buildings, still present to the spectator, from without, the appearance of a flourishing city; but, within, all is solitude, silence, and desolation. The deep moat, the double rampart, and the ruins of the splendid palaces in the citadel, attest the former magnificence of the court. The great mosque is a grand edifice, and the tomb of Ibrahim Adil Shah, already mentioned, is remarkable for its elegant and graceful architecture; but the chief feature in the scene is the mausoleum of Mohummud Adil Shah, the dome of which fills the eye from every point of view; and, though in itself entirely devoid of ornament, its enormous dimensions and austere simplicity invest it with an air of melancholy grandeur, which harmonises with the wreck and desolation that surround it." (Grant Duff, vol. i. p. 340.) One is at a loss, in seeing these ruins, to conjecture how so small a state could have maintained such a capital.

BOOK XI.

Aurangzíb breaks the peace with Golcónda.

No sooner had Bíjapúr fallen than Aurangzíb determined to break the peace with Golcónda; and the means he employed were as base as the design was perfidious. He drew his army near on pretext of a pilgrimage, and he obtained jewels and gifts of all sorts from the unfortunate king, anxious at any cost to purchase his friendship, or at least his compassion; but during all this interval he was intriguing with the ministers of Golcónda, and debauching the troops; and when his plot was ripe for execution, he published a manifesto denouncing the king as a protector of infidels, and soon after laid siege to his fort. From this moment Abul Hasan seemed to cast aside his effeminacy; and, though deserted by his troops, he bravely defended Golcónda for seven months, till it also was given up by treachery; and he then bore his misfortunes with a dignity and resignation that has endeared his memory to his subjects and their descendants even to this day.

A. D. 1687, September.

Takes the capital, and subverts the monarchy.

Imprisons Prince Móazzim.

During this siege, the unsleeping suspicions of Aurangzíb were stirred up by some indiscreet communications between Abul Hasan and Prince Móazzim. The object of this intercourse was to procure the prince's intercession with his father; but to Aurangzíb it appeared to afford a confirmation of all his former surmises, and he lost no time in securing Móazzim, who remained in more or less strict confinement for nearly seven years. Móazzim seems never to have given any cause for these alarms. All accounts give him credit for caution and moderation. Bernier says, no slave could be more obedient, or seem more devoid of ambition: he, however, hints that this was rather too like Aurangzíb's own conduct in his youth; and perhaps the same reflection may have occurred to the emperor.*

Effects of these conquests.

Aurangzíb had now attained the summit of his wishes, but had sown a harvest of which he and his posterity were to reap the bitter produce. The governments which in some degree kept up order in the Deckan being annihilated, the frame of society which depended on them was dissolved, and the scattered materials remained as elements of discord. Though the Patáns and foreign mercenaries may have obtained service with the emperor, the rest of the troops of both armies were obliged to join Sambají, or to plunder on their own account. The distant zemíndárs seized every opportunity to make themselves independent, and, among all the wars and robberies to which they betook themselves, were always ready to befriend the Marattas, whom they looked on as the patrons of anarchy: those most within reach of the Moguls were disaffected to their conquerors; and from this motive, and the new-born feeling of religious opposition, were always ready to assist their enemies: so that in spite of a short gleam of prosperity after the fall of Golcónda, Aurangzíb might date from that event a train of vexations and disasters which followed him to the grave.

Disordered state of the Deckan.

* Bernier, vol. i p. 120.

Aurangzíb takes possession of Bíjapúr and Golcónda, as far as Tanjore.

A. D. 1688.

He was not remiss in taking advantage of his present good fortune. He took possession of all the territories of Bíjapúr and Golcónda, even their latest southern conquests: he seized on Sháhjí's jágír in the Mysore, confining Véncají to Tanjore, and compelling the Marattas in Sevají's late acquisitions to fly to their forts; but in all these countries he had little more than a military occupation: the districts were farmed to the Désmuks and other zemíndárs, and were governed by military leaders, who received 25 per cent. for the expense of collecting, and who sent up the balance, after paying their troops, to the king; unless, as often happened, assignments were made for a period of years on fixed districts for the payment of other chiefs.

Inactivity of Sambají.

During all these great events Sambají remained in a state of personal inertness, ascribed by the Maratta historians to the enchantments of Calúsha, but naturally explained by the stupor and mental debility produced by a course of drunkenness and debauchery.

Prince Akber goes to Persia.

Prince Akber, disgusted with his manners, and hoping nothing from such an ally, quitted his court and repaired to Persia, where he lived till A. D. 1706. The chiefs exerted themselves individually against the Moguls, notwithstanding the inefficiency of their rája; but in spite of their resistance, the open country belonging to the Marattas was gradually taken possession of, and Aurangzíb was preparing for a systematic attack on the forts, when the activity of one of his officers unexpectedly

CHAP. III.

Sambají made prisoner.

threw his principal enemy into his hands. Sambají was enjoying himself, with a small party of attendants, in a favourite pleasure-house, at Sangaméswar in the Concan, when intelligence of his unguarded situation was brought to Tokarrab Khán, the Mogul officer at Colapúr.* Though this place is only fifty or sixty miles from Sangaméswar, it is separated from it by the range of Gháts; and as Tokarrab Khán was only a governor of a district, his neighbourhood (if it could so be called) gave little uneasiness to Sambají or those about him. Being an active and enterprising soldier, he set off with a small body of troops, and took his measures so well that he reached Sangaméswar before his march was suspected. Sambají might still have escaped; for, before his house was surrounded, some of his followers ran in with information of the arrival of the Moguls; but Sambají was in a state of intoxication, and replied by threatening them with punishment for such insulting intelligence. Soon after Tokarrab made his appearance; most of the attendants fled; Calúsha was wounded in endeavouring to save his master; and both were made prisoners and sent in triumph to the imperial head quarters.†

* Grant Duff. From a letter in the "Rakáimi Karáim" (the forty-first in the India House copy), it appears that the plan originated with Aurangzíb himself, and was executed in strict conformity to his orders. Tokarrab, by that letter, seems to have been besieging Parnála.

† Calúsha is generally, but erroneously, believed to have betrayed his master.

BOOK XI.

They were led through the camp on camels, amidst the din of drums and other noisy instruments, and surrounded by an innumerable multitude, who flocked to see their dreaded enemy; and, after being exhibited before Aurangzíb, they were ordered into confinement. Aurangzíb probably intended to spare his prisoner, for a time at least, as an instrument for gaining possession of his forts; but Sambají, now roused to a sense of his degradation, courted death, and replied to an invitation to become a Mussulman by language so insulting to the emperor, and so impious towards his prophet, that an order was given for his immediate execution. The sentence was probably issued on the ground of blasphemy; for it was attended with studied barbarity, very unlike the usual practice of Aurangzíb. His eyes were first destroyed with a hot iron, his tongue was cut out, and he was at last beheaded along with his favourite, Calúsha.

Put to death.

A. D. 1689, August.

Though his person had been despised by the Marattas, his fate was pitied and resented; and the indignation and religious hatred of the nation was raised to a higher pitch than ever.

Weakness of the Marattas.

Strong as was the animosity of the Marattas, their chance of resistance appeared to be very small. The overwhelming force of Aurangzíb, his personal reputation, even the pomp and grandeur which surrounded him, and the very name of the Great Mogul, struck them with an awe which they had not experienced in their former wars with his lieutenants. Their weakness became more con-

CHAP. III.

spicuous when Aurangzíb, remaining, himself, near Púna, sent a force to lay siege to their capital of Ráighar. The principal chiefs had assembled there on the death of Sambají, had acknowledged his infant son, afterwards called Sáho, as rája, and had nominated his uncle, Rája Rám, to be regent.

Aurangzíb sends a detachment to besiege Ráighar.

They then, after providing the fortress with a garrison and provisions, withdrew with the regent, to be ready for any service that might arise. Ráighar held out for several months, until a secret ascent was disclosed to the Moguls by a Máwalí chief, whom some personal disgust, combined with the general despondency, induced to this act of treason.* The infant rája was now in the hands of the enemy, and it was resolved that the regent, instead of exposing to risk the last representative of Sévají, should withdraw to the distant fortress of Jinjí in the Carnatic; while his forts in the Deckan were to be put in a good state of defence, and his troops dispersed in their villages, ready to profit by better times. Rám Rája accordingly

Regency of Rája Rám.

Ráighar taken.

A. D. 1690.

Rája Rám escapes to Jinjí.

* It seems unaccountable that these forts, which, at some times, are taken by a dozen at a time, at others held out for years against well-equipped armies: but they are often ill garrisoned, and without provisions; the garrison is often paid by lands which lie under the fort, and make them dependent on the enemy; even good garrisons are often surprised from overconfidence in the strength of the place, and sudden despair when they find difficulties overcome which they thought insurmountable. When such forts are in good order, with properly prepared garrisons and stores, it requires all the military resources and active courage of Europeans to make an impression on them.

BOOK XI.

proceeded with a few followers in disguise through the hostile provinces between him and Jinjí. When he reached that place, he proclaimed his arrival, and assumed the title of rája, on the ground of the captivity of his nephew. He was fortunate in an adviser in Prillád, one of the Bramin ministers, who had sufficient talents to gain an ascendancy over the other ministers and chiefs, and judgment to see that it was not desirable, even if it had been practicable, to do more than give a common scope to the general efforts.

Is proclaimed rája.

System of defence adopted by the Marattas.

Without the pervading genius of Sévají, the Marattas would never have been formed into a nation; but now, when all were animated by one spirit, the nature of the people, and their mode of war, required that it should be left to operate by individual exertions. The plan best adapted to them was, to bend before a blow, to offer nothing tangible for the enemy to attack, and to return to the charge with undiminished vigour whenever it suited them to take the part of assailants. Accordingly, their chiefs who were in possession of lands lost no time in making their submission to the Mogul, and none were louder in professions of zeal and attachment than they; but they almost all kept up a communication with the rebels, allowed their retainers to join them, even sent parties secretly under their own relations to share in plundering expeditions, and did more mischief as spies and hollow confederates than they could have done as open enemies. The soldiers, also, when they had no efficient government or regular treasury to look to, formed each his own plan for his individual profit. The thirst for plunder was always the strongest passion of the nation, from the first robbers under Sévají to the most opulent times of the monarchy. Their only word for a victory is, "to plunder the enemy;" and though they readily combine for common objects, yet even then the mass is moved by each man's eagerness for his separate booty. When this spirit was called into activity, it required but a moderate interference on the part of the government to give it a direction that rendered it more formidable than the courage of disciplined armies.

Zulfikár Khán sent to reduce Jinjí.

When the Maratta government appeared to have been expelled from the Deckan, Aurangzíb dispatched Zulfikár Khán, the son of Assad Khán, who had distinguished himself by the capture of Ráighar, to give it its death-blow by the reduction of Jinjí. Zulfikár, on his arrival, found that his force, though considerable, was not sufficient to reduce, or even to invest, the place. He applied to Aurangzíb for reinforcements, and in the mean time employed part of his army in levying contributions on Tanjore * and other southern countries. Aurangzíb was in no condition to furnish the reinforcements desired. He had sent his son, Cámbakhsh, with an army to reduce Wákinkéra, a fort not far from Bíjapúr, which, though only held by the head of one of the predatory tribes of the Deckan, was strong enough to baffle all his efforts.

* Called by the Marattas "Chandáwar."

BOOK XI.

Marattas renew the war by desultory operations under independent leaders.

A still greater demand for troops was created by the re-appearance of the Marattas themselves. No sooner was Rám Rája settled in Jinjí, than he dispatched his two most active chiefs, Santaji Gorpara and Danají Jádu, to make a diversion in his own country. Before they arrived, some bands of discharged Bíjapúr troops had begun to plunder on their own account, and as soon as these well-known leaders made their appearance, Maratta horsemen issued from every village, and flocked to join their standards. Rám Chander Pant, who was left at Sattára, in the civil charge of what little territory remained to the Marattas, had assembled some troops within his own districts, and by appealing to the predatory spirit before adverted to, he now called a new and most efficient army at once into
A. D. 1692. existence. His plan was, to confer on every man of influence amongst the soldiery a right to levy the *chout*, and other claims of the Maratta government, on all places not in its possession, and to plunder and lay waste every country that refused this tribute. The contributions were to go to the payment of the troops, the booty to the actual captors, and each chief was authorised to impose, for his personal benefit, a new exaction, called *ghás dána*, or *corn and hay money*. This invitation put every horseman in the country in motion. Most of the principal Maratta names appear (and many for the first time) as leaders of independent parties of various strength, which set out to enrich themselves at the expense of the Mogul's subjects; sometimes

each acting singly, and sometimes with a general concert, and fixed plans for rendezvous and retreat. The armies of Santají and Danají, though under the control of those chiefs, acted much on the same system: the Marattas spread, at once, in all directions, and the whole Deckan was filled with fire and rapine, terror and confusion.

Comparison of the Mogul and Maratta armies.

It was now that the Mogul and Maratta systems of war were fairly brought into competition, and it soon appeared with which side the advantage lay. The long tranquillity and mild government and manners established by Akber, and the greater mixture with the Hindús, first began to soften the character of the northern conquerors of India. The negligence of Jehángír's reign, and the internal quiet of Sháh Jehán's, were respectively unfavourable to discipline and to military spirit; and by the time we are speaking of, both were very sensibly impaired. The nobles had far advanced towards the sloth and effeminacy for which they have since been noted; and even those who retained their energy were unsuited to active service. They all went into the field in coats of wadding, that would resist a sword, and over that chain or plate armour, and were mounted on large and showy horses, with huge saddles, and ample housings of cloth or velvet, from which many streamers of different coloured satin, and often pairs of the bushy ox tails of Tibet, hung down on each side. The horse's neck, and all the harness, were loaded with chains, bells, and ornaments of the precious metals; and as each soldier imitated his superior as far as his means would admit, they formed a cavalry admirably fitted to prance in a procession, and not ill adapted to a charge in a pitched battle, but not capable of any long exertion, and still less of any continuance of fatigue and hardship.

To their individual inefficiency was added a total relaxation of discipline. In spite of all Aurangzíb's boasted vigilance, the grossest abuses had crept into the military department. Many officers only kept up half the number of their men, and others filled the ranks with their menials and slaves. Such comrades corrupted the soldiers by their example, and extinguished spirit by degrading the military character. The indulgence and connivance necessary for chiefs so conscious of their own delinquencies completed the ruin of their troops. They could neither be got to keep watch nor to remain alert on picket, and their sluggish habits would have prevented them ever turning out on an emergency, even if the time required to adjust their bulky housings and heavy defensive armour had not put it out of the question.*

The emperor's camp equipage was in all the pomp of peaceful times. Each nobleman endea-

* "The Frenchmen praised the high pay, and said the service was diversion: nobody would fight or keep watch, and only forfeited a day's pay when they failed to do either." (Gemelli Carreri, in *Churchill's Collection*, vol. iv. See also the Bondéla Narrative in *Scott's Deckan*, vol. ii.)

voured to imitate this magnificence; even private soldiers attended to comfort in their tents, and the line of march presented a long train of elephants, camels, carts, and oxen, mixed up with a crowd of camp followers, women of all ranks, merchants, shopkeepers, servants, cooks, and all kinds of ministers of luxury, amounting to ten times the number of the fighting men. This unwieldy host soon eat up a country, and the people suffered further from the insolence and licence of the soldiery.*

The Marattas, as has been said, were little active men, accustomed to hard work and hard fare. Their usual food was a cake of millet with perhaps an onion: their dress a small turban, tight breeches covering their thighs, and a scarf or sash rolled round their middle. When their body was not bare, it was covered by a light cotton tunic.

Their arms were a sword and a matchlock, but oftener a bamboo spear 13 or 14 feet long; their national weapon, which they used with extraordinary skill. Their horses were those of their own country; small, strong, and active; capable of enduring great fatigue; and taught to bound forward, or stop, or to wheel round when at full speed, on the slightest pressure from their rider's leg. They had a pad for a saddle, with a blanket folded over

* Gemelli Carreri saw Aurangzíb's cantonment at Galgala (March, 1695.) He describes it as an enormous assemblage, said greatly to exceed a million. The king's and prince's tents occupied a space of upwards of three miles in circumference, and were fortified with a ditch, palisades, and falconets.

it. When stationary, few except the chiefs had tents; and on their inroads, each man slept on the ground, with his spear stuck by him and his bridle tied to his arm, ready to leap on horseback on the slightest alarm of the approach of an enemy.

An assemblage of such troops never stood the heavy charge of a body of Moguls, but dispersed at once, and scampered off singly to the nearest hills or broken ground. If the enemy left their ranks to pursue them, they cut off single horsemen, or rapidly assembled behind a ravine, or in some other situation where it was not safe for small parties to attack them; and, when the disheartened pursuers turned back with their horses exhausted, the Marattas were upon them in a moment, charged in on them, if there was an opening or confusion, but generally hung loosely on their flanks and rear, sometimes dashing up singly to fire their matchlocks into the mass, or even to dispatch a straggler with their long spears. Their chief excellence, as well as their delight, was in the plunder of a convoy. The favour of the country people gave them full information, while it kept the Moguls in darkness, till they were suddenly assailed on the line of march, and saw the camels and cattle, carrying the grain and stores they were escorting, swept off in a moment. They would then form a compact body to protect those which were carrying treasure; but, with such a prize before them, the Marattas were irresistible: the party was generally obliged to take post; the Marattas cut off the communications, and perhaps even the water; and, at the end of a day or two, the Moguls were obliged to surrender; the men were stripped of their horses and their valuables, and the chiefs detained for a ransom.

As Aurangzíb drew a great proportion of his recruits and treasures from Hindostan, Santají and Danají threw themselves between his army and that country. They intercepted several convoys, defeated more than one detachment, and gained such a superiority that the Moguls began to change their contempt for them into fear and dread. A. D. 1693.

Siege of Jinjí committed to Prince Cámbakhsh.

In this state of discouragement Aurangzíb perceived the necessity of adopting some measure, which, if it did not bring the war to an end, might recover his reputation and restore the spirit of his troops. He resolved on the vigorous prosecution of the operations against Jinjí: he had withdrawn Cámbakhsh from Wákinkéra, and he now sent that prince with a fresh army to assume the conduct of the siege; but, according to his usual practice, he appointed Assad Khán, the father of Zulfikár Khán, to serve with him, and committed the real direction of all operations to those noblemen. A. D. 1694. This arrangement disgusted both parties: the prince was displeased at the little solid authority intrusted to him, and the others thought it hard that Zulfikár should be deprived of the dignity of the command and the honour of the victory.*

Disgust of Zulfikár.

So completely was Zulfikár led away by his re-

* Grant Duff; Kháfi Khán; and the Bondéla Narrative, in *Scott's Deckan.*

He obstructs the siege.

sentment, that he listened to overtures from the Maratta Bramins (ever on the watch to profit by such dissensions); and by indecisive operations on his own part, as well as by affording intelligence to the enemy, he enabled them to spin out the siege for no less than three years.

Santají Górpara advances to raise the siege.

A. D. 1697.

At the end of that time, Santají Górpara resolved on a bold attempt to relieve his rája. Leaving the rest of the Maratta hordes to keep Aurangzíb in occupation, he called in Danají Jádu, and set off for Jinjí with 20,000 of their best cavalry. He passed rapidly through the intervening country, and came on the besieging army with such celerity, that before they could arrange their cumbrous body for mutual support, his advance had surprised one of their divisions, plundered its tents, and made the commander prisoner; and he himself immediately after defeated a considerable body of troops sent out in haste to oppose him. He then drove in the outposts, destroyed the foragers, and cut off all supplies and intelligence from the camp. He next circulated reports of the emperor's death, which were easily believed in such a moment of calamity; and under favour of that rumour, he made proposals to Cámbakhsh to support his claim to the throne. Cámbakhsh, who seems to have apprehended sinister designs on the part of Assad and Zulfikár, gave ear to these communications, while his intercourse with the enemy in like manner alarmed those officers. One night Cámbakhsh ordered his immediate contingent to get under

Cámbakhsh placed under re-

CHAP. III.

straint by Zulfikár.

arms, and the two generals assuming (whether justly or otherwise) that this was a direct attempt to go over to the Marattas, immediately placed the prince under restraint.* This step increased the alarms and dissensions in the army to such a pitch, that they were soon compelled to blow up their cannon, abandon their batteries, and concentrate on one spot, where they intrenched themselves, and were besieged in their turn. At length an agreement was entered into between the parties; the Moguls were to be allowed to withdraw about twenty miles to Vandiwash, and were there to await the further orders of the emperor.

Retreat of the besiegers.

Aurangzíb cantons on the Bíma.

On the first advance of Cámbakhsh and Assad Khán, Aurangzíb had moved southward, and cantoned at Galgala on the Kishna. In the next year he retired to Birmapúri, near Panderpúr, on the Bíma, where he erected a permanent cantonment, and remained for several years. He now made a movement to Bíjapúr, and at the same time sent orders expressing his total disapprobation of the proceedings of his generals. He directed Cámbakhsh to be sent up to court, and received him with marked kindness†: at the same time he recalled Assad Khán; but, with unaccountable inconsistency, left the sole command of the army to Zulfikár Khán, whom, though the ablest of his

Releases Cambakhsh.

* Report of Assad and Zulfikár to Aurangzíb, quoted by the emperor in the forty-seventh note of the "Rakáim i Karáim:" also Grant Duff; Kháfi Khán; and Bondéla Narrative.

† Forty-eighth and forty-ninth notes of the "Rakáim i Karáim."

BOOK XI.

Increased disaffection of Zulfikár.

officers, he could not *now* expect to find the best affected. The war, when renewed, assumed a desultory character. Zulfikár levied contributions at Tanjore; and Santají totally destroyed a very strong Mogul detachment under an officer of rank and reputation near Chítaldrúg in the Mysore: other conflicts took place, with various success, in different parts of the country; but the general result must have been favourable to the Moguls,

A. D. 1697.

as they were able, in the end, to resume the siege of Jinjí.

He renews the siege, but protracts the operations.

During the operations in the field, Zulfikár performed the part of a zealous and able officer; but, on recommencing the siege, he renewed his intercourse with the Marattas, and evidently made it his object to protract the fall of the place.*

Resentment of the emperor.

But it was difficult to carry on such practices under a prince of Aurangzíb's penetration; and in the course of the next year Zulfikár found that he must either take Jinjí or expect to be recalled in disgrace. He performed a last act of friendship in advising Rája Rám to escape; and then, prose-

Jinjí taken. A. D. 1698.

cuting his operations with vigour and in earnest, he, before long, made himself master of the fortress.

* All Zulfikár's intrigues with the enemy appear from Maratta MSS. referred to by Captain Grant Duff, and are asserted (probably on similar authority procured at Mysore) by Colonel Wilks. They are unknown to the writers on the Mogul side; but the Bondéla accuses Zulfikár of purposely prolonging the war. His object, probably, was to retain his large command and important position until the death of the emperor, which his very advanced age made men expect to be of early occurrence.

CHAP. IV.

FROM 1698 TO THE DEATH OF AURANGZÍB.

CHAP. IV.

Dissensions among the Marattas.

THE unexpected recovery of Zulfikár's strength, which had put it in his power to renew the siege, was probably occasioned by dissensions among the Marattas, which now broke into an open quarrel. Danají Jádu had fallen out with Santají, and had received the support of the rája, who was jealous of the renown of the latter chief; and as Santají was unpopular, in consequence of his attempts to keep up discipline, a party was formed in his own camp, he was compelled to fly, and was at length overtaken and put to death on the spot.

Murder of Santají Górpara.

Before this catastrophe, Rája Rám had established his residence at Sattára, and he now assumed the active control of the whole government.

Rája Rám takes the field in person.

He took the field himself, at the head of the largest Maratta army that had ever yet been assembled, and, proceeding to the north of the Godáveri, levied the *chout* and other dues on such places as submitted, and ravaged the rest as far as Jálna in Berár. At this point his progress was checked in consequence of a change in the system of the Moguls.

New plan of Aurangzíb, — a besieging and pursuing army.

Hitherto Aurangzíb had, for the most part, had his head-quarters at Birmapúrí, sometimes sending a detachment under his son, Prince A'zim, to reduce a hill fort or repel an incursion, but generally trust-

BOOK XI.

ing the defence of the country to detachments stationed at different parts of it. At present his plan was to bring his whole force into efficiency, by leading one part, in person, against the enemy's forts, while another under Zulfikár Khán, nominally commanded by one of his grandsons, should pursue their field armies wherever they might direct their course. Had this plan been earlier adopted, it might have been attended with success; but disturbances had reached too great a height to be put down by any merely military dispositions. Although Zulfikár Khán began by driving back Rája Rám, as has been mentioned, and during the succeeding years repeatedly defeated the Marattas, and in some degree restored the courage of the Mussulmans, yet he found himself, at the end of that time, in a worse situation than when he began. A defeat to the Marattas was like a blow given to water, which offers no resistance to the stroke and retains no impression of its effect: their army dispersed at the moment to unite again on the same day or the next. But a defeat to the Moguls was attended with loss and humiliation; and even their partial success did not stop the waste of their resources and embarrassment of the finances of their government, which every day increased their difficulties and undermined their strength.

Exhaustion of the Moguls.

Sieges by the emperor in person.

Aurangzíb's personal operations gave a promise of more solid advantage. He quitted his cantonment, to the great regret of his officers, who had erected comfortable dwellings, and founded a sort of city; and, after reducing some other forts, he sat down before Sattára. By a dexterous feint he contrived to take that place unprepared: it nevertheless made a desperate defence, and did not surrender till the siege had lasted for several months.

Takes Sattára.

A. D. 1700, April.

Before it fell, Rám Rája had died, and had been succeeded by his son, Sévají, under the regency of Tára Bái, the widow of the deceased and mother of the young rája. This event had little effect on the war. Aurangzíb went on with his plan; and in the course of the next four or five years had taken almost all the principal forts possessed by the Marattas. Many of the sieges were long and bloody *, and various expedients and stratagems were employed by both parties in the conduct of them; but they were too monotonous to bear description, and the result was as has been stated.

Death of Rája Rám.

Aurangzíb goes on taking forts.

In reviewing these laborious undertakings, it is impossible not to admire the persevering spirit with which Aurangzíb bore up against the difficulties and misfortunes that overshadowed his declining years. He was near sixty-five when he crossed the Nerbadda to begin on this long war,

Spirit and perseverance of Aurangzíb.

* Aurangzíb writes thus of one of them to his son, Prince A'zim: "You will have received accounts of the calamities of the siege of Kélna, and of the unheard-of condition and intolerable sufferings of the followers of Islám. Praise be to God that the afflictions of this devout band have at length been brought to a conclusion." He then prays for happy results, and ascribes the past disasters to a judgment on his own wickedness and neglect. (Thirty-eighth note of the "Dastúr ul Aml.")

BOOK XI.

Difficulties and hardships to which he was exposed.

and had attained his eighty-first year before he quitted his cantonment at Birmapúri. The fatigues of marches and sieges were little suited to such an age; and in spite of the display of luxury in his camp equipage, he suffered hardships that would have tried the constitution of a younger man. While he was yet at Birmapúri, a sudden flood of the Bíma overwhelmed his cantonment in the darkness of the night, and during the violence of one of those falls of rain which are only seen in tropical climates: a great portion of the cantonment was swept away and the rest laid under water; the alarm and confusion increased the evil; 12,000 persons are said to have perished, and horses, camels, and cattle without number. The emperor himself was in danger, the inundation rising over the elevated spot which he occupied, when it was arrested (as his courtiers averred) by the efficacy of his prayers. A similar disaster was produced by the descent of a torrent during the siege of Parli, the fort he took next after Sattára; and, indeed, the storms of that inclement region must have exposed him to many sufferings, during the numerous rainy seasons he spent within it. The impassable streams, the flooded valleys, the miry bottoms, and narrow ways, caused still greater difficulties when he was in motion; compelled him to halt where no provisions were to be had; and were so destructive to his cattle as sometimes entirely to cripple his army. The violent heats, in tents, and during marches, were distressing at other seasons, and often rendered overpowering by failure of water: general famines and pestilences came more than once, in addition to the scarcity and sickness to which his own camp was often liable; and all was aggravated by accounts of the havoc and destruction committed by the enemy in the countries beyond the reach of those visitations. But in all these discouragements Aurangzíb retained his vigour. He alone conducted every branch of his government, in the most minute detail. He planned campaigns and issued instructions during their progress; drawings of forts were sent for him to fix on the points of attack; his letters embrace measures for keeping open the roads in the Afghán country, for quelling disturbances at Multán and Agra, and even for recovering possession of Candahár; and, at the same time, there is scarcely a detachment marches or a convoy moves in the Deckan without some orders from Aurangzíb's own hand.

His indefatigable industry.

His attention to details.

The appointment of the lowest revenue officer of a district, or the selection of a clerk in an office, is not beneath his attention; and the conduct of all these functionaries is watched by means of spies and of prying inquiries from all comers, and they are constantly kept on the alert by admonitions founded on such information. This attention to particulars is not favourable to the real progress of business, any more than it is indicative of an enlarged genius; but, combined, as it was in Aurangzíb, with unremitting vigilance in all the

BOOK XI.

greater affairs of the state, it shows an activity of mind that would be wonderful at any age.

His distrust of all around him.

These labours were the penalty he paid for his former offences against his father. The fate of Sháh Jehán seems never for an instant to have been absent from his thoughts. To avoid a similar destiny, he retains all power and all patronage, and by removing his chiefs from place to place prevents their forming permanent connections with anybody but himself. His sons are the constant objects of his observation and his management: he surrounds them with spies, gives them colleagues in command, places trustworthy persons in inferior situations about them, exercises an open control over all their proceedings; and at the same time never fails, by familiar and affectionate letters, and by constant presents and attentions, to conciliate their attachment and prevent their feeling the irksomeness of their situation. To similar motives also, though partly to his natural disposition, must be attributed the considerate manner in which he treats his officers, and the sort of court which he appears to pay to all of them: he condoles with their loss of relations; inquires about their illnesses; confers honours in a flattering manner; makes his presents more acceptable by the gracious way in which they are given; and scarcely ever passes a censure without softening it by some obliging expression. His extreme leniency to all offences that do not touch his power or his religious prejudices seems also

His management of his sons, and courtiers.

to have had its source in an unwillingness to make enemies, no less than in the real easiness of his temper. After all, he does not seem to have been successful in winning attachment; and with his sons, he seems at heart to have trusted much more to fear than affection. Though he released Móazzim after seven years' imprisonment (A. D. 1694), he seems always to have regarded him with dislike and apprehension. He sent him to the remote government of Cábul, constantly resisted his wishes to return, even for a time, and endeavoured to engage him in an expedition which might carry him to the most distant part of his province and might completely absorb his resources. He at first approved of the seizure of Cámbakhsh, though afterwards convinced of his innocence; and his behaviour on one occasion to his favourite, Prince A'zim, shows at once his policy in the management of his sons and his innate love of artifice and dissimulation. Having imbibed a suspicion that this prince was meditating independence, he sent for him to court; and as the prince made excuses and showed alarm, he offered to meet him slightly attended on a hunting party. A'zim, on this, set out, and Aurangzíb secretly surrounded the place of meeting with chosen troops: as the prince got more and more within his toils, the old emperor found a succession of pretences for requiring him gradually to diminish the number of his attendants, until, when he reached the place where his father was, they were reduced to three persons.

BOOK XI.

As nobody offered to undertake the duty, he was obliged to leave two of his companions to hold his horses; and he with the remaining attendant were disarmed before they were admitted to the royal presence. On this he gave himself up for lost, and had no doubt that he was doomed to a long or perpetual imprisonment. But when he was introduced to his father, he was received with an affectionate embrace. Aurangzíb, who was prepared for shooting, gave his loaded gun to him to hold, and then led him into a retired tent, where he showed him a curious family sword, and put it naked into his hand that he might examine it; after which he threw open his vest, on pretence of heat, but in reality to show that he had no hidden armour. After this display of confidence, he loaded A'zim with presents, and at last said he had better think of retiring, or his people would be alarmed at his detention. This advice was not premature: A'zim, on his return, found his whole camp on the point of breaking up, and his women weeping and lamenting his supposed fate. Whether he felt grateful for his easy dismission does not appear; but it is recorded that he never after received a letter from his father without turning pale, or recovered his composure until he had satisfied himself of the contents of it.*

Increased disorders of the state.

But all Aurangzíb' arts and all his industry were insufficient to resist the increasing disorders

* Kháfi Khán.

of the state, which now pressed upon him from every quarter. The Rájpúts were still in open hostility: their example had long since been followed by the Játs near Agra: against these last, as at a later period against some insurgents at Multán*, it had been necessary to send a force under a prince of the blood. Zulfikár's force began to be exhausted, and the inefficacy of his former exertions became more and more apparent. The Marattas seemed to multiply as the Mogul armies decayed: after reducing the Deckan to a desert, they had spread over Málwa and made a powerful inroad into Guzerát; leaving their traces every where, in pillaged towns, ravaged fields, and smoking villages.

Successes of the Marattas.

The grand army still went on taking forts; but its last success was scarcely less ignominious than a defeat: it was the taking of Wákinkéra, which, though only a fortified village, belonging to a chief of banditti, required the presence of the emperor and a siege of several months to subdue it. These acquisitions began at this time to be balanced by corresponding losses. The Marattas were in a condition to attempt the recovery of their strong holds, and the forts which it had cost so many labours to gain, were one by one falling into their possession. As the calls on the grand army increased, its power went on to decline. The troops became more timid than ever; the cattle were worn out

They begin to recover their forts.

Exhausted state of the army.

* Probably the Síks, under Guru Govind.

BOOK XI.

and could not be replaced from the wasted state of the country; provisions failed from the same reason, and the means of obtaining them from a distance were cut off by the emptiness of the treasury.

Disorder of the finances.

Notwithstanding vast remittances from Hindostan, the finances had long since fallen into confusion; and as their state became more painful, Aurangzíb withdrew his attention from them.* He was irritated by applications for arrears of pay, and used peevishly to answer such demands by saying that he did not want the troops, and if they were not pleased with his service they might quit it.† He even disbanded some bodies of horse, with the intention of easing the finances. But regular pay was indispensable to troops situated like his; and when it had been long withheld, they began to break into open mutinies, which were quieted by temporary expedients.‡

Grand army hard pressed by the Marattas.

All his difficulties were increased as the Marattas drew closer round the army. At times they plundered up to the very skirts of the camp, intercepted

* Aurangzíb's letters, and Kháfi Khán.

† Kháfi Khán. The army was for a long time very regularly paid. Gemelli Carreri, in 1695, says the troops were paid punctually every two months, and would not bear any irregularity.

‡ He writes, on one occasion, to Zulfikár Khán, that he is stunned with the clamours of "these infernal foot soldiers," who are croaking like crows in an invaded rookery. In another letter he reminds him of the wants of the exchequer, and presses him to search for hidden treasures, and to hunt out any that may have fallen into the hands of individuals. Many of his notes dwell on his pecuniary embarrassments.

CHAP. IV.

the supplies, carried off the cattle, cut up the foragers, insulted the pickets, and made it impossible for any one to show his head out of the lines without a powerful escort. If an ordinary detachment was sent to check them, they repelled or destroyed it. If a great effort was made, they vanished, and perhaps did not again appear till they had plundered some distant town, and left time for their pursuers to weary themselves by forced marches in a wrong direction.* They now treated the power of the emperor with derision. Those in his service mixed and feasted with those opposed to him, and on such occasions they used to mimic the pompous manners and devout ejaculations of the Mussulmans, and to pray with mock solemnity for long life to their best patron, Aurangzíb. So low was the emperor reduced, that he was persuaded by Cámbakhsh to authorise overtures to the enemy; and if the negotiations had not been broken off by the exorbitance and insolence of the Marattas, he would probably have agreed to release Sáho Rája, and grant (in such forms as might save his dignity) an annual per centage on the revenue of the Deckan.

Retreats to Ahmednagar.

Aurangzíb's last military operation was a retreat to Ahmednagar, the nature of which may be conceived from his exhausted cattle and dispirited troops. All hurried on in disorder and dejection, deafened with the incessant firing kept up by the

* Bondéla Narrative, in Scott's "Deckan," vol. ii.

BOOK XI.

marksmen, alarmed by the shouts and charges of the lancers, and every moment expecting a general attack to complete their dispersion and destruction. Such, indeed, was the fate of a portion of the army; and it is a subject of pious exultation to the Mussulman historians that the emperor himself escaped falling into the hands of the enemies whom he had once so much despised.*

Ahmednagar, from whence, twenty years before, he had marched in so much power and splendour on his conquests, received the remains of his ruined greatness, and was soon to witness the close of his earthly career.

Declining health of the emperor.

His health had, of late, become gradually impaired; he with difficulty overcame one illness that threatened his life; and although he continued his public appearance and his attention to business, his spirit at length began to sink under the accumulated burden of anxiety and disease. On reaching Ahmednagar, he said he had now come to the end of all his journeys; and from his last letters we perceive, at once, the extent of his bodily sufferings, the failure of his hopes in this world, and his dread of that to come. The remembrance of Sháh Jehán seemed to haunt him more than ever; he nowhere expresses remorse for his share in that monarch's fate, but he shows by all his actions how much he fears that a like measure may be meted out to him.

His fears of encountering the fate of Sháh Jehán.

* Grant Duff, vol. i. p. 409.

His suspicions of his sons.

Prince Móazzim having proposed some arrangements which common prudence required at such a crisis, he interprets them into a design to seize on the government while he was yet alive. When a letter from Prince A'zim was read to him, entreating permission to come to Ahmednagar, on the ground that the air of Guzerát was ruining his health, he abruptly remarked, "That is exactly the pretext I used to Sháh Jehán in his illness;" and added, that "no air was so unwholesome as the fumes of ambition:" and although afterwards prevailed on by A'zim's importunity to allow him to pay him a visit on his way to his new government of Málwa, yet one of the last exertions of his authority was, to compel the prince to proceed on his journey, and to prevent his finding any excuse for remaining about the court. He had just before sent off Cámbakhsh to Bíjapúr; but this seems rather to have been done to gratify A'zim than from any apprehensions of his own.

His alarms at the approach of death.

These measures had not been long completed before he became sensible that his end was approaching. In this awful moment he wrote, or dictated, a letter to Prince A'zim, in which his worldly counsels and his adieus are mixed with broken sentences giving utterance to the feelings of remorse and terror with which his soul was agitated, and which he closes with a sort of desperate resignation, — "Come what come may, I have launched my vessel on the waves." . . . "Farewell! farewell! farewell!"

BOOK XI.

He also wrote to his youngest, and, latterly, his favourite, son, Cámbakhsh. His letter, as to a much younger man, is more one of advice and admonition than that to A'zim. It shows that he retained his favourite habits to the last. "Your courtiers," he says, "*however deceitful*, must not be ill-treated: it is necessary to gain your views by gentleness and art," &c. Even in this letter, his sense of his own situation breaks out from time to time. "Wherever I look I see nothing but the Divinity." ... "I have committed numerous crimes, and I know not with what punishments I may be seized." ... The agonies of death come upon me fast." ... "I am going. Whatever good or evil I have done, it was for you."* It must have been about the same time that he drew up a sort of will, which was found under his pillow on his death. He there recommends that Móazzim should be recognised as emperor, and that he and A'zim should divide the empire, one taking the northern and eastern provinces, with Delhi for his capital; and the other, Agra, with all the country to the south and south-west of it, including all the Deckan, except the kingdoms of Golcónda and Bíjapúr. These last were assigned to Cámbakhsh.†

I have taken the translation in Scott's "Deckan," vol. ii. page 8. of the Memoirs, though the original of it must have differed in some slight particulars from the Persian copy at the India House.

† He left another will, seemingly prepared when under less agitation. It contains some general maxims of government, and

CHAP. IV.

His death,

He expired on the 21st of February, A. D. 1707, in the eighty-ninth year of his life, and fiftieth of his reign. *

and character.

A native historian, impressed with the courage, wisdom, and ability of Aurangzíb, is at a loss to account for the ill success of his reign. The real defect was in his heart. Had he been capable of any generous or liberal sentiment, he would have been a great prince; his subjects would not have been alienated by his narrow views in religion, nor would the powers of his officers have been cramped, and their zeal chilled, by a constant spirit of suspicion and distrust. † In alluding, for the last time,

---

instructions about his funeral; the expense of which was to be defrayed by a sum of four rupees and a half (about ten shillings), saved from the price of caps which he had made and sold. Eight hundred and five rupees, which he had gained by copying Koráns, was to be given to the poor. (See *Asiatic Register* for 1801.)

* These are solar years. He was born the 15th Zi Cáad, 1027, about the end of October, 1618. (*Kháfi Khán. Gladwin's Jehángír*, p. 45.)

† "Of all the house of Teimur, indeed of all the kings of Delhi, none since the time of Secander Lódi ever appeared so distinguished, in point of devotion, austerity, and justice; and in courage, patience, and sound judgment, he was without a peer: but as, from reverence to the injunctions of the Divine law, he did not inflict punishment, and as without punishment no country can be kept in order — in consequence, also, of the dissensions arising from rivalry among his nobles — every plan and design which he formed came to little good, and every enterprise drew into delay, and never attained its object. Though he had lived ninety years, yet none of his five senses were at all impaired, except his hearing in a small degree, but not so that others could perceive it." (*Kháfi Khán.*)

to his narrow views in religion, which contributed so largely to the ruin of his empire, it is well worth while to observe by how little direct persecution that evil result was produced. The Hindús seem rather to have been irritated by systematic discouragement than inflamed by acts of cruelty or oppression. They were excluded from office; they were degraded by a special tax; their fairs and festivals were forbidden; their temples were sometimes insulted and destroyed; and it was sufficient to procure the abolition of any ceremony or practice of the court that it seemed to give a countenance to their superstition: but it does not appear that a single Hindú suffered death, imprisonment, or loss of property for his religion, or, indeed, that any individual was ever questioned for the open exercise of the worship of his fathers. Yet such is the effect of mutual jealousy and animosity in matters of religion, that the most violent outrages have seldom raised up so obstinate a spirit of resistance as was engendered by the partiality and prejudices of this emperor.

Some hundreds of Aurangzíb's letters have been preserved, from which we may glean some particulars of his character, in addition to the great lines marked by his actions. With all his bigotry he was not superstitious. He cordially detests the Hindús, and has very little more good will towards the Shiás; but he lays out no money on mosques or endowments, shows no sign of being under the influence of the recognised clergy, and often expresses his contempt for the assumed sanctity of fakírs and dervises. CHAP. IV.

His government is a system of continual mistrust: every man's character is secretly investigated, and colleagues are so selected, that each may be a check on his neighbour; yet there never was a prince so much cheated or so ill served.

The coldness of his heart is conspicuous in the manner in which he receives the accounts of the death of his oldest and most intimate friends. In so long a life such events often occur, and they always draw forth some pious or philosophical reflection, followed up by strict orders to seize on the property of the deceased, to see that none is embezzled, to hunt out all deposits, and to be careful in recovering all outstanding debts.

His letters almost invariably include some poetical quotation, or some verse from the Koran. They are sometimes familiar, and even jocose, especially those to his sons. One, written after he was eighty, ends with some burlesque verses, of two or three words long, each of which gives a ludicrous description of the present occupations of some one of the principal people about his court.* His letters.

* There are three collections of his letters: — First, the "Kalámát i Táibát," published by one of his chief secretaries, Enáyat Ullah; second, the "Rokáimi i Karáim," by the son of another secretary; and, third, the "Dastúr ul Aml Agáhí," collected from all quarters, thirty-eight years after his death. The two first collections profess to be merely the rough drafts or notes which he wrote with his own hand for his secretaries. Most of the third collection have the same appearance. They

BOOK XI.

Gemelli Carreri, who saw Aurangzíb in the seventy-eighth year of his age, describes him as of low stature, slender, and stooping with age, with a long nose and a round beard, the whiteness of which was more visible on his olive skin. He was dressed in plain white muslin, with one emerald of great size in his turban. He stood amidst his omrahs, leaning on a staff; received petitions; read them without spectacles, endorsed them with his own hand, "and, by his cheerful smiling countenance, seemed to be pleased with the employment."*

Of all the kings of India, Aurangzíb is the most admired among the Mussulmans. There are few who are quite blind to the lustre of Akber's character, but fewer still whose deliberate judgment would not give the preference to Aurangzíb.

Miscellaneous transactions.

There are some unconnected events which should not be entirely omitted in an account of this reign.

The insurrection of the Játs has been mentioned; they are a Hindú people of the Súdra class, who inhabit a tract near Agra, of which the capital is Bhartpúr. Though in an open country, and close to Agra and Mattra, they occasioned much embarrassment to the government even during this reign, and rose to so much greater consequence in

---

are without dates or order, and are often obscure, from their brevity and our ignorance of the subjects alluded to.

* Gemelli Carreri, in Churchill, vol. iv.

those that followed, that at one time they were in possession of Agra; and were the last people in the plains of India that have offered any serious obstacle to the British power. CHAP. IV.

In the thirty-eighth year of the king's reign, A. D. 1693, a ship bound from Surat to Mecca with pilgrims, which Kháfi Khán describes as carrying 80 guns*, and furnished with 400 muskets, was attacked by an English ship of small size. A gun burst on board the king's ship; the English boarded, and "although the Christians have no courage at the sword, yet by bad management the vessel was taken."

On this Aurangzíb ordered the English factors at his ports to be seized, and directed the Abyssinians to take Bombay.

The English retaliated by seizing the king's officers, and the Abyssinians, who (by Kháfi Khán's account) where on a friendly footing with them, showed no inclination to break it off. At length Kháfi Khán himself was sent on a mission from the viceroy of Guzerát to Bombay. He describes his reception as being conducted with great dignity and good order, and with a considerable display of military power. He negotiated with elderly gentlemen in rich clothes, and, although they sometimes laughed more heartily than became so grave

* The number is probably not exaggerated, though the guns must have been light. Some of the Company's ships of 600 tons carried seventy guns. (See *Macpherson's Commerce of India*, p. 133.)

BOOK XI.

an occasion, yet he seems to have been favourably impressed with their acuteness and intelligence. The English alleged, apparently with truth, that the king's ship had been taken by pirates, for whom they were not answerable; and explained their coining money in their own king's name (which was another complaint against them) by stating that they had to purchase investments at places where the Mogul's money did not pass.

Nothing is stated to have been settled on this occasion; but it appears from other sources that the English compounded for some pecuniary payments.*

It is curious that Kháfi Khán (though, in this case, he relates a transaction of small moment in which he was personally engaged) takes no notice of the war made on Aurangzíb by the English on both sides of India, which was of so much consequence in the history of the East India Company. He did not foresee the future importance of those unskilful antagonists.

* Grant Duff

BOOK XII.

SUCCESSORS OF AURANGZÍB.

CHAP. I.

TO THE ACCESSION OF MOHAMMED SHÁH.

Bahádur Sháh.

CHAP. I.

Contest between Prince A'zim and his elder brother, Prince Móazzim.

As soon as Prince A'zim heard of his father's death, he returned to camp, and within a week was proclaimed sovereign of all India, in perfect disregard of the late emperor's will.

Prince Móazzim, with better reason, assumed the crown at Cábul, with the title of Bahádur Sháh; and both brothers prepared to assert their pretensions by force of arms. In spite of the exhausted state of the empire, they assembled very large armies, and met at length not far to the south of Agra. A bloody battle ensued, in which Prince A'zim and his two grown up sons were killed, and his youngest son, an infant, was taken prisoner. Prince A'zim had disgusted many of his principal officers by his arrogance: among others, Assad Khán, and his son, Zulfikár Khán, had quitted his camp, and remained spectators of the contest. When the event was known, they sent their submission to the victor. Bahádur Sháh received

Victory of Móazzim, henceforward Bahádur Sháh.

A. D. 1707, June.

A. H. 1119, Rabi al awal.

BOOK XII.

them graciously, and promoted them to the highest honours in the state. He showed like indulgence towards the other adherents of A'zim Sháh; but his confidence was chiefly reposed in Moním Khán, who had been his own principal officer at Cábul, and was now appointed vizír. Moním was an equally able and well-intentioned minister; and as the king's only fault was too great facility of temper, his accession was welcomed by the great body of his subjects, who looked to some relief from the religious austerity of Aurangzíb, and the sacrifices entailed on them by his obstinate wars.

Revolt of Prince Cámbakhsh in the Deckan.

Prince Cámbakhsh, though a vain and violent young man, had admitted the sovereignty of Prince A'zim, and had been confirmed in his appanage; but he refused to acknowledge Bahádur Sháh; and that king, after attempting in vain to win him over by concessions, marched against him to the Deckan, and defeated him in a battle near Heiderábád, where Cámbakhsh died of his wounds on the same day.

His defeat and death. A. D. 1708, February; A. H. 1119, Zí Cáad.

Bahádur's proceedings in the Deckan.

State of the Marattas.

Factions of Rája Sáho and Tára Bái.

The emperor's presence in the Deckan made it necessary to consider what course should be adopted towards the Marattas. It was easier at this time to effect an accommodation with them than could have been expected from the state of affairs at Aurangzíb's death. At that period, Sáho the rightful rája, was still a prisoner in the hands of the Moguls, and the government was carried on by Tára Bái, the widow of his uncle, Rája Rám, in the name of her infant son. But though the necessity of having an efficient chief had induced the Marattas to place Rája Rám on their throne after the taking of Ráighar, they had not forgotten the hereditary claim of his nephew, and were not pleased to see him again excluded without the same motive as before. With a view to profit by these contending claims, Prince A'zim, on his march against Bahádur Sháh, released Sáho, who was now grown up, and promised him peace on favourable terms if he should succeed in establishing his title. This plan was adopted at the suggestion of Zulfikár Khán, and completely answered its end. The Maratta chiefs took different sides; and instead of overwhelming their enemies, who seemed incapable of further resistance, they fell into civil war among themselves, and left the Moguls undisturbed at the moment of their greatest weakness When Bahádur Sháh turned his attention to the Marattas, Sáho seemed likely to prevail in the contest; and Zulfikár, who was now in great favour, was anxious that peace should be concluded with him, at the price of the concessions formerly offered by Aurangzíb. But Moním Khán, the vizír, though willing to agree to the terms, wished them to be granted to Tára Bái, and the whole negotiation fell to the ground.

Dáúd Khán Panni left in charge of the Deckan for Zulfikár Khán.

On Bahádur's departure, he gave the viceroyalty of the Deckan to Zulfikár; and, as that chief could not be spared from court, he left the administration of the government to Dáúd Khán Panni, a Patán

BOOK XII.

officer already distinguished in Aurangzíb's wars, who was to act as his lieutenant.

Makes a truce with the Marattas.

Dáúd followed up the views of his principal, and concluded a personal agreement with Sáho, consenting that the *chout*, or fourth, should be paid while he remained in office, but stipulating that it should be collected by agents of his own, without the interference of the Marattas.

Transactions with the Rájpúts.

This arrangement kept the Deckan quiet till the end of the present reign, and allowed Bahádur to turn his thoughts to other scenes where his exertions were scarcely less required. While he was on his march against Cámbakhsh, he had endeavoured to make a settlement of his disputes with the Rájpúts. He had entered into a treaty with the rána of Oudipúr, restoring all conquests, re-establishing religious affairs on the footing on which they stood in Akber's time, releasing the rána from the obligation to furnish a contingent in the Deckan, and, in fact, acknowledging his entire independence in every thing but the name.* He had concluded a treaty, apparently on similar terms, with Ajít Sing, the rája of Márwár, except that, in the latter case, the service of the contingent was still retained. On Jei Sing, the rája of Jeipúr, (who, though he had never asserted his independence, had joined with Prince A'zim in the late civil war,) he had imposed more rigorous terms. He had left a garrison in his capital; and, although he

* Colonel Tod's Rajasthan, vol. i. p. 395.

allowed him to command the Jeipúr contingent with the army, he seems to have deprived him of all authority in his own principality. By the time the army reached the Nerbadda on its advance, Ajít Sing also had received some cause of offence; and the two rájas went off together, with their troops, and entered into a league to resist the Mogul authority. As soon as the contest in the Deckan was put an end to by the death of Cámbakhsh, Bahádur Sháh turned his attention to breaking up the confederacy; but, before he reached the Rájpút country, he received intelligence of the capture of Sirhind by the Síks, and of such a state of affairs in the Panjáb, as left him no time for his intended operations.*

Peace with that power.

In these circumstances, he became anxious to make peace with the Rájpúts; and, as the great obstacle to an accommodation arose from their fears of treachery, he sent his own son, Prince A'zim u Shán, to accompany them to a meeting which took place on the emperor's line of march, and at which the rájas appeared at the head of their own armies. All their demands were agreed to, and they were probably left on the same footing as the rána of Oudipúr.

A. D. 1709, A. H. 1121.

Rise of the Síks.

The Síks, against whom the emperor was obliged to march, had originally been a religious sect; were then rising into a nation; and have, in our times,

* Scott's Memoirs of Erádat Khán, p. 58. Tod's Rajasthan, vol. ii. p. 77, &c.

BOOK XII.

attained to considerable political influence among the states of India.

Peaceful character of their sect.

Their founder, Nánik, flourished about the end of the fifteenth century. He was a disciple of Kabír, and consequently a sort of Hindú deist, but his peculiar tenet was universal toleration. He maintained that devotion was due to God, but that forms were immaterial, and that Hindú and Mahometan worship were the same in the sight of the Deity.* The spirit of this religion promised to keep its votaries at peace with all mankind; but such views of comprehensive charity were particularly odious to the bigoted part of the Mahometans; and accordingly, after the sect had silently increased for more than a century, it excited the jealousy of the Mussulman government, and its spiritual chief was put to death in A. D. 1606†, within a year after the decease of Akber. This act of tyranny changed the Síks from inoffensive quietists into fanatical warriors. They took up arms under Har Govind, the son of their martyred pontiff, who inspired them with his own spirit of revenge and of hatred to their oppressors. Being now open enemies of the government, the Síks were expelled from the neighbourhood of Láhór, which had hitherto been their seat, and constrained to take refuge in the northern

Persecuted by the Mahometans.

Their revolt.

* Professor Wilson, *Asiatic Researches*, vol. xvii. p. 233.

† Sir J. Malcolm, *Asiatic Researches*, vol. xi. p. 212.

mountains.* Notwithstanding dissensions which broke out among themselves, they continued their animosity to the Mussulmans, and confirmed their martial habits, until the accession (A. D. 1675) of Guru Govind, the grandson of Har Govind, and the tenth spiritual chief from Nánik. This leader first conceived the idea of forming the Síks into a religious and military commonwealth, and executed his design with the systematic spirit of a Grecian lawgiver.

Guru Govind.

He forms the Síks into a religious and military commonwealth.

To increase the numbers of his society, he abolished all distinctions of cast among its members, admitting all converts, whether Mahometan or Hindú, Bramin or Chandala, to a perfect equality; while, to preserve its unity, he instituted a peculiar dress and peculiar manners, by which his followers were to be distinguished from all the rest of mankind. Each was to be a vowed soldier from his birth or initiation, was always to carry steel in some form about his person, to wear blue clothes, allow his hair and beard to grow, and neither to clip nor remove the hairs on any other part of his body.

Their doctrines and manners.

Reverence for the Hindú gods, and respect for Bramins, were maintained, and the slaughter of kine was most positively forbidden; but all other prohibitions relating to food and liquors were abolished; the usual forms of worship were laid aside; new modes of salutation, and new ceremonies on the principal events of life, were intro-

* Sir J. Malcolm, p. 214.

BOOK XII.

duced*; and so effectual was the change operated on the people, that the Síks have now (after parting with several of their singularities) as distinct a national character as any of the original races in India. They are tall and thin, dark for so northern a people, active horsemen, and good matchlockmen: they are still all soldiers, but no longer fanatics; though unpolished they are frank and sociable, and are devoted to pleasure of every description and degree.

They are overpowered at first

Far different was their character under Guru Govind, when they were filled with zeal for their faith and rancour against their enemies, and were prepared to do or suffer any thing to promote the success of their cause. But their numbers were inadequate to accomplish their plans of resistance and revenge: after a long struggle, Guru Govind saw his strong holds taken, his mother and his children massacred, and his followers slain, mutilated, or dispersed. His misfortunes impaired his reason, or at least destroyed his energy; for so little formidable had he become, that he was allowed to enter the Mogul dominions unmolested, and was murdered by a private enemy, at Nándér, in the Deckan.† But although it is sometimes possible to crush a religion even after it has taken root, it can only be done by long

* Sir J. Malcolm, *Asiatic Researches*, vol. xi. pp. 219, 220. 284. 288.

† Sir J. Malcolm. Forster's Travels, p. 263. The latter author states that Guru Govind had a small command in the Mogul service; which is confirmed by Kháfi Khán.

and steady persecution; and *that* the internal disturbances of the Moguls prevented their applying.

Their fanaticism.

Their severities only exalted the fanaticism of the Síks, and inspired a gloomy spirit of vengeance, which soon broke out into fury. Under a new chief named Bandu, who had been bred a religious ascetic, and who combined a most sanguinary disposition with bold and daring counsels, they broke from their retreat, and overran the east of the Panjáb, committing unheard-of cruelties wherever they directed their steps. The mosques, of course, were destroyed, and the mullahs butchered; but the rage of the Síks was not restrained by any considerations of religion, or by any mercy for age or sex: whole towns were massacred with wanton barbarity; and even the bodies of the dead were dug up and thrown out to the birds and beasts of prey.

Their successes, ravages, and cruelties under Bandu.

The principal scene of these atrocities was Sirhind, which the Síks occupied after defeating the governor in a pitched battle; but the same horrors marked their route through the country eastward of the Satlaj and Jamna, into which they penetrated as far as Seháranpúr. They at length received a check from the local authorities, and retired to the country on the upper course of the Satlaj, between Lodiána and the mountains. This seems, at that time, to have been their principal seat; and it was well suited to their condition, as they had a near

BOOK XII.

and easy retreat from it when forced to leave the open country.

Their retirement, on the present occasion, was of no long continuance; and on their next incursions they ravaged the country as far as the neighbourhood of Láhór on the one side, and of Delhi itself on the other.*

Bahádur marches against them.

It was the extent of these depredations that made it necessary for Bahádur to come against them in person. He soon drove them within their own limits, and then obliged them to take refuge in the hills: to subdue them effectually, however, required a considerable exertion; and after Bandu had at length been reduced to take refuge in a fort, it was only by means of famine that the emperor could hope to take the place. A long and strict blockade was therefore set on foot; but, although the Síks endured the utmost extremities of hunger, and died in vast numbers, they still continued the defence. When further resistance became hopeless, a desperate sally was made by the besieged; many of the partakers in this bold enterprise were killed, and the Mussulmans took possession of the fort without further resistance. A person who seemed to be their chief, and had used every means of making himself conspicuous, was made prisoner, and carried off in triumph: when he arrived in camp, it was found that he was a Hindú

They are driven into the hills.

Escape of Bandu.

* The proceedings of the Síks, till their capture of Seháranpúr, is from Sir J. Malcolm, Foster, and Kháfi Khán: the subsequent narrative is from Kháfi Khán alone.

convert who had sacrificed himself to save his leader, and that Bandu himself had escaped during the sally. The emperor, though sufficiently struck by the prisoner's self-devotion to spare his life, was yet so ungenerous as to order him to be shut up in an iron cage and sent to Delhi.

After this success, the emperor returned to Láhór, leaving a detachment to watch the Síks, and to check their depredations. This object was not fully attained, and the power of the Síks was again on the ascendant, when Bahádur Sháh died at Láhór, in the seventy-first lunar year of his age, and fifth of his reign.

Death of Bahádur Sháh. A. D. 1712, February; A. H. 1124, Moharram.

The death of Bahádur Sháh was followed by the usual struggle among his sons. The incapacity of the eldest (afterwards Jehándár Sháh) had given a great ascendancy to the second, whose name was A'zim u Shán; and as he was supported by most of the nobility and of the army, he appeared to have an irresistible superiority over his competitors.

Contest between his sons.

But his three brothers joined their interests, and were kept together by the persuasions and false promises of Zulfikár Khán, whose love of intrigue was still as strong as ever. Their concord was of short duration, but lasted until the defeat and death of A'zim u Shán. Two of the surviving brothers soon after came to an open conflict, and the third attacked the victor on the morning after the battle: he was, however, repulsed and slain; and Je-

Artifices of Zulfikár Khán.

He secures the victory to Jehándár Sháh.

BOOK XII.

hándár Sháh remained undisputed master of the throne.

A.D. 1712, May or June; A.H. 1124, Jamádi al awal.

Jehándár Sháh.

Accession of Jehándar Sháh. His incapacity.

Immediately on his accession, Jehándár appointed Zulfikár Khán to be vizír. This crafty and able chief had supported Jehándár through the whole of the preceding contest; judging, from the low and slothful habits of that prince, that he was best suited for a tool in the hands of an ambitious minister.

Arrogance of Zulfikár Khán.

Accordingly, he assumed the control of the government from the first, and treated the emperor with the utmost arrogance and disdain. He could not have ventured to adopt this course, if Jehándár, besides degrading his own dignity by his vices and follies, had not provoked the nobility by his partiality for the relations of his favourite mistress. This woman had been a public dancer, and her family were of the same discreditable class: yet they were exalted to high stations, to the exclusion of the nobles, whom they were also allowed on several

General discontent.

occasions to insult with impunity. But though their disgust at such proceedings prevented the nobility from taking part with the emperor, it did not reconcile them to the pride and tyranny of Zulfikár, which soon came to be displayed towards all ranks; and it is not improbable that their discontents might have led to open opposition, if the attention of all had not been attracted by a danger from without.

One of Jehándár's first acts had been to put all the princes of the blood, within his reach, to death: among those whom he could not get into his power was Farokhsír, the son of A'zim u Shán, who was in Bengal at the time of Bahádur Sháh's death. After that event, and the ruin of A'zim u Shán, he threw himself on the compassion and fidelity of Seiad Hosén Ali, the governor of Behár, an old adherent of his father's who warmly espoused his cause, and prevailed on his brother, Seiad Abdullah, governor of Allahábád, to adopt the same course.

Revolt of Prince Farokhsír in Bengal.

He is supported by Abdullah and Hosén Ali, governors of Behár and Allahábád.

By the aid of these noblemen, Farokhsír assembled an army at Allahábád, repelled a force sent to oppose him on his advance, and had marched to the neighbourhood of Agra, when he was met by Jehándár and Zulfikár with an army of 70,000 men. The battle was fiercely contested; and Hosén Ali, the soul of Farokhsír's enterprise, was left for dead upon the field. But success at length declared for the rebels: the emperor himself fled in disguise to Delhi; whither Zulfikár retreated at the head of his remaining troops. Jehándár, on reaching Delhi, repaired to the house of Assad Khán the father of Zulfikár: this practised traitor immediately committed him to custody; and, on the arrival of Zulfikár, persuaded him, though at first unwilling to part with the instrument of his ambition, to endeavour to make his peace with the new emperor by the sacrifice of his rival.

Defeats the imperial army.

A. D. 1713, Jan. 1.; A. H. 1124, Zil Haj 15.

Accordingly, as Farokhsír approached the capi-

Zulfikár betrays

BOOK XII.

Jehándár Sháh to the enemy; but is put to death along with the emperor.

A. D. 1713, Feb. 4.; A. H. 1125, Moharram 17.

tal, both father and son went out to meet him, and delivered their late unfortunate master into his hands. Assad Khán's life was spared; but Zulfikár paid the penalty of his selfish and perfidious career, and was strangled before he left the imperial tent. Jehándár was put to death at the same time; and these severities were followed by many other executions.

Farokhsír.

Great power of Seiads Abdullah and Hosén Ali.

The accession of Farokhsír was naturally accompanied by the elevation of his protectors. Abdullah Khán, the eldest brother, was made vizír; and Hosén received the rank of amír at ómra (or commander in chief), which was the second in the state. These brothers were sprung from a numerous and respected family of descendants of the Prophet, who were settled in the town of Bára; and in consequence of this origin, they are best known in India by the name of the Seiads.

They had expected, from their services, as well as from the grovelling disposition of Farokhsír, and his submissive behaviour while courting their support, that they would be allowed to exercise all the real power of the state, leaving to the emperor only the pageantry, and such a command of wealth and honours as might enable him to gratify his favourites.

Jealousy of the emperor.

But neither Farokhsír nor his favourites were so easily contented. His principal confidant was a person who had been cázi at Dacca, in Bengal, and on whom he conferred the high title of Mír Jumla. This man, though devoid of capacity, had an obstinate perseverance in his narrow views, which was well suited to gain an ascendancy over a mind like Farokhsír's, incapable of comprehending a great design, aud too irresolute to execute even a small one without support.

It was no difficult task to make the emperor jealous of the authority which he was so incompetent to exercise, and the overbearing conduct of the Seiads gave him a reasonable motive for counteracting them.

His intrigues.

The first scheme contrived in his secret cabinet was to weaken the brothers by a division of their force. For this purpose Hosén Ali was sent against Ajít Sing of Márwár, while secret messages were transmitted to the Rájpút prince, intimating that he could do nothing more acceptable to the emperor than by offering an obstinate resistance to his lieutenant. But Hosén Ali was too well aware of the danger occasioned by his absence to insist on terms that might protract the war; and Ajít, when his own interests were secured, had no inducement to make sacrifices for those of the emperor. Peace was accordingly concluded, on terms, to appearance, honourable to Farokhsír; the rája engaging to send his son to Delhi, and to give his daughter in marriage to the emperor.

Hosén Ali sent against Ajít Sing, rája of Márwár.

Makes an honourable peace.

Increased distrust.

The mutual distrust of the parties at court was increased after Hosén Ali returned, and Farokhsìr, as destitute of prudence and steadiness as faith and

BOOK XII.

honour, was exactly the sort of person with whom it was least possible to feel secure.

The Seiads, conceiving (probably with good reason) that their lives were aimed at, assembled their troops about their palaces, and refused to go to court. It was now the king's turn to be alarmed, and the preparations of the contending factions threw the capital into the utmost confusion and distress; and there remained no alternative but an immediate conflict, or the submission of the least determined of the parties. The king was therefore prevailed on to allow the gates of the citadel, in which was his palace, to be occupied by the guards of the Seiads, while they waited on him for the purpose of settling the terms of a reconciliation. It was there agreed that Mír Jumla should be made governor of Behár, and removed from court: that Abdullah Khán should continue to exercise the functions of vizír, but that Hosén should undertake the government of the Deckan, and proceed immediately with his army to that distant province.

Submission of the emperor.

Harmony being to appearance restored, the emperor's nuptials with the daughter of Ajít Sing were celebrated with unprecedented splendour, and the Ráhtór rája, from his independent territory, saw his importance acknowledged at the capital whence he had in his infancy been conveyed with so much difficulty to escape the tyranny of Aurangzíb.

Hosén Ali marches to

After this ceremony, Hosén Ali set off for the

Deckan. He was well aware that his continued absence would be the signal for the recall of Mír Jumla, and he told the emperor, at parting, that if he heard of any attempt to disturb his brother's authority, he should be at Delhi with his army within three weeks of the intelligence.

CHAP. I.

settle the Deckan.

A. D. 1715, December; A. H. 1127, Zí Haj.

Farokhsír instigates Dáúd Khán Panni to resist him.

But Farokhsír did not trust to the ordinary chances of war for affording employment to his general. He had recourse for this purpose to Dáúd Khán Panni, who was renowned throughout India for his reckless courage, and whose memory still survives in the tales and proverbs of the Deckan. Dáúd Khán had been removed on the accession of Farokhshír to the province of Guzerát, to which that of Cándésh was now added; and, being an old fellow-soldier of Zulfikár Khán, could be relied on for zeal against the instrument of his ruin. He was secretly instructed to repair immediately to Cándésh, to carry with him all the troops he could collect, to exercise his influence with the Marattas and other chiefs of the Deckan, and, under pretence of co-operating with Hosén Ali, to take the first opportunity of accomplishing his destruction. Dáúd's manner of executing these orders was conformable to his established character. He at once set Hosén Ali at defiance, proceeded to engage him as an open enemy, and soon brought the question to a trial of strength in the field. The impetuosity of his charge on this occasion entirely disconcerted Hosén Ali's army; they began to disperse in all directions, while Dáúd Khán, at the

BOOK XII.

Defeat and death of Dáúd Khán.

A.D. 1716, A.H. 1129.

head of 300 chosen men of his tribe, armed with battle-axes, pushed straight at the person of his opponent. At this decisive moment, Dáúd received a ball through his head, and his fall immediately turned the fortune of the day. His wife, a Hindú princess, who had accompanied him to Cándésh, stabbed herself on hearing of his death.

Hosén Ali, after his victory, proceeded to his operations against the Marattas, without imputing to the emperor any share in the opposition which he had met with.*

Renewed devastations of the Síks.

Meanwhile, the long-continued dissensions among the Mussulmans had afforded an opportunity to the Síks to recruit their strength. Bandu had issued from his retreat, defeated the imperial troops, and ravaged the level country with greater fury than before. At length an army was sent against him, under an able chief named Abdusemed Khán.

They are defeated and nearly extirpated.

By him the Síks were beaten in repeated actions, and Bandu was at last made prisoner with a number of his men, and some of his principal followers. Most of these persons were executed on the spot; but 740 were selected and sent with Bandu to Delhi. They were paraded through the streets on camels, dressed in black sheepskins, with the wool outside (in derision of the shaggy appearance they affected), and were exposed to the maledictions of the populace, which, it must be owned, they had well deserved. Their punishment ex-

* The above account is from the "Seir Mutákherín" and Scott's "Deckan," who have both borrowed from Kháfi Khán.

ceeded the measure of offences even such as theirs. They were all beheaded on seven successive days, and died with the utmost firmness, disdaining every offer to save their lives at the expense of their religion.

CHAP. I.

Cruel execution of Bandu.

Bandu was reserved for greater cruelties. He was exhibited in an iron cage, clad in a robe of cloth of gold, and a scarlet turban; an executioner stood behind him with a drawn sword; around him were the heads of his followers on pikes, and even a dead cat was stuck on a similar weapon to indicate the extirpation of every thing belonging to him. He was then given a dagger, and ordered to stab his infant son; and on his refusing, the child was butchered before his eyes, and its heart thrown in his face. He was at last torn to pieces with hot pincers, and died with unshaken constancy, glorying in having been raised up by God to be a scourge to the iniquities and oppressions of the age. The Síks who were still at large were hunted down like wild beasts, and it was not till after a long interval that they again appeared in force, and once more renewed their depredations.

Progress of the Marattas.

But the Síks, when at the strongest, were not numerous, and they were never formidable beyond a certain not very extensive tract.* It was with a different sort of enemy that the Moguls had to contend in the Deckan. The removal of Dáúd

* The Síks have never been so flourishing as they are now (1839), and they are confined to the Panjáb and the neighbouring countries: their numbers do not exceed 500,000 souls;

BOOK XII.

Chín Kilich Khán (afterwards A'sof Jáh).

Khán (A. D. 1713) had dissolved his engagements with the Marattas. His successor, Chín Kilich Khán (afterwards so well known under the titles of Nizám ul Mulk and A'sof Jáh), was a man of much ability and more cunning; and as the feud among the Marattas now raged with more bitterness than ever, he contrived, by favouring the weaker party, not only to foment their internal dissensions, but to induce several of their chiefs to espouse the Mogul cause.

But these measures, though they prevented the increase of the Maratta power, had little effect in restoring the tranquillity of the country; and the removal of Chín Kilich Khán, to make way for Hosén Ali, put an end to the little good they had produced. Bands of Marattas ravaged the Mogul territory as before, and individuals of that nation seized on villages within its limits, and turned them into forts, from whence they plundered the adjoining districts.*

Ill success of Hosén Ali.

The most troublesome of these, at the time of Hosén Ali's arrival, was a chief whose family name was Dábári: he occupied a line of fortified villages in Cándésh, and, by his depredations on caravans and travellers, shut up the great road from Hindostan and the Deckan to Surat.

---

and they are supposed to have 3,000,000 subjects by no means well affected to their government. (*Burnes's Travels*, vol. ii. p. 256.)

* Grant Duff, vol i. p. 431. Briggs's Seir ul Mutákherín, vol. i. p. 141.

Soon after the defeat of Dáúd Khán, a very strong detachment was sent to remedy this pressing evil, and was opposed by the usual Maratta tactics. The villages were evacuated as the Moguls advanced, and re-occupied as soon as they had passed by; and Dábári, after affecting to fly till he reached a convenient scene of action, suffered himself to be overtaken, when his men dispersed in small parties among the hills and broken ground with which the place was surrounded. The Moguls, elated with their victory, broke up to pursue the fugitives. The Marattas allowed them to involve themselves in the ravines until they could no longer assemble, and then turned on them at once, cut the general and most of the detachment to pieces, and did not suffer one to escape till he was stripped of his horse, arms, and even clothes.* The further progress of the campaign corresponded to this inauspicious commencement; and the Marattas, in addition to the manifest inefficiency of their enemies, were encouraged by the intrigues of Farokhsír himself. At length Hosén Ali, finding that his presence could no longer be spared at Delhi, made a treaty with Rája Sáho, and agreed to acknowledge his claim to the whole of the territory formerly possessed by Sévají, with the addition of later conquests; to restore all the forts in his possession within that tract; to allow the levy of the *chout*, or fourth, over the whole of the Deckan;

He makes peace with Rája Sáho, and submits to pay the chout. A. D. 1717.†

* Seir ul Mutákherín, vol. i. p. 142.

† Grant Duff, vol. i. p. 446.

and to make a further payment of one tenth on the remaining revenue, under the name of sirdésmuki. This tenth, with the cession of part of the territory, was all that had been demanded in the last negotiation with Aurangzíb. In return, Sáho was to pay a tribute of ten lacs of rupees; to furnish 15,000 horse, to preserve the tranquillity of the country, and to be answerable for any loss occasioned by depredations, from whatever quarter.

Though Sáho had at this time a superiority in the Maratta civil war, a great part of the country thus acknowledged to be his was not in his possession, and he was entirely unable to check the depredations of the hostile party, if he could those of his own adherents. But Hosén Ali's object was attained by being enabled to withdraw his troops from the Deckan, and by obtaining the assistance of a body of 10,000 Marattas on his march to Delhi.* Farokhsír refused to ratify this disgraceful treaty. His refusal only served to hasten the crisis of the dispute between him and the Seiads. The ultimate occurrence of such an event had long become inevitable.

Farokhsír refuses to ratify the treaty.

State of the court of Delhi—Abdullah Khán.

Abdullah Khán, the elder of the brothers, though a man of talents, was indolent and fond of pleasure. His business of vizír, therefore, was left to his deputy, a Hindú named Rattan Chand, whose strict measures and arbitrary temper made his administration very unpopular. Encouraged by this

Plots of Farokhsír.

* Grant Duff, vol. i. p. 144, &c.

circumstance, and by Abdullah's want of vigilance, Farokhsír began to form schemes for the recovery of his independence; and reports arose of an intention on his part to seize on the vizír's person. These rumours seemed confirmed by the proceedings of some large bodies of troops who had been suddenly dismissed from the king's service, and by the unexpected appearance of Mír Jumla, who made a rapid and secret journey from Behár to Delhi. He represented himself as obliged to fly from the dangers to which he was exposed by the disaffection of the troops in his province: he was very coldly received by the emperor; and he ostensibly threw himself on the vizír's protection, professing to have renounced all thoughts of public employment. But these appearances did not satisfy the vizír. He assembled his adherents, and prepared for the worst that might occur. If the emperor had entertained the design imputed to him, he had not the courage to carry it through. Overawed by the vizír's preparations, he hastened to appease his resentment; protested his anxious wish to maintain the administration on its present footing, and dismissed Mír Jumla to his native town of Multán.

But this reconciliation was only superficial; the vizír retained a well-founded conviction of the emperor's insincerity; and the other almost immediately renewed his plots, which he took up with as much levity, and abandoned with as much

BOOK XII.

Combination of great nobles to support him.

pusillanimity, as before. His plan now was, to form a combination of the principal persons who were discontented with the vizír. Among these was Jei Sing, rája of Ambér. This chieftain had been previously employed against the Játs, and had, by a long course of operations, reduced them to extremities, when the vizír opened a direct negotiation with an agent whom they had sent to Delhi, and granted them peace in a manner very derogatory to the honour of Jei Sing. Chín Kilich Khán, who had been removed from the viceroyalty of the Deckan to the petty government of Morádábád, was also ready to revenge the injury, and was summoned to Delhi: he was joined by Sirbuland Khán, governor of Behár: Rája Ajít Sing, the emperor's father-in-law, was also sent for, but showed no inclination to embark in an enterprise directed by such unsteady hands, and soon after openly attached himself to the prevailing party. The other conspirators, however, were zealous; and it was determined to assassinate the vizír on the occasion of a great annual solemnity, at which the number of troops well affected to the king would much surpass that of Abdullah's guards. But Farokhsír had now got a new favourite, a Cashmirian of low birth and profligate manners, on whom he conferred the title of Rokn u Doulu. By this man's persuasion, which fell in with his natural timidity, he postponed the execution of the concerted plot, and he afterwards promised to his favourite the succession to the office of prime minister, and con-

His levity and irresolution.

ferred on him, as a private jágír, the very district of which Chín Kilich Khán was governor.

Disgusts his confederates.

Disappointed and disgusted with this preference, and convinced that Farokhsír's irresolution must be fatal to any plan in which he was an actor, his confederates, with the exception of Jei Sing, lost no time in making their peace with the vizír. That minister, whose fears had been awakened by the previous appearances, had already called for the assistance of his brother from the Deckan; and Hosén Ali, who kept his army at his devotion, by carefully excluding all persons appointed by the court from command, was now in full march on the capital. Jei Sing endeavoured to excite the emperor to take some decisive step during the short interval that was left, but was unable to animate that feeble prince even with the courage of despair; and Hosén Ali's first demand, on his arrival, was for the dismission of the Rája to his own territory. Farokhsír, thus at the mercy of his enemies, had recourse to the most abject submission. Hosén Ali remained encamped without the city; but the vizír's guards were admitted into the palace, and it only remained to the brothers to decide on the fate of its tenant. In this state of affairs, some nobles who remained faithful to the

Return of Hosén Ali, accompanied by 10,000 Marattas.

A.D. 1718, December; A.H. 1131*, Moharram.

* This is the date of his march from Cándésh, taken from Kháfi Khán; Grant Duff also confirms the year. The "Seir Mutákherín" (Briggs's translation, vol. i. p. 164.) makes the year A.D. 1719, A.H. 1132; and many of its subsequent dates differ, in the same manner, from all other authorities.

BOOK XII.

emperor, set out with their retainers to his assistance; and a rising of the townspeople for the purpose of massacring the Marattas took place at the same time. In consequence of the confusion which followed, Hosén Ali marched into the city, of which he took possession after some opposition.

Farokhsír deposed and put to death. A.D. 1719, February; A.H. 1131, Rabi u Sáni.

It seemed no longer safe to spare Farokhsír; and that unfortunate shadow of a king was dragged from his hiding-place in the seraglio and privately put to death.

Some of the fruits of Aurangzíb's religious policy appeared during this reign. Enáyat Ullah, who had been secretary to that monarch, being appointed to the head of the finance, endeavoured to enforce the capitation tax on Hindús with the rigour of his former master; but he was soon forced to desist by the public clamour, and the tax was formally abolished in the next reign.

There was a violent affray between the Shiás and Sunnis in the capital, and a still more serious one, in Ahmedábád, between the Hindús and Mussulmans, in which many lives were lost: on this occasion the Mussulman governor (Dáúd Khán Panni) took part with the Hindús

Nominal emperors set up by the Seiads. Rafí u Dirját. A.D. 1719, February; A.H. 1131, Rabi u Sáni. Rafí u Doula. A.D. 1719, May; A.H. 1131, Rajab.

On the deposition of Farokhsír, the Seiads set up a young prince of the blood, to whom they gave the title of Rafí u *Dirját*. He died in little more than three months, of a consumption; when another youth of the same description was set up under the name of Rafí u *Doula*, and came to the same end in a still shorter period.

CHAP. I.

These princes had been brought up in the recesses of the seraglio, without any prospect of the succession, and had the ideas of women superinduced on those of children. Their deaths must have been inconvenient to the Seiads, and they pitched on a healthier young man as their successor. This was Roushen Akhter: he had no advantages in previous situation over the others; but his mother was a woman of ability, and had perhaps helped to form his character, as she subsequently influenced his conduct.

Mohammed Sháh. A. D. 1719, September; A. H. 1131, Zí Cáda.

He was raised to the throne by the title of Mohammed Sháh.*

* At Mohammed's accession it was determined that the names of his two predecessors should be left out of the list of kings, and that his reign should commence from the death of Farokhsír. (*Seir Mutákherin*, vol. i. p. 197. *Grant Duff*, vol. i. p. 450. Marsden, *Numismata Orientalia*.)

CHAP. II.

TO THE DEPARTURE OF NÁDIR SHÁH.

Mohammed Sháh.

BOOK XII.

A. D. 1719, September; A. H. 1131, Zí Cáda.

General indignation against the Seiads.

The murder of Farokhsír (in spite of his personal character, and the familiarity of such a catastrophe in Asia) produced a general feeling of horror, and led to suspicions regarding the premature deaths of his successors. The frequent change of pageants also drew attention to the moving power which they were intended to veil.

Internal dissensions of their party.

The authority of the Seiads, thus shaken in the public opinion, was further impaired by their own disagreement, as well as by the discontent of some of their principal adherents, and soon began to show signs of weakness in the inefficiency of the internal government.

Insurrections.

The governor of Allahábád (a Hindú) rebelled; and, although Hosén Ali went against him in person, he only gave up his province on condition that he should receive that of Oud in exchange: the tributary state of Búndi required a strong force to settle some disturbances that broke out there; while the Afghán chief of Kosúr, in the south of the Panjáb, revolted, defeated the royal troops, and was not subdued without an effort. A furious contest between Hindús and Mussulmans also took place in Cashmír, in which the efforts of the government to maintain tranquillity were unavailing, until some thousand persons had fallen on the two sides, and much loss of property had been sustained.

Proceedings of Asof Jáh.

The most alarming sign of the times was in the proceedings of Chín Kilich Khán. This chief (whom, anticipating the title, I shall henceforth call Asof Jáh, and whose descendants are known to Europeans as Nizáms of the Deckan) was of a respectable Túrk family, and was the son of Ghází u dín, a favourite officer of Aurangzíb, under which emperor *he* also distinguished himself. He showed spirit in maintaining his dignity during the depression of the nobility by the mistress of Jehándár Sháh and her relations *; and subsequently rose to importance (as has been related) by his services as viceroy of the Deckan. He had quitted the party of Farokhsír because he found he was not to be prime minister; and yet on the success of his new allies, he was not even restored to his viceroyalty, but made governor of the single province of Málwa.

The disturbed state of that country gave him a pretence for raising troops; and he became so for-

* Being rudely stopped in a narrow street, to make way for a woman who had unbounded influence with the mistress, and through her with the emperor, he ordered his attendants to repel force with force, dispersed the favourite's retinue, and compelled her to quit her elephant, and escape on foot to the palace.

BOOK XII.

midable to the Seiads, that they made a feeble attempt to remove him, offering him the choice of four other governments. This only showed Asof Jáh that the time for dissembling was passed; and as he saw the difficulty of establishing a permanent control at the capital, he determined to lay the foundations of his power on a firmer basis, and turned his first attention to the conquest of the Deckan. He had there many old connections both with the Mussulmans and the Marattas.

A.D. 1720, April; A.H. 1132, Jamádi u Sáni.

He establishes his power in the Deckan.

Defeats the armies of the Seiads.

Immediately on his revolt he marched to the Nerbadda. By intrigue and money he obtained possession of the fort of Asírghar, and procured the junction of several officers of the province. He was pursued from Hindostan by a force under Diláwer Khan (a Seiad of Bára), and another under A'lam Ali Khán (the nephew of the usurping brothers) was awaiting him at Aurangábád. Taking advantage of the impetuous character of Diláwer, he drew him into an engagement before he could be supported by his colleague, and totally defeated him in a battle fought near Burhánpúr; Diláwer Khán himself was among the slain. He then turned against A'lam Ali, whose force, though weakened by the desertion of some chiefs gained by Asof Jáh, was still very powerful. A battle took place at Bállapúr in Berár, in which large bodies of Marattas were engaged on both sides, and which terminated in the defeat and death of A'lam Ali.

A.D. 1720, June.

A.D. 1720, July.

Alarm at Delhi.

These events threw the Seiads into consternation, and, though secretly agreeable to the emperor and many of the nobility, filled the minds of reflecting men with dismal forebodings of the ruin of the empire. This gloom was rendered deeper among a superstitious people by a violent earthquake which occurred about this time, and seemed to threaten the existence of the capital; and in these depressing circumstances the brothers betrayed those signs of irresolution which are often the forerunners of great calamities.

Prudent conduct of Mohammed Sháh.

Mohammed Sháh (tutored by his mother) had carefully avoided any opposition to the Seiads, and patiently waited for some change of circumstances favourable to the assertion of his own authority. He now began, with the utmost secrecy, to deliberate what could be done to accelerate his deliverance. His counsellor in this dangerous undertaking was Mohammed Amín Khán, one of the noblemen who had deserted Farokhsír when he proved a traitor to his own cause, and who had since adhered to the Seiads, though full of envy and disgust at their power and arrogance. He was in the habit of conversing in Túrki with Mohammed, and by means of that language, which was unknown to Indian Seiads, he was able to ascertain the sentiments of the emperor, although closely surrounded by the connections and creatures of the brothers. Hints interchanged in this manner paved the way to more private communications, and a party was gradually formed, the second place in which was occupied by Sádat Khán, originally a

His plans against the Seiads.

Mohammed Amín Khán.

Sádat Khán.

BOOK XII.

merchant of Khórasán, who had risen to a military command, and was the progenitor of the present kings of Oud. These combinations, however secret, did not fail to excite obscure apprehensions in the minds of the Seiads, and occasioned much perplexity about the manner of disposing of the emperor during the approaching contest with Asof Jáh. It was at length decided that Hosén Ali should march to the Deckan, and should carry the emperor and some of the suspected nobles along with him, while Abdullah should remain at Delhi, and watch over the interests of his family at home.

Hosén Ali marches against Asof Jáh, accompanied by the emperor.

After much hesitation the brothers quitted Agra, and each marched off towards his destined station. The separation was judged by the conspirators to afford an opportunity for executing their designs. It was determined to assassinate Hosén Ali, and Mír Heider, a savage Calmuc, who (though a man of some rank in his own country) was ready for the most desperate enterprise, was pitched on to strike the blow. He waited for his victim as he passed in his palankin, and attracted his attention by holding up a petition. Hosén Ali made a sign to his attendants to allow him to approach, and was about to read the petition, when Mír Heider plunged his dagger into his body. The blow was fatal; Hosén Ali rolled out a corpse from the opposite side of the palankin, and Mír Heider was cut to pieces in an instant by the fury of the attendants. The death of this powerful minister threw the whole camp into commotion. A fierce

Assassination of Hosén Ali.

A.D. 1720, October; A.H. 1132, Zí Haj 6.

conflict took place between his adherents, many of whom were Seiads like himself, and the partisans of the conspirators, who were joined by numbers whose only object was to protect the emperor. Mohammed was with some difficulty prevailed on to show himself at the head of his own friends, and his appearance materially contributed to decide the fate of the day. The party of the Seiads was driven from the field, and many of its members, with all the neutral part of the army, made their submission to the emperor.

The emperor assumes the government.

The intelligence of this event reached Abdullah Khán before he entered Delhi. Painful as it was in itself it was as alarming in its consequences. Abdullah had now to oppose his sovereign without either right or any popular pretext in his favour; and he was made aware of his situation by the immediate breaking out of disturbances in the country around him. But his energy rose with his danger. He proclaimed one of the princes confined at Delhi king, conferred offices and dignities in his name, and applied himself with vigour to strengthening his cause by securing the services of troops and officers.

Difficult situation of Abdullah Khán.

He sets up a new emperor.

Few men of rank adhered to him; but by means of high pay he drew together a large, though ill-disciplined, army. He marched in little more than a fortnight after his brother's death, and was joined as he advanced by Choráman, the rája of the Játs, and by many of his brother's soldiers who deserted after having submitted to the emperor.

Assembles an army.

BOOK XII.

On the other hand, Mohammed was reinforced by the arrival of 4000 horse, hastily sent forward by Rája Jei Sing, and of some chiefs of the Rohilla Afgháns. The armies met between Agra and Delhi. Abdullah was defeated and taken prisoner; his life was spared, probably from respect for his sacred lineage. Mohammed Sháh immediately proceeded to Delhi, which he entered in great pomp, and celebrated his emancipation by an extensive distribution of offices and rewards. Mohammed Amín was made vizír; but he had scarcely entered on his office, when he was taken ill, and died in a few hours.

A.D. 1720, November; A.H. 1133, Moharram.

Is defeated and taken prisoner.

A.D. 1720, Nov. or Dec.; A.H. 1133, Safar.

Sudden death of Mohammed Amín, the new vizír.

A.D. 1721, January; A.H. 1133, Rabi al Awal.

In most cases, the sudden death of a prime minister would have been attributed to poison; but in this instance there was a manner of accounting for it still more acceptable to the popular love of wonder. An impostor had made his appearance at Delhi some years before, who produced a new scripture, written in a language of his own invention, framed from those spoken in ancient Persia, and had founded a sect in which the teachers were called Békúks and the disciples Ferábúds. He had become so considerable at the accession of Mohammed, that the new vizír sent a party of soldiers to apprehend him. Before he was taken into custody, the vizír was seized with a violent illness, and his family, in alarm, endeavoured by presents and entreaties to avert the anger of the holy man. The Békúk boldly avowed the miracle, but said his shaft, once shot, could not be recalled.

He was nevertheless left undisturbed, and lived for some years after.

The office of vizír was only filled by a temporary substitute, being ultimately designed for Asof Jáh.

Rapid decline of the monarchy.

Meanwhile, every day brought some fresh proof of the decline of the monarchy. The government of Guzerát had been conferred on Rája Ajít Sing as a reward for his adherence to the Seiads; the addition of that of Ajmír had been secretely promised by Mohammed, as the price of his friendship or neutrality in the contest between himself and those brothers, and a grant for life of both governments had been delivered to him under the royal seal. In spite of these engagements, Ajít was now removed from Guzerát; and although his deputy, a Rájpút, endeavoured to keep possession by force, he was driven out by the Mussulmans of the province, and compelled to take refuge with his master at Jódpúr. Ajít Sing, on this, occupied Ajmír with a large army of Rájpúts, took and plundered Narnól, and advanced his parties to Rewári, within fifty miles of Delhi. All attempts to check his progress had been rendered ineffectual by the dissensions of the generals ordered against him, and their reluctance to undertake the duty; and when, at last, the commander-in-chief moved out to protect the capital, he was glad to agree to the terms originally proposed by Ajít, that he should submit to the loss of Guzerát on condition of being confirmed in Ajmír.* A. D. 1721, A. H. 1133.

* Seir Mutákherín. Tod's Rajasthan.

BOOK XII.

Asof Jáh, vizír.

A. D. 1722, January; A. H. 1134, Rabi u Sáni.

Soon after this, Asof Jáh arrived at Delhi, and took possession of the office of vizír. Though he had for sometime been apprised of his appointment, he thought it of more importance to secure his independence in the Deckan than to seize on the authority held out to him at the capital. He had been engaged in many transactions with the Marattas, who were rapidly assuming the form of a regular government, and it was not till he had settled affairs in that quarter to his satisfaction that he repaired to Delhi. He found the court in a state of the utmost weakness and disorder. The emperor was given up to pleasure; his favourite advisers were young men of the same pursuits, and his mistress had such an ascendancy over him, that she was allowed to keep his private signet, and to use it at her discretion. This state of things gave great disgust to Asof Jáh, brought up at the austere court of Aurangzíb, and, in spite of his predilection for intrigue, both able and willing to conduct a vigorous administration: but he had neither the boldness nor the power to seize the government by force; and he made no progress in gaining the confidence of the emperor, who felt himself constrained by his grave manners, and importuned by his attempts to draw attention to public business, and who had no greater pleasure than to see his antiquated dress and formal courtesy burlesqued by his own dissolute companions.

Indolence of the emperor.

His favourites.

His dislike to Asof Jáh.

Asof Jáh sent against the refrac-

After some months of mutual dissatisfaction, the emperor and his favourites thought they had devised a plan to free themselves from their troublesome counsellor. Heider Cúli, the governor of Guzerát, though one of the principal actors in the revolution which restored the royal authority, was offensive to the cabal for his proud and inflexible disposition; and they hoped, by embroiling him with Asof Jáh, that both might be rendered more dependent on the court. They accordingly directed Heider Cúli to give up his government to Asof Jáh; on which the former chief, as they expected, repaired to his station, and made ready to defend his position of it by force of arms. But this deep laid scheme ended in sudden disappointment; for their subtle adversary so well employed his talents for intrigue and corruption, that his rival's army deserted almost in a body, and he speedily returned to Delhi, strengthened by the addition of a rich province to his former exorbitant command.

tory governor of Guzerát.

Quells the insurrection, and retains the government of the province.

No event of importance succeeded to Asof Jáh's return, except the murder of the deputy governor of Agra by the Játs; on which Rája Jei Sing*, the old enemy of that people, was appointed governor of Agra for the purpose of revenging the outrage. Choráman, the aged rája of the Játs, happened to die during the expedition; and Jei Sing, by dexterously supporting his nephew against his son and successor, brought about a

Expedition against the Játs of Bhartpúr.

* Kháfi Khán. Scott's Deckan, vol. ii. p. 187. Briggs and Grant Duff make it Ajít Sing, as does the old translation of the "Seir Mutákherín;" but probably all on one authority.

BOOK XII.

division among the Játs, and at last placed the nephew in possession on condition of his paying tribute to Delhi.

Disgust of Asof Jáh.

The mutual aversion of the emperor and his vizír were not diminished after the return of the minister; and it was probably, at the moment, a relief to Mohammed, when Asof Jáh, after securing his safety, by removing, on some pretence, from the capital, sent in his resignation and marched off for the Deckan. But this measure amounted, in reality, to a declaration of independence, and was viewed in that light by the emperor himself, who, although he graciously accepted Asof Jáh's resignation, and conferred on him the highest titles that could be held by a subject, did not on that account remit his active hostility. He sent orders to Mobáriz Khán, the local governor of Heiderábád, to endeavour to dispossess the viceroy and assume the government of the whole Deckan in his stead. Mobáriz entered zealously on the task imposed on him; and by the sanction of the emperor's name, joined to his own influence and the enmity of individuals to his rival, he succeeded in collecting a powerful army. Asof Jáh, always more inclined to art than force, protracted his negotiations for several months, during which he endeavoured to sow sedition among Mobáriz's adherents. As he made little progress in this mode of hostility, he at last came to open war, and soon gained a decided victory over Mobáriz, who lost his life in the battle. As the emperor had not avowed the

He resigns his office, and sets off for the Deckan.

A.D. 1723, October; A.H. 1136, Moharram.

The emperor instigates Mobáriz Khán, governor of Heiderábád, to supplant him.

Mobáriz defeated and slain.

attack which he had instigated, Asof Jáh, not to be outdone in dissimulation, sent the head of Mobáriz to court with his own congratulations on the extinction of the rebellion. He then fixed his residence at Heiderábád; and, though he continued to send honorary presents, on fixed occasions, to the emperor, he thenceforth conducted himself, in other respects, as an independent prince.

A. D. 1724, October; A. H. 1137, Moharram.

Asof Jáh's policy towards the Marattas.

But, although he was beyond the reach of attack from his former sovereign, he was by no means equally secure from his neighbours the Marattas. Their power, being now concentrated and in able hands, was too great for any resistance that he could oppose to it, and all the refinements of his artful policy were for a time employed to divert it from himself and to turn it against his enemies at Delhi,

Consolidation of the Maratta government.

The change in the state of the Maratta government had been gradually brought about during a considerable period, and requires to be taken up from the commencement. Though Sáho had been set up as rája by the Moguls, it suited the policy of Asof Jáh, during his first government of the Deckan (A. D. 1713 to A. D. 1716), to assist his rival, Samba, at that time the weaker of the competitors. Other circumstances tended, soon after, to depress the party of Sáho, who would never have recovered his superiority, but for the abilities of his minister, Bálají Wiswanát.

Bálají Wiswanát, péshwa.

This person (the founder of the Bramin dynasty of Péshwas) was the hereditary accountant of a

BOOK XII.

village in the Concan. He afterwards entered into the service of a chief of the Jádu family, whence he was transferred to that of the rája. He distinguished himself by many services; the most important of which was his bringing over A'ngria (a powerful chief as well as famous pirate), in the Concan, from the side of Samba to that of Sáho.

His merits were at length rewarded with the office of péshwa, at that time the second in the state; the pírti nidhí, or *delegate of the rája*, being the first.

It was through his means that the cession of territory and tribute was obtained from Hosen Ali Khán (A. D. 1717), and he was joint commander of the Maratta force that accompanied that minister to Delhi. At that time Sáho (without in other respects laying aside the titles or the independence assumed by his predecessors) was content, in his intercourse with the Mogul court, to acknowledge himself a vassal of the empire. It was professedly in this quality that his troops accompanied Hosén Ali; and the fall of that chief did not necessarily make any change in their relation to the government. Under this view Bálají remained at Delhi after the death of Farokhsír and ultimately obtained a ratification of the treaty by Mohammed Sháh (A. D. 1720). This recognition of his authority, together with other advantages, had established the ascendancy of Sáho over his rival; and Bálají, before his death,

Establishes the government of Sáho.

(which happened in October, 1720,) had the satisfaction of seeing him placed above the assaults of enemies, either foreign or domestic.

Dies.

His complicated revenue system.

The cessions by the treaty having given legality to what before was mere robbery, enabled Bálají to introduce some degree of order into the Maratta mode of collection. It appears extraordinary, at first sight, that he did not prefer a solid territorial possession to assignments on other proprietors, such as the *chout* and *sirdésmuki;* or that he did not, at least, consolidate those dues, by throwing those on the same territory into one head, and uniting it with the land revenue where that also belonged to the Marattas. But it was by no means his object to simplify the claims of his government. He knew, from the relative power of the parties, that the rája would be a gainer in all disputed points with the Moguls, and was more anxious to obtain a pretext for interference and encroachment over an extensive territory than clearly defined rights within a small one. In furtherance of this policy, he claimed, as *chout*, one fourth of the permanent revenue fixed by Tódar Mal and Malik Amber, of which but a small portion was now realised from the exhausted country; and, although he did not enforce this principle to its full extent, it still served to keep his claim undefined. It was not in dealing with the Moguls alone that he profited by keeping up this system of confusion: by granting the *chout* and *sirdésmuki* to different persons, and even

His motives.

BOOK XII.

inventing new subdivisions, so as to admit of further partition, he parcelled out the revenues of every district among several Maratta chiefs; so that while each had an interest in increasing the contributions to the general stock, none had a compact property such as might render him independent of the government. The intricacy produced in the affairs of the Maratta chiefs, by these innumerable fractions of revenue, led to another effect that Bálají had quite as much at heart: it threw them entirely into the hands of their Bramin agents, and strengthened the péshwa's power by increasing that of his cast. But, though this system of subdivision was general, it was not universal; some chiefs had already landed possessions in the old territory; and similar grants, more or less extensive, continued to be made from special favour. Every chief required a village or two for his head quarters, and all were anxious to possess the government claims on those of which they were natives or hereditary officers.

Báji Ráo péshwa.

His enterprising policy.

Bálají Wiswanáth was succeeded by his son, Báji Ráo, the ablest of all the Bramin dynasty, and of all the Maratta nation, except Sévají. Báji Ráo did not at once enjoy the whole authority that had been possessed by his father. He had a powerful rival in the pírti nidhí, and the interests of those politicians were not more opposed than their opinions. The pírti nidhí was sincerely apprehensive of the effects of a further diffusion of the Maratta power: and he strenuously contended for the necessity of consolidating the rája's present possessions, suppressing civil discord, and acquiring a firm hold on the countries in the south of the peninsula, before attempting to make any conquests in Hindostan. Báji Ráo took a wiser as well as bolder view. He saw that the hordes of predatory horse, who were so useful in an enemy's country, would be utterly ungovernable at home; and that it was only by forming an army, and establishing a military command, that an efficient internal government could be brought into existence. He therefore counselled an immediate invasion of the northern provinces, and pointed out the inward weakness of the Mogul empire, which was nowhere so rotten as at the core: "Let us strike," said he, "the withered trunk, and the branches will fall of themselves." The eloquence and earnestness with which he pressed his advice overcame all the doubts of the rája; and when urged by Báji Ráo to allow him to carry his standard beyond the Nerbadda, he exclaimed, with enthusiasm, "You shall plant it on Hémaláya."*

The results of these debates gave Báji Ráo a preponderance in the councils of the rája, and his ascendancy daily increased from the necessity for his assistance. Though Sáho was not destitute of abilities, his education in a Mussulman seraglio was alike unfavourable to hardiness of body and activity of mind; while Báji Ráo, born in a camp

Character of Sáho.

Of Báji Ráo.

* Grant Duff, and Maratta MSS. quoted by that author, vol. i. p. 482—486.

BOOK XII.

and trained up a statesman and diplomatist, combined the habits of a Maratta horseman with an enlarged judgment and extensive knowledge. Unlike his cold-blooded brethren of the priestly class, his temper was ardent and his manner frank; he never flinched from fatigue or danger, and could make a meal of dry grain rubbed out of the husks between his hands as he rode along on a march.

His designs on the northern provinces were aided by the Moguls themselves. Shortly before the battle with Mobáriz, Asof Jáh was removed from his governments of Málwa and Guzerát. Rája Gírdhar was appointed to the former province, and found no difficulty in occupying it, while the troops were drawn off to the contest in the Deckan; but was unable to defend it from the incursions of Báji Ráo; and in Guzerát, Hamíd Khán, Asof's uncle, not only offered a strenuous resistance himself, but directly called in the aid of the Marattas. In return, he gave up to them the *chout* and *sirdésmuki* of the country under him; and Sirbuland Khán, the lawful governor, though successful in expelling Hamíd, was, after a long struggle, obliged to confirm the grant.

Báji Ráo ravages Málwa.

Obtains a cession by the governor of the chout of Guzerát.

A. D. 1725, A. H. 1138.

Asof Jáh foments the dissensions of the Marattas.

Notwithstanding the loss of these governments, Asof Jáh's power was now so well established in the Deckan, that he thought he might venture on an attempt to reduce that of his formidable neighbours. For this purpose, he again availed himself of their internal dissensions. He first applied himself to the pírti nidhí, and by his means had nearly concluded a treaty, by which the chout and sirdésmuki on the country round his new capital were to be commuted for a territorial cession and a fixed pecuniary payment; but Báji Ráo, faithful to his system of indefinite claims, and no doubt offended by the interference of his old rival, gave his decided opposition to the execution of the agreement; and Asof gained nothing by the negotiation, except the advantage of exasperating the jealousies of the Maratta ministers.

His next attempt of the same nature was of more importance. Samba, the claimant to the Maratta throne, though eclipsed by the superior fortune of Sáho, had fixed the seat of his government at Cólapúr, and retained the southern part of the dominions of his family, while he continued to assert his claim to the whole. Asof Jáh, without formally espousing his cause, affected to be in doubt to whom he ought to pay the money due from his country to the Marattas, and called on the parties to exhibit the grounds of their respective claims. This demand was highly resented by Sáho, and his anger found a willing instrument in Báji Ráo. At the end of the rainy season, the péshwa invaded Asof's territories, and first threatened Burhánpúr; but when Asof Jáh (now openly joined by Samba) moved to the relief of that city, Báji Ráo changed the direction of his march, made a rapid incursion into Guzerát, where the chout had not at that time been con-

He is attacked, and compelled to make concessions.

A. D. 1727, A. H. 1140.

BOOK XII.

firmed), and after ravaging the province with fire and sword, returned with equal celerity to the Deckan. He now laid waste the country round Asof's army, and so straitened his supplies, by the usual Maratta means, that he was obliged to renounce his connection with Samba, and to concede some other advantages to the Maratta government. After this adjustment, Báji Ráo crossed the Nerbadda to ravage Málwa, and to extort Sirbuland Khán's confirmation of his predecessor's grant of the chout of Guzerát.

A. D. 1729, A. H. 1141-2.

Accommodation between Sáho and his rival Samba.

During his absence the pírti nidhí surprised and defeated Samba, and at last compelled him to sign a treaty acknowledging Sáho's right to the whole Maratta country except a tract round Cólapúr, bounded on the west by the sea. This portion he was himself to retain, with the title of rája, and the same dignity as that assumed by Sáho. Though this success raised the reputation of the pírti nidhí, it did not enable him to enter the lists with the péshwa, and Asof was obliged to look out for some other instrument to disturb the Maratta government.

A. D. 1730, A. H. 1142.

Renewed intrigues of Asof Jáh.

Dábári, a great Maratta chief in Guzerát.

He found one in the head of the family of Dábári, the hereditary sénapati or commander-in-chief. This leader had been the principal means of establishing the Maratta power in Guzerát, and saw with indignation the fruit of his labours carried off by another. His jealousy derived additional bitterness from the ascendancy acquired by the péshwa, who now conducted the government with out the least control on the part of the rája. Incited by these feelings, and the promise of powerful co-operation from Asof Jáh, Dábári assembled an army of 35,000 men, and set out for the Deckan, with the professed object of delivering the rája from the thraldom of his minister.

Marches to depose the péshwa.

Bájí Ráo had not an equal force at his disposal; but what he had was composed of old troops, and he saw the advantage of promptitude in acting against a combination. Without allowing time for Asof Jáh to declare himself, he crossed the Nerbadda, entered Guzerát, and encountered Dábári not far from Baródra. The superiority of his veterans over Dábári's less experienced troops decided the victory in his favour, and he used it with prudence and moderation. Dábári having fallen in the action, he conferred his office, in the rája's name, on his son, and left him in possession of the Maratta rights of Guzerát on condition of his paying half the produce, *through the péshwa*, to the government. As the son was an infant, his mother was appointed his guardian, and Guzerát was to be administered in his behalf by Pilaji Geikwár, an adherent of his father's, and ancestor of the Geikwár family that still rules in Guzerát.

Is anticipated by Bájí Ráo, defeated and killed.

A. D. 1731, April; A. H. 1143, Sháwál.

Moderation of Bájí Ráo, in settling Guzerát.

Most of the other great Maratta families had also their origin a little before this time. When Bájí Ráo began his incursions into Málwa he gave commands to U'daji Puár, Malhár Ráo Hólcar, and Ránaji Sindia. The first of these was a chief before his connection with the péshwa: he soon

Origin of the families of Puár, Hólcar, and Sindia.

BOOK XII.

acquired a territory about Dhár, on the borders of Guzerát and Málwa; but never rose to such power as his colleagues or their descendants. Hólcar was a shepherd on the Níra, south of Púna; and Sindia, though of a respectable family near Sáttára, was in such abject poverty as to be a menial servant of Báji Ráo's. These chiefs, and others of this period, were no longer adventurers warring at the head of their own retainers, but officers of the péshwa, commanding divisions of *his* troops, and acting under *his* commission.

Compromise between Báji Ráo and Asof Jáh.

Báji Ráo had now the means of punishing the machinations of Asof Jáh; but both parties began to perceive the advantages of a mutual good understanding: Báji Ráo saw how much his supremacy at home would be endangered, during remote expeditions, by the enmity of so powerful and so insidious a neighbour; and Asof, besides other grounds of apprehension, felt by no means secure that the emperor might not revenge his defiance of the royal authority by transferring the viceroyalty to the péshwa, in whose hands such a title would not be inoperative. Accordingly, not long after Báji Ráo's return, the two usurpers entered into a secret compact, by which it was settled that Asof should support the government of Báji Ráo, while the other carried his arms into Málwa, and pushed his conquests over the emperor's remaining dominions.

Rája Abhi Sing of Márwár,

Báji Ráo had, at this period, strong motives of his own for extending his views in the country

CHAP. II.

beyond the Nerbadda. Immediately after his departure from Guzerát, the court of Delhi refused to ratify the grant of chout, removed Sirbuland Khán from the government, and conferred it on Abhi Sing, rája of Jódpúr. viceroy of Guzerát.

The appointment of an independent prince to such a charge would have been objectionable at any time; and the profligate character of Abhi Sing, who had acquired his power by the murder of his father, Ajít*, did not promise much fidelity on his part; but he possessed resources not enjoyed by the Mogul government, and seemed able by his own means, both to expel Sirbuland, and to defend the province against the Marattas.

The first of these objects was attained in one campaign; the second was not so easy of accomplishment. A.D. 1730. Pilají Geikwár, though driven out of Baródra, still continued so formidable that the unprincipled Abhi Sing saw no means of overcoming him except by procuring his assassination. A.D. 1732. Procures the assassination of Pilají Geikwár. This crime only roused the indignation of the Marattas, without weakening their power. The son and brother of Pilají appeared in greater force than ever, and not only ravaged Guzerát themselves, Retaliation of the Marattas. but raised all the surrounding hill tribes of Bhíls and Cúlis, and threw the whole province into revolt and confusion. While the Rájpút prince was completely occupied by these disturbances, the Geikwárs made a sudden irruption into his hereditary terri-

* Tod's Rajasthan, vol. ii. p. 91.

BOOK XII.

tory, and penetrated to the neighbourhood of Jód-púr, itself. This attack, and the threatening aspect of the Maratta force in Málwa, compelled Abhi Sing to withdraw to his own principality, and the deputy whom he left in Guzerát could make but a feeble stand against the Marattas.

Abhi Sing retires to Márwár.

The affairs of that nation were not less prosperous in Málwa. Gírdhar Sing, the governor of that province, had fallen in a battle with Báji Ráo's officers (in 1729); and his nephew, Deia Rám, who succeeded him, and had opposed a gallant resistance till this time, was defeated by Chimnají, the péshwa's brother, and lost his life in the battle.

A. D. 1732.

Successes of Báji Ráo in Málwa.

When Báji Ráo entered Málwa in person (1732), the government was in the hands of Mohammed Khán Bangash, an Afghán chief, who was also governor of Allahábád. He was at that period employed against a rája in Bundélcand, which lay between his two provinces; and the rája, reduced to extremities, had recourse to the aid of the Marattas. Báji Ráo immediately obeyed the summons, came suddenly on Mohammed Khán, and before long compelled him to take refuge in a fort. The government of Delhi was too weak to afford him any relief, and he must have surrendered at discretion, but for the exertions of his own family. His wife sent her veil (the strongest appeal to Afghán honour) to her countrymen in Rohilcand. His son put himself at the head of the volunteers thus assembled, and by these means he was delivered from his difficulties and escorted to Allahábád. But this rescue of his person did nothing for his province. The rája of Bundélcand ceded the territory of Jánsi on the Jamna in return for the services of Báji Ráo; and afterwards, at his death, left him rights in Bundélcand, which in time led to the occupation of the whole of that country by the Marattas.

Obtains possessions in Bundélcand.

Mohammed Khán's ill success procured his removal from Málwa, and the province was conferred on Rája Jei Sing of Ambér.

Rája Jei Sing II., viceroy of Málwa.

This prince, whose love of science makes him one of the most remarkable persons of his nation, was by no means so distinguished for his firmness or decision. His hereditary connection with the Marattas, although not sufficient to induce him to betray his trust, facilitated an accommodation after he found resistance desperate; and the result was, that, in the succeeding year, he surrendered his province to the péshwa, with the tacit concurrence of the emperor, on whose behalf the territory was still to be held.

A. D. 1734. His tacit surrender of the province to the Marattas.

But if the Moguls thought to obtain permanent forbearance from Báji Ráo by concession, they knew little of him or his nation; for though he for a time turned his attention to the internal affairs of the Deckan, he continued to press the formal cession of the chout and sirdésmuki of Málwa and Guzerát, and directed the chiefs whom he had left behind him to carry their incursions up to Agra. The Moguls on their part made

BOOK XII.

great demonstrations, and sent out unwieldy and feebly conducted armies, whose operations served only to expose them to the contempt of the enemy.

Báji Ráo increases his demands. A.D. 1736.

After some lapse of time Báji Ráo again took up the negotiation in person; and in proportion as the progress of it disclosed the weakness of his adversaries, he continued to rise in his demands, until at length he insisted on the grant of a jágír, comprising the province of Málwa and all the country south of the Chambal, together with the holy cities of Mattra, Allahábád, and Benáres. The emperor, though all his attempts at open resistance proved futile, was not reduced quite so low as to submit to such terms. He endeavoured to pacify the Marattas by minor sacrifices, and those they accepted without receding from their great object.

Further cessions by the emperor.

Among the concessions were a right to levy tribute on the Rájpúts, and to increase that already due from the territories of Asof Jáh. These were, doubtless, given with a view to embroil the Marattas with the last named powers, and they did

Alarm of Asof Jáh.

not quite fail of their purpose; for Asof Jáh began to perceive that he was pushing his present policy too far, and that he had now as much to fear from the weakness of the emperor, as he formerly had from his enmity. At the same time he was assiduously courted by the cabinet of Delhi, who no longer looked on him as a rebellious subject, but as a natural ally, capable of rescuing them from the danger that hung over them.

He is reconciled to

The result of this state of circumstances was to

CHAP. II.

determine Asof Jáh to support the emperor; but while he was engaged in these deliberations, Báji Ráo was advancing towards the capital. By the time he had himself arrived within forty miles of Agra his light troops were ravaging the country beyond the Jamna, under the command of Malhár Ráo Holcar; and while so employed they were attacked and driven back on the main body by Sádat Khán, governor of Oud, who, with a spirit very unlike his contemporaries, issued from his own province to defend that adjoining. This check, which was magnified into a great victory, and accompanied by reports of the retreat to the Deckan of the whole Maratta army, only stimulated Báji Ráo to wipe off the disgrace, and (as he said himself) to show the emperor that he was still in Hindostan. An army had been sent out to oppose him under the vizír, Kamr u dín Khán. While it lay inactive near Mattra, Báji Ráo suddenly quitted the Jamna, passed off about fourteen miles to the right of the Mogul army, and, advancing by prodigious marches, all at once presented himself before the gates of Delhi.

the emperor.

Báji Ráo appears before Delhi.

A. D. 1737, A. H. 1149.

The consternation produced by his appearance may easily be imagined; but as his object was to intimidate, and not provoke the emperor, he forebore from further aggression, and endeavoured to prevent the destruction of the suburbs. He was unable entirely to restrain the devastation of his followers, and he made that a pretext for drawing

BOOK XII.

off to some distance from the city. This retrograde movement induced the Moguls to attempt a sally, and they were driven back into the town with heavy loss. By this time, however, the vizír had been joined by Sádat Khán, and was on his march to relieve the capital; and Báji Ráo deemed it prudent to commence his retreat, a step involving no dishonour, according to the Maratta rules of war. His intention, at the time, was to have crossed the Jamna lower down, and to have plundered the country between that river and the Ganges; but the approach of the rainy season, and the advance of Asof Jáh, determined him to return at once to the Deckan, where his presence was also required for other objects. After the péshwa's retreat Asof Jáh pursued his march to Delhi, and was invested with full powers to call out all the resources of the state; while the governments of Málwa and Guzerát were conferred on his eldest son, Gházi u dín. But to so low a point was the power of the empire reduced, that, with all the means at his disposal, he could only complete the army under his personal command to the number of 34,000 men.

He retreats.

A. D. 1737, A. H. 1150. Arrival of Asof Jáh at Delhi.

Marches against Báji Ráo.

He was, however, furnished with a fine train of artillery, and supported by a reserve under the command of Safdar Jang, the nephew of Sádat Khán of Oud. With this force he advanced to Serónj, while Báji Ráo crossed the Nerbadda at the head of an army said by himself to be 80,000 strong, and probably superior in numbers to that of Asof Jáh.* This disparity ought not to have deterred the Mogul general from an engagement; for the Marattas had never been formidable in pitched battles; and with them, more even than with other enemies, it was of importance to assume a superiority at the commencement of a campaign. Asof Jáh, on the contrary, probably from reliance on his artillery, as well as the caution natural to his disposition and his advanced age, determined to await an attack in a favourable situation, close to the fort of Bópál. The strength of his position availed him nothing against such an enemy: the Marattas laid waste the country round him, intercepted his supplies, attacked every detachment that attempted to show itself beyond his lines, and completely broke off the communication between him and his reserve.

A.D. 1738, January. Is attacked by Báji Ráo, near Bópál;

The effects of these operations so straitened Asof Jáh, that at the end of a month or six weeks he was obliged to attempt a retreat towards the north. He had probably lost many of his cattle, and, although he left his baggage at Bópál, he had still a heavy train to drag along with him. His movements, in such circumstances, were slow, and were further impeded by the Marattas: though deterred by his artillery from attempting a general attack, they harassed him with rockets, and hung

* According to the present way of speaking among the Marattas, "lak fouj," which ought to mean 100,000 horse, will seldom be found to imply more than 10,000 or 15,000 fighting men.

BOOK XII.

on his rear with their cavalry, until, after some marches at the rate of three or four miles a-day, he was obliged to submit to his fate, and enter into terms with the péshwa. By this convention, he engaged to cede all the country from the Nerbadda to the Chambal (including all Málwa), and to use his best endeavours to procure from the emperor a confirmation of the cession, and a payment of fifty lacs of rupees.*

and constrained to make great cessions on the emperor's part.

A. D. 1738, February; A. H. 1150, Rámzán.

Asof Jáh was then permitted to pursue his retreat to Delhi, and Báji Ráo took possession of his conquests: but before he could receive the promised confirmation from the emperor, the progress of the transaction was arrested by one of those tremendous visitations which, for a time, render men insensible to all other considerations.

Invasion of Nádir Sháh.

The empire was again reduced to the same state of decay which had on former occasions invited the invasions of Tamerlane and Báber; and a train of events in Persia led to a similar attack from that country.

Previous transactions in Persia.

The family of Safavi, after having reigned for 200 years (about the usual duration of an Asiatic dynasty), fell into a state of corruption and decay, and was at last dethroned by the Afgháns of Candahár.

Western Afgháns.

An account has already been given of the north-eastern portion of the Afghán nation †; but the western tribes, who were the actors in the revolu-

* 500,000*l.*

† Page 250.

tion in Persia, differ from those described, in more points than one.

Their country is on the high table land * which is supported on the east by the mountains of Sóli-mán, and separated by them from the plain on the Indus. On the north, a similar bulwark is formed by the range anciently called Caucasus, which overlooks the low level of the Oxus and of the Caspian Sea.† The part of this table land westward of Herát belongs to the Persians; and that eastward of the same city, to the Afgháns.

There are fertile plains in this tract, and on the most extensive of them are the cities of Cábul, Ghazni, Candahár, and Herát ‡; but the greater part consists of high downs, ill-suited to agriculture, and inhabited by pastoral tribes, who live in tents. They have the same government and the same character as the north-eastern Afgháns, except that they are much less turbulent and contentious. In the pastoral tracts, the Afgháns, are almost unmixed; but a great part of the population of the plains, including the cities, consists of Tájiks, who speak Persian, and are the same

* The city of Cábul is 6000 feet above the sea. (*Burnes's Travels*, vol. i. p. 151.)

† See an essay by Mr. J. Baillie Fraser, in *Transactions of the Royal Geographical Society*.

‡ Herát is just beyond the ridge which divides the waters that run to the south from those that flow northward to the Oxus; but it is on the same level with the rest of the table land, and may be regarded as forming a part of it.

BOOK XII.

people that occupy similar situations in Persia and Transoxiana.

The plains alone formed the conquests of the Persian and Indian kings. The Afghán tribes remained independent; though those near the possessions of the two great monarchies must no doubt have been influenced by their power.* The greatest of the western tribes were the Ghiljeis, who inhabited the country round Candahár, and the Abdális †, whose original seat was in the mountains of Ghór, but who chiefly resided at the time now spoken of in the country round Herát. These tribes were always rivals, and often at war with each other.

Ghiljeis.

Abdális (or Duránis).

Revolt of the Ghiljeis.

During the reign of Sháh Hosén (the last of the Safavis), the Ghiljeis had given such offence to Persia as to provoke a formidable expedition against them. Gurgín Khán, the prince of Georgia (a convert from Christianity to the Mahometan religion), was sent to Candahár with an army of upwards of 20,000 men ‡, a force his opponents were unable to withstand. But so galling was the yoke of the Persians, that the Ghíljeis, ere long, resolved to run all risks to throw it off. They were headed by Mír Weis, their hereditary chief, a man of talents and enterprise, and well aware of the feeble con-

* The Abdális agreed about the beginning of the seventeenth century to pay tribute to Persia on condition of protection against the Uzbeks.

† Now called Duránis.

‡ Malcolm's Persia, vol. i. p. 601.

dition of the Persian empire. Conducting his operations with equal caution and boldness, Mír Weis surprised Candahár, expelled the Persians from the surrounding country, and formed his acquisitions, with the original possessions of his tribe, into an independent state. This achievement took place in 1708, and was followed by repeated attempts of the Persians to recover Candahár, in which they were at one time assisted by the Abdális. In A. D. 1716 that tribe joined the Ghiljeis against them, and took Herát, and overran the greater part of Persian Khorásán. The two tribes however, continued their mutual hostilities: the Persians profited by their disunion, and persevered in operations against both until 1720; when the chief of the Ghiljeis formed the bold resolution of carrying the war into Persia, and striking at once at the existence of the government which had oppressed him and his people.

Conquest of Persia by the Ghiljeis.

Mír Weis had died in A. D. 1715, and was at first succeeded by his brother; but his son, whose name was Mahmúd, before long seized on the government; and it was by him that the invasion of Persia was planned. The Persians had before this been defeated in a great battle with the Abdális, who now threatened Meshhed, and whose progress was assisted by the incursions of the Uzbeks from the Oxus.

The north-western part of Persia, also, had been invaded by the Lezgis, from Mount Caucasus;

BOOK XII.

and the misconduct of the government itself made it weaker than those foreign attacks.

Mahmúd left Candahár with 25,000 men. He first marched to Kirmán, and thence to Yezd, from which place he moved directly on Isfahán.*

He was opposed at Gulnábád, in the neighbourhood of that capital, by an army of very superior numbers, admirably equipped, and furnished with twenty-four pieces of cannon.† But the spirit of the Persians was declined and their councils divided: the Afgháns obtained a complete victory, and soon after began operations against the town. Isfahán had at this time attained to its highest pitch of magnificence and population.‡ The last advantage became a calamity on the present occasion; for the Afgháns, finding themselves unable

* He had before been, for a time, in possession of Kirmán, while in a temporary alliance with Persia against the Abdális. (*Jones's Histoire de Nádir Shah*, introduction, sect. 6.)

† "The Persian soldiers looked fresh and showy, and all their equipments, from their tents in which they reposed, and the dresses they wore, to the gold and enamelled furniture of the sleek horses on which they rode, were rich and splendid. The Afgháns had hardly a tent to cover them, their horses were lean from fatigue, the men were clothed in tatters, and tanned by the rays of the sun; and, throughout their whole camp, it was emphatically observed, nothing glittered 'but their swords and lances.'" (*Malcolm's Persia*, vol. i. p. 623.)

‡ Hanway, following Chardin, states the inhabitants at 600,000 souls (vol. ii. p. 164.); and although the comparisons drawn by travellers between this city and those of India render so great a population incredible, yet it cannot be unreasonable to admit one third of it, or 200,000 souls.

to make an impression on the walls, had recourse to intercepting the supplies. It seemed a wild project to blockade so extensive a city with 20,000 men, to which amount the Afgháns were now reduced; yet so well did Mahmúd supply the want of numbers by vigilance and activity, that the inhabitants before long began to suffer all the horrors of famine. The extent of this calamity, and the miseries endured by the besieged, are described by most writers as surpassing the greatest extremities ever known on such occasions.* This disproportioned contest continued for no less than six months; a proof of the prostration of the courage of the Persians as well as of their powers of endurance. At length, after all their sallies had been repulsed, and all the attempts of troops from the provinces to force in convoys had failed, the necessity of submission became apparent. The king went forth with all his principal courtiers in deep mourning, surrendered himself to Mahmúd, and with his own hand placed the diadem on the head of the conqueror (October, 1722).

Their tyrannical government.

Mahmúd's government was, at first, exercised with unexpected leniency; but his garrison in Cazvín having been surprised and massacred by the inhabitants of that city, he became alarmed for his own safety, put several of the Persian chiefs to

* The poet Mohammed Ali Hazín, however (who was in Isfahán during the siege), contradicts these statements, and doubts if any man actually died of hunger. (*Belfour's Memoirs of Hazín*, p. 122.)

BOOK XII.

death, and compelled all the armed part of the population to quit the city on pain of a similar fate. Though the cruelties of the Ghiljcis have been extravagantly exaggerated *, it is easy to imagine the insolence and barbarity of a tribe of shepherds suddenly raised to uncontrolled power over their former oppressors, and rendered deaf to compassion by a consciousness of numerical insignificance which could find no protection but from terror.

* An example may be found in the different accounts of the transaction just mentioned. Hanway, who is by no means given to exaggeration, but who sometimes drew his information from popular rumour or from worse authority, asserts that Mahmúd extirpated the whole of the nobility, and hunted down their children, turning them out, one by one, like beasts of chase; and that he afterwards ordered the slaughter of every man, civil or military, who had received pay (in however humble a capacity) from the former government, commencing the massacre by the execution of 3000 of the late king's guards. On the other hand, the author of the "Nádirnámeh," whose statement may almost be considered as official, and who certainly had no wish to extenuate the atrocities of Mahmúd, relates that "he formed a design to massacre the Persians; and, on the same day on which the Afgháns arrived from Cazvín, he caused *one hundred and fourteen persons* to be put to death, confounding the good with the bad, and the small with the great." (From Sir W. Jones's French translation, vol. v. of his Works, p. 12.) The same author relates that soon afterwards his evil genius led him to massacre all the princes of the blood, and that he put them to death, to the number of thirty-nine. These statements are not very consistent with the idea of a massacre by thousands; and it may be observed, that, during all this time, Shah Hosén was left alive, and so far from being cruelly treated, he complained of his condition because he was confined to a small palace, and only attended by five male and five female servants. (*Malcolm's History of Persia*, vol. i. p. 644.)

Mahmúd had not reigned two years when the agitation and anxiety he was exposed to, together with the effect of religious austerities and penances which he superstitiously imposed on himself, unsettled his reason. He became raving mad, and either died or was put to death; when he was succeeded by his nephew, Ashref (April, 1724).

Their wars with the Turks and Russians.

The new king was a man of talents and vigour. Before he had completed the conquest of Persia, he was assailed at once by the Russians and Turks, who had entered into a confederacy for dismembering the kingdom. The western provinces were to belong to the Porte, and the northern, as far as the Araxes to Russia. Ashref turned his attention in the first instance to the Turks: he defeated them in repeated actions, and compelled them to acknowledge his title; but he was not able to expel them from the conquests they had made. The Russians, though led by the czar Peter in person, were less dangerous from the strong country through which they had to advance: they had, however, made their way to Resht, on the south of the Caspian Sea, when their career was interrupted, and afterwards abandoned, in consequence of the death of the czar.

Rise of Nádir Sháh.

But Ashref's most formidable enemy was now rising nearer home. Tahmasp, the son of Hosén, had fled from Isfahán, and had remained under the protection of the tribe of Kajar, on the shore of the Caspian, with nothing of the royal dignity but the name. The first sign of a change of fortune

BOOK XII.

was his being joined by Nádir Cúli, the greatest warrior Persia has ever produced.

This chief, who had first collected troops as a freebooter, now appeared as the deliverer of his country. He raised the courage of the Persians by his example and his success, called forth their religious zeal, and revived their national pride, until, by degrees, he elevated them from the abject condition into which they had sunk, to as high a pitch of military glory as they had ever before enjoyed.

He drives out the Ghiljeis, and recovers Khorásán from the Abdális.

His first exploits were the capture of Meshhed and the recovery of Khorásán from the Abdális and Mohammed Khán of Sistán, who had seized on part of that province: he afterwards engaged the Ghiljeis under Ashref, who advanced to the northern frontier to attack him, drove them, in a succession of battles, to the southern limit of the kingdom, and so effectually wore down their army that they at last dispersed, and gave up the possession of their conquest, which they had retained for seven years. Most of their number were killed in the war or perished in the desert on their return home. Ashref was murdered by a Belóch chief between Kirmán and Candahár (January 1729).

Nádir next marched against the Turks, whose treaty with Ashref left them in possession of part of the Persian territories. He had already recovered Tabríz, when he received intelligence of a rising of the Abdális, and was obliged to return to Khorásán.

On his former successful expedition against that tribe, he had followed up his victory by measures of conciliation. By those means, and from their common enmity to the Ghiljeis. he gained a strong party among the Abdális, and to its leader, he confided the charge of Herát. The other party had now gained the ascendancy, had overrun Khorásán, and laid siege to Meshhed, then held by Nádir's brother, I'brahím, whom they had just before defeated in the field. They had even formed a connection with the Ghiljeis: but the new allies had no sooner met, than their old enmities broke out, and they separated more estranged than ever. This war was more tedious than the former one, the siege of Herát alone occupying ten months; but the Abdális were this time completely subdued. Nádir again took measures to attach them to him after his victory, and as he not long after embraced the Sunni religion, they became the most devoted of his followers.

Renewed invasion of the Abdális.

Nádir takes Herát,

and gains the attachment of the Abdális.

The length of time occupied in these operations produced a crisis in the affairs of Persia. While the sole function of the government was the employment of the army, the king naturally remained a mere pageant in the hands of the general; but when restored to the capital, and acknowledged throughout the kingdom, he became a person of more importance; and, during the absence of Nádir, he took upon him the exercise of all the royal prerogatives.

He deposes Tahmasp Sháh.

Nádir was not at all disposed to acquiesce in

BOOK XII.

such a transfer of authority, and, as soon as he had settled the affairs of Khorásán, he repaired to Isfahán, and, taking advantage of the odium created by an unfavourable treaty with the Turks, he deposed Tahmasp, and raised his infant son to the nominal sovereignty. This may almost be considered as the avowed commencement of his own reign; but it was not till he had gained many victories over the Turks, recovered the whole of the territory occupied by that nation and the Russians, and made peace with both powers, that he formally assumed the title of King of Persia. Before he was invested with that dignity, he repaired with his army to the plain of Móghán, to which place he summoned the civil and military officers, the governors of districts, the magistrates, and all the other men of distinction in the empire, to the number of 100,000 persons. By the unanimous voice of this assembly he was offered the crown, which, after some affected reluctance, he accepted, on condition that the Shía religion should be abolished, and that of the Sunnis established throughout Persia (1736).*

Is himself elected king.

He suppresses the Shía religion.

By this change of religion Nádir hoped to eradicate all attachment to the Safavis, whose claims were founded on their being the champions of the Shía sect; but as the Persians remained at heart as much devoted as ever to the national faith, the

* Nádirnámeh. Jones's Works, vol. v. p. 237. Hanway represents Nádir as only stipulating for a toleration of the Sunni religion, and *subsequently* abolishing that of the Shías.

real effect of the measure was to produce an alienation between the new king and his subjects, and led to consequences equally calamitous to both.

Though little aware of this result at the time, Nádir felt that a throne established by a succession of victories must be maintained by similar achievements: he therefore determined to gratify the pride of his countrymen by retaliating on their former conquerors, the Ghiljeis, and restoring Candahár to the Persian monarchy.

Invades the Ghiljeis.

He made great preparations for this expedition, and set out on it at the head of an army estimated, by some authorities, at 80,000 men.* He had, on this occasion, the hearty co-operation of the Abdális, while the Ghiljeis were dispirited and disunited. But they had not so far lost their martial character as to yield without a struggle; and it was not till after a close blockade of nearly a twelvemonth that Nádir ventured on an assault of Candahár: even then he was more than once repulsed before the city fell into his hands (March, 1738). While the siege was pending, he settled the greater part of the surrounding country; and, at the same time, his son, Reza Cúli Mirzá, who had marched from Meshhed against the Uzbeks, not only conquered the province of Balkh, but

Takes Candahár.

* Malcolm's History of Persia, vol. ii. p. 68. Hanway (vol. ii. p. 355.) says that this army of 80,000 men was closely followed by another of 30,000; but these great numbers do not seem probable to the west of the Indus, where the vast armies, common in India, are very seldom seen.

BOOK XII.

gained a victory on the Oxus, over the king of Bokhára, in person.

His conciliatory policy.

Nádir's conduct towards the Ghiljeis was moderate and politic: he took no vindictive measures in retaliation for the invasion of Persia; he treated the Ghiljeis like his other subjects, and enrolled many of them in his army; but he removed a portion of the tribe from their lands round Candahár, which he made over to the Abdális, and particularly to that part of them who had been settled about Níshapúr, in the west of Khorásán.*

His difference with the government of India.

The acquisition of the Ghiljei territory brought Nádir to the frontier of the Mogul empire. The extreme weakness of that monarchy could not escape his observation; and the prospect of repairing the exhausted resources of Persia from so rich

* Jones's Nádirnámeh, Works, vol. v. p. 275. The account of the Ghiljei conquest is almost entirely drawn from Hanway and the "Nádirnámeh:" that of Nádir Sháh's proceedings chiefly from the latter work. Hanway is himself a man of judgment and veracity, but his facts seem sometimes to rest on the authority of the "Dernière Révolution de la Perse," a sort of version, we are told, of the notes of Father Krusinski, a Polish Jesuit, which, though founded on good information, is too fanciful and highly coloured to be at all depended upon. It bears a considerable resemblance, in these respects, to Catrou, formerly mentioned (in the reign of Sháh Jehán). Krusinski's own work has since been published in Germany, but I have never seen it. The "Nádirnámeh" is a Persian history, by Mírza Mehdi, who is stated by Sir J. Malcolm to have been confidential secretary of Nádir Sháh. Though a minister and a panegyrist, he is a much more faithful historian than Abul Fazl, and his style, in Sir W. Jones's French translation at least, is much clearer and more compact.

a mine was scarcely a greater temptation than the means of employing the warlike tribes now subject to his authority, and combining their rival energies in an undertaking so acceptable to them all.

While engaged in the siege of Candahár, he had applied to the court of Delhi for the seizure or expulsion of some Afgháns who had fled into the country near Ghazni. The Indian government was probably unable to comply with this demand, and they seem also to have had some hesitation in acknowledging Nádir Sháh's title: for these reasons they allowed a long period to elapse without returning an answer. Nádir Sháh remonstrated in strong terms against this neglect of his application, and without further delay advanced on Ghazni and Cábul. Another messenger, whom he now despatched to Delhi, having been cut off by the Afgháns in the mountains, Nádir thought himself fully justified in an invasion of India. Cábul had fallen into his hands with little difficulty; but he remained in that neighbourhood for some months for the purpose of settling the country, and did not commence his march to the eastward till near the approach of winter. The court of Delhi had been too much absorbed in the dread of the Marattas and its own internal factions to pay much attention to the proceedings of Nádir. As long as he was engaged in a contest within the old territory of Persia, they looked on with total indifference; and even when he had invaded their own territory and taken Cábul, they still expected that

A. D. 1738, May; A. H. 1151, Safar.

A. D. 1738, October; A. H. 1151, Shábán.

Supineness of the court of Delhi.

the mountain tribes between that city and Péshávar would check his further advance. But the money, which, in regular times, was paid for the purpose of keeping up an influence with those tribes, had for some years been withheld; and they had no inclination, if they had possessed the power, of interfering in favour of the Moguls. It was therefore with dismay proportioned to their former supineness that the Moguls learned that Nádir had passed the mountains, had defeated a small force under one of their governors, had thrown a bridge of boats over the Indus, and was advancing into the Panjáb.

Nádir invades India.

A. D. 1738, November; A. H. 1151, Rámzán.

Notwithstanding a faint show of opposition attempted by the governor of Láhór, Nádir met with no real obstruction till he approached the Jamna, within one hundred miles of Delhi, when he found himself in the neighbourhood of the Indian army.

Defeats Mohammed Sháh.

Mohammed Sháh had at length exerted himself to collect his force: he had been joined by Asof Jáh, and had moved to Carnál, where he occupied a fortified camp. Sádat Khán, the viceroy of Oud arrived in the neighbourhood of this camp about the same time with Nádir Sháh; and an attempt to intercept him by the Persians brought on a partial action, which ended in a general engagement. The Indians would in no circumstances have been a match for the hardy and experienced soldiers opposed to them; and they were now brought up in confusion and without concert, Asof

Jáh having, from some real or pretended misconception, taken no part in the action.*

The result was the rout of the Indian army; Kháni Dourán, the commander-in-chief, was killed, and Sádat Khán taken prisoner; and Mohammed had no resource but to send Asof Jáh to offer his submission, and repair, himself, with a few attendants, to the Persian camp. Nádir Sháh received him with great courtesy, and allowed him to return on the same day to his own encampment. He did not on that account desist from pressing his advantages; for he soon after obliged Mohammed to join his army, and in this manner the two kings marched on towards Delhi. Different accounts are given of the negotiations carried on during the interval, which were embarrassed by the rivalry of Asof Jáh and Sádat Khán; but such intrigues could have no result of consequence, for Nádir had the power completely in his own hands, and required no prompter to tell him how to exercise it.

A. D. 1739, Feb. 13.; A. H. 1151, Zí Cáda 15.

Advances to Delhi. A. D. 1739, March; A. H. 1151, Zí Haj.

The army reached Delhi in the beginning of March, when both kings took up their residence in the royal palace. Nádir distributed a portion of his troops throughout the town; he ordered strict discipline to be observed, and placed safeguards in

* The journal translated by Fraser (*Life of Nádir*, p. 154.) makes Nádir's whole army, with the followers, who were all armed, amount to 160,000; but an enumeration, by a news-writer in his camp, states his whole force, *when at Péshávwer*, at 64,500 fighting men, and 4000 followers. (Ibid. pp. 140, 141.)

BOOK XII.

different places for the protection of the inhabitants.

Insurrection of the inhabitants.

These precautions did not succeed in conciliating the Indians, who looked on the ferocity of these strangers with terror, and on their intrusion with disgust.* On the second day after the occupation of the city a report was spread that Nádir Sháh was dead, on which the hatred of the Indians broke forth without restraint. They fell on all the Persians within their reach; and from the manner in which those troops were scattered throughout the city, a considerable number fell sacrifices to the popular fury. The Indian nobles made no effort to protect the Persians; some even gave those up to be murdered who had been furnished for the protection of their palaces.†

Nádir Sháh at first applied his whole attention to suppressing the tumult, and, though provoked to find that it continued during the whole night, and seemed rather to increase than diminish, he mounted his horse at day-break, in the hope that his presence would restore quiet. The first objects that met his eyes in the streets were the dead bodies of his countrymen; and he was soon assailed with stones, arrows, and firearms, from the houses. At last one of his chiefs was killed at his side, by a shot

General massacre by the Persians.

* Fraser.

† Hazín states the number cut off at 700 (p. 281. of Mr. Belfour's edition of the original; in the translation, p. 299., it is 7000, but doubtless from an error of the press). Scott (vol. ii. p. 207.) makes it 1000.

aimed at himself; when he gave way to his passion, and ordered a general massacre of the Indians.* The slaughter raged from sunrise till the day was far advanced, and was attended with all the horrors that could be inspired by rapine, lust, and thirst of vengeance. The city was set on fire in several places, and was soon involved in one scene of destruction, blood, and terror.

At length Nádir, satiated with carnage, allowed himself to be prevailed on by the intercession of the emperor or his prime minister, and gave an order to stop the massacre; and, to the infinite credit of his discipline, it was immediately obeyed.†

* Fraser, p. 183.

† The authentic accounts differ about the suspension of the massacre. It is said that Nádir, during the whole period, sat in gloomy silence in the little mosque of Rokn u doula, in the Great Bázár; where Mohammed Sháh and his nobles at length took courage to present themselves. They stood before him with downcast eyes, until Nádir commanded them to speak; when Mohammed burst into tears, and entreated Nádir to spare his subjects. I wish there was better authority than Dow for this not improbable anecdote. The best accounts of the massacre are that of Hazín, who was an eye-witness, and whose narrative is copied, almost verbatim, by the author of the "Seir Mutákherín;" and the journal of a native Indian, who was secretary to Sirbuland, given by Fraser, in his "History of Nádir Sháh." The succeeding transactions (in some of which the writer must have been an actor) are minutely recorded in the same journal. Hazín informs us the massacre lasted for half the day, and that the numbers slain were beyond calculation. Fraser makes the amount from 120,000 to 150,000; but the author of the "Nádirnámeh" seems nearest the truth, and probably below it, in stating that the slaughter continued for almost the whole day, and that about 30,000 persons were put

BOOK XII.

Nádir's extortions.

But the sufferings of the people of Delhi did not cease with this tragedy. Nádir's sole object in invading India was to enrich himself by its plunder, and he began to discuss the contributions from the moment of his victory. His first adviser was Sádat Khán: that nobleman died soon after reaching Delhi, when the work of exaction was committed to Sirbuland Khán and a Persian named Tahmasp Khán; and their proceedings, which were sufficiently rigorous of themselves, were urged on by the violence and impatience of Nádir.

They first took possession of the imperial treasures and jewels, including the celebrated peacock throne. They afterwards seized on the whole effects of some great nobles, and compelled the rest to sacrifice the largest part of their property as a ransom for the remainder. They then fell on the inferior officers and on the common inhabitants: guards were stationed to prevent people leaving the city, and every man was constrained to disclose the amount of his fortune, and to pay accordingly. Every species of cruelty was employed to extort these contributions. Even men of consequence were beaten to draw forth confessions. Great numbers of the inhabitants died of the usage they received, and many destroyed themselves to avoid

His rapacity and violence.

to the sword during the course of it. Scott (vol. ii. p. 207.) restricts the number to 8000, but he does not give his authority; and it is incredible that so small a result should be produced by many hours of unresisted butchery by a detachment of 20,000 men, which was the body employed on it.

the disgrace and torture. "Sleep and rest forsook the city. In every chamber and house was heard the cry of affliction. It was, before, a general massacre; but, now, the murder of individuals." *

He prepares to return.

Contributions were also levied on the governors of provinces; until Nádir was at length convinced that he had exhausted all the sources from which wealth was to be obtained, and prepared himself to return to his own dominions. He made a treaty with Mohammed Sháh, by which all the country west of the Indus was ceded to him. He married his son to a princess of the house of Teimúr, and at last he seated Mohammed on the throne, invested him, with his own hand, with the ornaments of the diadem, and enjoined all the Indian nobles to obey him implicitly, on pain of his future indignation and vengeance.

The country west of the Indus ceded to him.

Mohammed Sháh restored.

Amount of the treasures carried off by Nádir Sháh.

At length he marched from Delhi, after a residence of fifty-eight days, carrying with him a treasure in money, amounting, by the lowest computation, to eight or nine millions sterling, besides several millions in gold and silver plate, valuable furniture, and rich stuffs of every description; and this does not include the jewels, which were inestimable. He also carried off many elephants, horses, and camels, and led away the most skilful

* The words between inverted commas are drawn from Scott (vol. ii. p. 210.); but the substance is the same in all the narratives.

BOOK XII.

workmen and artisans, to the number of some hundreds.*

* The various sums of *money* enumerated by Scott amount to between 8,000,000*l.* and 9,000,000*l.* The "Nádirnámeh" says fifteen crores of rupees; Fraser, thirty crores of rupees; and Hanway, thirty crores, which he estimates at 37,500,000*l.*; and all these sums are the *money* alone. The imperial treasures must have been greatly encroached on since the reign of Sháh Jehán: the peacock throne, which Tavernier estimated at 6,000,000*l.*, is only valued, in the "Nádirnámeh," at 2,000,000*l.*, and in Scott, only at 1,000,000. Many stories which were current at the time, about the causes of this invasion, are preserved in Dow's "Hindostan." According to those narratives, Nádir was invited to India by Asof Jáh and Sádat Khán, and the loss of the battle of Carnál was concerted between those chiefs. Nádir Sháh rewarded their treachery by spitting on their beards, and ordering them to be driven from his court. The two nobles, thus disgraced, agreed to end their shame by a voluntary death; but, as they were rivals, and each suspected the sincerity of the other, they sent spies to discover whether the resolution was carried into effect. Asof Jáh, the more crafty of the two, took an innocent draught, and soon after pretended to fall down dead; on which Sádat, deceived by the artifice, swallowed real poison, and forthwith expired. These fictions, like many others which are believed in times of agitation, disappear when full light is thrown on the period.

CHAP. III.

TO THE DEATH OF MOHAMMED SHÁH.

CHAP. III.

Deplorable condition of the capital,

For some time after Nádir Sháh's departure, the inhabitants of Delhi remained in a sort of stupor. They had not yet recovered the terror of the past, and the destruction of their fortunes: many of their houses were in ruins; much of the city was entirely deserted, and the whole infected by the stench of the bodies which still lay unburied in the streets. It was not till long after Nádir was gone, that the court awoke as if from a lethargy.* The view of the empire which presented itself was as full of ruin and desolation as the capital. The army was destroyed, the treasury emptied, the finances all but annihilated; the Marattas still threatened on the south, and the only provinces which had not been laid waste by their ravages had now been destroyed by Nádir's army.

and of the empire.

Internal dissensions.

To these unavoidable evils the court added internal dissension. The prevailing faction was formed of a few great families who, from their Túrk descent, were called the Túráni nobles: the heads were the vizír Kamr u dín Khán and Asof Jáh; and they were connected by intermarriages as well as by party. To them were opposed all those de-

* Fraser.

BOOK XII.

sirous of supplanting them, or jealous of their ascendency; among which number the emperor himself was thought to be included.

This divided government would have fallen an easy prey to the Marattas, had not circumstances procured it a respite from the encroachments of those invaders.

Proceedings of the Marattas.

If the power of Nádir Sháh had been underrated by the Moguls, it was probably quite unknown to Báji Ráo: and he seems to have been struck with amazement at the appearance of this terrible antagonist, in a field which he expected to have traversed unopposed. His first thought was to suspend all his plans of aggrandizement, and form a general league for the defence of India. "Our domestic quarrels (he writes) are now insignificant: there is but one enemy in Hindostan." ... "Hindús and Mussulmans, the whole power of the Deckan, must assemble."* When he was relieved from the fear of Nádir Sháh, he returned to his old designs.

Báji Ráo resumes offensive operations.

He had a ground of quarrel with the Moguls, as the agreement made by Asof Jáh had not been formally ratified by the emperor, and the obvious course for him was to have enforced his claim at Delhi: but he was led to choose the Deckan for the theatre of the war, that he might be at hand to watch the proceedings of the Bosla of Bérar and the Geikwár of Guzerát, who were plotting to overthrow his power under pretence of emancipating the rája.

Attacks Asof Jáh's possessions.

He disposed of the Bosla

* Grant Duff, vol. i. p. 547.

by engaging him in a remote expedition into the Carnatic, and then attacked Násir Jang, the second son of Asof Jáh, who had been left in charge of his father's government, and was encamped with 10,000 men at Burhánpúr. Báji Ráo at first surrounded him, and probably expected the same success as he had lately met with against Asof Jáh himself; but the young viceroy showed a vigour unusual to the Moguls of that day; and, being joined by a reinforcement, he attacked the Marattas, broke through their army, and had advanced to Ahmednagar on his way to Púna, when Báji Ráo thought it prudent to come to an accommodation with him. The péshwa seems now to have been reduced to perplexity by the variety of embarrassments which he had brought on himself*: and was returning to Hindostan (for what purpose is not known), when his plans were arrested by his death, which took place on the Nerbadda.

A. D. 1740, A. H. 1153.

Is repulsed by Asof's son, Nasir Jang.

Perplexed affairs of Báji Rao.

His death. A. D. 1740, April 28.; A. H. 1153, Safar.

He left three sons: Bálají Ráo, who succeeded him as péshwa; Rágonát Ráo, or Ragoba, who was at one time much connected with the English, and was the father of the last péshwa; and Shamshír Bahádur, to whom (though an illegitimate son by a Mahometan woman, and brought up in his

His sons.

* He writes thus to his spiritual guide: — "I am involved in difficulty, in debt, and in disappointments; and like a man ready to swallow poison: near the rája are my enemies, and should I go at this time to Sattára, they will put their feet on my breast. I should be thankful if I could meet death." (*Grant Duff*, vol. i. p. 559.)

mother's religion) he left all his possessions and pretensions in Bundélcand.

Wars in the Concan before Báji Ráo's death.

During the last years of Báji Ráo's administration he had been engaged in wars in the Concan. They were chiefly conducted by his brother, Chimnají; and, from the position of his enemies in forts and islands, protected on one side by the sea, and on the other by hills and jungles, required extraordinary exertions, and were attended with imperfect success.

With A'ngria.

These enemies were A'ngria of Colába, the Abyssinians of Jinjera, and the Portuguese. A'ngria, after his acknowledgment of Sáho Rája, remained in nominal dependence on the Maratta state, but employed his own resources with little or no control. His piracies (which he called "levying *chout* on the sea") rendered him formidable to all his neighbours. The English made repeated attacks on him with considerable naval forces; and, on one occasion, with the co-operation of the Portuguese (A. D. 1719); yet failed in all their attempts. The Dutch also sent a strong force against him at a later period (A. D. 1724) with equal ill success. The péshwa interposed in a dispute between two brothers of the family, and received from one of the competitors two forts which they possessed in the Gháts (about A. D. 1734). The contest, however, continued; and the péshwa, though latterly assisted by an English fleet, was unable to bring it to a conclusion till the time of Báji Ráo's death.*

* Grant Duff.

The war with the Abyssinians was still less successful. Those Mussulmans were as powerful at sea as A'ngria. They were, besides, in the practice of ravaging the Maratta territories on the main land, and had even seized on some of their forts. The utmost result of the péshwa's efforts was to procure forbearance from those aggressions (A. D. 1736).* (margin: With the Abyssinians of Jinjera.)

The war with the Portuguese originated in the contest between the A'ngrias (A. D. 1737). It ended in the loss of the Portuguese possessions in Salsette, Bassein, and the neighbouring parts of the Concan (A. D. 1739). The difficulties encountered by the Marattas in this conquest may be estimated from their loss at the siege of Bassein, which they themselves admit to have amounted to 5000 killed and wounded.† (margin: With the Portuguese.)

The storms which were gathering round Báji Ráo at his death might have been expected to overwhelm his successor; but Bálají, however inferior to his father in other respects, was at least his equal in address; and the skill with which he availed himself of some favourable circumstances effected his deliverance from the difficulties with which he was surrounded. (margin: Bálají Ráo.)

The dangers felt by Báji Ráo, besides his ill success against Násir Jang, were caused by his financial embarrassments and his domestic enemies. The chief of his enemies were, the pírti nidhí, Ragují (margin: Domestic enemies of Báji Ráo.)

* Grant Duff. † Ibid.

BOOK XII.

The pírti nidhí.

Ragují Bosla.

Bosla, and Damají Geikwar. The first was the old rival of his family*; and, though much depressed, was still formidable. Parsojí, the founder of the Boslas, afterwards rájas of Berár, was a private horseman from the neighbourhood of Sattára: though he bore the same name with the house of Sévají, there is no proof that he was of the same descent. He, however, rose to distinction; and, being one of the first to join Rája Sáho when he returned from Delhi, was further advanced by that prince, and invested with a right to collect all the Maratta dues in Berár and the forest country farther to the east. Ragují, his cousin, who was a favourite of Sáho, and married to his sister-in-law, was raised to his station on his death, in preference to his son, who ought to have succeeded him. Ragují had given offence to the péshwa by levying contributions to the north of the Nerbadda, in the tract which had been appropriated to the latter chief: he was likewise an object of jealousy, from the apprehension that he might prevail on Sáho to keep up the name of Bosla by adopting him. The Geikwár had been the guardian, and was now the representative, of Dábári, the chief of Guzerát, another of the péshwa's rivals, whose own ignorance and debauchery incapacitated him for business.*

Damají Geikwár.

The last of Báji Ráo's difficulties arose from the enormous debts incurred in his military expeditions, which, from the exhausted state of the country,

* See p. 562.

and some changes in the mode of war, no longer paid their own expenses.

His principal creditor, Bárámatiker, was himself a man of some consequence, and of immense wealth: his unsatisfied demand had led to quarrels with Báji Ráo, and Ragují secured his co-operation by promising to support his claims, and even to procure for him an indemnity, in the succession to the high office lately held by his debtor.

Their intrigues to prevent Bálají succeeding to the office of péshwa.

Ragují, as has been mentioned, was on an expedition to the Carnatic, and was besieging Trichinopoly, when he heard of the péshwa's death; and, although he instantly hastened to Sattára to oppose Bálají's succession, he was obliged to leave the greater part of his army behind him: his views, also, were as inconsistent with those of the pírti nidhí as with the péshwa's; and he had, therefore, no concert with that minister. Dámají Geikwár was not ready to take the field; and Násir Jang, who soon after rebelled against his father, was too much occupied to profit by the Maratta dissensions. On the other hand, Bálají was already near the capital: he had been joined by a portion of his father's troops under his uncle, Chimnají, and the rest were disposable and at hand: the rája was surrounded by his creatures; and, above all, he was the head of the Bramin party; and as all the business, even of his enemies, was in the hands of that class, he had a prodigious advantage in every contest. He was accordingly appointed péshwa in spite of all opposition, and Ragují returned to his

A. D. 1740, August.

BOOK XII.

army at Trichinopoly, whither Bárámatiker, in this change of circumstances, was glad to accompany him. Bálají, however, did not fail to apply himself to the liquidation of his debts; a task for which he was much better fitted than his father.

Success of Bálají.

Bálají marches into Málwa.

After more than a year spent on internal arrangements, Bálají turned his attention to his claims on Hindostan which had been encroached on by Ragují Bosla. For this purpose he procured from the rája a distinct assignment of all the Maratta rights and all tribute that might be collected to the north of the Nerbadda, excepting in the province of Guzerát. To give reality to this grant, Bálají marched towards the point from which he could most easily check the interference of Ragují: he crossed the Nerbadda, took Garra and Mandala, and was about to move on Allahábád, when he was recalled by an invasion of Málwa by Damají Geikwár from Guzerát. Damají, who, perhaps, had no object but to make a diversion in favour of Ragují, retired on his approach; and Bálají took advantage of his position in Málwa to press the court of Delhi for a confirmation of the grant of that province extorted by Báji Ráo from Asof Jáh, which had remained in suspense during the Persian invasion. His views on this subject were facilitated by those very encroachments of Ragují which it had been so much his desire to check.

Revives his father's demands on the court of Delhi.

Invasion of Bengal by Ragují Bosla.

This chief had, on his return from the Carnatic, sent a force into Bengal, under his Bramin minister, Básker Pandit, which had ravaged the province, threatening the viceroy himself when his troops were dispersed, and retiring into the southern and western hills when he was in force. Ali Verdi Khán *, then viceroy, maintained a good resistance to Básker Pandit; but he was alarmed at the advance of Ragují in person, and besought the emperor to afford him immediate assistance, if he did not wish to lose the province. The emperor conscious of his own weakness, ordered Safder Jang (who had succeeded his father, Sádat Khán, as viceroy of Oud) to undertake the task; at the same time, he took the more effectual measure of calling in the aid of Bálají Ráo, and purchased it by a confirmation of the grant of Malwa.† Nothing could be more agreeable to Bálají Ráo than this invitation. He immediately marched by Allahábád and Behár, and reached Murshidábád, the capital of the province, in time to protect it from Ragují, who was approaching from the south-west. He here received from Ali Verdi the payment of an assignment granted to him by the court of Delhi on the arrears of the revenue of Bengal; and being now zealous in the cause which he was so well paid

The emperor purchases the aid of Bálají by the formal cession of Málwa.

* Called also Mohábat Jang.

† Captain Grant Duff states that the grant was not confirmed until after the expulsion of Ragují, in A. D. 1743; and it may not have been formally delivered over till then; but his own abstract of the grant (vol. ii. p. 15.) bears the date of Jamádi ul Awal, in the twenty-fourth year of Mohammed Sháh's reign, which would be about May, 1742. Bálají, on his part, was to furnish 4000 horse at his own cost, and 8000 more to be paid by the emperor.

BOOK XII.

for espousing, he marched against the invader. Ragují retired before him, but was overtaken, and suffered a rout, and the loss of his baggage, before he was completely driven out of the province. After this success Bálají returned to Málwa, whence, after some time, he set out for Sattára.

Bálají defeats and drives out Ragují.

A. D. 1743, A. H. 1156.

Fresh combinations against the péshwa.

His presence was at no time more required; for Ragují, on his return from Bengal, determined to profit by Bálají's absence, and was on full march for the capital. Damají Geikwár was also approaching from Guzerát, and the agent of the pírti nidhí (who was himself disabled by sickness) was in active preparation to assist him. Bálají must have formed a high estimate of the power of this combination, since he thought the dissolution of it worth the sacrifice of those exclusive rights beyond the Nerbadda for which he had so successfully contended. He conceded to Ragují the right of levying tribute in all Bengal and Behár, if not also in Allahábád and Oud. By this adjustment the other confederates were left without support; but it suited the péshwa's projects to temporise with them, and the storm which threatened so much disturbance was thus quietly dispelled. The concession to Ragují seems to have been dictated by sound policy: his views were henceforth turned towards the east, and his designs on the succession to the rája appear to have been laid aside. Bengal, indeed, soon afforded him sufficient employment.

He buys over Ragují by liberal cessions.

A. D. 1744, A. H. 1157.

Ragují again invades Bengal.

Básker Pandit was again sent into that province: his operations in the field were successful; but he suffered himself to be inveigled into an interview with Ali Verdi, by whom he was treacherously murdered, and at the same moment his army was attacked and dispersed. Bengal was thus, for a time, delivered from the Marattas. But Ali Verdi's chief support in his wars had been a body of Afgháns, under a celebrated leader named Mustafa Khán; and with them he now quarrelled. A serious revolt ensued, of which Ragují took advantage; and, although the revolt was at last subdued, and many other vicissitudes befell the contending parties, yet Ragují was so far successful in the end, that, in A. D. 1751, not long before the death of Ali Verdi, he obtained a cession of Cattac (the southern division of Orissa), and an engagement for the payment of twelve lacs of rupees (120,000*l.*) as the chout or tribute of Bengal.

His general murdered by the viceroy. A. D. 1745, A. H. 1158.

He ultimately obtains the chout of Bengal and a cession of Cattac.

During all this time the Marattas had been entirely free from disturbances on the side of the Moguls in the Deckan. Asof Jáh had been recalled from Delhi, in A. D. 1741, by a revolt of his second son, Násir Jang; and when it was suppressed, he was involved in disturbances in the subordinate government of Arcot, which occupied him till he died, at the age of 77.

Affairs of Asof Jáh.

Revolt of Násir Jang. Asof Jáh returns to the Deckan.

His death. A. D. 1748, June; A. H. 1161, Jamádi u Sáni.

His death led to contentions among his sons; which, being unconnected with events in the other parts of India, and chiefly influenced by the French and English, will be best understood when we come to relate the proceedings of those nations.

The death of Asof Jáh was followed, before the

Death of Sáho Rája.

BOOK XII.

A. D. 1749, (about Dec.).

end of the succeeding year, by that of Sáho Rája; and the latter event produced the crisis for which the péshwa had all along been preparing, and which was to decide the future fortunes of himself and his descendants.

Intrigues and contests for the succession.

As Sáho was without issue, it was necessary by the Hindú custom that he should *adopt* a successor; and the same custom restricted the choice to his kindred. The nearest kinsman, in this case, was the rája of Cólapúr; and his claim, in itself so difficult to set aside, was supported by a close alliance with Sawatri Bái, the wife of Sáho and the rival and enemy of the péshwa.

Though the government was entirely in the hands of Bálají, the personal conduct of the rája was almost as much under the control of his wife; the imbecility into which he had of late years fallen rendering him incompetent to judge for himself. There was, therefore, a continual danger of her prevailing on Sáho to adopt the rája of Cólapúr; and it was impossible for Bálají to anticipate her, as he was unprovided with a claimant, and could not yet venture to seize on the government in his own name.

Boldness and address of Bálají.

In this perplexity he had recourse to a stratagem well worthy of the subtlety of his class. Tára Bái, the widow of Rája Rám, who had so long maintained the claims of her son, Sévají II., in opposition to Sáho, was still alive at an advanced age; and although her enmity to the péshwa was not abated, she was tempted, by the prospect of recovering her influence, to enter into the designs

CHAP. III.

of that minister. In furtherance of their project, a secret intimation was conveyed to Sáho, that a posthumous son of Sévaji II. had been concealed by Tára Bái, and was still alive. Sáho made known his supposed discovery to the péshwa, and it was determined to question Tára Bái. It may be imagined that she readily admitted the fact; but the whole story was treated with ridicule by the other party, and Sawatri Bái redoubled her vigilance to prevent the rája from acting on the delusion produced by it. She was safe from an adoption which could not take place without a certain degree of publicity; but she was circumvented by a stroke of audacity for which she could not have been prepared: it was no less than an assertion that the rája had signed an instrument, transferring all the powers of his government to the péshwa, on condition of his maintaining the royal title and dignity in the house of Sévají through the grandson of Tára Bái. It is said that this important deed was executed at a secret interview between Bálají and the rája: but whether the signature (if genuine) was obtained by persuasion or fraud; *when* the deed was produced; and how far its authenticity was admitted at the time, are left in an obscurity which is rendered more mysterious by the conduct of Bálají and Tára Bái in circumstances which will appear in the sequel.*

Alleged abdication of Sáho in favour of Bálají.

* I possess no facts relating to this revolution but what are given by Grant Duff; but I have been led to conclusions somewhat different from that author, both with regard to the reality

BOOK XII.

Bálají takes possession of the government.

At the moment of the death of Sáho, the péshwa called in a fresh force to Sattára, and seized on the head of the opposite party. He then proclaimed the grandson of Tára Bái by the title of Rám Rája, and took measures to promote the influence of that princess, with the intention of turning it

A. D. 1750.

to his own use. After these preparations, he summoned the great chiefs to court, that the new arrangements might be confirmed by their recognition. Damají Geikwár did not attend, but Rágují Bosla appeared as an ally, and, after some affected inquiries, acknowledged the succession of Rám Rája. The former concessions to him were confirmed, and he received, in addition, a portion of the lands of the pírti nidhí, which were now confiscated. Various other chiefs received advantages calculated to bind them to the new government; and, among others, Sindia and Holcar received assignments of the whole revenue of Málwa, except a small portion granted to other chiefs.*

The establishment of the péshwa's authority was not effected without some attempts at insurrection, and was endangered by a temporary quarrel between him and his cousin, Sedásheo Bháo; but it was at length so fully completed as to leave Bálají at liberty to engage in the affairs of foreign states.

---

of Rám Rája's descent, and the *boná fide* consent of Sáho to the transfer of the sovereignty.

* Of 1,500,000*l.*, which formed the whole revenue, 750,000*l.* was allotted to Holcar, 650,000*l.* to Sindia, and 100,000*l.* to Púar and other chiefs. (*Grant Duff*, vol. ii. p. 40.)

CHAP. III.

Marches against Salábat Jang, the son of Asof Jáh.

He then undertook the cause of Ghâzi u dín Khán, the eldest son of Asof Jáh, against Salábat Jang, his third son, who was in possession of the family inheritance, after the death of two other competitors cut off during a civil war. He had before transferred his residence to Púna, and he now left Rám Rája at Sattára in perfect freedom, but under the control of Tára Bái. He then marched into the Nizám's territory, and was already in the neighbourhood of Salábat's army, when he received intelligence which obliged him to relinquish his undertaking, and to return by forced marches to his own country.

He is recalled by the insurrection of Tárá Bái and Damají Geikwár.

He had no sooner set out on his campaign than Tára Bái, whose ambition and violence were not tamed by age, secretly invited Damají Geikwár to march with his army to Sattára: at the same time she proposed to Rám Rája to assert his sovereignty; and finding the rája averse to her design, she took advantage of the approach of Damají to seize his person and confine him to a dungeon. She had it still in her power to have made use of her prisoner's name: instead of that she proclaimed him an impostor, and carried on the government without any ostensible authority but her own.

Notwithstanding the rapidity of the péshwa's return, his officers had already more than once encountered the Geikwár; and the advantage, after some alternations of success, was on their side, when Bálají arrived. But that wily Bramin trusted to other arms than the sword: he procured a

BOOK XII.

meeting with Damají, at which he treacherously made him prisoner; attacked his army, thus deprived of their leader; and, in the end, completely broke up and dispersed his force. Tára Bái, though stripped of military force, and founding no title on the rája's pretensions, had still some inexplicable influence which prevented the péshwa from crushing her. She derived aid at the present moment from the advance of Salábat Jang, who invaded the Maratta dominions in his turn, and was more formidable than any of his predecessors since Aurangzíb, being accompanied by a French subsidiary force of 500 Europeans and 5000 Sepoys under M. Bussy, the most distinguished of the officers of his nation that ever appeared in India. Though Bálají opposed the invasion with all the resources of Maratta war, he soon learned their inefficiency against his new adversary, who repulsed his assaults, beat up his camps, and, before long, established a general impression of his own superiority. By these means the army advanced to within twenty miles of Púna. Bálají probably felt little uneasiness about his infant capital, but was alarmed by the discovery that the invaders were in communication with Tára Bái and the rája of Cólapúr, and made overtures for peace; which were in the course of negotiation, when he was unexpectedly relieved from the presence of his enemies. However superior to all parties in the field, Bussy was dependent on the civil arrangements of the prince with whom he served; and the mismanagement of

Bálají seizes Damají by treachery.

Salábat Jang advances on Púna.

Superiority of the invaders — M. Bussey.

A. D. 1751, Nov.

Bálají is saved by a mutiny of Salábat's army.

Salábat and his ministers had embarrassed his finances, thrown his troops into arrears, and brought on such discontents that the army became nearly ungovernable : at the same time Ragují Bosla (who had just obtained the cession of Cattak and the tribute of Bengal formerly mentioned) broke into the Nizám's part of Berar, took the forts of Gáweilghar and Nárnála, and threatened further hostilities. Salábat was therefore well satisfied to make up an armistice, and move back to his own dominions; where new troubles, in which the Marattas were again actors, awaited him at no distant day.

A. D. 1752.

An armistice concluded.

Transactions at Delhi resumed.

The division of India into several states, and the necessity of pursuing their separate histories, make it difficult, at this stage, to preserve the order of time, and have carried us on in the Maratta transactions for several years beyond the date to which those of Delhi have been brought down. These last, however, were for a long time of little importance. On the departure of Asof Jáh for the Deckan (A. D. 1741), his place at court was taken by his son, Gházi u dín, whose political connection with the vizír, Kamr u dín Khán, was strengthened by his being married to the daughter of that minister. Their union enabled them to resist many intrigues and combinations, which were stained with treachery and assassinations, on both sides, beyond the worst epoch of former history.

Rise of the Rohillas.

The only event of importance within that period

BOOK XII.

was the rise of the Rohillas, an Afghán colony, which acquired possession of the country east of the Ganges from Oud to the mountains, and made a considerable figure in later times. Their chief was Ali Mohammed, a Hindú convert, adopted by an Afghán officer; and they were themselves mostly composed of Eusofzeis and other tribes of the north-east. Though no long period had elapsed since their appearance as a state, they had already attained to considerable importance; and it required an expedition headed by the emperor to bring them into temporary submission.

The emperor marches against them.

A. D. 1745, A. H. 1156.

Fresh invasions from the side of Persia.

But a far more formidable combination of the same people was forming within their native limits; and fresh invasions were prepared for India, by the death of her most dreaded enemy.

Revolutions in that country.

Tyranny of Nádir Sháh.

Though Nádir Sháh had not attained to sovereignty without incurring all the varieties of guilt by which that prize must be purchased in the East, and although he had more than once given instances of barbarous severity in his treatment of some offending towns, yet, on the whole, up to the taking of Delhi, he was, perhaps, less sanguinary than the generality of Asiatic monarchs, especially those of Persia. But the scenes of spoil and slaughter to which he was there habituated, together with the intoxication of uninterrupted success, appear to have commenced an alteration in his character which gradually changed him from a rigorous, but not unjust, master, into a cruel and capricious tyrant. These qualities did not at once disclose themselves to their full extent. The first years after his return from India were occupied in the conquest of the kingdoms of Bokhára and Khárizm, which he subdued and evacuated as he had done India; in an attempt to reduce the hill tribe of Lézgi; and in three campaigns against the Turks: but when this war was terminated by a treaty, and the mind of Nádir remained without a vent for its natural energy, it turned its powers against itself, and became the abode of dark suspicions and ungoverned passions. His chief uneasiness arose from the religious prejudices of his countrymen. Though he had endeavoured to render the Sunni religion more acceptable, and to give it something of a national character, by placing its establishment under the special protection of the Imám Jáfir, who was a descendant of Ali, and a favourite saint in Persia, yet he was aware that the people were still zealous Shías, and that the feelings of the sect were turned against him by the priests, whose lands and stipends he had confiscated immediately after his accession. He therefore looked on every Persian as his enemy; but was especially jealous of his eldest son, Rezza Cúli, who, he thought, was the fittest instrument for the purposes of the disaffected. He had been wounded in a forest, on one of his campaigns, by a shot from a secret hand; and although there was no reason to think that the assassin was not one of the enemy, yet he could not divest himself of the belief that he was an emissary of the prince. The working of

His fears of the Shías.

He puts out the eyes of his son.

these feelings at last led him to put out the eyes of Rezza Cúli; and his remorse, instead of softening his heart, exasperated his fury. He now taunted all who entreated him for mercy with their failure to intercede when his own son was in danger. His conduct became that of an open enemy of his species.

His intolerable cruelties.

His cruelties were equalled by his extortions; and both were accompanied by threats and expressions of hatred against his subjects. These oppressions led to revolts, which drew on fresh enormities: whole cities were depopulated, and towers of heads raised to commemorate their ruin: eyes were torn out; tortures inflicted; and no man could count for a moment on his exemption from death in torments. During the two last years of his life his rage was increased by bodily sickness, until it partook of frenzy, and until his subjects were compelled to lay plots for ridding themselves of a tyrant whose existence was incompatible with their own.

His favour to the Afgháns.

In his distrust of his countrymen, he had entertained a body of Uzbek mercenaries; and he had thrown himself, without reserve, on the Afgháns, taking a pleasure in mortifying his old soldiers by a marked preference of their former enemies and his own. He now began to harbour a design for employing these new allies in hostility to his own nation, of whom he lived in constant dread. On the day before his death, while labouring under some presentiment of evil, he leaped on his horse in the midst of his camp, and was on the point of flying from his own army to take refuge in a fortress.

When his mind was somewhat calmed, after this act of madness, he sent for the Afghán chiefs, appealed to their fidelity for the preservation of his life, and concluded by instructing them to disperse his Persian guards, and to seize on his principal nobles. These orders were not given so secretly but they came to the ears of those so nearly concerned; and as the night was to pass before their destruction was accomplished, they had time to anticipate it by the assassination of their enemy.

CHAP. III.

He is assassinated by the Persians.

A number of the conspirators, among whom were the captain of his guard and the chief of his own tribe of Afshár, entered his tent after midnight; and, although they involuntarily drew back when challenged by that deep voice at which they had so often trembled, yet they soon recovered their courage: one of them made a blow at the king with a sabre, and brought him to the ground; he endeavoured to raise himself, and attempted to beg his life; but the conspirators only redoubled their blows until he expired; — "the boast, the terror, and the execration of his country." *

A. D. 1747, June; A. H. 1160, Jamádi u Sani.

* Père Bazin (*Lettres Edifiantes*, vol. iv.). This Jesuit, who accompanied Nádir Sháh as his physician in the last years of his life, gives the best account of that period. The other authorities for his history are, Sir John Malcolm's "Persia," the "Nádirnámeh" (translated by Sir. W. Jones), and Hanway. Hanway gives a different view of the transactions relating to Rezza Cúli, but Bazin's is confirmed by the "Nádirnámeh," which, likewise, gives a lively picture of the tyranny and atrocities of Nádir Sháh. (Livre vi. chap. xix. p. 398. Jones's Works, vol. v.)

BOOK XII.

Retreat of the Afgháns.

On the next morning an attack was made on the Persians by the Afgháns, under the command of Ahmed Khán Abdáli, who was joined by the Uzbeks. It was made in the hope of being still in time to rescue the sháh; but, considering the inferiority of the numbers of the Afgháns, they may be reckoned fortunate in making good their retreat to their own country, near the frontier of which the death of Nádir took place.*

Ahmed Khán Abdáli.

Ahmed Khán was the son of Zemán Khán, the hereditary chief of the Abdális, who headed them on their first conquest of Khorásán. He was descended of the family of Sadduzei, which was looked on with a sort of religious veneration by their tribe; and although only twenty-three years of age, he had been distinguished by the particular notice of Nádir Sháh.†

* An animated description of this unequal contest, and of the valour and good order with which the 4000 Afgháns conducted their retreat, is given by Bazin, who was a spectator of the action, "au milieu des balles et des sabres."

† The person of a Sadduzei was inviolable, and no officer, of whatever rank, could put an Abdáli to death without the authority of a Sadduzei. I have been led to think that the common story of Ahmed's having been a macebearer of Nádir Sháh's originated in the circumstance that the word (chóbdár), which on the west of the Indus belongs to a few of the greatest officers of state (who carry wands or gold sticks), is in India applied to a common macebearer; yet it is not probable that one of those high offices would be conferred on the chief of a foreign tribe. Ahmed's early history is well known. He was a prisoner with the Ghiljeis when Candahár was taken by Nádir Sháh. That conqueror received him with favour, assigned him an honourable maintenance, and sent him to reside in Mázun-

Ahmed crowned king at Candahár. Oct. 1747.

He had, therefore, already, the command of his own tribe, which he hastened to confirm; and, extending his influence over the neighbouring tribes and countries, before the end of the year he was formally declared king at Candahár. From some superstitious motive he changed the name of his tribe from Abdáli to Duráni, by which it has been since known.* He modelled his court on that of Nádir Sháh, and assumed all the pretensions of that monarch, but exercised them with the moderation that was required by his circumstances. He was absolute in the plains and cities, as well as in Balkh, Sind, Cashmír, and other conquered provinces; he left the Afghán tribes to their internal government, retaining only power enough to secure their contingents of troops or money, and to preserve tranquillity. Belóchistán, Sístán, and some other places remained under their native chiefs, and owed allegiance and military service. The dissensions of Persia prevented his being disturbed on that side, and enabled him to take possession of most of

Changes the name of Abdális to Duránis.

His skilful management of his unruly subjects.

---

dérán (*Nádirnámeh*, vol. v. of Jones, p. 274.). His object probably was, to keep him at a distance from his tribe as long as the country was unsettled; for it appears, from a contemporary writer, who accompanied the Persian camp, that "Nádir Sháh always kept a watchful eye over him; but the officers of all ranks treated him, in private, with great respect." (*Memoirs of Abdoolkereem*, p. 176.)

* By an unaccountable confusion the Indians sometimes call the Duránis, Ghiljeis; in the north they are also called Khorásánis; but Duráni is the usual as well as the correct appellation.

BOOK XII.

Khorásán; but he saw the difficulties of further progress in that direction, and contented himself with protecting Sháh Rókh, the son of Nádir Sháh, in Meshhed, while his own immediate dependencies were confined to the east of that city.

His views on India.

It was to India that he looked for conquest, as well as for pecuniary resources and employment for his army; and his first operations in that kingdom took precedence, in point of time, of the settlement of several of the other countries just mentioned.

He occupies the Panjáb.

His coronation, indeed, was scarcely over, when he began his march for the east, and soon brought all the country up to the Indus under his authority. The circumstances of the Panjáb invited his further advance. The viceroy was in revolt, and had no aid from Delhi, so that he offered but a feeble opposition; and Ahmed, after taking possession of Láhór and other towns on the road, pursued his march to the Satlaj. When he reached that river, he found the fords occupied by the Mogul army, which had been sent from Delhi to oppose him, under Prince Ahmed, the heir apparent, and the

He is repulsed by an Indian

vizír, Kamr u dín Khán. Though his force did not exceed 12,000 men *, he saw that his best

* He marched with this number from Candahár; and although it was probably increased before he crossed the Indus, it would necessarily be again reduced by the garrisons in the Panjáb. The "Seir Mutakherín" says he had "*not more than* 67,000 horse;" which would be a greater army than that of Nádir Sháh: but the life of Háfiz Rehmet, translated by Mr. Elliott, gives the more reasonable number of 15,000 men (p. 25.).

chance lay in a vigorous use of it; he crossed the river where there was no ford, left the Indians in his rear, and took Sirhind, where their baggage and stores had been deposited. Among other advantages of this success, he got possession of some guns, with which he was before entirely unprovided. His boldness intimidated the enemy, who halted when they approached him, and intrenched their camp. A small body of horse could do little in such circumstances; and although the Mogul vizír was killed by a cannon ball, while at prayers in his tent, yet his army continued to repel the Duranís till the tenth day, when, after a general and desperate attack on the intrenchments, during which a party of them made its way into the midst of the camp, the assailants were totally repulsed and defeated, and compelled to march off homewards during the ensuing night.

CHAP. III.

army under Prince Ahmed, the heir apparent.

A. D. 1748, March; A. H. 1161, Rabi ul Awal 26.

The Mogul prince forthwith sent a viceroy to the Panjáb; but as he was immediately afterwards recalled to Delhi by the illness of his father, Ahmed Sháh turned back before he had reached the Indus, and did not quit the Panjáb until the new viceroy had engaged to pay a permanent tribute.

Death of Mohammed Sháh.

A. D. 1748, April; A. H. 1161, Rabi u Sáni 26.

Mohammed Sháh expired within a month after the battle of Sirhind, and was succeeded by his son, who bore the same name as his Duráni neighbour.

CHAP. IV.

TO THE EXTINCTION OF THE MOGUL EMPIRE.

Ahmed Sháh.

BOOK XII.

A. D. 1748, A. H. 1161.

Internal arrangements of the new king.

The return of the Afghán monarch to the Panjáb, combined with his well-known power and activity, kept the new sovereign in a state of continued anxiety, and obliged him to sacrifice a portion of his independence for the sake of such allies as might secure him from foreign conquest. He therefore offered the appointment of vizír to Asof Jáh; and on his declining it (which was soon followed by his death), he invited Násir Jang (who succeeded Asof in the Deckan) to move to his assistance with all the troops he could assemble. But it was not long before he learned that the Duráni king was occupied in the western part of his dominions; in consequence of which intelligence he was enabled to dispense with the aid he had solicited, and was left to make his internal arrangements in the way best suited to his own views. He appointed Safder Jang, the son of Sádat Khán, to be vizír; and as that nobleman retained his viceroyalty of Oud, the first efforts of the imperial government were directed to the suppression of the Rohillas, who had again become formidable in the northern part of that province.

Attempt to subdue the Rohillas by Safder Jang, the vizír.

A. D. 1748, December, A. H. 1161, Zi Haj.

Safder Jang's prospect was favourable, for Ali Mohammed was dead; and he engaged Cáiam Khán Bangash, the Afghán jágírdár of Farokhabád, to conduct the war against his countrymen: but Cáiam Khán, though at first successful, lost his life in battle; and Safder Jang, disappointed in his main object, turned his misfortune to account, by dispossessing the widow of his ally of the greater part of her territory. His ungenerous conduct brought him no advantage: the people of Cáiam Khán's country rose upon his agent, and called in the Rohillas, against whom the vizír was obliged to march in person. He was accompanied by a very numerous army; but so ill disciplined, that they sacked their own town of Bára (so famous as being peopled by descendants of the Prophet), and massacred many of the inhabitants who resisted the outrage. It is not surprising that such an army was routed by a very inferior force. The vizír himself was wounded; the Rohillas proceeded to carry their arms into his country; and, though beaten off from Lucknow and Bélgrám, they penetrated to Allahábád, and set the power of the vizír and the emperor alike at defiance.

The vizír marches against them in person, and is defeated. A. D. 1750, A. H. 1163.

He calls in the Marattas.

Safder Jang saw his embarrassments increasing, while his own power of resisting them was exhausted, and had recourse to the humiliating expedient of calling in the Marattas. He applied to Malhár Ráo Holcar and Jeiapa Sindia (whom the péshwa had recently sent back into Málwa), and induced them, by the promise of a large sub-

BOOK XII.

sidy, to join him with the greater part of their forces. By the same means he obtained a renewal of the services of Súraj Mal, rája of the Játs, who had been his confederate on the former expedition. With these auxiliaries, he defeated the Rohillas in a pitched battle, overran their country, and drove them into the lower branches of Hémaláya, which form their boundary on the north-east. To satisfy the claims of the Marattas, he authorised them to levy their subsidy from the conquered territory, and their ravages reduced it to a state from which it did not recover for years.

A. D. 1751, A. H. 1164.

Who compel the Rohillas to submit.

By the activity of these plunderers the Rohillas were reduced to such difficulties for subsistence, that they submitted to Safder Jang, and were content with the assignment of a few villages for the maintenance of their chiefs.*

Defeat of the imperial troops in Márwár.

The little advantage which the Mogul government gained by this success was more than compensated by the defeat of the governor of Ajmír, who had interfered in a civil war between two claimants to the principality of Jódpúr.

Second invasion of Ahmed Sháh Duráni.

While the weakness of the Mogul government was thus daily more displayed, intelligence arrived that Ahmed Sháh Duráni had again invaded the Panjáb; and it was soon followed up by accounts of his having obtained complete possession, and by an ambassador demanding a formal cession of the province. The visit of Nádir Sháh was still suffi-

* The "Life of Hafiz Rehmet" gives an account more favourable to the success of the Rohillas.

CHAP. IV.

Cession of the Panjáb.

ciently remembered to produce a ready compliance with the demand; and when the vizír arrived at Delhi with his Maratta allies, he found the arrangement concluded. There is no reason to doubt that he would himself have agreed to it if he had been on the spot, or that he would have disregarded it after it was made, if he had thought that he could gain by infringing it; but he had other grounds of dissatisfaction with the court, and he made this cession, which he represented as degrading, the pretext of his complaints.

Discontent of Safder Jang, the vizír.

During his absence in Róhilcand, his influence at court had been supplanted by a eunuch named Jawíd, who was favoured both by the emperor and his mother.

He assassinates the emperor's favourite.

Safder Jang, finding that his presence did not restore his authority, took a course which had become familiar at Delhi: he invited Jawíd to an entertainment, and had him murdered during the banquet. The emperor was naturally exasperated at this outrage, and he soon got a suitable instrument to avenge him on the vizír.

Ghází u dín the younger.

Ghází u dín, the eldest son of Asof Jáh, had remained at Delhi during the first part of the contest between his younger brothers; but, seeing an opening afterwards, he entered into a connection with the péshwa, and set off for the Deckan, accompanied by Holcar and Sindia. He died soon after his arrival at Aurangábád; and his son, a mere youth, whom he had left at Delhi, was promoted, by the vizír's favour, to the title of Ghází u dín, and the high office of commander-in-chief. It was this young man that now guided

BOOK XII.

the operations designed against his benefactor. He was a specimen of such of the Mogul courtiers as were not quite sunk in sloth. Restless and ambitious, as skilful in dissembling his passions as incapable of controlling them, he looked on perfidy and murder as the natural means of attaining his ends, and was as reckless of consequences, as regardless of principle.

Resists the the vizír.

The result of his measures was a civil war; not determined as usual, by a battle in the field, but carried on for six months in daily combats in the streets of Delhi. The factious hostility of the parties was embittered by religious fury: the vizír was a Shía, and the test-word of his sect, and that of the Sunnis, became the war-cries of the combatants on each side. At length, the vizír, finding his position becoming weaker, and alarmed at the approach of the Marattas under Malhár Ráo, whom Gházi u dín had called in as an auxiliary, consented to make peace, retaining possession of the provinces of Oud and Allahábád. Gházi u dín, thus relieved, and anxious to employ his Maratta friends, while he revenged himself on a partisan of the vizír, marched against Suraj Mal, the rája of the Játs, in the siege of whose strong forts, especially Díg and Bhartpúr, he found ample occupation for his army.

Calls in the Marattas, and expels the vizír.

The emperor plots against Gházi u dín.

But the emperor was by this time more disgusted with his arrogant and overbearing temper than he had ever been with Safder Jang; and moved out with what troops he could assemble, on pretence of hunting, but really to profit by the difficulties in which Gházi u dín was entangled. So little judgment was shown in his ill-concerted operations that no step had been taken to secure the co-operation of Safder Jang; and it did not require the acuteness and activity of Gházi u dín to turn the whole scheme against his enemy. Without discontinuing the siege on which he was employed, he sent his Maratta confederate against Ahmed; but when he heard that the emperor was taken prisoner in the battle which followed, he repaired in person to the camp, deposed the captive king, and put out his eyes, as well as those of the queen, his mother. He then fixed on one of the princes of the blood for successor to the throne, and proclaimed him by the title of A'lamgír II.*

Is defeated and deposed.

A. D. 1754, July; A. H. 1167, Shábán.

A'lamgír II.

Safder Jang died soon after this revolution, and Ghází u dín took the office of vizír to himself, leaving Shújá u doula, the son of Safder Jang, in possession of his father's provinces, of which he was unable to dispossess him. A longer period of tranquillity now elapsed than might have been expected from the restless ambition of the new vizír; but his internal government was still as arbitrary as ever. At length he provoked a numerous body of troops to mutiny, and made himself personally so odious, that he was seized by

A. D. 1754, September; A. H. 1167, Zí Haj. Ghází u dín, vizír.

His violent government.

His life in danger in a mutiny.

* The above account is from the "Seir Mutákherín," and Grant Duff's "History of the Marattas."

BOOK XII.

the insurgents and dragged through the streets without his slippers or his turban. Though threatened with instant death, he continued to revile his captors, and to say that they should pay for their insolence with their heads. At length he was rescued by the interposition of the officers; when he instantly ordered a massacre of the whole body, giving up their tents, horses, and property to plunder, so as not to leave a vestige remaining of the corps.

His suspicions of the emperor.

A'lamgír, on pretence of saving the life of Ghází u dín, had offered, while the disturbance was at its height, to pay to the mutineers a considerable sum of arrears, if they would deliver their prisoner into his hands; but the proposal served only to awaken the suspicions of the vizír, who took additional measures to guard against the possible intrigues of his nominal sovereign.

A. D. 1756, A. H. 1170-71.

His treacherous seizure of Ahmed Sháh Duráni's governor of the Panjab.

When interrupted by this adventure, Ghází u dín was on his march towards Láhór, and he now continued his progress. Mír Manu, the Mogul governor of the Panjáb, whom Ahmed Sháh had continued in his office after the cession, had died. His son had been appointed his successor by the Duráni monarch, but was an infant under the tutelage of his mother. This state of things presented an irresistible temptation to the young vizír: he immediately entered into a most amicable correspondence with the widow, claiming the hand of her daughter, to whom he had really been affianced, and advancing towards Láhór as if to celebrate the marriage: when he had completely lulled all suspicion, he surprised the town and made the governess prisoner in her bed. While they were conveying her to the camp she broke into invectives against the treachery of her son-in-law, and phrophesied the ruin of India, and the slaughter of its inhabitants, as the certain consequence of the vengeance of Ahmed Sháh. Her prediction was but too early accomplished; for Ahmed no sooner heard of the outrage offered to him than he flew to revenge it; and, speedily effecting his march from Candahár, passed through the Panjáb without opposition, and soon presented himself within twenty miles of Delhi. Gházi u dín, having contrived to pacify the widow of Mír Manu and to procure her intercession, repaired at once to the Duráni camp, and received pardon as far as his own person. Ahmed Sháh, however, insisted on pecuniary compensation, and marched on to Delhi to enforce his demand. Nearly all the horrors of Nádir Sháh's invasion were repeated on his arrival; for though not himself cruel like that monarch, he had much less command over his troops; and the city again became a scene of rapine, violence, and murder.

Third invasion of Ahmed Sháh.

He takes Delhi.

Nor were these sufferings cónfined to the capital; Ahmed Sháh sent a detachment of his army, with Gházi u dín, to levy a contribution from Shujá u doula, and marched, himself, with a similar intention against the Játs. He took a fort called Balamghar after an obstinate resistance, and put the garrison

Massacres and exactions.

BOOK XII.

to the sword; but the action which leaves the deepest stain on his character, or rather on that of his nation, was the massacre at Mattra. This city (one of the most holy among the Hindús) was surprised by a light detachment during the height of a religious festival, and the unoffending votaries were slaughtered with all the indifference that might be expected from a barbarous people, accustomed to serve under Nádir, and equally filled with contempt for Indians and hatred for idolatry. Meanwhile Ahmed himself was advancing towards Agra, to which city, as well as to one of the Ját forts, he laid siege. But by this time the summer was far advanced, and a mortality broke out among the Duránis, who are incapable of bearing heat: he was therefore obliged to be content with the money he had levied, and to direct his course towards his own dominions. Before he went he married a princess of the house of Delhi, and contracted another to his son, afterwards Teimúr Sháh; and having been entreated by the emperor not to leave him at the mercy of the vizír, he appointed Najíb u doula, a Rohilla chief of abilities and of excellent character, to be commander-in-chief at Delhi; in the hope that his own influence, even when at a distance, would render that nobleman a counterpoise to Ghází u dín.*

His return to his own dominions.

A. D. 1757, about June; A. H. 1171, Sháwál.

His arrangements for the protection of A'lamgír II. against Ghází u dín.

Najíb u doula, minister.

* The above account is chiefly from the "Seir Mutákherín:" it agrees, in most respects, with the Afghán accounts; but the latter state that Ahmed Sháh did not leave Delhi, and that the whole expedition to Agra, as well as that to Mattra, was commanded by Sirdár Jehán Khán.

Gházi u dín applies for the assistance of the Marattas.

But no sooner had he quitted India, than Gházi u dín once more set him at defiance. He was at Farokhábád when the Afghan king departed, and he immediately gave the appointment of commander-in-chief to Ahmed Khán Bangash, the chief of that place, in supersession of Najíb u doula. But as he was not sufficiently strong to effect another revolution by himself, he called in the aid of the Marattas, who were now in greater power than ever.

Previous transactions of that nation.

Although Bálají made peace with Salábat Jang (as has been stated) in the beginning of A. D. 1752, it was no obstacle to his entering into fresh intrigues with Gházi u dín *the elder*, the brother and competitor of Salábat. On the arrival of that prince from Delhi, Bálají joined him at Aurangábád with all his forces; and so numerous was the combined army, that even the aid of Bussy might have been insufficient to have saved Salábat Jang, if the danger had not been averted by the sudden death of Gházi u dín. After this Bálají became involved in affairs to the southward, and transactions with the French and English, which will be best related with the history of those nations. But as his government got settled at home, he ventured to release Damají Geikwár, and to avail himself of his assistance in settling the province of Guzerát. He made severe terms, involving payments and reservations which led to many disputes in the end: but at first all went prosperously. Damají set out in company with the péshwa's brother,

BOOK XII.

Ragoba (A. D. 1755), and they soon reduced the whole province to complete subjection and obedience. Ragoba next levied contributions on the Rájpút states, and returned through Málwa to the Deckan. In the end of A. D. 1756 he was again sent into Málwa; and it was to him that the present application was made by young Gházi u dín. Supported by this ally, the vizír advanced on Delhi, occupied the city, and laid siege to the fortified palace, which held out more than a month.

Ragoba, the péshwa's brother, marches to support Gházi u dín the younger.

Takes Delhi.

It was, nevertheless, evident that Najíb u doula could no longer withstand his enemies; and the emperor had already taken the precaution of sending his son, afterwards Sháh A'lam, to a place of safety; the escape of Najíb himself was the principal difficulty remaining, and it was accomplished by means of a bribe to Malhár Ráo Holcar. The emperor then opened his gates and received Ghází u dín as his vizír. Najíb u doula retired to his own country, which was about Seháranpúr to the north of Delhi, and divided from Róhilcand by the Ganges.

Escape of the heir apparent, and of Najíb u doula.

A. D. 1758, A. H. 1171. Ragoba takes possession of the Panjáb.

After the taking of Delhi, Ragoba remained encamped near that city, until he was called away to an important and easy conquest. When Ahmed Sháh withdrew from India in the preceding year (A. D. 1757), he left his son Teimúr in charge of the Panjáb, under the guidance of Sirdár Jehán Khán. Their most dangerous opponent was Adína Bég, a man of a turbulent and artful character, who had been deputy to Mír Manu, and whose intrigues had mainly contributed to the various disturbances and revolutions in the Panjáb. He had fled from the province when it was occupied by Ahmed Sháh, and now returned for the purpose of continuing his factious designs. He first employed his influence with the Síks, who had recovered their strength during the past disorders; but not finding their power sufficient for his purpose, he applied to Ragoba, and pointed out the ease with which he might gain a rich prize for his countrymen. Ragoba marched accordingly, took possession of Láhór in May, 1758, and occupied the whole of the Panjáb, the Duránis retiring across the Indus without attempting a battle. The government was conferred on Adína Bég; and on his death, which happened soon after, a native Maratta was appointed his successor. Before this change, Ragoba had set off for the Deckan, leaving the Panjáb in temporary security, and the Maratta affairs prosperous in other parts of Hindostan. A force had marched from Delhi under Datají Sindia, for the purpose of pursuing Najíb u doula into his retreat; and Najíb, unable to resist, left his country to be plundered, and took post at Sakertál, a defensible ford of the Ganges. He maintained himself with difficulty in this position through the whole of the rainy season: and during this period there was time to mature a combination, to which all the neighbouring princes were called by a common and urgent danger.

A. D. 1758, May; A. H. 1171, Shábán.

A. D. 1759, June to September; A. H. 1172.

The Marattas were already masters of the Pan-

Plans of the Marattas

BOOK XII.

for the conquest of Hindostan.

jáb: they had concerted with Gházi u dín a plan for taking possession of Oud; and they talked without the least reserve of their intended conquest of the whole of Hindostan.

General combination of the Mahometan princes.

The apprehensions excited by this state of things induced Shujá u doula to forget his old enmities, and to enter into a league with Najíb u doula and his former opponents the Rohillas, the most considerable of whom was Háfiz Rehmet Khán.

The Marattas invade Róhilcand.

As soon as Datají Sindia was apprised of this confederacy he detached Góvind Ráo Bondéla * to invade Rohilcand. So effectually was the order performed that 1300 villages were destroyed in little more than a month, while the Rohillas were obliged to retreat for safety into the mountains. They were relieved from this distress by Shujá u doula. He marched from Lucknow immediately on the invasion, surprised the Marattas, and drove them with heavy loss across the Ganges.

A. D. 1759, November; A. H. 1173, Jamádi ul Awal.

Datají Sindia's force was weakened by the losses of his detachment; but he had a stronger motive for desiring peace, in the reported approach of Ahmed Sháh from Cábul: terms were therefore proposed to Shujá u doula and the confederates, and a peace was concluded, which was of no long continuance.†

Fourth invasion of Ahmed Sháh.

The Afghán king was occupied in the northwestern part of his dominions, when his son was

* A Maratta Bramin, so called from his employment in "Bundélcand," and ancestor of the late chief of Ságar and Calpí.

† Seir Mutakherín, and Grant Duff.

expelled from the Panjáb (A. D. 1758); and, when about to march to recover that country, he was arrested by the revolt of Nasír Khán, the ruler of the Belóches, who made an attempt to establish his entire independence. The operations necessary to place the affairs of that country on a satisfactory footing delayed Ahmed Sháh for a considerable time; after which he moved by the southern road of Shikárpúr to the Indus; and, marching up that river to Péshâwer, he crossed it in the month of September, and advanced into the Panjáb. The Marattas offered no opposition, and he avoided the swollen rivers and exhausted country by keeping near the northern hills, until he crossed the Jamna opposite Seháranpúr. During the sháh's advance, Ghâzi u dín, mindful of A'lamgír's connection with that monarch and with Najíb u doula, took alarm at the thoughts of his intrigues and his vengeance. He therefore at once gave orders for his assassination, and raised another member of the royal family to the throne. This prince's title was never acknowledged: Sháh A'lam, the heir apparent, was absent on a scheme for getting a footing in Bengal; and the confederate princes carried on their operations without any ostensible head.*

A. D. 1759, September; A. H. 1173, Moharram.

Murder of A'lamgír II. by Ghâzi u dín. A. D. 1759, November; A. H. 1173, Rabi u Sáni 8.

At this time the Marattas, though not supported by their allies the Játs, had 30,000 horse of their own in the field; but they were in two bodies at some distance from each other; and the hatred of

The Maratta troops in Hindostan dispersed by Ahmed Sháh.

* Seir Mutákherín. Ahmed Sháh's proceedings are from Afghán accounts.

the country people, who were exasperated by their depredations, kept them in ignorance of the movements of the enemy. Ahmed Sháh came suddenly on the body under Datají Sindia, and so effectually surprised it that the chief and two thirds of the force were cut to pieces on the spot. The other division under Malhár Ráo Holcar was still at a distance, and commenced its flight towards the country south of the Chambal: it was drawn from the direct line by the temptation of plundering a convoy, and was overtaken and almost destroyed by a Duráni detachment which had made a prodigious march for the purpose.* Long before these reverses, Ragoba had arrived in the Deckan. The glory of his conquests did not reconcile the Maratta court to the financial results which they produced: instead of an ample harvest of plunder, as used to be customary, he had brought home near a million sterling of debt. This unproductive campaign appeared to more disadvantage when contrasted with that in which the péshwa's cousin, Sedásheo Ráo Bháo (best known in India as "the Bháo"), was engaged: he had remained as home minister and commander-in-chief in the Deckan, had just obtained possession of Ahmednagar, and was on the eve of a settlement, afterwards concluded at U'dgír, by which territorial and pecuniary cessions of great extent were obtained from Salábat Jang, and such a burden im-

* Scir Mutákherín. Grant Duff.

posed on the Mogul government in the Deckan as it never was able to recover. This contrast led to jealousy on the part of Ragoba, who, to Sedásheo's remonstrances on the profusion of his expenditure, replied that the Bháo had better undertake the next expedition himself, when he would find the difference between that and serving in the Deckan. Sedásheo took him at his word, and an exchange of duties was forthwith agreed on.

Power of the Marattas at its zenith.

The Maratta power was at this time at its zenith. Their frontier extended on the north to the Indus and Hémaláya, and on the south nearly to the extremity of the peninsula: all the territory within those limits that was not their own paid tribute. The whole of this great power was wielded by one hand: a settlement had been made with Tára Bái, by which the person of the rája was consigned to his nominal minister, and all pretensions of every description were concentrated in the péshwa.*

Their army.

The establishments of the Maratta government had increased with its power. Its force was no longer composed of predatory bands alone; it included an army of well-paid and well-mounted cavalry in the direct service of the state, and 10,000 disciplined infantry, who, though a very imperfect copy of that commanded by Europeans, were far superior to any infantry previously known in India.

The Marattas had now also a train of artillery

* Chiefly Grant Duff.

BOOK XII.

surpassing that of the Moguls, which they had so long regarded with awe and envy. They even endeavoured to assume the pomp which was characteristic of their rivals. Rich dresses, spacious tents, and splendid caparisons became common among them, and their courts and retinues were formed on the Mogul model.

This show of greatness did not seem misplaced in the péshwa and his ministers, who were Concan Bramins, a comely race, prepared by the mildness and gravity of their manners to take up dignity without any appearance of incongruity; but it sat very ill on the little active Marattas, whose sturdy figures and vulgar manners gave a ludicrous effect to their attempts at a stately demeanour.

Great preparations for the contest in Hindostan.

Whatever the nation possessed either of power or magnificence was brought forth to give weight to Sedásheo Bháo. The news of the misfortunes of Sindia and Holcar were only a fresh stimulus to exertion; and it seemed to be resolved, by one great and decisive effort, to put the finishing stroke to the conquest of Hindostan.*

Arrogance of the commander Sedásheo Bháo.

The prince thus elevated was naturally haughty and overbearing, proud of the new greatness of his family, and puffed up by recent success into an overweening confidence in his own abilities both as a statesman and a soldier. He was accompanied by Wiswás Ráo, the péshwa's youthful son and heir apparent, and by all the great Bramin and

* Seir Mutákherín. Grant Duff.

Maratta chiefs without exception. Many Rájpút detachments were sent to join him as he advanced, and Súraj Mal is said to have reinforced him with a body of 30,000 Játs.

This experienced old chief, who had long been accustomed to act with the Marattas, took occasion to advise the Bháo to leave his infantry and guns, and all his heavy baggage, in the Ját territory, where it would be protected by strong forts, to advance with his horse alone, to harass his enemies in the Maratta manner, and protract the war until the Duránis, who had already been many months in India, should be constrained by the climate to withdraw to their native mountains. This prudent counsel, though seconded by the Maratta chiefs, was at once rejected by their commander, who looked down on a victory obtained by such means, and who also attached an undue importance to his regular infantry and guns. This was not the only occasion on which he slighted Súraj Mal, whom he treated as a petty zemíndár, incapable of judging of politics on a large scale. He also offended his Maratta chiefs by his Bramin pride, as well as his imperious manner of exercising his command, and the absence of the freedom and familiarity to which they were accustomed in their leaders. In this manner he advanced to Delhi, which was held by a small garrison of Duránis and their partisans, Gházi u dín having taken refuge in the Ját country. The great extent of the city walls enabled a party of Marattas to climb up a neglected bastion, and

He takes Delhi.

BOOK XII.

the citadel yielded to the artillery after attempting a short defence. The Bháo made an injudicious as well as ungenerous use of this conquest. He defaced the palaces, tombs, and shrines, for the sake of the rich ornaments which had been spared by the Persians and Afgháns. He tore down the silver ceiling of the hall of audience, which was coined into seventeen lacs of rupees *, and seized on the throne (no longer so precious as of old), and on all other royal ornaments. He even proposed to proclaim Wiswás Ráo emperor of India, and was only prevailed on to postpone the measure until he should have driven the Duránis across the Indus. All these proceedings alarmed and disgusted Súraj Mal, who was unwilling to go to extremities with his own near neighbours. He soon after entered on a secret consultation with Shujá u doula, and withdrew to his own territory without openly renouncing his alliance with the Marattas. The Bháo affected to treat this defection as a matter beneath his notice.

Ahmed Sháh's negotiation with Shujá u doula.

During this time the sháh was cantoned for the rains at Anúpshehr, on the frontier of Oud, whither he had been drawn by an important negotiation. He was sure of cordial assistance from Najíb and the Rohillas, but the co-operation of Shujá u doula was by no means equally certain. Though that ruler could not declare against the Mahometans,

* 170,000*l.* Cási Rai's Narrative (*Asiatic Researches*, vol. iii. p. 97.). Grant Duff makes the 170,000*l.* include all the plate in the palace.

CHAP. IV.

his interests counselled neutrality, and he had a hereditary disinclination to joining Ahmed Sháh, to whom his father, Safder Jang, had been openly opposed. It was to influence him that the Sháh advanced to Anúpshehr; and this movement, with the persuasion of Najíb u doula, who paid him a visit for the purpose, succeeded in procuring his accession to the Mussulman cause.

Who joins the Mahometan confederacy.

A. D. 1760, July; A. H. 1173, Zil Haj.

He nevertheless kept up a constant communication with the Marattas, which might serve to secure an accommodation, if expedient, and was in the meantime a useful channel for overtures between that people and the sháh.*

Ahmed Sháh marches against Sedásheo Bháo.

After this arrangement was concluded, Ahmed was still prevented moving by the violence of the periodical rains: but before that season was well over, he broke up his cantonment, and marched towards Delhi. His movement was accelerated by hearing that the Bháo had set out with a picked force to attack Cúnjpúra, on the Jamna, sixty miles above Delhi, where there was a Duráni garrison, under an officer of distinction. On reaching that river near the capital, he found it still swollen and rapid: he proceeded up the banks in search of a ford, until he got near Cúnjpúra, where he had the mortification to hear that the place had been taken, and the whole garrison put to the sword. Enraged at this disgrace inflicted almost before his eyes, the sháh passed the river, between fording

His bold passage of the Jamna.

* Cási Rái, the author of the Narrative, was one of the agents in this intercourse.

BOOK XII.

A.D. 1760, Oct. 25. Marattas retire to Pánipat, and intrench their camp. Their numbers.

and swimming; and though he lost many men in this bold undertaking, it made so great an impression on the enemy, that they hastened to remove out of his reach, and soon retired to Pánipat, where they threw up works round their camp, encompassed by a broad and deep ditch, and protected by their numerous artillery. The Bháo's force consisted of 55,000 cavalry in regular pay, with at least 15,000 predatory Maratta horse, and 15,000 infantry, of whom 9000 were disciplined Sepoys, under I'brahím Khán Gárdi, a Mussulman deserter from the French service. He had 200 guns, with numerous wall pieces, and a great supply of rockets, which is a favourite weapon with the Marattas. These troops, with their numerous followers, made the numbers within his lines amount to 300,000 men.*

Force under Ahmed Sháh.

Ahmed Sháh had about 40,000 Afgháns and Persians, 13,000 Indian horse, and a force of Indian infantry estimated at 38,000, of which the part consisting of Rohilla Afgháns would be very efficient, but the great majority the usual rabble of Indian foot soldiers.† He had, also, about thirty

* Grant Duff agrees with Cási Rái in making the paid horse and infantry 70,000, as above, and estimates the predatory horse and followers at 200,000. Cási Rái states the whole number at 500,000. (*Asiatic Researches*, vol. iii. p. 123.)

† The accounts of the Duránis themselves make the number of the army that crossed the Indus 63,000; but, from a comparison with Nádir Sháh's force, and that of Sháh Zemán, in later times, as well as from the incorrectness of Asiatic muster-rolls, I conceive the amount to be much exaggerated. There

pieces of cannon of different calibres, chiefly belonging to the Indian allies, and a number of wall pieces.

Protracted operations.

The inferiority of the sháh's force making an attack on the enemy's camp impossible, he was obliged to encamp also, and to throw up lines round his army. The occurrence of a general action being thus suspended, the Bháo's prospects were by no means unfavourable. He had ordered Góvind Ráo Bondéla to collect what troops he could on the lower course of the Jamna, and that chief now appeared with 10,000 or 12,000 horse in the rear of the Durání camp. He kept at a safe distance from the army, but spread over the country in the Maratta manner, so as to intercept all supplies. It is probable that the Bháo employed his own light cavalry in the same manner; for before much time had elapsed, the Mussulman camp began to suffer severely from the scarcity of provisions.

Failure of the Maratta supplies.

But although the Duránis were not accustomed to the desultory warfare used by the Marattas, they made up for their deficiency by the bold and

must also have been a great reduction from garrisons in the Panjáb and other places, casualties in action, and deaths from the climate during the hot season and rains; so that I think 40,000 a sufficient allowance for the Afgháns. The Indian numbers are from Cási Rái: Shuja u doula had only 2000 horse and the same number of foot. Cási Rái's statement, that the Duránis had forty guns of their own, is quite contrary to their own account and to all probability.

rapid movements of their detachments; and on this occasion, a body of their horse under Attái Khán, the grand vizír's nephew, made a march of upwards of sixty miles, surprised Góvind Ráo's camp about daybreak, and completely destroyed his party, Góvind Ráo himself falling in the action. When the Duránis had got the command of the open country, the Bháo soon felt the difficulty of his situation, inclosed in a fortified camp with such a multitude as he commanded.

The Marattas are excellent foragers. Every morning at daybreak, long lines of men on small horses and ponies are seen issuing from their camps in all directions, who return before night loaded with fodder for the cattle, with firewood torn down from houses, and grain dug up from the pits, where it had been concealed by the villagers; detachments go to a distance for some days, and collect proportionately larger supplies of the same kind; and convoys, each of many thousands of oxen, are also brought in from remote countries by banjárras, a sort of camp grain dealers, who partake of the character of the soldiery more than of the mercantile body. All these resources were now cut off; and after the Marattas had entirely eaten up and consumed the town of Pánipat, which was within their lines, they began to feel the severest pressure of want.

While things were tending to this conclusion, neither party was inactive in its efforts to hasten the crisis. Continual skirmishes went on between the armies: the Marattas made three vigorous attacks on the Duráni lines; convoys were always attempting to make their way into the camp; and though one charged with treasure from Delhi fell into the hands of the Afgháns, others were secretly forwarded by Súraj Mal and the Rajput chiefs; and as the Bháo bore his difficulties with dignity and resolution, their extent and daily increase were unknown to his enemies. In these circumstances, the Indian allies lost all patience, and wearied Ahmed Sháh with their importunities that he would put an end to their fatigues by a decisive action: but his constant answer was, "This is a matter of war with which you are not acquainted. In other affairs do as you please; but leave this to me." He had a small red tent pitched in front of his intrenchment, to which he repaired every morning in time for prayers at day-break, and where he generally returned to dine in the evening. He was on horseback for the whole day, visiting his posts, and reconnoitring the enemy; and never rode less than fifty or sixty miles a day. At night he placed a picket of 5,000 horse as near as he could to the enemy, while other parties went the rounds of the whole encampment. "He used to say to the Hindostani chiefs, 'Do you sleep; I will take care that no harm befalls you;' and to say the truth, his orders were obeyed like destiny, no man daring to hesitate or delay one moment in executing them."*

* Cási Rái.

During this time, the Bháo's embarrassments became daily more urgent; and he made frequent applications to Shujá u doula through Cási Rái (the author of our Narrative) to mediate a peace between him and the Mussulmans. When his proposals were made known to the sháh, he replied that he was only an auxiliary, and had no views of his own; that he claimed the entire control of the war, but left the Hindostáni chiefs to carry on their negotiations as they pleased. The majority of those chiefs were well disposed to an accommodation, which would have been particularly acceptable to Shujá u doula; but Najíb always steadily opposed the overtures, and succeeded in impressing on the rest the ruin to which they would be exposed if the sháh left India while the Maratta power was still entire.

It is not difficult to conceive what must now have been the state of the Maratta host, cooped up amidst the stench of a blockaded camp, among dead and dying animals, surrounded by famished followers, and threatened with the terrible consummation of the evils which they already suffered. Among their last efforts, they sent out a foraging party, with innumerable camp followers, to endeavour to bring in some relief; but the helpless crowd was discovered by the enemy, and slaughtered in prodigious numbers. On this the chiefs and soldiers surrounded the Bháo's tent in a body; they said that they had entirely exhausted the last remains of their provisions, and that it was better to run any risk in the field than to perish in misery. The Bháo agreed to their wish: they all partook of bítel leaf, and swore to fight to the last; and orders were given to make the attack on the next morning before daybreak.

In this extremity the Bháo wrote to Cási Rái a short note with his own hand: "The cup is now full to the brim, and cannot hold another drop. If anything can be done, do it, or else answer me plainly at once; hereafter there will be no time for writing or speaking."

Battle of Pánipat.

Cási Rái was communicating this note to Shujá u doula about three in the morning, when his spies came to report that the Marattas were getting under arms. Shujá immediately repaired to the sháh's tent, and desired he might be awakened without delay. The sháh soon made his appearance, ready dressed; and, mounting a horse which always stood saddled by his door, he rode towards the enemy, ordering his own troops out as he advanced.

A. D. 1761, January 6.; A. H. 1174, Jamádi u Sáni.

One of his first steps was to send for Cási Rái, and interrogate him about the source of the intelligence he had communicated. This he did as he was moving forward, until, about a mile from the camp, he met some Duráni horsemen loaded with plunder, who reported that the Marattas had deserted their camp and fled. On hearing this, Ahmed turned to Cási Rái and asked him what he said to that? but while he was yet speaking, the Marattas announced their presence by a general discharge of their artillery along the whole of their line. "On this the sháh, who was sitting upon his horse smoking a Persian kallián, gave it to his servant, and with great calmness said to the nabob (Shujá), 'Your servant's news is very true I see.'" He then sent orders to hasten the advance of his own army. When objects became discernible, the colours of the Marattas were seen advancing slowly and regularly with their artillery in front. The sháh drew up his army opposite, and, himself, took post at his little red tent, which was now in the rear of the line.

The Mussulmans did not make much use of their guns; and as those of the Marattas approached, the shot went over the heads of their adversaries. The actual engagement was begun by I'brahím Khán Gárdi, who rode up to the Bháo, respectfully saluted him, and said, "You have often been offended with me for insisting on regular pay to my men; you shall now see that we have not earned it in vain." He then seized a colour with his own hand, and ordered his battalions to cease firing and charge bayonets. Their attack fell on the Rohillas, whose undisciplined valour only increased their loss, and who were broken after a prodigious slaughter. Their defeat laid open the right of the grand vizír, who commanded the centre of the Duráni line, and who was now charged by the Bháo and Wiswás Ráo with the flower of the Maratta army. In this charge, Attái Khán, the vizír's nephew, was killed by his side, and his

Duránis were forced to give ground; but he himself dismounted, and, with the few that were near him, determined to die at his post. Shujá u doula was next to the grand vizír's division, but could not see what was passing for the dust: finding the sound of men and horses in that quarter suddenly diminish, he sent Cási Rái to inquire the cause. He found the grand vizír on foot in full armour, in an agony of rage and despair, reproaching his men for quitting him, and endeavouring to bring them back to their ranks. "Ride to Shujá u doula," said he, "and tell him that if he does not support me immediately, I must perish." But Shujá, though he kept his ground, did not venture to take part in the action.

Meanwhile these transactions had not escaped Ahmed Sháh; and the reserve which he had ordered up arrived at the critical moment to prevent the destruction of the grand vizír. The battle now became stationary, but the advantage still inclined to the Marattas; until Ahmed, after rallying the fugitives and ordering all who refused to return to be cut down, gave orders for an advance of his own line, and at the same time directed a division on his left to wheel up and take the enemy in flank. This manœuvre was decisive; for though the closest combat was raging in the centre, where the Bháo and Wiswás were engaged on horseback, and where they fought on both sides with spears, swords, battle-axes, and even daggers, yet, "all at once, as if by enchantment, the whole Maratta

BOOK XII.

army turned their backs, and fled at full speed, leaving the field of battle covered with heaps of dead." The victors pursued them with the utmost fury; and as they gave no quarter, the slaughter is scarcely to be conceived; the pursuit continuing in every direction for fifteen or twenty miles. A large proportion of those who escaped from the enemy were cut off by the peasants; and great numbers, who fell alive into the hands of the Duránis, were cruelly massacred in cold blood. The sháh himself was not exempt from a share in these barbarities: for he not only took no means to prevent them, but, at the instigation of Najíb, he made a strict search for Jancojí Sindia, who was concealed by a Duráni chief, and who was made away with to prevent detection. He also compelled Shujá u doula to give up the gallant I'brahím Khán, who had been made prisoner; sent for him into his presence to reproach him; and then gave him over to the grand vizír to be placed in confinement, where he died of his wounds within a week.*

Destruction of the Maratta army.

The body of Wiswás Ráo was found, and a headless trunk which was believed to be the Bháo's; but the fate of the latter was so far from certain, that, many years after, an impostor obtained credit for a time by assuming his character. The whole

* Cási Rái says he was treated with the greatest cruelty, and that it was reported that poison was put into his wounds; but that was not a moment when vengeance (if there had been any motive for it) would have taken so indirect a course.

number of the slain is said to have amounted to near 200,000.* Almost all the great Maratta chiefs were killed or wounded, except those who had been left with a force at Delhi; and Malhár Ráo Holcar, who was accused of too early a retreat. Mahájí Sindia, afterwards the founder of a great state, was lamed for life; and Nána Farnavís, who long kept off the downfal of the péshwa's government, narrowly escaped by flight. †

Despondency of the Maratta nation.

Never was a defeat more complete, and never was there a calamity that diffused so much consternation. Grief and despondency spread over the whole Maratta people; most had to mourn relations, and all felt the destruction of the army as a death-blow to their national greatness. The péshwa never recovered the shock. He slowly retreated from his frontier towards Púna, and died in a temple which he had himself erected near that city. ‡ The wreck of the army retired beyond the Nerbadda, evacuating almost all their acquisitions in Hindostan. § Dissensions soon broke out after the death of Bálají, and the government of the péshwa never regained its vigour. Most of the

Death of the péshwa.

* Grant Duff, vol. ii. p. 156.

† The account of Sedásheo Ráo Bháo's campaign is compiled from Grant Duff, the Seir Mutákherín, and Cási Rái's account of the battle of Pánipat (in vol. iii. of the *Asiatic Researches*, p. 91, &c.). This last is, perhaps, the best specimen to be found of narrative by an Indian. The Afghán accounts of Ahmed Sháh's proceedings also furnish some information.

‡ Grant Duff.

§ Sir J. Malcolm's Malwa, vol. i. p. 120, 121.

BOOK XII.

Maratta conquests were recovered at a subsequent period; but it was by independent chiefs with the aid of European officers and disciplined Sepoys.

Dissolution of the Mahometan confederacy.

The confederacy of the Mahometan princes dissolved on the cessation of their common danger. Ahmed Sháh returned home without attempting to profit by his victory, and never afterwards took any share in the affairs of India.

Extinction of the Mogul empire.

The actors in the last transactions having now all left the stage, the history of the Mogul empire here closes of itself. Its territory is broken into separate states; the capital is deserted; the claimant to the name of emperor is an exile and a dependent; while a new race of conquerors has already commenced its career, which may again unite the empire under better auspices than before.

APPENDIX.

ON THE STATES FORMED ON THE DISSOLUTION OF THE EMPIRE OF DELHI.

*Bahmani Kings of the Deckan.**

BAHMANI KINGS OF THE DECKAN.

	A.D.	A.H.
Hasan Gangu (or Alá u dín) -	1347	748
Mohammed I. -	1358	759
Mujáhid - -	1375	776
Dáúd - -	1378	780
Mahmúd I. -	1378	780
Gheiás u dín -	1397	799
Shams u dín -	1397	799
Fírúz - -	1397	800
Ahmed I. - -	1422	825
Alá u dín - -	1435	838
Humáyun - -	1457	862
Nizám - -	1461	865
Mohammed II. -	1463	867
Mahmúd II. -	1482	887
NOMINAL KINGS.		
Ahmed II. -	1518	924
Alá u dín II. -	1520	927
Wali - -	1522	
Kalím - -	1526	

Founded by Hasan Gangu, an Afghán of Delhi.

Hasan Gangu†, the first king of the Deckan, was an Afghán of the lowest rank, and a native of Delhi. He farmed a small spot of land belonging to a Bramin astrologer, named Gangu, who was in favour with the king; and having accidentally found a treasure in his field, he had the honesty to give notice of it to his landlord. The

* The accounts of the inferior Mahometan dynasties, where not otherwise specified, are taken from Ferishta, who has written a separate history of each (vols. ii., iii., and iv. of Col. Briggs's translation).

† The royal title assumed by Hasan was *Alá u dín*; but to distinguish him from other kings of the same name, I have retained his original appellation.

APPEND. astrologer was so much struck with his integrity that he exerted all his influence at court to advance his fortunes. Hasan thus rose to a great station in the Deckan, where his merit marked him out among his equals to be their leader in their revolt. He had before assumed the name of Gangu, in gratitude to his benefactor; and now, from a similar motive, added that of Bahmani (Bramin), by which his dynasty was afterwards distinguished. He fixed his capital at Culbarga.

The revolt of the rája of Warangól, and the foundation of the new government of Bijáyanagar, were favourable to the insurgents at first, as they increased the embarrassments of Mohammed Tóghlak; the rája of Warangól also sent a body of horse to assist Hasan Gangu in his final struggle; but their establishment cut off a large portion of the Mussulman dominions towards the south, and soon led to boundary disputes which involved them in an unceasing war with the new monarchy.

Wars with the Hindús.

After the death of Hasan Gangu, these wars, especially that with Bijáyanagar, continued, almost without intermission, until the end of his dynasty. They did not for a long time make much alteration in the Hindú and Mahometan limits: the rájas of Orissa and Télingána, at one time, (A. D. 1461, A. H. 865.) made their way to the gates of Bidr, which was then the capital: but the Mahometans were gainers on the whole; they occupied most of the country between the Kishna and Tumbadra; and in A. D. 1421, the Bahmani king, Ahmed Sháh, took permanent possession of Warangól, and compelled the rája of Télingána to relinquish his ancient capital.

At length, in the reign of Mohammed II., the last of the Bahmani kings who exercised the functions of sovereignty, (A. D. 1471, A. H. 876.) Amber Rái, a relation of the rája of Orissa, applied to the Mussulman prince to assist him in asserting his right to that government, promising, in the event of success, to become his tributary, and to cede to him the districts of Rájamandri and Cóndapili at the mouths of the Kishna and Godáveri. Mohammed accepted the offer, and sent an army to support the pretender. Amber Rái was put in possession of Orissa, and the two districts were made over to the Mussulmans, and occupied by their troops. Amber Rái subsequently endeavoured to regain possession of the districts he had ceded; when Mohammed moved against him in person, invaded his country, reduced him to submission, and after settling Rájamandri and Cóndapili, carried his arms to the southward along the coast; annexed Masulipatam to his dominions, and pushed his incursions to the celebrated temple of Cánchí, or Conjeveram, near Madras, which he plundered.

A. D. 1477, A. H. 882. Conquest of Rájamandri and Masulipatam.

The same king met with equal success on the opposite coast of India, his minister having acquired possession of the Concan, the tract between the western Gháts and the sea from Bombay to Goa. The Bahmani kings had been occupied in this conquest for more than forty years, and had suffered severe losses in that rugged and woody country, and, after all, were never able perfectly to subdue it.

Partial conquest of the Concan. From A. D. 1469, to A. D. 1471, A. H. 874, to A. H. 876.

The Bahmani kings were several times engaged in wars with those of Cándésh and Málwa, generally on the frontiers of Berár: on one occasion (A. D. 1461-2), the king of Málwa advanced to Bidr, then the capital, and might have taken it, but for the timely aid of the king of Guzerát.

APPEND.

Dynasty of A'dil Sháh at Bíjapúr.

FOUNDED BY EUSOF ÁDIL SHÁH, A TURKISH SLAVE.

	A.D.	A.H.		A.D.	A.H.
Eusof A'dil Sháh	1489	895	Ali A'dil Sháh -	1557	965
Ismáel A'dil Sháh	1510	915	I'brahím A'dil Sháh II. -	1579	987
Mallú A'dil Sháh	1534	941			
I'brahím A'dil Sháh - -	1535	914			

Eusof A'dil Sháh claimed an illustrious descent, supported by a plausible history. The Indian historians represent him as son of the Ottoman Sultan Amurath, and brother to Mohammed II., the conqueror of Constantinople. They relate that he was an infant at the accession of Mohammed, that he escaped being put to death with the rest of his brothers by the contrivance of his mother, and was by her means conveyed to Persia.

Being obliged to fly from Persia at the age of sixteen, on account of some suspicion of his birth, he was inveigled to the Bahmani court, and there sold as a slave.

He rose, according to the course of Mamlúk adventurers, until he assumed the crown, as has been related.

From that time he was occupied in resisting Kásim Barid, the usurper of the Bahmani government, and in seizing the possessions of other chiefs around, who, like him, were endeavouring to assert their independence. He was also engaged in wars with the rája of Bijáyanagar, in which, on the whole, he was successful. His conquests acquired solidity from a sort of partition treaty with the other two new kings (of Ahmednagar and Berár), by which the title of each to his possessions was recognised.

Extent of the kingdom.

A notion of the extent of his kingdom may be gained by assuming the Bíma and Kishna rivers for his boundary on the east, the river Tumbadra on the south, the sea from

APPEND.

near Goa to near Bombay on the west, and perhaps the Níra river on the north.

Attempt to introduce the Shía religion.

He afterwards involved himself in fresh troubles by his zeal for the Shía religion, which he had imbibed in Persia from some of the immediate followers of Shékh Safi. He declared that faith to be the established religion of the state; and by a proceeding so unexampled in India, he caused much disaffection among his own subjects, and produced a combination of all the other Mahometan kings against him. He showed great resolution in supporting himself against this confederacy, and great skill in disuniting the members; but it was only by renouncing his innovations in religion that he was able, at last, to reconcile himself to all his opponents.

Religious factions.

His son Ismáel was a minor at his death. The minister who acted as regent planned the usurpation of the government; and with this view put himself at the head of the Sunni or native faction, and depressed and discharged the foreigners. His plan having failed, the young king became as violent a Shía, formed his army entirely of foreigners, and would enlist no Indian, unless he were the son of a foreigner, a Pitán*, or a Rájpút. He affected foreign manners, and always used the Persian and Túrki languages in preference to that of the Deckan.†

I'brahím, the fourth king (the third having only reigned six months), was a zealous Sunni, and discharged all the foreign troops. They were recalled by his son Ali, an enthusiastic Shía. During the minority of Ali's son, I'bra-

* A name often applied by the Indians to the Afgháns, but more generally to the Indian descendants of that people.

† Ferishta, vol. ii. p. 72. The remark shows that Deckani (a dialect of Hindostani) was the usual language of the Mussulmans in the beginning of the sixteenth century.

APPEND.

hím II., there was a struggle between the factions, in which, at length, the Sunnis prevailed.

Rise of the Marattas.

A change of more importance than these revolutions of sects was the rise of the Marattas. These Hindús, having fallen completely under the kings of Ahmednagar and Bijapúr, in consequence of the extinction of their own rája of Deógíri, were treated as subjects, and employed without distrust. Eusof, the first A'dil Sháh, is said to have given a command of 12,000 infantry to a Maratta chief*; and in the subsequent reigns they shared the fortunes of the natives, being entertained in great numbers whenever that party prevailed. They were known under the name of Bérgís, were often horse, and by their light and predatory operations contributed to introduce the system of defence to which the Bíjapúr government always had recourse when attacked.

A remarkable innovation was introduced by I'brahím (the fourth king). He directed the public accounts to be kept in the Maratta language instead of the Persian. Considering that this was the language of all the village accountants, and that the body of the officers of revenue and finance were also generally Hindús, it is surprising that the improvement was not introduced sooner, and more extensively copied.

Wars with the other Mahometan kings.

There were constant wars and shifting confederacies among the Mussulman kings; in both of which the rájas of Bijáyanagar often took a part, as did the kings of Cándésh and Guzerát, the latter with much weight. In all these wars the constant enemy of the A'dil Sháh was the Nizám Sháh of Ahmednagar, their hostility being caused by rival claims to the possession of Sólapúr and some other districts on the left bank of the Bíma.

League against Bijáyanagar.

At length, the four great Mahometan governments,

* Grant Duff, vol. i. p. 84.

A'dil Sháh, Nízám Sháh, Baríd, and Kútb Sháh, formed a league against Rám Rája, then ruling at Bijáyanagar, the result of which has been related in the text, page 183. APPEND.

Wars with the Portuguese.

Among the other wars of the A'dil Sháhi kings, those with the Portuguese are mentioned by the native historians with affected negligence. They state that Goa was lost under Eusof, retaken by that king in person, and lost again under his son Ismáel *; but as the kings of Bíjapúr and Ahmednagar afterwards made a simultaneous attack on the Portuguese at Goa and Choul (A.D. 1570), and were both repulsed, it is evident that they could not have been insensible to the formidable character of their antagonists. †

This confederacy, as well as the battle of Tálicóta, was subsequent to the accession of Akber. When that emperor first interfered effectually in the affairs of the Deckan, the last mentioned king, I'brahím II., had emerged from a long minority, and was taking an active part in the internal disputes of Ahmednagar. A.D. 1595, A.H. 1004.

Dynasty of Nizám Sháh at Ahmednagar.

FOUNDED BY AHMED, A HINDÚ CONVERT.

	A.D.	A.H.		A.D.	A.H.
Ahmed -	- 1490	896	Ismáel -	- 1588	997
Burhán -	- 1508	914	Burhán II.	- 1590	999
Husén -	- 1553	961	I'brahím -	- 1594	1003
Murtezza	- 1565	972	Ahmed II.	- 1594	1004
Mírán Husén	- 1588	996	Bahádur -	- 1595	1004

The father of Ahmed, the founder of the Nizám Sháhi

* This was the second capture by Albuquerque in 1510.

† Briggs's Ferishta, vol. i. p. 134. Grant Duff, vol. i. p. 77.

APPEND. dynasty, was a Bramin of Bíjapúr. Having been taken prisoner, and sold for a slave to the Bahmani king, he was converted, and rose to the first dignity in the state, and his son declared himself king (as has been related) on the dissolution of the Bahmani government. So far were his descendants from being ashamed of their origin, that they had frequent wars with the kings of Berár for the possession of Pátrí, a village in the latter country, to which their Bramin ancestors had been hereditary accountants. In the same spirit Burhán (who was the second king) appointed a Bramin, named Káwar Sein, to be his péshwa, or prime minister, and derived great advantage from the confidence he reposed on him. This dynasty imitated that of Bíjapúr in employing Marattas, but not to the same extent. Those in their service were chiefly infantry, and much employed as garrisons in hill forts.

Religious factions. A.D. 1537, A.H. 944. Their liberality to other religions did not save the Nizám Sháhs from the influence of the sects in their own. The second king openly professed the Shía religion; and, although assailed by tumults within, and a combination of the orthodox kings around, was more successful than his neighbour at Bíjapúr, and made good the establishment of his own sect.

A.D. 1568, A.H. 996. A change took place in consequence of the murder of Mírán Husén, the fifth king, the foreigners by whom that act was effected being massacred, and the Sunni religion introduced.

A feud, however, broke out among the Sunnis themselves under the sixth king, Ismáel, in consequence of a powerful prime minister declaring for a new sect called Mehdeví, or Gheir Mehdi, which is very odious to the
A.D. 1588, A.H. 997. other Mussulmans. It may have been owing to this division that we find the native Deckanis and the Abyssinians on different sides in the dissensions which ultimately de-

stroyed the monarchy; but those dissensions had not much of a religious character. APPEND.

The share of the Ahmednagar governments in the wars and confederacies of the other kings has been noticed. It had also wars of its own with Cándésh and Berár, the last of which kingdoms it subverted, in A.D. 1572, and annexed the territory to its own. Previous to this success, the Nizám Sháhi king was subjected to a great humiliation, having been besieged in his capital by Bahádur Sháh, king of Guzerát, and compelled to acknowledge his superiority, and to do homage to him in very submissive forms.* Wars with the other kings of the Deckan.

A still greater degradation awaited his successor, who was besieged in Ahmednagar by Rám Rája of Bijáyanagar, then combined with Bíjapúr, and reduced to accept an interview with him on terms of marked inferiority. A.D. 1530, A.H. 937.

It was the pride displayed by Rám Rája on this and some other occasions, that led to the general combination against him, the result of which has been already mentioned. A.D. 1565, A.H. 972.

It gives a great idea of the power of Ahmednagar, although on an unfortunate occasion, that in one campaign against the A'dil Sháh, the king lost upwards of 600 guns. Many of these may have been mere swivels, but one was the famous cannon now at Bíjapúr, which is one of the largest pieces of brass ordnance in the world.† Miscellaneous facts.

* On this occasion Bahádur Sháh showed his superiority by speaking Guzeráti, his own language, and the Nizám Sháh replied in Persian, which might be considered as common to both.

† Briggs's Ferishta, vol. iii. p. 243. This gun is four feet eight inches in diameter at the muzzle. The calibre is two feet four inches (Grant Duff, vol. i. p. 112.); it is only fifteen feet long (Colonel Sykes, *Bombay Transactions*), vol. iii. p. 62.); and weighs forty tons (Colonel Briggs, above quoted).

APPEND.

Ferishta mentions the great prevalence of duels (an uncommon practice in Asia) under this dynasty. They were occasioned by the most trifling disputes: it was reckoned dishonourable to decline them, and no blame was attached to the death of the parties, provided the combat was a fair one. Ferishta himself witnessed a meeting of this sort, in which there were three on each side, and five of the combatants grey-bearded men, and in considerable estimation at court. Three were killed on the spot, and the survivors died of their wounds.* These duels were always fought with sabres.

Extent of the kingdom.

At its greatest extent the kingdom of Ahmednagar comprehended all that is now called the Subah of Aurangábád, and all the west of that of Bérar. It also possessed a portion of the sea coast in the Concan, between the tracts belonging to Guzerát and Bíjapúr.

Dynasty of Kútb Sháh at Golcónda.

FOUNDED BY KÚTB KÚLI, A TÚRKMAN SOLDIER.

	A.D.	A.H.		A.D.	A.H.
Sultán Kúli -	1512	918	I'brahím - -	1550	957
Jamshíd - -	1543	940	Mohammed Kúli	1580	988
Subhán Kúli -	1550	957			

Sultán Kúli Kútb Sháh, the founder of the dynasty, was a Túrkman of Hamadán in Persia. He claimed descent from the head of his clan, and he certainly came to India a free man in quest of military service. He entered the guards of the Bahmani king, distinguished himself on many occasions, and was governor of Télingána when the mo-

* Briggs's Ferishta, vol. iii. p. 208.

narchy broke up. It is not certain when he assumed the royal title, but he was king in substance from A. D. 1512, A. H. 918.

Kútb professes the Shía religion.

He openly professed the Shía religion from his accession, and met with no opposition in introducing it into his dominions.

Extent of his kingdom.

At the end of a long reign he left a territory extending from the Godáveri to beyond the Kishna, and from the sea to a line drawn west of Heiderábád about the seventy-eighth degree of east longitude. The north-western districts of this territory were fragments of the Bahmani kingdom, and those on the south-west were gained from Bijáyanagar; but by far the greater part of Sultán Kúli's conquests were from the remains of the Warangól family and other chiefs of Télingána. He gained a great victory at Cóndapilli over all those chiefs united, with the addition of the rája of Orissa; and although the rája of Bijáyanagar afterwards endeavoured to support the cause of his religion, the government of Warangól was never restored, nor the Mahometan power disturbed within the limits above mentioned.

Conquests from the Hindús.

Wars with the other Mahometan kings.

Sultán Kúli was sometimes interrupted in his operations against the Hindús by attacks from his Mussulman neighbours, especially Ismáel A'dil Sháh. He however took a much less active share than the rest in the wars among the kings of the Deckan.

He was murdered at the age of ninety by his son, Jamshíd, who succeeded him, and reigned for seven years. The third king was a minor, and only reigned a few months; but I'brahím, the fourth of the line, reigned thirty years, and his time was marked by most of the few important transactions of the dynasty.

I'brahím, the fourth king.

He had a Hindú minister named Jagdeó, and most of his infantry and all his garrisons were composed of Te-

APPEND.

lingás of the same religion. Jagdeó quarrelled with his master, fled to Berár, and was there appointed to a great command. He afterwards went over to Rám Rája of Bijáyanagar, and by his influence a combination, formed between the rája, Ali A'dil Sháh and Ali Barid Sháh, was enabled to overrun a great part of I'brahím's country, and shut him up in his capital: peace was however restored, and I'brahím afterwards joined in the general confederacy against Rám Rája.

His wars.

The Kútb Sháhi kings took part in the wars and alliances of the other Mahometan monarchs in which they are generally connected with the kings of Ahmednagar; but these occasioned no permanent change in their condition: their aggrandisement was always at the expense of the Hindús. I'brahím took advantage of the disturbances in Orissa, and the invasion of that country from Bengal, to recover Rájamandri and the country north of the Godáveri up to Chicacól, which had been seized by the Hindús on the dissolution of the Bahmani kingdom; and his successor, Mohammed Kúli, carried on his conquests to the south of the Kishna, and added Gandicóta, Cadapa, and the rest of the country up to the river Penár, to his dominions.

Conquests on the coast of Coromandel.

It was this last king who built Heiderábad. He at first gave it the name of Bhágnagar (by which the Hindús call it still), and to it he transferred his capital from the neighbouring site of Golcónda.

Mohammed Kúli reigned for many years after Akber's capture of Ahmednagar, but his situation was little affected by those remote transactions.

APPEND.

Dynasty of Imád Sháhi in Berár.

FOUNDED BY FATTEH ULLAH, DESCENDED FROM A CONVERTED HINDÚ.

	A.D.	A.H.		A.D.	A.H.
Fatteh Ullah -	1484	890	Burhán (perhaps)	1560	968
Alá u dín - -	1504	910	Tufal.		
Deria (about)	1529	936			

The little that is known of this small kingdom has found a place in the history of the neighbouring states. It extended from the Injádri hills to the Godáveri: on the west it bordered on Ahmednagar and Cándésh, about the middle of the seventy-sixth degree of east longitude. On the east its limits are uncertain, but probably did not take in Nágpúr.

Though Fatteh Ullah exercised sovereign authority, yet Alá u dín seems first to have taken the title of king.*

During the minority of Burhán Imád Sháh, who probably succeeded about 1560, his prime minister, Tufal, usurped the government, and the state merged in that of Ahmednagar in A. D. 1572, A. H. 980.

Dynasty of Barid Sháh at Bidr.

	A.D.	A.H.		A.D.	A.H.
Kásim - -	1498	904	Kásim II. -	1569	997
Amír - -	1504	910	Mírza Ali -	1572	1000
Ali - -	1549	945	Amír II.		
I'brahím - -	1562	990			

The Baríds derived some importance at first from appearing as the ministers and representatives of the Bahmani

* This is variously related in different places of Ferishta; but see vol. iii. p. 350, 351.

APPEND.

kings; but the illusion was not kept up beyond the life of Kásim: neither he nor Amír took the title of king.

Their territories were small and ill-defined, and the period of their extinction is uncertain.

Amír II. was reigning in A. D. 1609, A. H. 1018, when Ferishta closed that part of his history.

Guzerát.

KINGS OF GUZERÁT.

	A.D.	A.H.		A.D.	A.H.
Mozaffer Sháh -	1396	799	Secander Sháh -	1526	932
Ahmed Sháh -	1412	815	Mahmúd Sháh II.	1526	932
Mohammed Sháh	1443	847	Bahádur Sháh -	1526	932
Kútb Sháh - -	1451	855	Mírán Mohammed Sháh Farukhí	1536	943
Dáúd Sháh reigned one week.			Mahmúd Sháh III.	1553	961
Mahmúd Sháh Bégara - -	1459	863	Ahmed Sháh II.	1561	969
Mozaffer Sháh II.	1511	917	Mozaffer Sháh III.	1561	969

Description of Guzerát.

Guzerát is bounded on the north-east and east by a hilly tract which connects the A'ravalli mountains with the Vindya chain; on the south it has the sea, which nearly surrounds a part of it, and forms a peninsula equal in extent to all the rest of the province; on the west it has the desert, including that portion called the Rin. The only open part of the frontier is on the north-west, where a plain between the hills and the desert connects it with Márwár.

The northern hills are steep and rugged; and the branches which they send out towards the south are covered with thick woods, as are the numerous ravines which run from their base to the principal rivers. The country gradually gets more open as it recedes from the mountains, and the lower part stretching for about sixty miles in depth along the sea is a plain of extraordinary fertility.

The peninsula is sometimes distinguished from the rest of Guzerát, and was formerly called Sóreth (or Sourashtra), now Kátiwár.

It is for the most part composed of low hills, and is, in general, naked and unfertile; but there are separate plains on the sea which extend to a great distance inland, and are rich and open.

Nearly in the south is a hilly district, called Bábriawár, which is covered with woods.

Original extent of the kingdom.

When Guzerát separated from Delhi, the new king had but a narrow territory on the plain. On the north-west were the independent rájas of Jhálór and Siróhí, from whom he occasionally levied contributions. The rája of I'dar, another Rájpút prince, was in possession of the western part of the hills; and though he was often obliged to pay contributions, and sometimes regular tribute, yet those advantages were seldom gained without a struggle; and he was a constant source of disturbance to the king of Guzerát, by joining his enemies and harbouring fugitives from his country.

The rest of the hilly and forest tract was held by the mountain tribes of Bhíls and Cúlis, among whom some Rájpút princes, mostly connected with Méwár, had also founded petty states.*

The peninsula was in the hands of nine or ten Hindú tribes, who had mostly come from Cach and Sind, at different periods, some centuries before. They were, probably, tributary; but by no means obedient. All these petty states preserved their existence during the ascendency of the Moguls, and were, within these few years, almost as independent as under the kings of Guzerát. The real

* Dóngarpúr, Bhánswárah, &c.: these subsist to the present day.

APPEND.

possessions of those kings, therefore, only included the plain between the hills and the sea; and even of that the eastern part belonged to an independent rája, who resided in the hill fort of Chámpanér. On the other hand, the Guzerát territory stretched along the sea to the south-east, so as to include the city of Surat and some of the country beyond it.

With these small means, the kings of Guzerát made, at least, as considerable a figure as any of the minor kings, except the Bahmani family, in the Deckan.

Mozaffer Sháh.

Founded by Mozaffer, the son of a Rájpút convert.

Farhat ul Mulk was appointed governor of Guzerát in the reign of Fírúz Tóghlak. Having given great offence to the Mussulmans of the provinces, and even excited the suspicions of the court of Delhi, by the means he took to court the Hindús, he was displaced by Mahmúd II., and

A.D. 1391, A.H. 791-2.

Mozaffer Khán was appointed in his room. Farhat opposed the entrance of the new governor with an army chiefly composed of Hindús; he was defeated, and Mozaffer took possession.* Mozaffer was the son of a Rájpút convert, who had risen from a low station about the court to the highest offices. He had himself been brought up a Mussulman and a nobleman, and appears to have been rather desirous of making his origin be forgotten by hostility to the Hindús.

It is uncertain when he took the title of king. His reign commenced in reality from the time when he became

A.D. 1391, A.H. 793. His wars.

governor. He was successful in his wars. He occupied I'dar, and brought the rája to submission. He fought

* Mr. Bird's History of Guzerát, p. 181. and notes.

a great battle in the peninsula; after which he took and retained Diu, on the sea coast: he went to war with the king of Cándésh, about the district of Sultánpúr; and although hostilities were often renewed in after reigns, yet, for his time, the question was favourably settled.

APPEND.

He once besieged Mandalghar, in Méwár, and extorted a contribution: he proceeded from that place to Ajmír, on a pilgrimage; and on his way back plundered Jhálór, and destroyed the temples.

His occupation and subsequent evacuation of Málwa.

His greatest war was with Málwa. Hushang Sháh, the second king, was suspected of poisoning his father; and as Mozaffer had been on very friendly terms with the deceased, he made the revenge of his murder a pretext for invading Málwa. He was successful beyond his hopes: he defeated Hushang, made him prisoner, and got possession of the whole of his kingdom. He soon found, however, that he could not retain his conquest; and perceiving that the inhabitants were about to set up another king, he thought it prudent to get what he could from his prisoner, and to restore him to the throne. During Mozaffer's government, Mahmúd Tóghlak came to Guzerát, on his flight from Delhi: he was ill received, and obliged to repair to Málwa.

A.D. 1407, A.H. 810.

A.D. 1408, A.H. 811.

Ahmed Sháh.

A.D. 1411, A.H. 814.

His wars with Málwa and his Hindú neighbours.

A.D. 1422, A.H. 825.

Hushang Sháh did not feel his restoration as a favour, for on the death of Mozaffer he took part with a faction opposed to the accession of that king's grandson, Ahmed Sháh, and began a series of wars between the two countries that lasted for many years. Ahmed Sháh thrice invaded Málwa, and once penetrated to Sáranpúr, in the east of the kingdom, where he gained a victory. On the other hand, the king of Málwa assisted Ahmed's enemies, Hindú as well as Mahometan; combined with the refractory rájas within the territory of Guzerát, and twice made his way to the capital, but without any important result.

APPEND.

And with other Mahometan kings.

Ahmed Sháh made, also, the usual expeditions against I'dar, Jhálór, and the peninsula; and had two wars with Cándésh. On one occasion, he marched as far as Nágór, in the north of Márwár, where his uncle was in revolt against Seiad Khizr, of Delhi. He was obliged to retreat

A.D. 1416, A.H. 819.

on the advance of that prince, and was pursued as far as Jhálór.*

A.D. 1429, A.H. 833.

He was also engaged with a new enemy, in consequence of the capture of the islands of Bombay and Salsette, by the Bahmani king of the Deckan, during an attempt to subdue the Concan.†

It does not appear how those places came into the hands of the king of Guzerát. It may be inferred that they were detached possessions, as the expedition to recover them was made by sea. The Bahmani king was driven out; but remained hostile, and more than once joined the king of Cándésh in his wars with Ahmed Sháh. Notwithstanding all these disturbances, Ahmed Sháh brought the interior of Guzerát into good order. He established forts in different places, to bridle the disaffected; and built the town of Ahmednagar (the solid and extensive walls of which still remain), as a check on the rája of I'dar. He also founded Ahmedábád, thenceforth his capital, and still one of the greatest cities in India, both from the number of the inhabitants and the magnificence of the buildings.‡

* Ferishta, vol. i. p. 509., vol. iv. p. 18., and Bird's Guzerát, p. 189.

† Briggs's Ferishta, vol. ii. p. 413. A somewhat different order is given to the same events in vol. iv. p. 27.

‡ Ahmed Sháh is said to have introduced the practice of giving to each soldier, land to the yearly value of half his pay, the whole having previously been issued in money. The measure is spoken of by the Guzerát historian with applause, al-

Ahmed Sháh was a zealous Mussulman. He destroyed temples, and built mosques; and is said to have greatly contributed to extend his religion among his subjects. APPEND.

The usual contests with Málwa and I'dar continued under the two next kings, Mohammed Sháh and Kútb Sháh. The second of them (Kútb Sháh) commenced a more serious war with Kúmbho, the rána of Méwár, whose capital was Chitór. Méwár had been invaded by Ahmed Sháh in the time of Mókal, the predecessor of Kúmbho; but the present war originated in the support given by Kútb Sháh to his relation in Nágór against the Rájpút prince, who was laying the foundation of that great power, afterwards employed by his grandson Sanga against Báber. In these wars the king of Guzerát had almost invariably the advantage. He gained two victories; besieged Chitór; took A'bú, a mountain celebrated for its sanctity, and subdued the rája of Siróhi, one of Kúmbho's allies. Mohammed Sháh. A.D. 1449, A.H. 153. Kútb Sháh. A.D. 1451, A.H. 855. His wars with Méwár. A.D. 1457, A.H. 861.

On the death of Kútb Sháh, his uncle, Dáúd Khán, was placed on the throne. He was deposed within a few days for incapacity, and became an eminent dervise. He was succeeded by Mahmúd, surnamed Bégarra, a brother of Kútb Sháh. Mahmúd was fourteen years old at his accession; reigned for fifty-two years, and was one of the greatest of the kings of Guzerát.* He soon showed his Dáúd Khán. A.D. 1459, A.H. 863. Mahmúd Bégarra. A.D. 1459, to A.D. 1511.

---

though it appears calculated to injure both the discipline and the comfort of the soldier. (*Bird's History.*)

* The European travellers of his day seem to have formed a tremendous idea of this monarch. Bartema (in Ramusio, vol. i. p. 147.) and Barbosa are both full of him. One of them gives (Ramusio, vol. i. p. 296.) a formidable account of his personal appearance, and both agree that a principal part of his food consisted of mortal poisons; and so impregnated was his system with his diet, that if a fly settled on him it instantly dropped down dead. His usual way of putting men of consequence to

APPEND.

His vigorous government.

He rescues the Bahmani king of the Deckan.

A. D. 1462, A. H. 866.

vigour in repressing the turbulence of his nobles; and at an early period of his reign he made a diversion in favour of the former enemy of his house, the Bahmani king of the Deckan, when besieged in his capital, and reduced to extremities by the king of Málwa.

Marches to the Indus.

His territory having been harassed by depredations from Cach, he crossed the Rin, overran that country, carried his arms to the Indus, and defeated a considerable body of Belóches on its banks.

Takes Girnár and Chámpanér.

His greatest exploits were, the reduction of Girnár, or Júnaghar, and of Chámpanér. The first of these places (Girnár) is in the south of the peninsula, and stands on a hill equally remarkable for its strength and sanctity.

These enterprises occupied several years *, and afforded examples of the usual desperation of the Rájpúts, and of more than ordinary bigotry among the Mussulmans. The rája of Girnár was compelled to embrace the religion of Mahomet, and the rája of Chámpanér was put to death for a firm adherence to his own.

His wars with Mahometan kings.

A. D. 1507, A. H. 913.

A. D. 1499, A. H. 905.

Mahmúd also quelled insurrections at home, and levied tribute on I'dar. In one of his wars with Cándésh, he marched as far as Asírghar; and, on a previous occasion, he had obliged the Nizám Sháhi king of Ahmednagar, in the Deckan, to raise the siege of Doulatábád.

---

death was to blow on them after he had been chewing bítel. He is the original of Butler's "Prince of Cambay," whose

"———— daily food
Is asp, and basilisk, and toad."

The fate of his wives is related with perfect seriousness by the above authors.

* Girnár was annually attacked from A. D. 1468 to 1470, A. H. 873 to 875, and Chámpanér was not taken till A. D. 1483, A. H. 888.

APPEND.

But what chiefly distinguishes him from former Mussulman princes is the number of his maritime expeditions. He took the islands of Jígat and Bét, then, as in recent times, nests of pirates; and sent out vessels mounting guns from Cambay, which defeated the pirates of Balsár in an action at sea.

His maritime power.

A. D. 1482, A. H. 887.

He also sent a sea and land force against Bombay, then occupied by a revolted officer of the Bahmani king. On this occasion, his fleet was destroyed in a storm, and he owed his recovery of Bombay to the co-operation of the king of the Deckan.

A. D. 1494, A. H. 900.

He co-operates with the Mamlúks of Egypt in a naval war with the Portuguese.

He had afterwards a more conspicuous opportunity for signalising his naval enterprise. The Mamlúk Sultan of Egypt had equipped twelve ships in the Red Sea, for the purpose of attacking the Portuguese in India, and Mahmúd entered zealously into his views. He sailed, himself, to Damán, and afterwards to Bombay; and at length sent a large fleet from Diú, under the command of A'iáz Sultáni, an officer who had distinguished himself at Chámpanér. The Guzerát vessels, though much inferior in size to those of the Mamlúks, were numerous; and the combined fleets were strong enough to attack the Portuguese squadron in the harbour of Choul, south of Bombay. The particulars of the operations that followed belong to the history of the Portuguese. It may be sufficient to say, here, that the Mussulmans were successful in this first action, and that A'iáz is mentioned with applause by the Portuguese writers for his humanity and courtesy on the occasion. The combined fleet was afterwards defeated, and the Mamlúk part of it annihilated, in a great battle close to Diú.*

A. D. 1508, A. H. 913.

* The Mahometan historians suppress this defeat, and say very little of their wars with the Portuguese, even when their

APPEND.

The Mamlúks, however, continued to send squadrons to the Indian seas, a practice which was imitated by the Turks after their conquest of Egypt. Their object was to open the navigation of the Red Sea and the Persian Gulf; and for this purpose they assisted the native powers of India in their wars with the Portuguese; but they never entertained any views towards obtaining possessions for themselves in that country.

Mozaffer II. A.D. 1511, A.H. 917.

The reign of Mozaffer II. opened with a splendid embassy from Sháh Ismáel, king of Persia. The same compliment was paid to most of the Indian princes, and was probably designed to conciliate their favour to the Shía religion, which Ismáel was so eager to introduce.

Generosity to the king of Malwa.

The next six years were spent in inglorious wars with I'dar. A more honourable enterprise presented itself at the end of that time. Mahmúd, king of Málwa, having been almost entirely deprived of his authority by Médni Rái, a Hindú chief to whom he had confided the management of his affairs, fled to Guzerát, and solicited the aid of Mozaffer, who went in person into Málwa, took the capital, compelled Rána Sanga, who was coming to the aid of the Hindú cause, to retreat; and, after restoring Mahmúd to his authority, withdrew to Guzerát without exacting any sacrifice in return. He had not long quitted Málwa before Sanga returned, defeated Mahmúd, and made him prisoner, but generously released him, and made an honourable peace. Sanga was now able to revenge himself

A.D. 1519, A.H. 924. War with Sanga, rána of Méwár.

---

own party was successful. Three or four years after this battle, an interview took place between Albuquerque and A'iáz, and the character of the latter, given by the Portuguese viceroy, is related in Faria (vol. i. p. 193.). "He said he had not seen a more perfect courtier, or fitter to deceive, and at the same time please, an understanding man."

APPEND.

on Mozaffer II., by marching to the assistance of the rája of I'dar, and plundering Guzerát as far as Ahmedábád.

Next year, Mozaffer II. retaliated by sending an army, under A'iáz Sultáni, against Sanga. A'iáz besieged the rána in Mandesór, and had granted him terms, when the king of Málwa arrived to co-operate with his army. The king earnestly pressed A'iáz to profit by this advantage; but A'iáz was steady to his engagement, and withdrew his troops in spite of the king's remonstrances.

Mozaffer II. died in A. D. 1526, after a reign of fourteen years. A. H. 932.

Bahádur.

The rapid disappearance of two sons and successors of Mozaffer (whose names were Secander and Mahmúd II.) left the throne open to Bahádur. This prince, though only the third of Mozaffer's sons, seems always to have been looked on as the probable heir of his father: on some discontent, however, he had left the court and gone to Delhi, where he remained with Sultán I'brahím Lódi until Báber's invasion. His absence occasioned his temporary exclusion; but the assassination of one brother and the deposal of the other replaced him in his station. He had still to encounter opposition from a third brother, who was assisted by Sanga and some other Hindú chiefs. This last pretender being killed in action, Bahádur remained the only claimant to the throne.

Takes part in the wars of the Deckan.

His first measure was to reduce the Rájpút princes of I'dar and the neighbouring mountains. He was soon after solicited by his nephew, the king of Cándésh, to come to his assistance, and that of the king of Berár, who had confederated against Burhán Nizám Sháh of Ahmednagar.

His supremacy acknowledged by the kings of Cándésh,

The whole conduct of the war was conceded to Bahádur, and his permanent supremacy was formally acknowledged by the other kings. So successful were his operations, that Nizám Sháh, though joined by Baríd Sháh, king of Bídr,

APPEND.

Berár, and Ahmednagar.

was obliged to yield the points in contest with Cándésh and Berár, and to gratify the vanity of Bahádur Sháh, by an act of personal homage, as has been mentioned in another place.

Conquest of Málwa, and its annexation to Guzerát.

Bahádur's next enterprise was attended with a still more splendid result. Mahmúd, king of Málwa, who had been restored to his throne by Mozaffer II., was not restrained by that obligation from intriguing against the son of his benefactor; and with equal ingratitude he seized the opportunity of Rána Sanga's death to attack his successor, Rána Rattan Sing. The rána was before in close alliance with Bahádur Sháh, and they now united to revenge their common injuries. Mahmúd was made prisoner in Mándu, his capital, and was sent to Guzerát. He was afterwards put to death; and his dominions were taken possession of by Bahádur Sháh, and annexed to his hereditary kingdom.

A. D. 1531, February; A. H. 937. Shábán.

Troubles in Málwa.

Bahádur had not sufficient moderation long to enjoy so much good fortune. One of the principal instruments of the revolution in Málwa was Silhadi a Rájpút, who had risen under Mahmúd to the government of Ráisín, Bhilsa, and other places in the east of Málwa, to which he had since added the possession of Ujén.

Bahádur Sháh appears to have thought his conquest incomplete, while so powerful a chief remained, especially as Silhadi was in some measure under the protection of the rána of Méwár. He therefore made him prisoner while on a visit to the royal camp; and, taking advantage of the surprise occasioned by this act of treachery, got possession of the city of Ujén: Bópat Rái, the son of Silhadi, fled to Chitór; and Ráisín, a strong hill fort belonging to that chief, held out under his brother.

It was long before Bahádur could overcome the opposition thus raised; and he might have entirely failed in doing so, if Rattan Sing, the rána of Chitór, had not died and been succeeded by his son, Vicramajít, under whom that government lost much of its energy. APPEND.

During Bahádur's absence on this expedition, a serious attack had been made on Diú by a great armament of the Portuguese, but had been repulsed by the valour of the garrison (Feb. 1531).

War with Méwár. A.D. 1532, A.H. 938.

Having taken whatever measures were necessary against this enemy, Bahádur Sháh again turned his attention to Chitór. So much was the power of Méwár diminished, that he commenced his operations with the siege of the capital: and at the end of three months constrained the rája to purchase peace by the payment of a heavy contribution.* It was about this time that Bahádur Sháh provoked the war with Humáyun, the result of which has already been related.† During Bahádur's abode at Diú, he entered into negotiations with the Portuguese. Among other concessions he gave them leave to build a factory; and they furnished him, in return, with a body of 500 Europeans, to assist him in recovering his kingdom. As soon as Guzerát was settled after the retreat of the Moguls, Bahádur Sháh again turned his attention to Diú, where the Portuguese were surrounding their new factory with a wall, and, as he conceived, converting it into a fortification. He there found Nuno de Cunha, the Portuguese viceroy, who had come with a fleet to secure his new acquisition. Remonstrances and explanations took place, to appearance

A.D. 1433, A.H. 940. War with Humáyun, and expulsion of Bahádur.

Bahádur recovers his kingdom.

Disputes with the Portuguese at Diú.

* Among the property given up on this occasion, was a girdle of jewels, which had been taken from a former king of Guzerát, and which was afterwards sent with Bahádur Sháh's family to Medina, and found its way at last into the treasury of the grand signor. (Colonel Briggs's note on Ferishta, vol. i. p. 141.) For the date of this first siege, see Bird's History of Guzerát, p. 216. note.

† P. 126.

APPEND.

on a friendly footing; but both the Mussulman and Portuguese historians justify the belief that treachery was meditated by both parties, and that each was watching an opportunity to execute his design. Nuno de Cunha, when invited to visit the king, feigned sickness; and Bahádur, to lull his suspicions, went on board his ship with a few attendants. When on board, Bahádur Sháh was alarmed at some whispering and signs which passed between the viceroy and his attendants, and, taking a hasty leave, got into his boat to go ashore. An affray took place, which the Portuguese represent as accidental, and the Mussulmans as designed; and the result was, that several lives were lost on each side, and that Bahádur Sháh threw himself into the sea, and, after being stunned by a blow of an oar, was dispatched with a halbert.

Interview with the Portuguese viceroy.

Death of Bahádur.

As both parties equally held that faith was not to be kept with infidels, neither has the slightest claim to a favourable construction; but Bahádur could have had no immediate act of perfidy in view when he came on board unattended; and as the object of the Portuguese must have been to seize and not to murder the king, it is unlikely that they would, if prepared for such a step, have allowed him to leave the ship. The affray, therefore, probably arose unintentionally from the mutual alarm of the parties: if either was guilty of premeditated treachery, the greatest weight of suspicion rests on the Portuguese.*

A.D. 1537, A.H. 943.

Bahádur Sháh's natural heir was his nephew Mahmúd, the son of Latíf Khán, who had formerly been his rival; but that prince was a prisoner in the hands of his cousin by the mother's side, Míran Sháh, king of Cándésh; and the latter availed himself of the circumstance to claim the

Mírán Mohammed Sháh.

* See a full and judicious examination of the accounts of both parties in a note on Colonel Briggs's Ferishta, vol. iv. p. 132.

crown for himself. He, however, died a natural death within six weeks; and, as his brother, who succeeded in Cándésh, though in possession of the same advantages, was not so fortunate in profiting by them, Mahmúd was at length set at liberty, and allowed to take possession of his right. APPEND.

Mahmúd III. A.D. 1538, A.H. 944.

He took the title of Mahmúd III., and had a reign of sixteen years, remarkable for nothing but the intrigues and factions of his chiefs. His death was attended with circumstances sufficiently out of the ordinary course: he was assassinated by his domestic chaplain, whom he had at one time ordered to be built up to the neck in a wall and left to starve, and had released when nearly dead, on his attempting, even in that extremity, to bend his head to the king as he passed. The chaplain, after the murder, sent for the principal nobles, and put each privately to death as he appeared. He then assumed the crown; but, as might have been expected, was put to death by the remaining officers the moment he presented himself in public.

A.D. 1553-4, A.H. 961.

Mahmúd III. built the castle of Surat, which still remains; and likewise enclosed a park of fourteen miles in circumference with a wall; an unusual work in a country where deer and game of all sorts are so abundant.

Ahmed II.

A supposititious child was now set up by a party, under the name of Ahmed II. He lived to grow up, and probably to have a will of his own, for he was assassinated after a reign of eight years.

A.D. 1561, A.H. 969.

Mozaffer III.

A similar pageant was next set up under the title of Mozaffer III., and the kingdom was partitioned among the leading conspirators. Dissensions broke out among them, and the country became a scene of continual war, confusion, and tumult, until finally settled by Akber, as will appear in his reign.

Guzerát conquered by Akber. A.D. 1572, A.H. 980.

APPEND.

Málwa.

FOUNDED BY DILÁWAR, OF A FAMILY FROM GHÓR.

KINGS OF MÁLWA.

	A.D.	A.H.		A.D.	A.H.
Diláwar Ghóri -	1401	804	Mahmúd Khilji -	1435	839
Husheng Ghóri -	1405	808	Gheiásu dín Khilji	1482	887
Mohammed Ghóri	1432	835	Násir u dín Khilji	1500	906
			Mahmúd II. Khilji	1512	916

It has been mentioned that Málwa became independent at the end of the reign of Sultán Fírúz Tóghlak. The first king was Diláwar Ghóri, whose ancestors were natives of Ghór, and who claimed through his mother a connection with the royal family of that country.

His successor founded the capital, Mándu, remarkable for its situation on a rich table land of thirty-seven miles circumference surrounded by rocky precipices, as well as for the magnificence of its buildings.*

Wars in Hindostan and the Deckan. From A. D. 1407, A. H. 810, to A. D. 1432, A. H. 835.

He was engaged in those constant wars with Guzerát, which have already been related in the account of that kingdom. His successors were generally at peace with Guzerát; but they had frontier wars with the king of Júanpúr on the Jamna, and with the king of Cándésh on the Taptí. They had also wars with the Bahmani kings in Berár; and they once laid siege to Bídr, the capital of the last named monarch (1461). One king, Mahmúd I., besieged Delhi, and was defeated by Behlól Lódi, as has been related. The same prince began a series of wars with Kúmbho Sing, the rája of Chitór or Méwár; but, although they lasted upwards of fifteen years, involved other Hindú princes, and led to many battles and sieges, they made no material changes in the extent of the Mahometan territory.

A. D. 1440, A. H. 844.

From A. D. 1443, A. H. 846, to A. D. 1458, A. H. 863.

* Sir J. Malcolm's Central India, vol. i. pp. 29. 40.

The reign of Mahmúd II. was more fertile in events than all that preceded it, and deserves to be more particularly noticed.

Mahmúd II.

Immediately on the accession of this prince he was engaged in a civil war with his brother, Sáhib Khán, in which his success was principally owing to the support of a Rájpút chief named Médni Rái, who joined him at the commencement with a considerable body of his tribe. The struggle was long and arduous, and was renewed, after an interval with assistance to the pretender from the king of Delhi; but the courage and talents of Médni Rái again prevailed.

A. D. 1512, A. H. 916. Ascendancy of Médni Rái, a Hindú chief.

These long-continued services gave the Rájpút chief a complete ascendancy over his master, and threw the whole administration of the government into his hands. The superiority thus conferred on a Hindú excited universal discontent among the Mahometans, and led to the rebellion of several governors of provinces, who were crushed in succession by Médni Rái.

By the results of these contests Médni Rái became all-powerful, removed every Mahometan from about the king's person, and filled the court and army with Rájpúts. Mahmúd at length became alarmed; and, after an unsuccessful attempt to recover his authority, he felt that he was a prisoner in his own capital, and seized an opportunity of escaping to Guzerát. Mozaffer Sháh, king of that country, came to his assistance. The war lasted for more than a year: Mándu, the capital, was taken after a desperate defence by the Rájpúts; and the king of Guzerát, having restored Mahmúd to his authority, returned to his own dominions. Médni Rái had retired to Chandéri, of which place he was perhaps the hereditary chief. Mahmúd marched against him, and found him strengthened by the alliance of Rája Sanga, who had come with the whole of his army to defend Chandéri.

A. D. 1517, A. H. 923. Mahmúd flies to Guzerát.

A. D. 1519, A. H. 924. Is restored by Bahádur Sháh.

APPEND.

Is defeated, taken prisoner, and released by Sanga, rána of Méwár.

A battle ensued, in which Mahmúd was defeated; and as, although weak in other points, he was distinguished for his courage, he endeavoured to maintain the combat until he was covered with wounds, unhorsed, and made prisoner. The Rájpút prince treated him with courtesy, and after a short interval generously released him.

His ingratitude.

The mean spirit of Mahmúd was incapable of imitating the magnanimity of his enemy. On the death of Sanga he thought to avail himself of the difficulties of a new reign by attacking Rattan Sing, the son of the late rája.

A. D. 1525, A. H. 932.

Rattan Sing applied to Bahádur Sháh, who had succeeded Mozaffer on the throne of Guzerát, and who had likewise reason to complain of the ingratitude of the king of Málwa.

He is defeated, and his kingdom annexed to Guzerát. A.D. 1531, A. H. 937.

Mahmúd, unable to withstand so powerful a confederacy, saw his capital taken by Bahádur Sháh, and was afterwards himself made prisoner: when the kingdom of Málwa was permanently annexed to Guzerát.

Cándésh.

FOUNDED BY MALIK RÁJA, A PERSON OF ARAB DESCENT.

FARÚKHI KINGS OF CÁNDÉSH.

	A.D.	A.H.		A. D.	A. H.
Malik Rája			A'dil Khán II. -	1510	
Nasír Khán (first king) - -	1399	801	Mírán Mohammed Sháh - -	1520	926
Mírán A'dil Khán	1437	841	Mírán Mobárik	1535	942
Mírán Mobárik -	1441	844	Mírán Mohammed Khán - -	1566	974
A'dil Khán I. -	1457	861	Rája Ali Khán -	1576	984
Dáúd Khán -	1503	909	Bahádur Shah -	1596	1005

The kingdom of Cándésh was merely the lower part of the valley of the Taptí (the upper part being included in Berár); on the south it had the hills which support the table land of the Deckan, and on the north the Injádri range. It was only separated from Guzerát by forests. It was a rich country, watered by innumerable streams. Its history is almost entirely comprised in the small portion which its wars and alliances contributed to that of the neighbouring countries.

The first prince who threw off his dependence on Delhi claimed a descent from the Calif O'mar. He was married to the daughter of the king of Guzerát, from whom his son received the title of king, and to whom both he and his successors acknowledged a sort of subordination.

There is nothing to mention in their domestic history, except the taking of the strong hill fort of Asírghar by treachery from a Hindú chief, and the founding of the city of Burhánpúr near that fortress. Burhánpúr was made the capital. It is still a large city; and the ruins of public edifices around it show it to have been formerly much more considerable. The whole of Cándésh, indeed, seems to have been in a high state of prosperity under its own kings: the numerous stone embankments by which the streams were rendered applicable to irrigation, are equal to any thing in India as works of industry and utility; and, whether they were made by the Hindús or the kings of Cándésh, they must have been in use under the latter, though now in ruins and buried in woods.

Prosperity of Cándésh.

Cándésh was reannexed to Delhi by Akber, in A. D. 1599.

Conquered by Akber. A. D. 1599. A. H. 1008.

APPEND.

Bengal.

	A.D.	A.H.		A.D.	A.H.
Fakhr u dín* -	1338	739	Fatteh - -	1461	866
Alá u dín - -	1340	741	Sháhzádeh -	1481	886
Haji Eliás (or Shams u dín) -	1342	743	Fírúz - -	1481	886
Secander - -	1357	759	Mahmúd - -	1493	899
Gheiás u dín -	1367	769	Mozaffer - -	1494	900
Sultán u Salátín -	1374	775	Alá u dín II. -	1497	904
Shams u dín II. -	1383	785	Nasrat - -	1521	927
Rája Káns - -	1386	788	Mahmúd - -	1534	940
			Shír Sháh -	1537	945
Jit Mal (or Jelál u dín) - -	1392	795	Selím - -	1545	952
			A'dili - -	1548	955
Ahmed - -	1409	812	Bahádur - -	1553	961
Násir u dín -	1426	830	Jelál u dín -	1560	968
Násir - -	1426	830	Sólímán Kiráni -	1563	971
Bárbik - -	1428	832	Báyazíd - -	1573	981
Eusof - -	1445	849	Dáúd - -	1573	981

The kingdom of Bengal went on for upwards of two centuries after its revolt from Mohammed Tóghlak, with frequent changes of dynasty, but without events worth recording. Among the usurpers was Rája Káns, a Hindú zemíndár. His son embraced the Mahometan religion.

This kingdom seems at one time to have comprehended North Behár. It included Sundergong (Dacca): Jájnagar (Tipera) was tributary: Assám was occasionally plundered: Catak and the adjoining parts of Orissa were not acquired till just before the extinction of the state.

It was conquered by Shír Sháh, as has been related, and was in the hands of a revolted officer of one of his successors at the time of Akber's accession.

* The early dates in this dynasty are uncertain. Ibn Batúta left Delhi, in A. D. 1342, and found Fakhr u dín alive in Bengal at least a year or two after.

Júanpúr.

	A. D.	A. H.		A. D.	A. H.
Khája Jehán -	1394	796	Mahmúd - -	1440	844
Mobárik - -	1399	802	Mohammed -	1457	862
I'brahím - -	1401	804	Husén - -	1457	862

Khája Jehán, the vizír at the time of Mahmúd Tóghlak's accession, seems to have been unable to retain his ascendency during the minority, and to have retired to his government of Júanpúr, and made himself independent. Four of his family followed him in succession, and carried on wars with the kings of Málwa and Delhi. They twice besieged the latter capital; but, at length, their government was subverted, and their territory restored to Delhi by Behlól Lódí in A. D. 1476.

It was soon occupied by Báber after his conquest; was taken by Shír Sháh; and, after the fall of his dynasty, passed through different hands till conquered by Akber early in his reign.

It stretched along the Ganges from Canouj, on the north-west, to the frontier between Bengal and South Behár on the south-east.

Sind.

After the expulsion of the Arabs (A. D. 750), Sind, from Bakkar to the sea, remained in the hands of the Sumera Rájpúts, until the end of the twelfth century; when the reigning family became extinct, and the government, after some changes, fell into the hands of another Rájpút tribe, called Sama.

It is uncertain when the Sumeras first paid tribute to the Mahometans; probably, about the beginning of the

APPEND.

twelfth century, under Shaháb u dín Ghóri, or his immediate successors.

The early Samas seem to have been refractory, for one was invaded by Fírúz Tóghlak, as has been related (about A. D. 1361). The Samas were soon after converted to the Mahometan religion; and kept the country till expelled by the Arghúns, who held it at Akber's accession.

Multán.

Multán revolted during the confusion which followed the invasion of Tamerlane. It fell into the hands of an Afghán family of the name of Langa, who held it for about a century.

Early in the sixteenth century, they were dispossessed by the Arghúns of Sind, who were, in their turn, expelled by Prince Cámrán, and Multán fell under the house of Teimur.

State of the other parts of India.

Of the other provinces once belonging to Delhi, it need only be said that they all became independent after the invasion of Tamerlane; and, although Behlól Lodi, Báber, Humáyun, and Shír Sháh had recovered many of them, yet at Akber's accession (with the exception of the Panjáb, the possession of which was contested by Secander Súr,) they were all in the hands of adherents of the Afghán government.

END OF THE SECOND VOLUME.

LONDON:
Printed by A. SPOTTISWOODE,
New-Street-Square.